For reference

Not to be taken from the room.

Voices of the
Asian American and Pacific
Islander Experience

Voices of the Asian American and Pacific Islander Experience

VOLUME 1

Sang Chi and
Emily Moberg Robinson, Editors

AN IMPRINT OF ABC-CLIO, LLC
Santa Barbara, California • Denver, Colorado • Oxford, England

Copyright 2012 by Sang Chi and Emily Moberg Robinson

All rights reserved. No part of this publication may be reproduced, stored in a retrieval system, or transmitted, in any form or by any means, electronic, mechanical, photocopying, recording, or otherwise, except for the inclusion of brief quotations in a review, without prior permission in writing from the publisher.

Library of Congress Cataloging-in-Publication Data

Voices of the Asian American and Pacific Islander experience / Sang Chi and Emily Moberg Robinson, editors.
   p. cm.
   Includes index.
   ISBN 978-1-59884-354-5 (hardcopy : alk. paper) — ISBN 978-1-59884-355-2 (ebook)
   1. Asian Americans—Interviews. 2. Asian Americans—History—Sources. I. Chi, Sang, 1974– II. Robinson, Emily Moberg.
   E184.A75V65 2012
   973'.0495—dc23   2011032187

ISBN: 978-1-59884-354-5
EISBN: 978-1-59884-355-2

16 15 14 13 12   1 2 3 4 5

This book is also available on the World Wide Web as an eBook.
Visit www.abc-clio.com for details.

Greenwood
An Imprint of ABC-CLIO, LLC

ABC-CLIO, LLC
130 Cremona Drive, P.O. Box 1911
Santa Barbara, California 93116-1911

This book is printed on acid-free paper ∞
Manufactured in the United States of America

Contents

Preface	xv
Introduction	xxiii
Chronology	xli

VOLUME 1

Part I General Asian American	1
1. The Page Law, 1875	1
2. National Origins Act, 1924	3
3. War Brides Act, 1945	8
4. McCarran-Walter Act, 1952	9
5. Indochina Migration and Refugee Assistance Act, 1975	11
6. Asian American Movement: The San Francisco State Strike	13
A. Third World Liberation Front, "San Francisco State University TWLF Strike Demands," 1968	14
B. Philippine-American Collegiate Endeavor (PACE), "State of the Philippine-American Collegiate Endeavor Philosophy and Goals," 1968	14
C. Research Organizing Cooperative of San Francisco, "SFSU TWLF Strike Injuries from Police Brutality," 1969	15
D. Richard Aoki, Speech at AAPA (Asian American Political Alliance, University of California, Berkeley) Rally, July 28, 1968	16
E. "INTERCOLLEGIATE CHINESE FOR SOCIAL ACTION," 1968	16
F. Asian American Political Alliance, "AAPA PERSPECTIVES," 1969	17
G. Flyer for the Yellow Symposium at the University of California, Berkeley, "asian experience/yellow identity," 1969	18
7. "The Story of *Hyphen*," 2003	19
8. Asian American Alliance, Political Committee, Columbia University, 2006	20
9. SAALT (South Asian Americans Leading Together), "Making the Case: Why Build a South Asian Identity," 2006	21

10. Mike Lee, "Why Asian Girls Go for White Guys," 2007   23
11. Mike Lee, "A Comment on Asian Christians: A Friend's Response," 2007   24
12. Belinda Dronkers-Laureta, "Asian Family Values," 2008   26
13. *AsianWeek,* "A New Hope for Asian Americans," 2008   27
14. jozjozjoz, "Buddha-chic!" 2008   28
15. Ernie Hsuing, "Rainbow Nation and Gay Asian Male Stereotypes," 2008   29
16. John, "Asian Americans Going on a Date in a Wells Fargo Commercial," 2008   30
17. Beverly Chen, "The Strength of Sisters," 2008   31
18. John, "ABC's Nightline Profiles Raymond Zheng, 'Brillant Kid,'" and Rob, "Raising Your Kid: Problems with the 'Raymond Zheng' Approach," 2009   32
19. Frances Kai-Hwa Wang, "Attack of the Asianphile," 2009   35
20. Timothy Chiu, "On Talking with or without an Accent," 2009   37
21. Kathy Wang, "Racism: An Amateur's Perspective," 2009   38
22. Timothy Chiu, "Where Are the Asian CEOs?" and "The Bamboo Ceiling," 2009   41
23. Rob, "Asians Can Be Just As Racist Too!" 2009   43
24. Jeff, "Asian-American Kids: Moving Back and Forth Between Asia," 2009   44
25. Jeff, "Tall, Short, and Segregated Asians: Six Lessons from a Basketball Season," 2009   45
26. Hindu American Foundation, "Yoga beyond Asana: Hindu Thought in Practice," 2010   48

Part II   American Samoa   53

27. Eni F. H. Faleomavaega, "Regarding the Minimum Wage in American Samoa," 2003   53
28. Help Samoa Disaster Relief Coalition Press Release, "How Samoans in America Got Together to Help Their People," 2009   58
29. Tafea Polamalu, "Diasporic Dream: Letter to Grandfather," 2009 and "Daddy Said," 2010   61

Part III   Bangladeshi American   65

30. Kanwal Rahman, Interview by Rajika Bhandari, July 15, 1999   65
31. Farah Akbar, "A Troubling Cultural Gap," 2010   67

Part IV   Cambodian American   73

32. United Cambodian Community Booklet, Long Beach, California, 1990   73
33. Karen Kauv Sun, Interview by Janean Baker, 1993   75
34. Kong Phok, Interview by Barbara Lau, 2000   78
35. Ran Kong, Interview by Barbara Lau, 2001   80

36. Leendavy Koung, "You Cannot Lose Your Spirit," 2001	82
37. Vatey Seng, *The Price We Paid*, 2005	85

Part V Chinese American — 91

38. *The Golden Hills' News*, "The Chinese Exodus," 1854	91
39. William Speer, "An Answer to the Common Objections to Chinese Testimony," 1857	92
40. Kwang Chang Ling, "Letters of Kwang Chang Ling: The Chinese Side of the Chinese Question," 1878	94
41. Woman's Union Mission of San Francisco, 1881	97
42. Transcript of Chinese Exclusion Act, 1882	99
43. "California Chinese Mission," 1882–1883	103
44. *Tape v. Hurley*, 1885	106
45. *Yick Wo v. Hopkins*, 1886	108
46. "An Address from the Workingmen of San Francisco to Their Brothers throughout the Pacific Coast," 1888	113
47. Tuck Wo & Company Bankruptcy Case, 1909	116
48. Angel Island Poem, by One from Ziangshan, Undated, between 1910–1940	118
49. The Case of Huey Jing and Huey Fong, 1913	119
50. Portland Tong Peace Agreement, 1917	144
51. Yee Wee Thing Betrayal Letter, 1920	146
52. Mary Young Chan, Marriage Certificate and Court Summons, 1921	147
53. C. P. Colegrave, "Among the Chinese," ca. 1930	150
54. Carol Green Wilson, *Chinatown Quest*, 1931	151
55. Charles Shepherd, "The Story of Lee, Wong and Ah Jing," 1933	156
56. Ruth Chinn, Interview by Stafford Lewis, 1938	158
57. Yee Bing Quai, Interrogation Files, 1938	160
58. Wing Luke, "Remarks," August 17, 1960	164
59. John Dong, Interview by Elizabeth Calciano, 1967	166
60. *Rosenberg v. Yee Chien Woo*, 1971	167
61. Esther Don Tang, "Memories of Mother and Father," 1995	171
62. Fred Pang, "Asian-Pacific Americans: Microcosm of Greater National Mix," 1997	172
63. Sifu Cheung Shu Pui, "Chinatown without Lion Dancers Would Be a Community Filled with Regret," 2001	176
64. Ted Tsukiyama, "Eulogy for Hung Wai Ching," 2002	180
65. Maggie Gee, Interview by Leah McGarrigle, Robin Li, and Kathryn Stine, 2003	184
66. Shuyuan Li, "Walking on Solid Ground," 2003	188
67. Esther Don Tang, "Thoughts on the Chinese Community Today," 2005	193
68. Daniel Yang, "To Live and Die in (or East of) LA: The Life of a Former Asian American Gang Member," 2006	194
69. Joy Wong, "The Whole Picture," 2008	196

70. Roland Hwang, "The Vincent Chin Case Remembered 25 Years Later," 2007	197
71. Eddie Fung, "Chinatown Kid, Texas Cowboy, Prisoner of War," 2007	201
72. Eddy Zheng, "Autobiography @ 33," 2007	203
73. John, "How Bruce Lee Changed the World," 2009	206
74. Frances Kai-Hwa Wang, "From a Whisper to a Rallying Cry," 2009	207
75. Adam Cheung, "Encounter with Crazy Ming," 2010	210
76. Alice Shi Kembel, "My Mother's Purse," 2010	213

Part VI Filipino American — 219

77. Excerpt from Angeles Monrayo's *Tomorrow's Memories: A Diary*, 1924–1928	219
78. Antonio E. Velasco, "Filipino Student Suffers from Pang of Race Prejudice," 1928	223
79. Mariano Guiang, Interview by Carolina Koslosky, 1976	224
80. Apolonia Dangzalan, Interview by Meri Knaster, 1977	226
81. Frank Barba, Interview by Meri Knaster, 1977	228
82. Rufino F. Cacabelos, "Autobiography," 1992	230
83. Excerpt from Evangeline Canonizado Buell's *Twenty-Five Chickens and a Pig for a Bride: Growing Up in a Filipino Immigrant Family*, 2006	232
84. Robert Bernardo, "Strangers Among Us," 2006, and Interview with Eliyahu Enriquez, 2009	236
85. Estella Habal, "How I Became a Revolutionary," 2007	244
86. JoAnn Balingit, Three Poems and an Essay, 2007	247
87. Catherine Ceniza Choy, "How to Stand Up and Dive," 2007	250
88. "An Asian-American in the Music Business: Interview with Ryan Buendia," 2009	254
89. Gem P. Daus, "Discovering Carlos Bulosan," 2010	256
90. Robert Francis Flor, "Alaskero Memories," 2010	259
91. Eliyahu Enriquez, "Inquisitory Karma" and "Mahogany Mantle," 2010	263
92. Cynthia Vasallo, "Most American," 2010	265

Part VII Guamanian American — 267

93. Hartley Ochavillo, "Leaving Guam," 2009	267

Part VIII Native Hawai'ian American — 269

94. Ke Ali'i Bernice Pauahi Paki Bishop, "Will and Codicils," 1883	269
95. Lili'uokalani, *Hawai'i's Story by Hawai'i's Queen*, 1898	270
96. U.S. Public Law 103-150, "The Apology Resolution," 1993	273
97. Hawaiian Constitutional Convention, 2008	277
98. M. J. Halelaukoa Garvin, "How Do You See Yourself?" 2009	278

99. Jeno Enocencio, "Surviving the Enemy," 2009	280
100. Native Hawaiian Government Reorganization Act, S. 381, 2009	282

Part IX Himalayan American — 285

101. Anonymous, "A College Graduate: To Be or Not to Be," 2005	285
102. Anonymous, "Migyul Youth" Questions and Answers, 2005	287
103. Sonam G. Sherpa, "My Identity" and "As American as Apple Pie. What's in a name?" 2005	291
104. Roshani Adhikary, "Nepali Grrl Blues," 2005	295
105. Tenzin Shakya, "Living as 'Other' in the U.S.A.," 2008	297
106. Shilpa Lama, "One Nepalese Woman's Journey to America," 2009	299
107. Prem and Kumari Tamang, Interview by Emily Moberg Robinson, 2010	300

Part X Hmong American — 307

108. Pang Xiong Sirirathasuk Sikoun, Interview by Sally Peterson, 2006	307
109. Chao Xiong, "Waiting, 'not knowing if they are even alive,'" 2007	308
110. Sheng Xiong, "Address to the United States National Press Club," 2009	308
111. Critical Hmong Studies Collective, "Persistent Invisibility: Hmong Americans are Silenced," 2008	312
112. Katie Ka Vang, "Uncle's Visit," 2008	314
113. Noukou Thao, "Dowry," 2009	317
114. Sheng Yang and Sami Scripter, excerpt from *Cooking from the Heart*, 2009	321
115. May Lee-Yang and Katie Ka Vang, Interview by *Bakka Magazine*, 2009	324
116. Bee Vang and Louisa Schein, "A Conversation On Race and Acting," 2010	327
117. Ly Chong Thong Jalao, "Looking *Gran Torino* in the Eye: A Review," 2010	330

Part XI Indian American — 335

118. Mary Bamford, *Angel Island: The Ellis Island of the West*, 1917	335
119. *U.S. v. Bhagat Singh Thind*, 1923	338
120. Mary T. Mathew, Interview by Rashmi Varna, 1999	344
121. Anita Chawla, Interview by Peggy Bulger, 2001	345
122. DJ Rekha, Interview by Demetrius Cheeks, 2007	347
123. Sweta Srivastava Vikram, "Racist or a Victim?" 2009	350
124. Athena Kashyap, Four Poems, 2009	351
125. Sandip Roy, "The Great Diwali Fight and Obama," 2009	353
126. Rajiv Srinivasan, "My Battle Within: The Identity Crisis of a Hindu Soldier in the US Army," 2009	355
127. Ainee Fatima, "To My Mother," "Blues from a Black Burqah," and "Graceland Part I," 2009	357

128. John, "ABCD's: American-Born Confused Desis," 2009 — 362
129. Sanjay Patel, Interview by Grain edit, 2010 — 363

Part XII Indonesian American — 367

130. Nadia Syahmalina, "Kamu Bukan Orang Sini," 2001 — 367
131. Peter Phwan, "Game of Chance: Chinese Indonesians Play Asylum Roulette in the United States," 2009 — 370
132. William Wright, "Indonesian Makes New Life in America," 2009 — 373

VOLUME 2

Part XIII Japanese American — 377

133. Joseph Heco, *The Narrative of a Japanese; What He has Seen and the People He has Met in the Course of the Last Forty Years*, 1895 — 377
134. George Henry Himes, "An account of the first Japanese native in Oregon," ca. 1904 — 379
135. The Gentlemen's Agreement, 1907–1908 — 381
    A. President Theodore Roosevelt's Executive Order, 1907 — 382
    B. Commissioner General of Immigration, Report, 1908 — 383
136. Alien Land Law, California, 1913 — 383
137. "Shall Japanese Americans in Idaho Be Treated with Fairness and Justice or Not?" 1921 — 385
138. Ryu Kishima, Deportation Documents, 1936 — 388
139. Executive Order 9066, 1942 — 393
140. Evacuation Poster, "Instructions to All Persons of Japanese Ancestry Living in the Following Area," 1942 — 393
141. 442nd Regimental Combat Team, 1941–1945 — 397
    A. 442nd RCT JULY 1945 MONTHLY REPORT — 397
    B. Commendation Letter from Brigadier General Francis H. Oxx, 1945 — 399
142. Hayao Chuman, Letters and Affidavit, 1946–1967 — 400
143. Territory of Hawai'i Legislature, House Resolution No. 61, 1955 — 403
144. Tak Kubota, "Japanese American Citizens League Memo About Failure to Repeal Alien Land Laws in Washington State," 1962 — 405
145. Biography of George Tsutakawa, 1978 — 407
146. Fred Korematsu, Writ of *Coram Nobis*, 1984 — 408
147. Hiroshi Shikuma, Interview by Randall Jarrell, 1986 — 420
148. Yuri Kochiyama, Interview by *The Revolutionary Worker*, 1988 — 421
149. Milton Murayama, *Five Years on a Rock*, 1994 — 425
150. Naeko Isagawa Keen, Interview by Daniel Clark, 1995 — 427
151. Alice Ohashi Kuroiwa, "Life and Education of the Older Children of Immigrant Parents (born between 1910–1925)," 1996 — 429
152. Brenda Wong Aoki, "Uncle Gunjiro's Girlfriend: The True Story of the First Hapa Baby," 1998 — 432

153. Ryo Imamura, Interview by Stephen Fugita and Erin Kimura, 1999	435
154. Richard Aoki, Interview by Dolly Veale, Undated (post-1999)	440
155. Bruce Yamashita, *A Most Unlikely Hero*, 2003	444
156. LaVerne Sasaki, "Tule Lake Pilgrimage Memorial," and Jeanette Shin, "Transformations," 2006	450
157. Fumitaka Matsuoka, "Benediction at GTU Graduates of Color Ceremony," 2008	455
158. Yumi Sakugawa, "An Asian American Wedding," 2009	457
159. University of California Senate Resolution to Award Honorary Degrees to Japanese American Internees, 2009	459
160. Patrick Hayashi, Honorary Degree Ceremony Remarks, 2009	464
161. Wendy Maruyama, Interview by Joyce Lovelace, 2009	468
162. Stuart Hada, "Small Satisfactions," 2009	472
163. Charlene Gima, "Odori Story," 2009	474
164. The Hawai'i United Okinawa Association (HUOA) History and Guiding Philosophies, 2010	479
165. Midwest Buddhist Temple, Ginza Festival, 2010	482
166. Dean Koyama, "The Fullness of Obon," 2010	485

Part XIV Korean American   489

167. Han Bong Soon, Immigration Interview, 1940	489
168. Lucy, "'Lucy' Sails for 'Frisco," 1954	493
169. This Life of Mine—Chong Chin Joe, 1967	496
170. Koreans in Mexico—Gail Whang Desmond, 1975	500
171. Sook-ja Kim, Interview by Myong-ja Lee Kwon, February–April 1996	502
172. Sonia Sunoo, Interview by Anna Charr Kim, January 17, 2001	505
173. Phil Yu, "Keepin' It Real with the Rice Fields," 2001	507
174. You Mi Kim, "Diary of a Sex Slave," 2006	508
175. Min Jung Kim, "Bi-Racial Couples—A First Person Account," 2007	512
176. Letters on the Korean "Lost Colony," 2009	514
177. Jee Suh, "Immigrants with Accents Still Being Treated with Disrespect," 2009	517
178. Korean American Adoptees	518
A. Jae Ran Kim, "Cooking Lessons," 2006	518
B. Jenny Ryun Foster, "Once Upon a Time in America: An Introduction," 2002	520
C. Kimberly Waters, "How to Be a Korean from the South," 2009	522

Part XV Lao American   525

179. Bounheng Inversin, "Laotian Americans in the News," 2001	525
180. *Lao Angelz Newsletter*, "Our Mission," 2001	525
181. Interview with Ou Chiew Saetern; Letter From His Sister, 2003	527
182. Bryan Thao Worra, "Asian-Americans Must Speak Up," 2005	531
183. Xuliyah Potong, "Adopted American," 2007	533

184. Takashi Matsumoto, "Finding Takashi," 2008 — 536
185. Nye Noona (Ginger), "The Face of Laotians (Americans) Are Changing," 2008 — 538

Part XVI   Malaysian American — 541

186. Shymala Dason, "Outside His Window," 2010 — 541

Part XVII   Pakistani American — 545

187. "Salman Ahmad in the News," 2006 — 545
188. Wajahat Ali, "The Perpoose Story: The Minority Preschool Experience," 2008 — 547
189. Asma Hasan, Interview by Nadia Mohammad, 2008 — 551
190. Mariam Malik, "We Are All Punjabi," 2009 — 554
191. Aliya Latif, Interview by Yara Souza, 2009 — 556
192. Aman Ali and Bassan Tariq, "Day 30: Celebration," 2009 — 558
193. Nadia Mohammad, "Date Me, I'm a Racist," 2009 — 560
194. Shazia Kamal, "Color-Coded Confessions: Background Shades of the Marriage Process," 2009 — 563
195. Sarah Jawaid, "Generational Change in Accepting Mental Health Needs," 2010 — 565
196. Asma Uddin, "Exploring Gender and Islam," 2010 — 567
197. Imrana Zaman, "My Sound of Music," 2010 — 573
198. Farha Hasan, "The Decree," 2010 — 574
199. Nyla Hashmi and Fatima Monkush, Interview by Nadia Mohammad, 2010 — 577

Part XVIII   Sri Lankan American — 581

200. Vasugi V. Ganeshananthan, "It's All in a Name," 1999 — 581
201. Poornima Apte, "9/11: A Mother Remembers," 2004 — 583
202. Dilini Palamakumbura, "My Dream," 2005 — 584

Part XIX   Thai American — 587

203. Jeffery Boonmee, Interview by David Tanner, 1995 — 587
204. Panrit "Gor" Daoruang, "Living in America," 2003 — 589
205. Pueng Vongs, "Unrest in the Homeland Awakens Thai American Community," 2006 — 591
206. Protests over the Berkeley Thai Temple, 2009 — 592
    A. Gino Baltazar, "The Berkeley Thai Temple: A Different Perspective," 2009 — 593
    B. Dionne Jirachaikitti, "Thai American Organizing and the Berkeley Thai Temple," 2009 — 594

Part XX   Vietnamese American — 597

207. Lang Ngan, Interview by Guy Kawasaki, 1993 — 597
208. Betty Tu Kwok and Henry Kwok, Interview by David Tanner, 1994 — 598

209. Club O'Noodles, "Laughter from the Children of War," Performance Program, 1996 — 604
210. Hi-Tek Demonstration Flyer, "America Has Freedom," 1999 — 606
211. Tuan-Rishard F. Schneider, "Adoptee Connection," 2001 — 607
212. Anh Do and Hieu Tran Phan, "Camp Z30-D: The Survivors: 1975–2001," 2001 — 609
213. Trista Joy Goldberg, "Trista," 2004 — 612
214. Diu Hoang, "The Back of the Hand: Vietnamese American Nail Salons," 2006 — 614
215. Sumeia Williams, "Memorial Inheritance," 2006 — 616
216. Kevin Minh Allen, "Eggroll," 2006 — 617
217. Bác Nguyễn Vân Phương, Interview by Xuan Thanh Le, 2008 — 619
218. Tuyet Duong, "Family Immigration Law: It's Broke So Let's Fix It," 2008 — 621
219. Andrew Lam, "SSH . . . Thanks-Givin . . . Thanksgiving," 2009 — 623
220. Julie Pham, "Modern Day McCarthyism: The Case of Duc Tan," 2009 — 625

Part XXI Multiheritage Asian American — 629

221. Onoto Watanna/Winnifred Eaton, *Miss Numè of Japan: A Japanese-American Romance*, 1899 — 630
222. Sui Sin Far/Edith Maude Eaton, "Its Wavering Image," 1912 — 635
223. Alison Kim, Interview by Jacquelyn Marie, 2001 — 639
224. "Interview with 'Peaches,'" by Eddy Zheng, 2004 — 641
226. David Fleming, "Hello, I'm Japanese: Scott Fujita Is Helping to Bring the Saints Back to Life. And That's the Least Surprising Thing about Him," 2006 — 644
227. Chloe Sun, "Against Overwhelming Odds: Chinese Women in Ministry," 2007 — 649
228. Jeff, "I want to be wasian!" 2008 — 652
229. Simone Momove Fujita, "Little Momo in the Big Apple," 2008 — 653
230. Laylaa Abdul-Khabir, "Living the Mixed Life: Growing Up as a Black Chinese Muslim in America," 2008 — 657
231. Jade Keller, "On Being Part Other," 2009 — 660
232. Deborah Jiang Stein, "What's with the Jewish Man-Asian Woman Connection, Anyway? Asian-Jewish Fusion: More Questions than Answers," 2010 — 661
233. Wardell Townsend, "Thoughts on Being Japanese African American," 2010 — 664
234. Sara Sarasohn, "I Cook Nothing Like My Mother," 2010 — 667
235. Yayoi Lena Winfrey, "Fire Lily," 2010 — 671

Bibliography — 675
About the Editors — 681
Index — 683

Preface

Voices of the Asian American and Pacific Islander Experience is a two-volume collection of more than 200 primary source documents, dating from the early 19th century to today. It covers multiple geographic areas of the United States and represents a diverse range of perspectives on religion, ethnicity, gender, sexuality, class, immigration, politics, and family and community life. Each document is prefaced by a short introduction providing information on the author, as well as a brief discussion of the historical and cultural context in which it was written. The anthology includes a wide variety of sources, among them interviews, poems, personal essays, eulogies, legislation, court records, recipes, selections from novels, and movie script excerpts. We have placed a heavy emphasis on contemporary voices, highlighting new forms of media like blog posts and e-zine articles. In addition to the documents, *Voices of the Asian American and Pacific Islander Experience* contains an introduction laying out some theoretical concepts and a short narrative of Asian American history; as well as a chronology, a selected bibliography of both books and websites, and an index. It is the most comprehensive collection of Asian American sources to date.

The majority of the documents are from Hawai'i, the West and Northeast Coasts, where the highest concentration of Asian Americans have historically resided and continue to live today. However, we also have included documents from Alaska, the Midwest, and the Southeast, which illustrate the unique experiences and perspectives of Asian Pacific Americans who live in these regions. The anthology has two sections; the first is organized chronologically by documents applicable to Asian Americans in general, and the second is organized by ethnicity. We have been careful to include more recent groups of Asian Americans, especially immigrants from Southeast Asia, Pakistan, and the Himalayas. Although they presently comprise a small percentage of the overall Asian American population, their histories, immigration experiences, and growing communities are adding both familiar and new elements to contemporary Asian Pacific America.

Although the majority of the documents are written by Asian and Pacific Americans, some of the sources, especially ones dating from the 19th century, represent outsider perspectives on different Asian ethnic communities. For instance, it is difficult to find English-language sources written by early Chinese immigrants. The majority of these immigrants, laborers and women who were often brought to America against their will, were illiterate and left behind no written record.

Nevertheless, there exist a few exceptions. Japanese sailor Joseph Heco (born Hizoko Hamada) published a diary chronicling his life in the United States and his 1858 naturalization. The *Golden Hills' News* is another unusual source. The first Chinese-language newspaper published in the United States, it provides a glimpse into the world of San Francisco's Chinatown merchants during the mid-19th century.

However, because these kinds of documents are rare, scholars must supplement them by using non-Chinese voices to fill the gaps left in the historical record. Therefore, we have included a variety of perspectives written by Anglo-Americans about the Chinese in America. These include speeches given by xenophobic labor organizers, newspaper articles spouting anti-Chinese vitriol, and pieces of legislation like the Chinese Exclusion Act, which all reveal the extent of the hostility Chinese Americans faced. In contrast, white missionaries—like Presbyterian minister William Speer; the mission worker Donaldina Cameron; and teacher Marian Bokee—reveal much more sympathetic and nuanced treatments of the Chinese Americans among whom they lived and labored. At the same time, these well-meaning people were not immune to mainstream assumptions about the inferiority of Chinese culture. Even the most sympathetic accounts are rife with rhetoric bemoaning Chinese barbarity, heathen behavior, and unmanly characteristics. In some ways, this racialized imagery affirmed romanticized visions of white missionaries hoping to play the role of heroic and virtuous redeemer rescuing godless heathens in Chinatown. It is essential to acknowledge such biases when studying outsider accounts.

In addition to these first-person documents, we also have included excerpts of court cases, ordinances, and laws, all of which, until recently, had been composed and enacted by Caucasian politicians and judges. We have been careful to incorporate both restrictive legislation, meant to exclude and discriminate against Asian Pacific Americans, as well as legislation meant to rectify past injustices and safeguard Asian Pacific Americans' constitutional rights.

As with any work that attempts to cover a category as broad and diverse as Asian Pacific Americans, difficult choices must be made about how to define said category. Among Asian Pacific American scholars, there continues to be considerable debate over whether Pacific Islanders, including Native Americans, should be categorized as Asian American. Some scholars argue that in terms of ethnicity, history, socioeconomic situation, and experience with colonialism, Pacific Islanders are more closely aligned with Native Americans. However, *Voices of the Asian American and Pacific Islander Experience* includes Native Hawai'ians, American Samoans, and Guamanians, for a few reasons. First, since there is no definitive consensus on the issue, we have decided to err on the side of inclusion. Second, in part due to the high levels of intermarriage and the prevalence of mixed-race identity, particularly in Hawai'i, some Pacific Islanders themselves identify as Asian American. All of the contemporary contributors to this anthology have submitted their work by choice. Nevertheless, for all the romanticized notions of Hawai'i as a cosmopolitan and racially harmonious place, the relationship between Asian settlers and Pacific Islanders has been fraught with ethnic tension, colonialism, economic exploitation, and political inequity. We have tried to reflect this in the documents we have selected.

The anthology is divided into 21 parts, most organized chronologically by ethnic group. While this may reflect much of the ethnic diversity of Asian Pacific America, it does not encompass the totality of Asian Pacific American identities. Therefore, we have included General Asian American and Multiheritage Asian American, documents that reflect APA identities not based on ethnic affiliation. Although we use ethnicity and chronology as the major organizational frameworks for this anthology, several important themes emerged that crossed both ethnic affiliation and time.

One major theme that runs through the anthology is the ways in which the immigration experience impacts both individual and community-based identity formation. Early Asian immigrants were mostly laborers, working on Hawai'ian plantations and on farms, on railroads, and in mines across the West Coast of America. They sought entry into a nation whose growing xenophobia found its voice in restrictive racist immigration policies that explicitly named them as unwanted intruders. U.S. Immigration Service interview transcripts of prospective Chinese immigrants, such as Yee Wee Thing, Huey Jing, and Huey Fong, paint a vivid picture of not only the struggles they faced, but also the strategies they employed to overcome racist, xenophobic policies. The decision to cross the Pacific was often not by choice. Many Asian migrants were fleeing deprivation, persecution, and war in their homelands. Pang Xiong Sirirathasuk Sikoun, whose brothers were killed by the Pathet Lao in the 1960s; Vatey Seng, who escaped from Cambodia during Pol Pot's regime in the 1970s; and Prem Tamang, who fled Nepalese Maoists in the 1980s, are three examples of people whose lives in America were shadowed by harrowing experiences in their homelands. Still others came as war brides, marrying American servicemen and settling in areas with little social or cultural support. Yayoi Winfrey's essay about her mother, a Japanese woman who married an African American pilot; and Daniel Clark's interview with his grandmother, who moved from the island of Okinawa to the mountains of rural West Virginia with her American husband, highlight the challenges these women faced. The diverse stories contained in *Voices of the Asian American and Pacific Islander Experience* raise questions about how different experiences actually impact immigrants' lives: their desire and ability to Americanize, how the effects of emotional and psychological trauma from war or persecution affect their communities, and the legacy these experiences leave for their children and grandchildren.

A second major theme that spans all ethnic groups is the desire for cultural preservation. Maintaining a certain level of cultural continuity and homogeneity is of great concern to immigrant and ethnic communities. Cultural continuity serves both to sustain ties with the homeland and to create a cohesive community that provides protection against an often-hostile society. Cultural preservation takes many forms, from the retention of language skills, to the maintenance of traditional gender roles and family hierarchies, to the upholding of religious beliefs and practices. All of these are fought for tenaciously by some—and are contested, adapted, redefined, and abandoned by others. Ultimately, however, the complicated process of preserving homeland culture in the United States results in the creation of something new. Over time, heterogeneous communities spanning multiple generations, mixing older traditions with new ones emerge.

For example, several authors in this anthology discuss their deliberate and concrete attempts to create tangible links to their past, preserving what they can of their Asian heritage in the United States. Sifu Cheung Shu Pui mourns the loss of the Chinese language and holidays in his immigrant neighborhood, but he teaches folk arts, including kung fu and the lion dance, in the hope that at least a small part of his cultural heritage may be passed down to American-born Chinese. Similarly, Shuyuan Li performs traditional Beijing opera in Philadelphia, and Charlene Gima learns traditional Okinawan Bon dances in Hawai'i. Perhaps the easiest and most maintained link to ethnic culture is food. Cultural foods themselves offer an intriguing physical link to liminal and tenuous identities. For some, such as Sheng Yang, food represents a concrete symbol of her Hmong identity. She cultivates and cooks with Hmong herbs and vegetables brought over from Laos, and she buys her chicken from Hmong farmers, who raise and butcher the animals using long-established techniques. For Sara Sarasohn, who is half Japanese, certain foods provide an emotional connection to her mother's family and history; and when Jae Ran Kim, a Korean American adoptee, learns to cook Korean food, she gets a small sense—a taste—of the culture she never had growing up in a Caucasian household.

Asian American families have attempted to maintain cultural cohesiveness in more intangible ways as well. Nevertheless, both external and internal forces have continually challenged their efforts at cultural maintenance, eventually shifting the very nature of Asian American family structures. For example, in early Chinese American communities, the very definition of family was constantly being reinvented. The Chinese Exclusion Act and laws restricting Chinese women from immigrating to the United States created mostly male communities of uncles and brothers, resulting in the construction of complex—and fictitious—kin networks of paper relatives. For example, Eddie Fung's mother came to the United States as the paper wife of his uncle, who then divorced her so she could marry his brother, her (real) husband. Fung's adopted brothers came over as paper sons of his uncle and never changed their names back to Fung after they reached the United States. Fung himself thought nothing of this convoluted arrangement, "because it was so common in Chinatown." For immigrants in transnational families, far from home with few close relations, extended family networks took on an even greater importance. This is as true today, for immigrants such as Shymala Dason, as it was in the 19th century. Dason writes about contemporary reverse migration, describing immigrants whose family ties are so strong and so compelling that they leave the United States and return to their ancestral homelands.

Conflicts over cultural maintenance most often manifest in friction over the second generation's dating and marriage choices. Kerala-born Mary T. Mathew talks about how she and her daughters navigate between American and Indian social mores, particularly with respect to dating. In their poetry, Indian American Ainee Fatima and Hmong American Noukou Thao explore the tension between their parents' expectations for them to enter arranged marriages and their own conflicted desires about choosing their own spouses and pleasing their families. In their essays, Sweta Srivastava Vikram and Shazia Kamal denounce the pressure for South Asian Americans to select "fair-skinned" spouses, and question media representations of Western romance. Imrana Zaman's father even goes as far as banning

The Sound of Music, fearing it will expose his children to liberal attitudes about picking a partner without parental approval.

Negotiating evolving gender roles has played an integral role in the development of Asian American families. In their own ways, Apolonia Dangzalan and Maggie Gee both challenged contemporary views about women and work: Dangzalan by embracing her uncommon status as a Depression-era Filipina entrepreneur and Gee by joining the elite World War II Women Airforce Service Pilots, one of only two Chinese Americans to be accepted.

Chloe Sun explains how women are breaking through the religious and cultural beliefs that circumscribe the role women are able to play in Chinese American churches. Sun's piece also brings to light interesting issues in religion in Asian Pacific American communities. In these communities, religion can function both as a means of assimilation and as a means of maintaining ethnic identity. Although Western missionaries originally brought Christianity to Asia and Asian American communities, over the last few decades Asian American Christianity has emerged as its own movement, self-consciously distinct from mainstream Christianity. Seminary professor Fumitaka Matsuoka's benediction for the Students of Color graduation ceremony reflects how the Asian American community's experience with racism colors their interpretation of Christ's message and the Christian mission. Joy Wong's assertion that her identity as an evangelical Christian is inseparable from her identity as an Asian American woman carves out an identity that refuses to be defined by either race or religion. Both these positions mark a deliberate departure from earlier white missionary philosophies, which held that Christian identity was nearly synonymous with American cultural identity, and that demanded Asian culture be sacrificed in the name of God.

Indigenous Asian religions also evolved once they were imported to the United States. For example, although Japanese American Shin Buddhism still retains a remarkably ethnically homogeneous cast and continues to emphasize Japanese history and cultural festivals, it has steadily transformed itself away from Japanese Shin Buddhism by adopting religious forms and practices from Protestant Christianity. Sanjay Patel's graphic novel version of the Hindu epic Ramayana is a contemporary retelling of an ancient story meant to engage and appeal to young people today. For others such as Rajiv Srinivasan, it is not religious transformation, but the continual struggle over how to reconcile his Hindu faith with his U.S. military career that is at stake. Asma Hasan, a "Muslim feminist cowgirl," defies stereotypes, assumptions, and expectations from all sides. However, these religious permutations do not go uncontested. Debates over authenticity are very emotionally charged when it comes to religion, especially since the line between religion and culture is often blurred in ethnic religious institutions and change represents challenges to first-generation immigrant authority. Farah Akbar notes how second-generation Bangladeshi Americans who attempt to mesh their Muslim faith with their American sensibilities are strongly opposed by traditional imams. Similarly, the Hindu American Foundation's position paper criticizes the "mainstreaming" and "Westernizing" of yoga, which increasingly denudes the practice of its fundamental religious significance. In the end, cultural, ethnic, and religious identities all are inextricably intertwined.

Finally, many of the documents in *Voices of the Asian American and Pacific Islander Experience* explore what happens when ethnic group boundaries are crossed, and assumptions about what it means to be Asian American are challenged. In fact, race and ethnicity have always been fluid categories that have shifted and morphed according to societal context. While the U.S. Naturalization Act of 1790 may have specifically targeted African Americans by restricting naturalization to "free white" immigrants, the Act was used to prevent Chinese immigrants from becoming citizens half a century. However, Japanese immigrants were not officially defined as nonwhite until the Takao Ozawa case in 1922. Joseph Heco, a Japanese sailor who came to the United States in 1837, took advantage of this loophole to become one of the few 19th-century Asian immigrants to obtain American citizenship. The laws generally worked against Asian Pacific Americans, like Bhagat Singh Thind, a Sikh immigrant from northern India. In 1923, the Supreme Court ruled that, geographic and scientific definitions notwithstanding, Indians were not Caucasian "in the common understanding." *United States v. Bhagat Singh Thind* retroactively stripped naturalized Indian immigrants of their citizenship and subjected them to racially restrictive Alien Land Laws. The Thind case is a perfect example of the socially constructed nature of racial and ethnic identities. In fact, laws have been used to redefine the boundaries of race since the 18th century.

Biracial and multiracial Asian Americans further complicate our assumptions about racial and ethnic categories. Historically rejected by both Asian and non-Asian communities alike, mixed-race people were labeled morally and physically deficient by 19th-century sociologists and dismissed as insufficiently Asian by 20th-century activists. The line between Asian and white was so rigid that those who were able would try to "pass" as white. However, over the last few decades, mixed-race Asian Pacific Americans have been speaking out with increasingly louder and more confident voices. Adopting the Hawai'ian name *hapa* as a term of pride, mixed-race Asian Pacific Americans claim and celebrate their multiheritage identities, while simultaneously acknowledging their continuing struggles to be accepted as legitimate members of their ethnic communities. Although the *hapa* movement is relatively recent, multiracial authors have been addressing this issue for over a century. As early as the 1890s, sisters Winnifred and Edith Maude Eaton were exploring their own biracial heritage and condemning American racism and exclusion in short stories and novels. Following in the Eatons' footsteps, a new generation of Asian Pacific Americans are pushing the boundaries of ethnic identification and definition. Simone Fujita, whose Asian American high school classmates did not accept her because of her African American ancestry, found acceptance in college. Blogger Jade Keller muses about what it means to be "authentically" Asian and about her place—and her children's place—in the Thai American community. We have collected these documents under their own "Multiheritage Asian American" category because we feel that these perspectives are unique and important. More importantly, it acknowledges not only the complexity and diversity of racial and ethnic identities, but also the right to self-definition.

This anthology also features the voices of many adopted Asian Americans. For decades, adoptive parents of Asian babies were encouraged to raise their children as if they were not from another country. The adopted children's own cultural and ethnic heritage was erased in the effort to encourage total assimilation. This precipitated deep identity crises for many Asian American adoptees once they were old enough to realize they were not Caucasian (the vast majority of adoptive families are white). With little or no connection to any Asian Americans who could have helped ease them through this transition, many Asian American adoptees felt lost and isolated. In response, Vietnamese adoptees Tuan-Rishard F. Schneider and Trista Joy Goldberg both traveled to Vietnam as adults, looking for connections with their birth country and biological families. Jenny Ryun Foster, adopted from Korea as an infant, also journeyed back to her birth country, where she discovered that although Americans see her as Asian, Koreans see her as American. And then there is the singular story of Scott Fujita, a Caucasian adopted by a Japanese American father. Fujita grew up celebrating Japanese holidays, eating Japanese food, learning about Japanese art and history, and listening to his grandparents' and father's stories about the internment camps. He considers himself to be half Japanese American, reminding us that identity is indeed socially constructed.

Taken together, the documents in this anthology raise the philosophical question: What does it mean to be Asian American? Is it race? Is it ethnic heritage? A common history of being "othered" in the United States? A deliberate embracing of particular cultural practices? Over 20 ethnic groups are represented in this book alone. Each group speaks its own language or dialect, practices its own religion, and creates its own art; each remembers its own distinct history, both in the ancestral homeland and in the United States. Thus, locating a common, unifying Asian American identity is a difficult task. It becomes even more challenging when you compare new Asian immigrants with families who have been in the United States for generations. It becomes even more challenging when you include people with multiple racial and ethnic backgrounds. And it becomes even more challenging when you include individuals who break away from their communities' respective definitions of traditional gender roles, religious beliefs, cultural practices, and sexuality.

Voices of the Asian American and Pacific Islander Experience does not provide an easy definition of what it means to be Asian American. Instead, we have included as many different perspectives as possible, in an effort to present a picture of an ever-evolving collection of individuals, families, and communities—a collection of people who are continually redefining what it means to be Asian Pacific American.

Introduction

How do we come to understand the richness, diversity, and complexity of the Asian American and Pacific Islander experience? This is the primary question that *Voices of the Asian American and Pacific Islander Experience* seeks to address. The Asian American experience cannot be summed up in easy platitudes about immigrants yearning for a better life, the difficulties of cultural adaptation, or proclamations about Asian American success. This is merely the political rhetoric and discourse that surrounds the most commonly pronounced and digested ideas about Asian Pacific Americans. The experience of Asians and Pacific Islanders in America is much more than an immigrant story, much more than a story about becoming modern-day Horatio Algers. It is a transnational story that crosses national, social, cultural, and political boundaries. To understand the Asian Pacific American experience in its totality, we must examine how the tectonic shifts in political economic systems, technology, and war were paralleled by correspondingly massive shifts in Asian Pacific American cultural forms, social institutions, family and community formation, and political organizing.

Yet before we can even begin to tackle this question, we must ask an even more fundamental question. What is Asian American? What does it actually mean to be Asian American or Pacific Islander? Until very recently, the term *Asian American* did not even exist. However, the idea of Asia has long existed in the Western imagination. As historian Gary Okihiro has observed, the constellation of cultural ideas that surround Asia and Asians in the West can be traced all the way back to Greek ideas about the Orient. Starting with Greek philosophers like Hippocrates and written texts about Alexander the Great's conquests in Asia, and continuing on in the writings of Marco Polo and the widely disseminated travel guide *The Travels of Sir John Mandeville*, Europeans created a powerful image of Asia. Even Christopher Columbus admired the Mandeville texts.[1] This imagined Asia was not merely a collection of randomly assorted stereotypes, but rather a way of knowing Asia and Asians.

Okihiro's work builds on the ideas of literary scholar Edward Said's immensely influential work. In 1979, Said published *Orientalism*, in which he argued that the West had essentially created the East. Through the complex of information produced by colonial administrators, writers, scientists, and others, Europeans came to believe they knew "Orientals" better than Orientals knew themselves. In essence, they became experts on the Orient, what scholars today call Orientalists. These experts defined what the Orient was, who was Oriental, and what Orientals were like. The knowledge that Europeans created gave them power. They defined the Orient and Orientals as everything Europeans were not. Orientals were mysterious, mystical, depraved, cunning, deceitful, feminine, and exotic. If Orientals were these things, Europeans were the opposite—civilized, masculine, honorable, and modern.[2] Although Said's work focused on 18th- and 19th-century British and French knowledge production about the Middle East (what they called the Orient), scholars have discovered similar processes in respect to European and American knowledge production about Southeast Asia, East Asia, the Pacific Islands, and South Asia. The creation of this imagined feminized Asia would become the basis of how Americans would come to think about and deal with Asians.

Europeans who arrived in the Americas during the 17th–19th centuries already came with preconceived notions about nonwhite people. These ideas were molded and shaped through the knowledge created through colonial conquest. Europeans brought these Orientalist ideas about the "darker races" with them to the Americas. In colonial America, these ideas were again reshaped in the context of conflicts with Native Americans and African slavery. Three years after the Constitution was ratified, Congress passed the Naturalization Act of 1790, which limited naturalized citizenship to free white men who owned property. This effectively marginalized Asians, Africans, women, and other nonwhite persons, ensuring they were politically disenfranchised in the United States. The most salient distinction in American society became the divide between free and unfree. In 17th- and 18th-century colonial America, *unfree* was a broad term that included white European migrants who arrived as indentured servants.[3] However, by the late 18th century, *unfree* became synonymous with African slavery. Asian Americans were effectively made unfree through the denial of citizenship rights.

The process of "othering" and marginalizing Asian Americans also served an important function in American society. According to historian John Kuo Wie Tchen, in mid- to late 19th-century New York City, P. T. Barnum and other entrepreneurs put Asian bodies on display for public consumption in dime museums. These were not museums in the modern sense. For instance, Barnum's American museum did not have paintings, sculptures, or geological rock formations and stuffed mammoths. Instead, it displayed people. People like Charles Stratton, known better as Tom Thumb, who was two feet and one inch tall, and Ursa the Bear Lady, whose stunted and stocky legs forced her to walk hunched on all fours like a bear. Alongside the elephant woman and the world's fattest man stood the Siamese twins Chang and Eng, the Chinese dwarf, and the Chinese giant. Barnum's American museum was not the only place that displayed Orientals as strange and exotic entertainment. Peters's Great Chinese Museum also featured exotic and strange Oriental people. The commercial success of such "museums" capitalized on the physical and cultural differences between white bodies and Oriental bodies. Asians were perceived as foreign, strange, and weird.[4] On the West Coast, Asian labor, particularly Chinese labor, became synonymous with unfree coolie labor during the late 19th century. In addition, Asian labor was seen as hyperefficient because it was believed Asians lived in an uncivilized state; rumors about Chinese eating rats and living 40 men in one tiny room abounded. Of course, Chinese decisions to work and live in the same place and living frugally had more to do with desires to save money than being uncivilized heathens.⁵

It is also important to remember that ideas about white superiority were created in the context of European and American imperialism. It was Europeans who struck out to Africa, Asia, and the Americas. Europeans developed a global colonial system built on exploiting the natural resources of their colonies, including the labor of colonized bodies. In this globalized market economy, European colonial powers were metropoles, the center of the colonial system, and colonies made up the periphery. The peripheral colonial states provided raw materials like cotton, spices, tobacco, and precious metals that were processed into commodities in the metropoles. These commodities would then not only be marketed in the metropoles but also shipped back and sold to wealthy elites in the peripheral colonies.⁶

In this sense, America's original 13 colonies were peripheral states in this global colonial system. The American colonies supplied Britain with raw materials like tobacco and furs. The colonies were, for the British, a source of natural wealth. However, extracting these natural resources required land and labor. The land was forcibly taken from Native American tribes, and the labor came initially from indentured workers but then increasingly from African slaves. After the Revolutionary War, Americans continued to wrest away land from native peoples and, in the 19th century, from Mexico. They also continued to exploit African American slave labor and increasingly European and Asian immigrant labor. The mythology of frontier farmers and the taming of the West exist in direct contradiction to the reality of American colonialism. Westward expansion was American colonialism. Once Americans reached the Pacific Coast at the end of the 19th century, they continued their imperial march by annexing the Hawai'ian Islands, Guam, and the Philippines.

When the United States entered the Spanish American War, it claimed to be fighting to free Cuba from despotic Spanish rule. The war, however, was fought on two fronts, in Cuba and in the Philippines. After soundly defeating the Spanish in 1898, the United States granted Cuba its independence, but American international trade interests in Asia resulted in Philippine colonization. The United States actually bought the Philippines from Spain for $20 million after the war. However, the Filipinos would not go quietly under American rule. Under the leadership of Emilio Aguinaldo, the Filipinos fought valiantly for their independence against overwhelming odds. The war turned brutally racial very quickly. Americans called Filipinos savage monkeys and used an early and more brutal version of water boarding on captured Filipino fighters. Though Theodore Roosevelt declared victory in the Philippine American War in 1901, sporadic fighting continued until 1914.

Beginning in 1901, the Americans quickly began building a colonial system in the Philippines. The American colonial system was based on the idea of benevolent assimilation. Filipinos were taught that all things American were good and modern, while everything Filipino was primitive and backwards. All social, cultural, and political institutions were modeled on American examples. Everything from schools to hospitals to local governing bodies was copied from American models. So when Filipinos began migrating in larger numbers during the 1910s and 1920s, many expected to be warmly welcomed as fellow Americans. What they found was racism and discrimination.[7] For example, we have reprinted an article from the *Filipino Forum*, a Filipino American newspaper from the 1920s, in which Filipino student Antonio E. Velasco describes the harsh sting of American racism he felt at a school dance when his female classmates repeatedly rejected his invitations to dance.

The American colonial experiment also resulted in the crossing of national and cultural boundaries, what scholars call *transnationalism*. During the Philippine American War, some of the African American soldiers sent to fight the Filipino rebellion ended up switching sides and fighting with the Filipinos against the Americans. African American soldiers saw that white Americans treated the Filipinos with the same racism and contempt as they did blacks in America. These men, known as buffalo soldiers, had been shipped from the southwestern United States where they had fought against Native Americans in the last of the Indian wars. Some of these buffalo soldiers remained in the Philippines after the war, eventually marrying Filipino women and assimilating into Philippine society. Some of these men returned to the United States with their Filipino brides in the 1920s and 1930s. Evangeline Canonizado Buell, a descendant of a buffalo soldier and his Filipino wife, provides readers a glimpse into this transnational, transcultural world. In "Excerpt from Evangeline Canonizado Buell's *Twenty-Five Chickens and a Pig for a Bride: Growing up in a Filipino Immigrant Family*," Buell recounts the story of her Filipino/buffalo soldier family and their amazing transnational story.

However, colonialism also had devastating results in the Philippines and in Hawai'i. In Hawai'i, the first Westerners began to arrive in the late 18th century. Contact with the West had catastrophic effects on native Hawai'ian society. Like American Indians, Native Hawai'ians had no immunity to Western diseases such as smallpox and measles, which devastated the native population. Americans, particularly missionaries, quickly came to dominate the political, economic, and social life of the islands. American missionaries acted as advisors to the royal court and nobility. By the mid-19th century, missionaries who had come with the intention of saving souls were forced to turn to more secular pursuits when church missionary boards stopped funding their missions in Hawai'i. Missionary families soon discovered that sugar and pineapples were profitable cash crops. The children and grandchildren of these missionaries soon came to form a ruling oligarchy in Hawai'i called the Big Five. It was the members of the Big Five families who forced King David Kalakaua, at gunpoint, to sign the Bayonet Constitution of 1877, which effectively stripped the monarch of most of his power. In 1893, members of the Big Five families plotted against the monarchy again. This time, they instigated a coup d'état and overthrew the Hawai'ian monarchy for good. The Big Five families took complete political control of the islands and pressed for Hawai'i's annexation by the United States, which was granted in 1898.[8] "Lili'uokalani, *Hawai'i's Story by Hawai'i's Queen*" highlights the tragedy of Hawai'i's annexation by the United States. In this document, the last reigning queen of Hawai'i recounts the massive economic, social, cultural, and political upheavals created by the American incursion into the islands. American annexation and the loss of Hawai'ian sovereignty devastated the native Hawai'ian population and culture.

What Americans discovered in the West and in Hawai'i were vast natural resources. Sugar and pineapples became sources of wealth for the descendants of missionaries in Hawai'i. In California and other western states, there were vast reserves of gold and precious metals, miles of arable farmland, and an abundance of both lumber and seafood. However, the natural resources of the West Coast required massive amounts of labor to extract. Fruit and vegetable agriculture, mining, lumber, sugar production, and fishing were labor-intensive industries. Much of the labor needed to harvest these natural resources came from imported Asian labor. In 1853, Hawai'ians and part Hawai'ians accounted for 97 percent of the population on the islands, whites composed 2 percent, and Chinese were less than .5 percent. Seventy years later in 1923, Hawai'ians and part Hawai'ians were 16.3 percent of the population, whites 7.7 percent, Chinese 9.2 percent, Japanese 42.7 percent, Portuguese 10.6 percent, Puerto Ricans 2.2 percent, Koreans 1.9 percent, and Filipinos 8.2 percent.[9] Life was hard on the plantations. Workers eked out a living, working and sending remittances to families back in their homelands. Meanwhile, in their new home, the plantation-owning employers created a paternalistic economic and social system that stratified workers and paid differential wages based on national background and gender. Conflicts between different ethnicities were common, although cooperation between groups existed as well. Workers often went on strike to protest working conditions and wage differentials. Though most strikes were ethnic specific, some involved interethnic cooperation, like the combined Japanese and Filipino strike of 1920.[10] In "Excerpt from Angeles Monrayo's *Tomorrow's Memories: A Diary*," 12-year-old Angeles Monrayo gives readers a first-person account of a 1924 strike by Filipino plantation workers in Hawai'i.

Unlike contemporary Asian immigration, these early migrants were heavily male. These men faced harsh working conditions, low pay, and open hostility and contempt from many Americans. While industrialists like Leland Stanford and large farmers wanted cheap Asian labor, many Anglos on the West Coast believed that the Asians were not only taking jobs from whites but were also social and moral pariahs. Much of the anger directed at Chinese laborers came from racializations that hinged on supposed Asian hyperefficiency. Chinese could work for less money than white workers because they needed less to survive. For example, it was commonly believed that Chinese needed less food to survive; they supplemented their diet with rats and other vermin so they needed less money to survive; and that Chinese lived 10 or 12 in a room because they did not believe in nuclear families. Many anti-Asian clubs and organizations, such as the Sons of the Golden West and the Asiatic Exclusion League, were established during the late 19th and early 20th centuries. In California, the hostility was so rampant that a political party called the Workingmen's Party was formed in 1877. Their sole political platform was "The Chinese Must Go." Ironically, the party's primary supporters were themselves first- and second-generation Irish, Slavic, and other non-western European immigrants who were not fully accepted by native-born Anglos of western European extraction. Readers can get a sense of this nativist hostility in "An Address from the Workingmen of San Francisco to Their Brothers throughout the Pacific Coast, 1888."

This popular anger manifested itself in a series of exclusion laws and racist legal strictures targeting Asians. California, in particular, passed a series of discriminatory laws against the Chinese. For example, the Foreign Miner's Act (1852) targeted Chinese miners and forced them to pay a tax of $3 per month. Chinese even had to pay a $2.50 poll tax in California, just for being Chinese. California also passed an Alien Land Law in 1913, the first of 10 western states to pass such a law. These state laws typically restricted aliens who were ineligible for citizenship from renting or owning property for more than three years. Three states later passed Alien Land Laws during World War II. These laws were aimed at Japanese immigrant farmers like Hiroshi Shikuma, who had found a niche in vegetable and fruit growing. Shikuma had become a prominent strawberry grower in Pajaro Valley, California, during the early to mid-20th century. Included in *Voices of the Asian American and Pacific Islander Experience,* is the excerpt "Hiroshi Shikuma, Interview by Randell Jarrell, 1986," in which Shikuma recalls his family's early farming efforts.

Many other discriminatory laws were instituted as well. In 1875, the federal government passed the Page Law, which severely restricted the immigration of Asian women into the United States. Several years later it passed the Chinese Exclusion Act of 1882, the only immigration law in U.S. history that singled out a specific racial or ethnic group and barred them from entry. The Chinese Exclusion Act was renewed twice. In 1902, the final renewal extended the ban on Chinese laborers indefinitely. There was also the Gentlemen's Agreement of 1907–1908, which was actually an informal treaty that severely restricted Japanese and Korean immigration into the United States.[11] The 1917 Immigration Act created an Asiatic Barred Zone, which stretched from India to Japan, and restricted immigration from any country within this zone. Finally, there was the 1924 National Origins Act, which was the most restrictive immigration law in U.S. history. This immigration law remained in place until 1965. Readers will find the original text of most of these laws in this anthology. Together, these texts reveal the level of political and government power that was mobilized against Asian immigrants.

However, Asian Americans did not just sit quietly. They responded to the hostility in many different ways. In "Letters of Kwang Chang Ling: The Chinese Side of the Chinese Question," Chinese American Kwang Chang Ling responds to the anti-Chinese hostility in San Francisco. Kwang Chang Ling's letters were published in the San Francisco *Argonaut* in 1878. Ling's letters are unique because documents by Chinese authors from this time were rarely written in English. The letter not only provides insight into a Chinese American perspective but also highlights one of the ways Chinese resisted their marginalized status.

While public responses like Ling's letters were rare, Asian Americans resisted discrimination and oppression in less recognizable ways as well. Chinese immigrants took the opportunity presented by the 1906 San Francisco earthquake to circumvent the Chinese exclusion laws. The fires that burned for three days after the quake destroyed virtually all the immigration records in San Francisco. This enabled the Chinese to claim citizenship, a practice seldom used before 1906. They claimed they had wives and children in China. These claimed children became known as "paper sons," and they became the primary conduit for Chinese immigration until 1965.[12] However, immigration officials suspected that the Chinese were falsely claiming citizenship and began extremely detailed interrogations of all Chinese claims. "The Case of Huey Jing and Huey Fong, 1913," reveals the extent to which Chinese Americans and immigration officials tried to outwit each other.

The "Yee Wee Thing Betrayal Letter, 1920," exposes another fascinating and often-untold aspect of the paper son story. In a letter to immigration officials, Dea Goon Foo accuse a fellow Chinese, Yee Wee Thing, of being a paper son. Despite Anglo-American assumptions that the Chinese were a secluded and tightly knit community, it is clear from this document that there were conflicts within the Chinese community. Moreover, it is clear that some Chinese were not afraid to use state authority to settle individual disputes.

Early Japanese and Korean immigrants, who were overwhelmingly male, circumvented restrictive immigration laws by utilizing the 1907 Gentlemen's Agreement stipulation that allowed them to bring over "picture bride wives." The advent of photography created a modern twist on traditional arranged marriages and allowed these men to start families in Hawai'i and the U.S. mainland. Men and women exchanged pictures and letters through a matchmaker and if both parties agreed, overseas migrants sent the money required for their new bride's passage to Hawai'i or the United States. Men saved up their money for years to pay for both the matchmaker and the passage. The women who came to America through this process became known as picture brides because of the exchange of photographs used in the marriage transaction.[13] A significant number of Japanese and Korean women arrived in America as picture brides. However, as American nativism grew in the early 20th century, this loophole was closed with the passage of the 1924 National Origins Act. Although this was a modern adaptation of the old tradition of arranged marriages, it is perhaps not that different from our modern-day Internet dating services.

The advent of picture brides also brings us back to the theme of transnationalism. Studying the records of picture brides and immigrants reveals how many Asian immigrants did indeed travel back and forth between their ancestral homelands and their new homeland. This is not surprising considering Asian American pioneers to both Hawai'i and the mainland did not arrive with dreams of settling permanently in the United States. Rather, the early Chinese, Japanese, Filipino, Korean, and Punjabi Sikh migrants came with visions of earning money and returning to their homelands as wealthy men. In addition, their families—wives, children, parents, siblings—remained in their ancestral homelands. The whole purpose of coming to America was to send remittances home to their families. In this sense, early Asian migrants were both looking forward and looking backwards. Their lives spanned oceans and continents. The immigration interviews we have included of Japanese picture bride Ryu Kishima and Korean picture bride Han Bong Soon illustrate perfectly the transnational nature of Asian immigrant lives. They also reveal the incredibly stringent criteria that the government used in deciding whether a migrant could reenter the United States or not. Picture brides and other early Asian immigrants often returned to their homelands to visit relatives and manage their personal and business affairs. When they returned, they faced immigration officials who were deeply suspicious of their legal status. In the case of Ryu Kishima, she lost her case for readmission. However, Han Bong Soon was able to reenter but only after a difficult appeals process. The transnational nature of Asian American lives was not limited to travel across national boundaries. For instance, in "Tuck Wo & Company Bankruptcy Case, 1909," the death of Leong Kung in July 1900 demonstrated that Tuck Wo, the business he managed, had several copartners, none of whom resided in the United States. Eventually, Tuck Wo & Company was declared bankrupt and all its possessions sold at auction to pay off its debtors.

On the other hand, Koreans and Punjabi Sikhs created transnational communities that focused on freeing their homelands from colonial rule. Overseas Koreans and Sikhs donated much of their earnings to organizations fighting for independence of their homelands. Korea had been colonized by Japan in 1910, while India had long been under British rule. Though their numbers were small, the early Punjabi Sikh migrants were active in the Gadar Party, a transnational Indian independence organization.[14] Similarly, Koreans joined independence organizations such as the Korean National Association (KNA) and saw education and hard work as essential components of the movement. The KNA not only collected donations to support the independence movement and the Korean Provisional Government in exile, but also served as a fraternal and community organization that helped new immigrants adjust to life in America.[15] Koreans in Hawai'i and the mainland organized around the three leaders of the overseas Korean Independence Movement: Dosan Ahn Ch'ang Ho, Pak Yong Man, and Syngman Rhee. The three leaders advocated different strategies for obtaining Korean independence and followers of each fought bitterly with each other.[16] The divisions created by the Korean independence movement are reflected in "Letters on the Korean 'Lost Colony,' 2009." In this letter, Dr. William T. Chu reminisces about this early life picking fruit in the Kim Brothers' orchard, his employers' fervent support of Dosan Ahn Ch'ang Ho, and the political divisions created by the movement.

Early Filipino immigrants found life in America just as difficult as their Asian compatriots did. They were increasingly recruited when the numerous exclusion laws effectively choked off Asian labor to the United States. Employers took advantage of Filipinos' legal status as U.S. nationals, which allowed them to enter the United States without restrictions. Their numbers peaked in the decade prior to the Great Depression. Many worked as seasonal laborers—as migrant farmworkers and fish and seafood packers in the Alaskan canneries. Many others were employed as domestic servants or as menial laborers. Jobs became increasingly scarce during the 1930s with the onset of the Great Depression and the thousands of Dust Bowl refugees who poured into the farmlands of California looking for work. However, the legacy of American colonial domination, the Great Depression, and racism produced very different responses from early Filipino migrants, or *manongs*. After having learned about American democracy and equality from their American teachers in the Philippines, they arrived fully expecting to be accepted as equals. They quickly found that most white Americans saw Filipinos as inferior "little brown brothers." Filipinos may have been disappointed, but they had learned their lessons about democracy well. This first wave of Filipino migrants became heavily active in labor organizing.[17]

The onset of World War II and later the Cold War became watershed moments for Asian Americans and Pacific Islanders. America's war against fascism and

President Franklin Delano Roosevelt's articulation of the Four Freedoms (freedom of speech, freedom of religion, freedom from fear, freedom from want) encouraged minority groups to demand their rights. Many Asian Americans joined the military and fought for America's freedoms. However, Japanese war propaganda repeatedly criticized the United States for its discriminatory exclusion and citizenship laws against Asians. In this context, American racism against Asians was disingenuous at best and hypocritical at worst. The U.S. government responded by repealing the Chinese Exclusion Act in 1943, ending the more than 70-year ban on Chinese immigration. Three years later the federal government also repealed the 1917 Immigration Act, effectively dissolving the Asiatic Barred Zone. Nevertheless, these moves were largely symbolic. The quotas from the 1924 National Origins Act were kept in place. Although Chinese, Koreans, South Asians, and Filipinos could now enter the United States legally, a 100-person quota was established for each Asian nation. The key change came in the form of naturalization rights. Chinese, Filipinos, Koreans, and South Asians were legally allowed to become naturalized citizens of the United States. The passage of the first War Brides Act in 1945 also opened the door for a new wave of immigrants, the wives of U.S. servicemen. Not only did Asian American veterans marry women from Asia, but as the Cold War progressed, interracial marriages between white and African American GIs and Asian women became more and more common. In many ways, America's international alliances with Asian nations raised Asian American hopes and status in the United States.

For Japanese Americans, World War II would have terribly different consequences. After the Japanese attack on Pearl Harbor, President Roosevelt signed Executive Order 9066 in February 1942. This order created the legal framework for Japanese American internment. The U.S. government, under the military's War Relocation Authority (WRA), created a network of 16 temporary detention centers and 10 permanent camps. More than 120,000 people of Japanese descent were forcibly removed from the West Coast and incarcerated in these camps for the duration of the war. More than half were U.S. citizens. The U.S. government claimed they had removed Japanese Americans for their own safety. Japanese American families lost their businesses, their homes, and everything they had worked so hard to build. The WRA notified the Japanese American community of their impending evacuation by posting notices in areas where Japanese Americans resided. Japanese Americans were told to bring only what they could carry. The document "Instructions to All Persons of Japanese Ancestry Living in the Following Area" gives readers an opportunity to look at these notices firsthand. The internment experience left the Japanese American community with emotional and psychological scars that would last for decades.

In fact, the collective trauma of the camp experience manifested into feelings of deep shame and fear that resulted in a collective community silence about internment. The absence of Japanese American voices obscured the truth about life in the camps, helping to foster the myth that Japanese Americans went quietly into the camps. In fact, there was immense turmoil within the community. Some community members fiercely objected to the violation of their civil rights. The document "Hayao Chuman, Letters and Affadavit, 1946–1967" presents readers with a new perspective on the internment experience. Hayao Chuman was part of the Tule Lake Defense Committee. He, along with his wife, Toshiko, was one of around 5,000 Japanese Americans who renounced their U.S. citizenship. However, many Nisei (second generation) and Sansei (third generation) men joined the military and fought to prove their loyalty—and by extension the loyalty of all Japanese Americans—to the United States as members of the 442nd all-Japanese American battalion. The 442nd is one of the most highly decorated units in U.S. military history. Their sacrifices went a long way in improving the image of Japanese Americans after the war. Others, such as Fred Korematsu, defied the evacuation order through the court system. Korematsu was arrested and tried in federal court. His was one of three court cases that challenged the constitutionality of internment.[18] All three men lost their cases. The courts agreed with the federal government's assertion that military necessity justified suspending the civil rights of its own citizenry.

It would be decades before the Japanese American community finally spoke out about their internment experiences. During the 1980s, the Japanese American community organized a redress and reparations movement to bring public attention to the grave injustice suffered by Japanese Americans and to heal the traumatic wounds caused by internment. Many Sansei (third generation) and Yonsei (fourth generation) Japanese Americans did not even know about internment until their parents and grandparents began speaking out in the 1980s. In 1982, Fred Korematsu applied for a *coram nobis* action to overturn his 1944 conviction. *Coram nobis* applies only to cases in which a "fundamental error" or "manifest injustice" has been committed. Korematsu's case challenged his conviction, claiming that the federal government not only deliberately omitted information but also submitted misleading information in his original case. Judge Marilyn Patel of the San Francisco circuit court agreed and vacated Korematsu's conviction in 1984. The Korematsu case is one of just a handful of successful *coram nobis* cases in U.S. legal history. *Voices of the Asian American and Pacific Islander Experience* includes excerpts of the court records from the case in "Fred Korematsu, Writ of *Coram Nobis*, 1984." These efforts eventually led the U.S. government to publicly apologize for Japanese American internment in 1988. The federal government also offered a restitution of $20,000 to each family that was interned.[19]

The post-World War II period quickly devolved into a budding cold war between the United States and the Soviet Union. The Cold War would come to radically reshape relations between Asia and the United States. Asia quickly became an area of tremendous concern for American leaders. In China, Mao Tse Tung and the Communists had defeated Chiang Kai-Shek's Nationalist Party in 1949. Kim Il Sung began a war on the Korean Peninsula, and Ho Chi Minh was fighting against French colonization in Vietnam. The need for allies to buttress the fight against the Communist threat required a much larger American presence in Asia. The U.S. government continued the dismantling of racist Asian exclusion laws that had begun during World War II. In 1952, the United States passed the McCarran-Walter Act, also known as the Immigration and Nationality Act (INA). Like the Chinese Exclusion Repealer and the removal of the Asiatic Barred Zone, the McCarran-Walter Act kept the National Origins Act quotas in place. The INA limited immigrants from the Asia-Pacific Triangle to a maximum of 2,000 per year.

This time the impetus behind the INA was not to combat Japanese propaganda, but to challenge Communist propaganda, which labeled the United States as a racist imperialist nation. Facing the massive worldwide decolonization of former European colonies, U.S. leaders sought to lure these newly independent nations into the American orbit. For Washington policymakers, racism became an increasingly dangerous national security threat. This resulted in federal support of the Civil Rights Movement, including the passage of the Civil Rights Act of 1964 and the Voting Rights Act of 1965.[20]

The Civil Rights Movement would have a huge impact on Asian America. Like so many young Americans at the time, many second- and third-generation Asian Americans were inspired by the Civil Rights Movement. Many of these young men and women would eventually gravitate toward the more radical Asian American Movement of the late 1960s. However, as African Americans increasingly demanded their political rights, mainstream media and social commentators began indirectly criticizing black communities by comparing them to Asian Americans. The first of these articles was published on January 9, 1966 in the *New York Times Magazine*. The author, William Petersen, argued that Japanese Americans, only 15 years removed from World War II internment camps, had overcome extreme racism and discrimination. The unspoken connotation was that African Americans were a bad minority, and Japanese Americans were a good minority, or a "model minority."[21]

Policymakers also began instituting a program of military, economic, and social aid programs that would eventually become known as the United States Agency for International Development (USAID). This agency, and its successors, not only provided foreign aid, but also oversaw academic exchange programs between Asia and the United States. Students, scholars, and experts in the United States and various Asian nations, as well as health professionals, engineers, scientists, educators, social workers, and many others, were encouraged to travel to each other's homelands in a free exchange of knowledge, training, and cultures. This was part of a process meant to create, or brand, an image of America for global consumption. However, winning the hearts and minds of Asia also meant a parallel shift in the ways Americans understood Asian people. As Americans increasingly traveled to Asia to help build democratic capitalism, they spoke of hard working, democratic Asians. Gaining Asian allies would have been difficult if Americans continued to think of Asians as dirty, diseased, barbaric people. In the Cold War context, Asians were no longer the Yellow Peril but rather dependable hardworking friends and allies, who with proper American guidance would eventually establish a modern capitalist states. Considering the negative images of Asian Americans before World War II were based on Asian hyperefficiency, it is fascinating that in the Cold War era Asian efficiency was considered a positive Asian characteristic.[22] The document "'Lucy' Sails for 'Frisco," highlights the feelings of excitement and anxiety that many Cold War Asian migrants experienced. In this newspaper article, a young Korean woman recounts how she embarked for San Francisco to continue her studies in the United States.

World War II and Cold War conflicts in Korea and Southeast Asia fostered a deep and continuing American presence in Asia. Two unintended and unforeseen consequences of American military intervention and continuing presence in

Asia are transnational adoptions and military brides.²³ In Naeko Isagawa Keen's interview, we learn about how a young Japanese woman met and married her white American husband, who was serving as a member of the American occupying forces in Okinawa after World War II. Tuan-Rishard F. Schneider's "Adoptee Connection" is a first-person account of an adopted Vietnamese man's struggles growing up in Minneapolis, Minnesota. Finally, Korean adoptee Kimberly Waters discusses her ongoing search for her identity growing up in the American South in "How to Be a Korean from the South."

The U.S. defeat in Vietnam also produced a new wave of migrants escaping the war, poverty, and political oppression in Southeast Asia. *Voices of the Asian American and Pacific Islander Experience* includes several oral histories about the Cambodian, Hmong, Laotian, and Vietnamese refugee experience. The Southeast Asian refugee experience was qualitatively different from that of other Asian migrants who immigrated during the Cold War. Refugees were forced to leave their homelands because they feared for their own lives. Many suffered extreme posttraumatic stress while trying to escape their homelands and again in the Thai and Filipino refugee camps where they waited for western nations like the United States, Britain, and Canada to grant them asylum. In response to this, the United States passed the first Indochina Migration and Refugee Assistance Act in 1975. The act was amended in 1976 and 1977 to include refugees from Laos and Cambodia. In 1980, the United States passed the Refugee Act of 1980, which created a comprehensive refugee migration system. For Southeast Asian refugees, their transition into American society was often fraught with difficulties, which were only exacerbated by an economic recession and racial animosity. They were initially resettled largely in the Rust Belt, an area hit hard by the economic downturn of the 1970s and 1980s. Despite this, they reconstructed their communities and identities in America, with many transmigrating to California during the 1980s and 1990s.²⁴ The excerpt from Vatey Seng's *The Price We Paid* gives readers a raw, unfiltered look into the psychological trauma that many Cambodian refugees experienced as they made their way from refugee camps to America. These traumas have had long-lasting effects on many Southeast Asian refugee families. In "SSH . . . Thanks-Givin . . . Thanksgiving," Vietnamese American Andrew Lam gives readers a unique perspective on Thanksgiving, from the point of view of a Vietnamese refugee experiencing this quintessentially American holiday for the first time. As Lam puts it, even after escaping the terrors of Vietnam, there was "an oppressive silence that hung as heavy as the monsoon rain."

The Cold War, and in particular, the war in Southeast Asia, also helped fuel the rise of the Asian American Movement. *Asian American* was a term first used by mostly second- and third-generation Japanese American, Chinese American, and Filipino American activists involved in the Asian American Movement of the late 1960s. Asian Americans, like other activists of the time, were inspired by nationalist movements of independence around the world. For many Asian American activists, their identity was a nebulous complex of ideas about national liberation, racism, and social justice. In her book *Asian Americans: An Interpretive History*, historian Sucheng Chan describes how these "activists tried to organize garment and restaurant workers; set up social services agencies; recruit individuals to leftist organizations, which mushroomed overnight; and protest against a variety of ills."[25] These young Asian American activists believed that the historical and continued marginalization, violence, exploitation, and oppression their communities suffered was really a form of domestic imperialism.[26] It was this unique cultural milieu that gave birth to a new Asian American identity. *Voices of the Asian American and Pacific Islander Experience* includes several documents from the Asian American Movement, including a pamphlet from the Third World Liberation Front (TWLF), a multiracial/multiethnic coalition of student groups at San Francisco State University, who staged the longest student strike in U.S. history; a speech given by Richard Aoki, head of the Asian American Political Alliance at Berkeley and founding member of the Black Panther Party; and statements by two Asian American organizations involved in the San Francisco State University strike. Together, these documents give readers a fascinating glimpse into the world of 1960s Asian American activism.

Although the Asian American Movement may have birthed a new panethnic racial identity, this identity has been called into question by new immigration waves. In 1965, the federal government passed the Hart-Cellar Act, completely dismantling the 1924 National Origins Act. It created a hemispheric quota system for immigration. Immigration from the Western hemisphere was limited to 120,000 annually, and immigration from the Eastern hemisphere to 170,000. The new immigration policies emphasized family reunification and created a preference system based on the economic needs of the United States. The new policies gave preference to immediate family members and people in occupational sectors with the highest labor shortages, such as health care, scientific fields, and other white-collar occupations. This was because the U.S. economy had begun shifting away from a Fordist manufacturing system to a service-based economy beginning in the 1960s. The oil crisis and stagflation of the 1970s only accelerated the shift. The new service-based economy created a segmented labor system that needed either highly skilled workers or unskilled labor. Many Asian immigrants came to fill both labor sectors. Refugees and poorer Asian immigrants filled the unskilled labor market while highly educated Asian professionals were able to enter through the occupational preference categories. Ironically, many of these immigrants were able to obtain their high educational levels as a direct result of the economic and aid programs instituted by the United States during the Cold War. These aid programs had been designed to help nations develop economically. However, the educational systems that were funded and supported by U.S. experts produced many more graduates than most Asian economies could absorb. This migration helped complete the transformation of Asians from Yellow Peril to model minority (smart, nerdy techies) that began in the early Cold War. Along with military brides, transnational adoptees, and refugees, these highly educated immigrants made up the bulk of early post-1965 immigration.

However, this is not how most Asians would eventually enter the United States. Because immigrants who entered under family reunification were not counted as part of the quota, most post-1965 Asian immigrants immigrated under the family reunification component of the Hart-Cellar Act. Many of these immigrants would come to fill the low-wage labor needs of exploitive industries such as garment manufacturing. On the other hand, many professional Asian immigrants experienced occupational downgrading. Immigrants with college degrees who had been doctors, lawyers, businesspeople, or nurses in their home countries took unskilled positions in America or turned to small business entrepreneurship because of language barriers and/or discrimination. These businesses were, and are to this day, often located in dangerous neighborhoods; they produce small profit margins and require long hours of work. Think of Korean grocers and liquor store owners in New York City, or South Asian convenience store operators. While on the one hand these are contemporary Asian stereotypes, on the other hand these trends and patterns demonstrate adaptations to real-life circumstances. The reason many Asian American immigrants turn to these difficult occupations is because they offer a path to security. They can make a living by working harder and longer even at the risk of their own lives or health. Still other Asian immigrants have been able to translate their skills into successful businesses, especially in high-tech industries and food services.[27]

These new migrations have dramatically altered the face of Asian American and Pacific Islander communities in America. There has been not only an explosion in numbers but also a diversification in gender, class background, educational attainment, and ethnicity. Unlike earlier waves of immigrants, which were predominantly male and poor, these new waves include more women than men and comprise people of all socioeconomic backgrounds and educational levels from dozens of countries. This new migration has also altered the ratio of immigrant to native born. As a result of massive geopolitical transformations, shifts in the political economy of the United States, technological advancements, and monumental cultural and social changes, new generations of Asian Americans and Pacific Islanders are creating new identities. Blogger Ernie Hsiung gives voice to the Asian American gay experience in "Rainbow Nation and Gay Asian Male Stereotypes." DJ Rekha talks about tapping into the South Asian musical traditions of Sangament and Bhangra and melding them with house and hip-hop beats and grooves in "DJ Rekha, Interview by Demetrius Cheeks, 2007." Karen Kauv Sun discusses her experiences being both Mormon and Cambodian, and Samoan American scholar, activist, and writer Tafea Polamalu explores the Samoan experience in his poems "Diasporic Dream" and "Daddy Said."

Nevertheless, even what we think of as new identities are not really new. Take, for instance, multiracial Asian Americans. An excerpt from novelist Winnifred Eaton's *Miss Numè* reveals the complexities of racial identity. Eaton and her sister were mixed-race Asian Americans (Chinese and British) writing around the end of the 20th century. Capitalizing on the turn-of-the-century popularity of the "Japonisme" genre, Eaton wrote under the vaguely Japanese-sounding pen name, Onoto Watanna. Her complicated identity was no less multilayered than that of National Football League linebacker Scott Fujita, who is Caucasian but was raised by a Japanese American couple. Rod Fujita, who was born in the Gila River internment camp, and his wife, Helen, adopted Scott as an infant. In David Fleming's "Hello, I'm Japanese: Scott Fujita is Helping to Bring the Saints Back to Life. And that's the least surprising thing about him," Fujita discusses how his Japanese American cultural heritage has impacted the way he plays football. Or consider

Laylaa Abdul-Khabir's story in "Living the Mixed Life: Growing Up as a Black Chinese Muslim in America." Amazingly while Eaton and Abdul-Khabir may be separated by 100 years, both still struggled to understand their own identities, cultures, and lives.

This brings us full circle to the question we began with: What is Asian American/Pacific Islander? The answer is not easily defined. Like all identities, what and who are Asian American and Pacific Islander is constantly changing and evolving. While Asian Americans and Pacific Islanders may have had less power to define those identities in the past, the old Orientalist ideas of foreignness, exoticism, and strangeness still linger today. Indeed, some of these images have shifted due to economic, political, or cultural transformations. The Yellow Peril transformed into the model minority. Interracial marriages and transnational adoptions created new types of Asian American and Pacific Islander families. Shifts in the global geopolitics and the political economy of the United States diversified Asian American and Pacific Islander communities. Yet these massive transformations also broadened our definition of what and who is American. This has created more fluid spaces, places of contestation, imagination, and vibrancy where cultures, ideas, identities, communities, the past, and the present are continually made, remade, reshaped, and recreated by a new generation of Asian Americans and Pacific Islanders.

NOTES

1. Gary Y. Okihiro, *Margins and Mainstreams: Asians in American History and Culture* (Seattle: University of Washington Press, 1994).
2. Edward Said, *Orientalism* (New York: Vintage Books, 1979).
3. Indentured servants were typically British migrants, but other Europeans as well, who signed three- to seven-year labor contracts with an employer in exchange for ocean transportation, food, clothing, lodging, and other necessities. Many were escaping the social dislocations created by a population explosion that clashed with the system of primogeniture that left little opportunities for those who were not firstborn males.
4. John Kuo Wie Tchen's *New York before Chinatown: Orientalism and the Shaping of American Culture* (Baltimore: John Hopkins University Press, 1999) presents an excellent account of P. T. Barnum and the commodification of Asian bodies during the mid- to late 19th century. Tchen also gives a brief account of Peters's Great Chinese Museum.
5. For more detail on anti-Chinese and anti-Japanese movements in California, see Alexander Saxton, *The Indispensable Enemy: Labor and the Anti-Chinese Movement in California* (Berkeley: University of California Press, 1971) and Roger Daniels, *The Politics of Prejudice, the Anti-Japanese Movement in California, and the Struggle for Japanese Exclusion* (Berkeley: University of California Press, 1962). Colleen Lye's *America's Asia: Racial Form and American Literature, 1893–1945* (Princeton, NJ: Princeton University Press, 2005) is an excellent study on the cultural ideas surrounding Chinese hyper-efficiency during the late 19th and early 20th centuries.
6. Immanuel Wallerstein best described this colonial system in his seminal work *The Modern World-System* (New York: Academic Press, 1974).
7. For more on American colonialism in the Philippines, see David Brody, *Visualizing American Empire: Orientalism & Imperialism in the Philippines* (Chicago: University of Chicago Press, 2010); Julian Go and Anne L. Foster, ed., *The American Colonial State*

in the Philippines: Global Perspectives (Durham, NC: Duke University Press, 2003); Vicente L. Rafael, "White Love: Surveillance and Nationalist Resistance in the U.S. Colonization of the Philippines," in *Cultures of United States Empire*, ed. Amy Kaplan and Donald E. Pease (Durham, NC: Duke University Press, 1993); Daniel B. Schirmer and Stephen Rosskamm Shalom, ed., *The Philippines Reader: A History of Colonialism, Neocolonialism, Dictatorship, and Resistance* (Cambridge, MA: South End Press, 1987); and Catherine Ceniza Choy, *Empire of Care: Nursing and Migration in Filipino American History* (Durham, NC: Duke University Press, 2003). For an excellent account of the racism, discrimination, and challenges early Filipino immigrants faced, see Dorothy Fujita-Rony, *American Workers, Colonial Power: Philippine Seattle and the Transpacific West, 1919–1941* (Berkeley: University of California Press, 2003). http://us.mg6.mail.yahoo.com/neo/launch?.rand=6qlltcuing6rr.

8. For more on American empire in Hawai'i, see Eric T. Love, *Race Over Empire: Racism and U.S. Imperialism 1865–1900* (Chapel Hill: University of North Carolina Press, 2004) and Davianna Pomaika'I Mcgregor, "Engaging Hawaiians in the Expansion of the U.S. Empire," *Journal of Asian American Studies* 7, no. 3 (October 2004): 209–22.

9. Ronald Takaki, *Strangers from a Different Shore: A History of Asian Americans* (Boston: Little, Brown, 1989).

10. For an excellent history on the interracial labor movement in Hawai'i, see Moon-Kie Jung, *Reworking Race: The Making of Hawaii's Interracial Labor Movement* (New York: Columbia University Press, 2006). For general information on the life of Asian plantation workers in Hawai'i, see Ronald Takaki, *Pau Hana: Plantation Life and Labor in Hawaii* (Honolulu: University of Hawai'i Press, 1984) and Gary Y. Okihiro, *Cane Fires: The Anti-Japanese Movement in Hawaii, 1865–1945* (Philadelphia, PA: Temple University Press, 1991).

11. At this time, the U.S. government considered Koreans to be U.S. nationals. Japan annexed Korea in 1905 and officially made it into a colony in 1910.

12. For a detailed account of the transnational lives of Chinese Americans, see Madeline Y. Hsu, *Dreaming of Gold, Dreaming of Home: Transnationalism and Migration between the United States and South China, 1882–1943* (Stanford, CA: Stanford University Press, 2000).

13. See Wayne Patterson, *The Ilse: First-Generation Korean Immigrants in Hawai'i, 1903–1973* (Honolulu: University of Hawai'i Press, 2000); Won-kil Yoon, *The Passage of a Picture Bride* (Loma Linda and Riverside, CA: Loma Linda University Press, 1989); Yoshiko Uchida, *Picture Bride: A Novel* (Seattle: University of Washington Press, 1997); and Erika Lee and Judy Yung, *Angel Island: Immigrant Gateway to America* (Oxford: Oxford University Press, 2010).

14. See Jane Singh, "The Gadar Party: Political Expression in an Immigrant Community," *Comparative Studies of South Asia, Africa and the Middle East* 2, no. 1 (1982): 29–38.

15. For more on the overseas Korean Independence movements, see Yong-ho Ch'oe, ed., *From the Land of Hibiscus: Koreans in Hawai'i, 1903–1950* (Honolulu: University of Hawai'i Press, 2007); Kingsley K. Lyu, "Korean Nationalist Activities in Hawaii and the Continental United States, 1900–1945 (I), (II)," *Amerasia Journal* 4, no. 1 (1977): 23–90; 4, no. 2 (1977): 53–100; Richard S. Kim, "Inaugurating the American Century: The 1919 Philadelphia Korean Congress, Korean Diasporic Nationalism, and American Protestant Missionaries," *Journal of American Ethnic History* 26, no. 1 (Fall 2006): 50–76; and Zihn Choi, "Early Korean Immigrants to America: Their Role in the Establishment of the Republic of Korea," *East Asian Review* 14, no. 4 (Winter 2002): 43–71.

16. Han-Kyo Kim, "The Korean Independence Movement in the United States: Syngman Rhee, Ah Ch'ang-Ho, and Pak Yong-Man," *International Journal of Korean Studies* 6, no. 1 (Spring/Summer 2002): 1–28.
17. For an excellent history on the Filipino colonial experience, migration, and labor activism, see Fujita-Rony, *American Workers, Colonial Power*.
18. Min Yasui and Gordan Hirabayashi did not directly challenge internment but rather the military curfews on Japanese Americans on the West Coast after the Pearl Harbor attack. For an excellent and detailed account of the internment cases, see Peter Irons, *Justice at War* (New York: Oxford University Press, 1983). There are also many accounts of the Japanese American internment. Some of the best include Roger Daniels, *Concentration Camps USA: Japanese Americans and World War II* (New York: Holt, Rinehart, and Winston, 1972); Michi Weglyn, *Years of Infamy: The Untold Story of America's Concentration Camps* (New York: Morrow Quill Paperbacks, 1976); and Alice Yang Murray, ed., *What Did the Internment of Japanese Americans Mean* (Boston: St. Martin's, 2000).
19. See Roger Daniels, Sandra C. Taylor, and Harry H. L. Kitano, eds., *Japanese Americans: From Relocation to Redress* (Seattle: University of Washington Press, 1991).
20. See Mary L. Dudziak, *Cold War Civil Rights: Race and the Image of American Democracy* (Princeton, NJ: Princeton University Press, 2000); and Penny M. Von Eschen, *Race against Empire: Black Americans and Anticolonialism, 1937–1957* (Ithaca, NY: Cornell University Press, 1997).
21. See William Petersen, "Success Story, Japanese American Style," *New York Times Magazine*, January 9, 1966, 20–21, 33, 36, 38, 40–41, 43, and "Success Story of One Minority Group in the U.S.," *U.S. News and World Report*, December 26, 1966, 73–76.
22. This process began with Japan after World War II. See Michael Schaller, *The American Occupation of Japan: The Origins of the Cold War* (New York: Oxford University Press, 1985); Gary Hoichi Tsuchimochi, *Education Reform in Postwar Japan: The 1946 U.S. Education Mission* (Tokyo: University of Tokyo Press, 1993); and Naoko Shibusawa, *America's Geisha Ally: Reimagining the Japanese Enemy* (Cambridge, MA: Harvard University Press, 2006). U.S. Cold War policies were designed to bolster America's image through economic aid programs and cultural exchange. For more on this, see David C. Engerman, Nils Gilman, Mark H. Haefele, and Michael E. Latham, eds., *Staging Growth: Modernization, Development, and the Global Cold War* (Amherst: University of Massachusetts Press, 2003); Nils Gilman, *Mandarins of the Future: Modernization Theory in Cold War America* (Baltimore: John Hopkins University Press, 2003); Ellen Wu, "America's Chinese: Anti-Communism, Citizenship and Cultural Diplomacy during the Cold War," *Pacific Historical Review* 77, no. 3 (August 2008): 391–422; James Sang Chi, "Teaching Korea: Modernization, Model Minorities, and American Internationalism in the Cold War Era" (PhD diss., University of California, Berkeley, 2008); and Gene Lyons, *Military Policy and Economic Aid: The Korean Case, 1950–1953* (Columbus: Ohio State University Press, 1961). For an excellent account about the impact of American popular culture on U.S. Cold War ideas and relations about Asia, see Christina Klein, *Cold War Orientalism: Asia in the Middlebrow Imagination, 1945–1961* (Berkeley: University of California Press, 2003).
23. For more on military brides and adoptions, see Klein, *Cold War Orientalism*; Arissa Oh, "A New Kind of Missionary Work: Christians, Christian Americanists and the Adoption of Korean GI Babies, 1955–1961," *Women's Studies Quarterly* 33, nos. 3–4 (Fall/Winter 2005); 161–88; Eleana Kim, *Adopted Territory: Transnational Korean Adoptees and the Politics of Belonging* (Durham, NC: Duke University Press, 2010); and

Ji-Yeon Yuh, *Beyond the Shadow of Camptown: Korean Military Brides in America* (New York: New York University Press, 2002).

24. For more, see Karin Aguilar-San Juan, *Little Saigons: Staying Vietnamese in America* (Minneapolis: University of Minnesota Press, 2009); Nazli Kibria, *Family Tightrope: The Changing Lives of Vietnamese Americans* (Princeton, NJ: Princeton University Press, 1993); and Jeremy Hein, *Ethnic Origins: The Adaptation of Cambodian and Hmong Refugees in Four American Cities* (New York: Russell Sage Foundation, 2006).

25. Sucheng Chan, *Asian Americans: An Interpretative History* (Boston: Twayne, 1991), 175.

26. For a general history of the racial movements of the 1960s, see Laura Pulido, *Black, Brown, Yellow, and Left: Radical Activism in Los Angeles* (Berkeley: University of California Press, 2006). For a detailed summary of Asian American activism, see Fred Ho, ed., *Legacy to Liberation: Politics and Culture of Revolutionary Asian/Pacific America* (Edinburgh, UK: AK Press, 2000); Glenn Omatsu, "The 'Four Prisons' and the Movements of Liberation," in *The State of Asian American Activism and Resistance in the 1990's*, ed. Karin Aguilar-San Juan, 19–70 (Boston: South End Press, 1994); Karen Umemoto, "On Strike! San Francisco State College Strike, 1968–1969: The Role of Asian American Students," *Amerasia Journal* 15, no. 1 (1989): 3–41; and William Wei, *The Asian American Movement* (Philadelphia: Temple University Press, 1993).

27. For more detail on the political and economic shifts that influenced post-1965 Asian immigration and the occupational patterns of Asian immigrants, see Paul Ong, Edna Bonacich, and Lucie Cheng, eds., *The New Asian Immigration in Los Angeles and Global Restructuring* (Philadelphia: Temple University Press, 1994). For more on ethnic entrepreneurship see Ivan Light and Carolyn Rosenstein, *Race, Ethnicity, and Entrepreneurship in Urban America* (New York: Walter de Gruyter, 1995); and Anna Lee Saxenian, *Silicon Valley's New Immigrant Entrepreneurs* (San Francisco: Public Policy Institute of California, 1999).

Chronology

1760s	Filipino sailors desert from a Spanish galleon and form a small community of "Manilamen" near New Orleans.
1790	The United States passes the Naturalization Law: Only "free white persons" with property can become naturalized citizens.
1848	Gold is found in California; Chinese immigration begins.
1848–1934	"First wave" of Asian immigration occurs.
1852	Foreign Miners Tax: California institutes its second Foreign Miners tax, which targets Chinese miners.
1860	About 41,000 Chinese reside in California.
1869	Transcontinental Railroad is completed. More than 90 percent of all Central Pacific Railroad workers were Chinese. Many were released after the railroad boom ended. The Chinese headed to the cities and worked in factories and eventually opened their own businesses, creating an ethnic economy in Chinatowns across the West Coast.
1875	Reciprocity Treaty: Hawai'i can export sugar to the United States duty-free, leading to the explosion of the sugar plantation industry and Asian immigration to Hawai'i.
1878	*In re Ah Yup*: U.S. Supreme Court case in which a Chinese immigrant sues for U.S. citizenship and loses. Ah Yup is declared nonwhite, making him ineligible for citizenship under the 1790 Naturalization Law.
1882	The first Chinese Exclusion Act is passed, halting most immigration (with exceptions for merchants, students, teachers, and diplomats).
	Consolidated Chinese Benevolent Association (CCBA), or the Chinese Six Companies, is established in San Francisco and a year later in New York City.

1885	*Tape v. Hurley:* Mary Tape successfully sues the city of San Francisco School District for denying her daughter Mamie entry into Spring Valley School. However, the school district quickly lobbied the California State Legislature to pass a provision establishing a separate "Oriental" school.
1886	*Yick Wo v. Hopkins:* A Chinese laundry guild successfully sues the city of San Francisco for discriminatory enforcement of a permit regulation requiring an additional permit for all laundry businesses in wooden buildings.
1888	The first Japanese laborers come to California.
April 1898	The United States declares war on Spain, beginning the Spanish American War. The United States wins the war in about three months. The war was fought both in Cuba and the Philippines. America purchases the Philippines from Spain for $20 million.
June 1898	The United States annexes Hawai'i.
August 1898	The United States takes military control of the Philippines.
1898–1902	Philippine American War. The United States declares victory in 1902 and begins a program of benevolent assimilation, but fighting continues until 1912.
1899–1914	First wave of Punjabi Sikh immigrants arrive.
1900–1924	Picture bride migrants, mostly Japanese and Korean, come to Hawai'i and the mainland.
1902–1907	First wave of Korean immigrants arrive.
1903	Japanese Mexican Labor Association of beet workers in Oxnard, California, successfully wins strike. It is one of the first major victories involving unskilled migrant farmworkers.
	Korean Americans in San Francisco establish the Korean National Association, one of the most important organizations of the Korean Independence Movement.
1903–1934	First wave of Filipino immigrants arrive.
1906	The San Francisco earthquake and subsequent fire burn down the immigration building. Chinese immigrants use the opportunity to claim citizenship and paper sons as a way to circumvent the exclusion laws. This technique had been used prior to the earthquake but not in such large numbers.
	Abiko Kyutaro founds the American Land and Produce Company, also known as the Yamato Colony, and settles 40 Issei (first generation) families to farm the land.

1908	Gentlemen's Agreement sharply restricts Japanese immigration.
1913, 1920	California Alien Land Laws prohibit "aliens ineligible for citizenship" from buying and owning land; 10 other western states soon follow suit.
1917	Immigration Act of 1917 (Asiatic Barred Zone Act) prohibits immigration from India and the Pacific Islands. Migrants from China, Japan, and Korea were already excluded under the Chinese Exclusion Acts and the Gentlemen's Agreement.
1920	Japanese and Filipino sugar plantation strike takes place on Oahu. It is the first major interethnic strike in Hawai'i.
1922	Cable Act is enacted: If an American woman marries an "alien ineligible for citizenship," she loses her own citizenship.
	Takao Ozawa v. the United States; Supreme Court case in which a Japanese immigrant unsuccessfully sues for American citizenship. The Court concludes that he is not Caucasian and thus is ineligible for citizenship under the 1790 Naturalization Act.
1923	*United States v. Bhagat Singh Thind*: The Supreme Court declares that Asian Indian immigrants are not white or Caucasian according to the "common man's" definition and thus are ineligible for U.S. citizenship; the citizenship of previously naturalized Asian Indians is retroactively revoked.
1924	Immigration Act of 1924 (Johnson-Reed Act, also known as the National Origins Act) bars entry of women from Asia, including wives of U.S. citizens.
1930	Watsonville Riots: Fueled by anger over job competition and the affront of Filipino men dancing with and dating white women, white mobs numbering in the hundreds hunted Filipino men, beating them in the streets. One Filipino man was shot and killed.
1933	Filipino Labor Union Strike: Filipino lettuce workers organized a successful strike in Stockton and Salinas.
1934	Tydings-McDuffie Act provides for the future independence of the Philippines, changing the status of Filipinos from "nationals" to "aliens" and thus rendering them largely ineligible for immigration to the United States.
December 7, 1941	Japan bombs Pearl Harbor; World War II begins.

1942	Executive Order 9066 removes "enemy aliens" from "military areas" on the West Coast; 120,000 Japanese Americans (aliens and citizens) are sent to internment camps.
1943	Magnuson Act repeals the Chinese Exclusion Act, allows Chinese immigrants in the United States to become naturalized citizens, and sets a quota of 105 Chinese immigrants per year.
1945	War Brides Act: Asian wives and children of U.S. servicemen are allowed to immigrate quota-free.
1946	Luce-Cellar Act: Filipinos and Asian Indians may become naturalized U.S. citizens.
1948	*Oyama v. State of California:* The Supreme Court declares certain parts of the 1913 and 1920 California Alien Land Laws to be unconstitutional.
1952	*Sei Fujii v. State of California:* The Supreme Court declares the 1913 Alien Land Law to be unconstitutional.
1952	McCarran-Walter Act removes the racial restrictions from the 1790 Naturalization Law; retains strict national origins quotas for Asian immigration.
1953	Refugee Relief Act extends refugee status to non-Europeans, enabling Chinese refugees fleeing Communism to claim asylum in the United States.
1965	Immigration and Nationality Act (Hart-Cellar Act) abolishes all national-origin quotas; raises the quota for migrants from Asian countries to 20,000 per year; and exempts spouses, parents, and children of American citizens from the quota.
1965–present	Second wave of Asian immigration.
1966	William Petersen's "Success Story, Japanese American Style" is published in the *New York Times Magazine*. His story marks the birth of the modern model minority myth.
1967	*Loving v. Virginia:* The U.S. Supreme Court declares antimiscegenation laws to be unconstitutional.
1968	Student strikes take place at San Francisco State and the University of California, Berkeley. The Yellow Power Movement begins.
1968–1977	Fight to save the International Hotel (I-Hotel): Community activists rally around the mostly Filipino and Chinese elderly residents of the I-Hotel. The I-Hotel was the last remnant of a once-thriving Filipino community (Manilatown) in San Francisco that had been decimated by urban redevelopment.

1975	Refugee Assistance Act opens the door to refugees from Southeast Asia and creates a framework of assistance programs in the United States.
1979	Orderly Departure Program allows Vietnamese family members of refugees already in the United States to enter at the rate of 20,000 per year.
1980	Refugee Act creates the Federal Refugee Resettlement Program.
1982	Vincent Chin is killed by two white autoworkers in Detroit, Michigan. American Citizens for Justice is established to protest their lenient sentences.
1984	Fred Korematsu, Gordon Hirabayashi, and Minoru Yasui, who were convicted as felons for resisting Japanese American internment, have their convictions vacated.
1987	Amerasian Homecoming Act admits 100,000 Amerasian children and their mothers into the United States.
1988	Civil Liberties Act is passed, mandating a presidential apology for Japanese American internment and the payment of $20,000 to each surviving family.
1992	Los Angeles's Koreatown is targeted in the riots following the Rodney King verdict.
1992	Hapa Issues Forum is founded.

Part I
General Asian American

1. The Page Law, 1875

Most Chinese immigrants in the mid- to late 19th century financed their trip using the credit-ticket system, under which American hiring agencies advanced money for steamship passage, which would be paid back with the wages the immigrant earned once he was in the United States. Partly because most laborers earned enough to pay off this loan but not enough to send back to China for a wife, a gender imbalance appeared in the Chinese American community—along with burgeoning prostitution and sex trafficking industries in Chinatowns. At the same time, the emerging Progressive movement reflected the mainstream American public's desire to police morality, family, and sexuality, especially in immigrant and working-class communities. All these factors, coupled with growing racial and labor antagonism toward the Chinese, contributed to the passage of the Page Law in 1875.

The Page Law prohibited certain classes of immigrants from coming to the United States. One clause limited contract laborers from Asia (this would be codified more thoroughly in 1882, with the Chinese Exclusion Act); another clause prohibited convicts; and a third clause—the most significant one—denied entry to Asian prostitutes. Plantation owners and farmers seeking cheap labor managed to circumvent most of the proscriptions on "coolie" laborers, and, in fact, between 1875 and 1882, the number of Chinese immigrants to the United States reached a historic high. However, the clause prohibiting prostitutes effectively halted Asian female immigration, particularly women from China. Immigration officials generally did not distinguish between women coming over as brides of Chinese Americans and women coming over as prostitutes.

The Page Law resulted in an even more extreme demographic imbalance among Chinese Americans (and, paradoxically, exacerbated the problem of prostitution), making it almost impossible for any family culture to develop. Chinatowns remained primarily bachelor societies. Furthermore, the stereotype of the sexually predatorial Chinese man who threatened white womanhood was cemented even more solidly in the imaginations of mainstream Americans. The gender imbalance in the Chinese American community would not be rectified until World War II, when the War Brides

Act enabled Chinese American soldiers to marry women they met while stationed overseas.

FORTY-THIRD CONGRESS. SESS. II. CH. 141. 1875.

CHAP. 141.-An act supplementary to the acts in relation to immigration.

Be it enacted by the Senate and House of Representatives of the United States of America in Congress assembled, That in determining whether the immigration of any subject of China, Japan, or any Oriental country, to the United States, is free and voluntary, as provided by section two thousand one hundred and sixty-two of the Revised Code, title "Immigration," it shall be the duty of the consul-general or consul of the United States residing at the port from which it is proposed to convey such subjects, in any vessels enrolled or licensed in the United States, or any port within the same, before delivering to the masters of any such vessels the permit or certificate provided for in such section, to ascertain whether such immigrant bas entered into a contract or agreement for a term of service within the United States, for lewd and immoral purposes; and if there be such contract or agreement, the said consul-general or consul shall not deliver the required permit or certificate.

SEC. 2. That if any citizen of the United States, or other person amenable to the laws of the United States shall take, or cause to be taken or transported, to or from the United States any subject of China, Japan, or any Oriental country, without their free and voluntary consent, for the purpose of holding them to a term of service, such citizen or other person shall be liable to be indicted therefore and, on conviction of such offense, shall be punished by a fine not exceeding two thousand dollars and be imprisoned not exceeding one year; and all contracts and agreements for a term of service of such persons in the United States, whether made in advance or in pursuance of such illegal importation, and whether such importation shall have been in American or other vessels, are hereby declared void.

SEC. 3. That the importation into the United States of women for the purposes of prostitution is hereby forbidden; and all contracts and agreements in relation thereto, made in advance or in pursuance of such illegal importation and purposes, are hereby declared void; and whoever shall knowingly and willfully import, or cause any importation of, women into the United States for the purposes of prostitution, or shall knowingly or willfully hold, or attempt to hold, any woman to such purposes, in pursuance of such illegal importation and contract or agreement, shall be deemed guilty of a felony, and, on conviction thereof, shall be imprisoned not exceeding five years and pay a fine not exceeding five thousand dollars.

SEC. 4. That if any person shall knowingly and willfully contract, or attempt to contract, in advance or in pursuance of such illegal importation, to supply to another the labor of any cooly or other person brought into the United States in violation of section two thousand one hundred and fifty-eight of the Revised Statutes, or of any other section of the laws prohibiting the cooly-trade or of this act, such person shall be deemed guilty of a felony, and, upon conviction thereof, in any United States court, shall be fined in a sum not exceeding five hundred dollars and imprisoned for a term not exceeding one year.

SEC. 5. That it shall be unlawful for aliens of the following classes to immigrate into the United States, namely, persons who are undergoing a sentence for conviction in their own country of felonious crimes other than political or growing out of or the result of such political offenses, or whose sentence has been remitted on condition of their emigration, and women "imported for the purposes of prostitution." Every vessel arriving in the United States may be inspected under the direction of the collector of the port at which it arrives, if he shall have reason to believe that any such obnoxious persons are on board; and the officer making such inspection shall certify the result thereof to the master or other person in charge of such vessel, designating in such certificate the person or persons, if any there be, ascertained by him to be of either of the classes whose importation is hereby forbidden. When such inspection is required by the collector as aforesaid, it shall be unlawful without his permission, for any alien to leave any such vessel arriving in the United States from a foreign country until the inspection shall have been had and the result certified as herein provided; and at no time thereafter shall any alien certified to by the inspecting officer as being of either of the classes whose immigration is forbidden by this section, be allowed to land in the United States, except in obedience to a judicial process issued pursuant to law. If any person shall feel aggrieved by the certificate of such inspecting officer stating him or her to be within either of the classes whose immigration is forbidden by this section, and shall apply for release or other remedy to any proper court or judge, then it shall be the duty of the collector at said port of entry to detain said vessel until a hearing and determination of the matter are had, to the end that if the said inspector shall be found to be in accordance with this section and sustained, the obnoxious person or persons shall be returned on board of said vessel, and shall not thereafter be permitted to land, unless the master, owner or consignee of the vessel shall give bond and security, to be approved by the court or judge hearing the cause, in the sum of five hundred dollars for each such person permitted to land, conditioned for the return of such person, within six months from the date thereof, to the country whence his or her emigration shall have taken place, or unless the vessel bringing such obnoxious person or persons shall be forfeited, in which event the proceeds of such forfeiture shall be paid over to the collector of the port of arrival, and applied by him, as far as necessary, to the return of such person or persons to his or her own country within the said period of six months. And for all violations of this act, the vessel, by the acts, omissions, or connivance of the owners, master, or other custodian, or the consignees of which the same are committed, shall be liable to forfeiture, and may be proceeded against as in cases of frauds against the revenue laws, for which forfeiture is prescribed by existing law.

Approved March 3, 1875.

Source: The Page Law of 1875 (An act supplementary to the acts in relation to immigration). *U.S. Statutes at Large* 18 (1875): 477. 43rd Cong., Sess. II, Chap. 141.

2. National Origins Act, 1924

In the years following World War I, the United States retreated into itself, rejecting international involvement and attempting to bring back a mythical golden age of a (racially, politically, and socially) pure America. To this end, Congress passed the Immigration Act of 1924, also known as the National Origins Act. A new quota for immigrants entering the United States each year was set: 2 percent of the total of each national group (including both immigrants and natural-born citizens) living in America, as reported in the 1890 census. This was aimed at restricting southern and eastern European immigrants, especially Jews; none of these groups had come to the United States in statistically significant numbers until after 1900.

However, the National Origins Act also barred entry to all aliens ineligible for citizenship—thus halting Asian immigration altogether. This impacted the Japanese in particular, as most other Asians had already been excluded by previous pieces of legislation. The Japanese government protested the National Origins Act as contrary to the terms of the Gentlemen's Agreement, but the United States was more interested in creating a racially homogeneous nation than in maintaining ties with Japan, and the legislation passed. Not until the 1965 Immigration and Nationality Act would the United States open its doors to all of Asia.

The following excerpt from the National Origins Act lays out the main quota system, establishes the specific exclusion clause, and calls for the prosecution of people who bring over illegal aliens. It also includes a description of people considered unfit to immigrate, the category in which Asian immigrants found themselves.

AN ACT

To limit the immigration of aliens into the United States, and for other purposes.

Be it enacted by the Senate and House of Representatives of the United States of America in Congress assembled, That this Act may be cited as the "Immigration Act of 1924"....

Application for Immigration Visa.

Sec. 7. (a) Every immigrant applying for an immigration visa shall make application therefor in duplicate in such form as shall be by regulations prescribed....

(d) In the application the immigrant shall also state (to such extent as shall be by regulations prescribed) whether or not he is a member of each class of individuals excluded from admission to the United States under the immigration laws, and such classes shall be stated on the blank in such form as shall be by regulations prescribed, and the immigrant shall answer separately as to each class.

(e) If the immigrant is unable to state that he does not come within any of the excluded classes, but claims to be for any legal reason exempt from exclusion, he shall state fully in the application the grounds for such alleged exemption....

Numerical Limitations.

Sec. 11. (a) The annual quota of any nationality shall be 2 per centum of the number of foreign-born individuals of such nationality resident in continental

United States as determined by the United States census of 1890, but the minimum quota of any nationality shall be 100.

(b) The annual quota of any nationality for the fiscal year beginning July 1, 1927, and for each fiscal year thereafter, shall be a number which bears the same ratio to 150,000 as the number of inhabitants in continental United States in 1920 having that national origin (ascertained as hereinafter provided in this section) bears to the number of inhabitants in continental United States in 1920, but the minimum quota of any nationality shall be 100. . . .

Nationality.

Sec. 12. (a) For the purposes of this Act nationality shall be determined by country of birth, treating as separate countries the colonies, dependencies, or self-governing dominions, for which separate enumeration was made in the United States census of 1890; except that (1) the nationality of a child under twenty-one years of age not born in the United States, accompanied by its alien parent not born in the United States, shall be determined by the country of birth of such parent if such parent is entitled to an immigration visa, and the nationality of a child under twenty-one years of age not born in the United States, accompanied by both alien parents not born in the United States, shall be determined by the country of birth of the father if the father is entitled to an immigration visa; and (2) if a wife is of a different nationality from her alien husband and the entire number of immigration visas which may be issued to quota immigrants of her nationality for the calendar month has already been issued, her nationality may be determined by the country of birth of her husband if she is accompanying him and he is entitled to an immigration visa, unless the total number of immigration visas which may be issued to quota immigrants of the nationality of the husband for the calendar month has already been issued. An immigrant born in the United States who has lost his United States citizenship shall be considered as having been born in the country of which he is citizen or subject, or if he is not a citizen or subject of any country, then in the country from which he comes. . . .

Exclusion from United States.

Sec. 13.

(c) **No alien ineligible to citizenship shall be admitted to the United States** unless such alien (1) is admissible as a non-quota immigrant under the provisions of subdivision (b), (d), or (e) of section 4, or (2) is the wife, or the unmarried child under 18 years of age, of an immigrant admissible under such subdivision (d), and is accompanying or following to join him, or (3) is not an immigrant as defined in section 3. . . .

Deportation.

Sec. 14. Any alien who at any time after entering the United States is found to have been at the time of entry not entitled under this Act to enter the United States, or to have remained therein for a longer time than permitted under this Act or regulations made thereunder, shall be taken into custody and deported in the same manner as provided for in sections 19 and 20 of the Immigration Act of 1917: Provided, That the Secretary of Labor may, under such conditions and restrictions as to support and care as he may deem necessary, permit permanently to remain in the United States, any alien child who, when under sixteen years of age was heretofore temporarily admitted to the United States and who is now within the United States and either of whose parents is a citizen of the United States. . . .

Penalty for Illegal Transportation.

Sec. 16. (a) It shall be unlawful for any person, including any transportation company, or the owner, master, agent, charter, or consignee of any vessel, to bring to the United States by water from any place outside thereof (other than foreign contiguous territory) (1) any immigrant who does not have an unexpired immigration visa, or (2) any quota immigrant having an immigration visa the visa in which specifies him as a non-quota immigrant.

(b) If it appears to the satisfaction of the Secretary of Labor that any immigrant has been so brought, such person, or transportation company, or the master, agent, owner, charterer, or consignee of any such vessel, shall pay to the collector of customs of the customs district in which the port of arrival is located the sum of $1,000 for each immigrant so brought, and in addition a sum equal to that paid by such immigrant for his transportation from the initial point of departure, indicated in his ticket, to the port of arrival, such latter sum to be delivered by the collector of customs to the immigrant on whose account assessed. No vessel shall be granted clearance pending the determination of the liability to the payment of such sums, or while such sums remain unpaid, except that clearance may be granted prior to the determination of such question upon the deposit of an amount sufficient to cover such sums, or of a bond with sufficient surety to secure the payment thereof approved by the collector of customs. . . .

Steamship Fines under 1917 Act.

Sec. 26. Section 9 of the Immigration Act of 1917 is amended to read as follows:
"Sec. 9. That it shall be unlawful for any person, including any transportation company other than railway lines entering the United States from foreign contiguous territory, or the owner, master, agent, or consignee of any vessel to bring to the United States either from a foreign country or any insular possession of the United States any **alien afflicted with idiocy, insanity, imbecility, feeble-mindedness, epilepsy, constitutional psychopathic inferiority, chronic alcoholism, tuberculosis in any form, or a loathsome or dangerous contagious disease,** and if it shall appear to the satisfaction of the Secretary of Labor that any alien so brought to the United States was afflicted with any of the said diseases or disabilities at the time of foreign embarkation, and that the existence of such disease of disability might have been detected by means of a competent medical examination at such time, such person or transportation company, or the master, agent, owner, or consignee of any such vessel shall pay to the collector of customs of the customs district in which the port of arrival is located the sum of $1,000, and in addition a sum equal to that paid by such alien for his transportation from the initial point of departure, indicated in his ticket, to the port of arrival for each and every violation of the provisions of this section, such latter sum

to be delivered by the collector of customs to the alien on whose account assessed. It shall also be unlawful for any such person to bring to any port of the United States any alien afflicted with any mental defect other than those above specifically named, or physical defect of a nature which may affect his ability to earn a living, as contemplated in section 3 of this Act, and if it shall appear to the satisfaction of the Secretary of Labor that any alien so brought to the United States was so afflicted at the time of foreign embarkation, and that the existence of such mental or physical defect might have been detected by means of a competent medical examination at such time, such person shall pay to the collector of customs of the customs district in which the port of arrival is located the sum of $250, and in addition a sum equal to that paid by such alien for his transportation from the initial point of departure, indicated in his ticket, to the port of arrival, for each and every violation of this provision such latter sum to be delivered by the collector of customs of the alien for whose account assessed. It shall also be unlawful for any such person to bring to any port of the United States any alien who is excluded by the provisions of section 3 of this Act because unable to read, or who is excluded by the terms of section 3 of this Act as a native of that portion of the Continent of Asia and the islands adjacent thereto described in said section, and if it shall appear to the satisfaction of the Secretary of Labor that these disabilities might have been detected by the exercise of reasonable precaution prior to the departure of such aliens from a foreign port, such person shall pay to the collector of customs of the customs district in which the port of arrival is located the sum of $1,000, and in addition a sum equal to that paid by such alien for his transportation from the initial point of departure, indicated in his ticket, to the port of arrival, for each and every violation of this provision, such latter sum to be delivered by the collector of customs to the alien on whose account assessed. . . .

General Definitions.

Sec. 28. As used in this Act—
(c) The term "ineligible to citizenship," when used in reference to any individual, includes an individual who is debarred from becoming a citizen of the United States under section 2169 of the Revised Statutes, or under section 14 of the Act entitled "An Act to execute certain treaty stipulations relating to Chinese," approved May 6, 1882, or under section 1996, 1997, or 1998 of the Revised Statutes, as amended, or under section 2 of the Act entitled "An Act to authorize the President to increase temporarily the Military Establishment of the United States," approved May 18, 1917, as amended, or under law amendatory of, supplementary to, or in substitution for, any of such sections. . . .

Saving Clause in Event of Unconstitutionality.

Sec. 32. If any provision of this Act, or the application thereof to any person or circumstances, is held invalid, the remainder of the Act, and the application of such provision to other persons or circumstances, shall not be affected thereby.

Approved, May 26, 1924.

Source: The National Origins Act of 1924. *U.S. Statutes at Large* 43 (1924): 153. 68th Cong., Sess. I, Chap. 190.

3. War Brides Act, 1945

The first War Brides Act, Public Law 271, temporarily allowed American soldiers to bring their foreign wives to the United States. The federal government amended the act in 1946 and 1947, extending the deadline. The 1947 Soldier Brides Act allowed the wives to enter the United States regardless of their racial background. Though temporary, the War Brides Act was the first step in legal recognition of marriages between American GIs and foreign wives. In 1952, the McCarran-Walter Act ended the severe immigration restriction of the 1924 National Origins Act and lifted the ban on naturalization for Asians, clearing the way for foreign military wives. Military brides became the foundation for a new wave of post-1965 immigrants from Asia. They were the largest group of women to ever arrive from Asia. From 1947 to 1964, about 72,700 Asian women immigrated to the United States. This represented a 20 percent increase for the entire Asian American population. Many of these women eventually sponsored family members to come to America. The United States began loosening immigration restrictions during the 1950s and 1960s in an effort to counter Communist claims of American racism during the Cold War.

AN ACT

To expedite the admission to the United States of alien spouses and alien minor children of citizen members of the United States armed forces.

Be it enacted by the Senate and House of Representatives of the United States of America in Congress assembled, That notwithstanding any of the several clauses of section 3 of the Act of February 5, 1917, excluding physically and mentally defective aliens, and notwithstanding the documentary requirements of any of the immigration laws or regulations, Executive orders, or Presidential proclamations issued thereunder, alien spouses or alien children of United States citizens serving in, or having an honorable discharge certificate from the armed forces of the United States during the Second World War shall, if otherwise admissible under the immigration laws and if application for admission is made within three years of the effective date of this Act, be admitted to the United States: *Provided,* That the time of arrival in accordance with the provisions of section 16 of the Act of February 5, 1917, and if found suffering from any disability which would be the basis for a ground of exclusion except for the provision of this Act, the Immigration and Naturalization Service shall forthwith notify the appropriate public medical officer of the local community to which the alien is destined: *Provided further,* That the provisions of this Act shall not affect the duties of the United States Public Health Service so far as they relate to quarantinable diseases . . .

Sec. 2. Regardless of section 9 of the Immigration Act of 1924, any alien admitted under section 1 of this Act shall be deemed to be a nonquota immigrant as defined in section 4 (a) of the Immigration Act of 1924.

Sec. 3. Any alien admitted under section 1 of this Act who at any time returns to the United States after a temporary absence abroad shall not be excluded because of the disability or disabilities that existed at the time of that admission.

Sec. 4. No fine or penalty shall be imposed under the Act of February 4, 1917, except those arising under section 14, because of the transportation to the United States of any alien admitted under this Act.

Sec. 5. For the purpose of this Act, the Second World War shall be deemed to have commenced on December 7, 1941, and to have ceased upon the termination of hostilities as declared by the President or by a joint resolution of Congress.

Approved December 28, 1945.

Source: War Brides Act of 1945. *U.S. Statutes at Large* 59 (1945) 659. 79th Cong., H.R. 4857; Public Law 79-271.

4. McCarran-Walter Act, 1952

The 1952 Immigration and Nationality Act (INA), also known as the McCarran-Walter Act after Senator Pat McCarran (D-Nevada) and Congressman Francis Walter (D-Pennsylvania), continued the restrictive national origins quotas created by the Immigration Act of 1924. Like the 1924 act, it strictly limited immigration based on race and nationality. Although it abolished racist exclusion laws against Asian immigration and naturalization (citizenship), the McCarran-Walter Act continued to favor European immigrants, granting only a token immigration quota for Asia. The act limited immigrants from the Asia-Pacific Triangle, described as all countries from India to Japan and all the Pacific islands north of Australia, to a maximum of 2,000 a year, with each country within the Triangle limited to 100 immigrants. The INA was largely a symbolic act, passed because of growing U.S. fears about Communist expansion in Asia, particularly in China after the 1949 Communist Revolution. American leaders feared that racist immigration and naturalization laws would make the United States look hypocritical, prompting more Asian nations to turn to Communism.

AN ACT

To revise the laws relating to immigration, naturalization, and nationality; and for other purposes.

Be it enacted by the Senate and House of Representatives of the United States of America in Congress assembled, That this Act, divided into titles, chapters, and sections according to the following table of contents, may be cited as the "Immigration and Nationality Act"...

Determination of Quota to which an Immigrant is Chargeable

Sec. 202...

(b) With reference to determination of the quota to which shall be chargeable an immigrant who is attributable by as much as one-half of his ancestry to a people or peoples indigenous to the Asia-Pacific triangle comprising all quota areas and all colonies and other dependent areas situate wholly east of the meridian sixty degrees east of Greenwich, wholly west of the meridian one hundred and sixty-five degrees west, and wholly north of the parallel twenty-five degrees south latitude-

(1) there is hereby established, in addition to quotas for separate quota areas comprising independent countries, self-governing dominions, and territories under the international trusteeship system of the United Nations situate wholly within said Asia-Pacific triangle, an Asia-Pacific quota of one hundred annually, which quota shall not be subject to the provisions of subsection (e);

(2) such immigrant born within a separate quota area situate wholly within such Asia-Pacific triangle shall not be chargeable to the Asia-Pacific quota, but shall be chargeable to the quota for the separate quota area in which he was born;

(3) such immigrant born within a colony or other dependent area situate wholly within said Asia-Pacific triangle shall be chargeable to the Asia-Pacific quota;

(4) such immigrant born outside the Asia-Pacific triangle who is attributable by as much as one-half of his ancestry to a people or peoples indigenous to not more than one separate quota area, situate wholly within the Asia-Pacific triangle, shall be chargeable to the quota of that quota area;

(5) such immigrant born outside the Asia-Pacific triangle who is attributable by as much as one-half of his ancestry to a people or peoples indigenous to one or more colonies or other dependent areas situate wholly within the Asia-Pacific triangle, shall be chargeable to the Asia-Pacific quota;

(6) such immigrant born outside the Asia-Pacific triangle who is attributable by as much as one-half of his ancestry to peoples indigenous to two or more separate quota areas situate wholly within the Asia-Pacific triangle, or to a quota area or areas and one or more colonies and other dependent areas situate wholly therein, shall be chargeable to the Asia-Pacific quota.

(c) Any immigrant born in a colony or other component or dependent area of a governing country for which no separate or specific quota has been established, unless a nonquota immigrant as provided in section 101 (a) (27) of this Act, shall be chargeable to the quota of the governing country, except that (1) not more than one hundred persons born in any one such colony or other component or dependent area overseas from the governing country shall be chargeable to the quota of its governing country in any one year, and (2) any such immigrant, if attributable by as much as one-half of his ancestry to a people or peoples indigenous to the Asia-Pacific triangle, shall be chargeable to a quota as provided in subsection (b) of this section.

(d) The provision of an immigration quota for a quota area shall not constitute recognition by the United States of the political transfer of territory from one country to another, or recognition of a government not recognized by the United States.

(e) After the determination of quotas has been made as provided in section 201, revision of the quotas shall be made by the Secretary of State, the Secretary of Commerce, and the Attorney General, jointly, whenever necessary, to provide for any change of boundaries resulting in transfer of territory from one sovereignty to another, a change of administrative arrangements of a colony or other dependent area, or any other political change, requiring a change in the list of quota areas or of the territorial limits thereof, but any increase in the number of minimum quota areas above twenty within the Asia-Pacific triangle shall result in a proportionate decrease in each minimum quota of such area in order that the sum total of all minimum quotas within the Asia-Pacific triangle shall not exceed two thousand. In the case of any change in the territorial limits of quota areas, not requiring a change in the quotas for such areas, the Secretary of State shall, upon recognition of such change, issue appropriate instructions to all consular offices concerning the change in the territorial limits of the quota area involved.

Source: McCarran-Walter Act of 1953. *U.S. Statutes at Large* 66 (1952): 82, pp. 163–282.

5. Indochina Migration and Refugee Assistance Act, 1975

On April 29, 1975, after approximately 13 years of military engagement, nearly 60,000 American casualties, and mounting public protest against the war, the United States's involvement in the Vietnamese conflict drew to a close. U.S. Marine and Air Force helicopters began a massive airlift of both Americans and South Vietnamese out of Saigon. The fall of South Vietnam to Ho Chi Minh's North Vietnamese Communists not only ended a brutal and controversial war, but also precipitated a new wave of Asian immigration to America. Soon Southeast Asian refugees, first from Vietnam, and later from Laos and Cambodia, began arriving in the United States.

The first wave of Vietnamese refugees, airlifted out of the country immediately after the fall of Saigon, differed substantially from subsequent waves of Southeast Asian refugees. As a group, they were more educated and wealthier and spoke more English; almost half were Christian, a good portion were former South Vietnamese military or government workers, and they arrived mostly as families. Those escaping Communist regimes dominated subsequent Southeast Asian refugee migrations. These latter waves of refugees tended to be less educated and poorer; a significant percentage were ethnic Chinese, and many had become separated from or had lost family members on their journey to America. Arriving largely during the late 1970s and early 1980s, these people became known as the "boat people" because of the sensational stories of escaping on rickety fishing boats, dodging both Mother Nature and Thai pirates, only to end up in refugee camps in Thailand and the Philippines. Initial resettlement plans intentionally dispersed refugees to prevent ethnic community formation and to integrate individuals into American society more quickly. However, within a few years there was a considerable secondary migration to California and Texas.

Passed in 1975, the Indochina Migration and Refugee Assistance Act set the terms for the initial refugee migration from Cambodia and Vietnam, designating refugees under special migration and parole status. The act was amended in 1976 to include refugees from Laos, and again in 1977 to extend the period of assistance provided to refugees. The Refugee Act of 1980 created a comprehensive refugee migration system, establishing the Office of Refugee Resettlement to administer refugee programs and services.

PUBLIC LAW 94-23—MAY 23, 1975

AN ACT

To enable the United States to render assistance to, or in behalf of, certain migrants and refugees.

Be it enacted by the Senate and House of Representatives of the United States of America in Congress assembled, That this Act may be cited as "The Indochina Migration and Refugee Assistance Act 1975".

SEC. 2 (a) Subject to the provision of subsection (b) there are hereby authorized to be appropriated in addition to amounts otherwise available for such purposes, $455,000,000 for the performance of functions set forth in the Migration and Refugee Assistance Act of 1962 (76 Stat. 121), as amended, with respect to aliens who have fled from Cambodia or Vietnam, such sums to remain available in accordance with the provisions of subsection (b) of this section.

(b) None of the funds authorized to be appropriated by this Act shall be available for the performance of functions after June 30, 1976, other than for carrying out the provisions of clauses (3), (4), (5), and (6) of section 2 (b) of the Migration and Refugee Assistance Act of 1962, as amended. None of such funds shall be available for obligation for any purpose after September 30, 1977.

SEC. 3. In carrying out functions utilizing the funds made available under this Act, the term "refugee" as defined in section 2 (b) (3) of the Migration and Refugee Assistance Act of 1962, as amended, shall be deemed to include aliens who (A) because of persecution or fear of persecution on account of race, religion, or political opinion, fled from Cambodia or Vietnam; (B) cannot return there because of fear of persecution on account of race, religion, or political opinion; and (C) are in urgent need of assistance for the essentials of life.

SEC. 4. (a) The President shall consult with and keep the Committees on the Judiciary, Appropriations, and International Relations of the House of Representatives and the Committees on Foreign Relations, Appropriations and Judiciary of the Senate fully and currently informed of the use of funds and the exercise of functions authorized in this Act.

(b) Not more than thirty days after the date of enactment of this Act, the President shall transmit to such Committees a report describing fully and completely the status of refugees from Cambodia and South Vietnam. Such report shall set forth, in addition—

(1) a plan for the resettlement of those refugees remaining in receiving or staging centers;
(2) the number of refugees who have indicated an interest in returning to their homeland or being resettled in a third country, together with (A) a description of the plan for their return or resettlement and the steps taken to carry out such return or resettlement, and (B) any initiatives that have been made with

respect to the Office of the High Commissioner for Refugees of the United Nations; and

(3) a full and complete description of the steps the President has taken to retrieve and deposit in the Treasury as miscellaneous receipts all amounts previously authorized and appropriated for assistance to South Vietnam and Cambodia but not expended for such purpose, exclusive of the $98,000,000 of Indochina Postwar Reconstruction funds allocated to the Department of State for movement and maintenance of refugees prior to the date of enactment of this Act.

(c) Supplementary reports setting forth recent information with respect to each of the items referred to in this section shall be transmitted not more than ninety days after the date of transmittal of the report referred to in subsection (b) of this section and not later than the end of each ninety-day period thereafter. Such reports shall continue until September 30, 1977, and a final report shall be submitted no later than December 31, 1977.

Approved May 23, 1975.

Source: Indochina Migration and Refugee Assistance Act, 1975. 94th Cong., H.R. 6755; Public Law 94-23. *U.S. Statutes at Large* 89 (1975): 87.

6. Asian American Movement: The San Francisco State Strike

The San Francisco State strike—the longest student strike in U.S. history—began in November 1968 and lasted for 167 days. It marked the beginning of the Asian American Movement. In March 1968, the Black Students Union, the Mexican American Student Confederation, the Philippine American Collegiate Endeavor, the Intercollegiate Chinese for Social Action, the Latin American Students Organization, and the American Indian student group formed the Third World Liberation Front (TWLF). By the summer of 1968, the San Francisco State University chapter of the Asian American Political Alliance, an Asian American student group formed in May 1968 across the bay at the University of California, Berkeley, joined the TWLF. The students demanded a separate Third World College that would be run by faculty of color and provide an education that would be relevant to their communities' issues and needs. The strike quickly spread to the University of California, Berkeley, where students of color also initiated a strike. Though the students did not win all their demands, their protests led to the founding of ethnic studies (first at San Francisco State University and the University of California, Berkeley) as a legitimate field of academic study.

The 1960s and 1970s were a time of unprecedented social protest and upheaval. Young Americans and young people all over the world spoke out, marched, and protested against war, racism, sexism, poverty, and exploitation, sometimes with violent results. Many students involved in the San Francisco State strike were also involved in other protest movements and community organizations like the Black Panther Party, anti-Vietnam War protests, and the fight to save the International Hotel. These excerpts document the struggle for equal rights, equal access, and the end of racism that students fought for during those turbulent times.

A. THIRD WORLD LIBERATION FRONT, "SAN FRANCISCO STATE UNIVERSITY TWLF STRIKE DEMANDS," 1968

1. That a School of Ethnic Studies for the ethnic groups involved in the Third World be set up with the students in each particular ethnic organizations having the authority and control of the hiring and retention of any faculty member, director, and administrator, as well as the curriculum in a specific area of study.
2. That 50 faculty positions be appropriated to the School of Ethnic Studies, 20 would be for the Black Studies Program.
3. That in the Spring semester, the College fulfill its commitment to the non-white students by admitting those that apply.
4. That in the Fall of 1969, all applications of non-white students be accepted.
5. That George Murray and any other faculty person chosen by non-white people as their teacher be retained in their position.

(George Murray was an English Department lecturer who was dismissed for his participation in the Black Panther Party. SF State Strike Committee. On Strike: Shut It Down. 1968. p. 3.)

Source: Third World Liberation Front. "San Francisco State University TWLF Strike Demands." 1968. In *Stand Up: An Archive Collection of the Bay Area Asian American Movement, 1968–1974*, edited and compiled by Asian Community Center Archive Group. Berkeley, CA: Eastwind Books of Berkeley, 2009. http://aam1968.blogspot.com/2008/01/san-francisco-state-strike-1968-twlf.html. Accessed November 2009. Reprinted with permission.

B. PHILIPPINE-AMERICAN COLLEGIATE ENDEAVOR (PACE), "STATE OF THE PHILIPPINE-AMERICAN COLLEGIATE ENDEAVOR PHILOSOPHY AND GOALS," 1968

We seek . . . simply to function as human beings, to control our own lives. Initially, following the myth of the American Dream, we worked to attend predominantly white colleges, but we have learned through direct analysis that it is impossible for our people, so-called minorities, to function as human beings, in a racist society in which white always come first . . . So we have decided to fuse ourselves with the masses of Third World people, which are the majority of the world's peoples, to create, through struggle, a new humanity, a new humanism, a New World Consciousness, and within that context collectively control our own destinies.

Source: Philippine-American Collegiate Endeavor (PACE). "State of the Philippine-American Collegiate Endeavor Philosophy and Goals." 1968. In *Stand Up: An Archive Collection of the Bay Area Asian American Movement, 1968–1974*, edited and compiled by Asian Community Center Archive Group. Berkeley, CA: Eastwind Books of Berkeley, 2009. http://aam1968.blogspot.com/2008/01/philippine-american-collegiate-endeavor.html. Accessed November 2009. Reprinted with permission.

C. RESEARCH ORGANIZING COOPERATIVE OF SAN FRANCISCO, "SFSU TWLF STRIKE INJURIES FROM POLICE BRUTALITY," 1969

The Research Organizing Cooperative of San Francisco published statistics gathered by doctors on injuries to arrested San Francisco State strikers (and innocent bystanders) inflicted by police between December 2, 1968, and January 30, 1969.

Number Type Of Injury

- 1 Ruptured spleen (removed)
- 2 Fractured skull
- 2 Concussion
- 15 Forehead, skull lacerations
- 3 Nose broken, bloodied
- 1 Fractured eye orbit
- 7 Eyes maced
- 2 Other eye damage (e.g., black)
- 6 Facial lacerations, swelling
- 18 Other head damage (bump, swelling, contusion)
- 8 Stomach badly clubbed, scratched or kicked
- 2 Broken, contused, fractured ribs
- 3 Broken fingers, thumb
- 1 Broken, fractured leg
- 1 Arm broken, fractured from surgery
- 1 Arm infected from surgery
- 1 Kidney infection
- 4 Other groin area damaged
- 2 Respiratory Infection
- 1 Contused lung
- 7 Other rib area damage (soreness)
- 12 Back, neck (clubbing, choking, welts, burns)
- 4 Blood vessel damage (massive bruises only)
- 15 Hand, arm, foot, leg laceration, swelling, lumps
- 5 Limb, finger, toe sprain, wrenched, contused
- 13 General bumps, bruises, soreness only
- 1 Nausea
- 80 Total number injured arrestees (many had more than one injury)

These do not include: (1) injuries sustained between November 6 and December 1; (2) injuries not reported; and (3) injuries to people who were not arrested. There might well be more of the latter than there were injured arrestees; it is impossible to tell how many.

Source: Research Organizing Cooperative of San Francisco. "SFSU TWLF Strike Injuries from Police Brutality." 1969. In *Stand Up: An Archive Collection of the Bay Area Asian American Movement, 1968–1974*, edited and compiled by Asian Community Center Archive Group. Berkeley, CA: Eastwind Books of Berkeley, 2001. http://aam1968.blogspot.com/2008/01/sfsu-twlf-strike-injuries-from-police.html. Accessed November 2009. Reprinted with permission.

D. RICHARD AOKI, SPEECH AT AAPA (ASIAN AMERICAN POLITICAL ALLIANCE, UNIVERSITY OF CALIFORNIA, BERKELEY) RALLY, JULY 28, 1968

We Asian-Americans believe that American society has been, and still is, fundamentally a racist society, and that historically we have accommodated ourselves to this society in order to survive . . .

We're sick and tired of being sick and tired of being sick and tired of relating to white standards of acceptability . . . We're tired of hearing the racist chant about "if you're white . . . " This has wreaked havoc upon our cultural identity . . .

We are sick of being used by the white racist power structure . . . Don't rock the boat . . . Used as an example . . .

We Asian-Americans support all non-white liberation movements and believe that all minorities in order to be truly liberated must have complete control over the political, economic and social institutions within their respective communities". We unconditionally, support the struggles of the Afro-American people, the Chicanos, and the American Indians in to attain freedom, justice and equality . . .

We Asian-Americans oppose the imperialist policies being pursued by the American government . . .

Professor Miyoshi has presented our views on the Vietnam war . . . We are unconditionally against the war in Vietnam . . . some of us view the war as another one of white racist America's trickbag. . . . They are committing double genocide over there. Dig, if a black, brown or yellow brother is sent to Vietnam he is being sent to kill his yellow brother . . if the black, brown *or* yellow brother kills the Vietnamese . . Mr. Charley comes out ahead, and if the Vietnamese kills the black brown or yellow brother, Mr. Charley again comes out ahead . . . This is a classical case of heads I win, tails you lose . . .

In conclusion, I would like to add that the Asian-American Political Alliance is not just another Sunday social club. We are an action-oriented group, and we will not just restrict our activities to merely ethic issues, but to all issues that are of fundamental importance pertaining to the building of a new and a better world."

Source: Excerpts from a speech written by Richard Aoki for the Asian American Political Alliance (AAPA) rally on July 28, 1968. In *Stand Up: An Archive Collection of the Bay Area Asian American Movement, 1968–1974,* edited and compiled by Asian Community Center Archive Group. Berkeley, CA: Eastwind Books of Berkeley, 2009. http://aam1968.blogspot.com/2008/01/aapa-rally-july-28-1968.html. Accessed November 2009. Reprinted with permission.

E. "INTERCOLLEGIATE CHINESE FOR SOCIAL ACTION," 1968

The following excerpt is taken from a student brochure published for the 1968 San Francisco State strike.

S. F. State, a community college, exists in a moral vacuum, oblivious to the community it purports to serve. It does not reflect the pluralistic society that is San Francisco—it does not begin to serve the 300,000 non-white people who live in this urban community in poverty, ignorance, despair. The Chinese ghetto, Chinatown, is a case in point.

1. S. F. State has a Chinese language department that isolates the "Chinese Experience" as a cultural phenomenon in language that 83% of the Chinese in the

U.S. don't speak. Realistically, we can expect that a Chinese woman living in the ghetto, who speaks Cantonese, cannot explain to the scholar that she is dying of tuberculosis because she speaks a "street language" while the scholar mutters a classical poetry in Mandarin. S. F. State does not teach Cantonese.

2. Chinatown is a ghetto in San Francisco, there are approximately 50,000 Chinese of whom the vast majority live in Chinatown. It is an area of old buildings, narrow streets & alleys, and the effluvia of a great many people packed into a very small space. At present, more than 5,000 new Chinese immigrants stream into this overpopulated ghetto each year, an area already blessed with a birthrate that is rising, and will rise more. Tuberculosis is endemic, rents are high and constantly rising, city services are inadequate to provide reasonable sanitation, and space is at such a premium as to resemble the Malthusian ratio at its most extreme. There are no adequate courses in any department of school at S. F. State that even begin to deal with the problems of the Chinese people in their exclusionary and racist environment.

Source: "Intercollegiate Chinese for Social Action." 1968. In *Stand Up: An Archive Collection of the Bay Area Asian American Movement, 1968–1974*, edited and compiled by Asian Community Center Archive Group. Berkeley, CA: Eastwind Books of Berkeley, 2009, p. 46. http://aam1968.blogspot.com/2007/12/blog-post_3620.html. Accessed November 2009. Reprinted with permission.

F. ASIAN AMERICAN POLITICAL ALLIANCE, "AAPA PERSPECTIVES," 1969

The Asian American Political Alliance is people. It is a people's alliance to effect social and political changes. We believe that the American society is historically racist and one which has systematically employed social discrimination and economic imperialism, both domestically and internationally, exploiting all nonwhite people in the process of building up their affluent society.

They did so at the expense of all of us. Uncontrolled capitalism has pushed all of the non-white people into a social position so that only manual jobs with subhuman pay are open to them. Consequently, we have been psychologically so conditioned by the blue-eye-blond-hair standard that many of us have lost our perspective, We can only survive if "we know our place"—shut up and accept what we are given, We resent this kind of domination and we are determined to change. The goal of AAPA is political education and advancement of the movement among Asian people, so that they may make all decisions that affect their own lives, in a society that never asks people to do so. AAPA is not an isolated group, and should never profess to be such. Its only legitimacy and value is in the effects it has on many people, not just a small group of people. In the same vein, AAPA is not meant to isolate Asians from other people; it is unhealthy as well as unwise to do such a thing. AAPA must constantly expand and grow, and reach out to other people and groups. At the same time, AAPA must meet the needs of its own members and deal with its own problems.

In the past political organizations have tended to subject themselves to rigid, traditional levels of structure in which a few make the decisions, present them to the body, and the body can vote either "yes" or "no." This hierarchic organization, however, is only a manifestation of the elite control, primeval structure mentality in which you are not capable of making your own decisions, an idea drilled into you from the foundations of this society.

AAPA is only what the people make it. We have adopted a structure which better fits the needs and goals of our alliance, not a structure to which we have to adjust ourselves. Furthermore, there is no membership in AAPA in the strict sense of the word. There are workers who for common interests join together with one or more people to intensify the effectiveness of an action.

Since May, 1968, AAPA has grown from a small group of students and community workers to a powerhouse for Asian thought and action. AAPA is now a member of the Third World Liberation Front, Asian Association, and Asian Coalition. Some past activities of Berkeley AAPA include: Free Huey Rallies at the Oakland Courthouse, Chinatown Forums, McCarran Act lobbies, MASC Boycott, Third World Liberation Front Strike, development of Asian Studies, and liaison with and development of other AAPA's throughout the state.

AAPA is only a transition for developing our own social identity, a multiplication of efforts. In fact, AAPA itself is not the important link but the ideas generated into action from it—that we Asian Americans are no longer going to kowtow to white America in order to gain an ounce of respect; that we must begin to build our own society alongside our black, brown and red brothers as well as those whites willing to effect fundamental social, economic, political changes; that we have the right for determining our own lives and asserting our yellow identity as a positive force in a new life based on human relationships and cooperation.

Source: Asian American Political Alliance. "AAPA Perspectives." *Asian American Political Alliance* vol. 1, no. 6, October 1969, p. 3. In *Stand Up: An Archive Collection of the Bay Area Asian American Movement, 1968–1974,* edited and compiled by Asian Community Center Archive Group. Berkeley, CA: Eastwind Books of Berkeley, 2009. http://aam1968.blogspot.com/2008/01/aapa-perspectives-october-1969.html. Accessed November 2009. Reprinted with permission.

G. FLYER FOR THE YELLOW SYMPOSIUM AT THE UNIVERSITY OF CALIFORNIA, BERKELEY, "ASIAN EXPERIENCE/YELLOW IDENTITY," 1969

Bring this, your invitation, to the 1st Asian Experience in America, Sat. Jan. 11, 1969, 9:00am-4:30pm Pauley Ballroom, ASUC Building UC Berkeley.

"If the Asian American is to live in a very complex American society and an even more complex world, and if he is to be able to assert his own humanity in these life spheres, he must know his own cultural history as an Asian American." 1968 An Asian American Student.

"theasianexperienceinamerica/identifiedyellowqueriesqueuesfriends"

"the asian flu in america, blackheads all; gardeners, cooks, laundrymen and toshiro mifune; the golden race, america the beautiful, glittering ghettoes, second class citizens with visiting rights; chinatown, manilatown, little tokyo relocated concentrated, beautification, hallelujah christian colonies; submissive females, passive males, mellow yellows, that strong silent type; run run shaw, made in japan, p.r. 95%; japanophiles, sinophiles, you likee chop suey, chop chop, me no savee; white paper, brown paper, yellow paper, black paper, red paper, if I were god I'd make everybody white; third world liberation front, all men are brothers, love is a many splendored thing, black eyed blondes; we all live in a yellow submarine, anti-queue law, call me yellow, no vietnamese ever called me a nigger, let's call a spade a spade, a jap a jap; buddhaheads transcendental meditation, Jesus is a'comin so get yourself ready for a hard day's night; reparations for the opium wars, christianity the whole world over, the asians get what they deserve, they breed like rabbits anyways; that fat jap, that skinny chink, chinatown my chinatown, my little houseboy, sayonnara suzie wong; Free University for Chinatown Kids, Unincorporated"

Source: Asian Students of Chinese Students Club and Nisei Students Club, University of California, Berkeley. "asian experience/yellow identity," 1968. In *Stand Up: An Archive Collection of the Bay Area Asian American Movement, 1968–1974*, edited and compiled by Asian Community Center Archive Group. Berkeley, CA: Eastwind Books of Berkeley, 2009. http://aam1968.blogspot.com/2008/01/yellow-symposium-1969-flyer.html. Accessed November 2009. Reprinted with permission.

7. "The Story of *Hyphen*," 2003

Created in 2003, *Hyphen* magazine is produced entirely by volunteers and is published three times a year. The following article gives a brief history of the magazine, founded in response to the dearth of Asian American media and the corresponding lack of complexity in how Asian American experiences, issues, perspectives, and culture were represented. *Hyphen* continues in the long tradition of ethnic media, which provides alternative voices and deeper community analysis than what is generally reflected in mainstream narratives.

In 2002, spurred by the shuttering of *A. Magazine*, a small group of 20-something-year-old journalists and artists got together to fill the void by envisioning the kind of magazine we always wanted to read: a publication that would go beyond celebrity interviews and essays about discovering our roots, which we found a long time ago, thank-you-very-much.

We began meeting around a kitchen table in San Francisco that spring, and over snacks and beer, a vision slowly emerged. The magazine wouldn't flinch at covering serious issues, but also wouldn't take itself too seriously. It would cover Asian Americans in Texas, Kansas and Minnesota, not just the critical mass living in California and New York. It would feature emerging artists, thinkers and doers, not only the few established Asian Americans who'd gotten mainstream approval. It would be a magazine that looked beyond identity—we'd explore cultural issues while tackling what is Asian American by accident, by tangent or by happenstance.

Our early efforts were infectious. Those at the first meeting told a few friends, and the gatherings quickly outgrew the kitchen table. During a year's worth of after-work meetings, we developed the publication's voice, elected leaders, debated content, threw (fundraising) parties, fought among ourselves and eventually learned to work together. A pair of staff members even fell in love and got married—all stuff worthy of a reality TV show.

Starting a magazine from scratch with zero funds is no easy task. But we were made mighty by bowls of Spam and kimchee over rice. Inspired by the passion and dedication that we saw in each other, and energized by the hi-jinks that ensue when you spend too many hours with the same people in enclosed spaces, we marched—steadily if improbably—toward the publication of our first issue.

Hyphen issue 1, which paid tribute to Asian American activism, was published in June 2003. The cover depicted a woman sitting on a stack of suitcases by the side of a road, just under a sign that read, "Welcome to Asian America, Population 11 Million." Since then, our numbers have grown to 15.5 million. And in tackling issues of culture and community with substance and sass, Hyphen has also flourished, becoming a media must for savvy Asian Americans.

The Asian American landscape has changed since we published our first issue, and we are proud that Hyphen has been a part of the dialogue. When we started Hyphen, we didn't know that we would create such a far-reaching community. When we first gathered around that kitchen table, it was simply because we were driven by a hunger for a more complex representation of Asian America. And when none presented itself, we decided to do it ourselves.

Source: "The Story of *Hyphen.*" http://www.hyphenmagazine.com/story-hyphen. Accessed June 2009. © 2009 Hyphen Magazine. All rights reserved. http://www.hyphenmagazine.com/about. Used with permission from Hyphen Magazine.

8. Asian American Alliance, Political Committee, Columbia University, 2006

The Asian American Alliance at Columbia University was founded in 1995 and is one of the campus's largest student organizations. Christina Chen, then-chair of the Political Committee, wrote the following mission statement in 2006. Chen lays out various issues of concern to Asian American students; in particular, she invokes the original Asian American Movement of the 1960s to highlight the contemporary struggle to maintain a viable Asian American studies program at Columbia.

The Asian American Alliance Political Committee seeks to . . .

- . . . heighten awareness of issues affecting the Asian Pacific Islander American community in New York City and beyond, issues such as affordable housing, education, LGBTQQI rights, mental health, voting rights/civic participation, labor reform, domestic violence, healthcare, environmental justice, etc . . .
- . . . become a catalyst for social change by organizing around such issues and, by the same token, support progressive APA (and non-APA) political candidates who advance such issues by means of legislation and public policy . . .
- . . . tackle cultural stereotypes and discrimination and eradicate them by facilitating open and honest dialogue about the causes of such bias in the media, literature, and other societal milieu . . .
- . . . build coalitions with like-minded campus organizations and ally with other students of color . . .
- . . . research, study and chronicle the history of Asian Americans in the United States, thereupon promoting the awareness of APA history among our fellow students and allies . . .
- . . . and lastly, though perhaps most importantly, explore what it means to be Asian American (whether we believe this term to be legitimately applicable to all APA's or otherwise) and what it means to be an "Asian American" in society today.

Asian American Studies Campaign

"Join us. Support the demand for Asian American Studies! Don1t let the Man divide us from our Third World brothers and sisters! We have a right to learn about our own history, not just the history of Whites! We are not the Model Minority! We want relevant education that meets the needs of our community!"—November 6, 1968: SF State Ethnic Studies Strikes

Asian American Studies emerged from grassroots movements that attempted to critically resist the Eurocentric historical narratives dictated by people outside of our communities. Asian American activists advocated for forms of scholarship that could counter the oppressive schema employed by educational institutions before the Third World Strikes of the 60's and 70's. Recognizing the need for community-controlled education and popular pedagogy in our classrooms, as well as the lack of spaces for Asian American students to confront issues of power, privilege, inequality, and oppression on our campus, the Asian American Alliance Political Committee fights for the resources necessary to maintain a truly sustainable Asian American Studies program at Columbia University.

Source: Chen, Christina, chair of Columbia University Asian American Alliance Political Committee, 2006–2007. Asian American Alliance Political Committee mission statement. August 2006. http://www.columbia.edu/cu/aaa/pc.html. Accessed April 2010. Used with permission of Columbia University's Asian American Alliance.

9. SAALT (South Asian Americans Leading Together), "Making the Case: Why Build a South Asian Identity," 2006

People from the South Asian diaspora in the United States come from all over the world: India, Pakistan, Bangladesh, Nepal, Tibet, Bhutan, Sri Lanka, and the Maldives, as well as from the Caribbean, Africa, Asia, and Europe, where their forebears had immigrated. South Asians in the U.S. number approximately 2.7 million and are very diverse in terms of language, religion, and socioeconomic and residency status. In 2000, a group of first- and second-generation South Asians formed SAALT (South Asian Americans Leaders of Tomorrow; later changed to South Asian Americans Leading Together) to address the needs of their communities. In subsequent years, SAALT has created a documentary about anti-Asian hate crimes, released reports on the post-9/11 backlash against South Asians, and advocated for immigration reform. SAALT's document "Making the Case," published in the early days of the organization, lays out their rationale for a broad South Asian identity, finding a common history in the United States and arguing for the need for an engaged and unified voice in American politics.

WHY USE THE TERM "SOUTH ASIAN" TO DESCRIBE SUCH A DIVERSE COMMUNITY?

The use of the term "South Asian" is fairly recent. Progressive activists in the 1980s began using the word to reflect their belief that people from the same geographical area should ignore their historical divisions for the sake of building a unified political identity in the United States. During the 1990s, the term became increasingly used, especially by activists, and artistic organizers who sought to bring together individuals tracing their roots to South Asia.

SAALT's work is rooted in the development of coalitions that bring together groups and individuals from all parts of South Asia and the diaspora. Our common experiences as immigrants and people of color in American provide the foundation for a South Asian political identity. The South Asian community empowers itself by working together to address issues that affect us all.

While we come from diverse backgrounds, South Asians in America have many common problems that require immediate attention and broader, community-wide responses. These issues include hate crimes, racial profiling, immigration policies, education inequity, and poverty. Moreover, in the post-9/11 world, many of these issues have been greatly exacerbated to the point where Indians, Pakistanis, Bangladeshis and other South Asians are seen as a collective "other." By coming together to respond to stereotyping, discrimination, and other matters, we establish a more visible and powerful presence.

IS IT POSSIBLE TO UNIFY SUCH A COMPLEX AND DIVERSE COMMUNITY?

While it is a daunting task, there remain clear reasons for South Asians to unite and to project our influence on America through active civic and political engagement. There have been precedents in America of such unity. China, Japan, and Korea all have very long, distinctive, and intertwining histories that have created animosity towards one another. Yet in the 1960s, Chinese, Japanese and Korean Americans began to build coalitions for the purpose of political power. As a result, Asian American Studies classes emerged at universities in California. Groups organizing Asian Americans around legal rights, unionization, domestic violence, and other issues took on a visible role in the American fabric. Such unity was based on the understanding that Asian Americans, through shared experiences in America dealing with immigration, access to benefits, and discrimination, would have greater power to influence and change policy—from university curricula to immigration law—if they worked together.

Similarly, South Asians have a myriad of issues around which we can organize and unite. The post September 11th backlash, which included hate violence and immigration policies, had a significant impact on South Asians. Hundreds of immigrants—mainly from Pakistan—were detained in the aftermath of September 11th; many have either chosen to seek asylum in Canada or return to Pakistan, or have been deported.

WHAT IF I PERSONALLY AM NOT AFFECTED BY THE ISSUES YOU MENTIONED?

There are many reasons why these issues affect ALL of us, instead of only the individual person or ethnic or religious group to which we belong. Racism is not logical. It does not discriminate in terms of educational attainment, place of residence, or income level. Marginalization and discrimination can affect any member of our community.

While certain issues may personally affect particular members of the South Asian community more so than others, this also means that those who are not affected are generally more able to create change. For example, citizens may be less affected by certain immigration measures that hurt non-citizens. However, this also means that citizens have a certain degree of power that non-citizens do not have to challenge discriminatory laws and regulations, and petition for change without the fear of losing their rights or livelihoods.

By articulating our common experiences in America, South Asians can identify issues and points of interest around which we can work together.

SOUTH ASIANS ARE FREQUENTLY SINGLED OUT AS A "MODEL MINORITY." WHAT ARE THE PROS AND CONS OF THIS REPRESENTATION?

While many South Asians fall within the higher than average socioeconomic bracket of this country and tend to be educated, it would be an oversimplification to believe that all South Asians are the same. The average incomes and education levels often hide significant problems of many South Asians, and obscure the fact that South Asians are prone to marginalization and discriminatory treatment in America. For example, according to the Asian American Federation, New York City's Pakistani Americans experience greater poverty, earn less, speak less English and live in larger households than other city residents. With the per capita income of these New Yorkers ($11,992) being almost half the citywide average, and a fourth of the Pakistani population living in poverty, the assumption of South Asians being a very wealthy population proves to be incorrect.

WHY SHOULD SOUTH ASIANS BE MORE ENGAGED IN THE COMMUNITY AROUND US?

Active participation and engagement in the community around us are vital civic acts that will improve and empower the lives of South Asians in the United States. Civic engagement involves taking an active role towards the betterment of one's community. It can be defined as one's capacity to

- work with others to bring about common goals;
- see oneself as a stakeholder in public life; and
- believe that individuals have a responsibility to contribute to the range of communities in which they interact.

By actively being civically engaged—whether it is in the political process, in the academic context, or in the South Asian community itself—we join ourselves with a larger collective voice to bring about equality and justice for all.

Source: South Asian Americans Leading Together (SAALT), "Making the Case: Why Build a South Asian Identity." http://www.saalt.org/attachments/1/Making%20the%20Case.pdf. Accessed June 2009. Reprinted with permission.

10. Mike Lee, "Why Asian Girls Go for White Guys," 2007

Mike, an aspiring entrepreneur, web geek, and wannabe writer, is a former New Yorker, now a resident of the San Francisco Bay Area. Mike asks readers a question that is oft repeated in the Asian American community, "Why do Asian girls go for White Guys?"

The answer to this question has been a contentious one in Asian American communities. Some Asian American men feel that Asian American women often prefer to date white men because they have been influenced by Hollywood images that depict white men as confident, handsome, wealthy, and attractive while portraying Asian men as either sexually predatory or geeky, bumbling, weak, and sexually undesirable nerds. The images of Asian men as smaller, weaker, less athletic, and less well-endowed remain widely accepted stereotypes in America. Conversely, there are similarly strong stereotypes about the exotic, sexually available, submissive Asian woman.

Interestingly, a 2006 Massachusetts Institute of Technology study ("What Makes You Click" by Günter J. Hitsch, Ali Hortacsu, Dan Ariely) analyzing online dating preferences found that men of color needed considerably higher incomes than white men to receive the same level of interest (users browsed and first contact emails). Latino American men needed to make $77,000 more than a white male, African American men needed to make $154,000 more than a white male, and Asian American men needed to make $246,000 more than a white male. A 2005 Columbia University study found that Asian men received the lowest ratings for attractiveness by all women, including Asian women. However, Asian women were also rated as the least attractive by men of every racial background.

So, the age-old question: Why do Asian girls go for white guys? A friend (who happens to be Caucasian guy and married to an Asian American girl) asked if there really are more interracial couples than intra-racial couples out there. "Asian guys complain about all this interracial dating, but is it really all that common? Or are they just noticing the few interracial couples out there and making a big thing out of it?"

Hmm. So I did an informal poll amongst my friends and found that 27% of them are in interracial relationships, within all of which the girls are Asian American. They all happen to be in the San Francisco Bay Area too.

(BTW, his is a highly unscientific poll and really doesn't mean squat, except to show that 27% of my friends are in interracial relationships. Do a poll amongst your friends. See what you get.)

(Also check out Why Asian Girls Go For White Guys: A Response and Why Asian Guys Can't Get White Girls for more juicy coverage.)

So why do you think Asian girls go for white guys?

Source: Lee, Mike. "Why Asian Girls Go for White Guys." August 10, 2007. http://www.8asians.com/2007/08/10/why-asian-girls-go-for-white-guys/. Accessed September 2009. Reprinted with permission.

11. Mike Lee, "A Comment on Asian Christians: A Friend's Response," 2007

In this essay, Mike Lee, a Bay Area blogger, comments on his friend's blog about Asian Christians. His friend had suggested that Asian American Christians sometimes seem to demonize Asian American non-Christians, implying that Asian religions and philosophies are inferior to Western ones. Mike asks what is the connection between Christianity and imperialism.

Today, a common sight across college campuses is the Asian American Christian student group. These range from pan-Asian American Christian groups to ethnic specific Asian American Christian groups. These groups are typically Protestant and evangelical. The increasing visibility of Asian American Christians has prompted academic interest in the religious practices and meanings of spirituality in Asian American communities. In many ways, churches are one of the last strongholds of segregation. Americans have less aversion when it comes to working, socializing, and living next to people of another race. Considering Christianity's racial dividing lines, this blog asks if Christianity is merely a tool of cultural imperialism, or if instead it is a source of strength for Asian American communities. Are Asian American Christians merely unwitting pawns spreading Western imperialism to other countries, or has the growth of ethnic churches provided a vehicle for Asian American social and political activism? Historically, the answer has been yes and yes.

I was talking to a friend about Akrypti's article "A Comment on Asian Christians" earlier this evening.

"I'm surprised that all of the comments so far are supportive of the article. I expected a strong backlash."

"Why?" asked my friend. "What she says is entirely true. It is an utter fact that Christianity has been a tool of Western imperialism. Just look at any history book."

I nodded. "True enough. I guess I figured there'd be at least one Asian Christian reading that article and writing a counter-argument."

"This is probably un-PC to say, but one ironic example of this is the incident with the Korean Christian missionaries in Afghanistan. That was where a group of them were taken hostage by the Taliban. The Taliban has since agreed to release the hostages, but have killed two of them already."

My friend sat back in his head and shook his head. He continued, "This is an ironic case because here you have an imperialistic religion that has so successfully penetrated a culture that it's resulted in that culture sending out missionaries of its own. And into an openly hostile environment, no less."

"But that's what Christian imperialism is—the extension of its beliefs and dominance, sometimes through force, and sometimes through more subtle methods like evangelism. In the case of these Korean missionaries, they unfortunately and tragically encountered a group who didn't take kindly to their evangelism: the Taliban."

After the conversation, I went online to research this incident. So far, two of the twenty-three hostages have been released. And like my friend said, two have been executed. The Taliban and South Korean negotiations have recently reached a deal to release the rest of the hostages.

According to the above link, the South Koreans were not there for evangelism; instead, "the group of volunteers was only offering free medical services to poor Afghans."

Also, "South Korea is currently the world's second largest missionary sending nation after the United States."

I don't mean to make light of this incident. My heart goes out to the hostages; I can't even begin to imagine what they've been through and what they've sacrificed. But as an example of Christian imperialism, I can see my friend's point.

What do you think?

Source: Lee, Mike. "A Comment on Asian Christians: A Friend's Response." September 8, 2007. http://www.8asians.com/2007/09/08/a-comment-on-asian-christians-a-friends-response/. Accessed September 2009. Reprinted with permission.

12. Belinda Dronkers-Laureta, "Asian Family Values," 2008

Invoking the history of Asian American activism and struggles for equality, Filipina American Belinda Dronkers-Laureta cofounded API Family Pride to address the specific needs and concerns of Asian American families. Many gay Asian Americans face additional challenges when coming out: Cultural and community stigmas frequently characterize homosexuality as a "white disease." For the same reason, their family members often feel that they need to keep their loved one's identity a secret. Often shame prevents many gay APIs from attending the mainstream gay community's already-established support groups. API Family Pride reaches out to Asian American families in culturally sensitive ways by employing translators, relying on more individualized settings such as one-on-one sessions with parents, and making connections with other ethnic organizations.

In her "Beyond Borders" post from *Asian Week*, Dronkers-Laureta, on behalf of API Family Pride, describes the isolation felt by many homosexual Asian Pacific Americans and their families and how her organization seeks to overcome that isolation.

Belinda co-founded an organization (Asian & Pacific Islander-Family Pride) dedicated to end the isolation of APA/API families with lesbian, gay, bisexual, or transgender children. In her workshops, power-point presentations, and dinner speeches Belinda cites the central importance of family in the lives of APA/API individuals. We read the research that supports the claims she makes in her workshops and it is beyond question, family is a principal value in Asian culture and APA/APIs derive much of their identity from being members of their family.

Our experience is also that when a child "comes out" to parents, often the parents reject that child. Rejection takes several forms; for example, parents withdraw financial support, banish the child from family gatherings, or even deny access to the home. But now there is a contradiction, does not rejection of a child violate the paramount importance of family? We have not satisfactorily worked out the answer, but are developing several threads.

Thread one is that family is the basic unit of analysis for Asian cultures and the central focus of an APA/API's life; there is no smaller unit, there are no individuals. The behavior of an individual family member reflects on the entire family. The family unit is part of a larger social network that imposes norms developed over a long time. Our experience is that when a child tells parents that he or she is lesbian, gay, bisexual, or transgender, the reaction more often than not is shame. A sexual orientation other than the accepted norm is not acceptable. In fact, many Asian languages have no word for alternative sexual orientations and in some [Asian countries] it [homosexuality] is illegal.

Thread two is that harmony is another is highly praised Asian value. In fact, the clinical psychologist Sam Chan writes that for Asians harmony is the keynote to existence. A lesbian, gay, bisexual, or transgender child violates a social norm that reflects on the family and disturbs social harmony. Belinda reports that often parents agonize over what their family will think. Will their friends think them bad parents?

The explanation is, of course, too facile for so complex a phenomenon. The implication for our work, though, is clear. If we want to end the isolation of APA/API families with lesbian, gay, bisexual, or transgender children, then talking to families is not enough. We have to somehow reach the whole community.

Source: Dronkers-Laureta, Belinda. "Asian Family Values." *Asian Week*, April 12, 2008. http://beyondborders.asianweek.com/?p=7. Accessed on February 2010. Reprinted with permission.

13. *AsianWeek*, "A New Hope for Asian Americans," 2008

Established in 1979, *AsianWeek* was the oldest continuous English-language Asian American newspaper until it stopped its print production in 2009 and moved solely online (asianweek.com). This lead editorial, published three days after the election of Barack Obama, expresses the optimism many Asian Americans felt when the first person of color became president of the United States.

Asian Americans woke up to a new day this week—a day when the tallest racial barrier was broken, when a person of color could take a seat in the highest office of the land, when we as a country took one large step away from our racist past.

The election of Barack Obama as the 44th president of the United States is a historic moment for all Americans, and Americans of color in particular. He gives us hope that this is indeed a country of equality, that racial progress is happening, that an Asian American can become president one day.

In fact, as *San Francisco Chronicle* columnist Jeff Yang suggested, Obama may very well be the first Asian American president: Note his youth spent in Asian-majority populated Hawai'i as well as Indonesia; his sister Maya, of Indonesian descent, and her husband Konrad, a Chinese Canadian; his foreign-sounding name that branded him an outsider throughout his life; and his emphasis on education, hard work and personal responsibility.

It was impossible to ignore the truly multi-racial nature of Obama's campaign, in addition to its overwhelming diversity in terms of age, class and background. We are hopeful that it will predict the future of campaigns for all candidates regardless of race.

We are also buoyed by the fact that Obama was the first presidential candidate to care enough about Asian Americans to pen a platform addressing issues in the Asian American Pacific Islander community.

But we must temper our dreams with reality. History is littered with our community's dashed hopes and with promises unfulfilled: Ask the Chinese American railroad workers who were thanked for their backbreaking work with racist legislation, the Filipino veterans of World War II who today are pleading for benefits with their last breaths, the Japanese Americans who were herded into internment camps in the 1940s or the Hmong soldiers who fought the CIA's secret war in Laos only to face hate crimes and poverty in the United States.

Change was promised and now we must ensure that it is delivered. With Obama in the White House, our hopes are high that the refrain of his campaign will become the refrain of this century for all Americans of all colors: Yes, we can.

Source: "A New Hope for Asian Americans." *AsianWeek.* November 7, 2008. http://www.asianweek.com/2008/11/07/a-new-hope-for-asian-americans/#more-9344. Accessed April 2010. Used with permission of *AsianWeek.*

14. jozjozjoz, "Buddha-chic!" 2008

jozjozjoz is an Asian American blogger who lives and works in Los Angeles, California. In this blog, she asks whether or not the home-decorating trend of using "Asian" influences is a sign of positive cultural exchange and understanding or whether it belittles Asian cultures and religions. This trend of "Asian chic," things from Asia being associated with luxury and exoticism, has a long history. As historian John Tchen has described in his seminal work *New York before Chinatown,* wealthy white Victorian Americans in New York City were very fond of snuffboxes, rugs, paintings, china (dishware), and other consumer products or things they obtained through the very lucrative China trade. The luxury goods from China symbolized wealth and status because they were expensive and difficult to obtain. However, the desire for things from Asia did not necessarily translate into an acceptance of Asian immigrants. Globalization is not only a contemporary phenomenon. The question is whether or not this sort of cross-cultural exchange really resulted in cross-cultural understanding. In the late 19th century, it did not. Instead, Chinese cultural things were not celebrated for their cultural value, but as commodities that represented wealth. While we could easily ascribe this type of cultural insensitivity to the past, jozjozjoz's blog raises an important question: Has globalization really made us more culturally sensitive or less? Are we doing the same thing as Victorian Americans when we buy spiritual symbols like wooden Buddhas and use them to decorate our bedrooms?

I was surfing around when I found this slideshow on the LA Times site: Buddha in home decor.

A related article entitled "Buddhamania" goes into detail about how the religious symbol of Buddha has become "decorative" and is used by interior designers as a "visual shorthand" to exemplify "zen."

The article describes the popularity of buddha-shaped items like bars of soap, table lamps, and wind chimes:

The trend has even spawned the inevitable spoofs, including the sage dog in the classic contemplative pose—paws poking out of its monk robe—for $25 at the Pilgrims Way Community Bookstore & the Secret Garden, a Carmel shop that sells mostly serious items representing world religions. When a Japanese Buddhist monk saw the concrete canine, he laughed out loud, store owner Cynthia Fernandes says. "So I figure it can't be offensive."

Indeed, Buddha has become such a ubiquitous element in living rooms and on patios, the questions are inescapable: Has Buddhamania gone too far? What is the proper way to showcase such pieces? And at what point is the religious symbol reduced to a decorating tchotchke?

I don't consider myself to be religious, but I am definitely more Buddhist than anything else. Personally, I am not interested in "decorating" my house with Buddhas, save for maybe one or two very special pieces. And even so, I know that I would place the Buddha very purposefully and respectfully, but that's just me.

I guess other people can do what they want in terms of decorating their own houses, but being a non-Christian, I could not imagine putting Jesuses around my home, but it sounds like a lot of non-Buddhists like having Buddha in their homes. More power to them, I guess. What do you think?

Source: Wang, "Jocelyn" Joz. "Buddha Chic!" June 13, 2008. http://www.8asians.com/2008/06/13/buddha-chic/. Accessed September 2009. Reprinted with permission.

15. Ernie Hsuing, "Rainbow Nation and Gay Asian Male Stereotypes," 2008

Public discussions about sexual orientation seldom occur in communities of color. Queer voices are often silent, particularly in immigrant communities; it is almost as if gay, lesbian, bisexual, and transgender individuals do not exist. Of course, this is not true. Ernie Hsuing, the San Francisco Bay Area creator of the blog site 8Asians, examines the intersection of race and sexual orientation. In the following essay, Hsuing asks what it means to be an Asian American gay man. How do ethnic and sexual identities affect each other? How are Asian gender stereotypes applied (do they change or stay the same) when they are attached to gay men, and how are gay stereotypes applied to Asians?

That's a way to get a response from me; create a video that starts out with the line, "Asian men have a lot of diseases [and] small penises."

Gimmicky way to start off a documentary aside, some interesting points are raised by this video: stereotypes of Gay Asian men exist—that they're skinny, smooth, only date white guys and that they are effeminate and thus passive. The pod also asserts that non-Asians feel that the stereotypes of Asians are justified because that's all they see when they walk around in the Castro or go on chat rooms.

Usually it's easy to write my own personal opinions on the matter, but for this post I'm having a strangely difficult time on this one. Maybe it's because I'm definitely not a gay Asian stereotype—I'm definitely NOT skinny, I can't dress for shit (ask my friend Royce; he'll tell you stories) and I don't think I'm THAT effeminate (other 8A writers, feel free to shoot me down if I assume wrong.) While fighting stereotypes sounds like a noble thing, when you're coming out of the closet you WANT to fit in somewhere, be in a tribe, look and act like everyone else as a way to not feel ostracized. I had huge self-esteem issues where I've felt like the only way I could ever find a boyfriend is if I were to somehow magically lose fifty pounds and dress in DKNY, because that's the only thing I saw—horrible, but true. As a result, I hung out with the bear subculture for a while, but that didn't make things any better—an experience with discrimination there is one of the reasons why I started 8Asians.

Now I'm a little older and I know that if someone is trying so hard to live up to a certain label that they're not really worth my effort anyway. Dating is still a challenge but if someone is not into me, then their bad. Gaysians, what are your experiences?

Source: Hsuing, Ernie. "Rainbow Nation and Gay Asian Male Stereotypes." February 10, 2008. http://www.8asians.com/2008/02/10/rainbow-nation-and-gay-asian-male-stereotypes/. Accessed September 2009. Reprinted with permission.

16. John, "Asian Americans Going on a Date in a Wells Fargo Commercial," 2008

In this column, Bay Area blogger John discusses recent Asian American faces on television. He also talks about the lack of Asian American couples in American media. Historically, there has been a lack of Asian American representation in the media. During the height of the Hollywood studio system in the 1930s, the studios instituted a Motion Picture Production Code that banned any on-screen romances between white and nonwhite actors and actresses. Usually Caucasian actors and actresses in yellowface (makeup and taped eyes) portrayed Asian characters in films. Though more Asian Americans are seen in today's entertainment industry, they are still underrepresented.

I saw this television ad for Wells Fargo last week and realized that this was depicting an Asian American man about to take an Asian American woman on a movie date. I think this is the first time I've seen an Asian American couple in a TV ad. If you slow down the commercial (at least on my DVR), you can see the woman's facial expression of surprise and bewilderment as she sees how old and torn up the couch is, which is pretty funny.

I had blogged previously about an Asian American man in a, what I thought was a funny, CareerBuilder.com commercial. We at 8Asians.com have also blogged about Lucy Liu's character dating and kissing a fellow Asian American in Cashmere Mafia—shocking, I know, to actually see an Asian American couple on a major television network show.

We know Asian Americans aren't really represented well in the media. I had previously posted about Entertainment Weekly's write-up on the issue: EW: Diversity in Entertainment: Why Is TV So White? So even something as minor as having an Asian American couple in a TV commercial, well, it's a small big deal, at least for a post on 8Asians!

And my least favorite television commercial featuring an Asian American in recent years—Kaiser Permanente's "Thrive" campaign, titled "Entourage": In general, I have liked Kaiser Permanente's "Thrive" commercial campaign. It's just that in this particular ad, the only ad to feature a couple, they highlight a White male, coming home after a hard day's work, to his subservient welcoming Asian wife and head immediately to the bedroom so they can make a baby. Maybe I am being oversensitive, but this commercial just rubbed me the wrong way.

Source: John. "Asian Americans Going on a Date in a Wells Fargo Commercial." July 27, 2008. http://www.8asians.com/2008/07/27/asian-americans-going-on-a-date-in-a-wells-fargo-commercial/. Accessed September 2009. Reprinted with permission from John@8asians.com.

17. Beverly Chen, "The Strength of Sisters," 2008

Experts have pointed to many factors leading to depression and mental illness among Asian Americans. Underemployment in the United States can lead to depression over the loss of economic and social status. Refugees often suffer from posttraumatic stress disorder, which can persist decades after arriving in America. Conflicts over gender roles, cultural expectations, and assimilation can also stress family relationships. Experiencing prejudice, discrimination, and racism is particularly stressful for second- and third-generation Asian Americans who identify strongly with mainstream culture, but find it difficult to reconcile the dislocation between their self-image and their treatment by other Americans. Compounding these factors are cultural stigmas about mental illness in Asian Pacific American communities. Many Asian Americans tend not to talk about psychological problems or even recognize them as existing, focusing instead on physical symptoms. Moreover, language barriers and lack of insurance make it difficult for people to access services (according to the Surgeon General's report, rates of uninsured among Asian Americans and Pacific Islanders are 25 percent higher than the national average).

Beverly Chen, the Assistant Dean of Student Emotional Health at Harvey Mudd College, talks about her own experience growing up in an immigrant household, the specific challenges faced by Asian American families struggling with mental health challenges, and the often-accompanying tragedy of domestic violence. She sees her involvement with Asian American Women on Leadership (AAWOL) as a way to bring these issues into the open.

I met many challenges as the oldest child of immigrant parents. One of the major challenges was being forced to take on parental responsibilities for my younger sister because my parents were busily working long hours at their restaurant. Their business had placed tremendous emotional toll on their marriage and on their relationship with their children. My sister and I had to take care of ourselves without much guidance or supervision. While I became the caretaker and peacemaker in the family, my sister voiced her frustration and anger with the family by acting out in various ways in high school. In many ways, her behavior served as a wake-up call for the whole family. It forced us to be honest and real with one another. It gave us permission to examine the various underlying unmet needs, frustrations and emotional isolation we had all experienced for many years.

These challenges were the impetus for my desire to pursue psychology in college and eventually a career in mental health. In college, I was deeply impacted by a course on Asian American families. At the time, the course felt very much like God's gift of personal therapy. It opened my eyes to the many hidden shame and struggles common to many Asian American families. It was such a relief to know that I was not alone in my identity and family struggles! I became aware of the array of mental health issues that exist in the church when my professor shared her research on the secret presence of domestic violence in many Korean American Churches. I felt my heart break over the things I experienced and heard. At the same time, I also felt convicted in my desire to see God's healing go forth in my family and other Asian American families in the church. I am grateful that throughout my college, graduate school and professional journey, I have seen the awesome transformative power of God to heal and restore individual lives and family relationships.

I got involved in AAWOL because I believe that there is still a lot of shame and stigma towards mental health in Asian American churches and families. AAWOL creates a place for me to give voice and to empower other Asian American women in the church to obtain the support and healing they need. It has been exciting to have the professional network to serve alongside other AAWOL sisters in our respective spheres of influence, but more importantly, I have appreciated the personal friendships and mentoring that I have been able to cultivate with my sisters in AAWOL. The times that I've spent with them—whether formally at a retreat or informally over a meal—have strengthened and renewed our soul. Through our personal stories and prayers, we have been able to connect on a deeper level and I have felt energized to serve and lead in greater capacity. . . .

Source: Chen, Beverly. "The Strength of Sisters." 2008. http://aawolblog.blogspot.com/2008/08/strength-of-sisters_19.html. Accessed July 2009. Reprinted with permission.

18. John, "ABC's Nightline Profiles Raymond Zheng, 'Brillant Kid,'" and Rob, "Raising Your Kid: Problems with the 'Raymond Zheng' Approach," 2009

In 1999, Raymond Zheng was a 14-year-old college freshman; his academic career, profiled in April 2009 by ABC's *Nightline* news show, generated a great deal of discussion in the Asian American community. 8Asians bloggers John and Rob explore the issues surrounding the extreme pressure many Asian American children feel to succeed academically. This pressure has resulted in higher suicide rates among Asians than among whites, blacks, or Hispanics. Asian American women between the ages of 15 and 24 have the highest suicide rates of any demographic group. These pressures are not always just parental in nature but sometimes societal.

John and Rob also point out how Zhen's story reinforces the societal perception of Asian Americans as model minorities. The model minority myth is a contemporary stereotype that assumes all Asian Americans are academic powerhouses who excel in school and in fields like law, medicine, science, engineering, and math. This myth emerged in the 1960s, when African American demands for civil rights prompted depictions of Asian Americans as hardworking, successful examples for other minorities to follow. Conservative politicians also pushed this image during the 1980s when they successfully lobbied for huge cuts to social welfare programs. However, most proponents of the model minority myth did not take into account that Asians' higher than average household incomes were a result of most Asians living in cities where salaries and standards of living were higher; that Asians had more workers per household than other Americans; and that certain Asian American populations, like Southeast Asian refugees, suffered six times the poverty rate of other Americans.

JOHN, "ABC'S NIGHTLINE PROFILES RAYMOND ZHENG, 'BRILLANT KID'"

This past week, ABC's Nightline did a news segment on Genius School—Inside an innovative class for some of the world's most brilliant kids (video: 7 minutes. 40 seconds) and profiled Raymond Zheng, a fourteen year old freshman at the University of Washington. The news segment also profiled current middle school-aged students—mostly thirteen year old's—in a one-year program at the "Transition School," officially known as the The Halbert and Nancy Robinson Center for Young Scholars, which Raymond attended prior to entering college.

Young, precocious kids such as Raymond are fascinating, and sometimes I wish I were so bright. But why focus on Raymond? Maybe his parents were the only ones to agree to have their child profiled. But when Raymond says during his interview that "I find that I like math and science quite a bit," I wonder if Nightline is reinforcing the stereotypical Asian American "model minority." Raymond even performed piano recitals in kindergarten, currently has a 4.0 grade point average, and his favorite past-time is, yes, doing homework.

As an Asian American kid growing up in a white suburb in Western Massachusetts, I kind of identified with the model minority myth. Since moving to California, I understand much better the consequences and unfair expectations this myth imposes on Asian Americans.

The profile of the "Transition School" interviews students of this select sixteen student program that seemed like a fairly well balanced of students interested in a variety of topics beyond math and science, but I wonder also how kids like Raymond adjust socially to a college environment, given their age; do most of these kids adjust well? I have to imagine that there some social and peer issues that these Doogie Houser's have to come to grips with.

Rob, "Raising Your Kid: Problems with the 'Raymond Zheng' Approach"

Recently John posted about Raymond Zheng, a precocious 14 year old college freshman. Although I know nothing about Raymond beyond the video that John sent out, I'd like to use him as a starting point to explore a topic that I find fascinating: education philosophy, or in plainer terms, how to raise your kid.

Now, I should start by disclosing that I do not have any children of my own, as I'm 24 and spend my weekends drinking aggressively with my friends. That said,

I feel that I've experienced enough of life to have a rough idea of what skills and values lead to success, which means that I have an opinion on how to educate a child to instill those things.

I disagree with what I will term as the "Raymond Zheng" approach to education for two reasons: first, it seems to poorly provide for the types of interpersonal skills that are critical for success. Schools are about more than transferring academic knowledge; they are communities where people bond, form relationships, and go through the process of maturing into adulthood together. This program misses that by thrusting these kids into impersonal lecture halls with students who they can't possibly relate to in any meaningful way. It's telling that when the reporter asked Raymond to explain his computer program, Raymond gave the wrong answer. Not wrong in a technical sense, but wrong in that it failed to take into account the reporter's level of understanding of the subject and was thus useless. It lacked a level of human understanding that you can't learn by taking more advanced classes but which comes naturally to anyone who has spent time meeting people and making friends.

Similarly, the girl who dismissed going to prom completely missed the point; yes, she can still go with her friends (although I question how close she can remain with her friends given that she won't see them in school anymore and is going through a completely different set of experiences as they are). But prom is a communal ritual, and she is no longer part of that community. It is a step towards adulthood—it's no accident that so many high schoolers choose to lose their virginity at prom—that has a certain collective emotional resonance that she will likely miss out on.

Kids who grow up going through the normal education system are getting a lot more out of it than just an academic education. By being constantly surrounded with other people who are their same age and going through the same maturation process as them, and going through communal school events like prom, they are developing the ability to interact with other human beings. This is critical to success, not only because most careers involve a high amount of collaborative work, but more importantly because being a content, well adjust human being requires forming good relationships with other people. When I said earlier that I have a rough idea of what skills lead to life success, one of the things I meant is that I have never met a single person who is happy but does not have a lot of friends.

The Raymond Zheng approach also emphasizes the knowledge acquisition over creativity, when in most real life settings (at least the settings a high powered achiever like Ray is likely to get involved in) the latter is far more important. Creativity is a nebulous subject, but everything I've witnessed, read about, or experienced first hand suggests that it starts with play (there is an excellent book on improvisational acting called Impro that goes into this subject in more depth.) Watching Raymond, you don't get the sense that he plays very much, which makes me wonder how he'll do once he's gotten through all the academic knowledge that he's learning and moves on to the real goal of adding to knowledge and creating something new.

Raymond seems like a nice kid, and for all I know I might have the specifics of his story wrong. But I do want to call attention to and indict a way of thinking that is prevalent within Asian and Asian American communities—the exclusive emphasis on academic performance creates real problems and prevents children from growing up into successful, well-adjusted human beings.

Sources: John. "ABC's Nightline Profiles Raymond Zheng, 'Brillant Kid.'" April 16, 2009. http://www.8asians.com/2009/04/16/abcs-nightline-profiles-raymond-zheng-brilliant-kid/. Accessed September 2009. Reprinted with permission from John@8asians.com; Robert. "Raising Your Kid: Problems with the 'Raymond Zheng' Approach." April 27, 2009. http://www.8asians.com/2009/04/27/raising-your-kid-problems-with-the-raymond-zheng-approach-to-education/. Accessed September 2009. Reprinted with permission.

19. Frances Kai-Hwa Wang, "Attack of the Asianphile," 2009

Although originally outlawed in most states, interracial marriages became increasingly common in the years following World War II, the Vietnam War, and the Korean War. Under the terms of the 1945 War Brides Act, American servicemen began marrying Asian women and bringing them to the United States; correspondingly, antimiscegenation laws began to be overturned piecemeal (although they would not be deemed unconstitutional until 1967). Today, the vast majority of Asian–white interracial marriages are between white men and Asian American women. Sociologists and historians debate the causes of this imbalance, citing everything from historical colonial relationships between the United States and Asian nations, to pervasive gender and racial stereotypes in both communities, to levels of Americanization in various populations.

These conversations occur in the Asian American community as well, among people holding a wide range of perspectives. Frances Kai-Hwa Wang is a second-generation Chinese American author, public speaker, and activist. She is an editor for IMDiversity.com's Asian American Village, where she writes on family, arts, and culture, and she is the outreach coordinator of the Ann Arbor Chinese Center in Michigan. Wang's article, "Attack of the Asianphile," originally published on IMDiversity.com, humorously illustrates the intersection of gendered and racial stereotypes, expectations, and relationships.

I watch with nervous dread as he makes his move. The older bearded man—maybe a professor, maybe a street person—casually picks up his magazine and walks across the Borders café to sit in the chair next to the beautiful young Asian woman, at least thirty-five years his junior. No way. He is out of his league. What is he thinking?

He leans over and begins to make small talk. She begins to inch away in her chair, as far to the right as she can go. She smiles and nods politely, while burying her nose deeper and deeper into *The Audacity of Hope*. Still, he rambles on.

I am reminded of when I was the Manager of the UC Berkeley Glee Club Women's Chorus. One of my jobs was to intercept and redirect these Asianphiles* from young, inexperienced freshmen who might not yet know how to recognize and handle them. I remember crossing the large choir rehearsal room so many times, sometimes running down the risers, to physically put myself across the path of Known Asianphiles from the Men's Chorus as they walked in the door and beelined straight to the newest undergraduate Asian woman. "Hey Nick," I distracted him by taking his arm, "Would you mind helping Eric here with that new tenor passage?"

Meanwhile, back at Borders, I overhear snippets of "Where are you from?" and "When I first studied Chinese," and "My sensei at the dojo says . . ." I want to groan. Could this be any more stereotypical?

I catch the woman's eye from across the room and make an "OMG this guy is so crazy" face. She smiles imperceptibly and does not let him see. We have made contact. We are sisters. She is not alone.

I have recently met a few anti-Asianphiles—men who do not go out with Asian women because they do not want people to think they are Asianphiles. A curious breed, I am not really sure what to make of these. I suppose I should be glad to have found men who have no interest in me and are safe with whom to be just friends—the Asian equivalent of a gay friend. Yet, to be rejected out of hand because I am Asian feels almost as creepy as being desired simply because I am. There is no nuance. I am more than my race, the color of my skin. Is this borderline racist? Or simply a function of desire? I remind myself what Cybil Shepherd says, "Some people just don't like chocolate." At least it is more upfront than those men my father warned me about in college, white men who are happy to date Asian women, but will never marry them.

I feel I should rescue this poor woman somehow, but I am also afraid of attracting the Asianphile's attention. What if he then talks to *me* for an hour? Is that a risk I am willing to take for a stranger? Maybe I can deflect him better than she can, as I am American-born and more willing to not be polite, but I know that my body language will be like hers, illegible to him. Why doesn't she just get up and walk away? Why should she have to?

Last week, a friend affectionately called me "China girl." I did not have the energy to explain how offensive that was. I know he meant well, he simply did not understand the politics of his words, politics in which I live and work every day. So instead I rationalize, "At least it was not 'China doll,'" which has all sorts of worse fragile inanimate object connotations.

Finally, the Asianphile disappears, and the woman is free once again, her body relaxed as she returns to her Barack Obama book. However, I have been thrust into a whirlpool of doubt. How I long for friends who get me and take me as I am, in spite of and also not simply because of my race. My Asian and Asian American girlfriends get me, with little translation or explanation. I have a few male friends of color, but they have their own issues with white women. I sometimes wonder if it is possible for us to really have meaningful relationships across the borders of race (and gender). I am not talking about mere tolerance of people of different races (and gender), but real understanding and meaningful friendships. I have to believe that it is, that our differences of experiences are not insurmountable. Yet sometimes I really wonder if it is worth the effort, I cringe at the first sign of disjuncture (again!), and I hesitate.

Note

*The joy of writing for the ethnic media is that I do not have to define every single one of my terms. You already know what an Asianphile is: A man who likes Asian women *simply because they are Asian women, who cannot differentiate between Asian women who are smart, dumb, beautiful, ugly, skinny, fat, tall, short, fair, dark, outspoken, quiet, immigrant, American born, liberal arts, engineer, etc. Also known as someone with "yellow fever" and a "rice king." The offense is not that he likes Asian women, but that he likes Asian women without any sort of filter or discrimination. He sees what he wants to see and so any Asian woman is as good as another because they are all the same. He never really sees her. It is like the model minority stereotype. Yes, it is better to have a good stereotype than a bad one (here, better to be liked than not), but it is still a stereotype that is limiting and that denies us our individuality.*

Source: Wang, Frances Kai-Hwa. "Attack of the Asianphile." http://www.imdiversity.com/villages/asian/dialogue_opinion_letters/wang_asianphiles_0409.asp. Accessed November 2009. "Attack of the Asianphile" originally was published by IMDiversity.com, Asian American Village, and is used with permission of the author. Wang can be reached at fkwang@aol.com.

20. Timothy Chiu, "On Talking with or without an Accent," 2009

What is in an accent? This is the question that California blogger, Timothy Chiu addresses in this 2009 blog. Accents have always posed a difficult challenge for immigrants. In many ways, accents are a symbol of foreignness. For Asian Americans, who were historically denied citizenship rights, their accents mark them as perpetual foreigners. This idea of foreignness is a peculiar construction of Asian racializations in America. In his blog, Timothy muses about how people react to different accents highlights how much our assumptions about race are tied to how we speak.

I recently read a blog post from Louis Yap, an 18 year old Malaysian, on the topic of putting on a fake American accent when talking to foreigners. Apparently a lot of Malaysians drop their typical Malay accent and go for an American or English accent when approached by a non-Asian.

His reflections on this topic made me think about how the way I talk has been a major influence on how people react to me when they first meet me. While I was born in Taiwan, I moved to the U.S. when I was just shy of three years of age. I picked up American English easily, and while Chinese was my first language, I speak English completely accent free.

When I was younger and I lived on Long Island, I would regularly have people approach me, and say things like "Wow you speak English so well". I always had the immediate gut reaction of wanting to say "Of course I do you dimwit, I was raised here", but usually kept my mouth shut instead. These people were clueless, because there were few Asians if any on Long Island at that time (unlike today).

So, I grew up thinking I didn't have an accent, until I went to college in Philadelphia, a short 2 hour train ride from New York City. As soon as I stepped foot in my freshman dorm, I was teased mercilessly for having a Long Island accent. So much so, I learned to speak with out it by the time I graduated. Like Louis Yap, who affected an American accent to non-Asians; even I learned to speak differently to fit in to what was expected to come out of my mouth.

But it wasn't until I was older that talking without an accent really affected the way people treated me. In the working world, other Chinese, would automatically assume I was ABC (American Born Chinese) based on my lack of an accent, and that was enough for them to leave me out of their social circles. While the native Chinese speakers hung out in cliques, I always felt like an outsider, even if I could speak a dialect of Chinese flawlessly.

Of course there's also an upside to speaking perfect English. Everyone assumes I have no knowledge of Chinese, and will tend to make remarks they don't want me to hear in Chinese. This too has happened to me on more than one occasion, usually when I'm traveling in Asia, and has led to quite some embarrassment for the other party.

So, what's the moral of the story? Don't judge a person based on their accent. You may get more than you bargained for.

Source: Chiu, Timothy. "On Talking with or without an Accent." May 7, 2009. http://www.8asians.com/2009/05/07/on-talking-with-or-without-an-accent/. Accessed September 2009. Reprinted with permission.

21. Kathy Wang, "Racism: An Amateur's Perspective," 2009

Ever since they began settling in the United States, Asian Americans have faced the problem of "racial lumping." Mainstream Americans, unable to differentiate between Asian ethnic groups and their distinct histories and cultures, labeled everyone "Orientals," attributed the perceived vices of one ethnic group to all of the rest, and indiscriminately lobbed ethnic-specific slurs at Asian Americans of all ethnicities. Today, the model minority myth functions as an ostensibly more benign form of racial lumping. However, assuming that all Asian Americans are hardworking, successful, and do not need any government assistance results in struggling individuals and communities being erased from the public's consciousness, and their needs and concerns being ignored.

One response to racial lumping was ethnic disidentification, a self-conscious distancing of one group from another, in order to avoid being associated with their stereotypes and affected by their exclusion. This happened in Hawai'i, as successive waves of Asian immigrant groups tried to prove themselves to be different, of higher quality, and more desirable than the others, in a futile attempt to stave off exclusion. A second response to racial lumping was the deliberate creation of a pan-ethnic Asian American identity during the 1960s, which invoked the experience of exclusion and discrimination common to all Asian American ethnic groups.

Kathy Wang was born in Beijing, China, and immigrated to the United States with her family when she was five years old. She is a recent graduate of the University of California, Berkeley, where she studied psychology. Wang wrote "Racism: An Amateur's Perspective," for *Hardboiled,* Berkeley's Asian American issues newsmagazine. In her essay, she discusses the insidious effects of racial and ethnic stereotypes, assumptions, and biases and demonstrates how racial lumping still occurs today.

I used to be flattered to get attention when people asked me how to say things in Chinese . . . or Japanese . . . or Korean. It meant that they thought I was an expert on something, right? They wanted to learn something from me! However, since coming to Berkeley, I have realized that being asked how to say something in an "Asian language" is not always a compliment. In certain instances, such a request is an ignorant assumption about my ethnicity, my culture, my background, and my knowledge. Bet you didn't think a simple question could contain so many important implications, huh?

While I was walking on Sproul last Thursday, a pamphleteer tried to pass me a flyer. Unfortunately for me, his propaganda was accompanied by a "Ni Hao".

What the heck.

It gets worse. "Arigato" followed. First of all, fool, I can speak English. Second, good job for somehow guessing that I was born in Beijing, but I'm going to wager that you didn't figure that out by my mannerisms, my way of speaking, or the content of my words. No, because you didn't stop for one second to let me get a word out of my mouth.

FOB: Fresh Off the Boat. Sorry to break it to you, but the preferred means of transportation overseas nowadays is an airplane.

Is this term a point of Asian pride? Or is it a derogatory label that perpetuates the "Asians as outsiders" view? Until I was asked to consider this issue, I had never given the acronym "FOB" much thought.

It's common for Asian Americans to refer to themselves as "fobby-looking." This descriptor basically means that they are sporting hairstyles or clothing or accessories that are more commonly seen on Asian idols than on teenage kids from California. But what about those students who do come from Asian countries? Hey, I'm one of them. Isn't it okay for us to use that term? I mean, we're legit, right?

After quite a bit of pondering, I can honestly say that I have no idea what my stance is on the word "FOB". I guess it's a matter of interpretation. On the one hand, you can argue that reinforcing the idea that someone is "Fresh Off the Boat" means that we're also reinforcing the belief that he or she can never assimilate into American society. On the other hand, why shouldn't we of Asian descent and heritage reclaim a word that has been used to segregate and exoticize us? Pick your poison.

Let's consider the fraternal twin of fobbiness—being whitewashed. I've never been accused of being too "Americanized," but I'm pretty sure that it's always been on the back of people's minds. Although I was born in Beijing, I moved to the States when I was five and haven't really looked back since. I can probably rattle off *People Magazine*'s top five Hollywood scandals faster than I can name ONE Chinese celebrity. I've eaten more fries in my lifetime than pot stickers.

Here's the question that we've all been waiting for: Does being assimilated into one culture mean that one has to give up another culture? I don't know. I'd like to say no. But recently, I've been noticing how much longer it takes for me to find the right words when speaking in Mandarin with my parents. Those Chinese characters that used to be roll right off of the pages into my brain have acquired a more unnatural tone. In my mind, it's not about choosing sides. Life is about balance. Sure, I might fall in my great balancing act, but I'm trying . . . okay?

Work with me here.

Angry Asian Man, the moniker for the writer of a blog that goes by the same name, concludes certain news items with the exclamation: "That's racist!" . . . I can't do that. I'm not angry enough. I get it though, I really do. Racism still exists. It sucks majorly to be defined by the color of your skin and sometimes (if they care enough to look past the yellow), your physical features. The problem is, it happens too often and too subtly for a stray eye or comment to faze me anymore. Numbed by the avalanche of little, ignorant comments that threaten to bury me, I have begun to adopt a stoic stance towards cultural assumptions or ethnic biases expressed through looks, words, and actions.

And hey, here's a question for those of you who've ever cracked an Asian joke involving the phrase "me love you long time": What makes you think that you have the right to sexualize me based on the color of my hair or alienate me because my eyes aren't the same shape as yours?

In their Def Poetry Jam performance, the lovely ladies of Yellow Rage conclude: "Don't talk to me anymore, don't fuck with me anymore, because I am done talking to you."

But is blocking out the problem really the cure?

No.

We can bash racists all we want, but dialogue is necessary if we want to bring about change. Okay, I know that sounds idealistic and unfeasible. But hey, I'm not asking for some kind of world summit on racism here. I don't expect everyone to agree with me on an issue of this gravity. But let's talk it out. If we don't try to promote education about the pervasive problem of racism, we're screwed.

Recently, in my Asian American Studies class, we were posed the question: Does racism still exist?

That's a difficult question to answer. I am already overwhelmed by the deluge of criticism and disagreement that I can see looming in the minds of the readers.

My initial reaction is to say "yes". Maybe it's not overt, as some people may argue. No, it's more insidious. It's in the way that a school administrator treats me, giving me the benefit of the doubt because I am a good little Asian girl. It's in the way that strangers approach me, hesitating to speak English because they are afraid that I will open my mouth and blare out unrefined Chinglish back at them despite the fact that I have no Chinese accent. And that's even worse. Because people whom I don't know, and whom I will probably never get to know, assume that there is something that inherently makes me the unapproachable "other".

Racism is not skin deep anymore. It has penetrated us to the core.

So listen up. Look around. Stop assuming. We're all unique. Really, we are. And I'm sure you'd love me, or at least understand me, if you gave me a chance. Talk to me.

Source: Wang, Kathy. "Racism: An Amateur's Perspective." *Hardboiled*, vol. 12, no. 4, March 2009. http://hardboiled.berkeley.edu/issues/124/124-4-racism.html. Accessed September 2009. Used with permission of the author and *Hardboiled*, the Asian American issues newsmagazine at UC Berkeley.

22. Timothy Chiu, "Where Are the Asian CEOs?" and "The Bamboo Ceiling," 2009

Timothy Chiu was born in Taiwan and moved to New York in 1970 when he was only two years old. He grew up on Long Island. Chiu's blog posts, two of which are included here, explore the obstacles that Asian Americans face in the corporate world. Many of these issues stem from the model minority myth stereotype, which falsely assumes all Asian Americans are hardworking, college-educated, and technically proficient. Though many may believe that these are positive attributes, the myth essentializes Asian Americans, saddling them with unrealistic expectations. As Chiu suggests in his blog postings, not all Asians are good at math and science, and teachers who believe the myth may be unjustly harsh with Asian American students who do not meet their expectations. According to new research from the University of Washington, young Asian Americans between 18 and 34 have the highest rates of thinking about, planning, and attempting suicide of any age group (*Science Daily*, August 18, 2009).

The myth also assumes that Asians, though hard workers, are neither very creative nor possess the people skills to be good leaders. Some Asian Americans have found that these perceptions have negatively influenced their ability to get promotions. This subtle form of racism goes unnoticed by many who feel that Asian Americans are quite successful. In his blog, Chiu reinterprets the concept of the glass ceiling, renaming it the "bamboo ceiling" to refer to the invisible barrier that many Asian Americans face in corporate America. They can see advancement but can never reach it because of racism. They also struggle with mainstream society's inability to recognize this type of racism, oftentimes denying such racism even exists.

"WHERE ARE THE ASIAN CEOS?"

The question of Asians in executive row is the topic of an upcoming panel discussion, titled "Where are the Asian CEOs?" in Santa Clara, California. On May 20th, the Asia Society Northern California (ASNC), Ascend Bay Area and Corporate Executive Initiative, with event partners AAMA (Asian American MultiTechnology Association), CAAEN (Corporate Asian American Employee Network) and TiE (The Indus Entrepreneurs) are sponsoring the panel at the TiE Conference Center.

The panelists include Vish Mishra, Partner at Clearstone Ventures and President TiE Silicon Valley; Brian Schipper, Senior Vice President/HR, Cisco Systems; Chris Min, Vice President/Finance, Intel; and Susan Wang Wade, Board Member, Nektar, Altera and Avanex.

The meeting will cover topics including: why have only a handful of Asians have reached the highest corporate levels; the reasons behind their under representation on corporate boards and senior executive levels; what executive skills are required in large, complex organizations; and what companies are doing to develop and retain their best employees, including Asian employees.

In addition, a new study by Buck Gee, Project Director of the Corporate Executive Initiative and former Cisco Vice-President, will be released at the panel discussion. This study of large Bay Area companies found that Asian Americans continue to be substantially underrepresented at the highest levels of corporate management. While discussing this panel in a recent article, Asianweek also reported these statistics on Asian representation at the executive level:

2008 corporate reports have found that while Asians represented over 23% of the Bay Area population, they comprise only 5.5% of the Board members and 9.3% of the executive officers in the 25 largest companies with headquarters in the Bay Area. Furthermore, fourteen of these companies had no Asian board members and eight had no Asian corporate officers. Even in Silicon Valley, where Asians are over 30% of the population, Asians were only 9.7% of the corporate officer population. Top Bay Area companies Chevron, McKesson, the Gap and Symantec reported no Asians as board members or corporate officers in 2008.

This panel discussion is timely, given that 8Asians covered the topic of the perceived glass ceiling for Asians less than two months ago. Unfortunately, the number of Asian executives at my company hasn't improved since I wrote that post in March.

"THE BAMBOO CEILING"

I've written in the past about the glass ceiling for Asians in corporate America, but until I found this recent article on Asian scientists, I didn't realize there was a specific term for the ceiling when referring to Asians, specifically the Bamboo Ceiling.

The article I found was specifically referring to the inability of Asians scientists to move up into the management roles in academia and federal research institutes. Apparently Asians have as tough a time there as they do in the corporate world.

This article also introduced another new term I had not heard of before when referencing the inability to move up in an organization, sticky floors.

Here are some of the problems found by the recent study:

Problems raised by this Asian American community boiled down to three categories: employment, lack of support, and failure to file complaints.

"We found that most federal agencies didn't even look at Asian American numbers—they've become the forgotten minority," says Gazal Modhera, chair of the EEOC's Work Group. . . . while Asian Americans represented 23 percent of those holding tenure-track positions [at the NIH], they were only 12 percent of those at the tenure or senior scientist level. In the higher administrative positions the numbers further tapered off, with only 6 percent holding lab chief positions. Currently out of the 27 scientific director positions there is only one Asian American scientific director. There are no Asian Americans running any of the 27 Institutes, although one recently retired.

The study found Asians themselves to be part of the blame, by failing to file complaints when discrimination does occur in the work place.

From the article again:

> Despite the plethora of stories that were heard, official complaints remain few. A December 2005 EEOC Gallup Poll revealed that, although Asian Americans had the highest reports of discrimination (31 percent) of all the minority groups, only 3 percent of official charges were filed by them.

This article is a good reminder that as Asians we need to remember to stand up for our beliefs and our rights, since no other group is looking out for us.

One final note, the term Bamboo Ceiling is not new, as Jane Hyun used it in her book Breaking the Bamboo Ceiling: Career Strategies for Asians in 2005. So, I'm the one behind the times and need to catch up on new fangled terms like sticky floors.

Sources: Chiu, Timothy. "Where Are the Asian CEOs?" May 1, 2009. http://www.8asians.com/2009/05/01/where-are-the-asian-ceos/. "The Bamboo Ceiling." June 1, 2009. http://www.8asians.com/2009/06/01/the-bamboo-ceiling/. Accessed August 2009. Reprinted with permission.

23. Rob, "Asians Can Be Just as Racist Too!" 2009

Can people of color be racist? What is the relationship between Asian Americans and African Americans and Latino Americans? These are the questions that New York City blogger Rob confronts in this piece. While there is plenty of public discussion and scholarly research on racism directed at Asians Americans and other people of color by Caucasians, in comparison there is relatively little about race relations between people of color. If Rob's conclusions prove correct, being a person of color does not automatically make a person any less racist.

There seems to be a lot of discussion within the Asian American community about acts of racism against Asians, but very little about Asians acting racist themselves. It occurs frequently and seems to me to be a real problem. For example: the other day I was at a dinner party with a group of Asians, most of whom were in their 40s and 50s. At some point my friend's parents began discussing her boyfriend with me (who wasn't present). They weren't enamored with him, and began listing out the reasons why. When they were done, one of the other guests asked, "So what is worse in your eyes? If your daughter continues dating her current boyfriend, or if she begins dating a black man?" They then had a long, serious conversation about this, and while not reaching a firm conclusion, also made it clear that the black man wasn't winning any brownie points in their book.

The next day I was getting coffee with a friend of mine from Taiwan, and I mentioned this story to her. Her response: "Yeah! My parents do the same thing!" I got the same response from the next four Asian people I mentioned this to, so I don't think this is uncommon. Also, all the people who were discussing this at the dinner party were intelligent, caring people, yet none of them seemed to think that there was anything wrong or even strange about disliking someone on the basis of race.

So, what's the extent to which these problems exist? I'm reasonably convinced that amongst first generation Asian immigrants, racial stereotypes abound (especially against other non-Asian, non-white minorities), in large part because the homogeneity of most Asian countries doesn't really prepare immigrants for the racial and cultural diversity that is America. Also, based on everything I've ever heard, non Asian non-white races are treated in Asian countries with at best, amused curiosity and at worst, outright disdain (as hard as it is for a Chinese person to deal with racial issues in America, imagine how much harder it is for a black man to deal with racial issues in China). But I'm curious what happens to immigrant children, people of my generation. Do they tend to adopt the attitudes of the society they grew up in, or does racism pass on through the family?

And what's the impact of this to the Asian community? The most immediate impact is that it makes the Asian community a bit hypocritical—the same dinner guests who didn't want their daughter dating a black man also complained about racial glass ceilings in the workplace, and while that point might still be valid, it's harder to make persuasively when you are essentially guilty of the same behavior. It also has the effect of isolating the Asian American community. I don't think my parents have any non Asian non white friends, and I don't think any of their Asian friends do either. When others complain about Asians being insular, this strikes me as being one of the root causes.

What are your thoughts?

Source: Rob. "Asians Can Be Just as Racist Too!" April 7, 2009. http://www.8asians.com/2009/04/07/asians-can-be-just-as-racist-too/. Accessed September 2009. Reprinted with permission.

24. Jeff, "Asian-American Kids: Moving Back and Forth Between Asia," 2009

As our world speeds toward the digital age, it seems more and more people are talking about globalization. Though the term is new, globalization is not a new phenomenon. The world has been interconnected for quite some time, though in different ways than today. European colonialism created a world economic system that connected the slave trade to the signing of unequal treaties in Asia, and massive global labor migrations from East to West and back. The advent of modern technology has created new migratory patterns in which U.S.-born and -raised Asian Pacific Americans are increasingly going back to their parents' homelands. However, these are not permanent migrations; rather, they are transnational movements back and forth between different nations. Many American-born Asian Pacific Americans are finding fame as actors, actresses, and singers in Asia, something they find difficult to achieve in America because of racial stereotypes marking Asian Pacific Americans as model minorities who are "uncool". Conversely, Americanized Asian Pacific Americans have injected their own interpretations of American culture into Asian pop cultures. The relationship comes full circle with Asian Pacific Americans in the United States consuming Asian pop culture, watching Asian soap operas and films, and listening to Asian pop music. Silicon Valley blogger Jeff discusses the phenomenon of American-born Asian Pacific Americans moving back and forth between United States and Asia.

My boss has been living in India (I like to joke that my management has been outsourced), but he is moving back to the United States. One of his concerns is how his daughter will deal with the move. She originally lived in the US, moved to India, and is now moving back again. This article from the Mercury News talks about Asian-American kids who move from the United States to India and their experiences. When I was growing, going back "home" (that's how the parents called it) was a rare and special event. Asia was a place your parents immigrated from and that you visited on rare occasions. It certainly wasn't a place to where you moved. With the growth of India and China and other Asian economies, a growing number of Asian American kids are moving to Asia, or at least visiting much more often. In addition, those trips back to Asia were looked at as a pain, a visit to an unpleasant and backward place. Talking to a lot of The Daughter's friends, they don't look at it that way, and often talk about what a wonderful time that had going to Vietnam or China.

The article talks about how this new generation of kids will be able to move easily between East and West. Some of the kids profiled spend their summers in the US and the rest of the year in Asia. I have known kids like that. The article doesn't mention this, but a lot of Asian-American kids I know spend a lot of time in Asia—sometimes going there every Christmas or summer. Philippe Nover, the Filipino-American MMA fighter, did that. This kind of traveling back and forth was practically unknown in my youth, but is common at my sons' mostly Asian-American school. Those trips generated so many missed school days that the administration asked parents not to take extended trips while school is in session.

A number of Asian Americans have gone back to Asia to start careers, often in entertainment. Yoobin Kim (pictured—thanks for the picture, Jun) of the Wonder Girls spent time in San Jose. Sam Milby is successful in the Philippines. Jero went to Japan to start a career doing Enka. My nephew who does hip hop and electronic music and one of the last people I would expect to go to Asia, goes to the Philippines and other parts of Asia to perform almost every year. I am sure that there are many others that I did not mention.

I have occasionally thought about making that career move to Asia, but never that seriously. I do regret not taking my own kids there. It will be interesting to see how this new generation of Asian American kids evolve. Will they become totally assimilated into American culture, as some people say, or will they start forming a new hybrid global culture combining Asian and American?

Source: Jeff. "Asian-American Kids: Moving Back and Forth Between Asia." January 1, 2009. http://www.8asians.com/2009/01/01/asian-americans-kids-moving-back-and-forth-between-asia/. Accessed September 2009. Reprinted with permission from Jeff@8asians.com.

25. Jeff, "Tall, Short, and Segregated Asians: Six Lessons from a Basketball Season," 2009

One of the most pervasive stereotypes about Asians in America is the model minority stereotype. This stereotype centers on the idea that Asians are nerdy, asexual computer geeks who possess very few social skills, romantic charm, and even less athletic ability. Asians are often seen as short, weak, and uncoordinated. When combined with gender identities that idealize masculinity with heterosexual men who are strong, tall, athletic, and sexually desired by women, these stereotypes leave many Asian Pacific American men feeling emasculated. In this blog, Jeff, husband, father, and Silicon Valley computer systems researcher, tackles these stereotypes in humorous and insightful ways through his observations about his sons' basketball league.

My sons finished their very long basketball seasons last month, and I was surprised how some of my own views on sports, basketball, and Asian-Americans changed after what seemed to be an endless season. Here are six lessons that I learned:

Lesson 1: There are tall Asian-Americans out there
I find that the Asian-Americans are generally shorter.

I said that (so did Barack Obama), but after this season, I'd have to qualify that statement to "some groups of Asian-Americans are shorter." Number One Son's 6th grade basketball team had a non-league game scheduled against "School T". Both teams were mostly Asian-American, but School T's Indian and Chinese kids were taller than our Filipino kids. The real shock came when my sons' schools' 7th grade team played School T's 7th grade team. While both teams were mostly Asian, their 7th graders towered over our 7th graders, with a Chinese forward and an Indian forward who were each close to 6 feet tall.

I have noticed that more and more tall Indian and Chinese kids are playing basketball. This discussion points out that some provinces in China are known for having tall people. Moreover, the Asian-American basketball league Dreamleague has 6 feet and over divisions. One thing, though, is that when there is a tall Chinese kid, he gets referred to as "Yao Ming." "Yao Ming just got the rebound!" Annoying.

More lessons after the jump . . .

Lesson 2: Some teams don't take Asian-American teams seriously

Teams that aren't used to playing Asian-Americans teams often don't take them seriously. Number One Son says that when some teams see his team of shorter Asian kids, they think that they will win easily. These teams are surprised when his team isn't as easy as they think. The weak nerdy Asian stereotype is there, but it can be useful when it lures teams into overconfidence.

Lesson 3: Asian-American kids can play basketball as well as anyone

Number One Son's team of smaller Asian American kids took first place at their last tournament, beating almost totally white teams. They make up for being shorter by being faster, scoring lots of points on fast breaks. School T's 7th grade team was at the same tournament. They played against 8th grade teams and just destroyed their opponents.

Lesson 4: Silicon Valley is seriously segregated

Number One Son's team played against more teams of mostly one ethnicity than against truly diverse teams. Number Two Son's team had an African-American majority, and all of the mostly African-American and Hispanic teams they played were from our local NJB district. His team also had a similar experience to his brother's team with their opponents, playing undiverse teams. Despite hype about Silicon Valley's diversity, it's still is a pretty segregated place, and you really see it with youth sports teams.

Lesson 5: Asian-American parents are starting to treat athletic experience as something you can buy, just like tutoring sessions

As Asian-American parents become aware that colleges and selective high schools are not going to admit their kids if they stick only to academics and perhaps music, I see more and more Asian-American parents making their kids do sports. I am reminded of this comment on why few Asians-Americans are in the NBA:

That's because American born Asians have it easy. Try playing against native-born Filipinos, who honed their skills playing on concrete or dirt courts while playing barefoot or in flip-flops. They may not be as tall or jump as high, but they've got incredible ballhandling skills and can change directions like a deflating balloon.

The way get good in a sport is to concentrate exclusively on it, playing on well coached club teams in the off season. The playground stuff is good to an extent, but having a knowledgeable coach and practicing and playing real games year round is the most effective strategy for getting good (you are unlikely to learn things like press breaks on the playground). School T is an academically oriented private school that doesn't even have its own gym, but it's clear from the way their kids played that their parents also pay for club team experience. Many school teams form their own club and AAU teams to play together in the off season. Whether this is good for kids, leads to the next lesson . . .

Lesson 6: Sports should be about fun, exercise, and participation

On a previous post, there was the **following comment**:

I'm going to say something politically incorrect: Asians don't have the genes to play basketball, they don't have the height, the fast twitch muscles to make it to the big time basketball league like NBA. Jeremy Lin might be an exception so is Yao Ming.

I don't understand the part about fast twitch muscles, especially after seeing Asians in Olympic level badminton or table tennis. We discussed height above, and frankly, everyone in the NBA, some 450 players out of the whole planet, is going to be an exception. The point about the post about Jeremy Lin is even though he is an exceptional player, he didn't get recruited or taking seriously because he was Asian-American.

Now my turn to say something that might be considered politically incorrect. While watching pro sports like basketball may be entertaining, getting butts off the couch and actually doing sports is, IMHO, far more important. I recall one quote saying that a football game was "22 men desperately needing rest watched by 22,000 desperately needing exercise." Diabetes and obesity are real problems in the Asian-American communities and beyond. Overemphasis on winning, as seen by parents making their kids drop all sports in order to specialize in only one, really kills the desire to participate in sports and to be active. In Number One Son's last tournament, we the coaches (I was an assistant) were so eager to win that we didn't put all of the players in the championship game. Even though the team won and everyone there played in all the other games, the kids who didn't play were really unhappy. Although we later apologized, I think we forgot the point of why youth sports exist—to be active and to learn to love a sport that they can do the rest of their lives. It's wonderful that organizations like Dreamleague exist, promoting basketball for Asian Americans of all ages, heights, and skill levels as something you do and not just something you watch passively.

Source: Jeff. "Tall, Short and Segregated Asians: Six Lessons from a Basketball Season." April 22, 2009. http://www.8asians.com/2009/04/22/tall-asians-short-asians-segregated-asians-six-lessons-from-a-basketball-season/. Accessed September 2009. Reprinted with permission from Jeff@8asians.com.

26. Hindu American Foundation, "Yoga beyond Asana: Hindu Thought in Practice," 2010

The Hindu American Foundation (HAF), a multiethnic, progressive advocacy group, was formed in 2003. It supports reform efforts in public policy and education, works to highlight and eradicate the persecution of Hindus, and advocates for fair media representations of Hinduism, both in the United States and globally. The HAF has released reports on anti-Hindu hate crimes, testified in the Supreme Court case on public displays of the Ten Commandments, and won a lawsuit against the California State Board of Education for its misrepresentation of Hindus and Hinduism in the textbooks it had adopted. In addition, their lobbying on behalf of House Resolution 747 and Senate Resolution 229 led to their successful passage in 2007; the United States now recognizes Diwali as a nationally significant holiday.

The HAF released the following position paper on the importance of yoga's foundation in Hinduism. Like many religious communities in the United States, the HAF is recognizing the tensions that often arise between religious and American identity, especially as religious forms increasingly are adopted—and adapted—by the mainstream. "Yoga beyond Asana: Hindu Thought in Practice" argues against the despiritualized version of this essential Hindu practice.

"There is no physical yoga and spiritual yoga. If it is exclusively physical, it won't be yoga. Yoga is dealing with the entirety; it is a union."—*Prashant Iyengar, son of B.K.S Iyengar*

Yoga, from the word "yuj" (Sanskrit, "to yoke" or "to unite"), refers to spiritual practices that are essential to the understanding and practice of Hinduism. Yoga and yogic practices date back more than 5,000 years—the Indus Valley seals depict figures in yoga poses. The term covers a wide array of practices, embodied in eight "limbs," which range from ethical and moral guidelines to meditation on the Ultimate Reality. Yoga is a combination of both physical and spiritual exercises, entails mastery over the body, mind and emotional self, and transcendence of desire. The ultimate goal is *moksha*, the attainment of liberation from worldly suffering and the cycle of birth and rebirth.

With the popularity of Yoga skyrocketing throughout the world, particularly in the West, there arise two main points in need of clarification. First, that which is practiced as "Hatha Yoga"—a form of Raja Yoga—in much of the Western world is but merely a focus on a single limb of Yoga: *asana* (posture). From Yoga studios that recommend room temperatures to be maintained at 105 degrees to 90 minute Vinyasa flow classes that prescribe one Suryanamaskar (Sun Salutation) sequence after another, this "*asana* heavy" form of Yoga—sometimes complimented with *pranayama* (breathing)—is only a form of exercise to control, tone and stretch muscles. Ignored are both the moral basis of the practice and the ultimate spiritual goal.

Second, there is the concerning trend of disassociating Yoga from its Hindu roots. Both Yoga magazines and studios assiduously present Yoga as an ancient practice independent and disembodied from the Hinduism that gave forth this immense contribution to humanity. With the intense focus on *asana*, magazines and studios have seemingly "gotten away" with this mischaracterization. Yet, even when Yoga is practiced solely in the form of an exercise, it cannot be completely delinked from its Hindu roots. As the legendary Yoga guru B.K.S Iyengar aptly points out in his famous *Light on Yoga*, "Some *asanas* are also called after Gods of the Hindu pantheon and some recall the Avataras, or incarnations of Divine Power." It is disappointing to know that many of the yogis regularly practicing *Hanumanasana* or *Natarajasana* continue to deny the Hindu roots of their Yoga practice.

In a time where Hindus around the globe face discrimination and hate because of their religious identity, and Hindu belief and practice continues to be widely misunderstood due to exoticized portrayals of it being caricaturized in "caste, cows and curry" fashion, recognition of Yoga as a tremendous contribution of ancient Hindus to the world is imperative. Yoga is inextricable from Hindu traditions, and a better awareness of this fact is reached only if one understands that "Yoga" and "*Asana*" are not interchangeable terms.

Asana aka Yoga

A perusal of a few of the best known Yoga texts, such as Swami Svatmarama's *Hatha Yoga Pradipika* or Patanjali's *Yoga Sutras*, will quickly demonstrate that *asana* (posture) is only one component of Yoga. The *Pradipika* is divided into four main sections, of which 25% of only the first section focuses on *asana*. The *Yoga Sutras* are also divided into four parts, with a total of 196 sutras. The second part, composed of 55 sutras, briefly mentions *asana* as one of the eight limbs of Raja Yoga.

In his forward to an English translation of *Pradipika*, Iyengar aptly describes, "Hatha yoga . . . [to be] commonly misunderstood and misrepresented as being simply a physical culture, divorced from spiritual goals . . . Asanas are not just physical exercises: they have biochemical, psycho-physiological and psycho-spiritual effects."

In a 2005 interview published in *Namarupa* magazine, Prashant Iyengar, son of B.K.S. Iyengar, clearly espouses a similar view when he said, "We cannot expect that millions are practicing real yoga just because millions of people claim to be doing yoga all over the globe. What has spread all over the world is not yoga. It is not even non-yoga; it is un-yoga." The undue emphasis, particularly in the West, on *asana* as the crux of Yoga dilutes the essence of the spiritual practice and its ultimate goal of *moksha*.

B.K.S. Iyengar again reminds readers of the purpose of *asanas* in his *Light on Yoga*, when he states, "Their [*Asanas*] real importance lies in the way they train and discipline the mind . . . The yogi conquers the body by the practice of *asanas* and make it a fit vehicle for the spirit . . . He does not consider it [the body] his property . . . The yogi realizes that his life and all its activities are part of the divine action in nature."

The Hindu American Foundation (HAF) concludes from its research that Yoga, as an integral part of Hindu philosophy, is not simply physical exercise in the form of various *asanas* and *pranayama*, but is in fact a Hindu way of life. The ubiquitous use of the word "Yoga" to describe what in fact is simply an *asana* exercise is not only misleading, but has lead to and is fueling a problematic delinking of Yoga and Hinduism, as described further in the section below.

This attempt to clarify Yoga as far more complex than just *asanas* is not intended to discount the array of health benefits gained by practicing *asanas* alone. Beyond increasing muscle tone and flexibility, regular practice of *asana* has been associated with lower blood pressure, relief of back pain and arthritis, and boosting of the immune system. Increasingly, many believe *asana* practice to reduce Attention Deficit Disorder (AD/HD) in children, and recent studies have shown it improves general behavior and grades. But the Foundation argues that the full potential of the physiological, intellectual and spiritual benefits of *asana* would be increased manifold if practiced as a component of the holistic practice of Yoga.

Reversing the Efforts to Decouple Yoga from Hinduism

Although the Western Yoga community fully acknowledges Yoga's Indian roots, and even requires study of Hindu philosophy and scripture in most of its teacher certification programs, much of it openly disassociates Yoga's Hindu roots. While HAF affirms that one does not have to profess faith in Hinduism in order to practice Yoga or *asana*, it firmly holds that Yoga is an essential part of Hindu philosophy and the two cannot be delinked, despite efforts to do so.

Shyam Ranganathan's analysis gets to the crux of the issue when he writes, "Though some modern atheistic minds and aspiring yogis may disagree, textually there is no getting around the fact that Patanjali uses words, that in the context of Hindu culture, have obvious theological implications." Patanjali describes the goal of Yoga as *chitta-vritti-nirodha* or "the cessation of mental fluctuations", a core concept also expounded in Hinduism's *Bhagavad Gita:* "Thus always absorbing one's self in yoga, the yogi, whose mind is subdued, achieves peace that culminates in the highest state of Nirvana, which rests in me [Lord Krishna/Brahman/Supreme Reality]."

Similarly, Swami Svatmarama's opening line in the *Pradipika* is in honor of the Hindu God Shiva (Siva): "Reverence to Siva the Lord of Yoga, who taught Parvati hatha wisdom as the first step to the pinnacle of raja yoga."

In the same 2005 interview cited previously, Prashant Iyengar expounds upon Yoga with references to both Hindu epics and Hindu philosophy: "*Mahabharat* has so many aspects of yoga like yama (restraint), niyama (observance), sama (calmness) . . . *Ramayana* gives us so many beautiful aspects of bhakti yoga and karma yoga. Essential yoga starts with karma yoga . . . Without karma-consciousness, there will be no progress in yoga."

The Hindu American Foundation (HAF) reaffirms that Yoga, "an inward journey, where you explore your mind, your awareness, your consciousness, your conscience," is an essential part of Hindu belief and practice. But the science of yoga and the immense benefits its practice affords are for the benefit of all of humanity regardless of personal faith. Hinduism itself is a family of pluralistic doctrines and ways of life that acknowledge the existence of other spiritual and religious traditions. Hinduism, as a non-proselytizing religion, never compels practitioners of yoga to profess allegiance to the faith or convert. Yoga is a means of spiritual attainment for any and all seekers.

Source: Hindu American Foundation, "Yoga beyond Asana: Hindu Thought in Practice," http://www.hafsite.org/media/pr/yoga-hindu-origins. Accessed September 2010. Used with permission of the Hindu American Foundation.

PART II
American Samoa

27. Eni F. H. Faleomavaega, "Regarding the Minimum Wage in American Samoa," 2003

American Samoa is a group of Polynesian islands in the South Pacific; they comprise an unincorporated territory of the United States, administered by the Department of the Interior. Westerners have had sustained contact with (what is now called) American Samoa since the mid-19th century. During the 1899 Tripartite Convention, the United States and Germany divided control of the Samoan islands. Although the western group of islands gained their independence in 1962, calling themselves the Independent State of Samoa, the United States has retained control of the eastern islands. American Samoans are U.S. nationals. They may travel to and from, and live and work in, the United States without needing special visas, but they may not vote, and they must apply for American citizenship like any other foreign national. American Samoans have enlisted in the U.S. military in numbers disproportionate to their population, primarily due to the dearth of economic opportunities in their homeland.

The honorable Eni F. H. Faleomavaega is the at-large representative from American Samoa. (If a state is too small to have more than one congressional representative, they have an "at-large representative" who speaks for the entire state rather than for a particular district.) He was born in Vailoatai, a town in southwestern American Samoa, and he grew up in Oahu, Hawai'i. He served in both the U.S. Army and the Army Reserves, fought in Vietnam, and was elected to office in 1989. Faleomavaega's surname signifies his position as the chieftain of the Faiivae family in American Samoa. Faleomavaega is vice chair of the Congressional Asia Pacific American Caucus; in this capacity, he supported the Akaka Bill, which would give federal recognition to Native Hawai'ians.

In 2003, at a U.S. Department of Labor Special Industry Committee meeting convening in Fagatogo, the capital city of American Samoa, Faleomavaega argued that tuna cannery workers in American Samoa should receive the standard national minimum wage. The tuna cannery industry is American Samoa's primary source of jobs and revenue. In 2002, some major food industries lobbied to have tuna included under the terms of the Andean Trade Preference Act, which would have given preferential treatment to South American countries exporting tuna to the United States. On behalf of American Samoa, whose economy would have been devastated, Faleomavaega lobbied successfully against this. However, the next year, StarKist began claiming to the Special Industry Committee that it could not afford to pay the minimum wage to its American Samoan workers. In the following excerpt from his testimony to the U.S. Department of Labor, Faleomavaega argues that, given the favorable tax credits they receive for operating in American Samoa, StarKist either should raise their workers' wages or subsidize their health care.

JUNE 16, 2003

According to a 1954 U.S. Congressional House Report, "from January through April 1954, Van Camp Co. and the Tokyo Marine Products Corp., with whom the former had entered into contract, carried out in American Samoa the first joint American-Japanese venture in the history of Central Pacific tuna fishing. A fleet of 7 long-line boats, manned by Japanese fishermen, based in Pago Pago, with the logistical support of 2 American freezer ships, fished in a several hundred mile radius of American Samoa."

"During 1954, the cannery was in operation for only 6 months, yet over 200 tons of fish were processed and another 400 tons of frozen fish were sent to the United States. The results indicate[d] that a continuing and expanding tuna fishery in American Samoa [was] a distinct possibility, providing certain basic problems of supply and organization [were] met and solved."

Forty-nine years later, American Samoa is home to the largest tuna cannery in the world and since 1975 Chicken of the Sea/Samoa Packing and StarKist have exported billions of dollars worth of canned tuna from American Samoa to the United States. But our history with the industry has been tangled and our future is in no longer certain due to tremendous competition from foreign nations that catch and produce canned tuna at lower labor costs.

Only last year, American Samoa faced one of its most critical hours as a result of aggressive efforts by the H.J. Heinz Co., and its then subsidiary StarKist Seafoods, to include canned tuna in the Andean Trade Preference Act (ATPA). As part of the ATPA and in an effort to curb drug production in Latin America, the U.S. agreed to provide preferential, mostly-duty-free treatment to certain products exported to the U.S. from Bolivia, Colombia, Ecuador, and Peru. In my honest opinion, had StarKist been successful in its effort to include canned tuna under the provisions of the ATPA, American Samoa would have faced massive unemployment and insurmountable financial difficulties.

Briefly, the economy of American Samoa is more than 85% dependent either directly or indirectly on the U.S. tuna and fishing processing industries. Two canneries, Chicken of the Sea and StarKist, employ more than 5,150 people or 74% of the workforce. American Samoa processes about 950 tons of tuna per day which is equivalent to 228,000 tons of tuna or 20.5 million cases per year.

On the other hand, the Andean Pact countries control more than 35% of the catch in the Eastern Pacific Tropic (EPT) and, in the past ten years, the Andean tuna fishing fleet has also grown from about 20 to 90 fishing vessels. Ecuador and Colombia now have the capacity to jointly process 2,250 tons of tuna per day which is equivalent to 540,000 tons of tuna or 48.6 million cases per year.

It should be noted that the U.S. only consumes 48 million cases per year while the Andean countries have the production capacity to supply the entire U.S. market and wipe out the economy of American Samoa. Additionally, labor rates for cannery workers are $0.69 per hour and less in the Andean countries but on average $3.26 per hour in American Samoa. With these differences in wage rates, I did not believe then and I do not believe now that StarKist's interest in the ATPA was to curb drug production in the Andean countries. More likely, I believe StarKist fought the matter for one reason and one reason only–to displace $3.26 workers in American Samoa and exploit $0.60 labor in Ecuador.

I do not believe this is what fair trade should be about and I am pleased to state that my colleagues in both the House and Senate agreed with me on this point and excluded canned tuna from the ATPA. Parenthetically, I am also pleased that StarKist has since changed ownership and I am hopeful that our new corporate partner, Del Monte Foods, will work with us to rebuild the heap of stones that has collapsed. E ta'ape a fatuati, or the collapse of the heap or structure of stones, is a Samoan proverb which refers to the practice of setting up a heap of stones under the water to attract fish. Sometimes the structure collapses as a result of deliberate acts or accidental causes. Either way, when the heap collapses, the fishermen will come to rebuild it for the good of the community which is solely dependent on the fishing industry.

For more than forty-five years, American Samoa's economy has been dependent on a structure which is also used to attract and protect investment in the Territory. This structure, known as the U.S. tariff or tax structure, provides duty-free treatment for canned tuna entering the U.S. from American Samoa. This structure also assesses a low duty of 6% and a high duty of about 12% on canned tuna packed in water entering the U.S. from foreign countries. For tuna packed in oil the tax is about 30%. Whether 6%, 12%, or 30%, foreign countries must pay a U.S. duty, or tax, to send their canned tuna to the U.S. while American Samoa's canned tuna enters the U.S. free of charge.

Fortunately, this tariff or tax structure levels the playing field for American Samoa and allows us to compete against countries with lower wage rates of $0.60 and less per hour. This tax structure safeguards us. It protects us. It maximizes the profits of our canneries and without it American Samoa's canneries cannot survive. This is why I am disappointed that H.J. Heinz, the once parent company of StarKist, fought so hard to give Ecuador the same trade advantages as American Samoa. Thanks to H.J. Heinz, Ecuador can now send tuna packaged in pouches to the U.S. free of duty but the U.S., including American Samoa, must pay a duty rate of 20% or more to export canned tuna to Ecuador. Again, this is neither free nor fair trade and, although Heinz was unsuccessful in its attempt to eliminate duties or collapse tariff and tax rates for canned tuna, I am concerned that American Samoa's canneries are at risk. . . .

Now StarKist is testifying before Special Industry Committee No. 25 once again stating that it cannot afford to pay our workers a decent standard of living. What kind of sense does this make when StarKist (under previous and present leadership) spent hundreds of thousands of dollars trying to do away with the 12% duty protection that keeps our canneries in business? If StarKist can live without the millions in savings that the 12% duty provides who is to believe that StarKist cannot afford to increase the minimum wage for its workers in American Samoa....

My friends, I support business and the need for business to make a reasonable profit. But to paraphrase President Franklin D. Roosevelt, I will not let calamity-howling executives with million dollar incomes tell me that wage increases will have a disastrous effect on the U.S. economy or that we must exploit labor in developing countries to remain competitive. Neither will I support the notion that businesses are to maximize their profits without a moral obligation to also increase the wages of our cannery workers....

As I said two years ago in my statement before Special Industry Committee No. 24, I also believe that the right to live is higher than the right to own a business. Furthermore, I believe a business has an economic, legal, and moral responsibility to pay its employees enough to enable them to live and I believe this should be the basic idea that guides the actions of all major businesses, including those of the tuna industry.

Quite frankly, it is an insult to our people for executives who are paid top dollar to recommend that there be no increase to the minimum wage and to suggest that their only obligation is to their investors or stockholders. If this is the basic idea that guides StarKist or Del Monte, so be it. But I believe that higher laws should guide our actions and that we have a moral responsibility to do unto others as we would have them do unto us.

Indeed, I do not believe one corporate executive at Del Monte, StarKist, or Chicken of the Sea/Samoa Packing would oppose minimum wage increases if their mothers, fathers, sisters, brothers, sons or daughters toiled day in and day out in tuna canneries here or abroad. If suppressed wages are not good enough for their families and low yields are unacceptable to their stockholders, why should wages of $3.26 and less per hour be sufficient for our cannery workers? Furthermore, why should low wages be acceptable for cannery workers anywhere? This is not the way the world should be and I will do everything I can to make sure this is not the way things will be in American Samoa.

Nevertheless, I do not have a vote in these proceedings and neither do the people of American Samoa. The U.S. Department of Labor picks and chooses its Special Industry Committee and, for the most part, the outcome is determined before we testify. In some ways, it is unclear to me why the U.S. Department of Labor bothers to hold these hearings. If the Department of Labor was serious about minimum wage then it would be serious about conducting a study to determine the cost of living in American Samoa. If it was serious about minimum wage it would be serious about making the tuna industry declare its margin of profit. Simply put, until we know what the canneries are making we cannot determine what a fair wage is for our workers.

Having spent the past year and half fighting to protect the interests of American Samoa in the U.S. Congress, I can tell you that I understand what our canneries are up against when it comes to competing against countries with low wage rates.

I understand the realities of supply and demand. I understand that production will leave high cost locations when low cost alternatives exist. I also understand that these are the same words the U.S. tuna industry has been regurgitating for the past 47 years.

In 1956, as part of its lobbying effort to suppress wages in American Samoa and pay Samoan workers only 27 cents per hour, Van Camp (now Chicken of the Sea/Samoa Packing) said that "a minimum wage of $1 per hour, as required under present laws, is unrealistic, unwarranted, and unquestionably will have a deleterious effect upon the economic and social structure of the islands." Forty-seven years later, neither Samoa Packing nor StarKist thinks any more or less of our cannery workers and I can assure you that neither will think any more or less of cannery workers in Papua New Guinea or Ecuador, for that matter....

Workers in American Samoa are the backbone of the U.S. tuna industry and I believe that men and women of conscience will agree with me that businesses are also obligated to act in the interest of its workers. After 47 years of working against us, I believe it is time for our canneries to work with us and I am pleased that the U.S. tuna industry has united in support of H.R. 1424—a bill I introduced in Congress to make permanent or extend the federal IRS section 936 tax credit to American Samoa for another ten years....

Finally, if the minimum wage cannot be increased, I believe our canneries should subsidize medical care at the LBJ Tropical Medical Center. In any other U.S. location, the tuna industry would be required to provide health care benefits for its employees. In American Samoa, however, ASG subsidizes the tuna industry by providing health care for sick or injured employees and their families. In itself, this is a savings of at least $5 million per year to our canneries and it is time for our canneries to return this money to LBJ and assume responsibility for the medical care of its employees.

It is also time for our canneries to increase pensions for our workers and I believe something needs to be said on and in behalf of Samoans who stand for 8 hours a day cleaning fish and after 20 years of service only get a pension of approximately $120 per month. This is not right and this is simply un-American.

For 47 years, the U.S. tuna industry has told us it would leave American Samoa if wages were increased. Forty-seven years later, both canneries are with us and only last year StarKist erected a statue and declared that American Samoa is the permanent home of Charlie the Tuna. Maybe I missed it but I did not see any fine print beneath the statue stating that Charlie the Tuna's home is conditional on whether or not we raise the minimum wage. In fact, as I recall, StarKist's Vice-President was emphatic in stating that StarKist had no intention of leaving American Samoa. However, he also said StarKist was not up for sale and only a few months later it was sold to Del Monte.

Given these nonsensical statements, I have come to believe that the only thing we may know for certain is that our future with the industry is uncertain. But with the Andean Trade agreement behind us and the minimum wage hearings before us, I am again reminded of a Samoan proverb—O le upega e fili i le po ae talatala i le ao—which means that the net that became entangled at night will be disentangled in the morning. In other words, I am hopeful that when the night passes and the morning comes we will settle our differences and work together to protect American Samoa's tuna industry.

Source: Eni F. H. Faleomavaega, "Statement before Special Industry Committee No. 25 U.S. Department of Labor Wage and Hour Division Regarding the Minimum Wage in American Samoa." June 16, 2003. http://www.house.gov/faleomavaega/speeches/2003_06_16_minwage.shtml. Accessed September 2010.

28. Help Samoa Disaster Relief Coalition Press Release, "How Samoans in America Got Together to Help Their People," 2009

The Samoan archipelago was divided into two separate territories in the late 19th century. Germany gained control of the western islands, while the United States retained territorial control of the eastern islands. Eventually, the western islands became known as Western Samoa (present-day Samoa), and the eastern islands became American Samoa. The U.S. Navy took administrative control over the islands in 1900 and came to dominate the economy of the islands. During World War II, naval operations expanded rapidly, transforming the city of Pago Pago. When the Pago Pago naval base was decommissioned in 1951, many Samoans who worked for the U.S. Navy, either as servicemen, administrative workers, or the like, began relocating to the mainland. Since 1970, Samoan immigration to the United States has steadily increased, and between 1990 and 2000, about 35 percent of the Samoan American population was foreign born. Today, most of the estimated 130,000 Samoans or part Samoans residing in the United States live in Hawai'i, California, and Washington. In general, Samoans have higher levels of poverty, and lower rates of home ownership, educational levels, and employment than the general population. Samoans living in California tend to have a higher standard of living than Samoans in Hawai'i.

On September 29, 2009, an 8.0 magnitude earthquake struck off the coast of American Samoa. The quake triggered a monster tsunami that devastated the islands, killing more than an estimated 120 people. In the immediate aftermath of the disaster, Samoans in Southern California banded together to send medical aid, food, and basic necessities for the victims. They formed the Help Samoa Coalition. Because Samoans strongly value family, hospitality, community, and the Christian faith, the outpouring of generosity from the community was overwhelming. The press release reprinted here describes the efforts of the Help Samoa Coalition.

A day after the tsunami devastated Samoa and America Samoa, the Samoan community in Carson California began to organise a relief effort to assist the victims of the tsunami in the two Samoas.

On the 30 September, in excess of nine different non-profit/profit organisations coalesced to form a relief organization call Help Samoa Disaster Relief Coalition. This was initially organised by the office of Samoan Affairs and a group of young Samoan entrepreneurs' organisation call PacBiz. These initial organisations started to recruit other non profit and for profit Samoan organisations in Southern California to join in mobilising the community for assistance for the tsunami victims.

Among the many organisations included, the Samoan Federation of America, Inc. and Aiga both non profit organisations joined the Tsunami Disaster Relief effort.

A website Helpsamoa.com was immediately launched to reach other Samoans across the 50 states of the United States of America. It should be noted, that about 200,000 Samoans living in the United States. Of this, in excess of 38,000 live in the Southern California area second only to the State of Hawai'i, the largest concentration of Samoan in the United States.

In addition to the community organisations mentioned above, the California States and local political organisations (mayor of Carson City and State Legislators) and the office of the Congresswoman Laura Richardson also joined the Help Samoa coalition to help mobilise the community resources for the relief effort.

A 24/7 assembly line process was immediately put into operation to receive the goods and supplies, record, resort, and repack the items (clothing, food, health and hygiene items, etc) into containers to prepare for shipment to Samoa and America Samoa. The primary objective is to ensure these items are properly examined and repacked to meet Homeland Security and Custom regulations and to insure transparency across the process.

The response to this calling for help was and is overwhelming. The donors of the local communities across the southern California area from Los Anglers all the way to San Diego physically delivered the aid supplies to the Help Samoa head quarter drop off point.

Additionally aid supplies and goods were shipped in from other states as far as Texas, Idaho, Oregon and Washington and other near by states were transported to the dropoff zone in Carson California.

Simultaneously a Call Centre and the Website—www.helpsamoa.com were busy with calls and emails coming from across the United States expressing their condolences and empathy for the victims and extended their willingness to help.

The leadership provided by the Chairman of the Relief Coalition Hon. High Chief Loa Faletogo (Fagamalo, Tutuila), President and CEO of Samoan Federation of America and Vice Chairman Pat H. Luce, Executive Director of The Office of Samoan Affairs, and special assistance by Ms. June Pouesi also Director of The Office of Samoan Affairs and the rest of the coalitions organisation have yielded the delivery of the 15 20ft (equiv.) containers that have just arrived in Samoa and America Samoa on 30 October. This relief effort is made possible by the many volunteers via donated labour, money, and materials including transportation from all points of origin delivery.

This, of course, includes transportation from Long Beach and Oakland California to Samoa and America Samoa. In particular, the donated cost of shipment including vessel transportation cost, Port fees, loading and unloading of containers in these international Ports were made possible by the International Longshore Warehouse Union Local 13 members of which many are Samoans and/or Samoan decedents [sic].

An example of how people in America were profoundly affected by the news of the disaster caused by the Tsunami, the day the Help Samoa Coalition sign went up along the side of the headquarter, a "homeless" gentleman that walked by stopped at the assembly line operation reached into his pocket and pulled up and gave his only 35 cents with his condolences saying that "he is a friend of many Samoans that he has known for many years".

There were many instances of display of compassion and empathy including a group of Primary School students of Samoans and non Samoans that collected money from their lunch allowances in a bottle and a hand made well wishes card for the young victims of the Tsunami. These are only a few of the many instances of the impact of the Tsunami in this part of the world. It affected the old, the young, the rich and the poor who have felt the Tsunami in a deep and profound psychological impact in their hearts.

An approach by the Help Samoa Coalition to achieve transparency is to work with local non profit organisations in both Samoa and America Samoa in the distribution of the donated items directly to the victims in the affected villages.

And as such the Coalition selected SUNGO, PPSEWA, Seventh Day Adventist and Malua (EFKS), Native Samoa Advisory council (America Samoa) as distribution agents in Samoa.

A special assistance by Congresswoman Laura Richardson (democrat, 37th Congressional district), and Representative of American Samoa, Hon. Faleomavaega were working with Secretary of State of the United States of America, Hillary Clinton worked diligently to facilitate transportation, Custom and Homeland Security requirements for the movement of the cargos across international water. This represents the second part of the American's assistance to the victims of the tsunami of Samoa and American Samoa. The first part was the Faith-base initiative shipment directed by Rev. Ma'ilo and Rev. Liki of Carson, California that were shipped via aircraft that arrived in Samoa on the 18th Oct 2009.

A representative of the Help SAMOA COALITION, myself, Fata Letunu Ariu Levi overall Co-ordinator of the Coalition Operation and Salalau Mataali'i, member of the Coalition arrived in Samoa and America Samoa to work with the selected distribution agents to complete the objective of insuring transparency that was initiated in California.

The next face of the Coalition will focus on rebuild Samoa with building materials, tools and equipments that will assist in the restoration of the affected families and villages. While I'm in Apia, I will be gathering additional needs of the victims and the affected villages to take back when returning to the Help Samoa Coalition to better target the needs of the people and the generosity of the American people who are profoundly affected by the condition of those severely affected by the Tsunami.

The enigma of God's creation and love of human kind evidences that God is omnipresent, omnipotent, and omnificent and his love is everlasting.

It is trying times like this that reminds us that the Holy Spirit working through the hearts and minds of people that lifts the Human Spirit at levels that we can not imagine—that makes ordinary people do extra ordinary things.

Source: "How Samoans in America got together to help their people." Help Samoa Disaster Relief Coalition Press Release, 2009. *Samoa Observer*, 2009. Reprinted with permission.

29. Tafea Polamalu, "Diasporic Dream: Letter to Grandfather," 2009 and "Daddy Said," 2010

Tafea Polamalu is a Samoan American who grew up in rural Southwestern Oregon, hundreds of miles from the nearest Samoan community. Samoa is a group of Polynesian islands in the South Pacific that came under western political control in 1899, when Germany and the United States divided up the islands for themselves. While the German-controlled half gained independence in 1962, the U.S. retained control of the eastern islands. Polamalu traces his ancestral ties to the island of Ta'u in the Manu'a archipelago, part of U.S.-controlled American Samoa. Polamalu received his MA in Pacific Islands Studies from the University of Hawai'i at Manoa. He uses poetry, fiction, and painting to explore and express his relationship to Samoa and his identity and experiences as a Samoan American. In these two poems, Polamalu takes readers on a journey that crosses oceans, identities, and generations, and challenges our assumptions about what it means to be a Samoan, American, and an immigrant.

DIASPORIC DREAM: LETTER TO GRANDFATHER

I am the final result of your foresight:
The end product of opportunity

I am what they call
"Second-Generation US Samoan:"
That generation who has
Never been to Samoa

I am "First-World"
"Fully-developed"
"Fully-civilized"

I come from no island
I come from "The Mainland"

I was born among them
Raised among them
Melted into them
Fluent in their language and ways

I am "Educated"
"Modernized"

"American"

I am the quintessential neo Samoan:
A walking wealth of Western knowledge

I know my Pledge of Allegiance
I know my presidents
I can name all fifty state capitols

I can solve quadratic equations
Formulate a thesis
Type over 60 words per minute

I can dissect a frog and identify all of the vital organs
I can spot a dangling modifier
I have read the works of countless classic European writers

I can tell you the difference between
Polynesia, Micronesia, Melanesia
I am well versed on the Lapita Theory

I know all about Samoa:
Population
Climate
Average life expectancy
Margaret Mead

I am the vision
I am progress
I am a masterpiece of assimilation

I have forgotten what is useless
I have learned what matters
The world is at my finger tips

I am the future:
Woven of fear and survival
I am the "fully-evolved" immigrant
The Diasporic dream

I am what eventually becomes of those who left:
Not native like you
But settler like them
But not one of them
Nor one of you

I am lodged perfectly between worlds
In the war zone where razor wire
And minefields connect cultures

I wish I would have known you
I would like to show you this place
But I do not remember you

I do not speak your language
I do not know your ways
I do not know why I am here
I feel gone from you
Lost to you

I know nothing of Samoa

I sometimes think
it is too late

DADDY SAID

Son,
I prunk you hea
pecause tis is ta lan of
opprotunity

In Samoa,
te is nofing
To you heard me Son?
Nofing

Hea in Ameika,
ta worlt is at
yo finka tip
and ta sky is ta limits

You know why I nefa
teach you Samoan Son?
cause Samoan no ket you
anyfing in life

tis is ta white man's worlt
an Enklish is
only fink tat matta

You heard me Son?

Tis is ta white man's worlt
an at ta en of ta tay, we all haf
to walk fru his toor

at ta en of ta tay, we all haf
walk fru his toor
cause he sign ta check Son

look at me,
my whole life i strukle wif
fo try speak ta Enklish

i strukle my ass off Son
so tat you can ket you
pestes echucation

So i make tamn sure
my sons masta Enklish
pecause tis is what pestes

You see what I'm said Son?

Tis is why it pisses me when
te say, 'How come I nefa teachet
you speak Samoan?'

What ta hell te fink I prunk you here fo eh?
tes stupit hets know
nofing apout Samoa

Rememper sumfing Son,
Ameika is ta pestes place in ta worlt
so ket ta echucation

pe ta tocto
pe ta lawya
tis is my tream fo you
tis is why fo i prunk you hea

fo to kif you ta
opprotunity to haf ta
fings i nefa haf

You see what I'm said Son?

Okay, koot talk
alu su'esu'e
ko prush ta teef
an to ta maf homewok

Sources: Polamalu, Tafea. "Diasporic Dream: Letter to Grandfather." In *The Space Between: Negotiating Culture, Place, and Identity in the Pacific*, ed. A. Marata Tamaira, Honolulu, HI: Center for Pacific Islands Studies, School of Hawaiian, Asian & Pacific Studies, University of Hawai's at Manoa, 2009 and Polamalu, Tafea. "Daddy Said." In *Mauri Ola: Contemporary Polynesian Poems in English Whetu Moana II*, ed. Albert Wendt et al., Honolulu, HI: University of Hawaii Press, 2010.

Part III
Bangladeshi American

30. Kanwal Rahman, Interview by Rajika Bhandari, July 15, 1999

Kanwal Rahman came to the United States from Bangladesh in August 1991 to study public health and policy and administration at the University of North Carolina, Chapel Hill. She had worked as a dental surgeon for the Ministry of Health in Bangladesh. At the time of this interview, Rahman had been living in North Carolina for eight years, working in public health and insurance research. She speaks about the difficulty she had when she first arrived in the United States, her determination to persevere, the ways she has evolved personally since immigrating, her occasional feelings of alienation from mainstream American culture, and her strong desire to live a transnational life. The interviewer, Rajika Bhandari, notes that South Asian "men and women . . . go through very different experiences when they come [to the United States]. . . . they evolve very differently." Rahman highlights this trend when she discusses her views on gender roles. While influenced strongly by Bangladeshi traditions, her perspective also has been colored by her commitment to universal ideals of independence and liberation.

RAJIKA BHANDARI: Did you, when you were on your way here, did you ever imagine you would be here—what—eight years now?

KANWAL RAHMAN: I said [to myself] it's maybe, it's my wanderlust, and, if I don't make it, fine, I'll come back. But I never imagined I would stay eight years. . . . My heart still wants to go back to Bangladesh. That's where my home is, and I think, America will always be a home—a second home—but never my first home.

RAJIKA BHANDARI: Could you talk a little bit about your experiences [in America]? And have they largely been positive, or negative, or mixed?

KANWAL RAHMAN: Well, I had a very hard time the first year too. I don't really have a hard time with making friends but I do feel that I still have to explain a lot about myself. . . . I still feel that there are certain things that make me feel I am one of them but I'm still an outsider. . . . I don't know, it isn't anything to do with race or people; I think it's the American—, Americanness. . . . Of course, my expectations of very closeness is

RAJIKA BHANDARI: different from the expectations of an American person. . . . It's a more independent culture and I guess independence is taught from the very childhood, which we [immigrants] are not taught, but thrown into.

RAJIKA BHANDARI: Do you think that that sense of community that you had back in Bangladesh is reflected here in any way? In the life that you live?

KANWAL RAHMAN: I would say there's no resemblance to what the life I left, lived back home. Even the sense of community—. Sure, I was a newly graduated dental surgeon, but I was still living with my parents and I had relations distant and close, dropping in all the time. You're having interactions of community festivals, wwherever everyone goes regardless of any religion. . . . Here, more or less, it has been isolated because people spend time with their own families and not go out of their way to invite, outsiders for the family . . . reunions during Christmas or Thanksgiving. There the life was more protected. Here the life is totally independent.

RAJIKA BHANDARI: I was wondering if you could talk a little about, a) how you feel you've changed as an individual, and b) how you've changed as a woman?

KANWAL RAHMAN: Well, of course, eight years in a culture without going back home. It has changed me a lot. It has made me mature. In Indian cultures—regardless whether it's Pakistan, Bangladesh, or India—girls, or daughters of relatively upper middle-class families, or upper class families, are sort of encouraged to be . . . "dependent." You are not allowed to drive, because your father forbade you, so you come to the United States not being able to drive. You can't go out and do grocery shopping, because you've never done it, so you have to learn that. You have never cooked in your life because somebody had always cooked—whether it's your mother, or whether it was somebody [else]. So, those are the things that you learn very fast. How to be on your own footstep, and also, not to expect the world to do it for you, or give it to you. . . . You end up learning to respond the way they [Americans] expect you to. Not necessarily giving up your identity, but basically, you end up behaving and acting in a way that is more common with Americans, and that's also giving out the image that you're very confident and mature, and responsible. . . . But inside, you can still be insecure, regardless of the fact that you have developed all these other aspects, too. The feeling of insecurity as a single Asian woman in America, for the future, or for anything or, you know, the fact that we don't have a support system—is there.

RAJIKA BHANDARI: Do you feel that the American experience has made a difference to how South Asians from each of the different South Asian countries respond and react to each other?

KANWAL RAHMAN: . . . The way I feel every time I see a South Asian—, doesn't matter if he's from Burma or Sri Lanka and, you know, and I can just tell that he's from South Asia, I feel immediately bonded and I also feel that the other person bonds because they have a common basis of, if not language, a common cultural basis, common food habit basis—those are very strong aspects of a culture, food and other cultural aspects of, living and family life—that I think makes us feel more unified together in America. . . . A lot of friends say, "You're very Americanized"—but I don't perceive how Americanized am, because I don't feel as American as them. I'm not as American as apple pie, because I wasn't born or raised here, but I feel the bonding immediately with any South Asian person I see, regardless of the background.

RAJIKA BHANDARI: So, are you happy [in the United States]?

KANWAL RAHMAN: [pause] No, I'm not. . . . At this stage of my life, I'm looking, you know, looking for more, in just a career, and a good living. I'm looking for a meaning. Looking for a meaningful career which would give out, rather than take in. Like, you know, like public health, have a family. Those things are becoming more and more crucial as the years are going by. . . . And I guess I would define myself completely complete only when I have a meaningful career and a conducive home life and being able to step back into my country every two years. I think, right now, that is what I would strive as my ideal situation of living.

Source: Excerpted from interview with Kanwal Rahman by Rajika Bhandari, July 15, 1999 (K-0817), in the Southern Oral History Program Collection (#4007), Southern Historical Collection, Louis Round Wilson Special Collections Library, University of North Carolina at Chapel Hill.

31. Farah Akbar, "A Troubling Cultural Gap," 2010

Religion often plays a key part in immigrant identity, facilitating cultural continuity and community cohesiveness in an unfamiliar and unsettling environment. The lines between culture, ethnicity, and religion are blurry, however, and as immigrants and their children begin to adapt to and incorporate aspects of American life, these demarcations begin to be questioned and challenged. For Asian American Muslims, the issue is particularly fraught, as people wrestle with the Americanization of Islam.

Farah Akbar was born in Bangladesh, moved to the United States when she was a child, and grew up in Queens, New York. She is a freelance author who writes about civil rights and immigrant issues and the Muslim American community. Her essay "A Troubling Cultural Gap," written for Salon.com, explores second-generation Asian American Muslims: how they struggle to reconcile widely disparate questions of sexuality, radicalism and liberalism, and popular culture with Islam; how they attempt to mesh their evolving religious, ethnic, and national identities; and how they answer for themselves what it means to be "truly" Muslim in America.

Ishak Khan, 17, wants to know if it's OK to get a tattoo in his religion. He also wants to know if it's OK to write rap songs and if it's OK to have a Muslim girlfriend.

Like many of his Muslim American contemporaries, Ishak isn't quite sure how to balance his religion with American culture. He does talk to friends about these issues, but he'd really like to speak with an adult who understands both American culture and Islam. But he can't really talk to his parents because they're very traditional, and he's definitely not going to that imam "straight out of Bangladesh" who gives the boring sermons at the Queens, N.Y., mosque he attends once a month.

"I don't think I can connect or talk to him, because he's not from here," says Ishak, who was born here to Bangladeshi parents. "I can't even tell him that I write music, 'cause he's just gonna tell me that it's bad. And if I tell him about getting a tattoo, he's gonna tell me that it will look dirty." And about the girlfriend? "He's gonna say it's haram [forbidden]."

Says the aspiring rapper: "I just want a cool person who I can ask questions to and who can give me a reasonable response."

Ishak's dilemma is one familiar to many Muslim Americans of his generation. Going to a mosque to pray or to receive Islamic education is an integral part of their lives. Though not all young Muslims are mosque-goers, those who do go often look to their local imams for guidance, only to be turned off by the cultural gap that exists between them. This has caught the attention of some Muslim community members, who fear that too many young American Muslims are left feeling alienated and frustrated.

Some Muslims are voicing their opinions and calling for change. They would like imams, who tend to be older, male and "imported," to be able to connect with a generation of Muslims raised in America. They also want mosques, which have the potential to develop leadership and community-building skills among young Muslims, to make youth outreach a priority. Failing to address these issues, they fear, could sever the connection between a generation of American Muslims and their religion.

There may be another fear, too. Abdul Malik Mujahid, an imam and author, has written that young people who feel marginalized or alienated can constitute "a breeding ground for extremism."

A common frustration among young Muslim Americans is that many imams speak to their congregations in languages other than English, often to accommodate immigrants who are more comfortable with their native tongue. (Some imams themselves may be more comfortable speaking in their native tongues as well.) This can leave the younger generation, which often has limited or no knowledge of its parents' mother tongues, uninterested.

Muntasir Sattar, 30, who works with many Muslim youths as a program coordinator at the South Asian Youth Action organization in New York, has seen how this causes the imam's message to go right over the heads of younger congregants—even when it's aimed straight at them.

"A lot of Khutbahs [sermons] on Fridays are about youth, about vices and virtues and the importance of staying on the right path," he says, "but from a youth's perspective, they're like, 'OK, that's great, but you're talking in Arabic, or Urdu or Bengali, and I don't speak that language!'" he says.

Ishak admits that he's dozed off more than once during sermons, usually when they've been delivered in Bengali. "I speak Bengali, but it would be better if it was in English. I'd understand it better," he says. He does remember one time hearing a great sermon in English about how praying to Allah can make life less stressful during trying times. "I had exams and I was so worried. I prayed to Allah that I would pass them and I did," Ishak recalls. He would like sermons to be about issues closer to his life.

Tania Ahmed, a 17-year-old high school senior, agrees that language is an issue. (Tania is not her actual name, which she asked be withheld.) "I don't care where [the imam] comes from, as long as he can communicate," she says. If the imam cannot speak in English, it hurts the youth who are seeking answers about their faith, Tania says. And she feels that some imams are too judgmental. "I know that some of them would react in a certain preachy way if I were to ask them about personal issues," she says. "They might even just shun you," she says. "I wouldn't really go to anyone outside my circle of friends."

But many imams believe it's their job to provide a rigidly Islamic viewpoint on issues and that even stylistic concessions to American culture are out of the question. Ben Yahya Abdel-Ghani, the director of the Flushing Muslim Center in Queens, says that when young people ask him for his advice, he has to answer according to the rules of Islam. Abdel-Ghani, 45, is from Morocco and has been living in the United States since 1997. Should a young person ask about whether it was OK to drink alcohol, his answer would be swift. "All kids know that alcohol is wrong," he says in slightly accented English. "Alcohol is prohibited—so the discussion is almost closed."

Abdel-Ghani admits that youth don't often go to him for advice about personal matters, but, for example, if a young person were to confide to him that he or she might be gay (a situation he says he's never encountered), he would reply that being gay in Islam is not accepted. "Youngsters know that the answer will be that it is wrong," he insists. "They have to find a way to solve the problem. I don't think they will have the urge to say it to someone who is older."

Another issue complicating youth outreach is financial, with many mosques struggling just to pay their rent. Immigrant mosques in New York, for instance, are often run by working-class individuals and limited funds tend to be an issue. Sattar, the SAYA program coordinator, understands this and empathizes with these mosque officials, but he stresses that mosques should try to find room for youth programs even in their tight budgets. "Youth need opportunities to be active in their religious institutions," he says. "They need those roles, those opportunities, to shape the world."

Dr. Mahbubur Rahman, a professor of political science at the City University of New York who teaches a course called Islam and Democracy, agrees. He thinks that this is a way young Muslims can steer clear of fringe Muslim groups that may have extremist agendas or whose teachings are not in line with mainstream Islam. For example, the "Lackawana Six," a group of young Muslim American men from Buffalo, ended up in a militant training camp in Afghanistan. They were apparently recruited by a man named Kamal Derwish, who preached a radical brand of Islam and who won them over through meetings in his apartment. (Derwish was ultimately killed in a CIA mission in Yemen.)

A symbol of hope for Muslim American reformers can be found in the heart of Manhattan's West Village, the home base of a man who epitomizes the kind of spiritual leadership that so many young American Muslims yearn for.

Khalid Latif, 27, serves as the first-ever Muslim chaplain at the school's Islamic Center, a place that he boasts of running on progressive values rooted in authentic Islamic sources. Latif graduated from New York University with degrees in political science and Middle Eastern studies and attended the Hartford Theological Seminary briefly, then became the executive director of the Islamic Center at 24. He is also the youngest chaplain ever hired by the New York Police Department, brought in to cater to the spiritual needs of Muslim officers and civilian employees.

Latif says he understands why some young people don't feel comfortable going to religious places. Born and raised in New Jersey, he doesn't have fond memories of the local mosque he attended as a teenager. Back then, he had long hair and no beard, a violation of Muslim tradition, and congregants would accuse him of attending services just to mingle with the girls. "People weren't very nice to me," he recalls.

Membership at NYU's Islamic Center has increased significantly since he took over. He is well-liked and popular among students. One Pakistani-American student named Raza, after finishing his afternoon prayers, wrote "I love the I.C." on a whiteboard near the center's entrance. Raza credits Latif for uniting Sunni Muslims and Shia Muslims in prayer, something the student, who is of the Shia sect, had never experienced before. "It was really special," he says. "It was an incredible feeling."

Students come to Latif to seek his advice about any and all issues, including some that are traditionally deemed "haram," or forbidden, in Islam. They appreciate his easygoing attitude and feel comfortable enough to talk to him about sexuality, depression, mental-health issues, domestic violence, relationships and even experiences of rape.

So is Latif a rare breed of imam? "I'm not like Nemo, alone in this ocean of loneliness," he says. As the Muslim community begins to respond to the needs of its diverse members, he believes, more imams who espouse progressive values that are in line with Islamic teachings will emerge. "As needs have changed, as dynamics have changed, I think it's just a logical trend to a people who are well versed in how this society functions that they are going to be stepping into roles as community activists and leaders and specifically, at times, even imams," Latif says.

Sitting on the floor of the large prayer room located in the basement of a white church that serves as the Islamic Center, he says: "What it means to be an imam is contingent upon a community's needs at the time." He is wearing blue jeans, a blue button-down shirt, has a trimmed beard and is wearing a black skullcap called a "kufi." "In some Muslim countries and in immigrant mosques, the idea isn't that the imam will be a community leader," he adds. "He's expected to just lead the prayers."

Latif isn't sure if it matters whether an imam was raised in the U.S., or if he's young or old. "It's hard to create an archetype on what an individual needs to be like that can deal with the diversity of some 8 million Muslims [in the U.S.]," he says. "Different people have their own preferences."

If a student confides to Latif that he or she might be gay, he won't claim that homosexuality is permissible in Islam. "But, like, it doesn't change the fact that we have kids or adults who are homosexuals," he says. "An outright denial of its existence causes us to have more issues than solutions."

After listening to a student talk about his or her background, he encourages the student to understand what his or her "life choice" means. "Some people will be nice to you, some people will treat you like garbage," Latif might say.

"With any issue, it's about, 'Where do we go from here?'" he says. "In Islamic tradition, you see numerous instances with men and women going to the prophet Mohammed, peace be upon him, about their sins. The relationship with the Prophet was such that you could speak with him and he wouldn't be judgmental. He would respond in a way that made the most sense for the person coming to him with the issue."

Being a young and progressive imam has its challenges, too. "Especially in religious communities, when somebody comes in and does it differently, you kind of have to legitimize yourself," says Latif. "You have to prove to people that they can take you seriously. Because you're dealing with religion. And if you're wrong, Muslims perceive that wrong means hell."

At first, he says, people thought that NYU's Islamic center was too liberal. But now he claims that those same people simply see the center as "accepting."

Young Muslims in America are clearly hungry for some spiritual guidance from the right people, and they're asking for some specific things. For one, they say, imams should be raised or should at least understand what it's like growing up in America. They also shouldn't be quite so judgmental. And being on the younger end, though not required, is desirable. They should also be able to speak English and be reasonably current with American culture and technology. Ishak, the 17-year-old aspiring rapper, says he's met another imam, a young, American man, who showed him some Islamic prayers on YouTube that he liked a lot. "I don't think my imam [from the Queens mosque] even knows what YouTube is," he notes.

Tania once heard Latif speak at a conference and she absolutely loved what he had to say. Latif spoke about peer pressure and about the challenges of being a Muslim teenager in America. Still, she doubts that she'd ever confide in any imam about her personal life. "Except," she says shyly, "maybe for Khalid Latif."

Source: Akbar, Farah. "A Troubling Cultural Gap." May 16, 2010. This article first appeared on Salon.com, at http://www.Salon.com. An online version remains in the *Salon* archives. Reprinted with permission.

PART IV
Cambodian American

32. United Cambodian Community Booklet, Long Beach, California, 1990

The roots of Cambodian migration to the United States can be traced to America's involvement in the Vietnam War. During the war, the United States conducted secret carpet-bombing campaigns targeting North Vietnamese troops and supplies in Cambodia. The death and destruction caused by the bombing campaigns created strong anti-American feelings and increased support for the Communist Khmer Rouge. When Saigon fell in 1975 and the United States withdrew from Vietnam, the Khmer Rouge quickly defeated the Lon Nol's U.S.-supported government. When the Khmer Rouge, under their leader Pol Pot, came to power, they instituted a radical program intended to create an agrarian socialist state. The vehicle for this societal restructuring came in the form of a brutal forced labor program that eliminated political opposition, ethnic minorities, religious groups, the professional and educated classes, and any other groups that posed a threat to Khmer Rouge rule. The result was murder on a genocidal scale. During the Khmer Rouge's five years in power, one-third of the Cambodian population was killed (2 million people), mostly by starvation and disease, in what became known as "the Killing Fields." In 1979, Vietnam defeated Cambodia in a war that ended the Khmer Rouge rule. Though some Cambodians migrated to America after the fall of Lon Nol's government, it was not until the end of the Khmer Rouge that Cambodians began arriving in the United States in significant numbers. Many Cambodians headed for refugee camps across the border in neighboring Thailand. From there, they applied for asylum in the United States and other nations. To help facilitate rapid acculturation, the U.S. government initially settled Cambodians in various communities throughout the country during the 1980s. However, Cambodians soon began remigrating within U.S. borders, creating substantial communities in Long Beach, California; Fresno and Stockton, California; Providence, Rhode Island; and Lynn and Lowell, Massachusetts.

The following excerpt comes from a pamphlet about the United Cambodian Community, a Cambodian American organization located in Long Beach, California. Founded in 1977 by a group of Cambodian refugees, the United Cambodian Community supports the Cambodian American community in and around the Long Beach, California, area. Published by the

United Cambodian Community in 1990, this booklet describes the organization's mission, programs, and goals.

A TRADITION OF SUPPORT—A DREAM OF INDEPENDENCE

In 1977, as Southeast Asian refugees continued to flee from their homelands, a small group of Cambodian refugees who had already settled in Southern California founded the United Cambodian Community (UCC). Established as a self-help group and operated initially with modest funds raised primarily from within the refugee community, UCC quickly grew into one of the leading refugee service agencies in the country.

Today UCC has a full time staff of over sixty management and program specialties, 80% of whom were once refugees. In addition to Southeast Asians, UCC's multicultural staff also counsels, trains, and places people in need from Eastern Europe, Central America, Mexico, and Africa. In little more than a decade, UCC has provided job training and counseling for over 25,000 refugees and immigrants and has placed over 10,000 in permanent, full-time employment.

The agency also takes great pride in its multifaceted approach to community service. Through projects specializing in health, education, child care, art, English-as-a-Second Language, and technical assistance, UCC strives to serve the community on many levels. Due in large part to UCC assistance in areas such as child care, employers who hire UCC trainees report minimal turn over. Both agency and employer records indicated that 85% of the trainees UCC places remain with the same companies for at least six months.

List of Services and Programs

Bilingual Vocational Training
Central Intake Unit (Case Management)
Child Care Program
Community Economic Development Program
Drug Abuse Program
English as a Second Language
General Education Preparation
Job Placement
Khmer Women Weavers Project
Mental Health Program
Minority Aids Education
On the Job Training
Remediation
Social Adjustment Counseling and Referral Services
Southeast Asian Health Project
Summer Youth Employment Project
Technical Assistance
Traditional Music Program
Translation

Vocational Training:
   Electronic Assembly Training
   Auto Mechanics Training
   Dental Assistant Training
Youth and Family Services

Partial List of Donors and Funding Agencies

Ahmanson Foundation
American Association of International Aging
Atlantic Richfield Foundation
California Arts Council
California Community Foundation
California State University, Long Beach
Community Development Department, City of Los Angeles
County of Los Angeles
County of Orange
Department of Education, State of California
General Telephone
Health & Human Services Department, City of Long Beach
James Irvine Foundation
John Porter Trust
Knight Foundation
Long Beach Medical Association Auxiliary
Long Beach Press Telegram
Long Beach Unified School District
Private Industry Council, City of Long Beach
Private Industry Council, SELACO
Public Corporation for the Arts, City of Long Beach
St. Mary Medical Foundation
UCC Track Team
United Way
US Department of Education

Source: Southeast Asian Archive, vertical file collection, Special Collections and Archives, The University of California Irvine Libraries. http://www.calisphere.universityofcalifornia.edu/. Accessed July 2009. Reprinted with permission.

33. Karen Kauv Sun, Interview by Janean Baker, 1993

Karen Kauv Sun, born and raised in the Cambodian countryside, moved to the capital city of Phnom Penh in 1964 after graduating from high school. While living in Phnom Penh, Sun worked as a nurse, married a professor, and had three children. Then, the Khmer Rouge took power in 1975 and began implementing its sociopolitical engineering programs to transform Cambodia into a Communist agrarian society. The Sun family was caught up in the anti-intellectual purges. They were sent to the reeducation camps, where Sun's husband was killed. In 1979, Sun escaped to Thailand along with her children; and the next year, they were sponsored over to the United States by her cousin, benefiting from the newly passed Refugee Act. A few years later, she met some Mormon missionaries and became a convert.

In the following excerpts from her interview with Brigham Young University's Janean Baker, Sun talks about the similarities and connections she sees between Mormonism, her own life history, and Cambodian culture. She speaks extensively about the practical aspects of being part of the church: specifically the community and social aspects, and the help she received in navigating the unfamiliar American culture, crucial for all immigrants and particularly for refugees. However, Sun is equally adamant about her commitment to and love of the church; she frames the sincerity of her faith as entirely separate from the pragmatic benefits of being a Latter-Day Saint.

S: After I lived with my cousin for three months [after arriving in the United States], I got money from the government to help me. I got an apartment by myself. It had two bedrooms. I started to go to school. . . . I finished the English class. The lady teacher said, "You are writing good. Everything is good for you in English but speaking. You need to communicate with the people. You need to go to get a job." I was a nurse. They found a job at nursing home for me. . . .

God blessed me. I moved to another apartment. I met the missionaries of our church, the Mormon church. It was 1984. This is how I met the missionaries. . . . Mr. Brown and Sister Brown . . . talked about teaching me about the gospel and about Book of Mormon. I understood them. They showed a movie. I felt something. I thought, "These two are not like Cambodian family. They like to live together. They like family together." After the movie, I said to Elder and Sister Brown, "Why don't you come to visit me? I want to show my children the movie." She asked me my address and phone number.

She came to my house. She taught me about the gospel. I learned. After that I was baptized. Elder Brown baptized me. It was in 1984. It was in June or July, something like that.

B: Were all three of your children baptized?

S: Yes, all three together. They learned, and then they were baptized, too.

I learned more English. It is the true church. It is the same as my country people. They like the family together. I believed. I learned more and more so I start believing in the church. It is the true church. The Bible is true. It's real. Book of Mormon is very interesting. It is the same way that I escaped.

I worked very hard. I'm so happy. I am very proud of myself. I can remember my husband. I can do my job as a housewife and work. I can take care of three children, go to school, and go to work. I feed my children. I know that God loves me. I'm in good health. I take care of everything. I go to church all the time and teach my children.

After I learned in my Bible and Book of Mormon, I knew it was a good way to send children to church. I am by myself. If they go to church, they learn more about good things. They can help me because I'm a single parent. The Church can help me learn good things. . . .

B: Has the culture been an adjustment for you and your children?

S: I was born in Cambodia country. My children grow up here. It's very hard for me. It's very different.

B: In what ways?
S: This country is too free. Over there they are very strict with the kids.
B: In what ways?
S: We train the kid. We can spank a little bit. It is not too much. It is just a little bit to let them know, "Don't do this wrong." They respect the parents more. My generation respects the family more, brother and sister.

    We come here. We cannot do anything. We train them how to be good. Sometimes they do not listen to us. We cannot spank them and hit them. I hit the children a little bit, and they say, "I don't want to do anything to get spanked a little bit."

    It's hard. When they go to school, they know if a teacher hits them it is child abuse. They call police. We cannot do anything. It's happened with children in this country. It's very hard. . . .

B: How did your relatives respond to your joining the Church? What did your cousin who sponsored you do when he found out you joined the Church?
S: He said, "It's good. Find a church for your children. It is up to you. It's okay. It's freedom. This country is a free country. If you think it's a good way to go, you go." He didn't say anything. . . .
B: How do you feel non-member Cambodians feel about the church?
S: Most people that come over here are Buddhist. It's hard to change from Buddhist to Christian until people learn. But some people come from Cambodia. Educated people are being killed. Most people are killed. I heard two million people were killed by hunger and by sickness. Of the rest of the people, some don't know how to greet Cambodian. They never went to school. Those people came over here to United States.

    It's hard for them sometimes. They need a translator when a missionary goes to the house. Not too many people have free time to go along every Sunday. There were not too many members when I became a member.

    Some Cambodians believe and some do not. Now more people come. They have become members of the Church. They believe strongly that they need to go to church. But some people are uncomfortable by not understanding English.

    But now more missionaries know how to speak Cambodian. I heard in the Asian branch now that more people come now. I don't know in the future. . . .

B: Do the Cambodians like them or dislike [the Mormon missionaries]?
S: In general, they like them. Sometime they don't like the missionaries knocking on the door and going right away. Sometimes they have privacy, too. It is better if the missionaries have started to know them already. They should call and make a time. They knock on the door and see the house is messy. They cooked and spilled. They don't like that. They want to inspect the carpet and they prepare everything.

    One lady came to my house. She's a member of the church, too. She said, "Missionaries always go to my house, but sometime I feel like I don't want to go to the house because my house is messy. It smells. I cooked some Cambodian food. It has a Chinese food smell." It's good if they go to the house and call first.

B: Are there any other things that you think the missionaries could do to improve their missionary work among the Cambodians?
S: If they go to their houses, they invite you to eat their food. . . . I know sometimes it is different food. Some may not like that. They should at least drink the water.

Then we are happy. We don't force them to eat, but sometime we feel, "The missionaries don't like my family and Cambodians."

My people are very friendly especially when they were in Cambodia, but now they are mixed up. If missionary do that, maybe they will be happy. The missionaries should be kind, friendly, smiling, and talking. We like people that are friendly. If people don't talk to us, we say that is discrimination or prejudice. They don't want to get close with them and go to church. . . .

B: Tell me about your children's dating and social experiences. Have the Church's teachings have helped them? Do you think that being members of the Church has helped your children?

S: Yes, I think it has helped a lot. For me as the mother, the parent, it's hard to teach them. We didn't have dating over there. They come to church and they teach them about dating. I think it helps a lot. I teach them, but I've never been to an American school. It's hard for me to teach them. They know better than me. I teach them the Cambodian ways. It's not right how to grow up in this country.

For me, a parent, it is very hard to be from Cambodian culture to American culture. But I learn a lot from going to church and from going to work. Everywhere I ask what to do when my children grow up to teenager and how to deal with them.

I don't tell my daughter anything. If you go out and bring problems to the home, it's okay. If you go somewhere, call wherever you are. I teach my children, "Just let me know where you are. If you report, I'm happy. You go out, then tell me with whom."

I like to do the middle, not too tight, not too loose, not too easy. I know my children grow up with different culture. I went to the high school. I saw a lot of teenage boyfriends and girlfriends kissing at school. It is hard for me to see. I am thinking about my children. Maybe they do the same thing.

I don't know why in this country they are not a little bit stricter for the teenagers. They're too easy for the kids. . . .

B: Overall has the Church influenced your life?

S: I think it's good for me. I learn a lot. It is better than staying home and not know about the war going on. I go to church. Every time something new come up. They tell me about a storm coming up. They told us how to change the time back. That would be something new especially if I didn't speak English. I didn't know about the change of time. I like going to church.

Source: Karen Kauv Sun Oral History Project. Interviewed by Janean Baker, April 1, 1993. LDS Asian American Oral History Project, Charles Redd Center for Western Studies, L. Tom Perry Special Collections, Harold B. Lee Library, Brigham Young University. Used with permission of the Charles Redd Center.

34. Kong Phok, Interview by Barbara Lau, 2000

Kong Phok was born in Battambong, Cambodia, in 1976. When the Khmer Rouge took over Cambodia, Phok, his parents, and two of his siblings escaped, fleeing to refugee camps in Thailand and the Philippines. In

1985, sponsored by an American Lutheran family, they joined Phok's uncle in Greensboro, North Carolina. Following his graduation from high school, Phok got a job as a machine operator at Guilford Mills, a textile factory in North Carolina. After a few years, he was promoted to supervisor; however, the mill then closed down operations in Greensboro and moved to Mexico. In following excerpt of his interview with Barbara Lau, Phok describes how he negotiates his identity as both a Cambodian and an American.

BARBARA LAU: We were talking about how you think about yourself—you think about yourself as Cambodian-American?
KONG PHOK: Yes.
BARBARA LAU: Why that instead of Cambodian? How do you figure that out?
KONG PHOK: Because I spend so many my life—I mean, you can say more of my lifetime in America than Cambodia, but I am always Cambodian, would never change. But I celebrate every holiday like American people do. Actually, I'm doing everything almost exactly the same like American. That's how I consider myself as Cambodian-American, because I spend more of my lifetime [in the United States], more than in my own country. But I'm Cambodian.
BARBARA LAU: Do you sometimes feel like there's a struggle there, or you're being pulled in different directions?
KONG PHOK: No, never. I never had that problem.
BARBARA LAU: You just kind of bring it all into the center?
KONG PHOK: Yeah, just I have people ask me all the time, just say, how you feel? You think you're American or Americanized, or whatever. I think I say I'm both. I'm Cambodian and American, I guess. That's how I feel. Maybe it's not like that, but that's how I feel.
BARBARA LAU: What kind of people ask you that question?
KONG PHOK: Friend[s], workers, people who you know. See some people, they won't admit to themselves, you know. They don't believe themselves like Cambodian or Cambodian-American or Americanized Cambodian or whatever, because that's two different thing. I am Americanized Cambodian, and like I said, I'll respect, I'll cherish, I'll do everything Cambodian, but right now I consider myself as Cambodian-American, because America is like my country too.
BARBARA LAU: What do you think about your son? What will you tell him?
KONG PHOK: I'm not going to tell him. I'm just going to tell him that you both. You're Cambodian, Laos [Phok's wife is Lao American], and I'm not going to teach him what, hey you are Cambodian, you're not Laos or anything. It's up to him. It's not up to him if I keep on telling him, yeah, you're Cambodian or whatever. Like myself, I am Cambodian, Laos and American, you know. I mean, it's not Cambodian only; I'm Laos because my wife is Laos. I have, you can say, two different blood because I'm not really American blood, but I consider myself American. But my kid has, you know, two different bloods, and he is Cambodian, Laos and American. I know this might be hard for him when he grow up.

Source: Excerpt from interview with Kong Phok by Barbara Lau, December 19, 2000 (K-0273), in the Southern Oral History Program Collection (#4007), Southern Historical Collection, Louis Round Wilson Special Collections Library, University of North Carolina at Chapel Hill. Reprinted with permission.

35. Ran Kong, Interview by Barbara Lau, 2001

Ran Kong, originally from Cambodia, was 21 years old and a student at Salem College in Winston-Salem, North Carolina, when the United States was attacked on September 11, 2001. A month later, she spoke with Barbara Lau from the American Folklife Center's "September 11, 2001, Documentary Project." Kong recalled being mistaken for an Arab and explained how her family members' reactions to the attacks were conditioned by their memories of wartime Cambodia, their continuing ties to family in the homeland, and their ambiguous position as immigrants in the United States.

BARBARA LAU: Did [the attack] make you think differently at all about your own future?

RAN KONG: Yes, my initial thought was, "OK, they'd already suspected it was going to be terrorists." Then the name Osama Bin Laden came up, and "Arabics," and my impression was, *You know what? Americans right now probably aren't going to like foreigners. And even though I'm a US citizen, they're not going to know that. They're not going to be able to tell just by looking at me.* And, this was actually confirmed [wry laugh] when I went to work on the following Saturday . . . I went to work [at a local hospital] the next day, and this lady, the first question that she asked me was "Are you Arabic?" She was on a ventilator, so I couldn't tell—was she asking me this? So I read her lips again, and was like "What?" and she said, "Are you Arabic?"—she mouthed it again—and I said, "No. I'm not Arabic." And she said, "Well, what are you?" And I said, "I'm Cambodian." And she said again, "Is that Arabic?" . . . I told her "Cambodia's in Southeast Asia; it's Asia, but it's not the Middle East, and it's not really anywhere near where Osama Bin Laden is from . . ." And so from a *patient*, who was on a ventilator, who couldn't get up and do anything to me, I felt really uncomfortable. But then I stepped out of the hospital after work, and I just thought, "If it had been a guy, on the street, that had approached me and asked me that, what was I to do?" You know, would he have believed me? And so, I just can't imagine being in New York City, and looking like me. Or anybody with brown skin and black hair. Of Asian descent.

BARBARA LAU: Do you think your reaction to it was similar to your family's or was yours different?

RAN KONG: I think it's different, simply because my parents actually lived through a war; they lived through all the atrocities. So for them, immediately: "There's going to be a war. You know, war is really bad. We remember what war is like. The hunger, the fear—feeling unsafe all the time." For me, I think I have more belief in the American government; I have a working knowledge of how America might handle things. Just being able to keep up with the news, and being able to understand what's going on—but for my parents, who are not going to understand everything that's broadcast on the station—they just see the American people's reactions. For them, their immediate fear is: "They're not going to like us. They're not going to want us here anymore. What's going to happen to us, what's going to happen to my family? I'm not a US citizen. You know, my kids are [citizens]—what's going to happen with that?"

BARBARA LAU: ... What do you think people in the Cambodian community did as a result of this?

RAN KONG: I think their first thought was, "OK ... what happens in a war time, well: there's no food. There's no money." I don't know how many people actually went out to the banks and withdrew money. But for my parents, their first thought was "Well, how much cash do we have at home right now? And we need to go to the store, let's go ahead and buy some stuff." We went to our store, bought like 15 more bags of rice, to keep at home ... And I think that to a certain extent that other families are doing the same thing. The Cambodian store, the only Cambodian store in Greensboro, by Tuesday night: no more bags of rice. The owner herself was like, "Wait, we were supposed to keep some for our family. We don't even have some for our own family! It's all gone." And I just thought that was really funny.

BARBARA: LAU: Do you think that your family or other families in this community are afraid that the war's going to come to Greensboro, that things could happen here?

RAN KONG: I think so ... People in Cambodia heard about this, and ... are afraid, because, we are their backbones, here, and if we're gone, then what's going to happen to them? ... Yes, maybe you can take care of your family here, but what's going to happen with your family over in Cambodia? What if we can never fly again, to go visit them; what if we never ever get to see our native country again?

BARBARA: LAU: What do you think about the choices that have been made about how to respond to what happened last September 11th?

RAN KONG: ... It wasn't until recently that Bush gave the go-ahead to start bombing Afghanistan, and just seeing the situation, the country—from a refugee standpoint: just seeing the images of the Afghani people living in the refugee camps, and dying in the refugee camps, that that really—it really bothers me ... I personally disagree with just bombing a country, even though you say, "Oh, you know, in the end it's going to help the Afghani people to have the Taliban taken out, and have all the terrorists rid of." But ... we're doing what the terrorists did, by bombing these people. We're killing innocent civilians, too ... Maybe the world needs to stop, and ... just look, look at your foreign policy, look at how you treat the other countries, look at how other countries treat smaller nations . . . I know that America—Nixon—bombed Cambodia too, during the Vietnam War, and we were a neutral country; we weren't really directly involved with the Vietnam War, yet we were bombed also. And so just taking—stepping back and maybe re-examine everything instead of just reacting out of anger.

Source: Excerpted from interview with Ran Kong, conducted by Barbara Lau, Greensboro, North Carolina, October 14, 2001, for the September 11, 2001, Documentary Project Collection (AFC 2001/015), Archive of Folk Culture, American Folklife Center, Library of Congress. http://hdl.loc.gov/loc.afc/afc2001015.sr320a01. Accessed June 2009. Reprinted with permission from Ran Kong.

36. Leendavy Koung, "You Cannot Lose Your Spirit," 2001

Defying traditional Cambodian mores, which stipulate that only men can become professional musicians, Leendavy Koung's father taught her to play Khmer musical instruments when she was a child. After the Vietnam War reached Cambodia, in 1969, the Koung family fled their country to escape Pol Pot, Cambodia's brutal dictator. They carried their father's handcrafted instruments through the jungles to Thailand and brought them with them to the United States, where they settled in Philadelphia.

Today, Koung is a teacher in her immigrant Philadelphia community, working to preserve Cambodian music and dance in the United States. In 2001, Koung spoke with Debora Kodish from the Philadelphia Folklore Project, a 20-year-old independent public folklife agency that documents, supports, and presents Philadelphia-area folk arts and culture. In her interview, Koung talks about how arts and culture give immigrants a strong sense of identity and about the importance of the younger generation taking responsibility for cultural preservation.

Back then, when I was a child, music never interested me. I always wanted to learn to dance. When you are dancing you get to interact with other children, wear nice clothes, be out there on stage, and look beautiful. Dancing was more fun and exciting than being a musician.

Playing music, you had to sit still, and you didn't get to dress up nice! And, especially, I didn't like it because my dad would wake me up at four or five o'clock in the morning, when everybody else was still having good dreams. There I was, out there early in the morning, trying to hit the instruments and trying to find all the sounds. Sometimes I practiced in tears, but I had to do it because he wanted me to. He forced me to learn! In fact, none of my brothers and sisters wanted to learn music either, but the thing was, we had the gift. We were talented at it, and we could learn so much. . . .

In Cambodian music, I did not learn by reading notes. Everything is in your head. You have to remember the sounds. You have to remember where the sounds are at. That's how I was taught. When I was learning to play the *khim* [a Cambodian hammered dulcimer], my father would tell me where to hit with the hammers. So pretty much you have to recognize where all the sounds are at. From learning the khim,

I kind of got the sounds in my head, so then I could pick up any instrument. Now, I can learn any instrument on my own, any song or music, as long as I can hear the music. The basic learning is in my head already. I have the sounds. All I need to do is to use that sound and turn it to music. That's how I learned and that's how I still learn.

So when I was little, I went along and tried to learn. And it came in my head that the way to make my dad stop teaching me was to learn everything, so he would have nothing left to teach. That way, I thought I could get some free time! If he taught me one thing, the next day I'd learn three different things! He would teach me one instrument. I'd catch up—learning two or three other instruments, sometimes on my own. He would teach me one, two or three songs—I would learn five or 10 songs over the next week or month or so. I caught up so fast that now I know almost more instruments, songs and music than he does, which is weird.

One thing that has always motivated me to learn, even when I didn't love music, that I always have wanted to challenge myself. Always. If I see an instrument, I try to see if I can play it. And I find I can do it! I don't always play music because I love it—I do it because I want to know. I want to find out what it is, and how I can learn it, and if I have the ability to learn it.

It was only later on in my life that I came to recognize the importance, the value, of music. Now, I really, really, appreciate my dad so much for teaching me all that he did. Now, I am so happy that he forced me to learn all that music and all those instruments. Because now I understand that it is very important. Especially when you come from a country like Cambodia, where not a lot of artists survived the killing fields.

I have come to realize that in our culture, music is the most important thing of all. Everything we do—weddings, funerals—everything has to have music. The sad thing about it is that now we have to dance to taped music instead of live music. It makes it more difficult for the dancers to learn, because they have to follow the tape. And sometime we have to cut out some of the hand gestures that a dance is supposed to have, and dancers have to fit themselves into the amount of time on the taped music that we got from wherever! You don't feel like you are doing a full performance. It's following something that's not real. That's the sad thing about it nowadays, for us, is doing any performance here.

As a teacher, I want the children of this generation to recognize their arts and culture. A lot of the Cambodian parents who went through the war and who came to live here don't have great communication with their children. If Cambodian children are going to wait to learn about their culture and their history from their parents, forget it! It's not going to happen. For one thing, the parents are working hard making enough money to support the family. There are so many expenses here. In their country, there were no taxes. And we could grow vegetables around the house to support the family. Here, everything is money. So it's hard to blame the parents if they don't have enough time to teach their children anything about who they are. The children in this generation learn about who they are from the influence of outsiders. And sometimes they pick up bad things. Sometimes what they pick up is not really who they are, so sometimes they are lost.

Some of them feel that it is degrading to be called Cambodian. They'd rather be called American. I want to really help these children recognize who they are, where they come from, why their arts and culture are so important, and why they need to see that and appreciate it, for themselves. From arts and culture, you learn a moral standard. You also learn how to identify yourself, and you get a little background about where you come from. It helps you so you don't get lost too much. These things give you an identity. If you don't know your arts and culture, who are you? How are you going to explain to other people who you are? When people ask you, what are you? If you say, "I'm Cambodian," then what is Cambodian? If you can't tell them that, then you are empty behind your own face. If you can't tell people about who you are, how are they going to appreciate you? First, you got to appreciate yourself. And you learn to appreciate yourself through your arts and culture, through your tradition. And that's how I look at it.

Whenever I teach, I am teaching them something for the long run. When I teach dance, it's not just for a one-time performance, or something that will be used once in a while. I am also teaching students to learn about the outfit of our traditional costume. (And how long it takes to make the costume, first of all!) So they need to appreciate that. And from there, the songs for dance speak in a different language, at a level that they don't understand. So I talk to them about it. And the history of the dance—Why? How did this dance start? Who created it? And that will bring us back to the history of where dance comes from, and that will give credit to our ancestors and all those older generations that came before. And dance also has a moral standard with it. Because every movement in the dance shows how a Cambodian woman is supposed to be—going far back. The slow movement is all coming from a very respectful way, the way we walk, we talk—all of this goes to the movement of our dance. The song also speaks in a language of royalty. . . . In the dance, and in our language, there are certain words you can speak in referring to other people. In American English, there's only "you" and "me"—so it's very general and it's all at the same level. But in our language we have many different words. You speak one way to those who are older, another way to those who are younger. These are the things that students have to understand.

Teaching Cambodian arts and culture does not mean that I don't want Cambodian children to learn about American culture. It's not that. You're going to be here for so many years, you're going to learn about American culture, and you need to learn about it. You live here. No matter what. So you have to get along. But at the same time, you have to learn about yourself, too, so you won't be lost. Right now, we depend on the older generation to help us plan New Year celebrations, to marry us, and to do whatever it is that needs to be done for us culturally. But someday we are going to be the ones to carry on those traditions. And if we lose the knowledge, it is worse than losing your country. You lose yourself. You lose your spirit. Who is going to know what is Cambodian any more? If we lose our identity, we lose everything, and Cambodia will be completely history.

I came back to teach arts and culture for the younger generation who know nothing about these things. I did it because I cannot depend on their parents to teach them and to keep the arts alive. I didn't see other people teaching, or caring much about it. So I had to make a decision, somehow, for me, for my community, and for my children. And I don't regret what my decision has been. I love what I am doing.

I was taught so much, and have accomplished so much. I survived the war and overcame so many tragedies in my country, and the war, and here. For all this, I feel that I should do my best to return the favor to my country, my homeland, and my father. I must return the favor given to me by trying to continue to carry on our arts and culture.

[S]ee how important it is to keep the spirit alive. We lost our country. And I know that anybody can lose their country over anything. But one thing you have to remember is that you cannot lose your spirit. And as long as you have your spirit, your country will still be around you. Now, I understand the value and importance of arts and culture. That's what really motivates me to continue to do this.

I was away from it, but arts and culture never did leave my mind. My soul was gone, but my spirit was still here. That's what got me to come back. That's who I am. It doesn't matter how far you try to get away—you can never get away because you are already attached to it. I think I was put in a position to explode! I was put in a position to help carry on these things, whether I like it or not. I had a choice either to fix my personal relationships or to fix my arts and culture, and I had to choose between that. And it's not easy, you know. Especially, it's at a point where—are you willing to give up your family? Or are you willing to give up everything else that you have that was given to you to give to others or to share with others?

Source: Koung, Leendavy. "You Cannot Lose Your Spirit." Recorded and edited by Debora Kodish. *Works in Progress*, Philadelphia Folklore Project, vol. 14, no. 1/2, Summer 2001, pp. 26–29. http://www.folkloreproject.org/folkarts/resources/pubs/wip/summer01.pdf. Accessed August 2009. Used with permission of the Philadelphia Folklore Project.

37. Vatey Seng, *The Price We Paid*, 2005

Vatey Seng was 15 years old when the Khmer Rouge took power in Cambodia. As educated, light-skinned Chinese Cambodians, Seng's family faced intense persecution from the nationalistic Communist regime. The next year, they were imprisoned in a reeducation camp. There, they worked as slaves for the regime until 1979, when they were liberated by Vietnamese troops. After fleeing to refugee camps in Thailand and the Philippines, Seng, her mother, and her siblings eventually immigrated to the United States. They left behind many other family members, including her father, who had disappeared or were killed during the years of turmoil.

Three decades after the devastation of her homeland and her family, Seng wrote her memoir, *The Price We Paid: A Life Experience in the Khmer Rouge Regime, Cambodia*. The following excerpts highlight the trauma of the refugee immigrant experience for her family and the powerful impact the memory of Cambodia has on Seng's personal and political identity in the United States.

Refugee Camps

In July 1979, my family decided to flee to the Cambodian-Thai border to be with Uncle Sok. We wished we could go back to our house in Phnom Penh City, but Mae [Seng's mother] said she would not look back without Pa. In addition, she didn't trust the new government backed by the Vietnamese. We couldn't afford to take any more risk. We had to get out of this country as soon as we could, and this was a good opportunity.

Many people traveled on the road and most of them headed our direction. Traveling by foot and carrying heavy belongings, it took us two days to reach Srok Svay Sisophon, Battambang province [in northwestern Cambodia], which was about 35 miles away. This district was the meeting point of all traders and salesmen. Some salesmen delivered goods from Thailand and sold here, and some salesmen bought goods and sold in Battambang city. Since Mony [Seng's older brother] had been to the refugee camp before, he knew where to meet other people that were headed our way. My family waited with a big crowd of a hundred people until dark, to avoid the Vietnamese patrol. Our escape would be led by a group of men who knew the way well. They didn't charge us anything because they had to go to refugee camps, too, to do their trading business. They did not allow anyone with babies to travel with the group. There were a couple reasons why babies and small children could put the group in jeopardy during an escape. If they cried, robbers could spot us and robbed us. They said there were two to three groups of thieves that waited for travelers at about mid-point. Besides, we had to walk across the thick forest and mine fields. They told us to meet them at a certain place before sunset. . . .

[The Sengs settled in at Nong Mak-moon refugee camp, located in the disputed borderlands between Cambodia and Thailand. In April, 1980, Seng got married; she soon became pregnant.]

In July 1980, the Old Camp was attacked heavily. One night, Mony got information from one of Uncle Sok's secret agents that thousands of the Vietnamese troops were marching toward our camp. They planned the attack after midnight. Mony immediately went to get Sothan [Seng's oldest brother] from his workplace, but Sothan didn't believe that information because his office was the headquarters which was supposed to receive all secret information first. Mony returned home and told us to pack our belongings. Only the children could sleep that night. We hoped the information would be false.

A few minutes after midnight, we could hear gunfire from surroundings of the camp. This sounded like popping corn but much louder. Refugees got trapped in the middle of the battle zone between Vietnamese troops and Thai soldiers. Everywhere was gunfire and bombardment. Normally, refugees could escape to the Thai village, but this time, Thai soldiers fired at refugees and prevented us from entering their land. Hundreds of refugees got killed and there were many casualties. We could see blood everywhere.

Since Sothan usually stayed at his workplace, he was separated from my family at that time.

My family and our neighbors moved from one hut to another in order to stay away from the battlefield. Few hours later, one of the bombs dropped right nearby the place we were hiding. A piece of shrapnel grazed the left side of Mony's abdomen. Chhora [Seng's younger sister] was also got hit on her right cheek. They were bleeding a lot. Mae and Mony's wife cried out in fear. Mony and Chhora put pieces of cloth on top of their wound to minimize bleeding.

Since this place was not safe anymore, Mony said we had to get out the camp as soon as we could because it seemed like both troops attempting to kill all refugees. So, other survivors and my family crawled through disgusting sewage filled with worms, and walking passed dead bodies. We hid behind any small hills or barriers and headed towards the thick forest away from the camp. All the way, we prayed to God to protect us from bombs and gunshots. . . . [Seng and her family fled from one camp to the next, eventually ending up at Thailand's Keo I Dang Camp.]

A Road to the Third Country

I gave birth to twin boys on February 5, 1981. It was the greatest event in my life. They were so precious little babies. The older weighted 5.28 pounds, and the younger weighted 4.18 pounds. Mae and my husband were with me during the labor. I was thankful to two young French doctors and Cambodian nurses who took good care of me and helped me through my first experience of my life in delivering babies. Moreover, a young French Catholic nun named Denise du Bois came to visit me and other young moms and taught us how to take care babies. She provided me baby clothing, baby supplies, and some money. She even named my twins: Jean and Jacque.

Sister Denise and another sister . . . came to this refugee camp to help children and new moms by providing supplement food and clothing. They made many trips every day to visit those families without the feeling of weariness.

To honor Sister Denise, I named my twins by combining French and Cambodian names. I named the older Jean Kavey. Kavey means a poet or a writer. I named the younger Jacque Vithey. Vithey means a road that leads people to the right direction, like a leader. Unfortunately, the immigration worker wrote their names wrong. Jean Kavey became Jankavey, and Jacque Vithey became Jakvithey. I didn't request to make any changes because it could delay my case up to a year or two.

Fifteen days later, our family was accepted to migrate to the United States of America based on the political status because my dad was in former military. Normally, my husband used to check the listing whether our names were on it or not. With despair, he didn't go to check on that day until someone came to tell us with joy. It was the greatest news to my family. Finally, our hope in having better and safer lives in the third country came true! . . .

Before we immigrated to the United States, all refugees were transported to the camp in Chun Borei province, in Thailand. We were screened for any contagious diseases before we departed to a camp in the Philippines.

We arrived at the refugee camp in Morong, Bataan, in the Philippines, in May 1981. The camp was a beautiful site near waterfall and near the beaches. We stayed in wooden buildings which were organized into section. Fresh vegetables and seafood fish were adequate and provided every day. Besides, Filipinos could come in to trade food for clothing or jewelry. Refugees were allowed to travel outside the camp if they had money.

This camp was also known as the processing zone. All refugees, young and old, were required to go to school to learn the English language for three months, and then they had to attend a class for learning American culture for a week. If anyone missed the last class, that person would not be allowed for departure.

With twin babies, it didn't stop me from studying and doing my homework assignments. I did well in my English language class. Chhora and Sotheavy [Seng's sister] would bring Jean and Jacque to my class and let me breastfeed them, and my Filipina teacher Mrs. Guevara was happy to hold one while I breastfed another. My classmates and my teacher were proud of me because I consistently scored the third among youngsters, Cambodian English teachers and interpreters who took the same class.

In the culture class, we were taught that American people didn't like the smell of most Asian food. So, we had to be careful not to cook food that had stinky smell like pickled fish. We learned that most American women were independent and could stay single in the late 30s whereas women in our culture liked to get married in early age. We also learned that American liked to keep things personal. Being aware that our culture was so different from American culture. It made us have fear of what we could confront when we came to live in America. . . .

America, America

[Seng's family, nine people in all, landed at the San Francisco Airport on February 19, 1982. They relocated to Illinois, sponsored by a Catholic church in Peoria.] When the first Cambodian worker came, he brought us lots of clothes and shoes. His name was Chhun. He told us that the supplies were donated by members of his church. He also told us that our sponsor was Catholic Church and that they were paying for all our expenses. We were so grateful and wished to meet them, but our worker said we didn't have to.

Chhun was in charge of taking us to see the doctor, enroll in school, and bring us food—plenty of food. He demanded that we finished one chicken a day, which made us feel so fortunate because we didn't have this much food before. It was almost overwhelming for us to finish a chicken a day. To us, one chicken could be enough for a week. To add to our happiness, Chhun got us all kinds of Asian food, especially rice, and we were so happy about it. We were not used to American food, in both quantity and quality. . . .

[In 1985, the family moved to California, joining the extended family, including Sothan and Mony, who finally had arrived from Cambodia.] I gave birth to a baby girl on September 1, 1989. When I was in delivery room before giving birth, Wendy Tokuda, a television reporter, came to conduct an interview concerning healthcare of Alameda County that faced budget crisis. I was so excited to see her in person although I was in pain. After I delivered the baby, the nurse asked what the baby's name was.

I already chose her name Amanda; somehow, I changed my mind at the last minute.

"Wendy. Wendy Seng."

I hoped my daughter would grow up to be a reporter like Wendy Tokuda. This career was one of my dreams. However, I would give freedom to my daughter in deciding what she wants to be.

She was a cute little baby. The most unique thing about Wendy was that she always smiled every time she woke up. Most babies would cry so often. She grows up to be a happy and funny girl with self-confidence. She is like the sunshine brightens my life and helps to ease my pain.

***

My whole extended family lives in California now. We enjoy being together at Mae's house on most weekends. Although we all got married and have children of our own, we still feel as close as when we were young. Sometimes, we talk about our past in the Khmer Rouge regime. We make fun of each other: Sothan was so skinny that he couldn't walk straight. Chhora looked like a beggar and she always ran away to avoid work and ate all kinds of wild vegetables and even small fish heads thrown away at the communal kitchen. Sotheavy looked cute in her worn-out clothes with many patches and a big pocket in front of the shirt so that she could put her rice ration. Although she was skinny, her cheeks were pink and plumy. Tevy [Seng's youngest sister] was chubby while other children were so skinny due to lack of food.

Actually, during those horrible years, we endured all the difficulties, pains, starvation, and deadly diseases. The bond of affection between parents and children, brothers and sisters, kept us strong. We stood by one another in order to survive. The most painful part of this experience was that we lost our Pa, whom we admire and love very much. How we wish he had made it through those days and be with us now. Twenty years later, pain still exists in our hearts. It's like a wound that cannot be healed.

Although I live freely and have a good life in the United States, I always think about other Cambodians who struggle every day back home, just to put food on the table. I remember what Pa told me, "You're lucky because you didn't have to suffer through World War II as I did." Contrarily, my generation was the worst and most destructive in the history of Cambodia. Whenever leaders of political parties fight each other for their own power, we the people are the ones who suffer, sacrifice, and die for them. Those powerful leaders do not care about their people—it is all about their personal interests. Cambodia is a poor country. Its size is approximately the state of Nevada. Today, because of corruption and poor leadership its economy is probably even worse than it was during the old regime before the Khmer Rouge regime. We the people want to live peacefully. We demand liberty and justice for all, and we need leaders who enhance the country towards prosperity. We need leaders who believe in a country for the people and by the people.

It is painful to have these memories in the deep recesses of my mind, and I learn to forgive and have no feelings of hatred or retaliation toward those who have hurt me. I just wish that my story could help the new generation understand what happened in the past and stop attempting to put people through the terror again.

Source: Excerpted from Seng, Vatey. *The Price We Paid: A Life Experience in the Khmer Rouge Regime, Cambodia.* New York: iUniverse, 2005, pp. 227–252.

PART V
Chinese American

38. *The Golden Hills' News*, "The Chinese Exodus," 1854

Kim Shan Jit San Luke, or the *Golden Hills' News,* was North America's first Chinese-language newspaper. The *Golden Hills' News* was established in 1854 by American Methodist missionaries in San Francisco. This venture was closely connected with the denomination's overseas missions efforts, which had grown quickly in the wake of the Opium Wars and the 1842 Treaty of Nanking. The wars and the treaty forced China to not only open itself to more trade from Western nations, but also to Western churches. The first Methodist missionaries arrived in Foochow, China, in 1847.

The *Golden Hills' News* covered a wide variety of topics, from shipping information to local news to updates on the political situation in China—including the Taiping Rebellion, which had reached Guangdong province from where most Chinese immigrants to the United States originated. Although it ran for only a few months, the *Golden Hills' News* served as a model for future ethnic press publications in the United States. The majority of the newspaper was lithographed in Chinese characters, but the May 27, 1854, edition included the following publisher's column written in English. The publishers called for Americans to embrace the Chinese immigrants, for reasons of commercial and economic self-interest, and from principles of common humanity.

The people of San Francisco are a great people—great in the rapidity of their growth, great in the aspect of enterprise and determination, which their cities, villages and Institutions present, and in the original characteristics of their inhabitants. They are great by origin—they are sui generis—they are a commingelment based on Liberty, which fuses all into oneness. They are great by their love of freedom. They hold no seven by nine creed, which, like that of some of the Press, would cry privilege for themselves and despotism for others. They are great in the "Constitution," which declares, that all men are free and equal. The people and eschutchon of California are things to rejoice over—they are DEMOCRACY.

But the California picture is unique—their tout ensemble is the history of Civilization. The "Eastern States" have their Irish exodus, their German exodus, and hordes of Saxons, Danes, Celts, Gauls and Scandinavians, but we have all these, and the most wonderful of all a CHINESE EXODUS! The great wonder of the century is the astonishing flight of the hitherto immobile Chinamen across the

Pacific ocean, to seek refuge and liberty in the bosom of the "Golden Hills." It actually tickles the fancy to even think of Chinamen quitting the celestial empire—the paradise of earth—the garden of green Byson [?]—the Flowery Land, beyond which was supposed to lay outer darkness, and to come and mingle in the search for yellow gold, instead of remaining at home to fight and struggle for the "yellow robes of office."

Yes, John Chinaman disregarding the threats of the bastinade, and the tortures said to await his return to the "Flowery abode," for having forsaken the habits of his forefathers, joins the tide of Progress, and the Rubicon once passed, where shall his exodus end? The days of Chinese exclusion, small feet, and stand-still-ism, are ending—Chinese are no longer rare avis in terres—to see them is no longer to see "the Elephant." They are fast assisting to colonize California and various islands in Polynesia.

Statistics show, that the principle emigration of the Chinese is from the Canton river, and the rising port of Shanghai. The reverends Charles Taylor and M. P. Yates, both Missionaries at Shanghai, say that the latter port is thrown open, without restriction to the Foreigner, that Americans wander unmolested 40 miles into the interior, and that the Natives instead of calling Americans "outside barbarians," look up to them with profound respect. No Chinaman sneers at you in the streets; there is no hindrance whatever to your study of their character and habits; they will always look at you with an expression of goodwill," says Bayard Taylor. Is it too much to ask of a Christian population "to do unto them," at least, what it seems "they do to us," in their own land? Is it too much to ask of this Cosmopolitan state, in the veins of whose population flows the blood of a thousand tribes, to give freedom of growth and fair play to the Mongol element? Is it too much to ask of a Commercial People to give a generous and liberal encouragement to any means, that assist the Chinese to a knowledge of our laws and habits, and a sympathy with our interests? Surely not. Therefore Merchants, Manufacturers, Miners and Agriculturalists, come forward as friends, not scorners of the Chinese, so that they may mingle in the march of the world, and help to open for America an endless vista of future commerce.

Published by Howard & Hudson.

Source: "The Chinese Exodus." *The Golden Hills' News*, 1854. California Historical Society, Newspaper Collection. http://content.cdlib.org/ark:/13030/hb3j49n625/. Accessed May 2010. Courtesy of the California Historical Society.

39. William Speer, "An Answer to the Common Objections to Chinese Testimony," 1857

William Speer was born in Pennsylvania in 1822 and moved to Canton, China as a Presbyterian medical missionary in 1850. Upon his return to the United States, he moved to San Francisco, where he founded the Presbyterian Chinese Mission Church in Chinatown—the United States' first Asian American Christian congregation—in 1853. During his time in San Francisco, Speer frequently spoke out on behalf of the Chinese immigrant community. He called for the repeal of the Foreign Miners Tax; enacted in

1850 and reinstated in 1852, the tax applied only to foreigners and was aimed particularly at the Chinese. The system was also rife with abuse. Tax collectors were allowed to confiscate and sell the property of miners who could not pay. Speer also protested the law preventing Chinese from testifying against whites in court. In this excerpt from his 1857 pamphlet "An Answer to the Common Objections to Chinese Testimony," Speer points out the many ways in which Chinese Americans have been persecuted by unfair laws and unscrupulous men, and claims that Californians have a moral obligation to right these wrongs.

TO THE HONORABLE SENATE AND ASSEMBLY OF THE
STATE OF CALIFORNIA:

... The Chinese population, on the other hand, groan and cry out, though their articulations are little understood by us, with many and grievous burthens, hardships and troubles. Within the last two years, their condition has greatly improved; they are employed in many advantageous ways; the ignorant and filthy have ceased to spew, in the newspaper or the bar-room, upon their timid helplessness; and they are becoming more settled, prosperous, and contented. The greatest stumbling-block, a rock of offence in their way and in ours, is now the exclusion of their testimony from our courts of justice, in suits in which whites are parties. They are thus a tempting prey to all the depraved classes with which a new country, and especially a country rich in native precious metals, must abound. They are the spoil of villains of every race and hue. Our industrious classes are injured by their fluctuations and losses. Every branch of business suffers. Society is kept uneasy and shifting. All must feel the injuries of one member; as, if what appears to others an insignificant source of suffering continues to press and wound even a foot or toe, inflammation at length must ensue, and then constitutional disturbance, sickness, and the loss of a limb, or of life.

The settlement of the question involved in the grant to the Chinese of the privilege of testifying, on oath, against whites, is attended with some difficulties. And yet I have thought that the chief lay in, first, the want of popular information in regard to some of the tenets and practices of the Chinese; second, the not clearly discerning, and applying to a new case, some of the radical principles of our own system of justice. It is stepping out of my place to engage in the consideration of some of these points, and I regret that those better qualified have not elucidated them. But the claims upon me, in behalf of the Christian community, of the distressed race among whom my labors are spent, and of all who seriously think upon the present miserable and disordered state of things, are urgent. It is enough to fill any one with horror and anxiety. ...

If, Gentlemen, it be evident that the admission of Chinese testimony in cases where whites are interested is sanctioned by the Common Law, by our Federal laws, by the usage of various States, by an intelligent comprehension of the religion and the principles of justice prevalent in China, and by the principles of science and Christianity, the *conclusion* is easily reached, that before this Legislature adjourn, some act should be passed for its legalization. It is difficult to express in words the anxiety which multitudes of our citizens feel on this subject, or their distress that when it was brought up in the Senate at the beginning of the present sessions circumstances should have led to its indefinite postponement. The form of the Act is of little consequence, so that the end be obtained. Unless some relief be extended, new courage will be taken by a host of the most abandoned men to continue and increase their horrible acts of murder and crime. No doubt many expressions of opinion from the press and constituents have reached you. I need quote but one, from the *Mountain Democrat*: "A Chinaman was shot near the mouth of Big Canon, on the Sacramento road, on Monday last. The officers got a clue to the murderer, and started in pursuit, but have not arrested him. These are all the particulars we could glean. Chinamen are robbed and murdered *with impunity* because they are defenceless and have no remedy. Reports reach us daily of the hard treatment they are subjected to by cowardly and rascally white fellows. They justly complain that they pay for protection, yet never receive it. Since the indefinite postponement of the bill allowing them to testify in cases, they have been cruelly outraged...."

1. It [the admission of Chinese testimony in court] is *essential to the quiet, the prosperity, and the morals of the State*. Now one-sixth or seventh of the entire population is laid open to the practice of every species of fraud, trespass, violence, personal abuse, robbery, murder, wrong and injury. California possesses magnificent materials of greatness. Where can be equaled her mines, her soil, her climate, her timber, her commercial advantages! Well may we love this glorious State, and wish here to live and die. But it cannot be concealed that the land which God has so enriched with His gifts, man has fearfully polluted with his crimes. Painful as it is, we cannot deny that the name of "California" has become, in the New and Old World, a synonym for iniquity....

3. Regard for the *honesty and good behavior of officers of the State* requires stricter laws in regard to their treatment of the Chinese, and a more faithful administration of the laws. Scarce a man that reads this has not seen or heard of acts of barbarity and fraud on the part of "Foreign miners' tax collectors," that ought to have been severely punished; such as whipping, cutting, taking the blankets and tools of even those that have been sick, dating back their licenses one or two weeks in the month, snatching their dust when weighing out the amount due, charging $6 instead of $4 monthly, requiring one to pay for others, perhaps a stranger for a company of half-a-dozen, re-issuing old licenses, and the like....

Source: Speer, William. "An Answer to the Common Objections to Chinese Testimony: and an Earnest Appeal to the Legislature of California, for Their Protection by Our Law." San Francisco: The Chinese Mission House, 1857, pp. 1–2, 11, 14. xF870.C5.C51 v.1:5, The Bancroft Library, University of California, Berkeley. http://sunsite.berkeley.edu/cgi-bin/flipomatic/cic/brk4915. Accessed May 2010.

40. Kwang Chang Ling, "Letters of Kwang Chang Ling: The Chinese Side of the Chinese Question," 1878

In 1878, the United States was on the eve of passing the Chinese Exclusion Act, the nation's most restrictive piece of immigration legislation. Xenophobia, fueled by economic fears and racial prejudice, was rampant, especially in California. Anti-Chinese speeches and newspaper articles were circulated widely. Some people, however, spoke out against the racist propaganda, challenging mainstream assumptions and claims about both China and Chinese immigrants. In a series of letters written for the *San Francisco Argonaut,* a literary journal published in the late 19th century, Kwang Chang Ling argued that the Chinese were integral to California's economy. The following excerpt exposes American commentators' double standards concerning China and immigrant Chinese laborers, and the self-serving hypocrisy underpinning American denigration of Chinese morality.

WHY SHOULD THE CHINESE GO?

A Pertinent Inquiry from a Mandarin High in Authority

Letter 1

PALACE HOTEL, August 2, 1878

TO THE ARGONAUT:—You will doubtless gather from the superscription and general appearance of this letter that I am what Europeans, in the abundance of their vanity, would be very likely to regard as an anomaly—an educated Chinaman. In a word, I speak and write your language, as I believe, correctly. And it is because of this slight accomplishment that my general unworthiness has been overlooked by my countrymen residing in California, and I have been selected by them to communicate to the public the Chinese side of the Chinese question. The ARGONAUT has been especially preferred as the medium for the promulgation of these views on account of its reputed fairness to all.

The cry is here that the Chinese must go. I say that they should not go; that they can not go; will not go. More than this, that, were it conceivable that they went, your State would be ruined; in a word, that the Chinese population of the Pacific Coast have become indispensable to its continued prosperity, and that you cannot afford to part with them upon any consideration.

If this be true—and I believe I can demonstrate it even to your satisfaction—the truth is an important one. It concerns every element of the future social life of California; it lies at the basis of your industries; it is bound to subvert that demagogism by which politics, as you call it, have been degraded to a level scarcely higher than incendiarism, pillage and murder. . . .

Clothed in this dignity of discourse, I enter the lists without fear. I am upon your soil; I am surrounded at the best by unsympathetic spectators; my only buckler is the truth; my only weapon your language, the peculiarities of which can never be wholly mastered by a foreigner. Far from complaining of any disadvantage in these respects, I am free to own that no soil is freer, no assemblage more noble, no regulations more just than those which claim the proud title of American.

And now let the heralds be heard and my grievance stated. Hear, oh, ye just and valiant men, ye beauteous and compassionate women, the plaint of Kwang Chang Ling, a *literate* of the first class, a warrior and noble, a leader of the Chinese and a representative by authority. . . .

Letter II.

Palace Hotel, August 2, 1878,

... Under these articles [from the 1868 Burlingame Treaty, establishing friendly relations between the United States and China] a numerous body of your citizens have established themselves in China, possessed themselves of the coasting trade, and many other branches of navigation and traffic, and thus deprived thousands of Chinamen of employment. The complaints of these poor people are not conveyed to you; because our government has too much respect for its treaty obligations to permit you to be annoyed with any expression of regret concerning the working of its compacts with you. On the other hand, while the profits of which the Chinese coast and river junk trade have been deprived, by American steamers, go to swell the dividends of your navigation companies and afford employment to your maritime classes, your shipbuilders, and your machinists, your newspapers are filled and your halls of legislation resound, with outcries against Chinese labor in America.

Thus it appears that the United States maintains precisely the same position in respect to China as the other European nations do. You all desire to possess advantages in China which, at the same time, you would deny to Chinamen in America. You have bombarded our ports and forced us into an unwilling commerce with you, which now you desire shall be entirely one-sided. Your reason for this unfairness is not a sordid one. You are clear-headed enough to perceive that the benefit to commercial intercourse cannot be unilateral. But you fancy that the advantages of social intercourse may be monopolized by one party. You will not permit us to shut ourselves up. You demand every privilege for Americans in China, but you would deny the same privileges to Chinamen in America, because, in your opinion, the presence of the Chinese amongst you is a menace to your civilization. You shrink from contact with us, not because you regard us as mentally or bodily inferior, for neither fact nor argument will support you here—but rather because our religious code appears to be different from yours, and because we are deemed to be more abstemious in food, clothing and shelter.

If our religious forms, our daily bill of fare, and our demands for wages were the same as yours, it would be difficult to see what grievances, either real or fanciful, you would have to complain about. Since you profess in your political constitution, your pulpit declamations, and, more than all, in your manner of living, that you are not bigoted, and care nothing for religious forms, the menace to your civilization appears to resolve itself into a fear of losing your accustomed roast beef, white shirt-collars, and carpeted houses. It is a menace to the sensual indulgences to which you have been accustomed for the last three centuries—that is to say, since the opening of sea trade to the Orient. ...

Let me in this place, however, endeavor to correct one great misapprehension in respect to the Chinaman. You are continually objecting to his morality. Your travelers say he is depraved; your missioners call him ungodly; your commissioners call him uncleanly; and your *sans culottes* call him everything that is vile. Yet your housewives permit him to wait upon them at table; they admit him to their bed-chambers; they confide to him their garments and jewels; and even trust their lives to him, by awarding him supreme control over their kitchens and the preparation of their food. There is a glaring contradiction here.

The plain truth is, that what you have regarded as evidences of immorality and depravity are simply evidences of indigence and misery. China is in a feudal condition. Her nobles are enormously rich and powerful; her peasants are extremely poor and wretched. The unpleasant things which your travelers and missionaries have observed in China, are not common to Chinamen. They have never been observed in connection with rich Chinamen. They are peculiar only to poverty. They belong to the miserable—to the miserable of all countries. . . .

The nobles are the richest in the world; the peasants are the poorest. What little of the latter's habits and surroundings has provided repulsive to Occidental eyes, is the result, not of inferior morality, but of inferior wealth. The European peasant was in the same condition three centuries ago, and in some countries—for example, Russia, Eastern Germany, Roumania, Ireland, and parts of Italy and Portugal—he is very nearly in a similar condition today. Yet you not only tolerate him in America, you share with him your political privileges; you admit him to social communion; he is your brother; while the poor Chinaman you would drive away with blows and contumely. What if it should appear that, after all, there was nothing defensible beneath your hatred of Chinamen but ignorance and religious bigotry? Where would then stand the bases of your vaunted civilization?

Source: Ling, Kwang Chang. "Letters of Kwang Chang Ling. The Chinese Side of the Chinese Question, by a Chinese Literate of the First Class, Communicated to the *San Francisco Argonaut*, on the Dates of August 7th, 10th, 17th, and September 7th, 1878," pp. 2, 7, 8. California Historical Society, 325.251.Sa5a. http://www.oac.cdlib.org/ark:/13030/hb3m3n99bq/?brand=oac4. Accessed June 2010. Courtesy of the California Historical Society.

41. Woman's Union Mission of San Francisco, 1881

Middle-class American evangelicals became increasingly interested and invested in foreign missions in the years following the Civil War. Women in particular became very involved, supporting missionaries abroad, forming domestic mission societies, and, in some cases, going out into the field themselves. San Francisco Chinatown provided a close-to-home missions opportunity, and evangelicals sought to bring both Christianity and Western social mores to Chinese immigrants and their children.

The interdenominational Woman's Union Mission of San Francisco established a school in Chinatown. Their 1880 Annual Report includes a series of anecdotes about the interactions between Chinese individuals and the American teacher, Marian Bokee; a copy of the Mission's constitution; a short history of the Mission; and a list of members and supporters. The following excerpts reveal the contours of Chinatown tourism-voyeurism, complete with the obligatory visits to opium dens and reinforced notions of Western cultural superiority. They also demonstrate the ways in which 19th-century Progressive organizations encouraged assimilation among immigrants.

THE MARRIAGE CERTIFICATE

Chinese women are beginning to understand something of the dignity and rights of wifehood. They prize beyond expression the certificate of marriage, and both husband and wife secure one at the same time. Each keeps the valuable document, so that neither can run away without being overtaken with justice. As an illustration of this Mrs. Bokee says:

"As Jung Gow, our baby, did not come to school for several days I went after him, and while waiting for him, a woman in the building that calls the little fellow her 'heart's child,' motioned me to sit down and talk with her. She was busily engaged finishing off pants for a clothing store. On a low stool at her feet was Jung Gow's baby sister. The woman pointed to the child and said: 'Seen Sang, me love the children. Their mother not muchee sabee. Their father dead long time. You love children, me sabee. You wash Jung Gow's face, you love he. Me love he. Me work alle time, give money to husband. Seen Sang, you shuttee door—no man see, I likee show you;' and darting under the bed she brought forth a box, which she unlocked, and took out a certificate of marriage. Had she been displaying diamond solitaires she could not have manifested deeper pride, as she added: 'Seen Sang, you my dear sister; you kind to Chinese woman. Some time I have trouble, I come to Seen Sang, you help me? You take care me. I be kind to you—me heap smart.' I promised the poor woman that I would do all I could for her, should she ever need me, and she grasped my hand in grateful recognition. . . ."

Christian and Heathen Chinese Homes

I accompanied several ladies through the Chinese quarters recently. I first took them to the heathen homes in the narrow alleys, and showed them the opium-smoking and other vices allied to these homes. We then went to the Christian homes with their little suggestions of refinement and cultivation. The contrast was striking. The visit made a deep impression upon the party, some of whom were not especially interested in the Chinese.

A recent visit from the Census taker revealed the fact that nearly all the Chinese children in San Francisco are American born. We ought to at least teach these children to abandon the cruel and inhuman practice of mutilating the feet of their children, should they ever become parents. In speaking to one of my own Chinese mothers on this subject I asked: 'Why do you make your little ones suffer so?' She replied: 'When I go back to China, my girl have big feet, no rich man marry her—she marry only poor man. I no likee she marry poor man.' I concluded that folly was not confined to the women of any particular nation. . . .

Constitution

PREAMBLE—In view of the deplorable condition of heathen women and children of the Chinese race in San Francisco, a Woman's Society has been organized with the following Constitution, under which women of every Christian denomination may work together effectually by distinct, voluntary effort for the saving of these perishing ones.

ARTICLE 1. This Society shall be called "WOMAN'S UNION MISSION TO CHINESE WOMEN AND CHILDREN."

ART. 2. The object of this Society shall be the evangelization of Chinese women and children. For this purpose a Missionary shall be employed at a certain salary, to visit the houses of the Chinese, to hold a daily school for the instruction of children in the elementary branches of secular knowledge, and in Bible truths. . . .

To our Friends.

Eleven years ago a few ladies of San Francisco, irrespective of religious creed or denomination, formed a society called "THE WOMAN'S UNION MISSION TO CHINESE WOMEN AND CHILDREN." A competent teacher was employed, and a school for Chinese boys and girls has been kept in successful operation till the present time.

In addition to the school for children, the original design, as the name indicates, was to found an asylum for the Chinese women who might be anxious to escape from their life of servitude and shame; but church societies having subsequently taken up that distinctive work, this Woman's Union Mission has confined its efforts to the school, together with such missionary service as their teacher, and others appointed to co-operate with her, may be able to do, in visiting from house to house amongst the Chinese women.

The school is held in the Globe Hotel, on the corner of Jackson and Dupont streets, and is one of the points in "Chinatown" to which strangers are shown, and which they can remember as one of the most interesting features of this cosmopolitan city. Several hundred Chinese children, of both sexes, have been pupils in this school—the average attendance being about twenty-five—and there are always on the list, children of marked ability and great promise.

There are many reasons why this school should be continued and liberally supported:

First—We believe that work among the young, of whatever name or nationality, carries along with it the largest promise and the surest guarantee of success. The saving hope of the world rests in the children.

Second—This school affords the only means for secular and religious instruction which those gathered into it would likely be able to receive.

Third—The children born in this country will become American citizens, and some provision should be afforded for their education; or, should they return to China, what they learn in this school will fit them for becoming teachers of good things amongst their people at home.

Fourth—Chinese are not allowed to attend our public schools, and but for the benevolent efforts of philanthropies and Christians, no provision would be made for their education. . . .

Source: *The Annual Report of the Women's Union Mission of San Francisco to Chinese Women and Children.* San Francisco: George Spaudling & Co., Steam Boat and Job Printers, 1881, pp. 7–8, 11, 28, 29–30. xF870.C5.C51 v.3:13, The Bancroft Library, University of California, Berkeley. http://sunsite.berkeley.edu/cgi-bin/flipomatic/cic/brk5198. Accessed May 2010.

42. Transcript of Chinese Exclusion Act, 1882

Beginning in the 1850s, in the wake of the disruptions following the Opium Wars, Chinese began immigrating to the United States to work in the mines, on the railroads, on the farms, and in the forests of the West Coast. As more and more Chinese came looking for work, anti-Chinese sentiment began to rise, particularly among the white working class, who viewed the Chinese as competition for jobs. However, anti-Chinese sentiment was not merely a by-product of labor competition. Due to pervasive cultural stereotypes, many white Americans saw the Chinese as culturally backwards, dirty, unsanitary, diseased, sexually deviant, and addicted to opium. Chinese migrants faced tremendous discrimination. In 1852, California passed the Foreign Miners Tax, which targeted Chinese miners with a tax of $3 per month. By the 1880s, white hostility toward the Chinese became so great on the West Coast that Congress passed the first of three Chinese Exclusion Laws in 1882. The act banned Chinese laborers for 10 years. The federal government renewed the act for another 10 years in 1892 and then renewed it indefinitely in 1902. This is the only immigration law in American history that specifically targeted a racial or ethnic group.

AN ACT TO EXECUTE CERTAIN TREATY STIPULATIONS RELATING TO CHINESE.

Whereas in the opinion of the Government of the United States the coming of Chinese laborers to this country endangers the good order of certain localities within the territory thereof: Therefore, *Be it enacted by the Senate and House of Representatives of the United States of America in Congress assembled,* That from and after the expiration of ninety days next after the passage of this act, and until the expiration of ten years next after the passage of this act, the coming of Chinese laborers to the United States be, and the same is hereby, suspended; and during such suspension it shall not be lawful for any Chinese laborer to come, or having so come after the expiration of said ninety days to remain within the United States.

SEC. 2. That the master of any vessel who shall knowingly bring within the United States on such vessel, and land or permit to be landed, any Chinese laborer, from any foreign port or place, shall be deemed guilty of a misdemeanor, and on conviction thereof shall be punished by a fine of not more than five hundred dollars for each and every such Chinese laborer so brought, and maybe also imprisoned for a term not exceeding one year.

SEC. 3. That the two foregoing sections shall not apply to Chinese laborers who were in the United States on the seventeenth day of November, eighteen hundred and eighty, or who shall have come into the same before the expiration of ninety days next after the passage of this act, and who shall produce to such master before going on board such vessel, and shall produce to the collector of the port in the United States at which such vessel shall arrive, the evidence hereinafter in this act required of his being one of the laborers in this section mentioned; nor shall the two foregoing sections apply to the case of any master whose vessel, being bound to a port not within the United States, shall come within the jurisdiction of the United States by reason of being in distress or in stress of weather, or touching at any port of the United States on its voyage to any foreign port or place: Provided, That all Chinese laborers brought on such vessel shall depart with the vessel on leaving port.

SEC. 4. That for the purpose of properly identifying Chinese laborers who were in the United States on the seventeenth day of November, eighteen hundred and eighty, or who shall have come into the same before the expiration of ninety days next after the passage of this act, and in order to furnish them with the proper evidence of their right to go from and come to the United States of their free will and accord, as provided by the treaty between the United States and China dated November seventeenth, eighteen hundred and eighty, the collector of customs of the district from which any such Chinese laborer shall depart from the United States shall, in person or by deputy, go on board each vessel having on board any such Chinese laborers and cleared or about to sail from his district for a foreign port, and on such vessel make a list of all such Chinese laborers, which shall be entered in registry-books to be kept for that purpose, in which shall be stated the name, age, occupation, last place of residence, physical marks of peculiarities, and all facts necessary for the identification of each of such Chinese laborers, which books shall be safely kept in the custom-house.; and every such Chinese laborer so departing from the United States shall be entitled to, and shall receive, free of any charge or cost upon application therefore, from the collector or his deputy, at the time such list is taken, a certificate, signed by the collector or his deputy and attested by his seal of office, in such form as the Secretary of the Treasury shall prescribe, which certificate shall contain a statement of the name, age, occupation, last place of residence, persona description, and facts of identification of the Chinese laborer to whom the certificate is issued, corresponding with the said list and registry in all particulars. In case any Chinese laborer after having received such certificate shall leave such vessel before her departure he shall deliver his certificate to the master of the vessel, and if such Chinese laborer shall fail to return to such vessel before her departure from port the certificate shall be delivered by the master to the collector of customs for cancellation. The certificate herein provided for shall entitle the Chinese laborer to whom the same is issued to return to and re-enter the United States upon producing and delivering the same to the collector of customs of the district at which such Chinese laborer shall seek to re-enter; and upon delivery of such certificate by such Chinese laborer to the collector of customs at the time of re-entry in the United States said collector shall cause the same to be filed in the custom-house anti duly canceled.

SEC. 5. That any Chinese laborer mentioned in section four of this act being in the United States, and desiring to depart from the United States by land, shall have the right to demand and receive, free of charge or cost, a certificate of identification similar to that provided for in section four of this act to be issued to such Chinese laborers as may desire to leave the United States by water; and it is hereby made the duty of the collector of customs of the district next adjoining the foreign country to which said Chinese laborer desires to go to issue such certificate, free of charge or cost, upon application by such Chinese laborer, and to enter the same upon registry-books to be kept by him for the purpose, as provided for in section four of this act.

SEC. 6. That in order to the faithful execution of articles one and two of the treaty in this act before mentioned, every Chinese person other than a laborer who may be entitled by said treaty and this act to come within the United States, and who shall be about to come to the United States, shall be identified as so entitled by the Chinese Government in each case, such identity to be evidenced by a certificate issued under the authority of said government, which certificate shall be in the English language or (if not in the English language) accompanied by a translation into English, stating such right to come, and which certificate shall state the name, title or official rank, if any, the age, height, and all physical peculiarities, former and present occupation or profession, and place of residence in China of the person to whom the certificate is issued and that such person is entitled, conformably to the treaty in this act mentioned to come within the United States. Such certificate shall be prima-facie evidence of the fact set forth therein, and shall be produced to the collector of customs, or his deputy, of the port in the district in the United States at which the person named therein shall arrive.

SEC. 7. That any person who shall knowingly and falsely alter or substitute any name for the name written in such certificate or forge any such certificate, or knowingly utter any forged or fraudulent certificate, or falsely personate any person named in any such certificate, shall be deemed guilty of a misdemeanor; and upon conviction thereof shall be fined in a sum not exceeding one thousand dollars, and imprisoned in a penitentiary for a term of not more than five years.

SEC. 8. That the master of any vessel arriving in the United States from any foreign port or place shall, at the same time he delivers a manifest of the cargo, and if there be no cargo, then at the time of making a report of the entry of the vessel pursuant to law, in addition to the other matter required to be reported, and before landing, or permitting to land, any Chinese passengers, deliver and report to the collector of customs of the district in which such vessels shall have arrived a separate list of all Chinese passengers taken on board his vessel at any foreign port or place, and all such passengers on board the vessel at that time. Such list shall show the names of such passengers (and if accredited officers of the Chinese Government traveling on the business of that government, or their servants, with a note of such facts), and the names and other particulars, as shown by their respective certificates; and such list shall be sworn to by the master in the manner required by law in relation to the manifest of the cargo. Any willful refusal or neglect of any such master to comply with the provisions of this section shall incur the same penalties and forfeiture as are provided for a refusal or neglect to report and deliver a manifest of the cargo.

SEC. 9. That before any Chinese passengers are landed from any such line vessel, the collector, or his deputy, shall proceed to examine such passenger, comparing the certificate with the list and with the passengers; and no passenger shall be allowed to land in the United States from such vessel in violation of law.

SEC. 10. That every vessel whose master shall knowingly violate any of the provisions of this act shall be deemed forfeited to the United States, and shall be liable to seizure and condemnation in any district of the United States into which such vessel may enter or in which she may be found.

SEC. 11. That any person who shall knowingly bring into or cause to be brought into the United States by land, or who shall knowingly aid or abet the same, or aid or abet the landing in the United States from any vessel of any Chinese person not lawfully entitled to enter the United States, shall be deemed guilty of a misdemeanor, and shall, on conviction thereof, be fined in a sum not exceeding one thousand dollars, and imprisoned for a term not exceeding one year.

SEC. 12. That no Chinese person shall be permitted to enter the United States by land without producing to the proper officer of customs the certificate in this act required of Chinese persons seeking to land from a vessel. And any Chinese person found unlawfully within the United States shall be caused to be removed therefrom to the country from whence he came, by direction of the President of the United States, and at the cost of the United States, after being brought before some justice, judge, or commissioner of a court of the United States and found to be one not lawfully entitled to be or remain in the United States.

SEC. 13. That this act shall not apply to diplomatic and other officers of the Chinese Government traveling upon the business of that government, whose credentials shall be taken as equivalent to the certificate in this act mentioned, and shall exempt them and their body and house- hold servants from the provisions of this act as to other Chinese persons.

SEC. 14. That hereafter no State court or court of the United States shall admit Chinese to citizenship; and all laws in conflict with this act are hereby repealed.

SEC. 15. That the words "Chinese laborers", wherever used in this act shall be construed to mean both skilled and unskilled laborers and Chinese employed in mining.

Approved, May 6, 1882.

Source: An Act to Execute Certain Treaty Stipulations Relating to the Chinese, May 6, 1882; Enrolled Acts and Resolutions of Congress, 1789–1996; General Records of the United States Government; Record Group 11; National Archives. From ourdocuments.org, a website maintained by the National Archives and Records Administration. http://www.ourdocuments.gov/doc.php?flash=false&doc=47&page=transcript. Accessed February 2010.

43. "California Chinese Mission," 1882–1883

Great Britain compelled China to accept the crippling 1842 Treaty of Nanking after the first Opium War, imposing unequal trade agreements and forcing Chinese ports to open to British ships. Along with the military and economic consequences, the Opium Wars had cultural ramifications as well: China was required to allow Christian missionaries into the country, and over the next century they came in increasing numbers. When the Chinese began immigrating to the United States during the gold rush, many Protestants shifted their evangelistic work to the West Coast, establishing mission churches and parochial schools in Chinatowns and farm labor communities all over California.

The following three excerpts are from the Annual Report of the California Chinese Mission. The first two excerpts, written by Anglo-American members of the Mission, criticize the Chinese Exclusion Act (which reduced the number of potential converts coming to the United States) and demonstrate an investment in Chinese Americans taking leadership positions in the Mission. However, even though the missionaries' perspective is relatively nuanced and sympathetic, they are unable to avoid the yellow peril language that infused 19th-century rhetoric. The third excerpt outlines the regulations of the Chinese Christians associated with the Mission. All three excerpts illustrate the fluid nature of Chinese immigration: people moved back and forth between the United States and China, creating an evolving and transnational culture and religion.

"OUR WORK"

. . . We reported last year twenty-three as baptised; this year we report but sixteen, but we are glad to say that four more have already received baptism at Bethany Church since the fiscal year closed, and that it is probable that a goodly number will be ready to be baptised at the next Communion. We reported last year 156 as having ceased from idol-worship, and 106 as giving evidence of conversion; this year we report 175 and 121. But these numbers represent only such of those as were in attendance of the schools during August, or during the last month of each school—not by any means the total number of those whom we cherish the hope that they are believers. We trust that forty-three have been led to accept Christ as Saviour during the past year, and the total number who have seemed to turn from their darkness to the true Light which lighteth every man, from the commencement of our Mission till now, is about 400.

It is due to the truth to add that this increase in the number of our pupils, and this extension of our work, have not gone steadily forward from the beginning of the year to its close. On the contrary, for the last half of the year we have witnessed a decrease in the attendance which has sometimes been quite discouraging. Of course, under the operation of the Restriction Law the number of Chinese is diminished. Hundreds return to China by every out-going steamer, and very few can come this way. The effect of this is already perceptible in an increased demand for labor, and in a scattering of the Chinese from the centers where are Missions are located out into the country and the smaller villages, where the numbers accessible do not justify—with our present means—any attempt to establish schools. At the same time, at all the points where we have schools there are multitudes not reached as yet; more than 20,000, doubtless, in San Francisco alone. And the demand of the hour upon us is for greater diligence, greater zeal, greater aggressiveness and more prayer, that the white harvest perish not.

Last year we reported twenty-seven teachers, nine of whom were Chinese. This year our nineteen schools have called for the services of forty-two teachers, of whom fourteen were Chinese. Two of the American teachers labored with the helpers only, and were not concerned directly in the schools. At the close of this year, however, for reasons already referred to, our force is reduced to twenty American teachers and ten Chinese. We have said farewell to five of our faithful helpers who have returned to their native land, to labor there for Christ, we trust, in the presence of an even greater need, if not a grander opportunity, than they found on this side of the sea. Their places are partly filled, and we propose to continue to call into this work those whom the Spirit and Providence of God may point out to us, wiling to do the work of training, if the Master will use them, when trained, to testify for him among the swarming myriads in the villages and districts from which they came to this land. For we are fully convinced that China must be redeemed for Christ by its own sons. Men of other lands can aid, can guide; but the work itself must mainly be done by those to the manner born. No one can come into sympathy with a heathen Chinese—can look through his eyes, and speak to his thoughts—as the Christian Chinese, brought out of the same darkness and fear, can do. . . .

"In General"

He [Rev. C. R. Hager, an American missionary in Hong Kong] has one American and one Chinese helper employed. The latter, Lee Sam, went from our work in California. Four others from among our helpers, viz. Lem Chung formerly of Sacramento, Him Wong of Stockton, Low Quong and Hong Sing of the West and the Bethany Schools in San Francisco, are by this time working as self-sustained missionaries under his direction. Besides these, six other Chinese, some of them quite intelligent as Christians, though never employed as helpers here, are on their way to him. A little army of the Lord is thus being recruited and marshaled under his direction in that stronghold of heathenism, and it gives redoubled interest to our work here that we may see it contributing thus directly and efficiently to the Conquest of China for Christ.

"Regulations of the Congregational Association of Christian Chinese Connected with the California Chinese Mission"

Prepared by the Chinese themselves; originally written in the Chinese language, and in that form adopted unanimously; framed, and hung on the wall in the room of the Association, so as to be read and understood by every one proposing to join the Association; translated into English by Fung Affoo.

1st. The organization of this Society is to encourage morals and Christianity among its members. Each member is bound to respect the honor of the Association, and live, as far as possible, so as not to bring reproach upon its good name. The members are pledged to love one another, and to watch over, care for, and help one another.

2nd. Any one who desires to become a member of this Association must forsake idolatry and all bad habits, and prove himself to be a follower of Christ. He must bring references from one or more members. His name must be brought before the Society a week before he can be admitted, and he is received upon a vote of two-thirds of the members. He must himself sign his name, and pay the sum of two dollars as entrance fee, and twenty-five cents every three months, this money being used to defray the expenses of the Association. He is expected to do all he can to bring in new members, and to lead his countrymen to Christ.

3rd. The members are expected to take part in the meetings for worship, giving counsel and encouragement to one another. If any member does wrong, he is to be kindly entreated and led back to the right.

4th. The officers of this Association are President, Vice-President, Secretary, Treasurer and Librarian, to be elected once in three months. The duty of the President is to preside over the meetings of the Association. That of the Vice-President is to assist the President, and act in his absence. The duties of the

Secretary are to keep a written account of the doings of each meeting, and to carry on any necessary correspondence. The Treasurer must keep a strict account of the money matters of the Association. If any officer is obliged to be absent at any meeting, he must see that his place is supplied by a worthy member.

5th. Each week the President must appoint one or two members to prepare a talk for the next meeting. One speaker is allowed ten minutes; two are allowed fifteen minutes between them.

6th. If any member continue in the violation of the regulations of the Association after three successive remonstrances, he must be expelled from the Association. If he afterward repents and desires to come back, he is admitted without an entrance fee, his admittance depending upon the sincerity of his repentance, as judged by the members of the Association.

7th. If any member become engaged in a serious quarrel with an outsider, and injure him, the offender shall be sent to Court by members of the Association.

8th. If any member desire to go back to China, he must give notice to the Association one month beforehand. He must not go until he has paid all his debts here; if he is really obliged to go before he can pay his debts, he must find some one who will be security for him.

Source: Eighth Annual Report of the California Chinese Mission, Presented at the Annual Meeting Held at the First Congregational Church, Santa Cruz, October 11th. San Francisco: Bacon & Company, Book and Job Printers, 1883, pp. 13–14, 18, 27–28. xF870.C5.C51 v.3:14, The Bancroft Library, University of California, Berkeley. http://sunsite.berkeley.edu/cgi-bin/fli pomatic/cic/brk5217. Accessed May 2010.

44. *Tape v. Hurley*, 1885

Mary McGladery Tape was raised in an orphanage in Shanghai and moved to the United States with some missionaries when she was 11 years old. She married Joseph Tape, a Chinese American immigrant, in 1875. The Tapes had four children, all born in the United States. In 1884, the Tapes tried to enroll eight-year-old Mamie in Spring Valley School in San Francisco. The principal, Jennie Hurley, denied her entry, and her parents sued, citing the 1880 revised California Political Code, which stipulated that every school must be open to all children residing in the district. Both the Superior Court and the California Supreme Court ruled in favor of the Tapes; the text of the Supreme Court decision follows.

After the Tapes' victory, however, the San Francisco school board lobbied the California State Legislature for a special provision in the Political Code, establishing separate schools for "Chinese or Mongolian children." Despite her mother's impassioned protests, Mamie Tape, along with her brother Frank, was one of the first children to attend San Francisco's newly opened Chinese Primary School in 1885, only one month after they had won their court case.

MAMIE TAPE, an Infant, by her Guardian ad Litem,
JOSEPH TAPE, Respondent, *v.* JENNIE M.A. HURLEY et al., Appellants

SUPREME COURT OF CALIFORNIA

March 1885

SHARPSTEIN, J.—The main question in this case is whether a child "between six and twenty-one years of age, of Chinese parentage, but who was born and has always lived in the city and county of San Francisco," is entitled to admission in the public school of the district in which she resides.

The language of the code is as follows:

"Every school, unless otherwise provided by law, must be open for the admission of all children between six and twenty-one years of age residing in the district; and the board of trustees, or city board of education, have power to admit adults and children not residing in the district, whenever good reasons exist therefor. Trustees shall have the power to exclude children of filthy or vicious habits, or children suffering from contagious or infectious diseases." (Political Code, § 1667.)

That is the latest legislative expression on the subject, and was passed as late as 1880. Prior to that time the first clause of the section read, "Every school, unless otherwise provided by special statute, must be open for the admission of all *white* children between five and twenty-one years of age, residing in the district."

As amended, the clause is broad enough to include all children who are not precluded from entering a public school by some provision of law; and we are not aware of any law which forbids the entrance of children of any race or nationality. The legislature not only declares who shall be admitted, but also who may be excluded, and it does not authorize the exclusion of any one on the ground upon which alone the exclusion of the respondent here is sought to be justified. The vicious, the filthy, and those having contagious or infectious diseases, may be excluded, without regard to their race, color or nationality.

This law must be construed as any other would be construed. "Where a law is plain and unambiguous, whether it be expressed in general or limited terms, *the legislature should be intended to mean what they have plainly expressed,* and consequently, no room is left for construction." (*Fisher v. Blight*, 2 Cranch, 358, 399.) "When the law is clear and explicit, and its provisions are susceptible of but one interpretation, its consequences, if evil, can only be avoided by a change of the law itself, to be effected by legislative and not judicial action." (*Bosley v. Mattingly*, 14 B. Mon. 73.) This rule is never controverted or doubted, although perhaps sometimes lost sight of. In this case, if effect be given to the intention of the legislature, as indicated by the clear and unambiguous language used by them, respondent here has the same right to enter a public school that any other child has. It is not alleged that she is vicious, or filthy, or that she has a contagious or infectious disease. As the legislature has not denied to the children of any race or nationality the right to enter our public schools, the question whether it might have done so does not arise in this case.

We think the superintendent of schools was improperly joined as a defendant in this action, and that the court properly dismissed the action as to the board of education. In *Ward v. Flood*, 48 Cal. 36, the action was against the teacher alone. That it was properly brought, seems to have been conceded.

The board of education has power "to make, establish, and enforce all necessary and proper rules and regulations *not contrary to law*," and none other. (Stats. 1871–2, p. 846.) Teachers cannot justify a violation of law, on the ground that a resolution of the board of education required them to do so.

The judgment must be modified, so as to make the writ run against the defendant Hurley alone.

In other respects it is affirmed.

THORNTON, J., MYRICK, J., McKEE, J., McKINSTRY, J., ROSS, J., and MORRISON, C.J., concurred

California Supreme Court Case Summary

PUBLIC SCHOOLS—CHINESE CHILDREN ENTITLED TO ADDMISSION [sic].—Children between six and twenty-one years of age, of Chinese parentage, who were born and have always lived in the city and county of San Francisco, are entitled to admission into the public school of the district in which they reside. And teachers are not justified in excluding them, notwithstanding a resolution of the Board of Education purports to command them so to do.

ID.—PROCEEDING TO COMPEL ADMISSION—DEFENDANT.—The teacher of a public school is the only necessary defendant in a proceeding to compel the admission thereto of a child unlawfully excluded.

APPEAL from a judgment of the Superior Court—of the city—and county of San Francisco.

The respondent, through her guardian *ad litem*, applied to the appellant Hurley, the principal of one of the public schools of the city and county of San Francisco, for admission therein. The respondent is a Chinese child, and because of this fact Miss Hurley, acting in obedience to a resolution of the board of education of the city and county of San Francisco, refused to admit her as a pupil into the school. A writ of mandate was then sued out against Miss Hurley, A.J. Moulder, superintendent of public instruction, and the members of the board of education, individually. The Superior Court dismissed the writ as to the members of the board of education, and ordered it to issue against Miss Hurley and A.J. Moulder. From such judgment the appeal was taken. The further facts are sufficiently stated in the opinion of the court.

H.G. Platt, for Appellants.
William F. Gibson, and *Sheldon G. Kellogg*, for Respondent.

Source: Tape v. Hurley, 66 Cal. 473 (1885). http://www.learncalifornia.org/doc.asp?id=1037. Accessed November 2010.

45. *Yick Wo v. Hopkins*, 1886

Initially, Chinese immigrants arriving in California in the 1850s were welcomed, albeit with reservations, by Americans. But within a few years, racial and economic antagonism, both legally sanctioned and physically enforced, had come to define their way of life. Local and state legislatures passed laws and taxes singling out the Chinese: The 1852 Foreign Miners Tax levied a monthly fee on aliens "who did not desire to become a citizen" (applicable only to Asians, who were prohibited from naturalizing);

the California Supreme Court ruled in 1854 that Chinese and Chinese Americans could not testify against white citizens; newspapers up and down the West Coast ran articles denigrating the Chinese; and between 1850 and 1990, over 200 Chinese miners were lynched, and thousands more were driven out of their homes, neighborhoods, and towns.

Chinese Americans did not submit passively to this treatment, instead filing various lawsuits against cities for negligent protection against mobs and for discriminatory treatment. Yick Wo sued the city of San Francisco after he was jailed for refusing to pay a $10.00 fee. In 1880, San Francisco had passed an ordinance requiring a permit for laundries housed in wooden buildings. By this time, nearly two-thirds of the laundries in San Francisco were run by Chinese Americans—and not one of them was granted a permit. In contrast, all but one of the white laundry owners received a permit. Yick Wo, who had owned and operated his laundry for years and who had never incurred any fire safety violations, protested, brought his case all the way up to the U.S. Supreme Court, and won. In 1886, the Supreme Court unanimously ruled that the selective application of an ostensibly race-neutral law violated the Constitution's 14th Amendment.

Yick Wo v. Hopkins was not invoked to halt the Jim Crow laws and in fact effectively was bypassed in the 1896 *Plessy v. Ferguson* decision, which established the legality of the "separate but equal" theory. However, in the civil rights era and beyond, *Yick Wo* served as precedent for upholding minorities' rights to equal protection under the law. In the following excerpts from *Yick Wo v. Hopkins,* Supreme Court Justice Matthews provides the salient details of the case and argues that noncitizens are protected by the 14th Amendment and that the Constitution prohibits the discriminatory application of laws.

APPEAL FROM THE CIRCUIT COURT OF THE UNITED STATES FOR THE DISTRICT OF CALIFORNIA

Syllabus

In a suit brought to this court from a State court which involves the constitutionality of ordinances made by a municipal corporation in the State, this court will, when necessary, put its own independent construction upon the ordinances.

A municipal ordinance to regulate the carrying on of public laundries within the limits of the municipality violates the provisions of the Constitution of the United States if it confers upon the municipal authorities arbitrary power, at their own will, and without regard to discretion in the legal sense of the term, to give or withhold consent as to persons or places, without regard to the competency of the persons applying, or the propriety of the place selected, for the carrying on of the business.

An administration of a municipal ordinance for the carrying on of a lawful business within the corporate limits violates the provisions of the Constitution of the United States if it makes arbitrary and unjust discriminations, founded on differences of race between persons otherwise in similar circumstances.

The guarantees of protection contained in the Fourteenth Amendment to the Constitution extend to all persons within the territorial jurisdiction of the United States, without regard to differences of race, of color, or of nationality.

Those subjects of the Emperor of China who have the right to temporarily or permanently reside within the United States, are entitled to enjoy the protection guaranteed by the Constitution and afforded by the laws.

These two cases were argued as one, and depended upon precisely the same state of facts; the first coming here upon a writ of error to the Supreme Court of the State of California, the second on appeal from the Circuit Court of the United States for that district. The plaintiff in error, Yick Wo, on August 4, 1885, petitioned the Supreme Court of California for a writ of habeas corpus, alleging that he was illegally deprived of his personal liberty by the defendant as sheriff of the city and county of San Francisco.

The sheriff made return to the writ that he held the petitioner in custody by virtue of a sentence of the Police Judges Court, No. 2, of the city and county of San Francisco, whereby he was found guilty of a violation of certain ordinances of the board of supervisors of that county, and adjudged to pay a fine of $10, and, in default of payment, be imprisoned in the county jail at the rate of one day for each dollar of fine until said fine should be satisfied, and a commitment in consequence of nonpayment of said fine.

The ordinances for the violation of which he had been found guilty were set out as follows:

Order No. 156, passed May 26, 1880, prescribing the kind of buildings in which laundries may be located. "The people of the city and county of San Francisco do ordain as follows:"

"SEC. 1. It shall be unlawful, from and after the passage of this order, for any person or persons to establish, maintain, or carry on a laundry within the corporate limits of the city and county of San Francisco without having first obtained the consent of the board of supervisors, except the same be located in a building constructed either of brick or stone."

"SEC. 2. It shall be unlawful for any person to erect, build, or maintain, or cause to be erected, built, or maintained, over or upon the roof of any building now erected or which may hereafter be erected within the limits of said city and county, any scaffolding without first obtaining the written permission of the board of supervisors, which permit shall state fully for what purpose said scaffolding is to be erected and used, and such scaffolding shall not be used for any other purpose than that designated in such permit."

"SEC. 3. Any person who shall violate any of the provisions of this order shall be deemed guilty of a misdemeanor, and upon conviction thereof shall be punished by a fine of not more than one thousand dollars, or by imprisonment in the county jail not more than six months, or by both such fine and imprisonment."

Order No. 1587, passed July 28, 1880, the following section:

"SEC. 68. It shall be unlawful, from and after the passage of this order, for any person or persons to establish, maintain, or carry on a laundry within the corporate limits of the city and county of San Francisco without having first obtained the consent of the board of supervisors, except the same be located in a building constructed either of brick or stone."

The following facts were also admitted on the record: that petitioner is a native of China and came to California in 1861, and is still a subject of the Emperor of China; that he has been engaged in the laundry business in the same premises and building for twenty-two years last past; that he had a license from the board of fire wardens, dated March 3, 1884, from which it appeared "that the above described premises have been inspected by the board of fire wardens, and upon such inspection said board found all proper arrangements for carrying on the business; that the stoves, washing and drying apparatus, and the appliances for heating smoothing irons are in good condition, and that their use is not dangerous to the surrounding property from fire, and that all proper precautions have been taken to comply with the provisions of order No. 1617, defining 'the fire limits of the city and county of San Francisco and making regulations concerning the erection and use of buildings in said city and county,' and of order No. 1670, 'prohibiting the kindling, maintenance, and use of open fires in houses;' that he had a certificate from the health officer that the same premises had been inspected by him, and that he found that they were properly and sufficiently drained, and that all proper arrangements for carrying on the business of a laundry, without injury to the sanitary condition of the neighborhood, had been complied with; that the city license of the petitioner was in force and expired October 1st, 1885, and that the petitioner applied to the board of supervisors, June 1st, 1885, for consent of said board to maintain and carry on his laundry, but that said board, on July 1st, 1885, refused said consent."

It is also admitted to be true, as alleged in the petition, that, on February 24, 1880,

"there were about 320 laundries in the city and county of San Francisco, of which about 240 were owned and conducted by subjects of China, and of the whole number, *viz*, 320, about 310 were constructed of wood, the same material that constitutes nine-tenths of the houses in the city of San Francisco. The capital thus invested by the subjects of China was not less than two hundred thousand dollars, and they paid annually for rent, license, taxes, gas, and water about one hundred and eighty thousand dollars."

It was alleged in the petition, that "your petitioner and more than one hundred and fifty of his countrymen have been arrested upon the charge of carrying on business without having such special consent, while those who are not subjects of China, and who are conducting eighty odd laundries under similar conditions, are left unmolested and free to enjoy the enhanced trade and profits arising from this hurtful and unfair discrimination. The business of your petitioner, and of those of his countrymen similarly situated, is greatly impaired, and in many cases practically ruined, by this system of oppression to one kind of men and favoritism to all others."

The statement therein contained as to the arrest, &c., was admitted to be true, with the qualification only that the eighty odd laundries referred to are in wooden buildings without scaffolds on the roofs.

It was also admitted "that petitioner and 200 of his countrymen similarly situated petitioned the board of supervisors for permission to continue their business in the various houses which they had been occupying and using for laundries for more than twenty years, and such petitions were denied, and all the petitions of those who were not Chinese, with one exception of Mrs. Mary Meagles, were granted...."

Mr. JUSTICE MATTHEWS delivered the opinion of the court.

... The rights of the petitioners, as affected by the proceedings of which they complain, are not less because they are aliens and subjects of the Emperor of China. By the third article of the treaty between this Government and that of China, concluded November 17, 1880, 22 Stat. 827, it is stipulated: "If Chinese laborers, or Chinese of any other class, now either permanently or temporarily residing in the territory of the United States, meet with ill treatment at the hands of any other persons, the Government of the United States will exert all its powers to devise measures for their protection, and to secure to them the same rights, privileges, immunities and exemptions as may be enjoyed by the citizens or subjects of the most favored nation, and to which they are entitled by treaty."

The Fourteenth Amendment to the Constitution is not confined to the protection of citizens. It says: "Nor shall any State deprive any person of life, liberty, or property without due process of law; nor deny to any person within its jurisdiction the equal protection of the laws."

These provisions are universal in their application to all persons within the territorial jurisdiction, without regard to any differences of race, of color, or of nationality, and the equal protection of the laws is a pledge of the protection of equal laws. It is accordingly enacted by § 1977 of the Revised Statutes, that "all persons within the jurisdiction of the United States shall have the same right in every State and Territory to make and enforce contracts, to sue, be parties, give evidence, and to the full and equal benefit of all laws and proceedings for the security of persons and property as is enjoyed by white citizens and shall be subject to like punishment, pains, penalties, taxes, licenses, and exactions of every kind, and to no other."

The questions we have to consider and decide in these cases, therefore, are to be treated as invoking the rights of every citizen of the United States equally with those of the strangers and aliens who now invoke the jurisdiction of the court....

This conclusion, and the reasoning on which it is based, are deductions from the face of the ordinance, as to its necessary tendency and ultimate actual operation. In the present cases, we are not obliged to reason from the probable to the actual, and pass upon the validity of the ordinances complained of, as tried merely by the opportunities which their terms afford, of unequal and unjust discrimination in their administration. For the cases present the ordinances in actual operation, and the facts shown establish an administration directed so exclusively against a particular class of persons as to warrant and require the conclusion that, whatever may have been the intent of the ordinances as adopted, they are applied by the public authorities charged with their administration, and thus representing the State itself, with a mind so unequal and oppressive as to amount to a practical denial by the State of that equal protection of the laws which is secured to the petitioners, as to all other persons, by the broad and benign provisions of the Fourteenth Amendment to the Constitution of the United States. **Though the law itself be fair on its face and impartial in appearance, yet, if it is applied and administered by public authority with an evil eye and an unequal hand, so as practically to make unjust and illegal discriminations between persons in similar circumstances, material to their rights, the denial of equal justice is still within the prohibition of the Constitution....**

The present cases, as shown by the facts disclosed in the record, are within this class. It appears that both petitioners have complied with every requisite deemed by the law or by the public officers charged with its administration necessary for the protection of neighboring property from fire or as a precaution against injury to the public health. No reason whatever, except the will of the supervisors, is assigned why they should not be permitted to carry on, in the accustomed manner, their harmless and useful occupation, on which they depend for a livelihood. And while this consent of the supervisors is withheld from them and from two hundred others who have also petitioned, all of whom happen to be Chinese subjects, eighty others, not Chinese subjects, are permitted to carry on the same business under similar conditions. The fact of this discrimination is admitted. No reason for it is shown, and the conclusion cannot be resisted that no reason for it exists except hostility to the race and nationality to which the petitioners belong, and which, in the eye of the law, is not justified. The discrimination is, therefore, illegal, and the public administration which enforces it is a denial of the equal protection of the laws and a violation of the Fourteenth Amendment of the Constitution. The imprisonment of the petitioners is, therefore, illegal, and they must be discharged. To this end,

The judgment of the Supreme Court of California in the case of Yick Wo, and that of the Circuit Court of the United States for the District of California in the case of Wo Lee, are severally reversed, and the cases remanded, each to the proper court, with directions to discharge the petitioners from custody and imprisonment.

Source: Yick Wo v. Hopkins, 118 U.S. 356 (1886). 6 S. Ct. 1064, 30 L.Ed. 220. http://supreme.justia.com/us/118/356/case.html. Accessed November 2010.

46. "An Address from the Workingmen of San Francisco to Their Brothers throughout the Pacific Coast," 1888

The 1868 Burlingame Treaty established friendly relations between the United States and China and called for immigrants in each country to be treated fairly and equally. In 1880, the treaty was amended, and Chinese immigration to the United States was temporarily suspended; two years later, the Chinese Exclusion Act prohibited all skilled and unskilled Chinese laborers and miners from immigrating to America. The Chinese Exclusion Act was renewed many times over the following decades, in large part due to pressure from labor organizations.

The "Address from the Workingmen of San Francisco" was published by the California Workingman's Party in 1888. This labor organization, founded in the 1870s, consistently employed racist rhetoric against Chinese immigrant laborers, whom they viewed as their primary competition, especially for jobs on the railroad. The "Address" is a long political advertisement extolling the glorious history of the exclusion movement and calling for Californians to vote against Benjamin Harrison in the upcoming presidential election. The "Address" seeks to frame exclusion in terms of class: According to the pamphlet, men from the working class had seen their wages cut and jobs lost because of the influx of cheap Chinese labor. However, classic yellow peril rhetoric permeates the text, inciting racial fears and propagating stereotypes about Chinese culture and Chinese Americans.

FELLOW-CITIZENS OF THE PRODUCING AND WORKING CLASSES OF THE STATE OF CALIFORNIA:

We have met here in San Francisco to-night to raise our voice to you in warning of a great danger that seems to us imminent, and threatens our almost utter destruction as a prosperous community; and we beg each and every citizen of the State, without distinction of political party, depending on their own labor for the support of themselves and families, to hear us and to take time to examine with the utmost care the reasons and the facts we will give for believing a great danger to be now confronting us.

No consideration of a partisan character should weigh with us for a moment when our *all* is at stake. That *all* means the opportunity to work at some honest avocation which will insure us a respectable living and the support of our families in the reasonable comforts of life. The danger is, that while we have been sleeping in fancied security, believing that the tide of Mongolian immigration to our State has been checked and was in fair way to be entirely stopped, our opponents, the pro-China wealthy men of the land, have been wide-awake and have succeeded in reviving the importation of this servile slave-labor to almost its former proportions. So that, now, hundreds and thousands of Mongolians are every week flocking into our State. Let us go back, say, ten years in the history of our struggle against this heathen invasion which so plainly threatened the destruction of the white population of this coast.

The first outcry against them came from the mining districts of the State. The people of the large cities and agricultural districts were at first slow to follow in the demand made by the miners that the Mongolians must be driven back to their own country. Soon, however, as they spread over the entire State, the blight they brought wherever they located was recognized by all, even by those who gave them employment. The white laborers all over the State were not wanted except at starving rates of wages. The large cities soon became crowded with white men seeking employment.

Store-keepers in the country towns found that they sold no goods, for the white men had gone and the Chinese lived on rice, and made or imported their own clothes. All sorts of employment soon became monopolized by the Mongolian cheap workers; they began to farm extensively in the raising of all kinds of vegetables, always underselling the white farmer. A general stagnation of all sorts of business was manifestly the situation all over the State, our boys and our girls had no employment, and were becoming a scandal instead of a blessing to their parents; the values of real estate began to shrink. All this was so, and yet no one seemed to understand the cause. Then suddenly there came that never-to-be-forgotten cry from the San Francisco sand-lots, "The Chinese must go!" . . .

Now, what is our position to-day on this whole question? Are we through with the fight? No sensible or sane man will say we are. To-day we have two hundred thousand Chinese in the State, which is more than we had the day the miners first demanded their expulsion. Of these over forty thousand of both sexes live in San Francisco. We have a worse Chinatown now than we had then, with all the same filth, nastiness and other unspeakable horrors, dragging down to leprosy, shame and death, thousands of our white youths, who have been made idle vagabonds by the presence of the Chinese and the impossibility of finding work to make an honest living. All this is much worse than it was eight years ago. To-day every avenue to labor, of every sort, is crowded with Chinese slave labor worse than it was eight years ago. The boot, shoe and cigar industries are almost entirely in their hands. In the manufacture of men's overalls and women's and children's underwear they run over three thousand sewing machines night and day. They monopolize nearly all the farming done to supply the market with all sorts of vegetables. This state of things brings about a terrible competition between our own people, who must live, if they live at all, in accord with American civilization, and the labor of a people, who live like what in fact they are, degraded serfs under masters who hold them in slavery. We should all understand that this state of things cannot be much longer endured. . . .

We will conclude, fellow-citizens, by urging and imploring of you to calmly consider what we have said in this address. Merchants, mechanics, professional men, farmers, real-estate owners, dealers in real estate, bankers, dealers in money, as well as wage-workers, are all deeply interested. We ask you all to look back to the years 1878 and 1879, and ask yourselves if you want a possible return to that dark and gloomy time. We ask you to remember that the first dawn of returning prosperity appeared just as soon as all political parties became united in vigorous action against the influx of Chinese slave labor, and that that dawn broadened into sunshine brighter and brighter as our efforts at Washington seemed to grow hopeful and more hopefully that every succeeding session of Congress would result in the ultimate fruition of our struggle to drive the Chinese plague forever from our State.

Then came the vast immigration to California from the Eastern States, and with it prosperity beyond our most sanguine hopes, making us almost dizzy with the view it disclosed to our excited imagination of the future glory and grandeur of our State.

But now, fellow-citizens, observe that a check in our onward career of prosperity has undoubtedly appeared at this time—not much, so far—but enough to warn us of what it may come to, if we do not arouse ourselves from apathy and look the fact square in the face; that the Mongolian invasion has again commenced, and that if the people of California go back on their record on that all-important question on the 6th of November next, by casting the electoral vote of the State for a man with Harrison's record, the return of the dark days of the past seems inevitable. This must be the conclusion that every thinking man will come to on a calm reflection over the past history of our State.

We have shown you, fellow-citizens, beyond a question of doubt, that this cry about "free trade" is not sincere, but a lying fraud put forth by an unscrupulous partisan press in an effort to deceive the masses of the people. We ask you now, will the vile trick succeed?

Fellow-citizens: This question you will answer on the 6th day of next November. On that momentous day answer it as your patriotism and love of country will dictate to you. Answer it with your eyes on the fireside homes of your wives and your children, threatened with destruction by the Mongolian hordes. Your country is our country. Your prosperity is our prosperity. Your destruction will be our destruction; and in all we have said, you must believe us as only seeking for our united and common welfare.

Source: "An Address from the Workingmen of San Francisco to Their Brothers throughout the Pacific Coast," 1888, pp. 2–3, 4, 24. California Historical Society, 325.251.Sa5a. http://content.cdlib.org/ark:/13030/hb7199n8g9/?&brand=oac. Accessed May 2010. Courtesy of the California Historical Society.

47. Tuck Wo & Company Bankruptcy Case, 1909

In July 1909, Leong Kung (court records also name him as Leong Kim and Leong Kum) died in Oakland, California. Shortly thereafter, Tuck Wo & Company, the San Francisco business he managed and was a copartner in, went into receivership. It was determined that Leong Kum was the sole partner who resided in the United States. His copartners could not be located and allegedly resided in China. Judging from the surnames of the copartners, they were most likely blood relatives involved in the business. Chinese immigrants often held family businesses that were run by and for family members. The city and county of San Francisco declared the company bankrupt and took possession of property belonging to Tuck Wo & Company and sold it for $1,495. What ensued was a struggle between three of Tuck Wo's creditors to recover debts owed to them. The three creditors were (1) the South San Francisco Packing and Provision Company; (2) the American National Bank of San Francisco, the Anglo & London Paris National Bank, and F.B O'Reilly; and (3) Miller & Lux Incorporated. It appears the dispute formed out of the South San Francisco Packing and Provision Company's refusal to share the proceeds of the Tuck Wo property sale equally with Miller & Lux. The South San Francisco Packing and Provision Company, American National Bank of San Francisco, Anglo & London Paris National Bank, and F.B. O'Reilly filed for a petition of dismissal, probably after having divvied up the proceeds from the property sale. However, Miller & Lux objected to the dismissal, hoping to share equally in the sale.

This case was never resolved in the court system. On October 18, 1918, the case was closed without a final decision. No referee or trustee was ever named. The following excerpt is the affidavit given by Charles Gee, an employee of the American National Bank of San Francisco, on September 4, 1909, which helps to highlight the complexity of Chinese American communities. Early Chinese Americans were oftentimes participants in complex transnational economic ventures that drew family members and Anglo businessmen together in the name of profit. Charles Gee's testimony also reminds readers that Chinese Americans were not a monolithic community, but individuals pursuing their individual interests. Sometimes this meant siding with community members and other times not.

IN THE UNITED STATES DISTRICT COURT
NORTHERN DISTRICT OF CALIFORNIA

IN THE MATTER OF
Tuck Wo & Company, a co-partnership, IN BANKRUPTCY

State of California

City and County of San Francisco, ss

 Charles Gee, being first duly sworn, deposes and says:—That he is a resident of the City and County of San Francisco, State of California, and has been for a long time prior to the making of this affidavit; that he is not a party to nor interested in the above entitled matter, and is competent in all respects to become a witness therein; that he is regularly employed by The American National Bank of San Francisco, a banking corporation doing business within the City and County of San Francisco; that your affiant has made investigation among the Chinese and friends of the aforesaid Tuck Wo & Company, in the City and County of San Francisco, and as far as your affiant has been able to ascertain, and according to the best information and belief of your affiant, Leong Chuck, Leong Man Foo, Tom Yee Man, Low Sow and Leong Kung are the members of the said co-partnership of Tuck Wo & Company; that Leong Kung, otherwise known as Leong Kim, was a resident of the City and County of San Francisco, and was the acting manager of said co-partnership prior to the time of his death, July 30, 1909, in the City of Oakland, County of Alameda, State of California, and that the other members of said co-partnership, as far as your affiant has been able to learn, are Leong Chuck, Leong Man Foo, Tom Yee Man and Low Sow, and that the said Leong Chuck, Leong Man Foo, Tom Yee Man and Low Sow, each and all of them are residents of the Empire of China, and not within the State of California, and your affiant is informed and believes that the said Leong Chuck, Leong Man Foo, Tom Yee Man and Low Sow will not come to the State of California.

 That since the filing of the above petition, a large amount of goods has been shipped from China to the State of California, and that the same is now in the bonded warehouse of the United States Government, and that the same consists of fruits, preserved fruits and vegetables and like goods, all of which will perish or deteriorate in value within a very short time, unless the same are consumed, and for that reason your affiant alleges that it is necessary that the same be sold at as early a date as possible, in order that the same may not be totally lost or destroyed by deterioration; that at the present time no one is in charge of the said business of Tuck Wo & Company, as the book-keeper of said Tuck Wo & Company, Leong Kow, has left the City and County of San Francisco, and that a large amount of property will or is liable to be lost or destroyed because of no one else being in charge of the same.

Charles S. Gee (Signature)

Subscribed and sworn to before me this 3rd day of September 1909.

Charles Edelman (Signature)

NOTARY PUBLIC

In and for the City and County of San Francisco, State of California

Source: No. 6283, Tuck Wo Company; Bankruptcy Act of 1898 Case Files, 1898–1945; U.S. District Court for the Northern District of California, San Francisco; Records of District Courts of the United States, Record Group 21; The National Archives at San Francisco.

48. Angel Island Poem, by One from Ziangshan, Undated, between 1910–1940

In 1882, under pressure from xenophobic labor organizations, including the Knights of Labor, and racist political groups, such as the Supreme Order of Caucasians, the United States passed the Chinese Exclusion Act. Along with prohibiting Chinese laborers from entering the United States, the Exclusion Act, and its subsequent renewals, also made it difficult for Chinese immigrants residing in the United States to leave and reenter the country. However, the 1906 San Francisco fire destroyed the City Hall and all the government documents it housed—including birth certificates. Chinese immigrants seized the opportunity to claim that they were born in the United States and thus were American citizens. Prospective immigrants claimed fictitious family ties to resident Chinese American citizens, thus bypassing the strictures of the Exclusion Act.

The Immigration Station on Angel Island in the San Francisco Bay processed hundreds of thousands of immigrants from its opening in 1910 until it burned down in 1940. Upon disembarking at Angel Island, men and women were separated, subjected to medical examinations, and detained in barrack housing. Chinese immigrants often waited for months before appearing before the Bureau of Immigration's Board of Special Inquiry for interrogations. Some of the detainees carved poems into the wooden walls of the Immigration Station, mimicking classical Chinese poetry forms in their colloquial Cantonese. They wrote of their experiences and emotions on Angel Island, often bitterly castigating America for not extending to the Chinese its promise of freedom and opportunity. The following poem was written by an anonymous man from Ziangshan (Zhongshan), a city in Guangdong Province in southern China where most early 20th-century Chinese immigrants originated.

There are tens of thousands of poems composed on these walls.
They are all cries of complaint and sadness.
The day I am rid of this prison and attain success,
I must remember that this chapter once existed.
In my daily needs, I must be frugal.
Needless extravagance leads youth to ruin.
All my compatriots should please be mindful.
Once you have some small gains, return home early.

By One From Ziangshan

Source: Lai, Him Mark, Genny Lim, and Judy Yung. *Island: Poetry and History of Chinese Immigrants on Angel Island, 1910–1940.* Seattle: University of Washington Press, 1991, p. 66. Reprinted with permission from the University of Washington Press.

49. The Case of Huey Jing and Huey Fong, 1913

By the mid 1870s, there was a prevailing anti-Chinese sentiment among Euro-Americans on the West Coast, which resulted, in 1882, in the passage of the first of three federal anti-Chinese immigration laws. These Chinese Exclusion Acts prohibited nearly all Chinese from entering the United States, with the exception of some merchants, students, and diplomats.

Many Chinese found inventive ways to circumvent the Exclusion Acts by posing as "paper sons." Documented Chinese residents in the United States would journey back to China to visit their wives and family. The spotty birth and immigration records in both China and the United States also allowed some Chinese to falsely claim citizenship or legal residence in the United States. When these men returned to America, they would claim to have fathered as many children as was plausible given the duration of their time away. For example, someone who was in China for two years could claim he had two children, regardless of how many children he had in reality. Every claimed child that did not actually exist represented one immigration slot that could be used by a relative, friend of the family, neighbor, or even a stranger. These people became known as paper sons.

Immigration officials were well aware that the Chinese were falsely claiming familial relationships. To counter what they saw as outright fraud, immigration officials carefully scrutinized Chinese trying to immigrate into the United States. They conducted incredibly meticulous and detailed interviews with incoming Chinese immigrants and their alleged fathers once they landed in America. The following interview excerpts details from the case of Huey Jing and Huey Fong. Their case illustrates the plight that many Chinese immigrants faced and highlights why early Chinese American communities were so unstable.

On February 4, 1913, the Hueys arrived in San Francisco aboard the S.S. *Mongolia*. The two men claimed they were the sons of Huey Wah, a native citizen of the United States. Having come to the United States during the period of Chinese exclusion, the two brothers and their alleged father were interviewed to determine the validity of their relationship. Huey Wah's citizenship had already been established through an interview conducted with immigration officials when he entered the United States from China in 1898.

Although Huey Wah's U.S. citizenship was confirmed, Inspector J. B. Warner recommended both brothers be denied entry, basing his decision on what he saw as a number of serious discrepancies in their testimonies. The commissioner at Angel Island agreed, and denied Huey Jing and Huey Fong entry on March 3, 1913. Interestingly, Huey Wah requested that no adverse action be taken until he could be re-interviewed about the discrepancies between his interview, that of his alleged sons, and the statements of a witness, Gee Soon. He claimed he had been agitated by a collision of two steamers while on his way to Angel Island for his initial interview. One day later, Huey Fong filed an appeal to contest his denial through his attorneys Stidger and Kennah. However, Huey Fong's attorneys withdrew their client's appeal one day later, and requested that the two men be placed on a steamer to China the next day. Below are excerpts from the case file including the original statements (interviews) of Huey Wah, Huey Fong, Gee Soon (witness), and Huey Jing. There is also a report by Inspector J. B. Warner, the immigration commissioner's finding and decree, a statement by Huey Wah asking that adverse action not be taken, the official appeal form, and the letter withdrawing the appeal.

STATEMENT OF ALLEGED FATHER—HUEY WAH

UNITED STATES IMMIGRATION SERVICE
CHINESE DIVISION

Angel Island Station, San Francisco, California
February 14, 1913

#12505/2-11, Huey Jing, and Inspector J.B. Warner
#12505/4-2, Huey Fong, Sons of Native, ex ss "Mongolia" Stenographer S.W. Buchanan
2/14/13
Interpreter Ed. L. Park

Statement of alleged father _____ Sworn.
Witness speaks See Yip dialect; Interpreter Park originally
Speaks Sam Yup dialect and is qualified in See Yip dialect

Q What are your names?
A Huey Wah and Huey Sing. No other name.
Q How old are you?
A 38.
Q Where were you born?
A San Francisco—I forgot to bring my papers.
Q What papers have you?
A A Certificate of identity.
Q How many trips have you made to China?
A Three trips.
Q Tell us about those trips?
A First trip departed KS 6 returning KS 24 arriving 5th month ss "Doric"; landed as a native (May 17, 1898) under the name of Huey Wah.
   Second trip departed December 28, 1904 ss "Mongolia" returned on ss "Mongolia" November 22, 1908.
   Third trip departed ST 2 (January 9, 1911 returning as No. 329 ss "Korea" September 30, 1912)
Q In what village did you live while in China?
A Huey Oak village, S.N. District.

Q	How large is that village?
A	20 houses.
Q	Where is your house located?
A	2nd house 5th row counting from the east.
Q	Who lives in the 5th row 1st house?
A	Huey You Jung; married; natural feet; house is vacant.
Q	Who lives in the first house 6th row?
A	School house.
Q	Who is the teacher?
A	Chan Bow San.
Q	Does he live in your village?
A	No.
Q	6th row second house?
A	Huey Jung Chung; married; natural feet; one boy, I don't know his name, he is in a foreign country.
Q	Who lives in the second house 4th row?
A	Huey Sick Poy; married; natural feet; one girl, no boys. The girl is very small I do not know her name.
Q	4th row 1st house?
A	Huey Mon Nam; married; natural feet; no children.
Q	Who lives in the 3rd row second house?
A	Huey Jow; married; natural feet; one boy, Ah Heung, 18 or 19.
Q	How is your village supplied with water?
A	Well in front of the first row counting from the east.
Q	Any wall around your village?
A	No.
Q	Where is the entrance hate [sic]?
A	No gate.
Q	What is the nearest market?
A	Look Bo about one li[2] south.
Q	Name some of the nearby villages?
A	Nam Yung village to the rear of the village about one po.
Q	Any others?
A	Jock Mee also known as Lew Village about a li.
Q	Any ancestral halls?
A	No.
Q	Where is the nearest ancestral hall?
A	To the East there an ancestral hall but it does not belong to my village.
Q	What is the name of it?
A	Lew family ancestral hall.
Q	Where do your people worship?
A	Gee Lip Sing temple back of the village about 3 lis away.
Q	Did any one in your village own a water buffalo?
A	No one in my village owns one.
Q	What is your occupation in the United States?
A	Farming in East Sacramento near the levee.

Q   What is your father's name?
A   Huey Lai Kew alias Huey Yee Wah.
Q* Is he living or dead?
A   I do not remember when he died, 5 or 6 years ago.
Q   Where did he die?
A   In my house in China.
Q* What was your mother's name?
A   Lee Shee; natural feet; died more than 10 years ago.
Q   Have you any brothers or sisters?
A   No.
Q   Are you married?
A   Yes.
Q   When and where were you married?
A   KS 20-7-7, in China.
Q* Have you had more than one wife?
A   Only one.
Q   Is she still living in China?
A   Yes.
Q   What is her name, age, and what kind of feet has she?
A   Lew Shee; natural feet; 36 years old.
Q   Native of what village?
A   Hong How village, S.N. Dist, 3 or 4 lis away.
Q   What is your wife's father's name?
A   Lew Hay You; she [sic] is dead; died when I was in the United States, I don't know when.
Q   What is your wife's mother's name?
A   I don't know her name she is dead.
Q   Has your wife any brothers or sisters?
A   One younger, Lew Gip; never saw him.
Q   Do you know whether he is married or not?
A   I don't know.
Q   How many children have you?
A   5 boys and one girl.
Q   Names, ages and dates of birth?
A   Huey Fong; 19; born KS 21-11-17, applicant.
    Huey Jing; 17; born KS 23-1-15, applicant.
    Huey Heung; 16; born KS 24-5-22; attending school home village.
    Huey Sin; 9; born KS 31-12, I do not remember the day.
Q   You remembered a little over 4 months ago?
A   I was asked in a hurry and I gave some kind of date.
Q   Next boy?
A   Huey Toy; 6 years old; born KS 34-7, I do not remember the day.
Q   Girl's name?
A   Huey Ngook; 8 years old; born KS 33-1; I don't know the day.
Q   What have these applicants been doing in China?
A   Attending school in the home village.

Q Always in the home village?
A Yes.
Q When you were in China on this last trip they were attending school?
A Yes.
Q Where did they sleep?
A Always slept at home.
Q How old were these applicants when they started school?
A All started at age of 8 and continued until departure.
Q They were both attending school when you left China last year?
A Yes.
Q What place did you visit while you were in China?
A Canton and Hong Kong.
Q Any of the large market places?
A Yes, Look Bo market; that is the only market.
Q Did you take both of these applicants on any of these trips?
A No.
Q Did you ever take them to the market?
A No.
Q Where did you they have their photographs taken?
A Hong Kong.
Q Did they have them taken before you came to the United States?
A Yes.
Q Who went to Hong Kong with them?
A I took them to Hong Kong.
Q I thought you just stated you never took them to Hong Kong?
A I thought you were talking about the market places.
Q What year and month and day were you born?
A KS 2-1-15
Q Then you took both of these applicant's to Hong Kong?
A Yes.
Q Did any of your other children go with you?
A No.

   Note: Alleged father is asked to identify photographs: He identifies the photograph of Huey Fong as Huey Jing and Huey Jing as Huey Fong and Dong Leung Gow[3] as Huey Fong. He then identifies the applicants correctly and then the witness as Huey Fong.

Q Are there any marks or scars by which you might identify these applicants?
A I didn't pay much attention to any scars or marks.
Q They are your boys are they not?
A Yes.
Q And you have lived with them in your house from KS 30 to KS 34?
A Yes.
Q You lived in the same house with them for 4 years and then again for another year?
A I am not home much of the time.

Q   Where were you?
A   I go back to my store—I am not home all the time.
Q   You were not away all the time either?
A   I am away most of the time.
Q   Still they are your boys?
A   Yes.
Q   They were born before you left China KS 24?
A   Yes.
Q   They were living with you in China from KS 30 until KS 34?
A   Yes.
Q   And you were home most of the time for a year?
A   Yes.
Q   All the children lived at home?
A   Not home all the time sometimes they slept at the school.
Q   You just said they slept at home?
A   Maybe they sleep at home.
Q   Don't you know whether they slept at home or in the school house?
A   Maybe when I am not home the[y] sleep in the school house—I think they slept in the school house.
Q   You say you were not home much of the time—where were you?
A   I have my business in Gong Moon city, Sun Wooey District.
Q   What business have you in Gong Moon city? And in Sun Wooey District and your home is in Sun Ning District?
A   I could have business anywhere.
Q   What is that business?
A   Curios and fire works.
Q   What is the name of that firm?
A   Yee Bow Him Company.
Q   How long have you been interested in that firm?
A   About 7 or 8 years.
Q   How far is Gong Moon city from your village?
A   4 or 5 pos.
Q   How often did you visit home?
A   Sometimes once a month and sometimes twice a month; sometimes once in two months.
Q   How long would you remain at home?
A   Six or seven days, sometimes 8 or 10 days.
Q   Did either of these applicants ever visit your place of business in Gong Moon city?
A   No.
Q   Is your eye sight good?
A   Yes.
Q   You don't wear glasses?
A   No.
Q   Then you can say your vision or eye sight is perfect when you were examining these photographs?
A   I do not think I can see very good with my eyes today.

Q   What is the matter with your eyes? Were you up late last night?
A   No.
Q   You have not been drinking have you?
A   No.
Q   And you are perfectly sober this morning?
A   Yes, I am perfectly sober.
Q   Is there anyone now in the United States who has seen your boys in China?
A   Goo Soon[4]. He went to China in ST 2-6th or 7th month and I sent him $10 and a letter to my family.
Q   Is there anybody else that has seen your boys in China?
A   There was another man Dong Leong Gow.
Q   When where and under what circumstances did he see your boys?
A   He just visited my village when he was in China.
Q   Did Dong Leong Gow visit your home when you were in China?
A   No.
Q   Why did you have Dong Leong Gow sign an affidavit if you did not intend to have him for a witness?
A   I wanted him to come and testify but he disappeared and I can not find him.
Q   Why did you want him to come and testify?
A   He had been to my village.
Q   Was Dong Leong Gow home on a visit to China?
A   Yes.
Q   Do you know Dong Leong Gow personally?
A   Yes.
Q   You are well acquainted with him are you?
A   Yes.
Q   Still you can not identify his picture?
A   I haven't seen him for a long time—I could not recognize him.
Q   Have you anything further to state?
A   No.

(Interpreter Louis Fon called and he asked the witness whether he understood the interpreter in the case and he answered in the affirmative)

Signed Chinese Characters,
2/19/13—SWB

STATEMENT OF APPLICANT HUEY FONG

UNITED STATES IMMIGRATION SERVICE CHINESE DIVISION

Angel Island Station, San Francisco, California February 14, 1913

#12505/2-11, Huey Jing, and: Inspector J.B. Warner
#12505/4-2, Huey Fong, sons:
of Native, ex ss "Mongolia": Stenographer S.W. Buchanan
2/14/13:
:Interpreter Ed. L. Park

Statement of applicant—Huey Fong, _____ Sworn.
Applicant speaks See Yip dialect; Interpreter Park originally speaks Sam Yup dialect and is qualified in See Yip dialect.

Q What are your names?
A Huey Fong; no other names; not married.
Q How old are you?
A 19.
Q When were you born?
A KS 21-11-17.
Q Where were you born?
A Huey Oak village, S.N. Dist.
Q How large is that village?
A About 20 houses.
Q How is this village arranged?
A 10 houses to each row (2 rows).
Q Where is your house located?
A 5th row second house.
Q Who lives in the first house 5th row?
A Huey You Jung; married; wife has natural feet; no children.
Q Are they living or dead?
A Yes, living there when I left China: always lived there; he is about 60 years old.
Q Who lives in the first house 6th row?
A Huey You; married; wife has natural feet; one boy Huey Lin Woon; 12 or 13 years old; no girl.
Q Who lives in the second house 6th row?
A Huey Jung Chung; married; wife has natural feet; one boy Huey Fook; about 11 or 12 years old; no girl.
Q Is he at home?
A Yes.
Q Always lived there?
A Yes.
Q Who lives in the 2nd house 4th row?
A Huey Sick Poy; married; wife has natural feet; one girl about 3 years old, I don't know her name. No boys.
Q Who lives in the 1st house 4th row?
A Huey Gun Yee; married; natural feet; one boy, Huey Bo 15 years old; no girls.
Q Who lives in the 3rd row 2nd house?
A Huey Jow; married; natural feet; one boy Huey Hung; 18 years; one girl, I do not know her name; 11 or 12.
Q Where is the school located?
A 7th row, first house.
Q Do you know anybody in your village by the name of Huey Mon Nam?
A Yes, he lives 3rd row, first house.
Q Is that man married?
A Yes; wife has natural feet; one boy Huey Bo, about 10 years old.

Q How is your village supplied with water?
A Well opposite the first row.
Q Any wall around your village?
A No.
Q What is the nearest market?
A Look Bo market one li away to the east.
Q Name some of the nearby villages?
A Jock Mee to the east.
Q Has that village any other name?
A No other name. To the West is a Lew Village, I don't know the name.
Q Where is the nearest ancestral hall in your village?
A I don't know any.
Q Where do your family worship?
A I don't know.
Q Is there any temple near there?
A May be there is a temple there I do not know.
Q Why don't you know if you came from that village?
A Temple must be far away—I do not know about it.
Q Do you live in that village?
A Yes.
Q How is it that you do not know anything about the surroundings?
A I have never seen one.
Q Did you ever hear anyone talk of a temple?
A I never heard of it.
Q Are there any tablets in your house?
A No.
Q None of any description?
A Piece of red paper on the wall.
Q What name is written on the red paper?
A Just "ancestors"
Q What is your father's name?
A Huey Wah alias Huey Sing.
Q How old is your father?
A 41.
Q 41, that is right is it?
A Yes.
Q When did you last see your father?
A Last year.
Q Where did you see him?
A Home.
Q What was he doing while in China?
A Doing nothing—stayed at home.
Q Stayed at home all the time?
A Stayed at home a little over a year.
Q Did he have any business interests in China?
A No.

Q   You never heard of his having any business interests in China?
A   No.
Q   You are positive of that?
A   Yes, I am.
Q   Did your father remain at home during his entire stay in China on his last trip; that is most of the time?
A   Yes.
Q   Was he gone from 10 to 15 to 20 days a month?
A   Never away so long.
Q   He was never away 15–20– or 25 days at a time during his last visit home?
A   No.
Q   When did you see your father in China before his last trip?
A   KS 31.
Q   How long did he remain at home?
A   Until KS 34.
Q   Did he have any business interests in China during that stay to your knowledge?
A   No.
Q   Was he at home most of the time?
A   Yes.
Q   Did your father visit any market place while he was in China from KS 31 to KS 34 or during his last trip?
A   He might go in the morning and return the same evening; that is the longest stay he ever made.
Q   Did you ever hear your mother say that your father ever had any business interests in China? That is that he was connected with any firm?
A   No.
Q   Did you ever hear your father or mother speak of Gong Moon city?
A   Yes.
Q   In what respect?
A   I didn't hear them say Gong Moon; I have heard of Gong Moon through other parties.
Q   Do you know where Gong Moon is?
A   Quite a long ways.
Q   Were you ever there?
A   It is in a different district entirely, I have never been there.
Q   What is your paternal grandfather's name?
A   Huey Yee Wah; that is the only name I know for him.
Q   Living or dead?
A   Dead; I never saw him.
Q   What is your paternal grandmother's name?
A   Yip Shee.
Q   Did you ever see her?
A   She is dead.
Q   Did your paternal grandfather have more than one wife?
A   One only.
Q   And her name is Yip Shee?

A Yes.
Q Has your father any brothers or sisters?
A No.
Q What is your mother's name, age and what kind of feet?
A Lew Shee; natural feet; 36 years old.
Q Native of what village?
A Hong How village; 5 lis away.
Q What is her father's name?
A Lew Hee; I don't know his other name; he is dead; I never saw him.
Q What is your maternal grandmother's name?
A Dead; I don't know her name; never saw her.
Q Has your mother any brothers or sisters?
A One brother, Lew Lip Gip; I never saw him; he is married and has one boy; I have seen the boy; he has been to my village; his name is Lew Fook, 12 or 13 years old.
Q How many brothers and sisters have you?
A Four brothers and one sister.
Q Names, ages, and dates of birth if you know.
A Huey Jung, 17 years; applicant
   Huey Heung; 16; in China in the home village.
   Huey Sin; 9 years old; at home.
   Huey Toy; 6 years old.
   Huey Ngook; 7 years old; sister.
Q What have you been doing in China?
A Attending school in the home village.
Q How old were you when you started and when you quit?
A From the age of 8 until departure.
Q What is your teacher's name?
A Chan Bo San.
Q Where does he live?
A I do not know what village he is from; he sleeps in the school.
Q What was your brother Huey Jing doing in China?
A Attending school with me.
Q How many years did you go to school together?
A He started when he was 8 until departure.
Q You both attended the same school and had the same teacher?
A Yes.
Q Where did he sleep when your father was home?
A Home.
Q When your father was home did he ever take you and your brother Huey Jing anywhere?
A No.
Q Where did you have your photograph taken?
A Hong Kong.
Q When?
A When I left home to come to the United States.

Q Did you send your picture to the United States to your father?
A No.
Q Who attached it to the paper?
A My father wrote to the man who looked after my papers in Hong Kong and he pasted it on.
Q Who was that man?
A A man in the firm of Quong Lung Company, Hong Kong.
Q You are positive that you and your brother Huey Jing never visited Hong Kong with your father?
A Yes, positively never visited there.
Q How many scholars attended school with you and your brothers?
A 15.
Q Name some of them?
A Huey Mow, Huey Ing Bor; Huey Hen; Huey Fong; Huey Fook; Huey Shew; Huey Lin Woo; Huey Bo; that is all I can remember.
Q Is there anybody now in the United States who has seen you in China?
A Dong Leong Gow.
Q When and under what circumstances?
A He came to visit us the latter part of KS 32.
Q Did he come from the United States?
A Yes, came to visit my father while my father was home.
Q Did he visit the house more than once?
A Twice.
Q Was your father home both times?
A Yes.
Q Anyone else?
A Gee Soon.
Q When, where, and under what circumstances did he see you and your brothers in China?
A ST 1-6th or 7th month he brought a letter and $10 Mex. to my mother from my father.
Q Did he ever visit your village again?
A Yes.
Q What was the occasion of his second visit?
A He came to see if there was a letter to bring back to my father from my mother but <u>he didn't get any, we didn't give him any letter.</u>
Q He saw all the family members at that time?
A Yes he saw us all.
   (Identifies all photographs)
Q Have you anything further to state?
A No.

(Interpreter Louis Fon called and he asked the applicant if he had understood the interpreter in the case and he answered in the affirmative)

Signed Chinese Characters,
2/20/13—SWB

STATEMENT OF WITNESS—GEE SOON

UNITED STATES IMMIGRATION SERVICE CHINESE DIVISION

Angel Island Station, San Francisco, California February 14, 1913

#12505/2-11, Huey Jing, and Inspector J.B. Warner
#12505/4-2, Huey Fong, Sons :
of Native, ex ss "Mongolia": Stenographer S.W. Buchanan
2/14/13:
:Interpreter Ed. L. Park

―――――

Statement of Witness _____ Sworn.
Witness speaks See Yip dialect; Interpreter Park originally speaks Sam Yup dialect and is qualified in See Yip dialect

- Q What are your names?
- A Gee Soon alias Gee Chun Hung.
- Q How old are you?
- A 45.
- Q Where were you born?
- A Born in China.
- Q When did you first come to the United States?
- A KS 7
- Q How many trips have you made to China?
- A Two trips. Last trip departed ST 1-5-24 ss "Asia" returned ST 2-5-20 on the ss "Manchuria" on a merchant's certificate member of the firm Quong Lung Toy Kee Company.
- Q You were questioned concerning your wife and family on your return?
- A Yes.
- Q For whom are you here to testify today?
- A To testify for Huey Wah's sons Huey Jing and Huey Fong.
- Q In what village did you live while in China?
- A Wah Ping village, S.N. Dist.
- Q Where did Huey Wah's family live?
- A Huey Oak village, about one po from my village.
- Q How many times did you visit Huey Oak village?
- A Twice.
- Q Tell us about the circumstances?
- A I took $10 mex to Huey Wah's family.
- Q You are positive it was Mex?
- A Yes—Mexican dollars.
- Q Isn't it a fact that you were never in this village in your life and that you never saw Huey Wah's children and wife?
- A I was there.
- Q Isn't it a fact that he just took you on as a witness because his other witness failed to appear?
- A I was in his village and saw his boys.

Q You two can not tell the same story; he says he gave you $10 gold and you say $10 Mexican silver dollars; which are we to believe?
A I do not know why he said that because he gave me $10 in silver.
Q Did you see Huey Wah's wife?
A Yes.
Q What kind of feet did she have?
A Natural feet.
Q What is her name?
A Lew Shee.
Q How many children has Huey Wah?
A Six children; 5 boys and one girl.
Q Did you see all of them?
A Yes.
Q Can you give their names and ages?
A Huey Fong: 14 or 15 at the time; applicant.
   Huey Jing; 12 or 13; applicant.
   Huey Heung; about 10 or 11.
   Huey Sin; 6 or 7
   Huey Toy; one or two years old.
   Huey Ngook; girl; 3 or 4 years old.
Q What were the oldest two boys doing while you were in China?
A Attending school.
Q Did you see anybody else in this house?
A No.
Q What was the occasion of your second visit and when was it made?
A Second visit ST 2-3; I went there to get a letter to bring back
Q Did you get a letter?
A Yes.
Q Did you have any verbal message to deliver from either of these applicants?
A No.
   (Identifies all photographs correctly)
Q Have these boys any marks or scars by which you could identify them?
A I did not notice any.
Q Have you understood the Interpreter?
A Yes.

(Interpreter Louis Fon called and he questioned the witness as to whether he had understood the interpreter in the case and he answered in the affirmative)

Signed Chinese Characters,
2/20/13.—SWB

STATEMENT OF APPLICANT HUEY JING

UNITED STATES IMMIGRATION SERVICE CHINESE DIVISION

Angel Island Station, San Francisco, California February 14, 1913

#12505/2-11
#12505/4-2

Huey Jing, and Huey Fong,: Inspector J.B. Warner
Song of Native, ex ss: Stenographer S.W. Buchanan
"Mongolia" 2/14/13: Interpreter Ed. L. Park

———

Statement of applicant, Huey Jing _____ Sworn.
Applicant speaks See Yip dialect; Interpreter Park originally speaks Sam Yup dialect and is qualified in See Yip dialect.

Q   What are your names?
A   Huey Jing; no other name; not married.
Q   How old are you?
A   17, born KS 23-1-15.
Q   Where?
A   Huey Oak village, S.N. Dist.
Q   How large is that village?
A   20 houses.
Q   Where is your house located?
A   Counting from the East, 5th row, second house.
Q   How are the houses situated?
A   Two rows, 10 houses in each.
Q   Who lives in the 1st house 6th row?
A   Huey You; married; wife has natural feet; one boy Huey Lin Woon about 12.
Q   Who lives in the 2nd house 6th row?
A   Huey Jung Chung; married; wife has natural feet; one boy Huey Fook; 10 years.
Q   First house 5th row?
A   Huey You Jung; married; natural feet; no children.
Q   Has he always lived there?
A   He has always lived there and is still living there.
Q   Who lives in the second house fourth row?
A   Huey Sick Poy; married; wife has natural feet, one girl and no boy. I don't know her name, 3 years old.
Q   First house 4th row?
A   Huey Goon Yee; he is married; wife has natural feet; one boy, no girl. Huey Bo, 13 years.
Q   First house in the 3rd row?
A   Huey Mon Nam; married; natural feet; one boy, Huey Bo, 10 years old.
Q   Second house 3rd row?
A   Huey Gock Jow; he is married; wife has natural feet; one girl 2 or 3 years old; no boy.
Q   How is your village supplied with water?
A   Well opposite the first row.
Q   What is the nearest market?
A   Look Bo about one li away.
Q   Name some of the nearby villages?
A   Jock Mee village to the East about a li. To the west the Lew village about 5 lis.
Q   Is Jock Mee village known by any other name?
A   No.
Q   Where is the nearest ancestral hall?

A   I do not know of any ancestral halls anywhere near there.
Q   Where does your family worship?
A   Never worship.
Q   Is there a temple nearby?
A   No.
Q   Did you ever hear of one?
A   No.
Q   What is your father's name, age and occupation?
A   Huey Wah and Huey Sing; 41 years old; farmer in San Francisco.
Q   When did you last see him in China?
A   Last year 7th month.
Q   How long had he been in China then?
A   Little over a year.
Q   Did you ever see him in China before that time?
A   He was home in China from KS 21 to KS 24.
Q   Was he home from KS 24 until you saw him last year?
A   Only two times
Q   How old were you in KS 31?
A   9 years old.
Q   Did you see your father in KS 31 in China?
A   No, he was in the United States then.
Q   When did you see your father last before ST 2?
A   When I was two or three years old.
Q   You didn't see him when you were 9 years old?
A   No.
Q   Or when you were 10 years old?
A   no.
Q   Did you see your father in China during KS 31—32-33 or 34?
A   No, he was in the United States.
Q   You are positive that he was not in China during that time?
A   Yes, I am positive.
Q   When your father was in China ST 2-3 what was his business there?
A   Just visiting home, not doing anything.
Q   Was he away from home much?
A   He was home all of the time.
Q   Did he visit any market place or any cities while he was home?
A   If he did I don't know where he went.
Q   Was he absent for 15 or 20 days at a time during his stay in China on that trip?
A   No.
Q   Was he at home on an average of 6 to 10 days a month?
A   Yes.
Q   That was all he was home?
A   I meant to say he was home all the time excepting he took a walk down to Look Bo market and back the same day.
Q   While your father was home in China did he take you any place?
A   No, I was attending school all the time.

Q   Were you ever in Hong Kong before you embarked for the United States?
A   No.
Q   Where did you have your picture taken?
A   Hong Kong.
Q   When?
A   As soon as I came to Hong Kong to come to the United States.
Q   Did you go back to your village after having your picture taken?
A   No.
Q   Who attached that picture to this paper?
A   It was done in Quong Lung Company, Hong Kong.
Q   And you are positive that you never went to Hong Kong with your father?
A   I am positive.
Q   What is your paternal grandfather's name?
A   Huey Yee Wah; I do not know his other name.
Q   Is he living or dead?
A   Died before I was born.
Q   What is your paternal grandmother's name?
A   Yip Shee; she also died before I was born.
Q   Has your father any brothers or sisters?
A   No.
Q   What is your mother's name, age and what kind of feet?
A   Lew Shee; 36 years old; natural feet; still living in the home village.
Q   Is she your father's only wife?
A   Only wife.
Q   Of what village is she a native?
A   Lew village, I do not know the name, it is 5 lis away.
Q   What is your maternal grandfather's name?
A   Lew Hee; He died many years ago; I never saw him.
Q   What is your maternal grandmother's name?
A   I don't know her name; she died more than 20 years ago.
Q   Has your mother any brothers or sisters?
A   One brother, Lew Gip; I never saw him.
Q   Was he ever at your village?
A   No.
Q   Is he married?
A   Married; one boy Lew Fook, 11 or 12 years old.
Q   Did you ever see him?
A   Yes.
Q   How many brothers and sisters have you?
A   Four brothers and one sister.
Q   Names, ages, and dates of birth if you can?
A   Huey Fong, 19; born KS 21-11-17. Applicant. Huey Heung; 16; I don't know the date of his birth. Huey Sin; 9 years old. Huey Toy, 6 years old. Huey Ngook, 7 years old, my sister.
Q   Did you ever have any other brothers or sisters?
A   No.

Q   What have you been doing in China?
A   Attending school.
Q   How old were you when you started and when you quit?
A   Started at the age of 8 and attended until my departure.
Q   What is the name of the teacher?
A   Chan Bo San.
Q   Did he live in your village?
A   No; sleeps in the school.
Q   Did you attend school with your brother Huey Fong?
A   Yes.
Q   Did you have the same teacher?
A   Yes.
Q   Where did you and your brother sleep?
A   Slept at home?.
Q   Sleep at home all the time your father was home?
A   Yes.
Q   How many scholars attended that school with you and your brother Huey Fong?
A   12 or 13.
Q   Name some of them?
A   Huey Mow, Huey Ing Bor; Huey Hen; Huey Fong; Huey Fook; Huey Shew; Huey Lin Woo; Huey Bo; that is all I remember.
Q   Is there anybody now in the United States who has seen you in China?
A   Dong Leong Gow and Gee Soon.
Q   When and under what circumstances did Dong Leong Gow see you?
A   He came to my house twice; KS 21 and KS 24.
Q   Did he see you in KS 21?
A   No, I wasn't born yet.
Q   You do not remember him at all?
A   He came in KS 24.
Q   Do you remember him in KS 24?
A   Yes.
Q   Do you remember him distinctly?
A   Yes.
Q   How old a man is Dong Leong Gow?
A   I don't know, about 20 years.
Q   Then when he visited your house in KS 21 he must have been about one year old?
A   I made a mistake, it must have been KS 31.
Q   Then why did you say he came to your house before you were born?
A   I was dizzy in the head and got things all mixed up.
Q   Who was the other witness?
A   Gee Soon; he came to our house ST 1-6th or 7th month and brought a letter and $10 Mex to my mother from my father.
Q   Did he call the second time?
A   Yes in ST 2 he came to get a letter and my mother gave him a letter but I do not know whether he delivered it in person or mailed it.

Q   You are positive that your mother gave him a letter?
A   Yes.
Q   Are you also positive that you never knew of your father's having any interest in any mercantile establishment in China?
A   No, never had.
Q   Are you positive that your father spent most of his time at home while he was in China?
A   Yes, if he would go to the store I would go with him.
Q   You are also positive that you did not see your father in China between KS 24 and ST 2?
A   No I did not see him I am positive.
    (Identifies all photographs)
Q   Are any of your brothers married?
A   No.
Q   Have you anything further to state?
A   No.
Q   Have you understood the interpreter?
A   Yes.

(Interpreter Louis Fon called and he asked the applicant if he had understood the interpreter in the case and he answered in the affirmative)

Signed Chinese Characters,
2/21/13—SWB

ALLEGED FATHER RE-CALLED

Q   What are your names?
A   Huey Wah and Huey Sing.
Q   Will you kindly remember that you are under oath and that you have sworn to tell the truth concerning your alleged sons?
A   Yes.
Q   I will ask you to identify certain photographs?
    (Showing photograph No. 6 Doric May 17, 1898, Huey Way?[)]
A   Myself.
    (Showing No. 3 Mongolia November 22, 1908?[)]
A   That is myself.
Q   You stated that you had made three trips to China, is that correct?
A   Yes.
Q   Will you state what your occupation was from KS 30 to KS 34?
A   I didn't do anything.
Q   No occupation at all?
A   Just visiting.
Q   You had no business interests in China at all?
A   No.
Q   Have you any business interests in China now?
A   Yes.
Q   Where?

A   Gong Moon city.
Q   When did you acquire that interest in Gong Moon city?
A   KS 34 before I returned to the United States.
Q   Do you still retain that interest?
A   Yes.
Q   Did you take an active part in the conduct of that business in ST 2 and 3?
A   No active part.
Q   How much time did you spend in Gong Moon city in that store?
A   10 or 20 days each month.
Q   All the time you were in China on this last trip?
A   Yes.
Q   Were you absent from your village from 10 to 20 days a month each month during your stay at home during ST 2 and 2?
A   Yes.
Q   Your family, of course, knew that you had business interests in Gong Moon?
A   My boys would not know but my wife would.
Q   Why wouldn't your boys know?
A   I would not tell them.
Q   Why not?
A   They attended school—I would not want to tell them about it.
Q   What time was it last year that you took your boys to Hong Kong?
A   About the 4th or 5th month of last year.
Q   How long did you stay?
A   A few days.
Q   Where did you stop?
A   Quong Lung Company.
Q   Did Huey Fong and Huey Jing both have their photographs taken at that time?
A   I came out with them to the city but I did not take them to the photograph gallery; somebody from Quong Lung Company did.
Q   Did you bring the photograph back to the United States with you?
A   No.
Q   Did you ever see these photographs?
A   No.
Q   When did your father die?
A   I do not know. I was in the United States.
Q   Between what trips did he die?
A   Died after KS 24.
Q   When did [sic] were in China in KS 30 did you see him?
A   Yes.
Q   Why did you state this morning that your father died 5 or 6 years ago?
A   He died in KS 30 before I got to China.
Q   Did he die before or after your arrival?
A   He died before I got home.
Q   What is the name of your mother?
A   Lee Shee.

Q   Are you positive of that?
A   Yes.
Q   Did your father have more than one wife?
A   No.
Q   Did she die before or after your father?
A   She died first.
Q   When you were in China last year was the house in the same row as your's occupied?
A   Huey You Jung was living there.
Q   Was he living there when you left China CR 1?
A   He was there but I understand that he went away again.
Q   Had he been away before?
A   He went to some other part to the southern part of China.
Q   Did his family go with him?
A   Yes.
Q   When did he come back?
A   I don't know.
Q   Was he living in your village or was he in the southern part of China in KS 34?
A   Southern part of China.
Q   And was the house vacant then?
A   Yes.
Q   Why did you say this morning that the house was vacant when you were in China last?
A   Because there was trouble around the vicinity of my village and he moved out.
Q   Then he wasn't living in that house when you were last in China?
A   He used to go away and come back.
Q   Was he living in there in ST 3 and CR 1 when you were there last?
A   He was there.
Q   All the time?
A   He went away the 2nd or 3rd month and took his family with him.
Q   Where did he go?
A   Just a few day's trip by water.
Q   Did he return to your village before you left for the United States in CR 1?
A   No.
Q   Then the house was vacant when you left China?
A   Yes.
Q   When you were in China did you worship?
A   Gee Lip Sing temple.
Q   How far distant?
A   2 or 3 lis.
Q   Did you take your family to worship there?
A   No.
Q   Did your family ever go there to worship?
A   No, I do not think they have ever been there.
Q   How does it happen that you went there and did not take your children?

A   I just went there—I did not have to take my boys.
Q   Have you anything further to state?
A   No.

(Interpreter Robert Lym called and he asked the alleged father if he had understood the interpreter in the case and he answered in the affirmative)

Signed Chinese Characters.
2/21/13—SWB

REPORT BY INSPECTOR J.B. WARNER IN REGARDS TO HUEY CASE

Department of Commerce and Labor Immigration Service

Nos.
12505/4-2
12505/2-11

OFFICE OF THE COMMISSIONER
ANGEL ISLAND STATION
VIA FERRY POST OFFICE
SAN FRANCISCO, CAL.

February 24, 1913
Inspector in Charge,
Chinese Division,
Angel Island Station,
San Francisco, California.

In re Huey Jing and Huey Fong, Sons of native, ex ss "Mongolia"

2/4/13:

In my report on form 2020, I stated that I did not believe that the relationship existed between these applicants and their alleged father nor did I believe that they are brothers. In the first place, there is absolutely no resemblance between either of the applicants nor between the applicants and their alleged father. Again, the alleged father experienced considerable difficulty identifying the photographs of the applicants and finally did identify them correctly, and then identified the photograph of the identifying witness as his oldest son. This witness, however, did not testify and the alleged father did not know his whereabouts.

Huey Wah alias Huey Sing, states that he is 38 years of age; both of the alleged sons gave his age as 41.

He has made three trips to China, first returning May 17, 1898; second return November 22, 1908.; and third return September 30, 1912. Applicant Huey Jing states that he never saw his father from KS 24 until ST 2: that he, the applicant, was present in his village in his 9th, 10th, and 11th years, and that he is positive that he did not see his father in KS 31, 32, 33, or 34.

The alleged father states that his father died in KS 30 before he returned to China. Both of these applicants state that he died before they were born.

The alleged father states that his mother's name was Lew Shee; and that his father never had but the one wife. Applicants state that their paternal grandmother's name was Yip Shee.

The alleged father states that he took both of these applicants on a visit to Hong Kong; the applicants both say that he never took them to Hong Kong at any time.

The alleged father further states that he was not at home for from six to ten days a month during his last visit in China as he was interested in a store in Gong Moon city, Sun Wooey District, which is about 4 or 5 pos distant and is an entirely different district from his home. The applicants both say that the only time their alleged father was away from home was to walk to the market in the morning returning the same day in the evening.

These to my mind, are the most important discrepancies, but there are other discrepancies concerning the inhabitants of the home village, but I think those enumerated are enough to show the fraudulent nature of these cases[.]

I recommend that both these applicants be denied landing.

J.B. Warner
Immigrant Inspector

STATEMENT OF HUEY WAH

HUEY WAH, being duly sworn, does state: That he is the father of Huey Jing and Huey Fong, who arrived on the steamer Mongolia, February 4, 1913 (12505/2-11 — 4-2).

That he testified in these cases on February 14; That he was at that time much agitated and nervous for the reason that while en route to the Immigration office at Angel Island from San Francisco to testify a collision occurred close to the Immigration Steamer in which two steamers were sunk and the Immigration Steamer was obliged to stop and pick up many of the survivors. That affiant is not accustomed to travelling by water and this calamity occurring so close to the boat he was on, frightened him and rendered him so nervous that he may have made, in his agitation, some statements, unintentionally that are in conflict with the facts in these cases and that as no action has been taken admitting his sons, he fears such is the case.

That he, therefore, requests no adverse action be taken until he has been examined regarding any seeming contradictions while in a calm and normal state of mind, as these are his sons and both he and they should be able to—and can—answer any reasonable questions under normal conditions in such consonance as to show clearly the relationship.

<Huey Wah>
Subscribed and sworn to before me,
This 26th day of February, 1913.

Robert W. Jones
NOTARY PUBLIC
In and for the City and County of
San Francisco, State of California

COMMISSIONER'S FINDING AND DECREE

Department of Commerce and Labor Immigration Service

12505/4-2
12505/2-11

OFFICE OF THE COMMISSIONER
ANGEL ISLAND STATION
VIA FERRY POST OFFICE
SAN FRANCISCO, CAL.

In the matter of
Huey Fong and Huey Jing
ss Mongolia, Feb. 4, 1913
Applications to land as sons of native.

Finding and Decree.
The nativity and essential trip of the alleged father are satisfactorily established, as shown by prior landing records herewith.

One of the objectionable features of the cases is that (in the opinion of the examining officers) no physical similarity exists between the alleged father and the applicants. Another is that, although the applicants are 17 and 18 years of age respectively and have seen their father recently according to the claims made, they are unable to agree with him as to his age, he stating his age is 38, while they allege he is 41.

The alleged father departed on one of his trips for China KS 31 (1905) and returning KS 34 (1908), but applicant Huey Jing states positively he did not see his father while he was in China on this trip, irrespective of the fact that the alleged father states he spent most of his time at home and is corroborated in this by the other applicant.

It is maintained by the alleged father that his father died in his house in the home village five or six years ago. The applicants state they have never seen their paternal grandfather; and that he died before they were born.

The alleged father states his mother's name as Lee Shee, while the applicants declare their paternal grandmother's name was Yip Shee. It is maintained that the paternal grandfather only had one wife.

Another point which is unfavorable to the claims of the applicants is that the alleged father states positively that he was accompanied to Hong Kong by the applicants while in China recently, the applicants stating they never were in Hong Kong until their departure from the home village to the United States.

The alleged father states he has a business in Gong Moon city, Sun Wui district; that his business there is curios and fireworks, the firm name being Yee Bow Him Co.; that he has been interested in said firm about seven or eight years; that when he was home last he would sometimes visit home once a month, sometimes twice a month and sometimes only once in two months, remaining six or seven days and sometimes eight or ten days. Applicant Huey Fong states that from

KS 31 to KS 34 (1905 to 1908), while his father was home on a visit, he might go away from home in the morning and return the same evening; that that was the longest stay he ever made; that he never heard his mother state whether his father ever had business interests in China, i.e., whether he was ever connected with any firm; that he had never heard his father or mother mention Gong Moon, but that he has heard of Gong Moon through other parties. Applicant Huey Jing states that if his father was ever away from home for any length of time while on any of his visits to China he did not know his whereabouts; that he was not absent fifteen to twenty days at a time during his stay in China; that he was home except when he would take a walk to Look Bo market, returning the same day. This applicant too is positive that he never heard of his father being engaged in any business in China.

I note that the alleged father, under date of Feb. 26, 1913, has requested that adverse action be withheld until he has been examined regarding any seeming contradictions, he having been agitated and nervous during his original examination on account of a collision which occurred between two steamers while he was aboard the SS Angel Island on the trip from San Francisco to the station the morning of his examination. I feel, however, that he was given ample opportunity to state his case on the date set for hearing and that the ends of justice would not be furthered by granting him a reexamination.

In view of the foregoing contradictions and inconsistencies I am convinced that the relationship claimed does not exist and the applicants are accordingly denied admission and advised of their right to appeal.

> Dated this 3 day of March 1913 Samuel H. Backus
> Commissioner

FORM OF APPEAL

San Francisco, Cal., March 6, 1913

I hereby appeal to the Honorable Secretary of Commerce and Labor from the decision of the Commissioner of Immigration in case No. 12505/4-2, arriving ex S.S. #53 Mongolia on February 4, 1913, and agree to perfect appeal within three days by filing brief with Secty C & L. I will be represented before the Department by Attorney Stidger & Kennah.

> Attorney for Huey Fong,
> Denied March 3, 1913.
> Appellant

LETTER OF WITHDRAWAL FROM STIDGER AND KENNAH

San Francisco, Cal. February[5] 7, 1913
Commissioner of Immigration
San Francisco, Cal.,

Sir;—

In the cases of Huey Jing and Huey Fong, songs of native, ex S.S. Mongolia, Feb. 4, 1913, numbers 12505/2-11 and 12505/4-2, denied admission by you, we herewith withdraw the appeals in these cases and ask that the boys be returned to China by the steamer of the Pacific Mail S.S. Company sailing on Saturday March 8th (tomorrow).

Yours respectfully
Stidger and Kennah

[1] Stidger and Kennah, Attorneys, to Commissioner of Immigration, San Francisco, CA, February 7, 1913; 12505/4-2 [HUEY Fong]; Box 666; Immigration Arrival Investigation Case Files, 1884–1944 (ARC 296445); Records of the Immigration and Naturalization Service, Record Group 85; National Archives and Records Administration-Pacific Region (San Francisco)

[2] A traditional Chinese measure of distance, which has varied over time but today is standardized at 500 meters (half a kilometer).

* This question had an X written in pencil to the right of the Q in the original document. This most likely was placed here to indicate a discrepancy with the answers Huey Jing & Huey Fong gave over the next two days.

[3] Dong Leung Gow was one of two corroborating witnesses who signed affidavits claiming to have personal knowledge of the relationship of Huey Wah and his two sons Huey Fong and Huey Jing. He never appeared to testify, but another witness Gee Soon (alias Gee Chun Hun) did testify in his place.

[4] The witnesses name is spelled Gee Soon. This is most likely a typographical error or an error in how the name was pronounced by the interpreter or heard by the inspection officer.

[5] This is most likely a typographical error and was supposed to be March not February. The cover letter attached to this withdrawal letter states the appeal was withdrawn on March 7th.

Source: Statement of Alleged Father, Huey Wah, February 14, 1913; Statement of Applicant, Huey Fong, February 14, 1913; Statement of Witness, Gee Soon, February 14, 1913; Statement of Applicant, Huey Jing, February 14, 1913; J. B. Warner, Immigrant Inspector in Charge, Chinese Division, Angel Island Station, February 24, 1913; Statement of Huey Wah, February 26, 1913; Samuel H. Backus, Commissioner's Finding and Decree, March 3, 1913; Form of Appeal, March 6, 1913; Stidger and Kennah to Commissioner of Immigration, March 7, 1913. 12505/4-2 [HUEY Fong]; Box 666; Immigration Arrival Investigation Case Files, 1884–1944 (ARC 296445); Records of the Immigration and Naturalization Service, Record Group 85; National Archives and Records Administration-Pacific Region (San Francisco).

50. Portland Tong Peace Agreement, 1917

Early 20th-century Chinese immigrants to the United States encountered an intimidating environment: discriminatory laws and ordinances, economic antagonism, the ever-present threat of racial violence, and government reactions ranging from indifference to hostility. In response, the Chinese retreated into ethnic enclaves, using organizations and structures imported from their homeland to provide financial and physical support, as well as cultural continuity. Tongs were secret societies that originated in 18th-century China, sometimes engaging in violent political insubordination. These organizations resurfaced in 19th-century Chinese immigrant communities as mutual protection societies. However, many tongs became involved in organized crime activities in Chinatowns across the United States. They controlled international drug trafficking, money laundering, gambling, and prostitution rings, and exploited business owners in protection rackets. Intertong feuds over territory and profits often turned violent, and several "tong wars" took place across the United States between the 1860s and the 1920s. The following document records a peace agreement between several different Portland tongs.

It is hereby covenanted and agreed between the Hip Sing Tong and SUEY Sing Tong on the part of said societies, its officers and each and all of the members thereof and of all persons associated and allied with them, and the Bing Kung-Bow Leong and Hip Sing Tongs on the part of said societies, its officers and each and all of the members thereof and of all persons associated and allied with them, that they will maintain peace and order among their members and all persons mentioned in this agreement within the County of Multnomah, State of Oregon, for a period of thirty (30) days from the day of execution of these present, and it is further hereby covenanted and agreed that they will prevent each and all of their said officers and members of said societies and associated persons from entering into any quarrells [sic], disorders or unlawful acts with any of the members of the said societies or its officers or said persons associated or allied with them, and that they will not give aid, assistance, contenance [sic] or shelter to any of their members or others who shall violate any of the covenants herein contained or any other persons who shall within said period come into the County of Multnomah, State of Oregon, for any unlawful or disorderly purpose.

And we further hereby agree that we will make every effort to bring about permanent peace between the respective parties hereto and adjust all differences between us at the earliest possible date.

And we further hereby agree that in case either of the parties hereto shall violate any of the covenants or agreements herein contained we will forthwith furnish to the proper officers of the law, the information and evidence necessary to obtain redress for said wrongs in the courts of law.

IN WITNESS WHEREOF the said societies have caused these presents to be executed this 31st day of March, 1917, by the Secretaries of the said societies and have authorized the official seal of said societies to be attached to this compact.
WITNESS

By H.R. Albee
By HIP SING TONG, Secretary

Source: "Portland Tong Peace Agreement," 1917. Mss 190, Oregon Historical Society Research Library. http://kaga.wsulibs.wsu.edu/cdm-imls_2/document.php?CISOROOT=/wsuvan1&CISOPTR=1260&REC=5. Accessed March 2010. Courtesy Oregon Historical Society.

51. Yee Wee Thing Betrayal Letter, 1920

In 1907, Yee Guey, a Chinese American man living in San Francisco, signed an affidavit saying he was a U.S. citizen who wanted to bring his Chinese son, Yee Wee Thing, to the United States. Yee signed this document the year after all immigration, birth, and naturalizaton records were destroyed in the catastrophic fire following the 1906 San Francisco earthquake. Consequently, it was impossible to tell between Chinese Americans who were born in the United States and could legally bring their Chinese-born children into the United States, and Chinese who were immigrants, ineligible for citizenship and unable to sponsor relatives. Yee Wee Thing's actual relationship to Yee Guey is uncertain. However, in 1916, nearly 10 years after his alleged father filed his affidavit and after one day of interrogation at Angel Island, Yee Wee Thing was deemed Yee Guey's son and was allowed to enter the mainland.

Yee Wee Thing soon moved from California to Globe, Arizona, where he worked at the Sang Tai restaurant, owned by Dea Gin Foo of San Francisco. While in Arizona, Yee became entangled in a dispute between rival factions of the Dea family. One member accused Yee of being the child of the cook at the Sang Tai restaurant and actually sent a letter to the immigration office accusing the restaurant owner, Dea Gin Foo, of running a smuggling operation that brought Yee into the country under false pretenses. The immigration officer was not impressed with the story or the accusation and allowed Yee to stay in the United States. On September 23, 1923, Yee was granted a certificate of return, allowing him to go back to China for a visit. He returned two years later and claimed that he had married a woman and fathered a son in the interim. In 1938, Yee Bing Quai would arrive in Boston, claiming to be Yee Wee Thing's son.

The following is the letter written by Dea Goon Foo, the rival family member, accusing Yee of entering the United States illegally. Dea's letter illustrates the complexity of exclusion-era Chinese immigration. While U.S. laws created the context of institutionalized racism, the Chinese themselves took advantage of the unpredictable situation to make a living, settle rivalries, and create a space in America for themselves and their loosely defined family members.

833 Grant Ave.,
San Francisco, Cal.
March 2nd, 1920
To the Tucson Immigration Office.

Gentlemen: —

Am sending you this letter today for no other reason than to inform you that one Dea Gin Foo, a resident of Globe, has been assisting people to gain illegal entrance into the United States. There is now in Globe, in the Sang Tai restaurant, working as waiter named See Hoo Kay. He came to the United States on a paper which be bought, and admitted as a son of native. His real name is See Hoo and is not Yee. He is a grandson of Dea Gin Foo's wife's people. I can testify to that fact;

I can testify to the place where he belongs, his village, and whose son he is. If you have authority to deport him back to China, I am willing to serve as witness. If you need me to testify you will furnished me my railroad transportation then I will surely come, and give testimony before court.

You arrest and bring See Hoo Kay to Tucson then I will testify, but not in Globe. With kind regards.

(Signed) Dea Goon Foo (In English)
On envelope:

Sent by Wee Po.

I hereby certify that the above is a correct translation of the letter written in Chinese attached herewith.

Lee Park Liu
Chinese Intpr

Source: 24212/2-4 [YEE Wee Thing]; Box 2101; Immigration Arrival Investigation Case Files, 1884–1944 (ARC 296445); Records of the Immigration and Naturalization Service, Record Group 85; National Archives and Records Administration-Pacific Region (San Francisco).

52. Mary Young Chan, Marriage Certificate and Court Summons, 1921

In 1921, Mary Young Chan initiated divorce proceedings against Jack Chan, her husband of two years. Both native Californians, the Chans married in Oakland and lived in Alameda County. The records from the court proceedings include her 1919 marriage license and certificate, Mary Chan's court deposition, and the Superior Court of Alameda's summons to Jack Chan. The documents, while filtered through the attorney's interpretation, paint a descriptive—and harrowing—picture of Mary Chan's life with her husband.

The Superior Court of the State of California, in and for the County of Alameda.
Mary Young Chan, Plaintiff, vs. Jack Chan, Defendant.
Plaintiff complains and alleges:

I.

That said plaintiff and said defendant intermarried at Oakland, County of Alameda, State of California, on November 25th, 1919, and then and there became husband and wife, and ever since have been and now are husband and wife.

II.

That said plaintiff now is, and for more than one year preceding the commencement of this action has been, a bona fide resident of the State of California and of the County of Alameda.

III.

That said plaintiff is now pregnant with and is carrying, an unborn child, to which she expects to give birth within the next two or three weeks.

IV.

That said plaintiff and said defendant separated on or about June 9th, 1920, and that six (6) months and fifteen (15) days have elapsed between the date of said marriage and the date of said separation.

V.

That ever since said marriage, said defendant, disregarding his marital duties, has by his acts and conduct treated said plaintiff in a cruel and inhuman manner, and has wrongfully, cruelly, wilfully and inhumanly inflicted upon said plaintiff, and still does wrongfully, cruelly, willfully and inhumanly inflict upon said plaintiff great mental anguish and physical suffering more particularly as follows:

a) That said defendant is of a jealous, morose, and morbid disposition, and has frequently and continuously, on occasions too numerous to mention, the exact dates of which said plaintiff is not now informed, unjustly and without provocation or cause, wrongfully accused said plaintiff of improper familiarity with men other than said defendant, and has accused her of adulterous intercourse with said men.

b) That said defendant repeatedly, and on occasions too numerous to specify, the exact dates of which the said plaintiff is not now informed, unjustly and without provocation or cause, denied the paternity of the said child, and openly stated that said child was conceived as a result of intercourse with various white men.

c) That said defendant has refused to pay the necessary medical and hospital bills required in connection with the birth of said child, and has refused to support it after its birth, and has told said plaintiff that after the birth of said child, she should place it in a public park and there abandon it.

d) That during the entire married life of the parties hereto, said defendant has frequently and continuously and repeatedly gambled, and lost his earnings, and thereby been unable to contribute to the support of said plaintiff in a proper manner, and has stayed out nights and stayed away from home several days at a time, all without the leave, knowledge or consent of said plaintiff.

e) That said defendant has frequently, and on occasions too numerous to specify, the exact dates of which said plaintiff is not now informed, sworn, cursed, reviled and applied opprobrious epithets to said plaintiff, such as "whore" and other lewd and lascivious terms, and implied a want of chastity on the part of said plaintiff.

f) That frequently during the entire married life of said parties, said defendant, on occasions to[o] numerous to specific and the exact dates of which plaintiff does not now recall, has violently and brutally beaten, struck, mistreated and maltreated said plaintiff, and has violently struck her in the face and upon her body with great force and violence, and bruised and lacerated her body; that in this connection, said plaintiff particularly alleges that on or about February 20th, 1920, without cause or provocation, said defendant, with great force and violence, and in a fit of unwarranted rage and anger, repeatedly struck her with his fist about her body, and that on February 5th, 1920, said defendant grabbed her by the hair, without cause or provocation, and pulled her and pushed her to the floor with great force and violence, thereby causing great physical pain to be suffered by said plaintiff.

g) That in the latter part of February, 1920, said defendant told her to go away from the home of the parties hereto, and to go to the man that she wished, thereby implying a want of chastity on the part of said plaintiff; that in fear of the threats of said defendant, and forced thereby, said plaintiff did leave the home of the parties hereto, and did stay over night in a hotel in San Francisco.

h) That said defendant, on occasions too numerous to mention, and the exact dates whereof said plaintiff is not now informed, did frequent and consort with women of lewd and lascivious nature, and in this connection said plaintiff particularly alleges that during the week given up to the celebration of the Chinese New Years, in the month of February, 1920, said defendant did remain away from the home of the parties hereto, and did spend his time gambling, drinking, carousing and consorting with and cohabiting with fast women.

i) That frequently during their entire married life, said defendant would, at the home of the parties hereto, without any cause or provocation given to him by said plaintiff, fly into a violent rage and curse and swear at said plaintiff in loud and boisterous tones, and upbraid said plaintiff for imaginary wrong doings on her part, and would break the furniture and electric fixtures and threaten the life of said plaintiff.

VI.

That there is community property now in the possession of said plaintiff consisting of certain household furniture of a probable value of Two Hundred and Fifty ($250.00) Dollars.

VII.

That said plaintiff is a fit and proper person to have the care, custody and control of the said minor child; that said defendant is not a fit and proper person to have the care, custody and control of the said minor child.

WHEREFORE said plaintiff prays that she be granted a decree of divorce dissolving the bonds of matrimony heretofore existing between the parties hereto, granting to her said community property in her own right, and awarding to her the care, custody and control of the said minor child, and such other relief as may seem meet and proper in the premises.

Leon E. Gray [signature], Attorney for Plaintiff, State of California, County of Alameda

MARY YOUNG CHAN, being first duly sworn, deposes and says: that she is the plaintiff in the above entitled action; that she has read the foregoing Complaint and knows the contents thereof, and that the same is true of her own knowledge, except as to the matters which are therein stated upon her information or belief, and as to those matters she believes it to be true.

Mary Young Chan [signature]

Subscribed and sworn to before me this 2nd day of December, 1920. Helen G. Christiansen [signature], Notary Public in and for the County of Alameda, State of California.

Source: Marriage certificate & court summons: From Papers relating to Chinese in California. 1920, pp. 1–5. BANC MSS C-R 153: fol. 4, The Bancroft Library, University of California, Berkeley. http://sunsite.berkeley.edu/cgi-bin/flipomatic/cic/brk4703. Accessed May 2010.

53. C. P. Colegrave, "Among the Chinese," ca. 1930

Mrs. C. P. Colegrave, from the Methodist Episcopal Church in Cincinnati, Ohio, wrote "Among the Chinese" for the Home Missionary Society in the 1930s. The pamphlet gives a brief history of early Chinese immigration to the United States, and its halt in 1924. Colegrave then describes the Girls' Home, one of several rescue missions established by various church denominations in San Francisco's Chinatown to save Chinese women enslaved by traffickers. Colegrave presents a largely sympathetic picture of the mid-20th-century Chinese American community. Still, she does distinguish second-generation Chinese Americans from "our own young people," perhaps revealing an unconscious bias, and it is clear that both Colegrave and the Methodist Episcopal Church viewed the Girls' Home as a means of assimilation and Americanization, as well as a safe haven for oppressed and abused girls and women.

The Chinese problem in the United States is a diminishing one as far as numbers are concerned, but an increasing one when opportunity and responsibility are considered.

Gold mining and the building of the transcontinental railroad brought over many thousands of Chinese coolies. The last spike of this road was driven in 1869 by Gov. Stanford. As a result of this, thousands of Chinese were dumped into San Francisco and our first Chinatown was born. These people had to find jobs in order to live, and would work for next to nothing. Because of this displacement of white labor, much anti-Chinese feeling developed, especially among the Irish laborers. Riots and atrocities followed; many Chinese were killed. In 1875, Mr. Pixley, a prominent man and politician of San Francisco declared that the Chinese had no souls; if they had, they were not worth saving. So in 1880 Chinese laborers were excluded from the United States by an act of Congress. Other Chinese could still come until 1924, when Orientals were not included in the "quota basis" law, though this would have meant only 90 Chinese and 163 Japanese per year. Now the only Chinese who can enter here are the children and wives of merchants (not laborers), students, and other especially privileged classes here temporarily. . . .

In the early days they landed and *stayed* in California, but they are now widely scattered over the United States, thus dividing our responsibility. . . . Three out of ten in the United States are American born, and therefore citizens. This second generation is our challenge and our opportunity. Quickly assimilating American standards and ideals, they are as cock-sure and candid as our own young people. They are trying to understand and orient themselves, trying to face the problem of being American by birth, and yet practically outcasts among us. . . .

Our first Girls' Home was destroyed in the fire and earthquake of 1906. The children were quite miraculously saved and cared for in private homes in Berkeley until a separate temporary Home could be secured. The present fine four story brick building was opened in 1911, and accommodates about 40 girls, who now vary in age from two to eighteen. Originally because of the "slave traffic" many women were cared for. While this business is pretty well done away with, a girl child is still occasionally rescued. . . .

We still serve as a house of refuge in time of sickness or other trouble. Recently a mother, bruised and bleeding from the cruel beatings of her husband, a drug peddler, came to our door with her three little children asking protection. She had come from China eight years before to marry a man she had never seen. Efforts for reconciliation were made, while she stayed with us, through our lawyer. But the promises of no more beatings were not kept, and now our lawyer is trying for legal separation. She is a lovely young woman. Again comes a call to care for two little girls, because their mother, a widow, has suddenly been taken to the hospital. There are many of these emergency cases often requiring an interpreter, and sometimes court proceedings. . . .

DOES IT PAY? Nearly a thousand women and girls have passed through our Home. Many of them have married and established Christian homes. More than thirty have married ministers of various denominations. Most of these went to China as missionaries. Just as American women have entered the business world so have the Chinese women. Our girls have become nurses, teachers, workers in beauty shops, clerks in stores and banks. At least one is a dentist in San Francisco; one went to China as a Y.W.C.A. worker; another is the wife of a Professor of Mathematics in the California State University and so on. Our girls gladly come back to visit, or write expressing their love for and appreciation of the Home. Sometimes their children come to pay their respects to the only home their mothers may have known. Surely it is worth all it has cost in time, money, and labor to have ministered to the physical and spiritual needs of these people of another race.

Source: Colegrave, C. P. "Among the Chinese." Cincinnati, OH: The Women's Home Missionary Society, Methodist Episcopal Church, ca. 1930?, pp. 3–4, 8, 9, 13. xF870.C5.C51 v.3:6, The Bancroft Library, University of California, Berkeley. http://sunsite.berkeley.edu/cgibin/flipomatic/cic/brk5171. Accessed May 2010.

54. Carol Green Wilson, *Chinatown Quest*, 1931

Donaldina Cameron was born in New Zealand in 1869, the daughter of a Scottish emigrant who subsequently moved his family to California's San Joaquin Valley when she was two years old. Cameron's mother died a few years later, and the family moved yet again, first to a suburb of San Jose, then to Oakland, and finally to a ranch in the San Gabriel Valley, where Cameron spent the rest of her childhood. After finishing teacher's college, Cameron went to work at Margaret Culbertson's Occidental Mission Home for Girls in San Francisco. The Mission Home cared for female Chinese trafficking victims, brought to the United States to serve as house slaves or prostitutes. White San Francisco authorities turned a blind eye to the slave trade, protecting brothels from police raids and regularly accepting bribes from the Chinese tong members who brought the women in illegally. Culbertson, and then Cameron, conducted clandestine raids on the brothels, rescuing thousands of women who they then boarded, educated, trained and—most important—evangelized at the Mission Home (later renamed Cameron House).

In 1931, Carol Green Wilson published *Chinatown Quest,* a biography of Cameron. The following excerpts chronicle some of the daring rescues conducted by the Mission Home and highlight the plight of the Chinese women—made worse by the collusion of American judges, lawyers, and policemen in the trafficking business. *Chinatown Quest* also presents a highly romanticized view of Cameron and rehashes many of the anti-Chinese stereotypes so prevalent in early 20th-century popular literature. Even the most progressive reformers of the day, including Cameron herself, believed that the Chinatown sex trade originated in inherent Chinese immorality, rather than being a result of restrictive U.S. immigration laws that created an extreme gender imbalance in the Chinese American community. The excerpts also reveal Cameron's fundamental assumption that rehabilitation meant conversion to Christianity and the adoption of Western cultural forms.

"Now to get home, fast. Forget the speed laws."

The young immigration official glanced at the tightly pursed lips of the white-haired woman beside him; but he lost no time in obeying. He stepped his engine up to sixty as they sped into the blackness of the night. In the back seat of the closely curtained sedan a sobbing little Chinese girl was still shrieking, "Fahn Quai! Fahn Quai! ["White Devil"]" as she shrank away from the outstretched hand of the strange foreigner in the front seat. The calm interpreter beside her spoke in soothing native tongue: "But she is not Fahn Quai. She is Lo Mo ["old mother"]. She has come to protect you."

The young official could not turn his head as the road stretched out before him, but he could use his ears. This was the first raid he had taken part in with Miss Donaldina Cameron. Until now he had understood little of her eventful career in Chinatown: but as the whirring motor sped them from Stockton to San Francisco he had opportunity to understand why there was such a ring of authority in the quick-spoken command that had started their dash through valley and foothills to the securely bolted doors of the red brick dwelling on steep Sacramento Street where this gallant Scotch gentlewoman harbors her family of Chinese "daughters." . . .

It was a Chinatown that has long since passed into fanciful tradition that Donaldina Cameron came to live and work in on that gray, foggy morning in 1895—welcomed unexpectedly by Eleanor Olney, who sprang up to greet her from the carved teakwood chair in Miss Culbertson's anteroom. "Just for one year," her adoring family had reluctantly consented. In her early twenties, unsophisticated and untrained, she came, overflowing with something unexpressed within that poured out freely and fully to meet the need which greeted her on every hand.

"From the first," she says in reminiscence, "I loved Miss Culbertson. I loved the Chinese. I never remember feeling anything foreign about them. Never will I forget the laughing face of Ah Ying, the first Chinese girl I came to know, as she tapped so gently on my door to announce 'Lunch is ready.'"

Miss Culbertson's niece, Anna, was staying with her at the time, while she attended an art school. Her appearance, at the end of that first afternoon, with an armful of white rose[s] to welcome the new assistant so near her own age is another bright memory of Donaldina's introduction to 920 Sacramento Street.

But it was not entirely a world of sunshine and family love where this girl from southern California had suddenly come to stay. Very soon after her arrival Miss Culbertson called her to the office.

"Are you sure you will not be afraid in this work?"

"Oh, no!" she answered quickly.

"It isn't too late to change your mind—there are dangers, you know."

Immediately her Scotch blood was aroused

"Why?"

Without raising her voice Miss Culbertson explained that on that very morning the girl who was cleaning the halls had found a strange-looking stick. Police were called and after a hasty investigation declared there was enough explosive in that "stick" to blow up a whole city block. This was unusual, for the Chinese seldom went this far with their bitter threats against the Home. But the latest slave girl rescued by Miss Culbertson had represented such a high purchase price that the owner had attempted to wreak direct vengeance.

Miss Culbertson turned quietly to her new helper.

"Now, are you going to stay?"

"Are you?" just as calmly returned Donaldina Cameron.

"Of course."

"Then I shall stay too."

Thus began a relationship between two women of finely tuned sensibilities which made it possible for the ideals of the older one to live on, transmitted through the devotion of the younger to hundreds of girls, who, though of another race, are one in spirit. Reared in the gentle refinement of a western New York home, Miss Margaret Culbertson had come to California as governess for the small boys of a brother of that well-known pioneer and empire builder, D.O. Mills. Because of their common cultural interests a friendship had sprung up between her and Mrs. P.D. Browne, that motherly friend of the Camerons.

Mrs. Browne had been early identified with a group of women who had sensed a unique need in old San Francisco. Hordes of Chinese, lured across the Pacific by that same glitter that had started covered wagons across the plains in '49, had poured into California to supply the labor needed for the development of mining camps and other industries of this pioneer land. By 1876, of the 148,000 Chinese in America, 60,000 were in California, one-half of these crowded into nine teeming, colorful blocks in San Francisco. In the year 1882, 40,000 Chinese immigrants came in. Bitter opposition began to arise. These thrifty Chinese, with their rice bowls and low standards of living, were considered a menace to white labor. Every reader of Bret Harte and Joaquin Miller is familiar with "the heathen Chinee" of those days, with his long, braided queue, and his stealthy, slippered feet, his reeking opium-den, as well as with "John," the ever-faithful servant appearing with his bowl of pungent China lilies blossoming for Chinese New Year or with the silk-coated gentleman merchants of old Dupont Street.

But perhaps not so many know the stories of the little slave girls kept behind barred doors of the labyrinthine dwellings of back alleys in old San Francisco's Chinatown. Easily forgotten bits of humanity they were, smuggled in like the opium their owners craved, bought and sold with the shining gold that gleams through all the history of these early days.

Ordinary domestic slaves sold for from $100 to $500; the pretty creatures bartered to the keepers of houses of ill-fame brought much larger sums. In the unequal population of these colonies of Chinese workmen, the lives of these children of the dark were pitiful beyond description....

From her window, barred and guarded as were all of the outlooks of this quiet citadel on the edge of Chinatown of the 'nineties,' Donaldina looked up "China Street," as Sacramento Street was known in those days, to Nob Hill, home of aristocrats, where the Hopkinses, Stanfords, Floods, and Huntingtons ruled the salons which their newly won wealth had ingrafted upon picturesque, pioneering San Francisco. Young and beautiful, with family ties that would have gained her entrée anywhere, Donaldina could easily have had her place in the functions that nightly blazed from this hilltop. The path, however, that led her into the heart of the city's night life followed another direction. Down the steep walk to Stockton and DUpont streets below, this young girl followed her courageous leader into dens that frightened the most adventurous of tourists. Here she beheld sights she had never dreamed existed.

"I'll need your help tonight," Miss Culbertson had said, as she glanced up from a tightly folded scrap of paper which had been slipped into her hands a few days after Donaldina's arrival. With three officers as guards they made their way to Spofford Alley, then one of the worst of the narrow by-passes of Chinatown. The door indicated in the note was heavily barred. No amount of pounding would bring an answer. Out came axes and sledge hammers. A shattered window, its iron gratings pried off by the powerful police, was opened, and in crept the rescue party.

They found an anxious girl nervously awaiting release. With true feminine regard for her possessions she begged the officers to help her get her jewelry and watch held in the safe-keeping of her mistress.

"Not here—I get," readily responded that individual, starting out of the house. An officer stepped to her side to insure her return. What she wanted, and accomplished, was to notify the master of the house in a gambling den a few basements away. "Native son of the Golden West," he was, educated in California public schools, and ready with his subtle answer.

"Let her prove she have property, then I give"; adding, "Madam, you know what these women are—how they tell lies, tell things not true."

"Yes," said Miss Culbertson, drawing herself up with stern dignity to stab this schemer with her piercing brown eyes. "We know these women are what you men make them. You compel them to lead these wretched lives while you live off their earnings."

"Madam, you shut up. You talk too much." He turned on his slippered heel.

No amount of persuasion could produce the missing jewelry; but the rescued slave girl went off to gain, through her redirected life, treasures which neither rust nor thieves could touch. . . .

An older slave girl who had made her own escape was safely installed as a member of the Nine-Twenty family. But her owner, who lived in Palo Alto, a new town sprung up in the shadow of the recently established Leland Stanford Junior University, soon discovered where his property was hidden. One cold March day he appeared at the Sacramento Street Home accompanied by a burly constable holding in his hand a warrant for the arrest of Kum Quai on the charge of stealing jewelry. He showed Miss Cameron a "picture" of the girl he wanted, but unaccustomed as she then was to all the subtle tricks, new with each case, she said quite frankly:

"You have made a mistake. We have no such girl here."

"Let us see for ourselves," demanded the constable, producing his search warrant.

The brass gong was rung, lessons were stopped, sewing was dropped to the floor, and brooms were stood in corners, as the excited family quickly gathered in the large chapel room. This was always the custom when a search was to be made; but usually the guardians knew which girl was wanted and she was carefully hidden between a double folding-door or under rice sacks back of the basement gas meter.

This time, however, no one knew. Miss Cameron was quite sure the searchers were on the wrong track. With horror, then, she saw Kum Quai's face pale at the sight of her leering owner, and she was quite helpless to prevent the course of the law as the constable served the warrant on the terror-stricken girl. She pleaded with him with all her usual force; but he was there to do his duty and earn his fee. No silly woman could stop him. Miss Cameron dismissed the other weeping girls and reluctantly turned the key that opened the heavy bolted front door. The biting wind from the Bay swept up the narrow street, sending added shivers over the thinly clad little girl clinging to Lo Mo's hand.

"Come along, we must be off," demanded the impatient officer jerking her from her protector's arm. For one instant Miss Cameron stood hesitant. Then a voice spoke in her heart: "Go with her—she is yours." And, hatless and coatless, she ran after the retreating trio, followed by Yuen Qui, the interpreter, supplying needed outer wraps. All the way to Palo Alto she sought to calm the despairing girl, who shrank trembling from the rough constable and the triumphant Chinese owner.

Even when the cell doors of the shack they called a jail were locked on her charge, Lo Mo stayed beside her. Two boxes were all the bed provided, but sleep was not to come that night. About midnight voices were heard talking excitedly in the corridor. The jailer appeared to open the cell. Kum Quai's "friends" had arrived with bail. Lo Mo knew this trick well enough. Miss Culbertson had told her too many tales of girls thus bailed out who had completely dropped from sight, or who had been found months later in conditions unspeakably worse than those of their former servitude. She barricaded the door with a piece of scantling, but the bailiff took out his ax. When he had succeeded in battering a hole big enough for his arm, he reached through, knocked down the barricade, and grabbed the girl from Lo Mo.

The exulting Chinamen lifted their pretty into a waiting buggy. Lo Mo climbed in too. But rough hands pulled her out and threw her into the tar-weed beside the road. Scarcely sensing whether she was hurt or not, the undaunted Lo Mo fled to the heart of the village for help. The only friend she could rouse was Dr. Hall, a druggist on a corner near the Circle. He introduced her to the proprietor of Larkin's Hotel, who gave her a blanket and allowed her to rest on a sofa in the lobby for the few remaining hours of the night. Dr. Hall then telephoned the San Jose sheriff to send a searching party after the fleeing Chinese.

In the meantime the Palo Alto justice of the peace, returning from a ride on the county road, had met the escaping trio. They asked as a special favor that he hold the trial then and there; and so in an improvised road-side court, at two-thirty in the morning, the frightened girl, waiving jury and counsel, pleaded guilty to the charge against her. One of her escorts acted as interpreter, while the other paid the five-dollar fine imposed by the judge, and off they galloped.

Source: Wilson, Carol Green. *Chinatown Quest.* Stanford University, California: Board of Trustees of the Leland Stanford Junior University Press, 1931, pp. 1–2, 10–12, 16–17, 26–28.

55. Charles Shepherd, "The Story of Lee, Wong and Ah Jing," 1933

Charles Shepherd, originally from England, had been a Baptist missionary in China before he moved to San Francisco's Chinatown in 1919. There, he met Donaldina Cameron, superintendent of the Presbyterian Church's Occidental Mission Home for Girls; the Mission Home served as a refuge for Chinese women and girls who had been smuggled into the United States and sold into sexual slavery. Cameron told Shepherd about the plight of orphaned and homeless Chinese American boys, many whose mothers had been rescued from prostitution by Cameron's organization.

In 1923, Shepherd founded the Chung Mei Home for Chinese Boys in Berkeley, California. In 1934, he moved the Home to El Cerrito, just north of Berkeley. The Home closed in 1954; by then, more than 800 boys had lived there. Chinese American memories of the Chung Mei Home are very mixed. Some, including many former residents, remember it fondly. Others see it as a site of ostensibly benign yet fundamentally coercive assimilation, run by people who disdained Chinese culture and viewed their U.S.-born charges as not quite American. The following excerpt from Shepherd's booklet tells the stories of two of the children, Ah Jing and Wong Kwai, who lived in the Chung Mei Home. Shepherd's words reveal his complicated perspective on the boys' Chinese American culture and community and their future as upstanding Christian citizens.

THE STORY OF AH JING

This little fellow was the unhappy victim of inhuman treatment on the part of the woman with whom he lived, and by whom he had been purchased from his real parents on account of the extreme poverty of the latter. In spite of his diminutive stature Ah Jing had considerable spirit which rebelled against this cruel treatment and caused him to run away. For several nights he slept in parks and doorways and in the day time begged his food wherever he could until the police found him and brought him to the Home. His body was terribly scarred and bruised from the beatings he had received. Tearfully he told his story. "This woman is not my real mother," he said. "I would rather go back to China and be a 'cowherd' than stay with her." But there is no way to send Ah Jing back to China, and so, because of the unfitness of this woman to care for him, he stays in Chung Mei Home, and there has become one of the most happy and sunshiny members of the family—always willing to do whatever task is assigned him, and ever ready with a cheery word. He is strikingly intelligent, and is doing excellent work at school.

An Averted Kidnapping

The story of Wong Kwai is one that is difficult to believe by Americans who are not familiar with the workings of certain groups of Orientals. The phone rang in the office, and the writer, picking up the receiver, placed it to his ear. Over the wires there came the agitated voice of Ah Leen, a young Chinese girl in her teens. "My step-mother has just passed away," ran the story. "She is a widow, and since her husband's death has fallen into the clutches of a group of evil men. These men want to take possession of my little half-brother, Wong Kwai, who is just six years old; but I know that they are planning to take him away from here and I shall never see him again, for my step-mother whispered this to me before she died, and begged me to save Wong Kwai. I know what kind of men they are. They will raise him and train him to do the things that they do. Won't you come and get him and take him into the Home?"

"Where is your little brother now?" asked the writer. "I will come and get him right away."

"You do not need to come now," said the quiet voice over the wire. "According to Chinese custom they must permit him to attend his mother's funeral. They are planning to be at the graveside, and to take him away as soon as the ceremony is over. Please come then, for I shall be unable to do anything alone."

They were there, these men, four of them, and they stood dark of countenance and menacing at the back of the little group that gathered about the grave of this woman. One of them had previously argued with the half-sister that they were able to give the boy better care than she; but she had said nothing, for she knew that other plans were being made for him. Thus, when the ceremony was completed and one of these men stepped forward to take possession of Wong Kwai, Ah Leen grasped one of his little hands and her American friend grasped the other. They brushed aside the would-be abductors, and stepping quickly into a waiting car drove away. Wong Kwai was taken to the Juvenile Court and there made a ward of San Francisco County. A few hours later he was joyfully received by the family at Chung Mei.

What Chung Mei Does for These Boys

Numerous boys who have gotten off on the wrong foot, so to speak, have been taken into Chung Mei, helped to find themselves and taught to stand on their own feet and walk straight. To such boys Chung Mei Home means a new start in life, an opportunity to forget the past and begin all over again, a chance to make good. Associated with a group of virile, happy, peppy boys, he comes to see boy life at its best. He learns that there are older men and women who are really his friends and are willing to go out of their way to help make a man of himself. He comes into a healthy stimulating school atmosphere where teachers are kind and sympathetic, where the Oriental boy is never oppressed with the feeling of inferiority. He gets abundance of fresh air, exercise, play and hard work. He finds himself an integral part of an institution that keeps ever to the front of its purpose, namely, THE PROMOTION OF HABITS OF REVERENCE, OBEDIENCE, DISCIPLINE, COURTESY, SELF-RESPECT AND ALL THAT TENDS TOWARD TRUE CHRISTIAN MANLINESS. He lives in an atmosphere which is good but not goody-goody, religious but not abnormally pious. The Christian religion is not rammed down his throat, but ever exemplified before him in an endeavor to make it attractive and winning.

Source: Shepherd, Charles. *The Story of Lee, Wong and Ah Jing.* San Francisco Bay Cities Baptist Union, 1933?, pp. 2–4. The Bancroft Library, University of California, Berkeley. http://www.oac.cdlib.org/ark:/13030/hb409n99qs/?brand=oac4. Accessed May 2010.

56. Ruth Chinn, Interview by Stafford Lewis, 1938

Ruth Chinn was born in Seattle in the early 20th century and went to China to study at Ling Nan University in Canton. In 1938, she was interviewed by Stafford Lewis from the Federal Writers' Project, a New Deal Works Project Administration program. In her interview, Chinn talks about Chinese American boys who were sent to Canton for their college education. Her description about the cultural conflicts between Chinese American students and their Chinese professors reveals the levels of Americanization among the second generation, even for those who grew up in the ethnic neighborhoods of Chinatown. It also gives a picture of the upper-class Chinese American community, composed primarily of merchants and diplomats; they enjoyed privileges not granted to the majority of Chinese Americans who belonged to the laboring classes. Chief among these included the ability to move relatively freely between the United States and China.

It was summer in Canton, China and very hot. So the American Born Chinese boys from Seattle changed to white linen suits and tropical clothing such as is worn in India and other hot countries. They had been sent to Ling Nan University to complete their education in the Chinese language and history. These boys were from wealthy or well to do families, their ages ranging from 14 to 10 years. Chinese boys from all over the world go to this University.

Professor Wong especially, didn't like the Seattle boys because they were mischievous and played practical jokes. Besides their manners were bad, they were frank and outspoken, they ate too much and spent money they should have saved, for extra meals and picture shows.

The true Chinese boys Professor Wong held up as an example were quiet and mild. They sat down thankfully to their meals in the mess hall that was poorly made up of loose boards and bamboo thatching, and were willing to leave the table half-filled and hungry, without protest. The Seattle boys thought the food was stale and scantily portioned out. So after eating in the mess hall they would use their money to take a launch across the water to Canton. They would go to a hotel and get a good meal, of fresh and plentiful food.

Wing was the leader of a little group of three Seattle boys, and Wing liked to correct Professor Wong whenever his American-gained knowledge gave him a chance, making Professor Wong very angry and leading him to use his position of Professor in charge of Wing's dormitory to teach Wing and the other Seattle boys good manners and the value of money through strict discipline.

So Wing was no longer allowed to play his guitar with American harmony and sing American songs after 10 o'clock at night, when all lights had to [be] out and silence was compulsory. Professor Wing thought Chinese music that cannot be harmonized, much more seemly than the discordant noises Wing and his companions took such delight in. Then, to correct the boys of extravagance, he forced the Seattle boys to put all their money in the treasury—and whenever they asked for their own money, they would only receive a dollar.

This wasn't enough; it cost 20 [cents] to cross the water to Canton in a launch, 20 [cents] cents for a show and at least 60 [cents] for a meal. After 6 in the evening, the boys would have to hire a sampan to get back to the University and this cost much more than the motor launch, 60 or 80 cents.

The boys said, we pay for our education and should be able to lead our own lives, as we do in America. We must all work together to force Professor Wong to break away from his severe rules.

Then the Seattle boys would slip out of the dormitory and play their guitars and sing American songs under the Professor's window as he was trying to sleep. But this only made Wong more strict. He gave Wing and his friends much extra work on studies the boys thought were very dry, tying them down even more.

In desperation, while the Professor was out of the dormitory, the boys took all his white linen out of the closet and spilled ink all over it. Then they put the suits back with a note saying,

"Try and find out who did this."

Professor Wong went to bed without noticing his clothing—but the next morning none of his clothing was fit to wear.

Of course, Wong knew who had spoiled his clothing as the resentment of the Seattle boys against his rules was not hidden from him. And only the American Chinese boys would have the courage necessary to attempt such a destructive trick.

Professor Wong called Wing and his two best friends in his office and gave them the choice of either buying a complete new outfit of clothing for him or being expelled. The boys decided to be expelled as they were all anxious to return to Seattle where there was good food and they could lead their own lives.

Source: Ruth Chinn, interview by Stafford Lewis, 1938. Library of Congress, Manuscript Division, WPA Federal Writers' Project Collection.

57. Yee Bing Quai, Interrogation Files, 1938

In 1938, 15-year-old Yee Bing Quai immigrated to the United States from China, landing in the port of East Boston. As the Chinese Exclusion Act would not be repealed for another seven years, Yee needed to prove that he was the son of a U.S. citizen in order to be allowed to enter and remain in the country. Like thousands of other Chinese "paper sons," Yee produced fabricated identity papers and a detailed family "history" to convince the immigration officer of his story: A Chinese American man had traveled to China for a brief visit to get married and had fathered a son—Yee—who was now petitioning to join his father in the United States. In fact, Yee's "father" actually was his older brother, Yee Wee Thing, who had come to the United States in 1916 as a paper son himself.

Both Yee Bing Quai and Yee Wee Thing, along with a third man, Jew Gong Fook, were interrogated in the Boston Immigration and Nationalization Service district office. Inspector Charles E. Golding, looking for inconsistencies in their testimonies, asked hundreds of questions about Yee Bing Quai's village, upbringing, education, and family members, paying particular attention to the details about Yee's childhood house. In the following excerpt from Yee Bing Quai's and Yee Wee Thing's interviews, Yee changes his story to match his brother's.

The full transcripts of Yee Bing Quai's interrogation files have been made available by his son, Byron Yee (www.paperson.com). Byron Yee is a comedian and actor, whose solo show, Paper Son, incorporates the voices of his father and uncle into an exploration of immigration, cultural identity, and personal history.

APPLICANT presents as a means of identification affidavit executed by his alleged father, YEE WEE THING, at Boston, Mass., on January 18, 1938, before Katherine Flynn, Notary Public. To this affidavit are attached two photographs which the applicant identifies as those of himself and his alleged father, YEE WEE THING.

DESCRIPTION: Age, 15 years; height, 5' 5½", American shoes; Occupation, student; Marks: Scar, in hair, right side of neck; pit about three quarters of an inch above inner corner of right eyebrow; small scar about two inches above outer corner of right eyebrow; line scar right side of neck, about one-inch and ahalf below ear; group of pits, left side of jaw; other marks.

APPLICANT—duly sworn—testifies:—

Q. What are all your names?
A. YEE BING QUAI, given name; only name I have; I have never been married.

Q: What are your age, date and place of birth?
A. 15 years old; born CR 13-10-21 (Nov. 17, 1924) in LEN MEE Village, SND, China.
Q. Have you always livedin that village and are you now coming from there?
A. No, when I was 3 years old our family moved to HIN Village, HPD, China, and I am now coming from there. . .
Q. Before leaving China, did you apply at any American Consulate for an Immigration Visa?
A. No.
Q. Who paid your passage to the U.S.?
A. My father.
Q. To whom are you destined?
A. To my father, YEE WEE THING. He lives in New York. I don't know his address . . .

Q. When did your alleged father first come to the U.S.?
A. I do not know. He came before I was born. (See San Francisco file 24212/2-4).
Q. Has your alleged father made any trips to China since he first came to the U.S.?
A. I have never seen my father—my mother told me that he returned to the U.S. in CR 14. (San Francisco file 24212/2-4).
Q. If you have never seen your alleged father, how do you recognize the photograph attached to the affidavit which you present, as being that of your alleged father?
A. YEE MON TOY of the JEW THING NGIN Store, Bonham Strand, Hong Kong, gave me the affidavit when I went to Hong Kong on my way to the U.S.; and he told me that that was a picture of my father.
Q. Did you ever see any photograph of your alleged father prior to the time you saw the photograph attached to the affidavit?
A. Yes, there is a bust photograph of my father, dressed in American clothes, enclosed in a frame with a glass front, about 6x8 inches, which is hanging on the back wall of the center room of my house in HIN Village, HPD, China. That photograph of my father has been hanging there as long as I can remember. My mother told me that it was a picture of my father which he sent to her a long time ago. She did not say just when he sent her the picture . . .

Q. Describe HIN Village, HPD, China?
A. There are 4 dwelling houses on 4 rows; the village faces the south; the headis to the west . . . [Yee drew a map of the village, which was attached to his file.]
Q. Describe your house in HIN Village, HPD, China?
A. It is a five-room house built of cement; with a large and small door; large door faces the head; small door faces the tail; ithas red-tile floors throughout the house.
Q. Are there any windows or skylights in that house?
A. There are 2 windows, one in each bedroom facing the lane; each window has 2 glass shutters on theoutside; and 5 vertical and one cross bar on theinside. In

each bedroom there is a double skylight covered with glass, and in each kitchen there is a single skylight covered with glass . . .

Hearing resumed June 16, 1939 before:
Inspector Charles E. Golding .... Examining Officer
Clerk Marion T. Lovett .... Recorder
Yee Sone Wo .... Interpreter

WITNESS, alleged father, holds CI No. 24376, in the name of YEE WING THING, Age 10, showing admission as the son of a native (Parol) and issued at the Port of San Francisco, Calif., on November 22, 1916. Photograph attached bears some resemblance to holder. CI endorsed and returned.

WITNESS—duly sworn—testifies:—

Q. What are all your names?
A. YEE WING THING, given name; YEE LAI TOM, marriage name; no others.
Q. What is your present age, occupation, and address?
A. 33 years old; I am the manager of the Canton Restaurant, 143 Dyckman Street, New York City, and I live on the first floor at 184 Nagle Avenue, New York City . . .

Q. Do you know how many houses there are in HIN Village, HPN, China?
A. My wife wrote and told me that there were only 4 houses in 4 rows in HIN Village, HPD, China. . .
Q. Did your wife write you a description of your house in HIN Village, HPD, China?
A. My wife wrote and told me that the house was built of burnt brick. She did not say how many rooms were in it.
Q. When did your wife and tell you that?
A. After she moved into that house.
Q. Why should your wife write and tell you what the house was built of and not tell you how many rooms were in that same house?
A. I don't know why.
Q. Didn't youthink it rather peculiar that your wife wrote and told you what the house was built of and not tell you how many rooms were in that house?
A. I don't know why—she should have told me how manyrooms were in it.
Q. Isn't it a fact that your wife never wrote you any such letter at all telling you about any such house in HIN Village, HPD, China?
A. Yes, she wrote me a letter telling me that thehouse was built of burnt brick, and that the house is located on the 1st lot, 1st row from the west.
Q. Did your wife ever write to you telling you that any alterations had been made in the construction of that house in HIN Village?
A. No.
Q. Are houses in China built of anything else but burnt brick?
A. Yes, some houses are built of concrete; some houses are built of clay; and some of stone.
Q. Can you give any reason why the applicant and you should disagree as to what your house in HIN Village, HPD, China, is built of?
A. I don't know why—I can't explain it.

Q. If the applicant said his house in HIN Village HPD. China was built of anything else but burnt brick would he be wrong?
A. I never saw my house in HIN Village HPD. China, all I know is what my wife wrote and told me, maybe I was told wrong about what it was built of . . .

[Yee Bing Quai is brought back and requestioned about the house]

Q. You testified here the other day that your house in HIN Village, HPD, China was built out of cement. Is that correct?
A. Yes.
Q. What color is your house?
A. Kind of a light yellow color.
Q. Is that the general color of the cement houses in China?
A. Yes.
Q. Did you ever see any burnt-brick houses?
A. Yes.
Q. What color are burnt-brick houses?
A. Kind of a light green color.
Q. Are all the house in HIN Village the same color as your house?
A. No, the other houses are built of burnt brick.
Q. Your alleged father testified here today that your mother had written him a letter after your family moved to HIN Village, HPD, China, that her house, that is the house to which you moved with your mother, was built of burnt brick; how do you explain that?
A. Only the outside of my house is covered with cement; the inside of it is made of burnt brick.
Q. Why is the outside of your house covered with cement?
A. I don't [k]now.
Q. Are any of the other houses in HIN Village covered with cement?
A. No.
Q. Why did you say your house was built of cement if it only has a cement covering on the outside?
A. From the outside it looks like it was built of cement, so I just said it was built of cement, but it is built of burnt brick on the inside.
Q. Have you any further statements or any corrections you wish to make in any of your testimony?
A. No.
Q. Have you understood the interpreter?
A. Yes.

NOTE: The applicant and his alleged father were compared in the flesh, at this point, and it is the opinion of the Inspector and the recorder that there is a marked resemblance between the two . . .

2500/11904......21....June 16, 1938.

From the evidence adduced, I am of the opinion that the relationship claimed has been reasonably established. I, therefore, respectfully recommend that the applicant, YEE BING QUAI, be admitted to the United States, as the son of YEE WEE THING, a citizen thereof.

[signature] Marion T. Lovett, Clerk and Recorder
[signature] Charles E. Golding, U.S. Immigrant Inspector

Source: Yee Bing Quai immigration file, pp. 1, 2, 6, 9, 13, 14, 19, 20, 21. http://www.paperson.com/YeeBingQuai/. Accessed July 2010. Used with permission of Byron Yee.

58. Wing Luke, "Remarks," August 17, 1960

Wing Luke was the first Asian American elected official in the Pacific Northwest. Luke was born in a small town near Canton, China, on February 25, 1925. His family moved to Seattle in 1930 when Luke was only six years old. The eldest of six children, Luke excelled in school but like others joined the U.S. Army when World War II began. He served in Guam, Korea, New Guinea, New Britain, and the Philippines, where he received a Bronze Star. After leaving the Army, he finished his schooling and became a lawyer. In 1952, he was appointed Washington State's Assistant Attorney General for Civil Rights. He was elected to the Seattle City Council in 1962. Luke gave this speech to a group of Chinese Americans interested in creating a political action group. Though no group was formed, it shows the increasing political power of Asian Americans in Washington. Luke's speech also gives a glimpse into Asian American cultural identity during the Civil Rights Movement.

REMARKS

(Remarks made by Wing Luke at the initial meeting held August 17, 1960, printed as a basis for consideration in deciding on the question of whether or not we should organize as a "group", and if so, the nature, function and purpose of such a group.)

It would appear to any reasonably observant person of Chinese extraction that there is a growing number of Chinese-Americans in this community who have little or no economic, social, or cultural ties with "Chinatown", Chong Wah, Chinese Baptist Church, family and fraternal associations and the rest of the institutions and cultural matrix usually nebulously classified as the "Chinese community".

In former years language barriers, racial discrimination and the concentration of housing in and around the Chinatown area created a close knit community for whom the older institutions and customs formed an essential haven of refuge for a minority who felt like aliens in the general social environment. Changes, accelerated by the general social and economic upheavals of World War II, have since acted to loosen these ties. Among the many reasons for the feeling of lack of community are the following:

1. greatly decreased racial prejudice against Orientals since the end of World War II;

2. aided by improved economic standards, so that Chinese Americans are moving out of the older districts and purchasing homes in more far flung areas of the city;
3. a general advance in the level of education, an increasing number of white-collar business and professional men;
4. The coming of maturity of 3rd and 4th generation Chinese-Americans, many of whom have had little or no cultural experience with the older cultural matrix.

All of the above movements act to create greater gaps in communication between the older and the younger generation, and between members of the same generation. The general acceptance by the general community results in lessening vitality for the older institutions that were formerly relevant because they were meaningful and havens of refugee in an alien society.

As Chinese-Americans, we should of course remember that we are Americans first. There should be no question that as citizens of this country that we owe her our allegiance. The greater acceptance of Chinese-Americans is a salutary development. However, preserving the ties and institutions that are part of our cultural heritage is not inconsistent with integration and one's duty as a good American citizen. In fact, the essential vitality of the American life is that it is constantly enriched by heterogeneous cultures. This fact is recognized in the freedoms protected under the Bill of Rights.

Reasons that argue for a continuing community are these:

1. The disappearance of our rich cultural heritage would be a tragic loss
2. For the foreseeable future, racial and cultural identity as groups will still be present;
3. As immigration laws are relaxed in the future, other Chinese will migrate to this country and there needs to exist institutions that will help them bridge the social and educational gaps in becoming naturalized citizens.
4. Greater acceptance by the general community has partially resulted from the co-hesiveness of the Chinese community that has resulted in social stability, low incidence of delinquency and crime and a cultural identity that commanded respect, although admittedly begrudgingly in the past.

The Japanese-Americans in this community furnish a good standard to measure ourselves by. They have managed to greatly improve their economic and social status in recent years, yet have managed to maintain their cultural ties and institutions. Several groups in particular are especially vital and far outstrip comparable Chinese groups in most areas of achievement. The Japanese-American Citizens League is an active and influential social and political force; the Japan Society has made tremendous public relations advances for their people; the Japanese Buddhist Church, and the several other Japanese-American Churches boast a far greater percentage of participation and support than does the one Chinese-Baptist Church.

One needs to only look at the daily papers to note the great prestige that has resulted from such projects as the tea-house gift to Seattle, the Kobe-Seattle sister city project. . . .

Source: Luke, Wing. "Remarks." August 17, 1960. "A History Bursting with Telling: Asian Americans in Washington State: A Curriculum Project for the History of the Pacific Northwest in Washington State Schools," Matthew Klingle, developer. Courtesy Wing Luke Museum of the Asian Pacific American Experience.

59. John Dong, Interview by Elizabeth Calciano, 1967

John Dong (born Dong Hong Goon) was the last Chinese cook at Cowell Ranch in Santa Cruz, California, in the early 1900s. His father was born in San Francisco but traveled to China several times to find a wife and start a family. Dong was born in Canton, China. When he was in grade school, he joined his father in California, who was then the Cowell ranch cook; he later took over his father's position. Henry Cowell had opened the cattle ranch to supplement his lime kiln and logging empire. By the time Dong arrived, however, cement was replacing lime, and the ranch was going into decline.

In his interview with Elizabeth Calciano, from the University of California, Santa Cruz, Regional History Project, Dong, then 58 years old, primarily described his daily life as the ranch cook, talking about the logistics of preparing meals with no electricity and on a woodstove. This particular excerpt, however, illustrates the transnational aspects of 19th- and 20th-century Chinese immigration. With very few Chinese women in the United States and strict laws prohibiting interracial marriage, many Chinese American "bachelors" had wives and families thousands of miles away in China.

Calciano: Even though [your father] was born in San Francisco, did he feel China was his homeland?

Dong: Oh yes. He do. He do. He like China very much. You know, when he was young, grandpa took him back.

Calciano: Do you know how your grandfather happened to come over to this country?

Dong: No I don't. I never even see my grandfather.

Calciano: So your father worked for Cowell from 1912 or 1915 until 1928?

Dong: Yes. Till 1928. Then he take me back to China again.

Calciano: Was there anything that made your father decide to go back in 1928 rather than earlier or later?

Dong: Well, I think he feel he wants to retire. He was almost sixty, you know. So finally he think China was more better than the United States, I think.

Calciano: I see you've got Chinese newspapers here. I gather you talk and read it as your native language.

Dong: Oh yes. I'm a pretty good Chinese reader. I didn't go to school too much in the United States, so I don't understand too much, but I went long enough to learn some things.

Calciano: When you go back to China, do you feel right at home?

Dong: Yes. After I stay in China three or four years, I almost lose everything before I come back to the United States.

Calciano: Oh. You have to learn the English language again?

Dong: Yes, yes.

Calciano: Oh dear. When you were the cook for the Cowell's, you lived right in the cookhouse, didn't you?

Dong: Well, that's the only place to stay. You board in a little room next to the kitchen.

Calciano: Were you married at this time?

Dong:	Yes.
Calciano:	You were married, but you had to live up there?
Dong:	Yes. But my wife is not here though. I didn't bring my wife over.
Calciano:	Oh, she was still in China?
Dong:	Yes, she was still in China. She just came over about three years ago.
Calciano:	Oh my goodness.
Dong:	Well, one thing, I hate to take her over here because my mother is still living, see. So we had to have a nurse with her. My mother just passed away about a couple of years ago.
Calciano:	So you made several trips back and forth to China?
Dong:	Yes. A couple or three times.
Calciano:	Were both your sons born in China, too?
Dong:	Yes. My boys were born in China.
Calciano:	I was wondering, since your wife and family just came over from China three years ago, how did they avoid getting caught in Red China?
Dong:	No, it was not that reason they stayed. My mother was still in China so it was all or nothing.

Source: Excerpt from "John Dong, The Cowell Ranch Cookhouse." Interview conducted by Elizabeth Spedding Calciano, 1967. Reprinted with permission from the Regional History Project of the University Library at the University of California, Santa Cruz. http://library.ucsc.edu/reg-hist/.

60. *Rosenberg v. Yee Chien Woo,* 1971

During World War II, China fought on the side of the Allied Forces with the United States. Americans saw the Chinese as heroic patriots, defending themselves against brutal Japanese imperialism. After the war, however, the situation changed dramatically. The decades-long Chinese Civil War, fought intermittently between the American-supported Kuomintang and the Soviet-supported Communist Party of China, came to an end in 1949, when Mao Tse-tung proclaimed the creation of the People's Republic of China. Suddenly, China was no longer a U.S. ally—instead, it had become one of the world's largest Communist nations. Chinese and American interference in the Korean War (1950–1953) ensured the continued mutual hostility, as well as prompted the United States to take China into consideration in its multivaried efforts to contain and combat Communism.

In 1952, the United States passed the Immigration and Nationality Act, which, among other things, provided for refugees fleeing persecution in Communist countries. This provision was meant primarily for Eastern Europeans fleeing the Union of Soviet Socialist Republics (USSR). However, the following year, Congress passed the Refugee Relief Act, extending refugee status to non-Europeans and thus enabling Chinese refugees fleeing Communism to claim asylum in the United States.

Yee Chien Woo was a Chinese businessman who fled to Hong Kong (then still under British control) from Shanghai in 1953, after the government confiscated his business and financial holdings. After several years in Hong Kong, he moved to the United States, where he eventually tried to claim refugee status. The Immigration and Nationality Service, under George Rosenberg, the district director, rejected his claim and initiated deportation proceedings for Woo and his family. Woo appealed, and, in 1971, the U.S. Supreme Court upheld his claim that Hong Kong was not his permanent residence, and that he faced further persecution by the Chinese Communist government if he were forced to return to his homeland. The following is an excerpt from the majority opinion of the court, delivered by Justice Hugo Black.

MR. JUSTICE BLACK delivered the opinion of the Court.

Respondent, Yee Chien Woo, is a native of mainland China, a Communist country, who fled that country in 1953 and sought refuge in Hong Kong. He lived in Hong Kong until 1959 when he came to the United States as a visitor to sell merchandise through a concession at a trade fair in Portland, Oregon. After a short stay, he returned to Hong Kong only to come back to the United States in 1960 to participate in the San Diego Fair and International Trade Mart to promote his Hong Kong business. Thereafter he remained in the United States although he continued to maintain his clothing business in Hong Kong until 1965. In 1965 respondent's wife and son obtained temporary visitor's permits and joined him in this country. By 1966 all three had overstayed their permits and were no longer authorized to remain in this country. After the Immigration and Naturalization Service began deportation proceedings, Yee Chien Woo applied for an immigrant visa claiming a "preference" as an alien who had fled a Communist country fearing persecution as defined in 203 (a) (7) of the Immigration and Nationality Act of 1952. . . .

The District Director of the Immigration and Naturalization Service denied respondent's application because "the applicant's presence in the United States . . . was not and is not now a physical presence which was a consequence of his flight in search of refuge from the Chinese mainland." On appeal within the Immigration and Naturalization Service, the decision of the District Director was affirmed by the Regional Commissioner on the ground that "Congress did not intend that an alien, though formerly a refugee, who had established roots or acquired a residence in a country other than the one from which he fled would again be considered a refugee for the purpose of gaining entry into and or subsequently acquiring status as a resident in this, the third country."

Respondent then sought review in the United States District Court for the Southern District of California which reversed the District Director's determination. That court, without ever deciding whether resettlement would have barred respondent's claim, found as a matter of fact that he had never firmly resettled in Hong Kong. The Immigration and Naturalization Service appealed to the United States Court of Appeals for the Ninth Circuit. That court affirmed the District Court because in its view whether Yee Chien Woo was "firmly resettled" in Hong Kong was "irrelevant" to consideration of his application for an immigration quota. It stated:

"Whether appellee was firmly resettled in Hong Kong is not, then, relevant. What is relevant is that he is not a national of Hong Kong (or the United Kingdom); that he is a national of no country but Communist China and as a refugee from that country remains stateless."

The Court of Appeals for the Second Circuit in a case decided after the Ninth Circuit decision below faced the issue of the relevancy of resettlement and expressly declined to follow the Ninth Circuit interpretation of the statute. We granted certiorari in this case to resolve the conflict. [A writ of certiorari is when the Supreme Court agrees hear an appeal from a lower court.]

Since 1947 the United States has had a congressionally enacted immigration and naturalization policy which granted immigration preferences to "displaced persons," "refugees," or persons who fled certain areas of the world because of "persecution or fear of persecution on account of race, religion, or political opinion." Although the language through which Congress has implemented this policy since 1947 has changed slightly from time to time, the basic policy has remained constant—to provide a haven for homeless refugees and to fulfill American responsibilities in connection with the International Refugee Organization of the United Nations. This policy is currently embodied in the "Seventh Preference" of 203 (a) of the Immigration and Nationality Act of 1952, 8 U.S.C. 1153 (a) (1964 ed., Supp. V), which provides in pertinent part:

"(a) Aliens who are subject to the numerical limitations specified in section 201 (a) shall be allotted visas or their conditional entry authorized, as the case may be, as follows . . . :

"(7) [A]liens who satisfy an Immigration and Naturalization Service officer at an examination in any non-Communist or non-Communist-dominated country, (A) that (i) because of persecution or fear of persecution on account of race, religion, or political opinion they have fled (I) from any Communist or Communist-dominated country or area, . . . and (ii) are unable or unwilling to return to such country or area on account of race, religion, or political opinion, and (iii) are not nationals of the countries or areas in which their application for conditional entry is made. . . ."

The Ninth Circuit supported its conclusion that the "firmly resettled" concept was irrelevant under 203 (a) (7) upon two bases. First, the court noted that the "firmly resettled" language was first introduced in the Displaced Persons Act of 1948, 62 Stat. 1009, and was then expressly stated in the Refugee Relief Act of 1953, 67 Stat. 400, both of which are predecessors of the present legislation. However, when the Refugee Relief Act of 1953 was extended in 1957, the "firmly resettled" language was dropped in favor of a formula defining an eligible refugee as "any alien who, because of persecution or fear of persecution on account of race, religion, or political opinion has fled or shall flee" from certain areas. 71 Stat. 643. The 1957 Act was then followed by the Fair Share Refugee Act of 1960, 74 Stat. 504, which defined "refugee" as one "not a national of the area in which the application is made, and (3) [who] is within the mandate of the United Nations High Commissioner for Refugees." Finally, the present legislation was added to the Immigration and Nationality Act in 1965. From the 1957 abandonment of the words "firmly resettled" the Court of Appeals determined that Congress had purposely rejected "resettlement" as a test for eligibility for refugee status.

Second, the Ninth Circuit gave particular significance to the statutory requirement that refugees "are not nationals of the countries or areas in which their application for conditional entry is made." Thus, in the court's view, Congress intended to substitute the "not nationals" requirement for the not "firmly resettled" requirement. For substantially the reasons stated by the Second Circuit in *Shen v. Esperdy*, 428 F.2d 293 (1970), we find no congressional intent to depart from the established concept of "firm resettlement" and we do not give the "not nationals" requirement of 203 (a) (7) (A) (iii) as broad a construction as did the court below.

While Congress did not carry the words "firmly resettled" over into the 1957, 1960, and 1965 Acts from the earlier legislation, Congress did introduce a new requirement into the 1957 Act—the requirement of "flight." The 1957 Act, as well as the present law, speaks of persons who have "fled" to avoid persecution. Both the terms "firmly resettled" and "fled" are closely related to the central theme of all 23 years of refugee legislation—the creation of a haven for the world's homeless people. This theme is clearly underlined by the very titles of the Acts over the years from the Displaced Persons Act in 1948 through the Refugee Relief Act and the Fair Share Refugee Act of 1960. Respondent's reliance on the Fair Share Refugee Act of 1960 to show that Congress abandoned the "firmly resettled" concept is particularly misplaced because Congress envisioned that legislation not only as the means through which this country would fulfill its obligations to refugees, but also as an incentive to other nations to do likewise. Far from encouraging resettled refugees to leave one secure haven for another, the Act established United States quotas as a percentage—25%—of the refugees absorbed by all other cooperating nations. The Fair Share Refugee Act, like its successor and predecessors, was enacted to help alleviate the suffering of homeless persons and the political instability associated with their plight. It was never intended to open the United States to refugees who had found shelter in another nation and had begun to build new lives. Nor could Congress have intended to make refugees in flight from persecution compete with all of the world's resettled refugees for the 10,200 entries and permits afforded each year under 203 (a) (7). Such an interpretation would subvert the lofty goals embodied in the whole pattern of our refugee legislation.

In short, we hold that the "resettlement" concept is not irrelevant. It is one of the factors which the Immigration and Naturalization Service must take into account to determine whether a refugee seeks asylum in this country as a consequence of his flight to avoid persecution. The District Director applied the correct legal standard when he determined that 203 (a) (7) requires that "physical presence in the United States [be] a consequence of an alien's flight in search of refuge," and further that "the physical presence must be one which is reasonably proximate to the flight and not one following a flight remote in point of time or interrupted by intervening residence in a third country reasonably constituting a termination of the original flight in search of refuge."

Finally, we hold that the requirement of 203 (a) (7) (A) (iii) that refugees not be "nationals of the countries or areas in which their application for conditional entry is made" is not a substitute for the "resettlement" concept. In the first place that section is not even applicable to respondent. He was applying for an immigrant visa, not a conditional entry permit to which part (A) (iii) of subsection 7 is expressly limited. He had already been granted entry to the United States as a business visitor. Second, even if the provision were applicable, the country "in which" respondent's application was made was the United States and he was certainly not a national of this country. Had he been a national he of course would have been entitled to remain here. Section 203 (a) (7) (A) (iii) applies only to applications for conditional entry into this country made to Immigration and Naturalization officers authorized to accept such applications at points outside the United States.

Because it was under the erroneous impression that resettlement was irrelevant to refugee status under 203 (a) (7), the Court of Appeals failed to review the District Court's finding that respondent had never firmly resettled in Hong Kong. The District Director is, of course, entitled to review of that determination under the legal test set out in this opinion and the appropriate standards for judicial review. Consequently, the judgment below is reversed and the case is remanded to the Ninth Circuit for further proceedings not inconsistent with this opinion.

Reversed and remanded.

Source: *Rosenberg v. Yee Chien Woo*, 402 U.S. 49 (1971). http://supreme.justia.com/us/402/49/case.html#58. Accessed November 2010.

61. Esther Don Tang, "Memories of Mother and Father," 1995

In 1906, Don Wah, a Chinese American born in San Francisco and working in a restaurant in Tucson, Arizona, journeyed to Hong Kong to get married. His wife, Fok Yut Ngan, originally was from Fujian Province in southwestern China. Don brought her back to Tucson, where they lived for the rest of their lives, raising their 10 children and running a chain of grocery stores. In 1995, Esther Don Tang, the Dons' third child, gave an interview describing some of the struggles the couple faced as they tried to make a life in the United States.

My father came from California, uncomfortable with the political climate and prejudices there. He worked as a cook for the Southern Pacific railroads as they laid the tracks across the southern part of Arizona.

In 1906, he went to China to marry my mother from Fukein [sic; Fukien, or Fujian]. She used to recount stories of her life. Her father, who was a wealthy gold smith and manufacturer of gun powder and fire crackers, had 8 wives. He housed them in separate houses and there was a common kitchen and patio. The complex had a ten foot wall with double gates to keep bandits out. Beyond the wall there was an orchard.

Mother's parents felt that their baby daughter from the first family was going to the Gold Mountain. Little did they know she had to learn to cook and worked in the bakery and store my father owned. At 3 in the morning she would carry me, papoose style, to the store and wrap bread. Dad would deliver his bread to stores in a horse and buggy. On his first delivery his horse spooked and the buggy turned over, spilling the bread all over Simpson and Convent streets. The neighbors scrambled into the street for free loaves.

Customers would buy their groceries and my mother would mark the amounts they owed in a *cartera* (notebook) and return the cartera to the customer. On pay day, everyone would return to the store to pay their bill and receive *pelon*, a gift of fruit or candy. That was really trust!

My father was always proud that he made the deciding vote as to where the Drachman Elementary School should be located. He was at the barbershop getting his queue cut off when some men pulled him from the barber chair to come and break the tie vote.

My mother put $2000 earnest money on a house in the Belmont subdivision on Country Club Road. The salesman did not tell her that originally the subdivision had been restricted to keep Orientals from living there. On revisiting the house, "No Chinks Wanted" was scribbled on the wall.

My mother and father gave the house up, and lost $1000 of earnest money, which was a great deal of money in those days. Subsequently they bought two lots from Abe Chanin, a writer for the Arizona Daily Star, and built a beautiful house in that neighborhood (Water and Vine Streets).

Source: Tang, Esther Don. "Memories of Mother and Father." 1995; *The Promise of Gold Mountain: Tucson's Chinese Heritage*, 1995. http://parentseyes.arizona.edu/promise/donwah.html. Used with permission of David Tang and the website The Promise of Gold Mountain: Tucson's Chinese Heritage.

62. Fred Pang, "Asian-Pacific Americans: Microcosm of Greater National Mix," 1997

Asian Americans have served in the U.S. military for over a century. There are records of "Manilamen" fighting with Andrew Jackson in the War of 1812. Chinese American men joined both the Union and Confederate armies during the Civil War. In 1901, President McKinley signed an executive order allowing Filipinos to join the U.S. Navy, and even after Philippine independence in 1946, a series of treaties ensured that Filipinos could continue to be recruited by the Navy. During World War II, Chinese Americans and Filipino Americans enlisted in large numbers, motivated in large part by anger at Japanese atrocities in China and the Philippines. Maggie Gee and Hazel Ying Lee flew with the Women Airforce Service Pilots (the WASPs), the first and only Chinese American women in the organization. Korean Americans were considered enemy aliens, as Japan was currently occupying Korea; nevertheless, roughly 100 Koreans managed to enlist in the Army. Japanese Americans, despite the indignity of internment, volunteered for service in large numbers; they served in the segregated 100th Battalion and 442nd Regiment and provided translation services in the Military Intelligence Service. Immigrant and American-born Asian American women and men have fought in every war since.

Fred Pang grew up in Honolulu, Hawai'i. He joined the Air Force, where he served for 27 years, and he was appointed assistant secretary of defense for force management policy in 1994. In 1997, Pang spoke at the Asian-Pacific American Heritage Month Commemoration. In the following excerpt, Pang talks about notable Asian Americans in the military.

The United States, it has often been noted, is a nation composed almost entirely of descendants of immigrants. We call ourselves Americans, but at the same time, we are proud of our roots—proud of where our parents, our grandparents and our great grandparents came from. We honor our heritage in many public and private ways—parades and festivals from St. Patrick's Day to the Chinese New Year; family recipes from sauerkraut to kimchee; and gatherings from the Knights of Columbus to grandma's Tuesday night mah-jongg circle. And even though our association with the old country fades a bit as the generations progress, I daresay there aren't many of us here that do not keep some of the old traditions of our ethnic backgrounds. And in many respects, the many nationalities which are collectively called "Asian Americans" are a microcosm segment of our greater national mix. Of course, like African Americans, we look a little different from the Pilgrims, so our ethnicity is necessarily more present in our lives than, say, Irish or Greek Americans. But even that will become less and less important as the color of America changes in the next century—when, collectively, what are now called minorities approach becoming a majority of the population.

How diverse are we as Americans? Well, quite frankly, I don't know of any ethnic group in the world that is not represented in our country. The fact is that there is no other country as diverse as we are.

About 3½ percent of that diverse population—almost 9 million people—trace their roots to Asia and the Pacific Islands. And according to the "National Population Projection," the Census Bureau expects Asian-Pacific Americans to be the fastest growing segment of our population. They predict that by the turn of the century, the Asian-Pacific-American population will expand to over 12 million, double its current size by the year 2010, triple by the year 2020 and increase to more than five times its current size, to 41 million, by the year 2050.

So if we are one piece of America's polyglot puzzle, we are certainly becoming a bigger piece. And our diversity within that diversity continues to grow. It may seem like a mouthful to say Asian-Pacific-American Heritage Month, but try saying Chinese-Japanese-Korean-Filipino-Vietnamese-Thai-Cambodian-Laotian-Hmong-Indian-Pakistani-Bangladeshi-Afghan-Polynesian-Melanesian-American Heritage Month. Now that is a very big mouthful, and those were just examples—I didn't even include all of us.

Is there harmony in our diversity? I think that the answer to that question for us, as Americans, is a qualified "yes." It has been over 130 years since we really had it out among ourselves, which is quite exceptional by world standards. And since then, our society has only gotten more complex and more diverse. Of course, it would be wrong to say we don't have problems that arise from our diversity, and at times these problems can get ugly. But in general, the principles of law and order and tolerance and freedom have won out in the end. We do not see the kind of extreme ethnic violence that has occurred, tragically, in the formerly communist parts of Europe or in Central Africa, for instance.

As a nation, our harmony in diversity is not an absolute, but it is something that we work toward and are getting better at achieving. I think that is because we share one thing in common. Whether our ancestors endured hardship to escape from the tyranny and poverty of a distant land or from the tyranny and poverty of slavery, they became American citizens to seek a better life for themselves and their families. This common goal ties us together in a relatively harmonious community that is unique in the world.

For Asian Americans, the story began in the mid-1800s, when Asian immigrant laborers were hired for the gold mines and railroad construction in the West and to work sugar and pineapple plantations in Hawai'i. Despite discriminatory laws, which restricted immigration and imposed economic inequities, our forefathers and mothers overcame the fear of a "yellow peril." They tenaciously fought for the rights to which they were entitled and proved to other Americans their loyalty as citizens of this nation.

We who have inherited the fruits of their labors, who have more easily joined into American society must be mindful and appreciative of the struggle that has brought us as a group to where we are today.

As part of this event, I would like to highlight the public service of Asian Americans, and I think it is fitting to start with the highest service any citizen can offer to his or her country—service in wartime. We should honor again the bravery of the famed 100th Battalion of the 442nd Regimental Combat Team, composed almost entirely of Japanese Americans, which became the most decorated unit in our country's military history.

These brave soldiers, who answered the call of their country in war, rose from the ashes of suspicion and fear—many from behind barbed wire in the internment camps—to fight with extraordinary valor in seven major campaigns during World War II. In less than two years, the soldiers of the 442nd received among other awards and citations a . . . Medal of Honor; 52 Distinguished Service Crosses; one Distinguished Service Medal; 560 Silver Stars plus 28 oak leaf clusters; 22 Legions of Merit; 15 Soldiers Medals; 4,000 Bronze Stars with 1,200 oak leaf clusters; 9,486 Purple Hearts for wounds sustained in battle; seven presidential unit citations; two meritorious unit service plaques; 36 Army commendations; 87 division commendations; 18 decorations from allied nations; and a special plaque of appreciation from their fellow soldiers in the "lost" Texas battalion, which the 442nd shed blood to liberate.

As President Truman pinned the final presidential unit citation on the colors of the 442nd, he remarked: "I can't tell you how much I appreciate the privilege of being able to show you just how much the United States thinks of what you have done—you fought not only the enemy but you fought prejudice—and you won. . . ."

While war is ugly and tragic, there is no question that many individuals display outstanding courage and valor in battle. The most supreme acts of heroism are recognized by award of the Congressional Medal of Honor. As part of the commemoration of Asian-Pacific-[American] Heritage Month, we in the Department of Defense pay special tribute to those of Asian-Pacific heritage who received the Medal of Honor. I'd like to read that honored list to you and ask you to join with me in paying humble recognition to their deeds:

In World War I:

- Pvt. Jose B. Nisperos, 34th Company, Philippine Scouts; and
- Fireman Second Class Telesforo Trinidad, U.S. Navy, USS San Diego.

In World War II:

- Pfc. Sadao S. Munemori, U.S. Army, Company A, 100th Infantry Battalion, 442 Regimental Combat Team; and
- Sgt. Jose Calugas, U.S. Army, Battery B, 88th Field Artillery, Philippine Scouts.

In Korea:

- Cpl. Hiroshi H. Miyamura, U.S. Army, Company H, 7th Infantry Regiment, 3rd Infantry Division;
- Pfc. Herbert K. Pililaau, U.S. Army, Company C, 23rd Infantry Regiment, 2nd Infantry Division; and,
- Sgt. Leroy A. Mendonca, U.S. Army, Company B, 7th Infantry Regiment, 3rd Infantry Division.

In Vietnam:

- Sgt. 1st Class Rodney J.T. Yano, U.S. Army Air Cavalry Troop, 11th Armored Cavalry Regiment; and,
- Cpl. Terry T. Kawamura, U.S. Army, 173rd Engineers Company, 173rd Airborne Brigade.

These individuals, through their gallantry, have secured a special place in our history and in our Asian-Pacific-American Heritage. . . .

The Asian-American contribution to public and private life is dynamic and growing. We are bound together by a common desire to improve our country. And it is a cause in which we must enlist our fellow citizens, especially the generation just now starting their careers.

This next generation will come of age as the expansion of the Asian-American population hits the national consciousness. The much-heralded Pacific century will be upon us, and American interdependence with the established and emerging economies of Asia will deepen. So this new generation of Asian Americans must be prepared to do their part to help lead this nation down the path of tolerance—to help the country capitalize on the strengths inherent in diversity. . . .

As a young man growing up in Hawai'i, I remember working as a summer employee in a pineapple cannery. During a break, I overheard a couple of regulars talking about their hopes and aspirations for their children. In the course of their conversation, they talked about how it would be if they never left the "old country" to seek a better life.

It was clear to me that their future and those of their children would have been much bleaker. As they concluded their conversation, I heard one of them say, "We lucky we come to America." So I want to conclude my talk today by echoing the simple conclusion of that conversation 45 years ago: Whatever our prefix—African, European, Hispanic, native or Asian—we are all lucky to be Americans.

God bless those who have gone before us, and God bless this wonderful country.

Source: Pang, Fred. "Asian-Pacific Americans: Microcosm of Greater National Mix." Prepared remarks of Fred Pang, assistant secretary of defense for force management policy, Asian-Pacific

American Heritage Month Commemoration, Asian/Pacific-American Council of Georgia, Atlanta, Saturday, May 17, 1997. *Defense Issues* vol. 12, no. 28. http://www.defense.gov/speeches/speech.aspx?speechid=726. Accessed August 2010.

63. Sifu Cheung Shu Pui, "Chinatown without Lion Dancers Would Be a Community Filled with Regret," 2001

Kung fu, strongly influenced by Buddhism and Taoism, has developed over thousands of years into many different schools and styles. The relationship between student and *sifu*, or "master," is of utmost importance in kung fu. *Sifu* is a term of respect; it takes on a more intimate, familial meaning when used by a student for his or her teacher. Sifu Cheung Shu Pui was trained in Hung Gar Kung Fu, a style originating in a 17th-century Shaolin temple in southern China. Cheung, born and raised in Hong Kong, entered the school as a young adult. In the early 1970s, he immigrated to the United States to teach traditional Chinese martial arts. In 1977, Cheung opened his own academy in Upper Darby, a Philadelphia suburb, where he teaches Chinese language, calligraphy, painting, and chess as well as kung fu.

In the following article, Cheung tells his immigration story and explains why these traditional folk arts play vital roles in preserving cultural identity in the Chinese American community. Even more important, to Cheung, these all are essential components of a holistic program meant to develop moral character. He traces his emphasis on the morality of kung fu back to his own *sifu*, drawing out the personal and spiritual connections between Hong Kong and the United States.

When I was young, life was very hard and difficult. My father worked in the Kaitek International Airport in Hong Kong as a fire department officer. I had five brothers and two younger sisters. In those days, the government had some dormitories for the workers inside Kaitek Airport, and we lived there in the government housing.

I studied at Chung Saan Middle School. The students were all very poor. At that time, my family didn't have any money. I studied and completed elementary school and graduated from Form One (which is the equivalent of about seventh grade in the United States) and after that, I didn't have formal schooling. I went out to work and started working at Kingwah Hotel where I opened doors and carried suitcases and things like that. I was about sixteen years old....

[Cheung began attending a kung fu school on Hong Kong island when he was 18 years old. Initially, he was taught by the older brothers at the school.]

After I had studied for four years, my Sifu started a National Martial Arts Special Class to teach the more attentive and obedient students. That class consisted of a few of my older brothers, a few of my younger brothers, and myself. Sifu began to teach us especially. There were 11 or 12 of us who were the heart of the school. We had to help the master, listen to what he said, follow him and study him, and we couldn't really oppose anything.

At that time, there were a lot of people who came to study for a short time, and then left. They didn't have the patience to stick it out and learn everything. To learn kung fu, you definitely need patience. That's the first requirement. And after patience you need to have time for yourself. After you determine you have the time, you need to practice hard—you can't fear difficulty or pain. Those are the important characteristics for studying kung fu. . . .

After the special class started, Sifu taught kung fu directly to me. And at that time, I took a lot of time to study *tit da*, Chinese herbal medicine that deals with bruises, sprains and contusions. Sifu gave me some recipes for herbal medicine. The prescriptions are complicated and consist of a lengthy list of ingredients. He gave the recipes to me and taught me how to cook the medicine. My Sifu didn't really teach. He told me to go stand aside and observe how to cook and wrap the medicine. He made us follow him and watch him. We lived together and slept at the school, so we could study everything with him all the time. At that time, we talked a lot about how to make the herbal medicine, how to prepare and organize the ingredients, and how to examine patients and take care of their wounds through performing surgery. I also helped my Sifu clean up the kung fu school. . . .

Every Sifu has his own kung fu values. Twenty or 30 years ago, very few of them had values. The vast majority of Sifus were not moral; a lot of them were corrupt, they were criminals. Many of the Sifus were really bad people. They really did know kung fu. But at the time the government was really messed up, and there was the KMT and the Communist party and the society was so chaotic. So lots of the Sifus just used kung fu for crime.

When I wanted to study kung fu, I went to Ho Lap Tin of course because I could see how he was and how he taught his students. If you studied for half a year anywhere, that's enough time to see if the Sifu is a good person. I discovered that my Sifu was a good person. He wouldn't teach anyone gambling. I trusted his conduct. . . .

. . . This other Sifu came from Hawai'i to Hong Kong and was looking for a few Sifus to come to America to teach kung fu. At that time in America, Bruce Lee was just becoming popular, and all these Americans wanted to learn kung fu. So this Sifu decided he would find partners in different cities who wanted to try and start a school. He came to Hong Kong and found my Sifu and asked him whether or not he had any students who would like to go to the United States to teach kung fu. My Sifu asked all the older brothers, but no one really wanted to go. They had careers that paid more than teaching kung fu. So they didn't want to leave their wives and children to go to America and teach kung fu. But it was right at that time that I didn't get the promotion, and so I thought I would go to Philadelphia for just one year.

After I came to America, it was so pitiful. I was alone and I didn't have any friends. I didn't speak English. I was extremely lonely. It was also winter, so it felt even more depressing. At that time, every place had a holiday vacation, and it was Sunday, and everywhere was closed. It wasn't anything like Hong Kong, where everything is so lively. So I would sit at home and wouldn't know what I should do. I couldn't drive and I didn't know how to go anywhere. It was really depressing.

After a year, I started to have a little disagreement with that boss because he kept telling me that I had to teach people how to fight. These American guys liked free fighting. Sparring. But I wanted to teach kung fu—fist forms, two-man forms and weapon forms. And I wanted to teach Westerners the heart—the real authentic Chinese kung fu. I didn't come here to teach Americans how to fight. So I told the boss, "You invited me here to teach kung fu. I cannot teach people to fight." So the boss was really unhappy.

This guy didn't know anything about kung fu. He didn't understand Chinese values or morality. He wasn't a Chinese guy, he was an American. I mean, the guy who came to Hong Kong to recruit us was a Sifu who taught in Hawai'i. But these two guys didn't really talk to each other. He just helped this American find people. So I was teaching people real kung fu, and he wanted to teach people to fight. I told him it was very dangerous to teach people to fight. If I hurt somebody, that would be bad. And if people hurt me, that would also be bad. I told him, "Why don't you buy some lions, some drums, some weapons, and let me teach." And he said, "Why should I buy that stuff? It's noisy." So I sat there and thought, "This is really wrong."

I had very few students. And I was teaching kung fu on the first floor. He lived on the second floor. He would smoke cigarettes, smoke cigars, drink beer. The whole school was dirty, messed up. I said, "What are you trying to do here? I am trying to teach kung fu and trying to teach people to be healthy and strong, to do good things for their bodies. You're always smoking cigars and cigarettes and drinking beer, the air is dirty." He and his friends would talk and laugh loudly. It made me really unhappy. He said, "This isn't a problem. It doesn't affect you." I said, "Of course it affects me. I am trying to teach kung fu. You're always making this unnecessary and annoying noise. How can I teach kung fu?"

And then there was another problem—the biggest problem. He was supposed to pay me 600 dollars every month. I told him to help me and send this 600 directly to my mom. One year later, I found out he hadn't sent her the money. Not even for one month. He cheated me. He was so hard-hearted. He had cheated me, and I didn't know. He personally went to the bank and told me he was sending the money. I believed him because he was my boss. But I found out, and then we fought even more.

After a year, my contract was done. And our relationship kept getting worse and worse. So he telephoned the immigration department, and the INS came and locked me up. They locked me up and took me to the headquarters on Race Street, and I was in jail for a night. At that time I was so depressed, I cried. The next day, I had to go to court. But I had a few students—Corney, Bob and Rick—these guys immediately went to try and help me to get immigration papers. The judge saw that I had so many students willing to help me. He gave me three months to find a job, and if I could find a job, he said I could apply for a green card. We thought Chinatown probably would like to offer me a job, so we all cooperated and supported each other and went down to Chinatown and asked the associations if there might be a possibility that they might hire me to teach kung fu.

Originally I wanted to teach at the CBA (Chinese Benevolent Association). But the CBA said they didn't have funding and couldn't hire me. They said, "Why don't you go to the On Leong Association. Maybe they'll hire you." So On Leong Association hired me to teach the children of their members. I started teaching there and taught there for about three years—1975 through 1977. During that time, almost all my students were Chinese. There were three, four, or five kids who were Americans. They were all the senior students. They followed me to On Leong Association and studied with all the other students there. By 1977, September, I started my own school in Upper Darby....

When I started teaching, Chinatown was small and there weren't many people there. There were only six or seven restaurants, and there were three or four grocery stores. At that time, when I taught students, I had to speak English 100 percent of the time. There were some language difficulties. After a while, the language difficulties lessened because my relationship with my students was a little more open. We played together and went out to eat together. We'd go out and see movies. We'd go to New York Chinatown and watch Chinese movies about Hung Hei Kuen and Fong Sai Yuk. I wasn't so stubborn or strict.

In the future, there will be fewer and fewer people studying kung fu. The future for Chinese martial arts doesn't look great. Children now like to play basketball and soccer. To tell them to do horse stance or to study fist forms—there are very, very few kids who will have this kind of talent. And making lion heads is almost a lost art in Hong Kong. The people who make lion heads and drums are all in China, in Canton. There are very few in Hong Kong. Fewer and fewer people will do it....

My school is very racially mixed. There are black, white, Latino and Asian students. They all get along. I try and teach some of the deeper things about Chinese culture to my students, but it is very hard. Some things about culture cannot be taught in a class, they have to be lived. So they can only understand some of the surface things, not the really deep things. And in the old days, the schools were supported by the community, and students didn't learn just for their individual enjoyment. They learned because the tradition is important for the community. But in the US, everything is about time and money. I have had to run my school like a business, and students come to learn more for themselves than for the connection they might have to Chinatown.

I have always had trouble maintaining Chinese students at the school. The lives of Chinese immigrants in Chinatown are very hard. They work 16 or 18 hours a day in low wage jobs. They have no time for their children. The children too have a hard life. Many of them have to work inside the house and outside as well as go to school. I have always wanted to have more Chinese students, but the pressures of paying my rent and keeping up the school mean I have had to charge tuition, and even when I charge very low tuition they have difficulty paying. Through my classes at Asian Americans United, through the Folklore Project, I now have a small group of Chinese students to carry on the traditions in Chinatown....

People who live in Chinatown or who own businesses in Chinatown are all from China, Taiwan or Hong Kong. After a while, they gradually forget their traditions. Even if they don't forget, there's no way they can celebrate every single holiday. But dragon dance, lion dance and kung fu are traditional Chinese folk arts. If there are none of these folk arts, people will feel disappointed or even unlucky. If the people from China never saw this kind of folk art in Chinatown, they would feel disappointment and carry regrets that such necessary folk arts are not continued here. There would be a sense of loss—the most meaningful folk art form disappears and is not passed on.

Chinatown without the lion dancers or dragon dancers would be a community filled with people with regrets. People have sacrificed so much to come here. People have lost so much—their culture, their language. Without the dances, it would be the final loss. Everything would be gone. Secondly, if they have children, the children won't know anything. They will completely forget everything. What is Chinese kung fu? What is a dragon dance or a lion dance? They've never seen it before. And for the adults, even if they saw it before in their childhood, they may not have a clear memory of what these traditional arts look like.

Source: Sifu Cheung Shu Pui. "Chinatown without Lion Dancers Would Be a Community Filled with Regret." Recorded, translated, and edited by Deborah Wei. *Works in Progress: Magazine of the Philadelphia Folklore Project*, vol. 14, no. 1/2, Summer 2001, pp. 18–23, 32. http://www.folkloreproject.org/folkarts/resources/pubs/wip/summer01.pdf. Accessed September 2009. Used with the permission of the Philadelphia Folklore Project.

64. Ted Tsukiyama, "Eulogy for Hung Wai Ching," 2002

In the aftermath of the bombing of Pearl Harbor in 1941, the Japanese American community faced racism and discrimination not only from mainstream America, but also from other Asian American groups as well. Historical antipathies brought over from Asia ran strong. Chinese Americans, whose memories of Japanese atrocities in Nanjing remained raw, joined the U.S. Army in the thousands, hoping to help defend China against further Japanese aggression. People wore buttons saying "I'm Chinese" (i.e., "I'm not Japanese"), and some families destroyed all products that were made in Japan. Korean American immigrants angrily protested their enemy alien status, doubly insulting because it resulted from Japan's 30-year-long brutal colonization of Korea. The Korean American National Association instructed its members to buy war bonds, volunteer, and wear badges identifying themselves as Korean (i.e., not Japanese). Some Korean nationalists even agitated for Japanese American internment, arguing that they were engaged in secret anti-American intelligence operations. Although other Asian American groups had experienced decades of legal, political, and cultural prejudice from the U.S. mainstream, a combination of fear and anger meant that there was little sense of pan-ethnic solidarity with Japanese Americans during World War II.

However, particularly in Hawai'i, certain Asian American individuals did stand up for Japanese Americans, protesting their treatment and working to reintegrate them into society. Hung Wai Ching was one such man. Born in Honolulu in 1905, Ching was the son of immigrants from Guangdong, China. He graduated from the University of Hawai'i and attended Yale Divinity School; he then moved back to Hawai'i and was working for the YMCA when the war broke out. Ching, deeply disapproved of the way Japanese Americans were being treated. He organized the Nisei Reserve Officers' Training Corps (ROTC) members (who had been dismissed due to their classification as enemy aliens) into what became known as the Varsity Victory Volunteers. In lieu of military training, the Varisty Victory Volunteers performed manual labor at Schofield Barracks. For the rest of the war, Ching traveled the country advocating on behalf of Japanese American soldiers.

Ted Tsukiyama was a Varsity Victory Volunteer, a veteran of the 442nd Regiment, and a member of the Military Intelligence Service. In his 2002 eulogy for Ching, Tsukiyama remembers his friend's tireless efforts to fight war hysteria, racism, and discrimination, both during and after the war.

Most of the 442nd boys don't know or remember this, but in early April 1943 when the U.S.S. Lurline pulled away from Pier 10 in Honolulu Harbor with 2,452 volunteers for the future 442nd Regimental Combat Team, one of the few persons permitted on the pier to see us off was Hung Wai Ching. When the Lurline pulled into San Francisco six days later, there was Hung Wai Ching again on the pier to welcome our arrival. After an arduous rail trip across the country, when our troop train pulled into the railroad station at Camp Shelby, there to greet us again was Hung Wai Ching! Just who was this person "Hung Wai Ching," and what is his connection to the 442nd?

Hung Wai Ching was born in 1905 in Honolulu, one of six children born of Chinese immigrant parents. At an early age his father was killed in an accident leaving his mother to bring up her six children under circumstances of extreme financial hardship, forcing Hung Wai to sell papers and do odd jobs to help his way through school. He lived in the predominantly immigrant neighborhood around the Nuuanu YMCA where he grew up in fellowship and tolerance with peers of Japanese and other races.

He attended Royal School and graduated in 1924 with the famous "McKinley Class of '24" which included Hiram Fong, Chian Ho, Masaji Marumoto and Elsie Ting to whom he was married for 60 years. He graduated from the University of Hawai'i (UH) in 1928 with a degree in civil engineering, earned a Bachelor of Divinity degree from Union Theological Seminary, and graduated from Yale Divinity School in 1932 with a Master of Divinity degree. From 1928 through 1938 he worked at the Nuuanu YMCA as a Boy's Secretary, and served as Secretary of the Atherton YMCA from 1938 through 1941.

In December 1940, one year before the Pearl Harbor attack, Hung Wai was invited to attend a meeting with the FBI, Army and Navy Intelligence and community leaders present to form the Council on Interracial Unity to prepare the people of Hawai'i against the shock of imminent war and to preserve the harmonious race relations among Hawai'i's multi-racial population. Many years later he found out his name had been suggested by Charles R. Hemenway who was his mentor during his University days. When the Japanese bombs fell on Pearl Harbor on December 7, 1941, the Military Governor appointed a Morale Division comprised of Charles Loomis, Shigeo Yoshida and Hung Wai Ching to put into effect the plans prepared by the Council of Interracial Unity. The Morale Division served a key role as a bridge between the Military Government and the civilian community, in particular with the Emergency Service Committee comprised of leaders of the local Japanese American community.

Hung Wai Ching reported to Col. Kendall J. Fielder of Army Intelligence charged with the internal security of Hawai'i and also reported to the FBI Chief

Agent Robert L. Shivers. There were any number of Japanese in Hawai'i, who, unbeknownst to them, were either not detained or were released from internment because of Hung Wai's intervention on their behalf. In the first few weeks of the war, the Military Governor assigned Col. Fielder a quota of Japanese to be picked up each day, but upon consultation with Hung Wai, Fielder refused to make indiscriminate quota arrests, even at the risk of court martial and his military career.

Through his Morale Division job Hung Wai met some very high and influential people, including President Roosevelt and Mrs. Roosevelt but he never used these contacts to benefit himself. During a 1943 visit to the White House, Hung Wai used the occasion to brief the President on the wartime situation in Hawai'i, how well Sen. Emmons and the FBI were handling the "Japanese situation" and assuring him that there was no necessity for a mass evacuation of Japanese from Hawai'i.

But while Japan continued to wage its fierce [war] in the Pacific, all persons of Japanese ancestry in Hawai'i remained "on the spot" and their loyalty to America suspect. Hung Wai had no question about the loyalty of Japanese he had known all his life, but he knew that the general American public would never be convinced of the loyalty of Japanese Americans until they could shed their 4-C (enemy alien) status, get back into military service, and to fight and even die for their country. The greatest contribution made by Hung Wai Ching washis outspoken affirmation of the loyalty of Japanese-Americans and the direct part he played in the long struggle of Japanese-Americans to regain that opportunity to bear arms and to prove their ultimate loyalty to America.

In January 1942 when all soldiers of Japanese ancestry were discharged from the Hawai'i Territorial Guard, comprised of UH ROTC students, Hung Wai Ching met, counseled and persuaded these confused, bitter and disillusioned Nisei dischargees to offer themselves to the Military Governor for war time service as a non-combat labor battalion. The petition of 170 Nisei volunteers was accepted by the Military Governor who assigned this group to the 34 Combat Engineers at Schofield Barracks as a labor and construction corps, popularly to become known as the "Varsity Victory Volunteers." As "Father of the VVVs" Hung Wai showed off the VVVs at every opportunity to military, intelligence and governmental officials. In late December 1942 Hung Wai was asked to escort Assistant Secretary of War John J. McCloy around military installations on Oahu and made certain that McCloy witnessed the VVV volunteers at work in the field. Was it mere coincidence that only a few weeks later in January 1942, the War Department announced its decision to form a volunteer all Nisei combat team. This is exactly what the VVV had been working for, so its members disbanded so that they could volunteer for the newly conceived 442nd.

Hung Wai then adopted the 442nd in place of the disbanded VVV and thereafter dedicated himself to seeing that the Nisei got every fair opportunity to prove their loyalty. With the Military Governor's blessing, the Emergency Service Committee sponsored Hung Wai's assignment to monitor the Hawai'i volunteers' movement to Camp Shelby and flew him up to the mainland. While the Lurline sailed to San Francisco, Hung Wai met with the infamous General DeWitt to urge the latter that "These are American soldiers, not prisoners of war" and not to insult and humiliate the Nisei by placing armed guards along the embarkation route. He also asked DeWitt to grant the boys an overnight pass to San Francisco Chinatown for a chop suey dinner. DeWitt thought this man was crazy! During the week the boys entrained overland to Camp Shelby, Hung Wai flew to Washington D.C. to persuade Secretary McCloy to change the training site of the 442nd outside of the South, but to no avail, but he was authorized to go to Camp Shelby to observe the initial organization of the 442nd.

Prior to the arrival of the 442nd volunteers the town of Hattiesburg, Mississippi was in an uproar over the news that "a Jap regiment would be trained at Shelby," generating "Japs Not Wanted" editorials and "Go home Japs" signs in town. Hung Wai met with the editor of The Hattiesburg American and the Hattiesburg chief of police to explain that "these boys were all Americans and that they had all volunteered to serve their country." Thereafter, the "Go home Japs" editorials and signs disappeared. Hung Wai convinced the brass that the 442nd should have its own USO, which should be located in the "white side of town" and "not across the tracks." Hung Wai raised hell about the Southern Baptist minister as regimental chaplain and insisted that the boys should have "their own kind." Soon thereafter, Hiro Higuchi and Chicken Yamada showed up at Shelby as the new chaplains for the 442nd.

When Hung Wai returned to Hawai'i, he went everywhere speaking to families, plantation camps, civic and business organizations about the Hawai'i volunteers and the progress of their training at Camp Shelby. His constant message was: when the boys come back home, treat them like full American citizens, save their jobs for them, let them finish school, and to "give them a square chance." And after the war was over and the boys came home, Hung Wai worked ceaselessly and tirelessly for their orderly rehabilitation and return to civilian life. Through the Veterans Memorial Scholarship Fund which he headed, many returning veterans got scholarship aid to complete their education and vocational training to supplement the inadequate finding from the G.I. bill. He was responsible for placing Nisei war veterans into jobs with the Big Five and other previously inaccessible and unavailable employment opportunities in Hawai'i.

No one ever asked or requested Hung Wai Ching to render all this support and assistance to the Nisei, nor was he ever adequately compensated for the same, for which he never asked. He did not have to speak up nor stand up to defend and affirm the loyalty of the Japanese in Hawai'i, when most others chose to remain silent, but he did so willingly and courageously, in the face of peer criticism, racial animosity and wartime anxiety directed against the local Japanese.

The history of wartime Hawai'i relating to the story of the fair, calm and reasoned treatment of the Japanese in Hawai'i, how the tragedy of mass evacuation and internment was avoided in Hawai'i, and how Americans of Japanese ancestry were restored the right to bear arms to fight for their country and given the opportunity to prove their loyalty to America, cannot be written or told without mentioning the service and contributions of Hung Wai Ching in that historical process. And this is exactly why Hung Wai Ching was one of the very first to be elected and accepted as an Honorary Member of the 442nd Veterans Club.

Source: Tsukiyama, Ted. "Eulogy for Hung Wai Ching." 2002. Used with permission of Ted Tsukiyama.

65. Maggie Gee, Interview by Leah McGarrigle, Robin Li, and Kathryn Stine, 2003

In 1944, three years after the United States entered World War II, Maggie Gee joined the Women Airforce Service Pilots (WASPs)—one of only two Chinese American women to achieve this status. Gee was the granddaughter of immigrants from Guangzhou, China; they moved to Monterey, California, in the mid-19th century to escape the depredations of the Taiping Rebellion. Gee's mother, born in Monterey, lost her U.S. citizenship when she married her Hong Kong–born husband. According to the 1922 Cable Act, a woman marrying an alien ineligible for citizenship—which, in effect, applied only to Asians—forfeited her own as well. Wanting to raise their children outside of Chinatown, Gee's parents moved the family to Berkeley, where she was born in 1923. Her father died soon after the 1929 stock market crash, leaving her mother to raise six children on her own.

When World War II began, Gee's mother took a job working as a burner in the Richmond shipyards. Gee followed in her mother's footsteps, leaving the University of California, Berkeley to train as a draftsman in the engineering department at Mare Island Naval Shipyard, north of San Francisco. She worked at Mare Island for a year, earning enough money along the way to pay for flying lessons. Once she completed 50 hours of flight time, Gee applied for the WASP program. The WASPs were civilian pilots who ferried military planes to different airbases across the United States and flew bombers on mock dogfights to train (male) pilots heading overseas. Although they were flying under military command, the WASPs were classified as civilians and were offered no military benefits. Out of 25,000 applicants, only 1,900 were accepted. Two were Native American, and two were Chinese American (including Gee); the rest were Caucasian. A children's book based on her life was published in 2009, Marissa Moss's *Sky High: The True Story of Maggie Gee*.

Leah McGarrigle, Robin Li, and Kathryn Stine, from the University of California, Berkeley's Rosie the Riveter World War II American Homefront Oral History Project, interviewed Maggie Gee on several different occasions in April and May 2003. Gee talked about the Chinese American communities in Monterey and San Francisco, her diverse neighborhood in Berkeley, the impact of World War II on Chinese Americans, her year flying with the WASPs, and the ways in which her political philosophy was shaped by her experiences with discrimination. In the following excerpts, Gee reflects on Chinese Americans' responses to Pearl Harbor, and on their conflicted relationships with their Japanese American neighbors. She then talks about her time as a WASP.

April 29, 2003

Li: How did Pearl Harbor affect Chinese Americans in particular, in terms of their treatment?

Gee: America's always had a love affair with China. Why it's had, there are various reasons, but I always felt that particularly the missionaries who went to China, because there's no religion in China, really, they converted all these Chinese to be Christians. But I don't know whether that's the real reason but I think that had a lot to do with it. I think that the Chinese here became more proud of themselves, because they were Chinese and it was the Japanese that were our enemies. You let people know that you were Chinese. I wish I had whatever I wore at that particular time; I don't know if they're around, saying "I'm Chinese." I don't see whether you had Chinese American. I don't think there was that expression, Chinese American. Just Chinese. I mean, they must have been around, a dime a dozen, like little Mao red books that you probably can't find anymore. So we wore them. We were proud.

Stine: Did you wear those throughout the war?

Gee: Oh, I didn't wear them throughout the war, but around here if you went over to San Francisco on the Bridge you wore them, but it was obvious after a while because all of the Japanese were moved out, then.

Stine: I remember being very struck last time—we didn't get it on tape, but you had talked about how in your house you had thrown and broken things made in Japan. I wonder if you could talk about that a little bit.

Gee: Yes. I mean, it's so ridiculous, though. There were a lot of things in this country that were made in Japan. Not a lot of things, but a lot of china-type things. One thing I remember about Japanese goods, they were poor quality. They do such fine quality things, but whatever they imported here, a lot of it was children's toys and little dishes and things. The workmanship, in fact, I will show you something I have that is Japanese that is a plate that is just beautiful handwork, but the quality of porcelain or whatever they used was just so poor. So the idea of taking everything and breaking it that was Japanese was ridiculous, though. There was just a lot of junk that we had, bottom line. We had no money; these were the very ordinary, just common things that you would buy, dishes. That's the one thing I remember, dishes.

Li: Was everyone doing this in their homes? Was there an announcement on the radio?

Gee: How did people start doing this? I'm sure a lot of it, among the Chinese, was just word-of-mouth. Just break all these things; throw 'em away, and I think people did. There was so much—do you know how the dislikes are? Here, I'm speaking among my Japanese friends, part-Japanese friends. [laughs] There was really so much dislike of the Japanese, from the Chinese. Not the people you knew, because I lived in a town where there were as many Japanese as Chinese, and we all went to school together. We were friends. I guess you didn't think of them as being Japanese, though. Japan was the invasion of China and Manchuria, them coming in. The military was so cruel to the Chinese. You didn't see it in the newspaper necessarily in this country, but since everyone had relatives in China that they felt it very personally. So one of the worst things you could do, that I could remember, [was] my sister dating a young Japanese schoolmate. I remember someone said, it's better that she dates a black man than this Japanese young person. But it was really frowned down upon. It's interesting; it's really stuck in my mind in a sense, though.

	There are so many marriages now between people of Chinese ancestry and Japanese ancestry, and I think oh, that couldn't have happened with my generation. There aren't that many in my generation. I can't think of anyone...
Stine:	How did you seek out the opportunity to get involved with the armed forces and flying? How did that happen, that transition from Mare Island to flying? How did you make that choice?
Gee:	There were three women, three girls, and we were looking for something else to do that was joining one of the services, but we were too young. I don't know whether I was eighteen or nineteen at that particular time. I was too young. I was almost nineteen years old by then. I think that also was by chance in a way, too. But I went to learn to fly on my own, because I had enough money to buy the flying time. I went up to Minden, Nevada to learn to fly. The recruiters for the WASPs at that particular time were coming through Reno, Nevada, so at that time I got interviewed. I passed all the examinations and qualifications, and I was accepted. There were twenty-five thousand women that applied, and I felt very fortunate. About two or three thousand of us were accepted, and then half of us washed out of training. I didn't wash out of training, I was lucky to finish...
McGarrigle:	How were your duties defined, the women's duties?
Gee:	The initial duties, why the organization was started—that was for the women at the very beginning—was part of the Air Transport Command. It was to get a plane from here to there... We were pilots towing targets, doing mock gunnery missions, delivering planes, instructing, and test pilots. Also, testing planes out. So there was a variety of type of things that had to be done. It really gave you an opportunity to fly. I think the women who were with the Air Transport Command flew everything. Those were the very early ladies. Those were the ladies that really had lots of flying time, commercial. A lot of them had commercial pilot's licenses. So they flew every type of plane. Some of them were never checked out on them, though. Some of the stories that they tell are really quite exciting. They were asked to take this plane, never seen it before, from here to there, and they could do it. I admire them. So we have our hierarchy. We have the ladies who were very early and then as time went along, we became more service pilots. Instructing, and also flying mock gunnery missions. What is a mock gunnery mission? A mock gunnery mission is—I'll give you a phrase there—towing targets, so gunners could have practice. A mock gunnery mission is as if you're flying over Germany, a bunch of large planes, whether B-17s or -24s, flying in formation, going over to bomb whatever it is in Germany. These missions would have pursuits or fighter planes from the opposite side, really simple flying. Germans, making passes, trying to crash these planes. The gunners would try to shoot 'em down. So this was practice for the gunners in these big planes...

May 20, 2003

[After being accepted into the Women Airforce Service Pilots, Gee went to Sweetwater, Texas, for flight training. She then flew around to different airbases in the Southeast.]

Gee: . . . The Air Transport Command, when I graduated was no longer taking women, but the first group of women that did graduate, they went into the Air Transport Command. The idea of the organization was they picked up the planes at the factory, and the factories really were on the West Coast, and they flew 'em to the East Coast, all kinds of planes. All of the military planes, whether they were checked out on them, or not. So everyone had great adventures, great, great adventures. Then after you get the plane to the destination, then you got to find your way back to the base. Some of them partly by bus, hopping rides and trains and things. There were no commercial planes or anything like that to take you home. So that was part of the adventure of those days. For me, I was stationed at Nellis Airbase Field [in Nevada]. I did a bit of cross-country while in training, which was really nice. So I did get to see some of the Southeast, which I had never seen before, Atlanta, Georgia; Stuttgart, Arkansas, Greenville, Mississippi; all those places. So many of our airbases were in the South. It was nice. I had not seen that part of the world, and it's different. These small towns are very different than they are out here, at that time. I had no problems in these towns. If I were black, it would have been a different story. We had no black women in the WASPs. There were qualified black women, except Jacqueline Cochran told the women that she could not take them, because it was hard enough just being a woman in the service, but if you're black in the South, they'd have to have separate quarters for them. It just couldn't be done. It really was unfortunate, but in a sense, in those days it had to be that way. There were black women who were pilots at that time, with commercial licenses. Well, I think there were three. Not very many, though, but there were some. Some of them had applied. Two had applied, I think, and she turned them down. . .

McGarrigle: Did you see segregation in the parts of the South where you were?

Gee: In the little town that I was in, there were Mexicans, I think, but not too many. It was such a small town. It's a larger town now, because they found oil there after the war, but in that particular town it wasn't obvious. It's interesting; I'm sure that if you've been to the South, the Caucasians in the South are really very, very nice and warm people. They're inclined to be very kind, more so than in big cities. They spend a little time with you, as long as you're not black, I'm sure. So that's the one thing I remembered about the South. I didn't have any trouble. My brother, when he was traveling through the South, since he's dark like I am, a little darker, so he had to stay at all the black places. The black Y, because you look a little bit like you're a Mexican, and I guess the Mexicans weren't able to stay in public places where the Caucasians were. There aren't very many Asians, but I think that's where they put them.

McGarrigle: You and I have talked in the past about the difference for minority men, how being a minority male was different at the time we're talking about, then being a minority woman.

Gee: I even think that during World War II that was true. I just gave the example of my brother. I have found that it was much easier as a woman to mix with all groups. I guess that much is true today, too. You see with

	the African-American women, they can move ahead, where it's difficult for the male African- American. It was that way at that time with the Asians, too. So the reason why, I really don't know, but women aren't a threat to society as much as a male is, an economic threat or a sexual threat, I guess in a way. That's the feeling of a lot of white Americans...
McGarrigle:	And you lost women in your group, also. [Thirty-eight women were killed flying with the WASPs.]
Gee:	Yes. They were lost in various kinds of accidents. There was another Chinese woman who was quite well known—she's getting to be better known now, who was killed. Her name was Hazel Ying Lee. She was very early in the service. She was killed in an accident. She came in for a landing and someone landed on top of her. They were in Fargo, North Dakota and there was a big storm there, so lots and lots of planes were at this particular airport. They were trying to get them out very quickly, and there was just a lot of confusion. So women were killed different ways. Some were killed during the training, and some were lost. Some of them ran into other planes. There were thirty-eight that were killed...
McGarrigle:	Did the women who you were flying with want to fly the same missions as the men, or were they relieved not to have the same status?
Gee:	This is 1940, though. You have to remember we were so lucky that we were able to fly that we didn't even feel that we wanted to do the same things that men did. Just to have the ability to fly... We all felt we were very fortunate because we could do what we were doing.

Source: Rosie the Riveter World War II American Homefront Oral History Project: An Oral History with Maggie Gee conducted by Leah McGarrigle, Robin Li, and Kathryn Stine, 2003, pp. 52–54, 68, 74–75, 80–81, 88–89, 91, 93. Regional Oral History Office. The Bancroft Library, University of California, Berkeley, 2007.

66. Shuyuan Li, "Walking on Solid Ground," 2003

Generations of Shuyuan Li's family members, on both her mother's and father's sides, have performed with the Beijing Opera. Li herself began training when she was a child, and at age 12, she joined her father's company. In 1962, they were sent to Tibet to perform in China's remote border areas, and the next year, at the behest of an opera-loving Communist Party official, the troupe moved again to Inner Mongolia. They performed there for over a decade, and although they were classified as counterrevolutionaries, Li and her family escaped much of the persecution that other artists and intellectuals endured during the Chinese Cultural Revolution. After the Revolution, Li moved back to central China and performed with the Nanjing Beijing Opera Company until she retired. She then immigrated to the United States, where she founded the Philadelphia Chinese Opera Society.

In her interview with Debbie Wei of the Philadelphia Folklore Project, Li talks about the Cultural Revolution's impact on Beijing Opera and the future of this art form both in China and in the United States. Early in her interview, Li says, "To learn opera, you have to be able to endure hardship, to 'eat bitterness.' You must be diligent, work hard, and have endurance." She questions whether the new generations of Chinese Americans will practice this discipline.

When you learn Beijing Opera, you learn how to "walk on solid ground." You don't take shortcuts. You're down to earth. As a person you need to do things step by step—one step makes one footprint. You cannot just always think of taking short cuts or finding an easy way. Art is a real thing. It takes work and commitment.

To learn opera, you have to be able to endure hardship, to "eat bitterness." You must be diligent, work hard, and have endurance. It's not like you just finish going to class and that's it! You have to continue to work, study, and practice. You have to have self-discipline. A teacher can teach you, but if you want to become a successful performer, success depends on your self-motivation.

So this applies to real life. Especially for raising children. You cannot let them take short cuts. The easy way is not the right way. It's like building a foundation. If your foundation isn't any good, you cannot make a good building. And if you don't have a foundation in opera, there are a very limited number of things you can do when you perform.

In the Beijing opera community, my family is considered to be "Li Yuan Shi Jia," opera artists going back many generations, descended from performers of the Ming Dynasty. Many, many, members of my family continue in opera, in many different places.

On my mother's side, my grandfather and my grandmother and my aunts were all Beijing opera performers. One uncle taught in an opera school in Taiwan. Another was a famous television host. On my father's side four generations are all Beijing opera performers. They are also considered Li Yuan Shi Jia.

My father was a very famous Beijing opera artist. He used to have his own school, and he invited many teachers there. In his lifetime, he taught over 500 students. Senior students in the school changed their acting name to Ming. New students changed their middle name to Chun. Anyone who studied with my father could be identified as his student by their stage names. After the students graduated, they formed a performing arts troupe called Ming Chun Shi. (My mother also taught, but she didn't have many students. All of her students were women because they were studying the female roles.)

Since we were little, we were influenced by opera. My father's students all came to my house to study. So I saw how they trained. I watched how my uncle trained his students. One of the most famous Beijing Opera performers, Du Jin Fang, was one of my uncle's students. I always stood on the side and watched. Later on, he also taught me. Sometimes, I followed my parents to their performances. You can see, we trained from the time we were very little. You just live in that kind of environment.

When I was little, I didn't want to study opera. I wanted to be a doctor. But because of the environment in my family, sometimes they needed my help to perform small roles. One time they needed a little girl for a special role. So I went to perform and I went on the stage and I got on the train to go here and there to perform, and I felt it was a lot of fun. Just because of that, I slowly started to learn Beijing Opera. But my character is such that once I start learning something,

I want to do my best. Also, my family is one of the best in Beijing opera, so I felt like I needed to study.

My parents were very busy and had to perform all the time, so they never had time to teach me directly. Also, in the beginning, I studied only the very basic skills, so my parents didn't really need to teach me. A university professor would not teach a kindergartner! My father hired a martial arts teacher to teach me, but he always came to observe and to make sure that the teacher was teaching me correctly. My father would critique what I did. My mother did the same thing. She hired teachers for me and observed on the side, making sure I was taught correctly. My teachers worked with me on different things. I had physical training: how to stretch my legs, kick, use weapons—all the basic skills. Another teacher came to the house to train me in singing, to train my voice. Another teacher worked on my voice tone. I also trained my voice by following the sound of the jinghu, called the Chinese fiddle, a main instrument in opera. All of this training was after school.

There are four aspects to studying Beijing Opera: singing, recitation of monologues, acting and movement, and martial arts. This is different from a musical or a play or a dance performance. In a dance, you mainly just dance. In a play, you mainly just talk. But in Beijing Opera, you need to know all those things. When I was young, I had to undergo basic training: stretching, kicking, tumbling, and work with martial arts weapons like staffs and swords. You need to learn how to walk, move your hands, use your eyes, hold your body, and how to put all those things together. After you have the foundation, you find a teacher who can teach you how to act.

After I turned twelve, I started formal training. I joined a troupe and started to tour and perform. I used to get up at six o'clock and start by doing voice exercises. If you wanted to do better, you just got up earlier! Other students got up at seven o'clock but I got up at six. And I trained by myself. After the voice training, I did physical training until noon.

During the time I was in the troupe, we didn't have a breakfast hour. You studied voice training, then you did physical training, and then you had lunch. You had no breakfast. Nothing to eat or drink the whole morning. During the training, you weren't allowed to go to the bathroom. This was a way to train yourself. Let's say, you need to perform for two or three hours. You can't just stop and go to the bathroom in the middle! So that was how they trained us. Now, I still remember that time because inside the school there were too many students studying. So my teachers asked me to go out to the courtyard to train. Even if it was snowing really heavily, the teacher would clear a path in the snow to an area for me to go and exercise.

At the time I was learning, teachers weren't really beating students. But my father's generation got beaten all the time. My teachers were very strict. They didn't hit, but they pushed us and handled us very roughly. My parents didn't really care how strict the teachers were. They just would tell me to go and practice. Students always respected their teachers, one hundred percent, all the time. Whatever the teacher said, the students had to do it. The word "Sifu" (master) doesn't really mean just "teacher." "Si" means teacher, and "fu" means father. Sifu is really like a parent. Whatever sifu says, you listen. If sifu says you're wrong, you don't talk back.

When the teacher taught, you stood up and listened. You weren't even allowed to sit down. You had to be very, very, respectful to your teacher. The good thing about this kind of teaching is that you learn the importance of respecting your elders. Even now, there are some sifus who are older and I still respect them so much. You always keep that sifu and student relationship. My father, when he was very old and very famous, also had a teacher. Whenever my father went out to perform, when he came back, he always brought a present and went to visit his sifu. Whenever they took pictures, he always put his sifu in the center of the picture. What he did also set an example for me. I do the same thing to the senior performers and teachers. I respect them. . . .

Once I joined the opera company when I was twelve, I became a professional. I was performing on stage after that. In 1962, I was fifteen and we went to Tibet. The opera troupes in Beijing were asked to support the remote border areas because there were no Beijing Opera troupes there. At that time, the Dalai Lama had just left Tibet. Whoever was sent to Tibet had to be politically checked out and have a clear background. My father was considered a counter-revolutionary because he was a Beijing Opera artist. But because my father was such a high level performer, many high-ranking people in the government wanted to see him, so they cleared him and we were sent to Tibet for nineteen months.

Wu Lan Fu, a vice-chair of the Communist Party, Inner Mongolia, really liked my father's performances and he ordered us all to come from Tibet to Inner Mongolia in 1963. My whole family—the whole clan, the whole opera troupe of over 80 people—we all went, including musicians, performers, costume makers, and make-up artists. We stayed in Inner Mongolia for sixteen or seventeen years. We weren't allowed to return to Beijing. We were told that Inner Mongolia needed us. After 1978 and the end of the Cultural Revolution we were finally allowed to leave. But more than half of our troupe is still in Inner Mongolia. My uncle and my older brother all stayed there, and they passed away there.

Life was not as good in Inner Mongolia as it was in Beijing, but it was still okay. There wasn't much flour or rice. The food wasn't really what we were used to. If my family had been in Beijing during the Cultural Revolution, it would have been worse. We would have been in serious trouble. During the Cultural Revolution, we were considered counter-revolutionary forces, capable of strong influence because of our artistic skill and background. During the Cultural Revolution, our traditional costumes were all confiscated. When we knew they were going to take the costumes anyway, we cut a lot of them up and just used them for different things, to wrap things, and things like that.

We lived in the provincial capital in Inner Mongolia, but we always were sent out to remote areas, grasslands, to perform. These shows were a form of support for the local rural people and for the soldiers at the border. I play female heroines. My specialty is the role of White Snake, and Mu Gui Yin, a heroine. My mother also performed similar kinds of roles. But in Inner Mongolia during the Cultural Revolution, we only performed the Eight Model Plays. These are also part of Beijing Opera tradition, but they were written then, in the 1960s. The Eight Model Plays were repeated over and over again for over ten years. Everybody still knows how to sing those plays. Even little kids. Everywhere you went, here, there, at home, in the movies—everywhere they were playing the same thing. Actually, there are lots of good things about the plays. This kind of opera is a type of reform opera. Artistically, they combine Chinese and Western music and musically, they are very good. The government had a special group of people to write this kind of music. But normally, they are all credited to Jiang Qing, Mao Tse Tung's wife. Even up until now, they are still very valuable. . . .

I came here on a tourist visa to visit my sister. I went to a party and I sang some opera. I didn't know people here would still like opera so much! After they heard me singing, they wanted to learn. So slowly, gradually, the Philadelphia Chinese Opera Society (PCOS) started to develop. More and more people started to get involved.

I never thought I could have an opera troupe in the United States. I feel so pleased. In the beginning, people here could only sing the Eight Model Operas. Because of their age, they didn't know anything else. After they became members of PCOS, they slowly began to learn the traditional roles. The main two professional Beijing Opera performers in the troupe are myself and Teacher Zhenguo Liu, a jinghu master from Beijing. Some new young people who were also professional opera artists in China have also arrived and are working with us, including my nephew, Li Xin. I really hope I can organize a strong, professional program of a very traditional Chinese opera with all the elements: singing, recitation, acting and fighting. I want to do a good program with a good story. I really hope that we can make Beijing opera accepted by the American public. That's my real hope. I want to let Americans know about the real Chinese opera culture and tradition. But the main problem is financial.

Now, I work in a dental lab five days a week. Whenever I need to perform, I have to take a leave without pay. In China, when I performed, I got paid enough to live on. But here, if I don't do my job, I won't make money and I won't be able to perform. I want to stay here to make some contribution.

The question about the future of Beijing Opera is something that's been discussed for a long time. After the Cultural Revolution, there was a gap—a missing period of time. There was a broken generation where the tradition didn't continue. Not only was the training of performers discontinued. Even the audience was discontinued during this period. Now, it's difficult to reconnect the tradition. Chinese Opera also has been diffused by modern culture. I don't know if the younger generations will still accept Chinese opera. So it's difficult to say what the future developments will be. But this tradition must continue—it must be preserved. I do believe that Beijing Opera will exist forever. I don't know what the development will look like. I don't know if opera will ever be as popular as it was in the old days. It is difficult for young people here in this country to learn opera. You need to cultivate it. Even now in China, they try and teach young children in school.

Modern American culture for young people is a short cut culture. If you want to be a good opera performer, there's no way you can take a short cut. There are too many things you have to learn in opera. The reason why young people like this kind of short-cut culture is because they don't need to "eat bitterness." They can see results in a very short time. But Beijing Opera requires a long period of time. You can only have achievements a very little bit at a time. There is a saying in

Chinese Opera, "Three minutes on the stage requires three years of hard work off stage."

I have never regretted learning opera. Many times, when I feel upset or unhappy, I go and practice singing, and then I feel happy again. I am in my 50s, but my health is still good because of the training I had when I was young. The smallest return, ignoring everything else, is having good health.

Source: Li, Shuyuan. "Walking on Solid Ground." Interviewed and recorded by Debbie Wei; translated by Ming Chau. *Works in Progress: Magazine of the Philadelphia Folklore Project*, vol. 17, no. 1/2, summer/fall 2003, pp. 24–27, 41–42. http://www.folkloreproject.org/folkarts/resources/pubs/wip/summerfall03.pdf. Accessed November 2009. Used with permission of the Philadelphia Folklore Project.

67. Esther Don Tang, "Thoughts on the Chinese Community Today," 2005

In the early 1900s, the Chinese population of Tucson, Arizona, consisted primarily of single men, most of whom had worked on the railroads. After they were forced out of that market by racist labor groups and laws, many Chinese moved into vegetable farming, serving the multiethnic Mexican and American communities in Tucson. As Chinatown grew, businesses were established, and organizations and associations were formed, creating a vibrant community.

Esther Don Tang, born in 1917, grew up a few blocks from Tucson's Chinatown. Her early memories highlight the role Chinatown played in cultural preservation for the immigrants. In her 2005 interview, she reflects on the changes, both positive and negative, that she has seen in Tucson's Chinese American community.

I see a great change in the school situation today. My son and daughters, my nieces and nephews by and large participate in all school functions. They date students not of Chinese origin, and have married out of their race. This was not always the case. In the 1940's, my parents put a down payment on a house in the Belmont subdivision. The next day there was obscene writing, letting us know that Chinese were not wanted there. Today, the Chinese live all over Tucson. My own family is something like a United Nations: our son has a Polish wife, and our daughters married a[n] Irishman and a Portuguese.

I believe that our Chinese youth have equal, if not better opportunities than other ethnic groups. This has come about through a tradition that emphasizes excellence in education, performance, and positive attitude. Chinese parents continually plan financially for their children's education.

In celebrations, the Chinese community comes together. Otherwise, families carry out their own work and activities integrated into the general community workplace and community organizations.

There is still a Ying On Benevolent Society which cares and houses the eldest members of the community. The extended family still is very important. Relatives coming from the homeland are usually given jobs by their family or relatives, or recommended to friends. With the mobility of society and job opportunities elsewhere, families do separate, but the strong ties continue to exist, and visits are frequent. Concern for family members do not diminish with distance.

I believe the future of the Chinese in Tucson is as good as any other group. In fact, they are probably better off in Tucson than many places since they have all the advantages any other citizen has. The Chinese population will continue to grow with newcomers from Taiwan and the mainland. The approximate number today is 3000 individuals representing 500 families. However that does not count the students and trainees who come to Tucson.

Of course Tucson has changed from a small pueblo of a few thousand. Then everybody knew everyone. Doors were never locked. The air was clean, we swam in irrigation ditches, the traffic was not congested, water was not a problem, crime occurred infrequently (well, except when Dillinger came to town!).

Now I walk down the street and strangers wonder when I arrived by slow boat. We can't stop growth and progress, but we need planning and solutions to water pollution, air quality, education, crime and access to medical assistance, especially for the elderly. I'll always love Tucson, no matter what. My hopes for Tucson are the solutions for these problems. Hopefully our governments will resolve them with commitment to the community's future—and not through political pressure or greed.

My parents taught us early that the community is an extension of our home. We never stop caring and helping our family, no matter how much they go astray. And so it is, as long as I can walk and talk I will give my time and energy to public service—to preserve and to insure the possible best for my family and all of Tucson.

Source: Tang, Esther Don. "Thoughts on the Chinese Community Today." 2005. http://parentseyes.arizona.edu/promise/esthersthoughts.html. Used with permission of David Tang and *The Promise of Gold Mountain: Tucson's Chinese Heritage* website.

68. Daniel Yang, "To Live and Die in (or East of) LA: The Life of a Former Asian American Gang Member," 2006

Many 19th-century Chinese immigrants joined tongs and triads in the United States. Although these tongs and triads were modeled on existing organizational structures imported from China, in the United States they also served a protective role against an often hostile American society. These groups, while offering aid and community to struggling and alienated people, also controlled the black market, the vice trade, and ran extortion rackets in Chinatown. These organizations still exist today; many of them have expanded their scope and are involved in the international drug trade, illegal immigrant smuggling rings, and human trafficking.

In addition to these well-established and long-historied tongs are today's Asian American youth gangs. These emerged in the 1980s in the wake of refugee immigration from Southeast Asia, and although Asian Americans comprise the smallest percentage of ethnic gangs in the United States, this number is rising. Most gangs are located in large urban centers in the West and Northeast, and gang activity tends to be concentrated within the Asian

American community. Fear of retaliation, mistrust of police, past experience with corrupt officials in the homeland, and reluctance to expose community and family problems make Asian American victims less likely to report violent crime than any other group. And while gang members tend to be on the periphery, both socially and economically (as the following article reveals), a growing number of middle- and upper-class Asian American young people are becoming involved.

As part of an Asian American psychology course that he took at the University of Southern California in 2006, Daniel Yang interviewed Chris Shen, a former Wah Ching gang member from Los Angeles. Shen grew up in an upper-middle-class family, but got involved in the Asian gang subculture in high school. After being threatened by the Vietnamese boyfriend of one of his friends and then harassed by another group of Vietnamese men, Shen asked for help from a friend who was in the Wah Ching gang. He was told that he must join the Wah Chings in order to get protection. In this excerpt from his essay, Yang interweaves Shen's story with an analysis of the societal characteristics of Asian American gangs.

He [Shen] was introduced to an older man who was one of the local leaders. He was evaluated and told what he must do to join. Getting into the gang involved an initiation where he had to fight three other guys, which meant he was thoroughly beaten up. After that, the same gang members who beat him up would protect each other with their lives. One day a couple of weeks later, he received a phone call from someone crying, "I'm sorry, I'm so sorry." It was the Vietnamese guy from the cybercafe. The same man who had initiated Chris into the gang turned out to be a wildly violent thug. He and several *Wah Ching* boys had gone to the cybercafe and pulled a gun to the guy's head forcing him to call Chris and apologize. At the same time they had pulled a knife to the neck of the girlfriend. Chris had no idea that they were going to do this and would never have wanted this to happen, but it was too late and he started to realize what he had become a part of.

Most of the illegal activity was directed by the leadership comprised of adults in their 40s and 50s. The leaders of his *Wah Ching* chapter were poor immigrants from China who had become very wealthy through organized crime. They drove expensive sports cars and took care of the boys with girls and food whenever they met. The meetings were mostly conducted in Mandarin because of the leadership, though most of the boys were second generation bilingual Chinese. . . .

The gang members also used the societal perception of Asians as the model minority to their advantage by hiding the fact that they were gang members from police and authorities. . . . Most of the gang members used their youthful appearances and the stereotype to project themselves as harmless students, and to blend into the rest of the Asian American community.

. . . While most of the violence remained intergang, the fundraising activities were mostly protection, extortion, and home invasions. The victims were usually other Asian small businesses and families in the suburban community. In one case, Chris developed a feud with another gang member who threatened to invade his home. *Wah Ching* decided a preemptive strike was in order, and when that rival gang member went on vacation with his family, they rented trucks and completely emptied the guy's house of all possessions. This was so shameful to the victim that he never said anything about it. . . .

[Shen eventually was arrested on gang-related charges, to the shock of his unsuspecting family.] It was in jail that he awoke to the reality of what he had been involved with. He was the only Asian there surrounded by blacks and Latinos. The first things they asked him was "Hey Bruce Lee, what gang are you in?" and "Do you know kung fu?" He knew that to survive he would have to use his street instincts and act tough. Any sign of weakness and the other inmates would take away everything he had. All he knew was that he wanted to get the hell out of there. He watched as little boys barely in middle school from impoverished neighborhoods fought each other over the most trivial things like a piece of candy. They had nothing to lose. Some of the most troubled inmates were placed in isolation for weeks, and as soon as they got out they would get in a fight and go right back. Shen was lucky because his parents would come visit him every week giving him support. . . .

Shen served his time with good behavior and was released on parole with community service duties on Saturday mornings. He currently works for his uncle's business and plans to return to school while assisting a friend in starting an import/export business. He worries about his younger brother getting into trouble like he did, and uses his former gang reputation to scare his brother's friends into staying the straight path. They know that if Chris' brother were to get in trouble Chris would hold them responsible. Chris also tries to convince some current gang members to get out before they end up dead or in jail. However, he has learned that some people like himself just won't listen and will have to learn the hard way. Shen and his brethren have learned *To live and die in* (or east of) *LA*.

Source: Yang, Daniel. "To Live and Die in (or East of) LA: The Life of a Former Asian American Gang Member." 2006. http://www.danielyang.com/musings/asiangangs2.php. Accessed February 2010. Used with permission of Daniel Yang.

69. Joy Wong, "The Whole Picture," 2008

Asian American Christianity is a strong and growing force in the United States today. Many Asian American congregations are immigrant churches, offering services in two or more languages, and providing both a space for cultural maintenance and ethnic community solidarity, as well as nurturing spiritual growth and development. The place of women in Asian American churches is thus affected both by diverse theological beliefs and by different cultural expectations about gender. In response to these pressures and opportunities, a group of evangelical women formed a support group called the Asian American Women on Leadership (AAWOL) in 2004. Over the years, AAWOL has evolved into an organization providing mentorship, training, and a safe space for conversations about the place of women in the Asian American evangelical community. Joy Wong, M.Div., has worked with several Chinese and Taiwanese immigrant churches in Southern California and is a hospital chaplain in Los Angeles. In "The Whole Picture," originally published on AAWOL's blog, Wong talks about the importance of recognizing and honoring all aspects of identity—cultural, ethnic, family and religious—rather than privileging one over the rest.

As a hospital chaplain intern, I visit a diverse variety of patients. One particular patient who stood out in my mind was an 89-year-old Asian man who had suffered a stroke. When I first visited him, he seemed non-responsive. His eyes were open but fixed upon the corner of the room, not on the television or upon me. There was no indication that he knew I was in the room; he didn't acknowledge my presence. His patient chart noted that he was a Christian originally from Taiwan.

On my second visit, I decided to sing some Taiwanese songs to him. As before, his eyes were open but were not making any eye contact. I first sang a Taiwanese worship song, but that did not draw much of a response. I then sang a Mandarin worship song, which also did not evoke anything out of the ordinary. Finally, I sang an old, familiar Taiwanese folk song. As soon as I began singing the folk song, the patient began making noises with his mouth as his eyes welled with tears. I was startled, but happy that I had made some sort of connection with him.

This experience caused me to reflect on the significance of our identity. This patient was moved not by a Christian song, but rather a folk song, probably one that had been sung and heard many times throughout his life. Each of us has a cultural identity, whether it is a specific culture, a mix of two or three cultures, or some combination of various traditions of our childhood and upbringing. When we encounter something that speaks to that cultural identity, it moves us. I believe it is because it evokes emotions from our longing for familiarity, belonging, and our home.

God is our ultimate Parent and ultimate home and our identity as Christians is important, but our earthly, cultural identity is also God's intention. I believe our cultural identities need to be discovered and fully embraced in order to delve deeply into our knowledge of God. After all, our understanding of God must be grasped as who God made us to be, including our ethnicity, background, and upbringing. For Asian American evangelical women, the lens through which we see God will become ever clearer as we learn to love and embrace the entirety of who God made us to be.

Source: Wong, Joy. "The Whole Picture." Asian American Women on Leadership, 2008. http://aawolblog.blogspot.com/2008/08/whole-picture.html. Accessed July 2009. Reprinted with permission from Joy Wong.

70. Roland Hwang, "The Vincent Chin Case Remembered 25 Years Later," 2007

On June 19, 1982, Vincent Chin became a tragic victim in one of the most brutal hate crimes in modern American history. Chin was Chinese American had been adopted from China, and grew up in Detroit. On the night he was murdered, Chin was celebrating his bachelor party at the Fancy Pants strip club. In the club, Chin and his friends got into an altercation with another group of men. Witnesses stated that they heard two men, Ronald Ebens and his stepson, Michael Nitz, call Chin a "Chink" and "Jap." Ebens, a Chrysler plant superintendent, told Chin, "It's because of you little motherfuckers that we're out of work." Nitz had recently been laid off from one of the auto plants. During the 1980s, U.S. automakers began laying off large numbers of workers in response to increased competition from Japanese auto companies like Toyota and Honda. During this time, charities often had people publicly destroy Japanese cars in exchange for donations.

Both parties were thrown out of the club, and Ebens and Nitz went looking for Chin. They caught up with him in front of a McDonald's restaurant. Nitz held Chin down while Ebens swung for his head. Ebens shattered Chin's skull and bludgeoned him to death. Chin fell into a coma and died four days later in the hospital. Ebens and Nitz were convicted of manslaughter and sentenced to three years probation and fined $3,000 each.

The sentence set off a firestorm of protest, not only in Detroit's Asian American community, but also in Asian American communities across the country. Chin's death sparked the creation of a pan–Asian American movement and community.

This article, written for the Council of Asian Pacific Americans (CAPA), commemorated the 25th anniversary of Chin's death. The author, Roland Hwang, teaches for the Program in American Culture at the University of Michigan. Hwang was also the vice president of American Citizens of Justice, the civil rights organization created in the aftermath of Chin's death, from 1992 to 1994 and a board member of the Detroit chapter of the Organization of Chinese Americans. He served as president of the organization in 1983 and as vice president from 2005 to 2006.

Do you remember the details of the Vincent Chin case, the watershed Asian American civil rights case from 25 years ago? And what were the lessons learned from that important case? This article is to fill you in on the details and those lessons.

THE FACTS

On June 19, 1982, Vincent Chin, a 27 year old Chinese American was with three of his buddies for a bachelor party at the Fancy Pants Bar in Highland Park a few days before his upcoming wedding. By the end of the evening, Vincent Chin had been beaten by two white auto workers with a baseball bat and Chin was clinging to life, only to die four days later.

Vincent got into an altercation with Ronald Ebens and his stepson Michael Nitz. Vincent and his friends, and Ebens and Nitz were told to leave the bar. Ebens got a baseball bat from the trunk of his car, and Vincent and his friend Jimmy Choi ran away. Ebens and Nitz drove around for 30 minutes looking for Vincent. Ebens and Nitz caught up to Vincent Chin on Woodward Avenue outside a nearby McDonald's. While Nitz held Vincent, Ebens beat him with several swings of the baseball bat. Vincent Chin died on June 23, 1982 after he was taken off life support.

In a State criminal proceeding Ebens and Nitz were charged with second degree murder, but later plead guilty and no contest respectively to manslaughter in a plea bargain. Without any prosecuting attorney present at sentencing, Wayne County

Circuit Judge Charles Kaufman heard only from defense attorneys and sentenced the men to only three years probation and a $3,000 fine.

The Chinese American community and soon the whole Asian American community were outraged at the lenient sentence. On Leong President and honorary mayor of Chinatown Kin Yee called then OCA [Organization of Chinese Americans]-Detroit Chapter president Roland Hwang for a meeting to talk about the sentence. Combining the efforts of two groups would be a stronger force for the case. Hence, at that meeting at On Leong Hall, American Citizens for Justice, a newly formed Asian American civil rights group was born with a name to show broad support for justice for Vincent. Kin Yee, Marisa Chuang Ming, Helen Zia, and Roland Hwang were the first officers.

Attorney Liza Chan filed a motion to reopen the sentence, claiming misrepresentations were made during sentencing in front of Judge Kaufman. Appeals to reopen the sentencing in the State appellate courts were not successful. Later on, after investigation by American Citizens for Justice, and journalists, it was learned Racine Colwell one of the dancers in the bar overheard Ebens say "Nip", "Chink", and "because of you mother fuc---s, we're out of work."

Research revealed that the most viable option for justice for Vincent Chin was the pursuit of federal civil rights charges against Ebens and Nitz. Lily Chin, the mother of Vincent met with the Assistant Attorney General for Civil Rights William Bradford Reynolds, the FBI agreed to investigate the case, and a federal criminal trial proceeded. The federal trial before U.S. District Judge Anna Diggs Taylor resulted in a guilty verdict against Ronald Ebens and a 20-year sentence. The Sixth Circuit Court of Appeals overturned the verdict citing trial errors. Later, a change of venue motion was granted, and the case was moved to Cincinnati, Ohio. At a second trial in Cincinnati, Ohio, a jury found Ronald Ebens not guilty of a civil rights violation in the killing of Vincent Chin.

Lessons Learned

Those lessons are summarized below:

1. Identifying and interviewing all of the witnesses is crucial.

We cannot assume that law enforcement will always identify all of the facts and the motivations for an assault. Here, police investigation was lacking. The detective did not interview the dancers at the Fancy Pants where such interviews would have revealed the motivations of Ebens and Nitz, what was said, and what occurred about a half an hour before the beating.

2. Coalition building is important.

After the sentence of probation, American Citizens for Justice and the APA community could not get a meeting with the then-county prosecutor William Cahalan. It took the intervention of New Detroit, the urban coalition that arose from the 1967 Detroit Riot, and the Detroit Organization of Black Organizations, for a meeting to occur with the prosecutor.

The importance of coalitions cannot be overemphasized. Moving ahead twenty years after the beating death of Vincent Chin, representatives of New Detroit, the Detroit Branch of the NAACP, the American Arab Anti-Discrimination Committee Michigan branch, and the Anti-Defamation League, all participated in the 20th Year Remembrance in Detroit.

3. Pressure brings results.

Federal involvement is most often discretionary. Usually cases are left for local prosecution. The application of local hate crime tack on statutes (in Michigan, it is 2 years additional or $5,000 fine) is discretionary with the local prosecutor. Without community pressure, a local prosecutor may not apply the hate crime provision. Federal interest in a particular case or a set of facts likely will not arise without community pressure and media attention on a case, pointing out the egregiousness of the case facts, or the unfairness of the sentencing result without Federal involvement.

4. Sentencing is a crucial part of the case.

The county prosecutor's office did not treat the sentencing hearing as a very important part of the justice process. The cases were treated as complete after the plea bargain. Assistant prosecutors at the time of the Vincent Chin case routinely did not appear at sentencing. Since the Chin case, the county assistant prosecutors have more often appeared at the sentencing phase.

5. The media has an important role.

ACJ was very fortunate to have journalist Helen Zia, then a writer for the Detroit Free Press and Metropolitan Detroit, and later managing editor of Ms. Magazine, as its first secretary and later president. It was Helen who was able to gain the attention of the news desks of the media in Detroit and later the attention of a writer for the New York Times.

Without the scrutiny of the media, it is quite possible the later investigations in the case, the involvement of the FBI, and the Department of Justice decision to proceed with a civil rights trial involving an Asian American victim, all might not have occurred.

6. The victim's loss must be a matter of record.

At the time of the Vincent Chin case, the impact of the victim's death was not a matter of record. The Chin case became a cornerstone for the state statute that gives representatives of the victim's family an opportunity to make a statement about the impact of the loss on the victim's family at sentencing.

7. Changing venue changes results.

We now know after the Rodney King case how a change of venue (in that case to suburban Simi Valley from Los Angeles) can vastly affect the results of a case after a jury trial. The same held true in the Vincent Chin case when the second federal trial of Ronald Ebens in Cincinnati, rather than in Detroit, resulted in a not guilty verdict, rather than guilty.

8. The activists can wear different hats.

Many of the activist volunteers in the Vincent Chin case went on to wear different hats so their advocacy could take place in different forums. The Asian

American Bar Association of Michigan came into being during the Vincent Chin case. Many of the same volunteer attorneys were involved in ACJ and the founding of the Asian American Bar. Attorney Harold Leon, who appeared in the movie "Who Killed Vincent Chin?" went on to become the first president of the Asian American Bar Association of Michigan in 1985.

9. The case leaves a lasting legacy.

The legacy of the Vincent Chin case lives on today. What must we as leaders and activists remember?

Organize. To be ready to fight harassment and hate violence, the APA community wherever it may be must be organized. That is the matter of importance for OCA to have chapters in every state and every metropolitan area where sufficient numbers of Asian American reside.

Coalition build. Wherever there is an opportunity to identify and work on civil rights issues and to develop a common agenda, whether it is harassment, hate violence, or immigration reform, OCA and its chapters should explore working with other civil rights organizations, both locally and nationally.

Contact the Media. Never be afraid to contact the media with your story of harassment, discrimination or hate violence. If the case goes unreported, it will have an unsatisfactory result. Each chapter should identify its media point persons hopefully ahead of time, and identify media outlets that are willing to run those stories.

Source: Originally published in the OCA National's Newsletter. Reprinted on website of the Council of Asian Pacific Americans (CAPA). June 9, 2007. http://capa-mi.blogs.com/capami/2007/06/the_vincent_chi.html. Accessed November 2009. Reprinted with permission.

71. Eddie Fung, "Chinatown Kid, Texas Cowboy, Prisoner of War," 2007

Eddie Fung grew up in San Francisco's Chinatown, chafing against what he saw as his parents' strict traditionalism and yearning for adventure. Although he was born in the United States and was an American citizen, Fung's childhood in Chinatown, during the 1920s and 1930s, was lived in the shadow of Chinese exclusion. Many in the Chinese American community—including members of Fung's own family—were in the United States illegally, having immigrated as paper sons; this created an unsettled and fearful atmosphere in Chinatown's impoverished and crowded tenements. Moreover, for some like Fung, the benefits of the Chinese American community's strong sense of ethnic solidarity and family loyalty were counteracted by an ever-present awareness of insularity, boundary, and proscription.

At the end of the Depression, Fung ran away from home to become a cowboy in Texas and joined the Texas National Guard two years later. He became one of the 15,000 Chinese Americans to serve in the U.S. Army during World War II—and the only Chinese American soldier to become a Japanese prisoner of war in Burma. He spent many months in captivity, building the Burma-Siam railroad. In the following excerpts from his biography, cowritten by his wife, Judy Yung, a professor of Asian American studies, Fung describes his family background, complicated by the strictures of the Chinese Exclusion Act, and the way he came to terms with his Chinese American ethnic identity.

I had two older adopted brothers who were born in China, and four other sisters and a younger brother who were born at home like me. My father, being a progressive man, chose to use a lady doctor instead of a midwife. The reason we had two adopted brothers was because after my parents got married in China and before Pop came over to America, it was thought that Mom was barren. So since he was going to find his fortune in the West, he decided to adopt two sons to keep her company in China. But when he finally got her over here in 1914, one year later, my older sister Mary was born! How did Pop get his wife and two sons over here when he was illegal? He had a brother in San Francisco who had a wife and three sons in China. As a merchant, he could have brought them to America, but he never intended to do so. Instead, he sold the papers to my father. Mom came over legally as my uncle's wife, and my oldest adopted brother, Al, came as my uncle's ten-year-old son, Ho Li Quong. Somehow, Pop knew the Chinese consul general, and in 1939 the consul fixed it so that Mom and Uncle were divorced, and Mom and Pop got married. As to my second adopted brother, Francis, or Pee Wee as we called him, Pop was able to buy immigration papers for him to come in 1920 as Hom Sin Kay, the nine-year-old son of a native-born citizen. Both Al and Pee Wee retained their paper names because it would get too complicated. The consul general could do only so much.

This would create all kinds of problems for us later, like when I went overseas in November of 1941 and my mother said, "You stop in Honolulu and find out how Pee Wee is doing." At the time he was a seaman on the Matson lines. We had one day in Honolulu, so I went to the Seamans Union. I was in uniform, and I said, "I want to find out if my brother is in port." "What's your brother's name?" I said, "Hom Sin Kay." He said, "What ship is he on?" I said, "*Lurline*." And he said, "*Lurline* is not in." So he said, "Who are you?" I said, "I'm his brother." So I pulled out my dog tag. He said, "You're Fun, Edward. How can he be your brother when his surname is Hom?" I said, "I don't know, but he's always been my brother." This "paper son" business—I just never thought anything of it because it was so common in Chinatown....

My father died in September [of 1940].... I remember that the funeral was very old-fashioned and quite a departure from Pop's progressive ways, because we had a Chinese procession with official mourners. There was a Chinese marching band with the horns that play that strange wailing sound, and each family member was dressed in a white hemp cloak and a white pointed cap. We were each escorted, and my escort was my oldest sister Mary's husband, Tye. He had to lend me a suit jacket because I all had were ranch clothes. We marched along Stockton Street to the Chinese United Methodist Church at the corner of Washington and Stockton. Then we went upstairs to the second floor of the church, which was full with people—both relatives and business acquaintances of my father's—and Reverend T.T. Taam gave a long eulogy in English and Chinese about what an upstanding citizen my father had been, always trying to help other people. I thought it was quite a conglomeration of customs, because there was also the blanket ceremony, in which the children of the deceased lay blankets made of cotton cloth over their parent's body to provide warmth and comfort in the next life. As the first natural-born son, I covered my father's body with the first blanket. I didn't realize it then, but I took precedence over my older adopted brothers and sisters. In other words, I was now the head of the family. From there, we went to the Chinese cemetery for the internment, followed by a funeral meal at the Universal Café in Chinatown. My mother told us afterwards that instead of wearing the mourning armbands for three years, we would do it for one year, and that would be adequate. She said, "We're living in modern time, and one year is sufficient to show that we are in mourning." . . .

On a personal level, it was Dr. Hekking [the prison camp doctor in Burma] who helped me come to terms with my ethnic identity as a Chinese American. I remember when I first arrived in the jungle, Captain Fitzsimmons called me in one day and said, "Eddie, I can change your service record so it reads that you're half Chinese." And I said, "Why would we do that, Captain?" He said, "They [the Japanese] may not be as rough on a half Chinese." I told Captain Fitzsimmons, "My father would turn over in his grave if I did that. Let's just take our chances and leave it the way it is." That was when I realized that I was Chinese culturally and philosophically. There was nothing I could do to change that. I wasn't extra proud of it; I wasn't ashamed of it; I just knew that was the reality of it—I am Chinese, period.

Dr. Hekking reinforced this when he gave me a copy of Lin Yutang's *Importance of Living* to read. I think from our past conversations, he could sense my ambivalence about being Chinese. I told him I had left home twice, and he probably wondered, "What are you running from? After all, at sixteen years old, you haven't even gotten your education yet." Since he was born in Indonesia and had dealt with a lot of natives, he probably could see how the natives had suffered under the Dutch restrictions that were imposed on them. Maybe that was what he saw as the analogy to the restricted life I had experienced in San Francisco Chinatown, and the explanation as to why I felt almost ashamed of being Chinese. I think he gave me Lin Yutang's book because he wanted me to learn about China's rich culture and history.

Source: Excerpted from *The Adventures of Eddie Fung: Chinatown Kid, Texas Cowboy, Prisoner of War*. Edited by Judy Yung. Seattle: University of Washington Press, 2007, pp. 4, 73, 155–156. Reprinted with permission.

72. Eddy Zheng, "Autobiography @ 33," 2007

Eddy Zheng immigrated to California from China in 1982, when he was 12 years old. Speaking little English and alienated from his new Oakland community, Zheng allied himself with a few other Chinese immigrant youths and began sinking into crime. At 16, he was convicted of armed robbery and kidnapping; sentenced as an adult, he was incarcerated in San Quentin prison. There, he learned English, earned his general equivalency diploma (GED), and began a decades-long attempt to rehabilitate himself and work on behalf of other Asian American prisoners and at-risk youth. Although he was released on parole in 2005, changes in federal law mandated that noncitizens be deported for aggravated felonies and Zheng presently is in limbo. Zheng wrote the following poem during his time in San Quentin. *CCCMS* stands for correctional clinical case management system; *PC* stands for protective custody of prisoners.

I am 33 years old and breathin'
it's a good year to die
to myself
I never felt such extreme peace
despite being mired in constant ear-deafening screams
from the caged occupants—triple CMS, PCs, gang validated,

> drop-outs, parole violators, lifers,
> drug casualties, three strikers,
> human beings

in San Quentin's 150 year old solitary confinement

I don't want to start things over

@ 33

I am very proud of being who I am
I wrote a letter to a stranger who said

> "You deserve to lose at least your youth,
> not returning to society until well into middle age . . ."

after reading an article about me in the San Francisco Weekly
I told him

> "A hundred years from now when we no longer exist on this earth of human kind the seriousness of my crime will not be changed or lessened. I can never pay my debt to the victims because I cannot turn back the hands of time . . . I will not judge you."

whenever I think about my crime I feel ashamed
I've lost my youth and more
I've learned that the more I suffer the stronger I become
I am blessed with great friends
I talk better than I write

because the police can't hear my conversation
the prison officials labeled me a trouble maker
I dared to challenge the administration
for its civil rights violation
I fought for Ethnic Studies in the prison college program
I've been a slave for 16 years under the 13th Amendment
I know separation and disappointment intimately
I memories the United Front Points of Unity
I love my family and friends
my shero Yuri Kochiyama and a young sister named Monica

who is pretty wanted to come visit me
somehow I have more female friends than male friends
I never made love to a woman
sometimes I feel like 16
but my body disagrees
some people called me a square
because I don't drink, smoke, or do drugs
I am a procrastinator but I get things done
I've never been back to my motherland
I started to learn Spanish
escribió una poema en español
at times I can be very selfish and vice versa
I've never been to a prom, concert, opera, sporting event
or my parents' house
I don't remember the last time I cried
I've sweat with the Native Americans, attended mass with the Catholics, went
    to service with the Protestants, sat and chanted with the Buddhists
my mind is my church
I am spoiled
in 2001 a young lady I love stopped loving me
it felt worse than losing my freedom
I was denied parole for the ninth time
I assured Mom that I will be home one day
after she pleaded me to answer her question truthfully
"Are you ever going to get out of prison?"
the Prison Industrial Complex and its masters attempted to
control my mind
it didn't work

they don't know I've been introduced to Che, Yuri Kochiyama, Paulo Freire,
    Howard Zinn, Frederick Douglass, Assata Shakur, bell hooks, Maurice
    Cornforth, Malcolm X, George Jackson, Mumia, Buddha,

and many others . . .
I had about a hundred books in my cell
I was internalizing my politics
In 2000 I organized the first poetry slam in San Quentin
I earned my associate of art degree
something that I never thought possible
I've self-published a zine
I was the poster boy for San Quentin
sometime in the '90s my grandparents died
without knowing that I was in prison

@ 30
I kissed Dad on the cheek and told him that I love him for the first time
I've written my first poem
I called myself a poet to motivate me to write

because I knew poets would set us free
in 1988 I was granted parole
then it was taken away
the governor's political career superseded my life
some time in the 90s
I participated in most of the self-help programs
In 1996 I really learned how to read and write
I read my first history book "A People's History of the United States"
my social conscious mind was awakened
in 1992 I passed my GED in Solano Prison
I learned how to take care of my body from '89 to '93
in 1987 I turned 18 and went to the Pen from youth authority
the youngest prisoner in San Quentin's
Maximum Security Prison
I was lucky people thought I knew kung fu

@ 16
I violated an innocent family of four and scarred them for life
money superseded human suffering
I was charged as an adult and sentenced to life
with a possibility
no hablo ingles
I wish I could start things over
I was completely lost

@ 12
I left Communist China to Capitalist America
no hablo ingles
I was spoiled
in 1976 I went to demonstrations against the Gang of Four
life was a blur from 1 to 6
on 5/29/69
I inhaled my first breath

Source: Zheng, Eddy. "Autobiography @ 33." Originally published in *Other: An Asian and Pacific Islander Prisoners' Anthology*, a project of the Asian Prisoner Support Committee, 2007, pp. 37–41. *Other* is available at Amazon.com and AKPress.com.

73. John, "How Bruce Lee Changed the World," 2009

Bruce Lee's legacy in martial arts and film is enormous. Even 37 years after his death, Lee is still an international icon. His writings and teachings are still being read and taught the world over. He almost single-handedly introduced martial arts to the Western world through his films. Countless documentaries have been produced about his life and his legacy, and contemporary martial arts stars like Jackie Chan and Jet Li, Asian American actors like Jason Scott Lee and Cary-Hiroyuki, and ordinary people grew up idolizing Lee.

Lee was born in San Francisco on November 27, 1940, while his father was on tour with the Chinese Opera. However, Lee was raised in Hong Kong, where he began his training at age 13. Lee returned to the United States when he was 18, attending the University of Washington, where he was a philosophy major. He began teaching kung fu and later opened his own martial arts schools in Oakland and Los Angeles. Later, Lee privately trained many celebrities, including Steve McQueen, James Coburn, and Kareem Abdul-Jabar. He first appeared in the television series *The Green Hornet*, which caught the attention of Hong Kong movie producers. Lee returned to Hong Kong where his film career catapulted him into stardom. He quickly became a cultural icon, so much so that Hollywood came knocking, resulting in the renowned film *Enter the Dragon*. Lee died on July 20, 1973, in Hong Kong from cerebral edema caused by an allergic reaction to pain medication. He was 32 years old. In this essay, San Francisco blogger John, from 8asians, discusses the Asian martial arts stereotype and Lee's legacy.

I was watching The History Channel the other evening and saw a trailer for their 2 hour documentary, *How Bruce Lee Changed the World* which premiered this weekend.

Profiling Lee's influence on popular culture in fitness, cinema, music, sport, design, fashion, philosophy and other realms, the film showcases some rare family archival footage owned by the Bruce Lee Foundation, together with in-depth interviews with individuals who have cited inspiration from Lee, including Jackie Chan, comedian Eddie Griffin, rappers LL Cool J and RZA, Marvel Comics' Stan Lee, and renowned film directors John Woo and Brett Ratner.

Growing up in the 80's, I was [asked] my share of times if I knew kung fu or karate, and I am sure this is due to Bruce Lee's fame. Watching *Enter the Dragon*, I wondered if what Lee was doing was real, and if the bad guys in the film were really being pummeled by Lee or everything was just choreographed very well.

It's kind of shocking to think that Lee only lived to be 32 years old when he died in 1973, yet is still such an iconic figure today. Even one of the most popular Asian American blogs, *Angry Asian Man*, has a Bruce Lee action figure on its front page. It'll be interesting to see how this documentary highlights Lee's influence and I'm sure [it] will make us ponder how much more Lee would have accomplished if he had not died so prematurely.

Source: John. "How Bruce Lee Changed the World." May 19, 2009. http://www.8asians.com/2009/05/19/how-bruce-lee-changed-the-world/. Accessed September 2009. Reprinted with permission from John@8asians.com.

74. Frances Kai-Hwa Wang, "From a Whisper to a Rallying Cry," 2009

In 1982, Vincent Chin, a Chinese American engineer, was brutally beaten to death by two Detroit autoworkers wielding a baseball bat. Nine months later, Michael Nitz and Ronald Ebens were sentenced to three years' probation and $3,000 in fines for Chin's murder. Their light sentence outraged the Chinese American community in Detroit, and they began to mobilize. Soon, other Asian Americans joined the struggle, and in 1983 they formed American Citizens for Justice, a civil rights group campaigning for a federal trial for Nitz and Ebens.

In this excerpt from her remarks at the State Bar of Michigan's 34th Michigan Legal Milestone conference in June 2009, Frances Kai-Hwa Wang, the Executive Director of American Citizens for Justice, talks about how the media's coverage of the Vincent Chin case helped bring about a new Asian American Civil Rights Movement.

One of my favorite stories surrounding the Vincent Chin case is how it went from a local story about a barroom brawl to a national one about civil rights in America . . . at a car rental place. Helen Zia was a founding member of American Citizens for Justice and one of the lead activists, and her car was in the shop, so she had to rent a car. As she stood in line at the rental car agency, she noticed that the tall African American woman in front of her had both the *Detroit News* and The *Detroit Free Press* open to articles about the case, and she noticed that the woman was also holding a small notebook embossed with the words, "*New York Times*." So she leaned over and asked, "Are you interested in this case? I have some press packets right here, if you'd like." It turns out that when reporters are on vacation, if they can find some story to write about while they are there, they can get part of their expenses reimbursed. So this *New York Times* reporter, Judith Cummins, was in Detroit visiting family and looking for a story to do while she was here. I believe that this story caught her eye, in part, because she was African American and had some understanding that race and racism sometimes play into these things. And so from the beginning, this case has been about people recognizing across ethnicity and across race that this could have been any one of us, this could have been me, that the danger of racial stereotypes is that real people and real lives are reduced to caricature.

I have been asked to speak about the role of the media regarding the Vincent Chin case and the birth of the Asian American civil rights movement, and so I will talk about the role of the media at the time of the case, what has happened since that time, and what the future holds for American Citizens for Justice and civil rights.

When Judge Kaufman sentenced Vincent Chin's killers, Ronald Ebens and Michael Nitz, to a $3000 fine and three years probation, Asian Americans came together at the Golden Star Restaurant, and in the stunned silence that followed the lawyers' conclusion that legally there was nothing more to do, counterpointed by the sobs of Mrs. Chin, Vincent's mother, Journalist Helen Zia's voice broke the silence, "But we have to say something. We can't not say anything."

Before this moment, there were many Asian Americans who thought that if they just worked hard, laid low, and taught their children good English, that they would be able to quietly assimilate into the American dream. This case taught them that they cannot make such assumptions. And thanks in part to the leadership of American Citizens for Justice, Asian Americans woke up to the importance of being involved, speaking up, being visible, forming coalitions and building networks. There were protest rallies and remembrance vigils across the country—including Detroit, San Francisco, Los Angeles, Chicago—that brought together Asian Americans of all ethnicities. And these protests were well-covered by the media because they seemed so incongruous—the Model Minority waving protest banners?

In *Asian American Dreams*, Helen Zia talks about how the Chinese American scientists and engineers from Ford, GM, and Chrysler planning the protest in Detroit joked that this would be "the most precisely planned demonstration in history." The signs were all uniform, and the words were all in straight lines, and they had it choreographed down to 20-second intervals what people would chant and how they would turn.

This was the first time that Asian Americans spontaneously mobilized around a unified cause. It taught Asian Americans how to organize, network, build coalitions, fundraise. It created new organizations to watchdog and monitor civil rights issues for Asian Americans. This was the birth of the Asian American civil rights movement.

Key to this awareness and mobilization was education and media coverage—education of the Asian American community about their rights in America, education of the general public about what Asian Americans are really like, education of the legal community about whether or not Asian Americans are even covered by civil rights laws, education of elected officials about the impact of racially suggestive campaigns directed against Asian imports. Without this national mobilization, and national and international media attention, there never would have been a federal hate crime trial, and we would have been left with only Mrs. Chin's words:

"What kind of law is this? What kind of justice? This happened because my son is Chinese. If two Chinese killed a white person, they must go to jail, maybe for their whole lives & Some thing is wrong with this country."

Since then, the history of the Vincent Chin case has become a staple in Asian American Studies, Ethnic Studies, American Cultures, and law courses around the country. The Academy Award winning documentary film by Christine Choy and Renee Tajima-Pena, *Who Killed Vincent Chin?* has been shown to generations of college students. There have been remembrance events—vigils, dinners, conferences, poetry slams—organized around the country on the 10th, 20th, and 25th year anniversaries of Vincent Chin's death. Now there is a new documentary film produced by Asian Pacific Americans for Progress, *Vincent Who?* about how too many college students—who at this point are all born after 1982—do not know about this case or its importance, even as they take being Asian American and being a part of Asian American clubs and communities for granted. . . .

And so for the future, American Citizens for Justice will continue to educate the Asian American community about hate crimes, fair treatment, and civil rights; continue to educate the public, the legal community, and elected officials about Asian American civil rights issues; continue to build coalitions with other Asian American and civil rights groups; continue to do Court Watches and monitoring of cases that may have civil rights implications; continue to advocate and speak out against racially motivated injustice everywhere.

From a Whisper to A Rallying Cry, indeed.

Source: Wang, Frances Kai-Hwa. "From a Whisper to a Rallying Cry—The Role of the Media in the Vincent Chin Case and in the Birth of the Asian American Civil Rights Movement." June 19, 2009. http://www.multiculturaltoolbox.com/American_Citizens_for_Justice/MediaChin.html. Accessed February 2010. Reprinted with permission.

75. Adam Cheung, "Encounter with Crazy Ming," 2010

Boston's Chinatown was established in the early 1870s, after the transcontinental railroad was completed and Chinese laborers came to the East Coast to work in the manufacturing plants. Like most 19th-century American Chinatowns, the community in Boston began as a bachelor society. Over the generations, especially after 1965, when Asian immigration restrictions were lifted, the population of Boston's Chinatown grew. However, its physical boundaries were continually contested and limited by the city's urban expansion and major transportation projects.

Adam Cheung grew up in Boston and is a martial artist in Chinatown, specializing in White Crane kung fu. He writes for the *Chinatown Blog* (http://bostonchinatowngateway.com/). Originally a platform to provide information on land development in Chinatown, the *Chinatown Blog* now also includes articles on Chinese American social and cultural issues. The following essay gives an evocative picture of the culture and characters of Chinatown's kung fu community. According to Cheung, "Chinatown used to be a very small and tight community where everyone knew each other, so the man I am telling a story about in this article might be known to many of the old timers. His nickname was Crazy Ming or 'Ngau Ming.'"

I think I was in College when I met him. Jing, Sifu's son, told me Ngau Ming would be stopping in with his son so I should try to be at the school when he came so that we could do some forms for him. He was an old friend of the school and had brought us down to Worcester to do Lion Dance (He owned a restaurant there). Before we used to have people with sticks to barricade some space for the Lion Head to move. Apparently in Worcester, Ngau Ming had done this job himself by swinging a Gwan Do (Polearm Sword made famous by General Gwan) around hard. Needless to say people moved and obviously Ngau Ming had his nickname for a reason.

Upon going into one of the restaurants, the head waiter in the front had said, "Oh that's okay. We don't need a Lion Dance." Ngau Ming replied in angry tone dabbled with expletives about the man's mother, her reproductive organs, their age and smell, that he should get the owner out to the front right now, and did he know who he was talking to, etc.

In Chinatown Ngau Ming had quite a name for loving to fight. He would hang out at the bars, get drunk and get into fights with Americans, and then befriend them afterward. When I met him I realized more clearly why it was easy for him to get into a fight. He had a crazy stare that just looked off and made you nervous even if you were his friend. Whether he was born like that or became like that over a lifetime or a combination of both is unknown to me. He had met Sifu in China. And at that time I think he was already in "Collecting" business. He did the same sort of occupation in Hong Kong and probably in the States too. He saw a great deal of violence and talked with one of the other Chinese Workers associated with our school about just how disgusting those fights can look in real life, when hands are being hacked off etc. In other words he was a Gong Wu/Jiaghu person if there ever was one. And he also practiced various forms of Kung Fu.

In China he had actually questioned Sifu's skill. Sifu demonstrated a technique which passed/parried his attack and pushed him flying out the door. He came running back in and bowed down saying "Sifu!"

But for some strange reason I do not understand, when he came to the school with his son, he seemed to praise Jing's (the son) Kung Fu over the father, our Sifu, Woo Ching. All of us know that Woo Ching's power, fighting, skill, Gung Lik, and many other aspects of the art far exceeded Jing, especially when Woo Ching Sifu was in his prime. But Ngau Ming kept talking about Jing's sword form. When I performed a form, he said "That's alright, but it's not as intelligent as Jing's Kung Fu. I only want my son to learn from Jing." I should back up and say that by this time he had already written a large check to our Sifu.

Now all these events I describe didn't happen one after another, but rather all jumbled up, mixed together, repeated again in a very bipolar schizophrenic like fashion.

"Son bow down to Jing and let's take a picture of it!"

"Take a picture in the Lion Head!"

"Son show them that Karate form that Lo Fahn taught you. They don't have Kung Fu where we are so he has to do Karate. But you can't use that form if you're really fighting!

"See son block this punch." He threw a punch at his son and his son passed it and avoided. "See that's not what they taught you that's the hand techniques I showed you."

The techniques in the Karate form were a lot like Fukienese White Crane and were more straight in and a hard to hard philosophy of fighting. His son was very courteous and good at his form. I have heard that he has since grown very tall and done well in some fighting tournaments.

Then at some point he started praising my Kung Fu, saying that I was strong and young and should keep practicing, while touching my stomach. I stepped back he stepped forward. I sort of thought he was going to punch me in the ribs as hard as he could. Not to be mean, but just out of excitement, like "Wow you do Kung Fu!" Punch.

I said, "Hey what do you want to do first." I wasn't sure if he wanted to try hands or what, but I got the feeling he was going to start punching. I was getting a little on edge because he had already challenged my skill and now it looked like he was going to physically challenge me. At the same time, he had just donated a large sum of money to the school. Awkward situation, you had to be there. His wife told him to stop scaring people.

Suddenly the conversation shifted to story telling, "You know Master X?" (Master X is a Sifu who was quite well known in Chinatown for being a good fighter, and people say able to punch while holding 100 pound bags of rice. His name is not really Master X, but I will refer to him as Master X in this story unless he reads this story and tells me I can use his name.)

"Master X and me are sworn brothers. (geet bai hing dai) I was able to hit him like this!" and he demonstrated his Kung Fu (now at a distance from me.) A second ago I thought that if I went hard to hard with him at close range I would 90% win because he was old and short and skinnier than me. After seeing him demonstrate, if I had to fight him, I would definitely stay outside and be cautious.

His hands were so fast. The technique was to touch the attacking punch and then follow it in with a counter punch. Now many people practice this, but his hands were very fast. Real Kung Fu Fast. As in not just technique, and youthful quick hands, but the counter strike had gung. Even when I demonstrate this technique to others and they say "Wow that is fast," I have to explain that his hands were much faster.

Now if people ask me, do you think Ngau Ming could beat Master X in a fight, I would say I don't know, and maybe not. Ngau Ming often tied or even lost his bar fights. He also didn't always look where he was punching and hunched his head over much the same way boxers do, which can leave the back of the head open or leave you open to a tackle which would result in two people rolling on the ground.

But if you ask me, "Do you think Ngau Ming really was able to hit Master X?" I would reply yes, because of the speed of the hands, and the technique's philosophy. Especially if it was unexpected. Apparently Master X's reply was, "You are the first person able to hit me, and none of the students wanted to play hands with Ngau Ming. Again, he was also sworn brothers with Master X, which would explain the dynamic of the situation.

If I had played hands with Ngau Ming before seeing him demonstrate, I could easily have been knocked down, out, or dead, especially if the counter strike attacked the neck. He learned the techniques in China from Tong Bak (Grandfather Tong?) who other of our members have also talked to recently when they went back to China to visit family. That Kung Fu is supposed to be Hung Gar, but is recognized as the practitioners as completely different than any other Hung Gar, and is claimed by the practitioners to be more original than other Hung Gar. To us, the stances and philosophy is similar to Bak Mei or some Hung Gar Bak Mei mix. But who are we to judge since that is not the system we practice. (We practice White Crane. Both the Shaolin and Tibetan Branch. Sifu also absorbed the best of the Kung Fu of the surrounding Villages, and Masters he defeated in Guangzhou while hiding out there.)

As Ngau Ming left he continued to touch my stomach pushing on it with his fist even as we saw him off to his car. "Keep up! Keep Practice! More Power! Very Powerful." He kept telling me in English, despite the fact that we had been conversing in Chinese.

Meeting him was definitely an eye opener in many ways and a good experience. His was the true face of many of the average Kung Fu practitioners in China of that generation. They learned Kung Fu for fighting, but also were so excited by the joy of doing the moves that besides life or death fights, they might not be able to restrain themselves from challenging friends. I think if he was younger, he definitely would have started hitting me. Not that he would have meant anything bad by it, but simply because seeing how my Kung Fu was in the form, he would want to try and crack it's code, or solve the puzzle playing out the Kung Fu in real time fist to face.

The reason why he so respected Jing's Sword form, was because he saw no counter to those moves. They were too fast and smooth. Also, I think his real fights, the gang related ones, involved the long knives they used to hack away at each other and seeing that must have left a deep impression in his mind, as he spoke of regret of having been a part of that stuff now that he had dealt with those memories in old age.

I have heard since that he passed away in his sleep. Considering his life, which had much violence, drugs, and gambling in his youth, I would say he had a good and peaceful end, being survived by a strong son, and a good wife who was a good businesswoman as well.

I don't know where his son is now, but we would love to have him at our school if he would still want to learn with us.

Source: Cheung, Adam. "Encounter with Crazy Ming." March 13, 2010. http://bostonchinatowngateway.com/archives/666#respond. Accessed March 2010. Used with permission of the author and bostonchinagateway.com. Reprinted with permission from Adam Cheung, kung fu and chi gung instructor at Woo Ching Crane Chi Gung Institute.

76. Alice Shi Kembel, "My Mother's Purse," 2010

Taiwan, also known as the Republic of China (ROC), is an island off the southeastern coast of mainland China. In the aftermath of the 1949 Communist revolution, the proto-democratic Kuomintang government-in-exile took control of Taiwan, wresting power from the ethnic Taiwanese. The Republic of China and the mainland Communist People's Republic of China (PRC) clashed intermittently over the next three decades, fighting for physical control of the island, as well as for political legitimacy in the eyes of the world community. Motivated primarily by Cold War fears, the United States recognized the Taiwanese Republic of China as the legitimate government of China until 1971. However, as the Cold War waned, and relations with the PRC warmed, fewer than 25 countries now officially recognize Taiwan as independent nation. Moreover, the PRC has effectively blocked Taiwan from joining the United Nations.

Taiwanese immigration to the United States was slow before 1950. During the first wave of Asian immigration, plantation labor recruiters tended to skip the small island in favor of the much more populated Chinese mainland. After 1949, however, the PRC banned almost all emigration to the United States, so the bulk of Chinese immigrants came from Taiwan. Many of these emigrants were middle class and educated, especially from the 1960s on when Taiwan's rapid industrialization transformed it—along with Singapore, Hong Kong, and South Korea, into one of the "Four Asian Tiger economies." Included among these Taiwanese emigrants were thousands of young people who moved to the United States to study abroad; many would eventually send home for their spouses. Amazingly, fewer than 5 percent moved back to Taiwan after completing their education. The Taiwanese immigrants established new ethnic communities in America.

Instead of moving to urban Chinatowns like previous waves of immigrants, they formed Taiwanese suburban communities in places like Monterey Park in southern California and Flushing in New York City. By 2008, there were more than 340,000 Taiwanese in the United States, both aliens and naturalized citizens.

Alice Shi Kembel is a second-generation Taiwanese American living in northern California. She is a columnist for *The Redwood City Patch*. Shi's father immigrated to America in 1970, attending graduate school in New York. Her mother joined him in 1971, when they got married, and they had their first daughter in 1972 and their second (Kembel) in 1975. After her father graduated, the Shis remained in the United States. Today, Kembel's parents live in Southern California. Kembel's essay "My Mother's Purse" is a humorous reflection on her parents' lives as Americanizing Taiwanese immigrants and the ways in which their experiences have impacted her own habits and attitudes.

I was raised in a frugal family. My parents immigrated to the United States from Taiwan in their early twenties to attend graduate school in New York. Graduate students, in general, are already poor, but add to that the international travel, learning a new language, and my sister being born within eighteen months of their arrival, and they faced definite financial struggle. They both came from humble beginnings in the city of Jiayi: my father, one of seven children, grew up helping his family make peanut oil in their home to sell to families in the neighborhood. My mother, as a child, helped her father sell large bags of rice off the backs of their rickety bikes, falling often as she strained to pedal forward because the heavy bags weighed more than she did. The story goes that my parents arrived in the United States with only two hundred dollars and the promise of a better life. With the help of some kind families who loved helping international students, they were able to weather the transition, and always had a place to go to celebrate holidays that meant nothing to them. They were also savvy and sharp in their financial decisions, and that, combined with their extreme frugality, elevated them quickly to the upper middle class in the time span that it took for me to be born and develop long term memory. I have no recollection of being poor, just of pretending to live like we were.

When I was growing up, we never bought things full price. Our meals were determined by specials at the grocery store, our outfits consisted of end of season clothing from the sale racks or clearance items from K-mart or Ross. My parents would drive an extra twenty miles to buy gas for a few cents cheaper per gallon than the gas station around the corner from our house. The drawers in our kitchen were stuffed with packets of ketchup and hot sauce, plastic utensils, tiny cups of creamer, and sugar pouches pilfered from dining establishments that allowed their customers to help themselves. Our olive green napkin holder with a daisy painted on it, purchased at a garage sale, held thin, rough napkins that you could find only in the metal dispensers smudged with fingerprints at fast food restaurants. When my father returned home from business trips, he would unpack rolls of toilet paper and tiny bottles of shampoo, conditioner, and body lotion taken from the hotel bathroom rather than gifts for his daughters and wife. I don't remember ever owning a book until I was in middle school, as we made weekly Wednesday trips to the library, our arms laden with musty-smelling books to return. My parents even re-used dental floss, rinsing off the waxy green strands and carefully draping them in styrofoam cups on the bathroom counter, ready for use the next day. And while most families I knew spent their Sunday mornings having brunch or attending church, we spent ours sitting at the kitchen table, flipping through the ads and coupons that came with the Sunday paper. My mom was always armed with a pair of scissors, and my sister and I fought over who got to look at the Target ad first, as though there was some sort of victory in having first access to the thin pages of smiling faces and brightly colored products.

My mother always carried an enormous black purse. I didn't understand why, since it seemed only to contain her wallet bursting with coupons, her sunglasses, and her car keys, and she was forever rummaging around in the depths trying to find one of those three things. It made more sense one day when we went out to dinner at Souplantation, my mother clutching a "buy one get one free" coupon in her hand. My sister and I were thrilled—not only did we get to eat out, but it was American food! We grabbed our trays and slid them along the counter, our eyes barely able to peer over the edge to see the delicacies that awaited us in unlimited quantities. Spotlights mounted to the ceiling illuminated the rows of salads, pastas, muffins, and soups. With the help of our parents, we loaded our plates and made our way to a table. There, we gorged ourselves on food that had never crossed our kitchen table at home. We all went back for seconds, of course, to get our money's worth. My parents even went back for thirds, returning with their plates heaped with as much food as they had on their first run through the line. My sister and I stared at their plates, impressed. I was already bursting, but was determined to have a soft serve vanilla ice cream cone for dessert. I couldn't imagine, however, eating another entire plate of food. My dad dove in, wolfing down his food with singular focus, while my mom took only a few bites and said, "Oh, I'm so full! I just can't finish the rest!" She watched my father eat for a few more minutes, and then, to my horror, pulled out some plastic bags from the produce section of the grocery store and began surreptitiously stuffing food into the bags. I noticed that she had a disproportionate number of foods on her plate that traveled well: rolls, slices of congealed pizza, blueberry muffins, carrot sticks, cherry tomatoes. Seeing our dismayed expressions, she said, "They're going to throw it away anyway. I don't want it to be waste!" She finished loading the bags, tied them off efficiently, and stowed them in her purse.

Despite the embarrassment that my parents' thrifty habits often caused me, I seem to have inherited some of them. It is difficult for me to buy any clothing unless it's on sale, and at restaurants, I always look at prices first, before I can even consider ordering any of the dishes. I still love shopping at garage sales, and I always buy generic brands when I have the option. Being married to my husband, however, has opened my eyes to a new way of thinking. George grew up in a family in which finances were tight—they always had enough to eat, but never had leftovers. He and his three brothers have reacted to their financially strapped childhood differently. George and his twin brother, once they landed real jobs with healthy salaries after graduate school, loved to spring for indulgences—the latest technological gadget, expensive dinners with fine wine, clothes at full price. As George's wife,

I have benefited from his splurges, but I struggle with his flippant attitude towards saving and his ability to justify any purchase, big or small. In contrast, George's youngest brother is even more stingy than my parents. He was nicknamed "Bank" because he always had extra money in his savings account and was willing to lend it out to family members, with interest. When he first graduated from college and was living on his own, he lost nearly twenty-five pounds off his already lean frame. When I first saw his emaciated body, I worried that he had somehow developed an eating disorder, but it turned out that he was losing weight because he was eating ramen for almost every meal. It was the cheapest thing he could find at Safeway that tasted good, and for nineteen cents a pouch, who wouldn't?

Now, after ten years of marriage, George and I have struck a balance. He falls on the carefree spending side of things, and I often feel like the party pooper having to say, "We shouldn't go out for sushi tonight; it's not in our budget," but thanks to the other, we are both a little more thoughtful in our approach. He is sometimes willing to order one less glass of wine at dinner to save money, and I am sometimes willing to spend a little more on something I really love rather than buy things merely because they are an amazing deal. I am still very driven, however, by freebies. When I get coupons in the mail for a free pair of underwear at Victoria's Secret, or a free travel size lotion from Bath and Body Works, I take a special trip to the mall to get my freebie, even if it means lugging all three of my boys there with me, something I usually avoid. On the way into the mall, we stop at See's Candies and buy one chocolate after receiving four samples. Then I foil the marketing tactics of the retailers by marching into the store, picking out my free item, presenting my coupon, and leaving without having spent a single cent. On the way out, we stop by the cupcake store and get free cupcakes by whispering the secret phrase posted on Facebook that day. "Neopolitan," I whisper. "Neopolitan," says my six year old. "Neepowitan," says my four year old. "Knee un," says my two year old. And off we go with our four free vanilla cupcakes with strawberry frosting, dipped in chocolate ganache. As a reward for tolerating a trip to the mall, the boys each get half a cupcake. I treat myself to the remaining half, then save the other two cupcakes for George and me to eat later, after the boys have gone to bed. I once left the mall with a pair of underwear, a trio of mascaras, a travel size shower gel, four cupcakes, and one chocolate (with four samples already consumed), only having paid for the single chocolate.

Perhaps I have retained some of my parents' penny-pinching behavior because I witnessed how this approach to life benefited them greatly. They lived out the American dream, turning their two hundred dollars into significant wealth in a relatively short period of time. I also eventually discovered that they were willing to spend money on things they deemed worthwhile. They invested in violin lessons for us starting from the age of four. They never bought used cars once they could afford new ones, and they favored Japanese and German vehicles. They bought a lavender-colored house in a good school district when I was six years old, and kept their previous home as a rental property, later purchasing several other investment properties. They took us on vacation every summer, ranging from road trips to national parks when we were young to a bus tour in Europe when we were in high school. They paid for our education, putting both of us through Stanford, my sister through medical school, and me through graduate school. They travel several times a year to exotic international destinations. They have been incredibly generous to our family, helping us buy our first house, giving us money for every birthday, Christmas, and anniversary, and buying gifts for the boys constantly. Despite their financial success, however, my parents still rely on some of their old habits. On our most recent trip to visit them, as the boys scarfed down some Costco chicken nuggets purchased especially for them with a $3.00 off coupon, my father, his eyes magnified behind thick glasses, blinking slowly like an owl, said, "Tomorrow we need to go to McDonald's or Jack in the Box to get some more ketchup."

Source: Kembel, Alice Shi. "My Mother's Purse." 2010. Reprinted with permission.

Part VI
Filipino American

77. Excerpt from Angeles Monrayo's *Tomorrow's Memories: A Diary,* 1924–1928

Early Filipino immigration peaked in the second two decades of the 20th century. Before 1910, few Filipinos were entering Hawai'i or the mainland of the United States. However, the 1908 Gentleman's Agreement Act severely restricted Japanese and Korean laborers from entering the United States, limiting the supply of labor needed for West Coast agricultural fields and Hawaiian sugarcane plantations. With few options left, American employers began recruiting workers from the Philippines. The Hawaiian Sugar Planters Association (HSPA) began recruiting Filipino labor in earnest during the latter part of the first decade of the 20th century. However, it was not until after 1910 that Filipinos began entering Hawai'i in any significant numbers. By the late 1920s, they had replaced the Chinese as the second-largest group of workers on the plantations. The advantage of hiring Filipinos was their status as U.S. nationals, which allowed them to migrate freely between any U.S. territories. Plantation owners exploited their Asian immigrant workers, instituting a paternalistic labor system that included heavy fines for drinking, insubordination, and damage to equipment. Owners also created a stratified labor force, paying different wages to workers of different ethnic background. This created tensions among workers and discouraged them from striking. Despite this, workers soon began organizing for better pay and benefits. Typically, strikes were ethnic specific, though there were occasional multiethnic/multiracial strikes. A true multiethnic/multiracial labor movement in Hawai'i did not form until after World War II.

The excerpts below are from *Tomorrow's Memories*, a compilation of Angeles Monrayo's diary from 1924 to 1927. Angeles left the Philippines with her family when she was only three months old. They were part of the 5,234 Filipinos who arrived in Hawai'i in 1912. Most of these early Filipino immigrants were men. In 1924, Filipino plantation workers began a slow-growing strike that eventually involved about 60 percent of Filipino plantation workers. Their leader was Pablo Manlapit, the leader of the High Wages Movement. Manlapit came to Hawai'i as one of the earliest HSPA recruits in 1910. Plantation owners evicted their workers from their plantation homes in an attempt to break the strike. Like other Filipino workers, the Monrayo family relocated to the Middle Street strike camp in Honolulu. Her parents separated when she was six years old, and Angeles and her father and brother would eventually leave for San Francisco in 1927. The following excerpts illustrate the contours of Filipino community life during the plantation strikes of 1924. Life was difficult, but as one of only a handful of girls and women, she and other young girls found ways to help their families survive. Angeles was only 12 years old at the time she wrote these diary entries.

Waipahu, Oahu, T.H.
March 3, 1924

Dear Diary:
Mary and her folks had moved to Honolulu. I feel so lonely now without her. The reason why they went to Honolulu, because it's been heard that all Filipinos must strike for higher pay. Mr. Pablo Manlapit is the leader of this strike. Mr Manlapit says that all Filipinos must strike or else there will be many hurt. So I think that's why they left and moved to Honolulu to stay. Oh, why did this strike has to come up for. Now no one to pal with, now, I have to sleep all by myself from now on, go to school alone and I'll have to go to shows alone. Gee, I don't think I'll have any more fun, nowthat Mary is gone. I have other friends but they're not as close to me like Mary is. Speaking of the strike, I wonder, if Tatay [father] will go to Honolulu too. Gee, Tatya is making good here tho' he is steadily putting money in the bank. Anyway, I'll let you know if we do go to Honolulu. Oh Diary, before I forget, Father bought a new car. An Oakland Touring car. Boy, it's nice to have, I mean, own a car. A friend of ours will drive it for us. And my brother will learn from him. Faustino will drive the car—I'm scared of him somehow. I do not like him

Strike Camp, Middle St., Honolulu, T.H.
May 10, 1924

Dear Diary:
We have just arrived here today, here, at the Strike Camp. There are so many Filipinos here, married couples and unmarried men. They're from all parts of Oahu. There are five other young girls here too. I become friends with two of them already. Their first names are Esperanza and Victoria. They are both very nice girls. They showed me the place around here, as soon as we settled, I mean, found our sleeping quarters. You see, we all live in one big house, and so all we did was put curtains around our bed, and that will have to serve as our room, for how long, we don't know. I guess we have to stay here until this strike is over. And Manlapit is going to feed the whole crowd. We're suppose to go down to his office every other day to get our ration of food. Gosh, I hope this strike won't last long. You see, Diary, Mr. Manlapit wanted the plantation to give the laborers $2.00 a day and eight hours work. I certainly hope Manlapit wins, 'cause then it will be for our own good. Will tell you some more later on as the girls are draggin me. I told them I want to finish this.

Strike Camp, Middle St., Honolulu, T.H.
May 11, 1924

Dear Diary:
Another day had gone by. Do you know, as soon as we finished breakfast, I went over to Esperanza's sleeping quarters and she was just finishing breakfast.

I asked her if she has anything to do today. She said "No." And I asked her to show me the place again. We looked into everything. The bath room, the toilet, the kitchen and do you know there are so many mango trees close by. Boy! Wait until the mangoe season is in full blossom, by that I mean when they get ripe, and that's not far-off—it is next month, and Ill surely do some climbing again. I haven't climb trees for so long, it seems. Oh well, it won't be long now. I told Esperanza about it, and she says, "That's good, 'cause that means we don't have to ask any boys to get the mangoes for us. We can get them ourselves." And Esperanza introduced me to the other 3 girls—Sofia, Marcella, and Trinidad. I don't know which of this girls is the oldest, but I do know I am the youngest of them all. Triny is sort of snobbish—'cause she's better looking—but she has such mannish walk. But just so they are nice to me I'll be nice to them. And Diary, the men here play basketball and volleyball. And there are 3 women here that "cooks" and sells" "Maruya," you know, fried bananas and other good things to eat. Oh, I just love "Maruya." I bought four today and gave 2 to Esperanza. Somehow Esperanza kind of fill Mary's place; but I don't think I'll ever forget Mary. I do hope I'll see her soon. Well, Diary, that's all for now. If something new happens here I'll let you know.

Strike Camp, Middle St., Honolulu, T.H.
May 13, 1924

>Dear Diary:
>Say, there'll be something going on here on every Saturdays and Sundays from now on. You know what? Well, I'll tell you. It's this; there's going to be dances here every Saturdays and Sundays. Gee, won't that be fun. You see, Diary, I'm so crazy about dancing. And another thing, we are going to charge the men 10 cents for 3 minutes dance. Gosh, that's not bad is it? You know, Diary, someone thought of this idea, and it is for our own good, 'cause you see, we are very far from "show-houses." This dancing business is for our benefit so that the place here won't be as dull every Saturday and Sunday. And I know we girls are going to have lots of fun when that day comes around. Gee, I hope all the girls will be in it. I'm sure Esperanza and Victoria and Sophia will join in—including myself.

Strike Camp, Middle St., Honolulu, T.H.
May 20, 1924

>Dear Diary:
>Sorry, I couldn't tell you anything last night when the dance was over because I was so tired and sleepy, but I was happy, 'cause I made $7.20. I counted it before I went to sleep and I gave it to Father this morning. I kept just a dollar for myself to spend on something I'd like to eat. Gee, I didn't think I would make that much, but I did. And tonight there's going to be dancing again. Hope I'll make just as much as I did last night. Oh, there were only four girls that dance last night. The other two didn't join in 'cause they say nice girls don't dance at all. Marcela didn't say that but Trinidad did. Gee, I wish one of these days she'd be really jealous about us making some money and she won't, so that she will really join us. That way we'll

make her eat her words without us forcing her to. 'Cause she says too, that it's bad for us girls to dance, 'cause dancing will lead us to something else later on. She's just evil-minded, that's all. Gosh, we just dance. I don't see any harm in it, do you? These dancing isn't anything like they have in dancehalls. The dancing we have here is just-clean-good-fun, for all of us here. Oh well, if that's the way she feels about it, well, that's up to her, eh Diary?

Strike Camp, Middle St., Honolulu, T.H.
May 22, 1924

Dear Diary:

I've got to tell you this. Do you know Esperanza and I took in washing today from the men here in the camp, 'cause after all, we just play and play and so it so happened that one of our friends here brought this thing up about us washing his clothes 'cause he doesn't have any wife, he says, and, the laundry shops are so far-away; besides he says he's getting tired of washing his own clothes, and he say he'll pay us like he would pay the laundry-man. And so he says why don't you wash some of the boys clothes here, you'll make some extra money besides dancing on Saturdays and Sundays? And I says, "Gee, that is a very good idea." And he says "sure" and he says too, that I can wash clothes and iron them pretty good for a young girl like I am. And so I thank him so much for telling me about washing clothes, and to show he was in earnest, he gave me 4 shirts and 4 pair of underclothes. He says as soon as you wash them and iron, bring them to me and I'll pay you. Well, Diary, I put his clothes all bundled-up, and put his name on it and I ran out to find Esperanza 'cause I want her in it too. You know, her and I wash and iron and whatever we make, we'll divide it equally. I found her, she was talking to Victoria, and so I called her and says, "Let's go walking," and she came to me as soon as her legs could carry her. Then when we were far from everyone I told her of the good news. Gee, she was so happy as I was. So, we turned and walk towards the camp and asked a few more of our friends, all men, if they have any dirty clothes that they would like to be washed. At first they thought we were just joking but when they saw how earnest we were, they all say, "Sure, we have," but they say, "Be sure and return them nice and clean or else we won't pay you a cent," and I caught them winking at each other. Anyway, they know I can wash them, 'cause they always see the clothes I wash every Monday. Boy, they certainly gave us a great bundle. Anyway, we finished them in three hrs. We hung them late this afternoon about 2:30 but I think they'll dry before evening comes, 'cause the sun is shining so hot. Tomorrow we will iron again—'cause yesterday we iron our clothes, you know. Maybe it will take us about half day in iron all the clothes we washed today, but we don't care, 'cause we know we'll be paid well for our hard work. Gosh, I'm glad I could really wash, and Esperanza is too, 'cause she doesn't have much money. You know the money she earned last Saturday and Sunday, her father took nearly all of it. And so this money we earned washing, well, her father won't have to know about it. And that way she can keep every cent she'll get. About my father, well, he let me keep the money I earned, only I don't want to. One dollar out every dance-money I earned, is all I want. After all, he saves them and it helps to buy food too. So I don't worry about my father, he is so good to us. Esperanza and I are tired, but we don't care. After we finished washing I took her to the store and we had ice cream and vanilla snaps and we walked home slowly and we told stories all the way home. We laughed so much. It was fun, Diary.

Source: Monrayo, Angeles. *Tomorrow's Memories: A Diary, 1924–1928.* Honolulu: University of Hawai'i Press, 2003, pp. 15–21. Reprinted with permission.

78. Antonio E. Velasco, "Filipino Student Suffers from Pang of Race Prejudice," 1928

During the 1910s and 1920s, not all Filipino immigrants journeyed to America looking solely for good-paying jobs. Filipino students like Antonio Velasco came to America with dreams of completing their education. He and a handful of other Filipinos attended the Normal School in Bellingham, Washington. The school would later become Western Washington University. This article ran in the November 30, 1928, issue of the *Filipino Forum,* a biweekly Filipino American newspaper in Seattle. The *Filipino Forum* ran from 1928 to 1969. The paper called itself the "Independent Organ of Filipinos in the Pacific Northwest." The *Forum* covered a range of issues including Philippine independence, the struggles of Filipinos in America, labor unionism, poetry, and news about Filipino communities across the United States, as well as news about the Philippines as well. In this excerpt Velasco describes an incident of racial discrimination at a school dance. Some of the white female students did not want to dance with the Filipino students.

Among the biggest activities sponsored by the Freshman Class this quarter here in the Normal-by-the-mountain-and-by-the-sea, was the traditionally known, "Freshman Dance of the Nation," which was held on Nov. 10 at 8:30 p.m. in the big gym of the school.

A contribution of twenty-five cents was collected from every member. Those contributions have no doubt given something toward the success of the dance. I am proud to say that all the Filipino members had given their share heartily, although they knew that they didn't have any chance to enjoy the dance.

We were three among five Filipino members who bravely attended the dance. We did so with the idea of showing in particular our spirit in the activity of the Freshman Class of which we are members, and in general our spirit in any activity of the school. I, for one, admired the beautiful decorations of the hall, and appreciated the kind greetings of some friends. But nothing left on me a more lasting impression than Mrs. Fisher's attention to us Filipinos. She was the only lady in the hall who showed us that she was a woman. She was very kind indeed; a woman who possessed the spirit of sportsmanship.

We the Filipinos never aimed to dance with the charming white beauties in the hall, but Mrs. Fisher, wife of the president of the Normal School, inspired us to do so. We were feeling something in our hearts that made us so bashful. Somehow we tried to show that we know how to attend such gathering. By chance, one of us danced with one of the girls. Then after an hour or so, another companion of mine was inspired to approach a classmate of his to ask for a dance. I was near by when my companion said, "May I have the pleasure to dance with you Miss R. . . . . . . ? And Miss R. responded in quite harsh words, "no, thank you." Oh, what a pang I suffered although I was not the one addressed to. If only I had the divine power to disappear, I would have done so that very moment. If Mrs. Fisher had only witnessed the event, I would have told her that she put us in shame. For she had told us previously that the ladies were generous to welcome everyone. She encouraged us to dance. But that moment we found out that an attitude of race prejudice was being entertained by some of the girls. It was really a strange thing to me to know that such a discrimination prevail in this school. Some white friends consider themselves to be the best educated, most cultured, and above all they consider that all races other than theirs are inferior . . .

Source: *Filipino Forum*. November 30, 1928. University of Washington, Suzallo Library, Microforms and Newspaper Collection, A4137. Seattle Civil Rights and Labor History Project. Accessed March 2010.

79. Mariano Guiang, Interview by Carolina Koslosky, 1976

Mariano Guiang was born in the Philippines in 1904, in Ilocos Norte, the northwestern province on Luzon Island. He immigrated to Seattle, Washington, when he was 20 years old, joining his uncle who had moved there in 1918. Several years later, Guiang began a boxing career that took him all over the United States and the Canadian Pacific Northwest. In 1976, Carolina Koslosky, from the Washington State Oral History Project, interviewed Guiang. In the following excerpt, Guiang talks about his experiences as a boxer and the ways he maintained ties with his family in the Philippines.

"I came here by steamship, *President McKinley*. At that time, we landed on what they call Pier 91 now. It was just two piers in there. At that time there was no plane for coming from the Philippines. I was 19.["]

Coming To America

"[I came from] Norte, Ilocas Norte. I was raised—my mother died while I was 7 years old—we were lucky enough to be raised by our aunt. And when I went with my father to Manila, you know, when I went back from vacation, my aunt told me, 'All your friends are gone to America now, I think you better be going.' I didn't want it, I didn't want it. They finally convince me but they doubt if I wanted to come, see, because, you know, I refuse at first. Then my sister came with me to Manila and see [that] I really came. I didn't, in my mind, I was not willing to come. But they finally convinced me to come.

"I had my uncle [in Seattle], you know, Pedro Guiang, he got his doctorate of education I think in here, in the University of Washington. He was here then. He came here in 1918. I arrived at his apartment, see. But he was staying with somebody else, you know, so I went to a hotel in Chinatown, Panama Hotel.

"It was hard, the Depression was on at that time. I was lucky enough I arrived on June and July, I went to Alaska, see, for two months. And then when we came back we . . . I didn't have no work again, so I . . . went to Franklin High School. But I didn't stay very long again because it was very hard. You couldn't even find a schoolboy's work at that time, see. So I quit again and finally I drifted to going to boxing shows, you know.["]

Boxing Through Washington

"Every Friday they had boxing shows by 9th and Olive at that time. That's what they called the Austin and Bishop Gymnasium at that time. So I go there every Friday, they had a show. In fact, I was going while I was going to Franklin High School. Just to watch.

"But it was a funny thing that came up, you know, one guy named Ray Woods was beating everybody in his size, you know. One night I went over there and they asked me if I could fight. 'Sure, I could fight.' And they put me over him. And at that time I was not in very good shape, see, but I was strong because I was an athlete, I was a track man in Franklin High School. It's hard to believe. So, they put the gloves on, and said 'Are you going to fight?' I was not never scared or anything. I was never nervous, even the doctor, 'How come your heart never even, you know, vary in its beat?' Why should I? It's just a game to me, a sport, I should say. We fought over there but he got the decision. But that's how I got started.

"We boxed around Seattle, Everett, Mount Vernon, Yakima, and Wenatchee and Klamathe Falls, Oregon and so on. [I started] somewhere around 1927, '26, '27, yeah, I think it was '26. My name at that time was Young Marino. [The crowds] like Filipinos at that time because they were so many good Filipino fighters. They like me, they, in fact, I fought several good fights, but not money-wise, you know, I fought many men in Wenatchee. In fact, in 1931 I fought the champion of Eastern Canada and Toronto, Canadian, Territory of Alaska at that time. Bantam and Feather Weight. I fought mostly feather-weight. Sometimes, I even fought 129 pounders and I use to weigh 114 to 15. But I had to fight sometimes to live at that time. It was very hard, but what we can get, we could get something to eat and wash our clothes.

"They were quite a few [Filipino boxers], there's Clarence Corpuz, he was one of them. Johnny, Johnny, I forgot his name, he's a cook now . . . but there were quite a few Filipino boys before, but none of them took it . . . really serious like I did. I tried to learn because I didn't want to get beat.

"It's the opportunity that got me into [teaching] boxing, you know, when I got with the Navy, back in Bremerton --in Bremerton I didn't have nothing to do then. But when they transfer you to Pier 91, that is the time when I really taught boxing. That was Korean War, 1949, when I started teaching boxing. As a boxer, I quit in 1933.["]

Father Fighter

"I promise that when my son is born, that when I could go no place, I quit boxing then. I fought the same night he was born . . . So, well since I was a champion of Alaska, they book me to fight in Ketchikan, Alaska. But since my son was born, I wanted them to send me some money, you know, advance some money, so

I could leave them. They said, you come over here, we'll fix you. I said, No you're not going to fix me. So I give the ticket and accommodation to another Filipino boy that use to fight. They were surprise, you know, they had a band that meet him, they were surprised that was not me.

"When my son was eight years old, we was living over there in Greenwood and they had, they started a Greenwood Boys Club over there at that time . . . I think it was during the war, Japan war. So Dick Francisco was looking for me because my son said, 'My father was a fighter.' So he came to the house. 'Well, I like to help but I'm working, you know how it is at Bremerton. I started so early dark and I arrive here dark, I can't help you.' 'Well, I just wondered because your son is a natural fighter.' But after the war, just until 1944 . . . they transfer me to Pier 91 and that time, I met a colored boy and he ask me to train him. Freddy Brown. I know these kids because they were running around with my son then. 'Well, you come to the house with your mother and we'll talk.'

"So I trained him and he became good. And at that time they started, that was 1950, yeah, during the Korean War then. They have that KING's RING in television. Then I had so many boys that was winning all the time. I used to train, you know, we train them at the Professional Gymnasium, see over there by Fourth and Wall Street, that use to be a big K-Mart at one time.

"I exercise every morning. Me and my wife, I make my wife exercise too. It's doing her good. To tell the truth, my wife is my sister-in-law.

"She was the wife of my youngest brother that got killed during the Japanese war. But he was a member of the U.S. armed forces then. So, she was receiving pension when I married her. But when I married her it stopped. But when I first went over there [Mr. Guiang returned to the Philippines in '67, '71, and '74] I never think that we are going to . . . When my first wife died, I saw her over there then, well, 'How do you like to come to the states?' I said. Well she refuse at first but then . . . of course she got a sister you know, Mrs. Domingo Aurelia. That's her sister. So, she said 'I'll come see my sister.' Well, she came and she finally consented that she was going to marry me. It was alright, she's very nice, we get along fine. Well, I consider myself lucky . . . I'm fair with people, see.

So, that's my life here in America.["]

Source: Excerpt from Guiang, Mariano. Interview with Carolina Koslosky. September 24, 1976. Washington State Oral History Project. Washington State Archives, Olympia, Washington. Edited by Stacy Carlson, May 2000. http://www.historylink.org/index.cfm?DisplayPage=output.cfm&file_id=2428. Accessed September 2009. Reprinted with permission.

80. Apolonia Dangzalan, Interview by Meri Knaster, 1977

Apolonia Dangzalan emigrated from the Philippines to Hawai'i in 1924 and moved to San Francisco two years later. After a few years, she divorced her husband and moved to Watsonville, California, where she opened a restaurant, a pool hall, and a boardinghouse. Dangzalan then became one of the only female labor contractors in California, coordinating seasonal jobs for Filipino agriculture workers on Watsonville farms. Dangzalan faced many challenges in California: She was an Asian immigrant during a period of intense xenophobia; she was an entrepreneur looking for opportunities during the Depression; and she was a single woman in a primarily bachelor Filipino community. However, throughout her long life, Dangzalan remained an active and successful businesswoman he was still working in her grocery and liquor store at the time of her 1977 interview with Meri Knaster. In this excerpt, the 81-year-old Dangzalan describes her many business ventures, her social life in Watsonville, and her firm belief that she would have achieved success wherever she lived, regardless of the strictures of gender and ethnicity.

KNASTER: When you came to Watsonville and you started the business with the boarding houses . . .
DANGZALAN: Me and Frank did it. [Frank Barba was Dangzalan's nephew; she sponsored him to come to the United States from the Philippines.]
KNASTER: . . . were there other Filipino women in the community?
DANGZALAN: No, in 1927, not yet Filipino women in that time.
KNASTER: Were you the only one?
DANGZALAN: No, but I don't going around to see them, just meet them at the social, that's all.
KNASTER: Social. What is the social?
DANGZALAN: Well, we got the Filipino club here in Watsonville . . .
KNASTER: Oh, so when you first came, in 1927, were there some women here?
DANGZALAN: Yes.
KNASTER: Did you have friends?
DANGZALAN: I got some in Salinas and Watsonville, but I don't get them right away because I don't have too much time to go and look around. I take care of the kitchen, watch the cook.
KNASTER: Did you live in the boarding house?
DANGZALAN: Yes. I lived in the kitchen. My cook, Frank, and me stayed in the house, because I got three bedrooms, and kitchen and dining room, for eating the boys.
KNASTER: Was it considered unusual that a woman was in business at the time?
DANGZALAN: I don't remember.
KNASTER: Well, when you were dealing with people were they surprised? Did they not want to deal with a woman in business?
DANGZALAN: Well, some of the American people got surprised. Usually first time see the woman working like this. Especially when I am in camp, separate from Frank. Frank is in another place working under the company. Frank lived in Aromas, the place he now staying. There is the place he stay running the boarding house, too. I am to the Salinas Road to run my business, a boarding house . . .
KNASTER: So when you said you had the labor camp you also said you had a business you went to at night. Where was the business?
DANGZALAN: Main Street.
KNASTER: The same liquor store that you have now?
DANGZALAN: No. That is the first one I make in the building, Monterey Club. A Mexican runs it now.

KNASTER:	And you have the liquor store.
DANGZALAN:	Yes.
KNASTER:	What was it before, a restaurant?
DANGZALAN:	Restaurant, gambling. I run gambling too. I make that Monterey Club. I buy the dry cleaning business next door to the Monterey Club. I open a pool hall in 1936.
KNASTER:	Were there women, too?
DANGZALAN:	No Filipino women. Mexican women. American woman working under my beer parlor. And barber shop, Filipino, too.
KNASTER:	Was there music in the restaurant?
DANGZALAN:	Yes. I got some dancing, too. Then after that I buy license for nightclub. I run that, too. Soon after that I put a grocery to the place now I am. After that I reopen for nightclub . . .
KNASTER:	Do you think that if you had stayed in the Philippines that you would have been able to do as much—houses and business and everything.
DANGZALAN:	Yes.
KNASTER:	The fact that you are a woman would not have prevented you?
DANGZALAN:	Not at all.

Source: Excerpt from "Apolonia Dangzalan, Filipina Businesswoman, Watsonville, California." Interview with Meri Knaster. Reprinted with permission from the Regional History Project of the University Library at the University of California, Santa Cruz. http://library.ucsc.edu/reg-hist/dangzalan. Accessed August 2009.

81. Frank Barba, Interview by Meri Knaster, 1977

Frank Barba was born in 1898, the year that the United States took control of the Philippines after the Spanish-American War. After attending American-influenced schools in the Philippines, Barba immigrated to the United States in 1924. He eventually joined his aunt, Apolonia Dangzalan, in California, where he took over a Filipino labor camp that she had been managing. Barba worked in the agricultural industry for the rest of his career, primarily as a labor contractor.

This interview, conducted by Meri Knaster in 1977, when Barba was 78 years old, illustrates the effects of American colonization on the Filipino school system and describes the ethnic community created by Filipino laborers in central California.

KNASTER:	What were you born?
BARBA:	In San Nicolas, Ilocos Norte, in the northern part of the Philippines. I attended school there until seventh grade. Then I went to the capital of the province, to high school. We've got Filipino teachers and an American principal. During my third year [of high school] I was sick and we moved to Manoag, Pangasinan. I went to Lincoln High School. Then I moved back to my hometown, and went to high school [until] my graduation in 1924 . . .
KNASTER:	What, in all of the years that you were going to school, did they teach you about the United States?

BARBA: Yes, we had the history of the United States.
KNASTER: Well, how did you picture the United States to be?
BARBA: Oh, we picture it as very rich. We would like to go. It's very exciting. A rich country and a beautiful country. I would like to see and maybe make a better living . . .

[Barba's aunt and uncle sponsored him to move to Hawai'i, where he worked on a sugarcane plantation for a month. He then moved to the mainland, staying with some relatives in San Francisco for six months before moving to Watsonville.]

KNASTER: Who were these relatives?
BARBA: Oh, my cousin and second cousin. They've been down here in the United States for a long, long time.
KNASTER: Do you remember when they migrated here?
BARBA: No, I don't.
KNASTER: Were they from the same town?
BARBA: Yes.
KNASTER: What were they doing in San Francisco?
BARBA: Well they were working . . . waitresses or busboy, dishwasher or cook.
KNASTER: Had they come here as single people, or as a family?
BARBA: Single people.
KNASTER: Were they only men, or were there women too?
BARBA: No, mostly men.
KNASTER: Most of the time it seems that Filipino people came to the United States as single people, and mostly men, rather than families.
BARBA: Right. Mostly men. Then after a while the man maybe go back and bring his wife.

When I liked the place, I wrote to my aunt in Hawai'i. So they came over and joined me here. They stayed for a while in San Francisco, but they didn't work. I stayed in San Francisco for a while. I went and visited them once in a while in Stockton. They were working on Sherman Island in asparagus . . .

One day when I went to visit them, my friend who was insurance agent was talking to me. He was a neighbor of mine where I was born. He said, "Why don't you come here and look for a job? They are looking for a night clerk. So I got the job in Stockton in a hotel, renting rooms. I worked there for more than a year. Then my aunt and my uncle moved to Watsonville.
KNASTER: Do you know why they came to Watsonville?
BARBA: They figure that there's lot's of work in agriculture . . . lettuce and whatnot. When they came here they rented a couple of big houses in town. Keeping of boys. There's a lot of boys wanting to work.
KNASTER: Filipino boys?
BARBA: Yeah, all Filipinos then. They had a camp, and about fifty-five boys, sending boys to work for everybody who needs some help. There was this one big company from Salinas. He has a camp at the foot of Warner Hill in Watsonville. [The company] told them if they want to move in, you stay in the camp and keep boys and board boys. One day when I came down from Stockton to visit them, they said, "You'd better come back here and keep this camp and we move to another."

Source: Excerpt from "Frank Barba: Filipino Labor Contractor: Watsonville, CA, 1927–1977." Interview with Meri Knaster. Reprinted with permission from the Regional History Project of the University Library at the University of California, Santa Cruz. http://library.ucsc.edu/reg-hist/barba. Accessed August 2009.

82. Rufino F. Cacabelos, "Autobiography," 1992

Rufino F. Cacabelos immigrated to Seattle from the Philippines in 1929. He worked in the Alaskan canneries, as a houseboy, and as a migrant farmworker for a Japanese farmer. He graduated from the University of Washington with an English degree in 1939 and began graduate school, but World War II interrupted his studies. He was drafted into the all-Filipino 1st Infantry Regiment. Cacabelos never completed his graduate studies, but found a fulfilling career as a distribution clerk in the U.S. Postal Service. He married and settled in Seattle, where he and his wife raised their only child, James. Throughout his life, Cacabelos was active in many Filipino American organizations in the Seattle area, including the Filipino Columbians, Columbianas, the Northern League, and the Narvacanian Club. In these two excerpts from his autobiography, Cacabelos recounts his first experience in an American school and his stint working for a Japanese farmer during the Depression.

Jason Lee Junior High School

I will always remember September 4, 1929, when I met an American High School principal for the first time. Mrs. Ross took me to the Principal's office herself. The school was 5 blocks from the Rosses. We walked. She enrolled me in the 8th grade, talked to the clerk and Principal and left. The principal kept looking at my report card which I brought with me from Vigan. I cannot figure out what he thought of it as he gave it back to me, anyway, I was enrolled. A lady clerk gave me a schedule and told me to go to room 108 my homeroom, she explained. I entered the room with boys and girls who were all taller than I was although I was seven years older than the oldest of them. Since it was the homeroom and being the first day of school that fall, seat assignments took over an hour. Mrs. Jessica Reed, our homeroom teacher must have taken psychology in college. She was very systematic. She made us stand up against the wall according to height. This way, the short ones were placed in the front seats, while the taller ones in the back rows regardless of sex. With this method, I occupied the 9th seat from the left, since she alphabetized each row from left to right. I was in the middle of the front row in front of her desk. She was very strict, but she liked me because I was the quietest pupil in the room.

During the first weeks of school, I had difficulty talking with my classmates because of my poor accent and enunciation. Gradually many of my classmates understood me well enough and a few became close to me. My teachers too were kind and generous because I believed that they graded me better than I deserved. So, I adjusted myself easily at school even easier than at washing the piled dishes of the day at the Rosses.

On school days Mrs. Ross rose early and prepared breakfast. Carolyn had to go to school, the doctor to his office and I to my classes. While Mrs. Ross was in the kitchen, I kept busy in the dining room, squeeze orange juice for Carolyn (7) and Bud (William Jr.—3), set the plates, silverware, glasses for juice and milk, cups for coffee, napkins, and place the morning paper by the Doctor's plate. Then I tidied the living room cushions, dusted a few of the furniture pieces and cleaned the cigarette ashtrays. Ate my breakfast and got ready for school. Coming home at four, I washed the morning and noon dishes waiting in the kitchen. Then helped Mrs. Ross peel potatoes for cooking. Mrs. Ross did all the cooking. I served dinner the way she taught me. After the family had eaten, I had mine, wash the dishes and then hit the books.

During Saturdays, I washed the Oldsmobile, helped Mrs. Ross with the laundry, mop the kitchen floor. I mowed the lawn, wash the big living room window on both sides and also Toby (brown family dog) besides washing the dishes. After that I was free for the day. I just had to wash the dishes when I came home at night. On Sundays, I rode with them and they dropped me at church while they attended Presbyterian services. As a rule I had Sunday off unless the Rosses entertained. I went to Mr. Bolong's house and visit where I would meet Narciso now and then, or go to a show with one or two friends. Then I walked home and studied for the Monday's assignment.

This went on for years since I entered Jason Lee Jr. High, then to Stadium High. I graduated from Jason Lee as an honor roll student, 9th grade on January 30, 1931. Immediately I enrolled at Stadium High School for the 1st semester in 1931. In Stadium High, I also got in the honor roll list in my first semester. That was the end of my honor roll laurels until Senior High. Dr. Ross and family went to Yakima for a better position where his specialty was in demand. The family, especially Mrs. Ross wanted me to go with them, so I accepted with joy. With Buddy and Carolyn, I learned English faster than I had expected. I read all the children books Mrs. Ross brought home from the Yakima Public Library. It was then 1932 and I was a junior at Yakima High. I graduated with honors from Yakima High School in June 1933. The family bought me a new suit for my graduation present. After graduation, I said farewell to the Ross family that had showed me kindness and a degree of affection. I always had pleasant thoughts when I remember the Ross family. Indeed, I lovingly treasured their good wishes for my well being.

The Depression

After graduation, I came to Seattle looking for a chance to go to Alaska, there was no luck. I went to work at Auburn in a Japanese farm. Once again I came in contact with mother soil, the giver and source of life. Japanese workers are superior in the fields. It was no contest for one to keep pace with any of them. I just plodded along from early morning until sunset. The Japanese farmer raised strawberries, tomatoes, lettuce, cabbage, carrots, asparagus, radishes and onions. All of good quality for market. All summer long, we start work by 6 am after breakfast. Stop an hour for lunch and resumed work until 8 pm. A 14 hour back-breaking farm laborer. It was in such times that I regretted leaving Apo Ramon. I kept saying to myself, "If I stayed, I would be in the U. of Santo Tomas by now." In a 14 hour day's work, I was paid an amazing 90 cents plus my board and lodging. The good thing about working for a Japanese family is soaking in a very large hot tub. At first, I felt scalded and did not particularly enjoy the soaking. In my third night in the water, I experienced the most pleasant feeling of the 30 minutes soaking. From then on until the end of summer, I looked forward for the intoxicating experience where my tiredness evaporated and a great feeling settled my entire body. The Japanese discovered a pleasant secret of living. I give credit to them. In 85 days I had earned 76.50 plus a bonus of ten dollars for being a diligent worker. A few of the other workers had a 12 dollar bonus. Years later, when Mr. Ted Yamari, a shrewd Japanese cannery contractor included me in his 80 man crew as a can reformer, I was to enjoy once more the ecstasy of that glorious hot tub soaking. That was 1938 in Port Arthur cannery.

I worked for the Japanese farmer from July 10, 1933 until Friday September 15th. When the University of Washington opened in the fall, I did not earn enough for a quarter's tuition because my ninety cents a day that I earned in the farm was spent in bus rides to Seattle or Tacoma on Sundays to visit acquaintances. I ended up at Mr. Mariano Bolong's house. There I met Leo de Leon from Cagayan who would someday have a daughter to become first lady in waiting in the Seattle Seafair.

Franklin Delano Roosevelt became President in 1933 and the NRA, CCC and many other agencies were created to put men back to work. I went to apply to the Civilian Conservation Corps, the WPA, etc. But the race prejudice was still strong against minorities. On top of that, I was told that I was not big enough to be hired. So that fall, many of us students were penniless. We steeraged with Pinoys who were lucky to have restaurant jobs such as busboys, dishwashers, cook helpers and elevator boys. They had rooms of their own, so we steeraged with their permission. When they went to work, we joyfully used their beds.

Tacoma had a red light district wherein the Chinese operated gambling. Pinoys frequented these places both the penniless and those who worked. The place was at least warm and so in winter we spent hours there inhaling their opium smoke. They often gave us dry biscuits to go with the hot tea which was accessible to everybody.

Source: Cacabelos, Rufino F. "Autobiography." 1992. http://cacabelos.us/home.html. Accessed November 2009. Reprinted with permission.

83. Excerpt from Evangeline Canonizado Buell's *Twenty-Five Chickens and a Pig for a Bride: Growing Up in a Filipino Immigrant Family*, 2006

On February 15, 1898, the U.S. battleship *Maine* exploded and sank in Havana harbor. The incident quickly devolved into armed conflict in spite of Spain's attempts to withdraw from Cuba. Half a century of Manifest Destiny and expansionist hunger fueled the desire for America's "splendid little war" with Spain. Though the American defeat of Spain spelled Cuban independence, it did not result in the same for the Philippine

Islands. The United States paid Spain $20 million for the Philippines in December 1898.

However, the Filipinos did not go quietly into the night. Under the leadership of Emilio Aguinaldo, the Filipinos waged a war of independence. The United States labeled it as an insurrection and after three years of fighting, officially proclaimed the rebellion over in 1902. The Philippine Organic Act of July 1902 established a Philippine Commission and a civilian government in the Philippines. Despite American proclamations, the war continued as elements of Filipino resistance groups continued to fight the U.S. military and Philippine Constabulary for another decade.

During the 10-year Philippine American War, African American regiments that had originally fought against Native Americans in America's last Indian Wars in the American Southwest were sent to the islands to fight Filipinos. The soldiers in these all-black regiments were known as Buffalo Soldiers, a nickname that is commonly believed to have come from the Cheyenne Indians, a reference either to the resemblance of black soldiers' curly hair to the buffalo's mane or to the fierceness of African American soldiers, which was likened to that of a cornered bison. Although these Buffalo Soldiers were sent to fight the Filipinos, some of these men found they shared a common experience with their Filipino enemies, namely racism and discrimination at the hands of white Americans. A few of these Buffalo Soldiers decided to throw their lot in with the Filipinos, switching sides and fighting against the United States. Others remained stationed in the Philippines after the fighting ended. Some of these soldiers voluntarily stayed in the Philippines and eventually integrated with the local populace.

In this excerpt from her memoirs, Oakland, California native and Filipino activist and writer Evangeline Canonizado Buell tells the story of her grandfather, a Buffalo Soldier who stayed in the Philippines after the war and eventually returned to America with his Filipino bride.

Grandpa Stokes was among 6,000 African-American soldiers who were sent to the Philippines in 1898 to fight in the Spanish-American War. Upon arriving in the Philippines, he became part of the Ninth Cavalry of the U.S. Army. My grandfather became sergeant in that unit consisting of African-American members, who were called "Buffalo Soldiers."

Grandpa Stokes could not escape racism even in a foreign land. He and the members of his division were put in the forefront of the battles and used as shields for the Caucasian soldiers. In order to survive, they used their cunning, toughness, and defiance.

The Spanish-American War ended in 1898, and Spain ceded its Philippine colony to the U.S. as part of the Treaty of Paris. About one hundred Buffalo Soldiers, including Grandpa Stokes, remained in the Philippines to fight in the ensuing battle between the American colonizers and the Filipino fighters for independence that became known as the Philippine-American War. During this conflict, the Buffalo Soldiers had benefited from the solidarity of Filipinos, who refused to shoot African American soldiers because they felt an affinity with them. The Caucasian soldiers had referred to both groups as "savages." This War, which lasted for three years, resulted in hundreds of thousands of Filipino casualties and successfully solidified American control of the Philippines. Like many of the surviving Buffalo Soldiers, Grandpa Stokes chose to remain on the island archipelago.

In 1902 Grandpa Stokes married Maria Bunag, the daughter of Gregoria Rodriguez, a native of Penaranda, Nueva Ecija. They had three daughters, who were born at Fort Stotsenberg (later known as Clark Air Base), located in the province of Pampanga.

Despite the prejudice that he still experienced in the U.S. Army, it seemed that Grandpa Stokes had finally fulfilled his dream to find a better life outside the United States. He loved the Philippines, its people, culture, and customs. Grandpa learned to speak Chinese and Spanish, and local dialects like Ilocano, Kapampangan, Tagalog, and Visayan. He communicated with Filipinos in their own dialect and enjoyed the local food, including the strong-smelling *bagoong*, a salty paste of fermented fish or shrimp. At home, he ate peasant-style, using his fingers to dip the grilled fish in *bagoong*, scoop it up with rice, and thumb it into his mouth with relish. He washed the dinner down with a glass of *tuba*, a potent local wine made of palm sap, and ended the meal with a satisfied sigh and a compliment to his wife, "Ay, *masarap ang pagkain*," "Oh, the food is delicious."

After my grandmother Maria died in 1917, Grandpa Stokes had to send his three daughters to stay with his late wife's relatives because he could not care for them while fulfilling his Army duties. Ten-year-old Felicia and five-year-old Theodora went to live with their Uncle Nicolas in Cabanatuan, Nueva Ecija, and eight-year-old Dominga stayed with her grandmother, Gregoria, in Penaranda. While Dominga found love and nurturing in her new home, Felicia and Theodora did not fare as well. Their uncle and other relatives treated them like servants because they were half black and did not look like their cousins with straight hair and fairer skin. Older male cousins repeatedly raped and beat the two girls, who endured physical, emotional, and sexual abuse for five years, until their father rescued them from this horrifying experience.

In 1923 Grandpa Stoakes met Roberta Dungca, a beautiful and vivacious 16-year old from Angeles, Pampanga, where his army base was located. She was thirty years younger than my grandfather, who was then in his late forties, and was only a few months older than his eldest child Felicia. Grandpa was deeply in love with Roberta and wanted to marry her and bring her back to the States. She was the first woman he had considered marrying since the death of his wife Maria, but he was wracked with doubts as to whether she would reciprocate his feelings or whether her parents would approve. Though Roberta was also unsure about Grandpa because of their age difference, she thoroughly enjoyed his company, appreciated that he spoke her Kapampangan dialect, and thought that he looked handsome in his uniform . . .

Grandpa Stokes, desperate to make Roberta his wife, decided to take matters into his own hands . . . Grandpa found the perfect opportunity to implement his plan. Fully aware that Filipinos forbade kissing during courtship and only marriage could save the family's honor if such a custom were violated, he grabbed Roberta, put his arms around her, and kissed her in front of her shocked parents. Her angry father blurted out the words that her daughter's suitor had been secretly wanting to hear, "You have to marry her immediately!"

While still reluctant to wed a much older man, Roberta knew that she could not break an honored tradition. Her parents also had misgivings about their daughter marrying Grandpa, but they had to save face and allowed the wedding to take place. Their biggest fear was that they would lose Roberta forever once she and Grandpa left the country. In 1928, Grandpa Stokes and Roberta sailed for the United States, and her parents' worst nightmare would be fulfilled. Their daughter would never have a chance to visit the Philippines and see her family again.

Grandma Roberta cried for days in her mother's arms before their departure and everyday on the ship bound for San Francisco. Once in the States, Grandpa helped his wife, who was illiterate, to write letters to her family and read their letters to her. He fulfilled his promise to make her happy and provide a stable home for her, but it took Grandma Roberta a long time to forgive him for kissing her in front of her parents. "We always had a chaperone whenever we went out together, and he never touched me, but he was worried that someone else might come along," she told me. "I learned to love your Grandpa only after we arrived her. It broke my heart to leave the country. I'm still very lonesome for my parents."

Like Grandpa Stokes, many of the African-American soldiers who had remained in the Philippines after the Spanish-American War eventually returned to the U.S. with their Filipino wives in the late 1920s and early 1930s. Among them were Grandpa's friends like Messieurs Brown, Hawkins, James, Jones, McQuinney, Nicholas, and Pitts who also settled in the Bay Area. The men taught their wives to play poker and they spent many evenings partying and playing cards together. Over the years, they often visited our home until they passed away, one after another. As a sign of deference for our elders, we children called the men "Grandpa" and their Filipino wives "Manang," a term of respect for an older sister or female relative.

The grandpas loved reminiscing about the Philippines and held the children's attention with stories about their adventures. One evening, while Grandma Roberta was still preparing dinner, one grandpa said, "Oh, how your Grandpa Stoked loved to make homemade gin . . ." Another raved about the culinary talent of my late grandmother Maria . . .

Grandpa Stokes and Grandma Roberta lived in West Oakland, together with my father Stanley and my mother Felicia. Grandpa had retired from the Army, and my father was in the Navy, stationed on Yerba Buena Island between Oakland and San Francisco. There were very few Filipinos and African Americans in West Oakland in the 1930s, and these minority groups had difficulty finding housing because of racial discrimination. Therefore, extended families tended to stay together to survive, especially during the Depression. After countless rejections from landlords, Grandpa and Grandma were able to rent the upper flat in an old Victorian home form a Portuguese family they had met through friends.

Although Grandpa and Grandma did not have children of their own, they had a household full of kids. They had adopted my cousin Rosario right after she was born in 1932 because she was abandoned by her mother, my Auntie Theodora. Because we were the same age, we were raised as sisters and dressed alike as twins. Grandpa would sit us on his lap and sing to us in Tagalog and Spanish, bouncing us up and down to the rhythm of the songs. He also taught us how to count in Chinese. When my sister Rosita was born in 1934, the whole family, especially

Grandpa, was thrilled to have another addition to the brood. While Grandpa took care of amusing the children, Grandma handled the task of nourishing the growing family.

Grandpa taught Grandma how to cook American, including Southern soul food from his native Tennessee and other cuisines, helping us to develop a multi-cultural palate. Fried chicken that had been soaked in buttermilk, mashed potatoes, cream gravy, sausage bread dressing, spaghetti, and lemon and sweet potato pies. Grandma learned to bake biscuits, but she always served rice, no matter what else was on the menu. Even now, my sister Rosita must have rice with every meal.

Grandpa died in February 1936, when I was just four years old. I was left with few but very fond memories of him. Two years later, Grandma married Manuel Unabia. Since Filipinos were barred from buying real estate property, one of Grandpa's friends helped Grandma and Uncle Manuel by placing his name on the deed for the house that the couple bought for $5,000. He said that before Grandpa Stokes died, he had asked him to take care of Roberta and the grandchildren in case anything happened to him. "Berta, Sergeant Stokes was like a brother to me, and I'm glad I can help you in this way. May you be happy and secure in this house," the helpful grandpa stated. When it finally became legal for Filipinos to buy homes, he turned over the deed to Grandma, who changed the title in her name . . .

Buffalo Soldier Ernest Stokes is buried in the Presidio in San Francisco, where in 1898 he trained as a soldier before sailing for his assignment to fight in the Spanish-American War in the Philippines. His brave journey to find a better life had begun and ended on a windy hill that now looks down on a monument honoring the Tennessee volunteers, who fought in foreign wars.

Source: Buell, Evangeline Canonizado. *Twenty-Five Chickens and a Pig for a Bride: Growing Up in a Filipino Immigrant Family*. San Francisco: T'Boli, 2006, pp. 17–22. Reprinted with permission from the author.

84. Robert Bernardo, "Strangers Among Us," 2006, and Interview with Eliyahu Enriquez, 2009

Forced to leave Spain during the 16th-century Inquisition, many Jews and Jewish converts (called *conversos* or *marranos*) fled to the Philippines, a Spanish colony where the Inquisition was not as strong. A small and covert Jewish community grew in the Philippines, and once the United States took over in 1898, Jews were allowed to practice their religion openly. Filipino Jews opened their doors to their brethren in China and Europe who were escaping the Germans during the buildup to World War II.

Filipino American Robert Bernardo is an activist, attorney, and former cochair of the Gay Asian Pacific Alliance (GAPA). He converted to Judaism when he was an adult, discovering his Sephardic Jewish ancestry through his Spanish grandmother's side. In 2006, Bernardo gave the following *drash* (sermon) for the Rosh Ha'shanah service at Congregation Sha'ar Zahav. "Strangers Among Us" is an exposition on the many meanings of "stranger," illustrated with examples from Bernardo's own life and experiences as a gay Jewish Filipino man.

That same year, Bernardo served as the Grand Marshal of the San Francisco Gay Pride Parade. Three years later, in an interview with Eliyahu Enriquez (author of the Bahay Shalom blog), Bernardo remembered his experience: "I was extremely proud to wear my Filipino Barong Tagalog shirt. It was lavender with traditional white embroidery. I also wore a Hawaiian Lei that was given to me by founding GAPA member and former Parade Grand Marshal, Hoover Lee. To represent my Jewish side, I wore a rainbow-colored yarmulke on my head. It felt truly liberating to show the different components that make me who I am." In this excerpt from his interview, Bernardo talks about the ties between Spain, the Philippines, and Judaism; the place of homosexuals in Israel; and his own multifaceted identity.

"Strangers Among Us," 2006

In 1974, when my family lived in San Francisco's Richmond District, I remember spending warm, summer afternoons walking along Ocean Beach with my father. Together, we would collect seashells and then head off to Playland, the nearby amusement park (at the time) near 48th Avenue. I remember one day as we were heading back to our apartment, a group of teenagers heading toward us with white flowers in their hair. They wore bright tie-die shirts, multi-colored beads, and sandals. As they walked, they laughed, giggled, smoked . . . cigarettes and sang songs. I was thrilled to see these young people because they all looked so happy. I looked up and smiled at one of them, as he kindly offered me a piece of candy. As I was about to reach out, my father said, "Wag ka tatanggap sa hindi mo kilala!" Don't take things from strangers. He smiled at the man, yanked me toward him, and we continued back to the apartment. My family had only been in the United States for four years.

That was my earliest experience with "strangers." Several years later, my notions were reinforced in Mrs. Roy's second grade class at Brown Elementary in Daly City. I remember a police officer coming into my class to talk about child safety issues. Officer Bob (yes, his name was Officer Bob) began to explain about never talking to strangers or taking things from strangers—in lessons that came to be known as stranger danger.

Understandably, there is a human tendency to fear strangers. Some bio-sociologists believe that we are programmed with a built-in mechanism to protect us from harmful situations. They say that our intuitive senses help keep us safe—and often times, help keep us alive. How many times have we looked down a dark street at night and seen suspicious people coming toward us, and we felt the urge to cross the street or walk a little faster?

What does Judaism teach us about "ger," or the "stranger?"

Parashat Mishpatim states, "You shall not wrong a stranger or oppress him, for you were strangers in the land of Egypt (Exodus 22:20)." One of the great teachings of Judaism is "hachnasat orchim," welcoming the stranger. The Torah provides over 30 guidelines about our behavior towards the stranger. That's even more than other mitzvot such as loving G-d, keeping the Sabbath, and refraining from eating forbidden foods. The treatment of strangers is one of those rare topics that is listed not only among the 248 commanded acts but also among the 365 prohibited acts.

The Torah also tells us that Abraham would sometimes seek out strangers and offer them a meal. In Parashat Vayera, while being visited by G-d, Abraham sees three strangers passing by his tent in the wilderness. He tells the Almighty that the travelers need his assistance, and so he puts G-d on hold, while he offers the strangers proper hospitality.

We derive an important lesson from this action, and the Talmud supports it: "Welcoming a guest can take priority over welcoming the Shechinah." Furthermore, Rabbi Yochanan teaches us that, "One is permitted to move heavy bundles on Shabbat in order to make room for guests."

Where else can we find similar teachings?

In Hebrew, Sodom means *Burnt* and Gomorrah means *A Ruined Heap*. Respectively, these names were given to the two cities after they were destroyed by G-d for their sinfulness. And while many religious fundamentalists use this well-known story to justify their homophobia, some Torah scholars believe that the truly wicked act was the fact that when strangers (in the form of angels) came to visit Abraham's nephew, Lot—these angels were not treated with respect and hospitality by the people of Sodom. As you may recall, the Sodomites demanded access to the strangers, and Lot denied them access. And as the story goes, the Sodomites were struck with blindness, allowing Lot and his family, who were then instructed to leave the city, to escape, while Sodom and Gomorrah were destroyed with fire by G-d.

Lot's need to protect the strangers came even before the protection of his own family. What Lot did was act as his culture expected him to. This was the norm. Hospitality, in these times, meant that if a person asked for assistance, you were completely obliged to help and protect your visitor—even if that meant losing your property, family or life. So, the real Sodom and Gomorrah lesson here is not, "G-d will be displeased if you're LGBTQQI", rather "G-d will reject you if you don't stand up for those among you who are strangers, those who are different—those who may need your help."

The prophets remind us that, "G-d wants you to love those who are outsiders, and protect those who are defenseless."

In order to fully understand the reasoning behind these teachings, we must remember that our people were a nomadic people who traveled and wandered in an often hostile environment. Weather conditions and suspicious neighbors made hospitality a matter of survival. Being welcomed in a stranger's home or tent could mean the difference between life and death.

Jews have a history filled with kindness to strangers. During Shabbat dinner, aren't we commanded to welcome strangers to join us for a meal?

And we must also remind ourselves that many times in our history, we were strangers ourselves. One such example is the Kaifeng Jews of China. During the so-called "Holy War Crusades" of the 1090s, many Jews living in small towns along the Eastern coast of the Mediterranean and throughout Persia saw their homes burglarized and their synagogues burned down. They were threatened: either convert to Christianity or die.

So, a handful of Jews headed east, down the Silk Road to China because they had heard that the Chinese people had a reputation for kindness and hospitality. It is believed that the original group of settlers included about 70 Jewish families, totaling approximately 500 people. By 1163 c.e., a great synagogue was built, where it remained standing for over 700 years. During the Ming Dynasty, which lasted until about 1644, the Kaifeng Jewry reached its peak with a population of about 5000. Clearly, their survival depended upon the kindness of Chinese strangers.

One only has to remember the events of September 11th to realize that the kindness of strangers can often determine who lives and who dies. Many average and ordinary people became heroes in the days that followed. After the devastating Hurricane Katrina in New Orleans, there were families around the country who opened their homes to complete strangers. Shortly after the hurricane, I remember hearing about Web postings by kind-hearted individuals who invited strangers to live with them, asking for nothing in return.

As we reflect upon the past year and as we take inventory of each moment, let's ask ourselves—what have we done to help the stranger? How have we helped another human being survive in this world?

If we examine the survival of modern Jews, don't many of us depend upon the kindness of strangers? The hostile desert environment that early Jews faced has been replaced with other hostilities: perhaps its discrimination in the workplace, or unfair housing, or perhaps unequal marriage laws.

And who exactly are the strangers of today? Who were the strangers 10 years ago? A hundred years ago?

As many of you know, Congregation Sha'ar Zahav was formed to welcome a new "type" of stranger in 1977. Lesbian and gay Jews found a home here. Since then, this congregation has continued a tradition of welcoming strangers from all walks of life. We were once considered "progressive" to acknowledge bisexual and transgender people. Today, it's a common thing at Sha'ar Zahav. Even the term sexual minority has evolved with the growing understanding of intersex, two-spirit, and genderqueer people.

In the mid-1990s, many Sha'ar Zahav members marched in support of immigrants' rights when the Governor supported a state proposition that would deny access to healthcare to the undocumented—many of whom were children. More recently, CSZ members stood in solidarity with other religious communities like the San Francisco Organizing Project (SFOP) to support access to universal healthcare.

I considered myself a stranger in that place that my parents called the Richmond District. Aren't we all strangers at some time or another? Aren't we all guests at one time?

I am reminded of a December night three years ago when I first stepped into this sanctuary. I very much felt like a stranger—not only because I am Filipino, but also because I was in the process of converting to Judaism.

Early rabbinic interpreters believe that the word, "ger" did not only mean stranger. They tell us that the word also can be interpreted as "convert." G-d so loves the stranger that Abraham's circumcision was postponed until Abraham was ninety years-old so that future Jewish converts would know that one can be a Jew at any age.

So, when I walked into this sanctuary for the first time, I really had no idea how I would be received. I wondered if I would meet other Filipinos, other Asian/Pacific Islanders, and other people of color.

I did, of course. In fact, I met a wide variety of people at Sha'ar Zahav—different people with unique philosophies, political beliefs, and traditions, but who still have much in common. One of those common values is "tikkun olam," repairing the world.

Tikkun olam is central to Reform Judaism—and to the Zohar, the most important book in kabbalah. It's the obligation to repair the world in the kingdom of G-d. It's what we pray every time we say the Aleinu. And don't we repair the world by welcoming strangers? We do this by taking in the widow for example, or the orphan, or the homeless—and caring for them.

As we take inventory of our actions during the past year, let us also reflect upon all of the times when we welcomed and cared for a stranger. As we embrace the New Year, let us also remember to embrace the stranger. How exactly can we do this? How can you embrace the stranger?

Some of the ways in which you can do this is by getting involved in activities and organizations that may seem "foreign" to you. For some, it may mean volunteering at the Transgender Law Center to challenge your gender paradigms and to gain a broader perspective on issues concerning transgender equality. For others, it may mean supporting the National Network for Immigrant and Refugee Rights in order to gain insight into the challenges of being an immigrant. It may mean taking a stroll at today's Folsom Street Faire to expand your understanding about the leather community.

One group that I support is LGBT seniors, so I attend monthly meetings with the San Francisco "Prime Timers" and the "Lavender seniors of the East Bay." There are many groups out there that need our help.

Earlier, I spoke of the Kaifeng Jews. I encourage you to visit the Jewish library this Fall because there will be an entire program on Asian Jews and Jews living in Asia. One of our members, Rose Katz was instrumental in bringing the Kaifeng photo exhibit to the San Francisco Jewish library for all of us to enjoy and learn. So, let's take this time to educate ourselves for the new year.

Together, let us continue our Jewish tradition of welcoming the gay man, the lesbian, the bisexual, the transgender, the gender queer, the straight person, the two-spirit, the single parent, the intersex, the child, the widow, the orphan, the poor, the oppressed, and everyone in between.

May your new year be sweet, and may it be filled with the kindness and sweetness of strangers.

INTERVIEW WITH ELIYAHU ENRIQUEZ, 2009

Bahay Yosef: There are approximately 30,000–60,000 Ha'Filipinim (Taglit/Tagalog-Hebrew for "The Philippines" or "The Filipinos") currently living and working in Eretz Yisra'el, a majority concentrated in Tel Aviv's Shuk Tahana Merkazit, otherwise known as "The Little Manila of Israel"; the city is also considered "The Gay capital of the Middle East" (*Out Magazine*). Since some Jews consider living in Israel a mitzvah, do you see yourself making aliyah [immigrating to Israel] one day?

Robert Bernardo: Yes, I do hope to visit our Holy Land someday, but not anytime soon because right now, I do have a genuine fear of terrorist activity due to the general instability in the region. I also realized that this fear is probably unfounded because so many Jews visit Israel without problems—including my own synagogue. Our Rabbi takes a group to Israel at least once a year, and one of these days, I will do it. But not right now.

Bahay Yosef: Tropical Goshen: Manuel Quezon—President of The Philippine Commonwealth, 1935–1941—assisted in harboring/resettling 1,200 Jewish refugees, escaping Nazi persecution, in the South-Eastern stronghold of Mindanao and posthumously honored with the title of "Righteous Among The Nations," as well as commemorative Israeli citizenship. Nevertheless, patriotic and hardworking Ha'Filipinim with children born in Israel currently struggle for benefits that come with official state recognition. If given the opportunity for advocacy, what steps would you take to advance the cause of Israeli Ha'Filipinim?

Robert Bernardo: Although I have neither lived in the Philippines nor in Israel, I still feel that I can make a difference by continually educating people about Filipino Jews—whether they are similar to my situation or not. I feel that Filipino Jews need to be respected and accepted within the larger Jewish family. There is plenty of room for Jews of all colors and nationalities.

Bahay Yosef: Since 1993, homosexuals have been allowed to openly serve in the Israeli Defense Forces, including special units (unlike the "Don't Ask Don't Tell" policy of the U.S. Armed Forces). Were Ha'Filipinim OFWs, as well as Filipino Jews, encouraged to serve in the I.D.F., how would this concrete act of solidarity transform societal perceptions of Filipinos in Israel and bring about lasting reforms?

Robert Bernardo: I feel that this act of inclusion would make a global statement that would boldly say: "We accept Filipino Jews because you are part of the Jewish family." Also, if Filipino Jews wish to risk their lives for the safety and security of Israel, that should be respected, honored and encouraged.

Bahay Yosef: On LiveJournal, you blogged about the discovery of Spanish Jewish roots on your Grandmother's side of the family. Ako rin [me, too]! To embrace dormant Jewish roots, dating back to the Inquisition, would understandably be a challenge for fundamentally-reared Filipinos. How extensive do you think this Hudyo-Matrix phenomenon of Sephardic/Ladino ancestry is within the Filipino diaspora? What would its significance be?

Robert Bernardo: I strongly believe that Filipino Sephardic ancestry is much more common than we have come to believe. The only challenge is that there is little research in this area because the Philippines is such a mega-Christian country. If studies were conducted, I feel that the significance of the findings would completely alter what the next generation of Filipinos believe.

Bahay Yosef: Your Rosh Ha'Shanah 5767 message, "Strangers Among Us" compliments the spirit of The Pilipino, whose kindness to strangers is also chronicled in Frank Ephraim's WWII biography, Escape to Manila: From Nazi tyranny to Japanese Terror. Diplomatic relations between Israel and The Philippines remain strong and dynamic, yet the two Democratic nations also share the burden of extremism and terrorism from within their respective borders. Could you describe how hospitality can be both a blessing and a curse, from a Filipino-Jewish perspective? As an openly-Gay Jewish man of color, how has anti-Semitism manifested itself in your life? Because of these existential risks, would you discourage Filipinos from converting to Judaism?

Robert Bernardo: Hospitality is always a blessing, regardless of how horribly we are treated sometimes. Whether we like it or not, we Jews have an obligation to both educate non-Jews as well as protect ourselves from slander and violence. I find that I have to educate people nearly every day, and although I feel tired and frustrated in having to teach people, I still believe that it is my job because as we decrease the ignorance around us, this allows the seeds of tolerance and acceptance to grow.

Bahay Yosef: Tiebreaker: The decisive vote in the United Nations on November 29, 1947 reviving Israel as a sovereign nation was cast by The Philippines (and was the only Asian nation to support Jewish Nationhood). What kind of impact would greater Filipino-Jewish identification—Pilipinong-Hudyo Pride, if you will—make in promoting peace and tolerance?

Robert Bernardo: Again, it's about education and teaching Filipinos around the world that their duty is not over . . . Our duty did not end with the tie-breaking vote. We have a daily obligation to help Jews around the world and to teach our children about Jewish history and Israeli history.

Bahay Yosef: Rob Schneider, arguably the most high-profile Filipino Jew in entertainment, quipped: "My mother's side had the better food, my father's side had the better jokes" to describe his Filipina Ima and Jewish Abba. Other notable Filipino Jews include Dean Devlin, Producer of Independence Day, Godzilla, and The Patriot; Nicole Scherzinger, lead vocalist of the Pussycat Dolls; Michael Schwartz aka Mix Master Mike, American Turntablist and contributing member of the Beastie Boys; Actress, Phoebe Cates (wife of Academy-Award winner, Kevin Kline); and Author, Geronimo Tagatac. We should all go out for merienda and Kosher Kamayan, diba? What makes Filipino Jewry unique from other burgeoning cultural kehilot [congregations], such as Beta Israel, The Kaifeng Jews, and B'nei Menashe? To my knowledge, a Filipino Jew has not yet been ordained as a Rabbi. Do you think Sefer Ha'Torah should be translated into Taglit-Tagalog? Is there a need to establish an authentic, Filipino-Jewish community-identity?

Robert Bernardo:	I feel that we are unique because Filipino culture is so heavily influenced by American culture. Just look at our pop idols. That's one of the reasons that most of the people you listed are pop stars (actors/singers/etc.) No, I do not believe the Torah should be translated. I believe Filipinos (and others who wish to learn Torah) should learn Hebrew. Also, I do not feel that an "authentic Fil-Jew community" identity needs to be established because by being Filipino and Jewish—one already exists. It exists in every shul across the country. I feel that to "create" a community means that you take something away from what already exists. I feel at home in my local community at Congregation Sha'ar Zahav. We have Filipinos at the shul, and that's MY community.
Bahay Yosef:	Gay and Lesbian Jews seeking Rabbinical ordination in Yeshivot are on the rise. And with Jewish Queer Cinema such as Bent, Trembling Before G-d, and Yossi & Jagger garnering accolades, significant strides have been made through a Jewish lens in combating homophobia, while maintaining halakhot relevant to the GLBTIQA community. You are active in a Gay-affirming synagogue in San Francisco, namely Congregation Sha'ar Zaav. How do you see the GLBTIQA Jewish community serving as a "Beacon to the Nations"?
Robert Bernardo:	I feel that Jews are natural ambassadors of peace in the world because our religion teaches us to embrace the stranger. Also, Judaism generally accepts homosexuality—unlike a lot of Christian religions which condemn it.
Bahay Yosef:	Paper Dolls is an award-winning documentary which follows the lives of transgender migrant workers from The Philippines who work as health care providers for elderly Orthodox Jewish-Israeli men. Furthermore, JDate has a flurry of Filipino men seeking Jewish men, myself included =) Can you explain the significance of this mystical magnetism?
Robert Bernardo:	Hmmm . . . I can't really explain this phenomenon because although there are many attractive gay, Jewish men, my partner is not Jewish. So, I can't say that I feel this "mystical magnetism." LOL! My only explanation is that it's like preferring strawberry ice cream over vanilla ice cream. It's a matter of taste and not something that can be explained . . .
Bahay Yosef:	If you were the Grand Marshal of the Jerusalem Gay Pride Parade, how would you envision such a landmark event?
Robert Bernardo:	Wow, I couldn't even imagine what that would be like! However, if it were to happen—I would try to include Filipinos, Jews and Gays in my contingent in the same way I did it in San Francisco when I was elected. I believe that I can be a BRIDGE to cultures, sexualities and religions. As a BRIDGE, the goal is always to bring people together . . .
Bahay Yosef:	Just as the Hebrews struggled with overcoming a slave mentality after being physically emancipated from Mitzrayim and Pharaoh, as

well as spiritual liberation of the giving of the Torah at the foot of Mount Sinai on Shavu'ot, to a certain extent the Wandering Filipino (estimates of Overseas Filipinos correspond to the population of Diasporic Jews) still struggles with an island mentality. With Pesakh and Shavu'ot approaching, how will you commemorate Liberation?

Robert Bernardo: During Pesach, I commemorated liberation by being the "Out, Gay, Filipino Jew" that I am . . . Being public about my sexuality and religion are the ways in which I feel liberated and how I feel I can help liberate others.

Sources: Bernardo, Robert. "Strangers Among Us." Congregation Sha'ar Zahav, Rosh Ha'shanah 5767 (September 24, 2006). http://www.shaarzahav.org/sites/default/files/HHD2006-Drash-RH2-Bernardo.pdf. Accessed June 2010. Used with permission of the author; Bernardo, Robert. Interview by Eliyahu Enriquez. May 2009. http://www.bahayyosef.com/2009/05/face-to-face-with-robert-bernardo.html. Accessed June 2010. Used with permission of Eliyahu Enriquez and Robert Bernardo.

85. Estella Habal, "How I Became a Revolutionary," 2007

Married when she was just 16 years old, Filipina Estella Habal struggled to complete high school while working as a farm laborer and raising two young children. In 1969, she began attending Long Beach State College, where she was introduced to the radicalizing minority student organizations that were emerging on campuses across the country. Two years later, Habal fled her unhappy and restrictive marriage and moved with her children to San Francisco. There, she became involved in the struggle to save the Filipino *manongs,* bachelor migrant laborers who had been living in the rent-controlled International Hotel (I-Hotel) for decades. Developers targeted the hotel for demolition, threatening to evict the *manong*; a decade-long legal battle ensued in which the tenants and their allies eventually lost.

In the following excerpt from her essay, Habal talks about her feelings when she discovered the Filipino movement and its celebration of the history and culture of the Philippines—so different from the assimilationist mindset of most Filipino Americans—and the ways she managed to combine being a mother and an activist.

At that time [the early 1970s], institutions like the media and schools exclusively projected White American culture and history, more specifically, European and American White Anglo Saxon Protestant culture. Most Filipino parents agreed with the status quo because they thought that was the way to get ahead. They felt that racial discrimination would not happen if their children became fully American and forgot their Filipino roots and culture. So, of course, young Filipinos learned to speak in impeccable American accents, ditched anything that resembled Filipino because it was considered inferior to European and white American values and culture. The new generation of Filipino youth was totally assimilated and spoke no Filipino languages or dialects.

It is hard to describe one's feelings when you discover that you do have a history worth studying and a culture to be proud of. The civil rights movement and the ideas of Black Power had influenced many of us who were willing to listen. We owe a debt to Black people in this country who opened the doors for us. Minority peoples became empowered. There was a tremendous pride in our own people's contributions to American society. We began to understand the role of racism and the inferiorization of Third world peoples. Anti-colonial movements around the world stirred us. Although I was not completely aware of all this at that time in my development, it was part of the background and atmosphere of the time. . . . [While in San Francisco, Habal worked with San Francisco Newsreel, an antiwar film collective. There, she met "Cynthia," who introduced her to Kalayaan, a Filipino anti-imperialist, anticolonialist revolutionary organization, which later became the Union of Democratic Filipinos, or the KDP.]

To me, Cynthia's greatest influence and contribution within the KDP was her ability to bridge the political and cultural differences between recent immigrants and Filipino Americans. She laid the cornerstone that allowed us to build a truly integrated organization of Filipino immigrants and Filipino Americans. Most of the Filipino Americans came from relatively poor, working class backgrounds, while the majority of the exiled student activists from the Philippines were from more privileged backgrounds. The class "chemistry" between the two groups was often not good, and at times the chasm seemed unbridgeable. Yet the confidence of the KDP that we could work with this contradiction and overcome much of the differences in pursuit of our common goal—in no small part was due to the role Cynthia played in the early, formative years of the organization. For example, Cynthia often suggested promoting persons of working class backgrounds to leading positions if they had potential. This situation sometimes would cause resentment by others of more privileged backgrounds because they felt "de facto" more qualified. Cynthia would smooth the state of affairs by explaining what our political tasks were and how each person complements our strengths. In the area of "mass work," she would explain that working class people had a deeper understanding of the conditions needed to lead the work, while the more privileged had the social ease to move in different social strata. She would talk about collective work that was greater than its parts. Her leadership usually got us moving forward.

Kalayaan's headquarters was in the back of a storefront in the International Hotel. Originally conceived as a propaganda/organizing team in 1971, Kalayaan's main purpose was to distribute, a Filipino newspaper with an anti-U.S. imperialist, anti-racist, and anti-national discrimination perspective nationwide. After a year of propaganda work, Kalayaan decided to become a more "all-sided" and disciplined "underground" collective. I didn't bat an eye at this development. In fact, I thought it exciting that I could participate in a movement that championed the working class and poor in both the United States and the Philippines. I remember quoting Marx to myself, that I had "nothing to lose but my chains."

I was still with the Newsreel Collective when I began attending the early meetings of the Kalayaan organization. I remember having both the pains of pregnancy and the anticipation of revolutionary activity in the Filipino community. My daughter was due the following fall, and I decided then to name her Kalayaan Guerrero, translated—"freedom fighter." When friends would ask how Kalayaan was, I always answered, "getting bigger everyday." You can imagine their shock when they discovered later that I was not talking about the newspaper!

But how was I going to deal with being a mother in a movement that was primarily composed of young people without children? Again I knew I was different, but that did not deter me. Taking my inspiration from stories about Communist China, I knew that childcare could and should be taken into account in order to encourage women's full participation. After all, even Chairman Mao said the "women hold up half the sky" . . . and in those days that was enough to settle any argument! At first I sought childcare in a Chinatown day-care center organized by leftists to care for their children and those of other working people in the community, but this did not work out for me. My persistence paid off though, when my comrades in the Kalayaan (and later the KDP) helped with childcare while I did my political work. I never entertained utopian ideas that the "collective" or even "socialism," could fully take care of children. I knew that I was the primary caregiver and that the burden of responsibility for raising my kids would still remain with me, regardless of the amount of help I received. Deep down I knew that being a mother would pose limitations on my political activity, no matter what. Difficult decisions regarding where to place my time and focus and attention were before me everyday . . . and at times I resented that others did not have to confront the same problem. The tensions created by the demands made by my leadership in the Movement and the needs of my children would remain constant throughout much of my life, a contradiction always to be negotiated and renegotiated again and again and again.

The first major decision that affected my participation because of my family conditions was at the first KDP National Council meeting in 1974. The Kalayaan organization was just one of the many local groups which decided to form a national organization of Filipino immigrants and Filipino Americans called the *Katipunan ng mga Demokratikong Pilipino* or the KDP. It had a dual program—support for national democracy in the Philippines and democratic rights for Filipinos in the United States. It was both anti-capitalist and anti-imperialist but explicit support for socialism came about seven years later in 1980. These politics reflected the conditions in the Philippines and in the United States. In the Philippine situation, a national democratic stage was needed before socialism. In the United States, minority peoples were part of the working class and we believed that democratic rights must be extended to minorities first. There was also a recognition that there was not a leading Communist Party in the United States and the task was to rectify and reestablish it. How that was to be done was tabled for the future.

The KDP was patterned after the form of the youth organization in the Philippines, a revolutionary mass organization, not a party cadre organization, as some may think. The process for arriving at decisions was called democratic-centralist, although at the time I never thought it might have been at the root of some errors. Even with our inexperience, we felt a collective leadership was necessary to lead the mass membership. If disagreements appeared, they were usually resolved at the leadership level. Democracy occurred on the chapter level and ultimately at national congresses, which occurred every other year.

At our Founding Congress in July, 1973, I was elected to the National Council. I was then nominated to become a member of the new National Executive Board, the day to day national leadership body of the KDP. I thought intently about my revolutionary tasks and how exciting it would be to build a national organization from the ground up. However, after much soul searching, I realized that the tasks would be too encompassing for a mother with three young children—so I declined the offer. The Council reluctantly acknowledged my conditions and chose someone else to fill the position, a young Filipina American woman who had similar working class credentials as myself, but no children. I was then assigned to help build the local KDP chapter in the Bay Area.

Source: Excerpted from Habal, Estella. "How I Became a Revolutionary." In *Legacy to Liberation: Politics and Culture of Revolutionary Asian Pacific America*, edited by Fred Ho. Oakland, CA: AK Press and Big Red Media, 2000, pp. 199, 202–203. Permission granted by Big Red Media, Inc.

86. JoAnn Balingit, Three Poems and an Essay, 2007

JoAnn Balingit is a Filipina American author, and Delaware's sixteenth poet laureate. She teaches poetry in community organizations and schools. "History Textbook, America," "Story I learn at forty-nine," and "My Mother Explains My Father to Her Girls" all are reflections on Balingit's Filipino and German American parents. In these poems, Balingit explores how cultures mix in marriage and family and the incomplete ways in which immigrants leave their lives behind. The subsequent personal essay provides additional background information on Balingit's parents' histories and relationship. She also discusses the impact of her father's upbringing in the American-colonized Philippines on his subsequent decisions both to immigrate to the United States and to turn his back on the language and culture of his homeland.

HISTORY TEXTBOOK, AMERICA

I'd search for Philippines in History class.
The index named one page, moved on to Pierce.
The Making of America marched past
my enigmatic father's place of birth.
The week he died some man we didn't know
called up. *This is his brother,* one more shock,
phoning for him. "He died three days ago."
The leaden black receiver did not talk.
My uncle never gave his name or town,
we never heard from him. Was it a dream?
The earpiece roar dissolved to crackling sounds,
a dial tone erased the Philippines.

And yet my world grows huge with maps, crisscrossed,
my history alive with all I've lost.

STORY I LEARN AT FORTY-NINE

Aunt Rita's lovely cursive
bares its hips, flinging words like
confetti, a story where my mother
delivers herself whole to my father—
elope they called it, a foreigner,
Filipino—old enough to be her
grandfather! Well not quite, Rita,
he was forty-nine and she nineteen
in all, but thirty years is still *one* generation even if
Joan was just a kid, all impulse and beauty, who
knew her mind before he sent the ticket—St.
Louis, a plane fare away! Rising past
midnight she must have worked quickly,
nickels tucked in pleat pockets, must have
opened her bag one last time, called Kitty to
pat the orange glow-in-the-dark before she fled
quietly into one or two a.m. on the moonlit
road. Barely can she make out her house on its hill,
saddle shoes tipping stones like skunks nosing
trash to steal, when Taxi pulls up, its driver, dazed
understudy for tonight's dramatic role,
Viceroy a-dangle as he grunts to slam her door but
"Wait!" she hisses, hand on headrest—as a phantom
X-acto knife slices this life off the next.
"You headed somewhere?" She nods. The Talon
zipper of her good jacket gapes. It's jammed.

MY MOTHER EXPLAINS MY FATHER TO HER GIRLS

Face from the radiant
other side of the globe. While mine grew dark,
his sky rose tropical, story-book, crammed with color
plates, Marco Polos, Magellans, palaces
    beyond the sea . . .

The Midwest's silver sky looked tarnished.
Some years we had six months of winter.
    Into the office wafts a man
from the islands with the climate of heaven
—warmth without heat, coolness without cold—

    who grew up wearing hand-woven linen
all seasons, was weaned by women in white
    gathered lawn and silk sleeves

lit from within like those star-shaped lamps
in festive doorways. What dreams I had
           of him. I painted
mango sunsets in a bowl.

How could a grown man's voice
       be fine as a line cast over water,
land and sink without a ripple? You know
at dusk how sky melts with ocean
           into one aqua plane from your toes
to the world's curve you can't tell

where you are from anything? So I fell
       into your father's voice—
tailored wool, silk tie, fedora. He glowed
like the boss's mahogany. I jumped aboard his liner
into his tiger's eye, his Mariana Trench, his valley
           carved of stone.

No, I do not forget our final disaster.
       I know his silence branded you
as a vine over time will tunnel the bark of a tree.
His beautiful syllables left him when he
came to master English and America
       and me.

       Yet girls, should you find some
few of his words survive your native jungles—
           let them forage like wild pigs!

PERSONAL ESSAY

I am first-generation Filipina-American, the third eldest of 12 children. My father, a Filipino immigrant from Macabebe, Pampanga, left his homeland at the age of 26 and never returned. My mother, a German-American woman from Canton, Ohio, was a Midwesterner whose ancestors fled Alsace-Lorraine in the mid to late 1800's.

My father arrived in San Francisco by ship in May of 1929, with a degree in Engineering from The University of the Philippines and money from his family to attend graduate school. Family lore says that he spent the money but did not complete his schooling. From his photo albums we know he travelled in California, Arizona, Missouri, Tennessee, Mississippi and Louisiana. His photos show pretty American sweethearts, corporate Christmas parties, bowling leagues, city sights—and familiar-looking children we do not know. Likely, long before he met my mother, my father had another family.

Extraordinarily private all his life, indeed taciturn about sharing personal history, Jesus Maglanoc Balingit divulged few details of childhood, friends, family or homeland in response to our questions. I know he became a naturalized U.S. citizen in 1946—the first year he could legally apply. I do not know the names of his parents or siblings.

From the 1930's through 1966, when my father suffered a disabling stroke, he worked for American corporations such as Bechtel, Joslyn & Ryan (Naval Architects), Martin-Marietta and Wellman-Lord. In 1951 he met my mother, Joan Carol Kuntz, at Arthur G. McKee Corporation in Cleveland, Ohio. A talented artist, Joan was 19, a year out of high school, and working at the engineering firm as a drafting apprentice. My father was 49. They married in 1952 and started a family life of moving from state to state, ever southward, babies in tow. They settled in Lakeland, Florida in 1963. I think my father was working all his life to get back to the tropics.

I believe the violent occupation and Americanization of the Philippines transformed my father's psyche even while he was in the womb. After all, he was born in 1903, just eight months after the U.S. government declared the Philippine-American War (1899–1902) officially over. Actually, Filipino armed resistance to the occupation went on for years. Reared and schooled during this era of intense and traumatic cultural change in his native land, my father eventually came to believe that he need not—perhaps must not—perpetuate Filipino culture in his American-born children's lives. For example, my father declined to teach us any of his native language, Tagalog. What little I know about Filipino culture and my particular heritage, I have gathered through research.

Though I am proud to be both Filipina and American, there are times I feel I am not fully either. Perhaps I have inherited from my father, and from my mother too, a dilemma familiar to immigrants. They perpetually search for home—in an effort to define the self.

Source: Balingit, JoAnn. "History Textbook, America," "Story I learn at forty-nine," and "My Mother Explains My Father to Her Girls." "History Textbook, America" originally appeared in *Best New Poets 2007*. Meridian: University of Virginia Press, 2007. Poems and essay used with permission of the author. Balingit can be reached through her website, http://joannbalingit.org.

87. Catherine Ceniza Choy, "How to Stand Up and Dive," 2007

For over a century, most people have thought of race in the United States in terms of black and white. This conception is gradually being eroded, in part by the growing Asian American population. Catherine Ceniza Choy, a second-generation Filipina American and an Ethnic Studies professor at the University of California, Berkeley, challenges the black-white racial paradigm in the following essay. "How to Stand Up and Dive" reflects on the importance of providing Asian American children with Asian American role models. Using her own daughter's experience as an example, Choy shows the power of enabling children to see the reality of a diverse America—one in which they can see their own faces reflected.

My six-year-old daughter Maya bobs up and down in the pool water smiling all the while. Her slender body makes the water gurgle and ripple just so. Thick strands of sopping wet hair stick to her face, partly covering an eye here, curling along the roundness of her nose there. She does not seem to mind. I enjoy watching her like this as if I can feel her joy of being in the water. Tired clichés of parenthood fill my mind. Yes, nothing can prepare you for being a parent. They indeed grow up so fast. Yes, learn to understand the power of now. While these statements hold truths, I find myself continually reflecting on the past in the present. As I smile and wave at her from the bleachers, I remember the way she made ripples in my womb. How her kicks made small half spheres that popped up from my then pregnant belly. Now her body makes waves in the water of Martin Luther King Pool, a public pool run by the city of Berkeley. How ironic, I chuckle uncomfortably to myself recalling a moment in February, Black History month.

I am standing next to Maya, who is perched on a step stool so that she can watch herself brush her teeth in the bathroom mirror. She swishes water in her mouth and spits it out, leaving a trace of toothpaste foam on her lips. "Mommy, are we black or white?" *Although I am physically and mentally exhausted, thoughts unfurl quickly. I have spent much of my career challenging the dual nature of U.S. race relations. I live in the Bay Area where the significant presence of Asian Americans complicates this binary. I teach on a campus where Asian Americans comprise the largest group of people of color. And yet here stands my daughter, toothpaste foam dribbling down her chin, thinking of the world around her in terms of black and white. The academic language I have become accustomed to—racialization, Orientalism, panethnicity—does not translate well in this situation. I tell her,* "We are neither. I am a second generation Filipino American. Daddy is a third generation Korean and Chinese American. You are a third generation Filipino American and a fourth generation Korean and Chinese American." *I know my response does not have the catchiness of "black" or "white" and sure enough Maya responds,* "But Martin Luther King said we were black or white." *Later when Maya is in her pajamas and lying in bed, I tell her that Martin Luther King believed in the equality of people of all colors. He stood up for the belief that we are and can be many things. I tell her that she is a talented artist, an amazing reader, an impressive dancer, and now a budding swimmer. I look into her eyes and whisper these truths:* "You are a wonderful big sister. You are my most perfect daughter." *I say to her as well as to myself this plea:* "Please do not forget this."

Maya is in a level one-plus swimming class. She is learning how to float on her belly and her back using what her instructors refer to as "starfish" moves, arms and legs spread out from her sides. "Watch me do the starfish, Mama," Maya would later say during a family swim day, proudly demonstrating her new swimming maneuvers. At the conclusion of the two-week intensive course, she will receive a progress sheet that lists 17 skills needed to pass level one-plus. None of the skills refer to starfish. Skill number three is the "back float with recovery (unsupported)" and skill number four is "front float with recovery (unsupported)."

The word "dive" also does not appear on the list of skills. But on one of the final days, the instructors tell the children to climb out of the shallow part of the pool and line up at its edge. They must take turns jumping feet first into the pool. When it is Maya's turn, I see some hesitation in her body. Instead of jumping up and over the edge, her body tenses, she crouches down and jumps in (well, scoots in, would probably be more accurate) barely making a splash. I do not think much of her hesitation until the following day when she and her classmates are instructed to climb out of the shallow end of the pool and walk over in a line to the deeper end. With two instructors in the water, they are supposed to take turns jumping in. I find myself nervous for Maya. I read fear in the way her body stiffens, the way her eyes cast downward. No joy here.

It is Maya's turn to plunge in the deep water. The instructors' voices are muffled, but I hear sounds of encouragement. Maya's toes curl against the rim of the pool's edge. She heeds the instructors' words, but fear jolts her shoulders back each time she leans forward preparing for her jump. I hear other parents coo as they watch her. "She's so small. She's so cute." But my body tenses too. When she first jumps in, her body is so stiff, that she lands almost face flat into the water making a huge splash, the water slapping against her hard. And yet Maya pulls her body up out of the water only to jump back in. Again and again. Her body continues to hesitate with each time. But she continues to stand up and dive.

A blowing whistle signals the end of class. I rush over to her and drape a towel over her shoulders. I tell her with the biggest smile I can muster, "I am so proud of you. You were terrific." I say this over and over as her body shivers and shakes from the coolness of the air as well as her struggle to fight back the tears. For the time being, she is not proud. She does not feel terrific. Later, she receives her progress report stating matter of factly that she has passed level one-plus and can move on to level two.

I know when something is wrong even though Maya laughs, tells stories, and plays games like nothing is wrong. I go along with the typically playful behavior until her eyebrows crinkle and tears well up and I know we will have to confront what's bothering her. And this time it is not difficult for me to predict that Maya is unhappy about moving on to level two. Because in level two you begin to learn strokes that move you from one end of the shallow pool to the other. You are almost in constant motion. You do not play water games like "Mr. Fox" and "Marco Polo." And with these certainties, comes uncertainty. How will you do in level two, where some of the kids are "big" kids who are in second and maybe even third grade? The tears stream down her cheeks and some mucous bubbles at the tip of her nose. "Please," she pleads, "I don't want to be in level two." She continues while choking back her tears, so that her voice sounds like gasps of air, "I don't want to go swimming anymore." "Not swim anymore?" I respond in disbelief. "You are so talented in the water," I tell her. "You look so natural as you bob and float and kick." I realize that I am raising my voice at her. And that does not help matters.

We do not continue to speak about this while Maya brushes her teeth and changes into her pajamas. But when she lies down on her bed, I tell her that swimming is much more than a level one or level two class. "First," I explain, "it's great exercise for the body." "You mean, swimming is a sport?!" Maya asks incredulously. I nod my head. I tell her how I did not learn how to swim until I was in college at the very relatively old age of twenty. By that time, I had had the opportunity to visit some amazing parts of the world: Belize in Central America and Kenya in East Africa. During both those journeys, my inability to swim impacted what I could experience. In Belize, I jumped off a boat with a friend thinking I would be able to tread or float in the water. But upon breaking the surface of the water, panic spread over me and I spent the rest of the afternoon desperately climbing back into the boat and nursing the bruises forming along the backs of arms. At the coast of Kenya, I was hanging out with two friends on a beach when they decided to explore an empty boat anchored close to the shore. The water was calm, but I told them to go ahead and they swam on without me. "So second," I continue, "swimming is more than something that's good for you. It can enrich your life. When I finally learned to swim a lap in college, when

I was twenty years old, mind you, I can still remember how good it felt, how good I felt when my hand touched the pool's edge. I had done something I was unable to do before, something I thought many times before I would never be able to do."

Maya is having trouble falling asleep from the stress of the impending level two class. So I reach for one more story to tell. "Once upon a time," I begin, "there was a girl who was born in San Francisco. Her name was Victoria Manalo. Victoria's daddy was from the Philippines. Her mommy was from England. Victoria did not learn to swim until she was about nine or ten. She was much, much older than you. Can you imagine? She was afraid of the water, which meant that she missed out on playing games in the water like 'Mr. Fox.' Can you imagine that? But when Victoria was much, much older, when she was a teenager, she was interested in learning how to dive. But in the 1920s and 1930s, people in California were not kind to Filipinos even though Filipinos did very difficult farm labor that other people did not want to do. A swimming and diving coach in San Francisco separated Victoria from the other swimmers and divers because she was part Filipino. And then he insisted that Victoria use her mother's English last name, Taylor, instead of her father's Filipino last name, Manalo. Victoria faced many challenges. But she faced her fears about being in the water and learned to love to dive in it. She faced people who did not like her because she was Filipino, but she continued to love herself and treasure both her Daddy's and Mommy's backgrounds. And, can you imagine, Victoria Manalo went on to win two gold medals in diving at the Olympic Games, a competition that includes swimmers and divers from all over the world. All over the world! In 1948, Victoria became the first woman ever in Olympic history to win two gold medals in two individual diving events. It's good to know who Martin Luther King was and what he stood for. It's also important to know who Victoria Manalo is and what she accomplished. Do not be afraid, little one. Just enjoy being in the water, moving across it, smiling as you bob in it."

The next morning as we walk over to the pool, I doubt that anything I said the previous night mattered. Maya whimpered and whined through breakfast and during our walk she does little different. When we arrive at that part of the pool where we must separate—I must go to the bleachers and she to the shallow pool's edge, I think about saying, "Remember the story I told you about Victoria," but I do not. I know that these stories do indeed matter, but I think that they must be told again and again in order for the worlds of the listeners to reshape, bend, look different. I tell myself, it takes time for these narratives to seep into the bones of our being. But then, as I watch Maya enter the pool, I think that perhaps it may not take as long as one might think. "Stand up and jump in," her instructor calls out to her. So Maya stands straight and plunges in, feet first, body straight. No hesitation. No fear. From the bleachers I can see that she is looking up at her instructor waiting for what comes next. And she is smiling.

Dedication Paragraph:
The narratives we construct and impart in academic teaching and research do matter in the "real world." They are integral to the continued success of social justice movements. Author, activist, teacher, and mentor Helen Toribio, who passed away in the fall of 2004, exemplified these truths throughout her life. And she continues to do so in her legacy. I feel privileged to have received a little bit of Helen's mentorship. I will always admire her scholarship and her commitment to Filipino American students and studies more broadly. Throughout her life, Helen encouraged students to bridge their education with social justice issues. The new "Helen

Toribio Legacy Fund" donates an internship grant to enable an organization to hire a young adult to work on progressive community issues.

Source: Choy, Catherine Ceniza. "How to Stand Up and Dive." Originally published in *Cheers to Muses: Contemporary Works by Asian American Women*. San Francisco: Asian American Women Artists Association, 2007, pp. 48–51. Used with permission of the author.

88. "An Asian-American in the Music Business: Interview with Ryan Buendia," 2009

Today there is still a dearth of Asian Pacific Americans in the music business. How many Asian American singers, emcees, or DJs can you name? However, Asian Americans are starting to make their presence felt. From apl.de.ap of the Black Eyed Peas to DJ Babu and Nicole Scherzinger of the Pussycat Dolls, Filipinos have been at the forefront of this movement. Perhaps the most well-known and influential Filipino musician and producer is Chad Hugo of the Neptunes and N.E.R.D. The Neptunes and N.E.R.D have worked with the biggest names in hip-hop and rhythm and blues (R&B) over the last 10 years—artists like N.O.R.E., Mystikal, Jay-Z, P. Diddy, Justin Timberlake, Snoop Dogg, Robin Thick, and Britney Spears, to name a few. In this interview, 8asians blogger Jeff talks with Bay Area American artist, performer, and music producer Ryan Buendia, who has worked with the Black Eyed Peas and the Jabbawockeez. Buendia is also a DJ and a turntablist. In the following interview, Buendia talks about the challenges and successes he has had as an Asian Pacific American in the music business.

How did you get into Sound Engineering?

Ryan Buendia: Well right after high school in 2000, I decided to make music my career. Instead of going to a 4 year college, I decided to take the Sound Arts program at Ex'pression Center for New Media, in Emeryville, CA. At the age of 18, I really didn't even know what an engineer was. I just knew I wanted to learn how to use all the equipment in a professional recording studio. I was driven to learn this and apply it to my own music.

What are the some of the difficulties of being Asian American in the music business?

Ryan Buendia: There are so many avenues in the music business, so avenues are difficult than others. If you're an Asian American getting into Engineering, it not so bad because technology in music has conformed from analog to digital. Most Asian Americans are pretty computer savvy, so that definitely helps. But for an Asian American recording artist, the chances are pretty slim here in the U.S. So far, out of the millions of Asian recording artists out there, we only have one mainstream, globally accepted, Grammy Award Winner, and that's Apl de Ap.

I recall you telling a story about a rapper asking you if you were Chinese or Japanese? Tell us about that story.

Ryan Buendia: When I first started working in the music industry, I had to work with these rappers out of the South for a whole month straight. They weren't used to seeing an Asian guy in the studio, so they used to call me "Chopsticks" as a nickname. At the time, I was very offended by this nickname, and thought they were racist. But as I got older, I realized that they were just ignorant. They really meant no harm, they actually thought it was a great nickname for me. hahaha

How did you first connect with Apl?

Ryan Buendia: I connect with Apl back in 2004. I was working at a famous recording studio called "Encore Studios." By this time, my music was circulating a lot around the music industry. One day a friend of mine came to the studio and introduced me to the Manager of the Black Eyed Peas, Polo Molina. He really liked my music alot and hooked me up with Apl. The rest is history.

Did you ever think as a kid that you would be traveling between the US and Asia on business?

Ryan Buendia: I never thought any of this as a kid. The dream even as a kid felt very far fetched. It goes to show you how much you really have to believe in yourself and not other's belief of yourself.

Where in Asia have you travelled with APL?

Ryan Buendia: Since 2004, I've been going to Philippines with Apl every Christmas to give gifts and money back to the poor. We also tour around Philippines and do gigs. I've also Djed in Taiwan by myself.

How many tracks do you have on the upcoming Black Eyed Peas CD?

Ryan Buendia: Well, I have 3 songs total. One song titled "Showdown" on the original Album pressing. And two more songs on the deluxe edition Album that they are doing exclusively with Target. Those songs are titled "Don't Bring Me Down" and "Mare". I'm really proud of my work on this album because I produced the entire beat on all three tracks, and have been working the last 9 years to reach this point in my career. I feel really blessed and humbled by the experience.

What's it like working with APL? Any particular stories that exemplify what that is like?

Ryan Buendia: Working with Apl is fun. We do work long hours, maybe 12–14 hours a day depending on which project. But sometimes we'll go to the nightclub and have a drink. Most might say that's not work, but we're actually studying what the people react to in clubs and it really shows on this next Black Eyed Peas Album. But trust me, after working all day, then going to a club until 2am, then going back to the studio to work until 6am, only to find out you have to start work again in a couple of hours is very draining.

Any stories about working with Will.I.am, Fergie, or Taboo that are noteworthy (and that you could tell without getting into any trouble)?

Ryan Buendia: Working with Will is amazing. Whenever I'm around him, I'm a sponge. I remember almost everything he has said about music. He's a true genius. I remember him saying in 2005 that the Internet is going to take over the Music Industry, and that there's not going to be a physical record store anymore. He explained how the only physical stores that are gonna be selling albums are places like Walmart, and he was right. . . .

How did you get into DJing?

Ryan Buendia: I got into Djing by being around hip hop. I was into all the elements of hip hop, whether it be art, dancing, or rapping. I loved every aspect of it.

What is the last set of work that you put out?

Ryan Buendia: The last mix I put out was this year with my crew the Fingerbangerz. We made it available for free download at www.myspace.com. Search for "The Bangerz" Its called the "Music Machine Mixtape."

Any new plans with the Fingerbangerz?

Ryan Buendia: We're are working on a new Album. You could find our last album on I-Tunes titled "VI.R.US" We also been developing a partnership with Will.i.am's new website www.dipdive.com. We have our own channel on this site, and you could learn more about us on there.

Any other new work coming out?

Ryan Buendia: I have two songs coming out on Kelis's new album. One song on Kid Cudi's upcoming album. And a song on Downtown Records recording artist Kid Sister's new album. Very excited.

How did you connect with the Jabbawockeez?

Ryan Buendia: The Jabbawockeez have been our (Fingerbangerz) brother crew before they became famous. We did their music ever since 2003, which ended up helping to develop their current style of dance.

Source: Jeff. "An Asian-American in the Music Business: Interview with Ryan Buendia." June 5, 2009. http://www.8asians.com/2009/06/05/an-asian-american-in-the-music-business-interview-with-ryan-buendia-part-1/. Accessed September 2010. Reprinted with permission from Jeff@8asians.com.

89. Gem P. Daus, "Discovering Carlos Bulosan," 2010

Carlos Bulosan was a Filipino American novelist and poet whose semi-autobiographical book, *America Is in the Heart,* remains a seminal work on the early Filipino immigrant experience. However, during his lifetime, he was best known for his 1944 publication *Laughter of my Father,* which gained mainstream notoriety in the United States. Though there is considerable debate over Bulosan's birth date, baptismal records reveal he was born in Pangasinan Province on November 2, 1911. His family leveraged their farmland to pay for his older brothers' passages to America. Bulosan would follow, immigrating to America as a young man in the 1930s during the height of Great Depression. He suffered dreadful conditions as a laborer and endured constant humiliations and discrimination because of his race. He became a labor activist and like other labor radicals was later blacklisted during the 1950s.

Bulosan was deeply affected by American ideals of equality being propagated by American teachers in the Philippines after the islands were colonized by the United States in 1898. The Americans instituted a colonial system based on the idea of benevolent assimilation. Americans did not see themselves as imperialists in the European manner. Americans opted to see their colonial project as a kinder, gentler, paternalistic attempt to remake Filipinos into their own image. American forms of governance; American-style schools; American social, political, and economic values; and even the language were instituted in the Philippines. However, while Filipinos were being taught about America's love of equality, no one bothered to tell them about American racism. The prevailing belief among white Americans was that Filipinos were primitive savages that needed to be civilized. As one American judge put it, Filipinos were "little brown men . . . only a decade removed from the bolo and breechcloth." When Bulosan and other Filipino immigrants arrived in America in the 1920s and 1930s, they received a crash course on American racism. In many ways, Bulosan's writings became a way for him to fight the injustices that he and his fellow Filipinos suffered in America. In the following article, Filipino American writer, activist, and teacher Gem P. Daus writes about his debt to Bulosan, who believed that being American was really a matter of the heart.

I became an American on February 19, 1975. But I think I was meant to be an American from birth. I was born in an American-engineered city (Baguio) in a former American colony (the Philippines). Yes, there were Filipinos in Baguio before the Americans. But when the Americans found this haven, on top of a mountain, a mile above sea level and a respite from the heat, they decided to build an "R and R" (rest and relaxation) station. Daniel H. Burnham, a famous architect and urban planner from Chicago, Illinois, came to Baguio in 1905 and laid out the plan for the city. The central park is named after him.

When I was born, on April 25, 1966, my father was fighting in an American war in Vietnam as a member of the U.S. Navy. (Well, actually, he was below deck cooking. Of course, "ya gotta eat," and every job is important, but most Filipinos "fought" in the job that American prejudice allowed at the time.) It's because he was away that I was born in Baguio and not our home town of Binalonan, Pangasinan, which is at the foot of the mountain leading to Baguio. While he was in Vietnam, my mother lived in dependent housing in Baguio. Good thing too because that meant she was close to proper maternity care: I was born breached at Notre Dame de Lourdes Hospital which is part of Saint Louis University. I don't think Binalonan would have had the facilities.

We immigrated to the U.S. on October 27, 1968 as part of the new surge of immigrants in the civil rights era. But it wasn't the immigration reform of 1965 that let us in, but rather the 1947 Military Bases Agreement, which allowed my father to serve, emigrate, and bring my mom and me over. We left on my grandmother's birthday. My mom was pregnant but I don't know if she knew that then. We settled in Long Beach, California where my sister was born. After two years, we moved to Pensacola, Florida. After another two years, my dad was transferred to Norfolk, Virginia. Contrary to what a lot of military families experience, families stationed in Norfolk tended to stay there. Every two years my dad alternated between ship duty and shore duty. Sometimes he was away for six months "in the Med" (Mediterranean). But we never had to move to another base, and I rarely lost friends to a father's reassignment. Except for kindergarten, I attended Norfolk Public Schools until I graduated from high school.

So in February 1975, I took a note to my third grade teacher excusing me from school the next day. I was going to be naturalized. She shook my hand after reading the note. All I remember from that day was waving a little American flag and saying the pledge of allegiance in a courtroom. I probably knew I was becoming a citizen, but I don't think I really knew what that meant. I was wearing a polka-dot shirt according to the picture on my naturalization certificate. I don't remember taking a test. Because I was a minor and in school, I guess they figured I'd be learning everything I needed to know.

I grew up with lots of Filipinos around. In fact, I grew up thinking all Filipinos were in the Navy. I couldn't imagine any other way of leaving the Philippines. But I didn't know anything about the Philippines, nor was I encouraged to. My parents had left it behind, and were more than content to do so (later, I found out this was partly due to family drama). But the upshot is that I became an English-only American kid who had no need of any other identity, just like the naturalization officials expected.

But America does not let us escape the burden of race for long. You either deal with it or deny it. But there's no ignoring it. I tried. I am American, I told myself. I'm even more American than white people because I had to earn it (yeah I got to take a shortcut but I did well in school; and never mind that I used white as the standard for comparison). My birthplace and race were incidental. America was in my heart and American was my identity.

I still believe that, but now I also believe that my birthplace and race are integral to my American identity. Of the various experiences that helped me realize that, my first trip back to the Philippines was the most transformative. In February 1995—28 years after leaving, 20 years after becoming an American citizen—my father, mother and I became "balikbayans". Homecomers. Returnees. It was stamped on our passports. All the sights and sounds and emotions I felt on that two-week trip are a story for another day. But I came back with new lenses from which to view the world. And in my search for new meaning, I found "America is in the Heart" by Carlos Bulosan. That seminal work of the Filipino American experience was not my family's experience, but it hurt to read, so it must be my story. I really connected when I read the passage where he described helping build the road to Binalonan. Wait! I was just there! That's my hometown! We're from the same place?! This pioneer who so eloquently described what it meant to be American while getting beat up for being brown . . . he was literally my kababayan. My townmate. It's kind of a goofy connection. Accidental. Coincidental. Or maybe it's fate. Whatever, it woke me up to a new self-image that embraced my heritage but also affirmed that I was meant to be an American.

Source: Daus, Gem P. "Discovering Carlos Bulosan." *Our Own Voices.* April 2010. http://www.oovrag.com/essays/essay2010a-5.shtml. Accessed August 2010. Reprinted with permission.

90. Robert Francis Flor, "Alaskero Memories," 2010

Robert Francis Flor is a Seattle native and the son of an immigrant Filipino. He is a published poet and coproduces the Pagdiriwang Festival's Words Expressed event, which hosts readings by Filipino American writers, poets, and dramatists. In his poem series "Alaskero Memories," Flor recalls his early years working in the Alaskan canneries. The Alaskeros were early migrant Filipino American laborers who worked in the canneries during the summers and on West Coast farms during the rest of the year. In 1933, the Alaskeros organized the Cannery Workers and Farm Laborers Local Union, the first Filipino American labor union in the United States. By the time Flor began working in the 1960s, the union was well established, fighting against the unequal treatment Filipino American workers received in the canneries. "Alaskero Memories" provides an evocative look at the everyday life of these Filipino American cannery workers.

Alaska Union—Seattle 1960s

In April and May, warm weather carries a wave of Filipinos north from Stockton, Delano and Watsonville fields. Sun companions them. They inhabit Chinatown hotels. Gamble underground dens. Shoot nine ball. Loiter 2nd, outside Local 37. Wait. Wish. Hope. Hope for assignments as sorters, butchers, slimers, fillers, or the catch 'n can. Hope-once again for an Alaska town . . . Falls Pass, Naknek, Bristol Bay, Chignik or Karluk. Hope for a salmon cannery with Kings, Reds, Humpies, Dogs and Silvers, their migrant brothers and sisters.

A compadre reunion, names float air . . . passed lips . . . Abaya, Torres, Navarro, Madayag. No longer young, some no longer able. Dreams deferred. Dreams suppressed. Unseen money changes hands under the table to pass the health check. A way of life. A receding journey.

Alaska Series No. 1

Boeing Field—1963

A summer evening, my folks drive us to Boeing Field.
Linda and I silently sit the back seat.
My first time to the canneries. Mahogany men cram the airport.
Their hard, brown Pinoy faces rim the waiting area.
"Young boys" like me cluster in close uncertainty.
I squeeze her picture tight against my chest.
In my duffle, the Four Tops and Righteous Brothers.
We hug goodbyes before I board for Cold Bay.

A final kiss. I cross the tarmac.
Fly north.

Alaska Series No. 2

Becoming Alaskero

We depart Boeing Field, wedged among
Manong migrants blown north to can salmon . . .
their summer hiatus from asparagus fields
and almond orchards. Our Reeve Aleutian circles
Cold Bay's fog-laced clutch of corrugated huts,
nestled on grizzled ground and shrub-terrain.
We descend into our frigid cloud breaths.
Huddle in warm pool hall. Like netted fish,
we wait a tender bound for King Cove.

Alaska Series No. 3

Bunkhouse

Cookie welcomes us to his mess hall.
A stocky Filipino, he wears an apron over t-shirt.
"Hot muck-a-lucka-sigh!" he laughs.
Coffee and lunch served, rooms assigned,
we climb to upper floor. Rummy and pai gow tables
full with seasoned Alaskeros greet us.
We unpack. Sweep. Carve our beings
into plywood walls.

"Bob loves Linda. 1963"

Alaska Series No. 4

5:30 a.m. King Cove

Mr. Acena, our foreman, wears Vaquero Stetson and Mackinaw.

Traipses hallway. Calls to each room—

"Get up boys! Get up! Time to go!"

Breakfast. Cookie prepares eggs, ham and hot *"mucka-lucka-sigh,"*
- colorful coffee word.

Mr. Acena orders, *"Young boys, you go slime!"*

We don rubber suits, waddle to stations. Three butchers straddle an Iron Chink, separating salmon heads and tails. Slimers gauntlet tables, gutting the remains.

"Blood money! Hard work!"

Alaska Series No. 5

The Fishhouse

Willie, head butcher, jerks the pneumatic lever for the overhead bin. Fish rush the counter like holiday shoppers. He whirls and twirls sockeyes, silvers and humpies . . . draws tails; spins bodies. Organizes them for processing. Musters them to line and guillotine.

Down chained conveyer, fish carcass rotate through a drum of knives. Circle, twist and turn . . . pirouette blades. Guts and fins shear. Flung upon a table, the final entrails cut away.

I admire Willie for the long hours he works 'til the cutting's complete.

One day he says: "Now, you try."

Alaska Series No. 6

Manong Ralph Agbalog

He enters our room. Perfumed and pomaded hair.
Sports a cardigan sweater. Seats himself on my bunk.
Eyes Linda's picture. *"You marry?"*

In conversation, I learn he'd killed a man
over a gambling debt. *"Punched him in the jaw.
Dropped him on a curb.
Hit his head. Manslaughter."*

He tries to teach me pai gow which I don't get.
"Better, you don't understand."

Alaska Series No. 7

Retorts

Steam soars 'round the catch 'n can.
Hot ovens brim with salmon.
Kings, Pinks an' Sockeye cookin'.
Soon to grace the country's pans.

Charlie Woods stokes the retorts.
Loves "Bird." Carried two .38 Police Specials.
"I'll never leave here. Wanted
in the lower forty eight."

Alaska Series No. 8

Packing and Shipping

Few fish today. Mr. Acena sends us to the warehouse. We toil the day to dusk. We pallet 50 pound salmon cartons. Backs break. Moling drives his blue Clark forklift. Careens like a carabao through rows of crated canyons. Chomping cigar, he stacks loads three high . . . longshore for distant tables.

Alaska Steamships anchor. We handpack cargo holes. Little time for sleep. America must be fed.

Alaska Series No. 9

Letter from Linda (1965)

The Blue Goose swoons over the town bringing mail. Descends on King Cove's rocky shore, delivering word from home. We collect in the bunkhouse, like hungry chicks in a nest, our hands stretch for sustenance. I gather my letters. Recline on my bed. Linda writes:

"My high school boyfriend's returned. I'm getting married. You weren't ready. Don't write. Mom reads my mail. Take care of yourself."

I slip on my waders. Wobble from the bunkhouse to the bank. Manongs clench bait-cans and metal rods, fishing the shallow lagoon. Lure octopus from submerged rocks.

I select a rod and wander into the water.

Alaska Series No. 10

Weekends

Saturdays, Aleut fishermen return. Our canning work complete, we shower and have dinner. Later, a movie or dance at the bunkhouse. Jimmy plays his sax. Freddie strums a washtub bass. The girls come to mingle and flirt.

Sundays, we climb the bluff north from town to fire our guns. I pack a .22 rifle and kill a gull. Kenny carries a .32 Barretta. By accident, he shoots himself. They send him home. I sell my gun.

We play ping-pong or shoot hoops in a warehouse where we hung a rim. Sometimes, we stroll King Cove's boardwalk to its sweet shop for shakes. Native girls hang out there.

Alaska Series No. 11

Laigo's "East is West" Tritych *(In memory of Val Laigo.)*

Mahogany artist of mahogany men fashions homage to Filipinos
who crossed the ocean of dreams. Articulated with Alaskeros,

sakadas, waiters, asparagus and hop pickers, nurses, pensionados,
barbers and boxers. Accented with gambling dens, cockfights,
dime-dances, brothels and bunkhouses. Affixed with in-laws and outlaws of
Spanish cross and Moorish moon.

Hearts in search of America,
Pinoys arrived with tamaraw and carabao memories.
Silent servants apprenticed in this new Eden.
Melting into the melting pot yet clinging to an adobo past,
they came . . .

Your east-west star celebrates their memory and yours.

Alaska Series No. 12

> *Source:* Flor, Robert Francis. "Alaskero Memories." 2010. Used with permission of the author.

91. Eliyahu Enriquez, "Inquisitory Karma" and "Mahogany Mantle," 2010

Eliyahu Enriquez is a Jewish Filipino author, poet, and playwright in New York City whose multimedia work examines the intersection of sexual identity and ethnic and religious diaspora. "Inquisitory Karma" is a short piece reflecting on the interplay between his Jewish and Filipino identities. "Mahogany Mantle," written for the 2010 Be'chol Lashon Media Awards competition, features portrayals of ethnic and racial diversity within Judaism and expands on the themes laid out in "Inquisitory Karma."

"INQUISITORY KARMA"

Inspired by Alex Epstein

In May, I turned 34. 6 weeks and 6 days of the Omer. My sister, Mercy flipped through Sephora, while her drowsy husband wrestled with Esau's Angel. There were no fireworks. No intoxication. That night, a Chamelion painted your plans, neon. And for the first time since my last cruci-fiction, we dreamed in Tagalog.

"MAHOGANY MANTLE"

> *"Tell me about your experience/upbringing as a Filipino Jew and the challenges you have confronted as a Jew of Color?"*—Akira Ohiso, Zinc Plate Press

Ima {Taglit-Tagalog for "Mother"} Virginia was the primary nurse for New Square's Rebbitzen during the 1980s. I distinctly recall her endearing smile and waving from her bedside. The curious neighborhood Orthodox Jewish children reminded me of the provincial squalor kids in Quezon City, Philippines. I'm not sure who threw stones at me anymore.

Ima worked the night shift for many years. I think I've inherited her alertness, in that respect. I take intermittent naps, throughout the day. I suppose I can wake up on time for mid-day prayers more often, actually.

Ima was really quite beautiful in her innocence and long, ebony bangs—upon immigrating Stateside. We don't talk much these days. A silent, bitter recognition. And her hair has had the appearance of a Sheitel [a Jewish woman who wears a wig] since (she's a cancer survivor).

Each year, she plants Ampalaya in her exotic garden [bitter melon, often used in the Philippines for medicinal purposes].

Then there's David Levi, an old soulful teen crashing in a Monsey basement, below a renovated Yeshiva-residence. One morning, a spattering of shocked students stand at attention, upon my fashionably-late, but desperate disruption, beside the bimah [platform from where the Torah is read]. The Rabbi puts his index finger to the lips, completes a prayer in whispers, while I catch my breath, then escorts me to where David was couch-surfing. From the top of the stairs, pre-pubescent kids peek in on our drowsy conversation, cajoling David to "daven with us." Unwavering, they shut the door, continue to shift their wooden chairs, back and forth, the shadowy ceiling screeching above us. He was cursing up a storm, really sore at the general state of things. We decide to sneak out and go on a simkha ride [joyride] to Brooklyn, chain-smoking Reds along West Side Highway (eventually ending up at an Egyptian Hookah bar on the Lower East Side) . . . Finally come home, the following foggy morning, where he proceeds to take the wheel of my ghetto vehicle, embodying Neo-Speedracer: papawheeling over suburban curbs, skidding DNA knots around the pristine block, all the while ignoring my pleas, lingol, and wrecking the breakpad in the process.

David told me he only dons a yarmulke when traveling through Monsey, as a sign of respect, honor; otherwise, he's just like any anonymous rebellious punk—Hasidic Hitchhiker—getting their kicks along this pearl-studded journey of ours known as Mabuhai [Tagalog for "live" or "thrive"].

I think that's why Eliyahu Ha'Navi ascended to Shamayim [Hebrew for "sky"] in a fiery chariot so hastily:

He needed a new kippah.

We're still rebuilding Bahay Yosef, where identifying as Filipin@ and Jewish is a work-in-progress, much like an impending marriage: Loneliness —a memory album of loved ones our only companion—until a Bamboo Ketubah exchange at the altar between Yesha-Efrayim.

And I miss giving complimentary Poi shows to off-duty IDF soldiers in Tel Aviv (aka The Little Manila of Israel), very, very much.

In the meantime, I cherish the company of Heavenly Birds—from Eagles to Pigeons to Sparrows to Ravens to Duchifat to Doves to Twitter-Anghélim.

Ibónim

I worked as a Mental Health Worker in Westchester, New York (home to Professor Xavier's Shul for Gifted Youngsters)—where I'd have a hasty smoke during lunch breaks. Remember the time, when the concentration camps were finally liberated? When the prisoners of hope were given cigarettes by the army companies: and ravaged them, they were so famished? One day, I realized I had no matches left in my book. Since Filipinim are known to scavenge for manna in wilderness shantytowns, I naturally bowed my head, my pearl vision cast to the ground, scanning the periphery about me, dejected. Like Aba. Suddenly, I notice a bird land on the stairs leading up to the entrance of the youth ward. I squint, as it pecked away, knocking on the concrete slab—weeds and tiny sticks and leaves, rustling. Instinctively, the bird soars, when I notice a single, unlit match buried among the thorns . . .

Source: Enriquez, Eliyahu. "Inquisitory Karma" and "Mahogany Mantle." 2010. http://www.bahayyosef.com/2010/05/babaylan-names.html. http://www.bahayyosef.com/2010/01/honey-brown-patches.html. Accessed June 2010. Used with permission of the author.

92. Cynthia Vasallo, "Most American," 2010

The United States colonized the Philippines in 1898, Americanizing its educational and political systems, undermining its economy, and paving the way for thousands of Filipinos to immigrate to America. Many Filipinos initially came to the United States as agricultural laborers and by joining the U.S. Navy, which recruited thousands of stewards and mess boys from its many bases in the Philippines. Filipinos were classified as nationals and were the only non-Americans allowed to join the U.S. military. In 1934, Congress passed the Tydings-McDuffie Act, reclassifying Filipinos as aliens and cutting off most Filipino immigration to the United States. However, the Act exempted members of the U.S. Navy from this restriction, and, in 1947, the year after the Philippines gained independence, the Military Bases Agreement allowed the Navy to continue to recruit and hire Filipinos. The Navy thus became the major vehicle for Filipino immigration to the United States, creating transnational communities of Navy families formed in both countries.

Cynthia Vasallo is a first-generation Filipina American, born in Manila and living in California. Several generations of men in her family have served in the Philippine Army (controlled by the United States following 1898) and the U.S. Navy. Her grandfather was a survivor of the Bataan Death March, and her father received his U.S. citizenship in the 1950s, after enlisting in the Navy; he later served in Vietnam. Vasallo's short story, "Most American," is a semi-autobiographical piece describing the Americanization process for an immigrant family, highlighting the unique—and profoundly disruptive—role of the military in the Filipino American community.

Kuya and I used to love playing this game called *Most American*. We invented it when we first came to the US—my brother was almost nine that year and I was six. Because we were the only players, we made up all the rules as we went along. The only prize was bragging rights and enthusiastic applause from our parents.

One of my earliest memories of the game was of Kuya walking around the house with his thumbs and forefingers pressed up against his eyelids in order to open them wider—as if he could reshape them by force. After a while, he convinced me it was working, and maybe to humor him, my parents had agreed. I couldn't really see any difference but because I believed everything they told me, he easily won that round.

Not too long after this, we begged Nani and Tati to shop at Sears, for clothes. If we couldn't exactly *look* like our classmates, at least we could dress the part. That's when Kuya started to wear blue jeans and t-shirts; I wore plaid jumpers over frilly blouses with chunky black Mary-Janes. It didn't matter that the old faldas and pantalones we brought with us from Manila resembled the new ones we had on. *Those* clothes came from *there*, *these* were from *here*—that's what mattered. Nani and Tati said because we both looked equally American in our new outfits, that round of the game ended in a tie.

Then for my birthday a couple of years later, they let me join the Brownies. I never let on that I didn't really like the tan colored vest—it was always stiff and scratchy. But I wore the uniform anyway. Not only because I threw such a huge tantrum in order to have it (something I would never have been able to get away with back home, under the quick eyes and sharp tongue of my lola), but mainly because of the merit badges. Those badges, like the one for safety, and another for good citizenship, were something I could put my hand on during the Pledge of Allegiance and be proud of. I still have a Polaroid that my parents took of me in that outfit, one of many they sent to the relatives back home. In the blank space beneath it, Nani wrote a caption that reads: *8 year-old María. New Brownie. Pic in front of apartment. Calif, USA.* For a couple of months that year, I was Most American. Until Kuya, just dying to have a uniform of his own, joined the Boy Scouts. Then we were tied once again.

As time passed, we found other ways to claim our victories. Like the year I started dating white boys. *Too American*, my parents had said frowning and shaking their heads. With that, I thought Kuya might concede. But then on his twenty-first birthday he enlisted in the Navy and that put a huge win in his column. My parents were so thrilled they pretty much left me alone—so in a way, I guess I won, too.

Now it's a half-dozen years later and we've stopped playing altogether. Our tongues have been so tightly wrapped by blue, red, and white, they've become clumsy, tripping and tumbling over Tagalog. We no longer call each other by our old names. Kuya is now big brother, I am Mary, and Nani and Tati are Mom and Dad. My parents have become sentimental. They've carefully put away our old clothes—even our Brownie and Boy Scout uniforms—saving them as hand-me-downs for grandkids that they hope will someday come along.

Today I'm clothed head-to-toe in black. Instead of my brother's favorite Levis and t-shirt he is shrouded in dress-blues, a suit as dark as midnight with six gold buttons marching in formation down the front, a medal for each year of his service. It's the uniform he was wearing when Mom and Dad used their new video camera to shoot footage of his academy graduation, the one he wore when he pledged his allegiance. It's the suit my parents have chosen for this occasion.

Mom and Dad are seated on either side of me, front and center in the midst of a tearful but silent crowd. We watch as members of my brother's division fold a flag into a perfect tri-corner before one of them salutes, then hands the bulky packet to my mother. Her shaky outstretched arms don't quite know what to do with it; she hugs it tightly to her breast before finally passing it to my father. He underestimates the weight of it and I catch it before it falls, claiming my brother's final prize.

Source: Vasallo, Cynthia. "Most American." 2010. Used with permission of the author.

Part VII
Guamanian American

93. Hartley Ochavillo, "Leaving Guam," 2009

Many people mark 1898 as the year that American imperialism began. However, American colonial expansion began the minute the 13 colonies ratified the Constitution. After subjugating the Native American peoples and forcibly acquiring huge swaths of Mexican territory, Americans continued their imperial expansion into the Pacific. The United States took possession of Guam, eastern Samoa, and the Philippines after they defeated Spain in the War of 1898. While the Philippine Islands were colonized for their economic potential, the eastern Samoan islands and Guam were taken for their strategic and maritime value. Because both the Philippines and Guam were U.S. territories and both colonies had a large military presence, many Filipinos found their way to Guam. Even after the Philippines was given its independence in 1934, Filipinos continued to arrive in Guam.

In this short oral history, Hartley Ochavillo speaks about why he left Guam and headed for the United States. His maternal grandparents emigrated from the Philippines years before when his grandfather was offered a job driving vehicles for the U.S. Air Force. His father's family moved to Guam in 1986 after fleeing from the Marcos regime. At the time, Ochavillo's father was attending Manila University, where he participated in the many college protests against President Marcos. Ochavillo's family fled the Philippines, fearing that they would be jailed. His parents met and married in Guam, and he was born and raised on the island. His family still resides in Guam, but Ochavillo left in 2007 to pursue his educational dreams. Today, he continues to live and study in the San Francisco Bay Area.

Guam is a beautiful place. The beaches, the landscape, the tropical weather, the coconut trees swaying slightly in the wind, mango trees in people's backyards, and flowers and butterflies all scatter the landscape of the little island I grew up in. It is a beautiful island, and the people there are some of the kindest people you will ever meet. Nobody knows hospitality like the people of Guam. And oh the people, in terms of ethnicity and what people looked like, you often couldn't tell what people were. Filipinos, Chamorros, Chuukese, Paloans, Yappese, Chinese, Koreans, Japanese, White, Black, Mexican, the island was diverse and welcomed all walks of life. The island I grew up in was a place where prejudice was not quite as apparent, and outright racism was very difficult to find. The idea that we were all "che'lu" (family) was pervasive. Most people just wanted to get by life and have a good time. Life was slow paced, relaxed, and lazy. Life was quiet, but occasionally (frequently) the silence was disrupted by a party. Good food, good music, good people, good times, why would anyone leave?

Well for one, the tourism based economy has been in a downturn for years, which leaves the island and the government with little to no resources to spend on infrastructure and things like roads, schools, and hospitals. To make matters worse, there are still many corrupt politicians in Gov Guam that take the money the government makes and uses it for their own personal purposes. What results then is a school system that struggles to keep its schools open and pay its teachers, a hospital that cannot staff the Emergency Room from midnight to 4 A.M., and the privatization of many of the services the government once provided. Couple that with the lack of job opportunities for most people, and you find quite a few reasons to leave. That, and the psych department down in UOG wasn't quite doing it for me. I wanted to see where breakthroughs and new things were happening. I felt like I wasn't going to get that in an insular community. So here I am, living in the Bay and loving it.

Source: Hartley Ochavillo. Oral History, interview by Sang Chi. November 14, 2009. Reprinted with permission.

Part VIII
Native Hawai'ian American

94. Ke Ali'i Bernice Pauahi Paki Bishop, "Will and Codicils," 1883

Ali'i (Chief) Bernice Pauahi Bishop was the last royal descendant of King Kamehameha I, who united the Kingdom of Hawai'i in 1810. Bishop grew up in a land increasingly taken over by Anglo-American businessmen and agriculture magnates. Over Bishop's lifetime, the native Hawai'ian population declined by over 50 percent, and three-fourths of privately held land was transferred to haole (white) ownership. Planters imported successive waves of laborers from all over Asia to work on the sugarcane and pineapple plantations and gradually took over both economic and political control of the Kingdom of Hawai'i.

Bishop, concerned for her people, deeded a large portion of her extensive estate for the establishment of a school for native Hawai'ian children. In the 13th article of her will, excerpted in the following, she specifies that all admitted students be of native Hawai'ian ancestry and that all teachers be of the Protestant religion. The Kamehameha Schools for boys and girls were founded in 1887, according to the terms of Bishop's will, four years after her death.

Know all Men by these Presents, That I, Bernice Pauahi Bishop, the wife of Charles R. Bishop, of Honolulu, Island of Oahu, Hawaiian Islands, being of sound mind and memory, but conscious of the uncertainty of life, do make, publish and declare this my last Will and Testament in manner following, hereby revoking all former wills by me made. . . .

Thirteenth. I give, devise and bequeath all of the rest, residue and remainder of my estate real and personal, wherever situated unto the trustees below named, their heirs and assigns forever, to hold upon the following trusts, namely: to erect and maintain in the Hawaiian Islands two schools, each for boarding and day scholars, one for boys and one for girls, to be known as, and called the Kamehameha Schools.

I direct my executive trustees to expend such amount as they may deem best, not to exceed however one-half of the fund which may come into their hands, in the purchase of suitable premises, the erection of school buildings, and in furnishing the same with the necessary and appropriate fixtures furniture and apparatus.

I direct my trustees to invest the remainder of my estate in such manner as they may think best, and to expend the annual income in the maintenance of said schools; meaning thereby the salaries of teachers, the repairing buildings and other incidental expenses; and to devote a portion of each years income to the support and education of orphans, and others in indigent circumstances, giving the preference to Hawaiians of pure or part aboriginal blood; the proportion in which said annual income is to be divided among the various objects above mentioned to be determined solely by my said trustees they to have full discretion.

I desire my trustees to provide first and chiefly a good education in the common English branches, and also instruction in morals and in such useful knowledge as may tend to make good and industrious men and women; and I desire instruction in the higher branches to be subsidiary to the foregoing objects.

For the purposes aforesaid I grant unto my said trustees full power to lease or sell any portion of my real estate, and to reinvest the proceeds and the balance of my estate in real estate, or in such other manner as to my said trustees may seem best.

I also give unto my said trustees full power to make all such rules and regulations as they may deem necessary for the government of said schools and to regulate the admission of pupils, and the same to alter, amend and publish upon a vote of a majority of said trustees.

I also direct that my said trustees shall annually make a full and complete report of all receipts and expenditures, and of the condition of said schools to the Chief Justice of the Supreme Court, or other highest judicial officer in this country; and shall also file before him annually an inventory of the property in their hands and how invested, and to publish the same in some Newspaper published in said Honolulu; I also direct my said trustees to keep said school buildings insured in good Companies, and in case of loss to expend the amounts recovered in replacing or repairing said buildings.

I also direct that the teachers of said schools shall forever be persons of the Protestant religion, but I do not intend that the choice should be restricted to persons of any particular sect of Protestants. . . .

In witness whereof I, said Bernice Pauahi Bishop, have hereunto set my hand and seal this thirty-first day of October A.D. Eighteen hundred and eighty-three.

BERNICE P. BISHOP (SEAL)

The foregoing instrument, written on eleven pages, was signed, sealed, published and declared by said Bernice Pauahi Bishop, as and for her last will and testament in our presence, who at her request, in her presence, and in the presence of each other, have hereunto set our names as witnesses thereto, this 31st day of October A.D. 1883.

F. W. MACFARLANE
FRANCIS M. HATCH

Source: Excerpt from Probate No. 2425, Bernice Pauai Bishop, from Probate Records of the First District Court [Series 007], Judiciary of Hawai'i. Hawai'i State Archives.

95. Lili'uokalani, *Hawai'i's Story by Hawai'i's Queen,* 1898

Lydia Kamaka'eha Kaola Mali'i Lili'uokalani was the last monarch of the Kingdom of Hawai'i. Lili'uokalani succeeded her brother, David Kalākaua in 1891. She was deposed two years later by a cabal of American and European businessmen and plantation owners who were supported by the U.S. Navy. They formed the Republic of Hawai'i, with Sanford Dole as president, and advocated strongly for U.S. annexation of the islands. In 1895, after an unsuccessful coup attempt, Lili'uokalani abdicated the throne and was placed under house arrest. Although President Grover Cleveland believed Lili'uokalani to be the lawful ruler of Hawai'i and refused to cede to the annexationists, his successor, William McKinley signed a Congressional joint resolution that made Hawai'i into an American territory in 1898.

Ostensibly her autobiography, *Hawai'i's Story by Hawai'i's Queen* is Lili'uokalani's impassioned defense of the sovereign rights of the Kingdom of Hawai'i. In this excerpt, she not only argues that the 1893 Treaty of Annexation, purportedly ceding Hawai'ian sovereignty to the United States, was illegal and unconstitutional, but she also petitions the U.S. Senate to deny its ratification.

MY OFFICIAL PROTEST TO THE TREATY

"I, LILIUOKALANI of Hawai'i, by the will of God named heir apparent on the tenth day of April, A.D. 1877, and by the grace of God Queen of the Hawaiian Islands on the seventeenth day of January, A.D. 1893, do hereby protest against the ratification of a certain treaty, which, so I am informed, has been signed at Washington by Messrs. Hatch, Thurston, and Kinney, purporting to cede those Islands to the territory and dominion of the United States. I declare such a treaty to be an act of wrong toward the native and part-native people of Hawai'i, an invasion of the rights of the ruling chiefs, in violation of international rights both toward my people and toward friendly nations with whom they have made treaties, the perpetuation of the fraud whereby the constitutional government was overthrown and, finally, an act of gross injustice to me.

"Because the official protests made by me on the seventeenth day of January, 1893, to the so-called Provisional Government was signed by me, and received by said government with the assurance that the case was referred to the United States of America for arbitration.

YIELDED TO AVOID BLOODSHED.

"Because that protest and my communications to the United States Government immediately thereafter expressly declare that I yielded my authority to the forces of the United States in order to avoid bloodshed, and because I recognized the futility of a conflict with so formidable a power.

"Because the President of the United States, the Secretary of State, and an envoy commissioned by them reported in official documents that my government was unlawfully coerced by the forces, diplomatic and naval, of the United States; that I was at the date of their investigations the constitutional ruler of my people.

"Because such decision of the recognized magistrates of the United States was officially communicated to me and to Sanford B. Dole, and said Dole's resignation requested by Albert S. Willis, the recognized agent and minister of the Government of the United States.

"Because neither the above-named commission nor the government which sends it has ever received any such authority from the registered voters of Hawai'i, but derives its assumed powers from the so-called committee of public safety, organized on or about the seventeenth day of January, 1893, said committee being composed largely of persons claiming American citizenship, and not one single Hawaiian was a member thereof, or in any way participated in the demonstration leading to its existence.

"Because my people, about forty thousand in number, have in no way been consulted by those, three thousand in number, who claim the right to destroy the independence of Hawai'i. My people constitute four-fifths of the legally qualified voters of Hawai'i, and excluding those imported for the demands of labor, about the same proportion of the inhabitants.

CIVIC AND HEREDITARY RIGHTS.

"Because said treaty ignores, not only the civic rights of my people, but, further, the hereditary property of their chiefs. Of the 4,000,000 acres composing the territory said treaty offers to annex, 1,000,000 or 915,000 acres has in no way been heretofore recognized as other than the private property of the constitutional monarch, subject to a control in no way differing from other items of a private estate.

"Because it is proposed by said treaty to confiscate said property, technically called the crown lands, those legally entitled thereto, either now or in succession, receiving no consideration whatever for estates, their title to which has been always undisputed, and which is legitimately in my name at this date.

"Because said treaty ignores, not only all professions of perpetual amity and good faith made by the United States in former treaties with the sovereigns representing the Hawaiian people, but all treaties made by those sovereigns with other and friendly powers, and it is thereby in violation of international law.

"Because, by treating with the parties claiming at this time the right to cede said territory of Hawai'i, the Government of the United States receives such territory from the hands of those whom its own magistrates (legally elected by the people of the United States, and in office in 1893) pronounced fraudulently in power and unconstitutionally ruling Hawai'i.

APPEALS TO PRESIDENT AND SENATE.

"Therefore I, Liliuokalani of Hawai'i, do hereby call upon the President of that nation, to whom alone I yielded my property and my authority, to withdraw said treaty (ceding said Islands) from further consideration. I ask the honorable Senate of the United States to decline to ratify said treaty, and I implore the people of this great and good nation, from whom my ancestors learned the Christian religion, to sustain their representatives in such acts of justice and equity as may be in accord with the principles of their fathers, and to the Almighty Ruler of the universe, to him who judgeth righteously, I commit my cause.

"Done at Washington, District of Columbia, United States of America, this seventeenth day of June, in the year eighteen hundred and ninety-seven.

"LILIUOKALANI.
"JOSEPH HELELUHE.
"WOKEKI HELELUHE } Witnesses to Signature."
"JULIAS A. PALMER.

Source: Liliuokalani. *Hawai'i's Story by Hawai'i's Queen by Liliuokalani, Queen of Hawai'i (1838–1917)*. Boston: Lee and Shepard, 1898, pp. 354–358. http://digital.library.upenn.edu/women/liliuokalani/hawaii/hawaii.html#LV. Accessed February 2010.

96. U.S. Public Law 103-150, "The Apology Resolution," 1993

In 1993, 100 years after the United States overthrew the Kingdom of Hawai'i, President William Clinton signed U.S. Public Law 103-150. Otherwise known as the "Apology Resolution," this document acknowledges the sovereignty and independence of the Kingdom of Hawai'i prior to 1893 and the collusion of the Church of Christ, Anglo-Hawai'ian planters, and William McKinley's government in deposing Queen Lili'uokalani and taking Native Hawai'ian lands. The following excerpt of the resolution outlines the historical context surrounding annexation, offers a formal apology, and calls for reconciliation. However, in delineating "Native Hawai'ian" as "a descendent of the aboriginal people" who inhabited the Kingdom of Hawai'i "prior to 1778," the Apology Resolution does not acknowledge the claims of today's Hawai'i Sovereignty Movement, which seeks redress at an international level rather than in a subnational or racial context.

To acknowledge the 100th anniversary of the January 17, 1893 overthrow Nov. 23, 1993 of the Kingdom of Hawai'i, and to offer an apology to Native Hawaiians on (S.J. Res. 19) behalf of the United States for the overthrow of the Kingdom of Hawai'i.

Whereas, prior to the arrival of the first Europeans in 1778, the Native Hawaiian people lived in a highly organized, self-sufficient, subsistent social system based on communal land tenure with a sophisticated language, culture, and religion;

Whereas, a unified monarchical government of the Hawaiian Islands was established in 1810 under Kamehameha I, the first King of Hawai'i;

Whereas, from 1826 until 1893, the United States recognized the independence of the Kingdom of Hawai'i, extended full and complete diplomatic recognition to the Hawaiian Government, and entered into treaties and conventions with the Hawaiian monarchs to govern commerce and navigation in 1826, 1842, 1849, 1875, and 1887;

Whereas, the Congregational Church (now known as the United Church of Christ), through its American Board of Commissioners for Foreign Missions, sponsored and sent more than 100 missionaries to the Kingdom of Hawai'i between 1820 and 1850;

Whereas, on January 14, 1893, John L. Stevens (hereafter referred to in this Resolution as the "United States Minister"), the United States Minister assigned to the sovereign and independent Kingdom of Hawai'i conspired with a small group of non-Hawaiian residents of the Kingdom of Hawai'i, including citizens of the United States, to overthrow the indigenous and lawful Government of Hawai'i;

Whereas, in pursuance of the conspiracy to overthrow the Government of Hawai'i, the United States Minister and the naval representatives of the United States caused armed naval forces of the United States to invade the sovereign Hawaiian nation on January 16, 1893, and to position themselves near the Hawaiian Government buildings and the Iolani Palace to intimidate Queen Liliuokalani and her Government;

Whereas, on the afternoon of January 17, 1893, a Committee of Safety that represented the American and European sugar planters, descendants of missionaries, and financiers deposed the Hawaiian monarchy and proclaimed the establishment of a Provisional Government;

Whereas, the United States Minister thereupon extended diplomatic recognition to the Provisional Government that was formed by the conspirators without the consent of the Native Hawaiian people or the lawful Government of Hawai'i and in violation of treaties between the two nations and of international law;

Whereas, soon thereafter, when informed of the risk of bloodshed with resistance, Queen Liliuokalani issued the following statement yielding her authority to the United States Government rather than to the Provisional Government:

"I Liliuokalani, by the Grace of God and under the Constitution of the Hawaiian Kingdom, Queen, do hereby solemnly protest against any and all acts done against myself and the Constitutional Government of the Hawaiian Kingdom by certain persons claiming to have established a Provisional Government of and for this Kingdom.

"That I yield to the superior force of the United States of America whose Minister Plenipotentiary, His Excellency John L. Stevens, has caused United States troops to be landed a Honolulu and declared that he would support the Provisional Government.

"Now to avoid any collision of armed forces, and perhaps the loss of life, I do this under protest and impelled by said force yield my authority until such time as the Government of the United States shall, upon facts being presented to it, undo the action of its representatives and reinstate me in the authority which I claim as the Constitutional Sovereign of the Hawaiian Islands."

Done at Honolulu this 17th day of January, A.D. 1893.;

Whereas, without the active support and intervention by the United States diplomatic and military representatives, the insurrection against the Government of Queen Liliuokalani would have failed for lack of popular support and insufficient arms;

Whereas, on February 1, 1893, the United States Minister raised the American flag and proclaimed Hawai'i to be a protectorate of the United States;

Whereas, the report of a Presidentially established investigation conducted by former Congressman James Blount into the events surrounding the insurrection and overthrow of January 17, 1893, concluded that the United States diplomatic and military representatives had abused their authority and were responsible for the change in government;

Whereas, as a result of this investigation, the United States Minister to Hawai'i was recalled from his diplomatic post and the military commander of the United States armed forces stationed in Hawai'i was disciplined and forced to resign his commission;

Whereas, in a message to Congress on December 18, 1893, President Grover Cleveland reported fully and accurately on the illegal acts of the conspirators, described such acts as an "act of war, committed with the participation of a diplomatic representative of the United States and without authority of Congress", and acknowledged that by such acts the government of a peaceful and friendly people was overthrown;

Whereas, President Cleveland further concluded that a "substantial wrong has thus been done which a due regard for our national character as well as the rights of the injured people requires we should endeavor to repair" and called for the restoration of the Hawaiian monarchy;

Whereas, the Provisional Government protested President Cleveland's call for the restoration of the monarchy and continued to hold state power and pursue annexation to the United States;

Whereas, the Provisional Government successfully lobbied the Committee on Foreign Relations of the Senate (hereafter referred to in this Resolution as the "Committee") to conduct a new investigation into the events surrounding the overthrow of the monarchy;

Whereas, the Committee and its chairman, Senator John Morgan, conducted hearings in Washington, D.C., from December 27,1893, through February 26, 1894, in which members of the Provisional Government justified and condoned the actions of the United States Minister and recommended annexation of Hawai'i;

Whereas, although the Provisional Government was able to obscure the role of the United States in the illegal overthrow of the Hawaiian monarchy, it was unable to rally the support from two-thirds of the Senate needed to ratify a treaty of annexation;

Whereas, on July 4, 1894, the Provisional Government declared itself to be the Republic of Hawai'i;

Whereas, on January 24, 1895, while imprisoned in Iolani Palace, Queen Liliuokalani was forced by representatives of the Republic of Hawai'i to officially abdicate her throne;

Whereas, in the 1896 United States Presidential election, William McKinley replaced Grover Cleveland;

Whereas, on July 7, 1898, as a consequence of the Spanish-American War, President McKinley signed the Newlands Joint Resolution that provided for the annexation of Hawai'i;

Whereas, through the Newlands Resolution, the self-declared Republic of Hawai'i ceded sovereignty over the Hawaiian Islands to the United States;

Whereas, the Republic of Hawai'i also ceded 1,800,000 acres of crown, government and public lands of the Kingdom of Hawai'i, without the consent of or compensation to the Native Hawaiian people of Hawai'i or their sovereign government;

Whereas, the Congress, through the Newlands Resolution, ratified the cession, annexed Hawai'i as part of the United States, and vested title to the lands in Hawai'i in the United States;

Whereas, the Newlands Resolution also specified that treaties existing between Hawai'i and foreign nations were to immediately cease and be replaced by United States treaties with such nations;

Whereas, the Newlands Resolution effected the transaction between the Republic of Hawai'i and the United States Government;

Whereas, the indigenous Hawaiian people never directly relinquished their claims to their inherent sovereignty as a people or over their national lands to the United States, either through their monarchy or through a plebiscite or referendum;

Whereas, on April 30, 1900, President McKinley signed the Organic Act that provided a government for the territory of Hawai'i and defined the political structure and powers of the newly established Territorial Government and its relationship to the United States;

Whereas, on August 21,1959, Hawai'i became the 50th State of the United States;

Whereas, the health and well-being of the Native Hawaiian people is intrinsically tied to their deep feelings and attachment to the land;

Whereas, the long-range economic and social changes in Hawai'i over the nineteenth and early twentieth centuries have been devastating to the population and to the health and well-being of the Hawaiian people;

Whereas, the Native Hawaiian people are determined to preserve, develop and transmit to future generations their ancestral territory, and their cultural identity in accordance with their own spiritual and traditional beliefs, customs, practices, language, and social institutions;

Whereas, in order to promote racial harmony and cultural understanding, the Legislature of the State of Hawai'i has determined that the year 1993, should serve Hawai'i as a year of special reflection on the rights and dignities of the Native Hawaiians in the Hawaiian and the American societies;

Whereas, the Eighteenth General Synod of the United Church of Christ in recognition of the denomination's historical complicity in the illegal overthrow of the Kingdom of Hawai'i in 1893 directed the Office of the President of the United Church of Christ to offer a public apology to the Native Hawaiian people and to initiate the process of reconciliation between the United Church of Christ and the Native Hawaiians; and

Whereas, it is proper and timely for the Congress on the occasion of the impending one hundredth anniversary of the event, to acknowledge the historic significance of the illegal overthrow of the Kingdom of Hawai'i, to express its deep regret to the Native Hawaiian people, and to support the reconciliation efforts of the State of Hawai'i and the United Church of Christ with Native Hawaiians;

Now, therefore, be it

Resolved by the Senate and House of Representatives of the United States of America in Congress assembled,

SECTION 1. ACKNOWLEDGMENT AND APOLOGY.

The Congress –

(1) on the occasion of the 100th anniversary of the illegal overthrow of the Kingdom of Hawai'i on January 17, 1893, acknowledges the historical significance of this event which resulted in the suppression of the inherent sovereignty of the Native Hawaiian people;

(2) recognizes and commends efforts of reconciliation initiated by the State of Hawai'i and the United Church of Christ with Native Hawaiians;

(3) apologizes to Native Hawaiians on behalf of the people of the United States for the overthrow of the Kingdom of Hawai'i on January 17, 1893 with the participation of agents and citizens of the United States, and the deprivation of the rights of Native Hawaiians to self-determination;

(4) expresses its commitment to acknowledge the ramifications of the overthrow of the Kingdom of Hawai'i, in order to provide a proper foundation for reconciliation between the United States and the Native Hawaiian people; and

(5) urges the President of the United States to also acknowledge the ramifications of the overthrow of the Kingdom of Hawai'i and to support reconciliation efforts between the United States and the Native Hawaiian people.

SEC. 2. DEFINITIONS.

As used in this Joint Resolution, the term "Native Hawaiians" means any individual who is a descendent of the aboriginal people who, prior to 1778, occupied and exercised sovereignty in the area that now constitutes the State of Hawai'i.

SEC. 3. DISCLAIMER.

Nothing in this Joint Resolution is intended to serve as a settlement of any claims against the United States.

Approved November 23, 1993
NOV. 23, 1993
103d Congress
Joint Resolution

Source: U.S. Public Law 103-150. 103rd Cong., 1st Sess. *Congressional Record* vol. 139, 1993. http://cwis.org/fwdp/Oceania/1_publaw.txt. Accessed April 2010.

97. Hawaiian Constitutional Convention, 2008

Ever since the United States took over the Kingdom of Hawai'i in 1898, people have fought for Native Hawai'ian sovereignty over the islands. Different groups hold very different opinions on how sovereignty should be achieved, what a sovereign land or territory looks like, and how the U.S. government should be involved in the process and outcome. In 2008, after years of activism around the sovereignty movement, a group called the Nation of Hawai'i called for a constitutional convention. They oppose the Akaka Bill, which calls for federal recognition of a Native Hawai'ian governing body, on the grounds that Native Hawai'ians are not indigenous to the United States and that the bill does not adequately address the United States' historical violation of international laws and conventions in its treatment of the Kingdom of Hawai'i. In this resolution, the Nation of Hawai'i calls for a Constitutional Convention for Hawai'ians, both native and "national," in order to have the full measure of self-determination.

Whereas, the fear of losing grants and entitlements for not supporting government programs or legislation, is the biggest threat and obstacle facing the native Hawaiian people (Kanaka Maoli) to freely determine the government of their choosing.

Whereas, the native Hawaiian people, will need a substantial period of time in which they can engage freely, and without fear of threat or intimidation, in the processes of educating themselves. They need the freedom to publicly debate amongst themselves, the various options of self governance available to them. It is imperative that they also have meaningful access to the mainstream news media in Hawai'i.

Whereas, the Hawaiian Constitutional Convention will automatically protect and preserve the *Sovereignty* of the native Hawaiian people over their National and Ancestral Lands.

Let it be known to All peoples, governments, financial institutions, multi national corporations, and affiliated entities, throughout the World, that the native Hawaiian people proclaim their right of self-determination, in accordance with Article 1 (2) of the United Nations Charter as well as the recent Hawai'i State Supreme Court Injunction, on January 31, 2008.

Be It Resolved That We, the undersigned native Hawaiian and non native Hawaiian people, Hereby Declare the Hawaiian Constitutional Convention in Session, on this, 27th day of May, 2008 @ 8:PM.

Source: Nation of Hawaii. "Hawaiian Constitutional Convention." 2009 h http://Hawaiianconstitutionalconvention.com/. Accessed June 2009. Used with permission.

98. M. J. Halelaukoa Garvin, "How Do You See Yourself?" 2009

Native Hawai'ians have struggled with health issues, impoverishment, and the loss of cultural identity since the colonization of their islands began in 1778. Anglo missionaries often imposed their cultural norms while spreading Protestantism, and they condemned Hawai'ian clothing, dance, and religious practices as superstitious and primitive. Businessmen and planters from the mainland also overturned the traditional Hawai'ian system of land stewardship. By introducing Western-style land ownership, based on individual ownership, haoles also managed to take possession of three-quarters of all privately held Hawai'ian lands by 1890. The legacy of colonization can still be seen today in the high incidences of chronic disease, substance abuse, and poverty among the Native Hawai'ian population.

M. J. Halelaukoa Garvin works with numerous Native Hawai'ian groups, including Malama Hawai'i and the Hokule'a Worldwide Voyage. In her short essay, Garvin reflects on and shows how institutionalized racism and stereotypes conditioned Native Hawai'ian self-perception, and she expresses her hope that today's Hawai'ian community will reject those images and embrace its true identity.

Recently, having lunch with friends, I was struck by how much Native Hawaiian self-image has changed over the years.

There was nothing particularly unusual about this lunch—a typical get-together of the cronies gathering for a highly anticipated talk story session. However, on this occasion we were lucky to be joined by one of our hui's Grandpa Joe.

A distinguished gentleman in his eighties, Grandpa Joe is one of those wonderful people you want at all of your parties. A raconteur at heart, his lifetime of experiences and wry wit combined to have us all rolling with laughter. Drawing us in as confidants, he would lean forward conspiratorially. His shock of white hair edging ever nearer and his eyes dancing, he wove amazing tales of the "old days."

During the course of the lunch, the conversation turned toward us. "What do you do?" he asked. A physicist, a lawyer, a writer, a professor and a flack (yes, I'm the underachiever of the bunch) were the answers.

"Wow, a group of smart Hawaiians," he said completely devoid of irony.

"Grandpa!" his namesake moʻopuna squawked. But, Grandpa Joe was nonplused. He had no idea why his grandson was upset.

Grandpa Joe wasn't being racist though; he was simply reiterating what he'd heard for a lifetime. Graduating from Kamehameha Schools nearly 70 years ago, his was a world in which native opportunities were few. What we now consider commonplace—a group of college educated Native Hawaiian professionals from ordinary backgrounds—was unheard of in his day.

But more interesting to me, he did not see the very incongruity of his thinking. Here was a man—a Hawaiian man—who without the benefit of higher education used his intellect and will to forge a highly successful international career. There is absolutely no question that Grandpa Joe is an extremely "smart Hawaiian." Yet, he was unable to place his own life example above the stereotypes embedded within him decades before. He continues to carry the century old bias that Hawaiians are somehow inadequate.

A generation later, my father followed along the same path of self-deprecation. A recurring conversation in our house went something like this.

Dad: "Hawaiians are lazy."
Child: "Dad, aren't we Hawaiians?"
Dad: "Yes."
Child: "Is anyone in our family lazy?"
Dad: "No."
Child: "So what Hawaiians are you talking about?"
Dad: Silence

Coming from a household of incurable workaholics, I never understood how my father could make such an outrageous statement. However, in speaking with Grandpa Joe, I began to better understand my own history. My father, like Grandpa, could not reconcile the gulf between his own experiences and the prejudices of long ago.

Yet—even though they could not see it within themselves—both of these smart, hardworking men are part of changing how Native Hawaiians are perceived. Amazing examples like theirs are the lens through which my friends and I view ourselves and our people.

Now, it is incumbent upon us to ensure that others of our generation, as well as the next, deliver on the potential we so clearly see.

Source: Garvin, M. J. Halelaukoa. "How Do You See Yourself?" January 16, 2009. http://ainaaloha.wordpress.com/2009/01/16/how-do-you-see-yourself/. Accessed July 2009. Reprinted with permission from M. J. Garvin.

99. Jeno Enocencio, "Surviving the Enemy," 2009

The issue of Hawai'ian sovereignty is very divisive. Individuals and organizations disagree on what role the United States should play in Hawai'i, on whether Native Hawai'ians should form a "nation within a nation" similar to Native American nations, on the administration and disbursement of ceded lands (land formerly belonging to the Hawai'ian monarchy, ceded to the United States in 1898), and on the role of race and bloodlines in designating Native Hawai'ian status. Oftentimes, loyalty to the United States is assumed to be incompatible with Native Hawai'ian identity.

However, Native Hawai'ian Jeno Enocencio does not see a conflict between being Hawai'ian and being American. As a young boy, he was raised by his extended family after his father died. As a young man, he fought in the Vietnam War like thousands of his peers. These experiences shaped Enocencio's unique views on identity. The following excerpt is from his column for the newsletter of the Office of Hawaiian Affairs (a government agency charged with improving the lives of Hawai'ians). In it, Enocencio asserts his belief that it is possible to embrace both Native Hawai'ian and American identity, to nurture Hawai'ian culture and at the same time be a loyal citizen of the United States.

THE FREEDOM TO CHOOSE: PROUD AMERICAN, PROUD HAWAIIAN—OR BOTH

Benjamin Franklin said, "Any society that would give up a little liberty to gain a little security will deserve neither and lose both." Another quote along those same lines, "Anyone who trades liberty for security deserves neither liberty nor security."

A couple of weekends ago, Caroline and I had the opportunity to attend my Disabled American Veterans convention in Līhu'e, Kaua'i. The weather was beautiful, though our room felt muggy when the eastern sun blazed mid-day through the patio window. It was an eventful convention of old men acting like 19-year-olds, a rejuvenating sauna of memories as veterans of three generational wars gathered and pondered their experiences. I gathered my thoughts on my war experiences during Vietnam but quietly ushered them out of my mind, replacing them with the solemn humbleness of being an American citizen—a Hawaiian warrior. This statement appears to be an oxymoron, an American citizen and Hawaiian warrior—one considered imperialistic and invasive, the other passive and welcoming by nature. Whatever the implication, I'm proud of being an American and very much of being Hawaiian.

Many have told me that I need to choose either or. I choose to be both. And that is what makes being an American great—I choose who I want to be. I get to choose where I want to go in life and what I want to achieve—the skies have no limits. I choose my words and share my ideals. I can express my perspective, which bears rights to argue and disagree. I choose the associates with whom I want to be; my life partner, the children that we raise. I can worship idols or express it in faith. I can write, and readers can criticize. We can reciprocate and not fear disparaging thoughts or retaliation. And we have the very laws that protect us embedded in our Constitution that affords us this freedom—which we enjoy, yet take for granted.

I wanted to write about a topic that we've been experimenting with at our 'ohana's ranch at Kalalau ahupua'a here in Hilo titled New Chicken v. Old Chicken, which concerns our efforts to introduce a new food that has been in Hawai'i for ages to feed our ever-growing population. But I'll save that for next month because this month's Fourth of July holiday provides the perfect time for expressing my patriotism to both flags (yet another example of my freedom to choose what I wish to share with my readers).

Not only do I celebrate the birth of America, July 4, 1776, but I also embrace the birth of my son, Orion-Independence Kahikina Enocencio, July 4, 1980. What an honor to have been blessed with a son born on this special day. Every fourth we make it out to Hilo Bay to have our family BBQ and celebrate his and our country's birthday; the cake often reads "Happy Birthday Orion-Independence and America, We Love U Both!"

On Aug. 21, 2009, a day after my birthday, we'll be celebrating 50 years of statehood—of being American. I'm sure many of you may wonder, "Eh, wot kine Hawaiian iz dis . . . I taught he wuz one of us?" I think if we wala'au one day, you may be able to understand my personal feelings on this sensitive issue.

One thing I will admit to all, I have taken a stand. I know in my heart that when our Queen was exiled from the throne, there were men and women who were ready to spill their own blood to reinstate her honor. But as Eve had partaken of the fruit from the Tree of Life, that mankind can become, so did the Queen relinquish her honor so Hawaiians can become. I believe that our Queen knew that in order for her children to advance in the forever-changed kingdom, she had to release her children by yielding her birthright. Had she not let go, I can only wonder how much further removed from our homeland and culture we'd become.

Yes, much has been sacrificed since with rampant disease, short life span, and lack of sovereign foods, poverty, and lack of education, homelessness, drug and alcohol abuse, domestic abuse, incarceration, and lack of agricultural lands. But in the onslaught for progression, Hawaiians have achieved and overcome great barriers through the efforts of schools at Kamehameha, Punahou, Maryknoll, Damien, St. Andrews and other high academic standing schools where many Hawaiians have taken the challenge and won.

Public charter schools have demonstrated how many of our Hawaiian youth have increased depth in knowledge and understanding through application when involved in culturally based means for education. An extension of that is what we do at Kalalau: Rediscovering the Ahupua'a Life System, where we express Native Hawaiian and culturally diversified survival and learning techniques, a totally hands-on application for better understanding of academics taught in school.

Today, Hawaiians are lawyers, nurses and physicians, astronomers, professors, diplomats, scientists, agronomists, teachers, judges, lawmakers, businessmen, entrepreneurs, mayors, governors, engineers, contractors, physicists, geophysicists, oceanographers, meteorologists, agriculturists, filmmakers, editors and writers and artists, farmers, ranchers and even more. I don't think this much could've happened for Hawaiians on a large scale had the Queen defended her birthright. It was a sad day for all to have seen the Queen step down from her throne. But I sincerely feel that our Queen realized that her children had to do more than just survive; they, WE, had to "thrive."

I'm thankful for the Queen for giving me a chance to survive in this new world. I'm thankful for America for allowing me to thrive beyond my imagination. I'm proud to be American and very proud to be Hawaiian—this is my stand. The canoe cuts sharply through the wave only when the paddle pushes forward, but only in unison with other paddlers and beat of the drum. It's time for you folks to take a stand too—that is, not to just survive, but to thrive. God Bless America, God Bless Hawai'i—God Bless our Queen.

Source: Enocencio, Jeno. "Surviving the Enemy." Originally published in *'Ka Wai Ola o OHA*, the newspaper of the Office of Hawaiian Affairs. http://www.oha.org/kwo/2009/07/col-enocencio.php. Accessed July 2009. Reprinted with permission from the author.

100. Native Hawaiian Government Reorganization Act, S. 381, 2009

Daniel Kahikina Akaka is the first U.S. Senator of Native Hawai'ian descent. Born in Honolulu in 1924, Akaka served in the U.S. Army Corps of Engineers during World War II; he became a Congressman in 1976 and was elected Senator of Hawai'i in 1990. In 2001, Akaka introduced the Native Hawaiian Government Reorganization Act, S. 381, which calls for the extension of federal self-governance and self-determination for Native Hawai'ians. A revised version of the Akaka Bill was passed by the House of Representatives in February 2010.

The bill is controversial among more radical sovereignty groups in Hawai'i, who believe that it will create a governing entity that implicitly legitimizes the 1898 overthrow of the Kingdom of Hawai'i. Akaka nevertheless believes this act will forward the process of reconciliation between the United States and Native Hawai'ians. The following two excerpts from the Native Hawaiian Government Reorganization Act discuss the importance of the ceded lands (over 1 million acres set aside for Native Hawai'ians in 1959, as part of the conditions for statehood) in maintaining Hawai'ian culture, reference the 1993 Apology Resolution (when the United States government took responsibility for the overthrow of the Kingdom of Hawai'i), and call for a reorganization and recognition of the Native Hawai'ian government.

SECTION 1. FINDINGS.

Congress makes the following findings: . . .

(9) Throughout the years, Native Hawaiians have repeatedly sought access to the Ceded Lands Trust and its resources and revenues in order to establish and

maintain native settlements and distinct native communities throughout the State.

(10) The Hawaiian Home Lands and the Ceded Lands provide an important foundation for the ability of the Native Hawaiian community to maintain the practice of Native Hawaiian culture, language, and traditions, and for the survival of the Native Hawaiian people. . . .

(13) The Apology Resolution acknowledges that the overthrow of the Kingdom of Hawai'i occurred with the active participation of agents and citizens of the United States and further acknowledges that the Native Hawaiian people never directly relinquished their claims to their inherent sovereignty as a people over their national lands to the United States, either through their monarchy or through a plebiscite or referendum.

(14) The Apology Resolution expresses the commitment of Congress and the President to acknowledge the ramifications of the overthrow of the Kingdom of Hawai'i and to support reconciliation efforts between the United States and Native Hawaiians; and to have Congress and the President, through the President's designated officials, consult with Native Hawaiians on the reconciliation process as called for under the Apology Resolution.

(15) Despite the overthrow of the Hawaiian government, Native Hawaiians have continued to maintain their separate identity as a distinct native community through the formation of cultural, social, and political institutions, and to give expression to their rights as native people to self-determination and self-governance as evidenced through their participation in the Office of Hawaiian Affairs.

(16) Native Hawaiians also maintain a distinct Native Hawaiian community through the provision of governmental services to Native Hawaiians, including the provision of health care services, educational programs, employment and training programs, children's services, conservation programs, fish and wildlife protection, agricultural programs, native language immersion programs and native language immersion schools from kindergarten through high school, as well as college and master's degree programs in native language immersion instruction, and traditional justice programs, and by continuing their efforts to enhance Native Hawaiian self-determination and local control.

(17) Native Hawaiians are actively engaged in Native Hawaiian cultural practices, traditional agricultural methods, fishing and subsistence practices, maintenance of cultural use areas and sacred sites, protection of burial sites, and the exercise of their traditional rights to gather medicinal plants and herbs, and food sources.

(18) The Native Hawaiian people wish to preserve, develop, and transmit to future Native Hawaiian generations their ancestral lands and Native Hawaiian political and cultural identity in accordance with their traditions, beliefs, customs and practices, language, and social and political institutions, and to achieve greater self-determination over their own affairs.

(19) This Act provides for a process within the framework of Federal law for the Native Hawaiian people to exercise their inherent rights as a distinct aboriginal, indigenous, native community to reorganize a Native Hawaiian government for the purpose of giving expression to their rights as native people to self-determination and self-governance. . . .

(22) The United States continually has recognized and reaffirmed that—

(A) Native Hawaiians have a cultural, historic, and land-based link to the aboriginal, native people who exercised sovereignty over the Hawaiian Islands;
(B) Native Hawaiians have never relinquished their claims to sovereignty or their sovereign lands;
(C) the United States extends services to Native Hawaiians because of their unique status as the aboriginal, native people of a once sovereign nation with whom the United States has a political and legal relationship; and
(D) the special trust relationship of American Indians, Alaska Natives, and Native Hawaiians to the United States arises out of their status as aboriginal, indigenous, native people of the United States. . . .

SEC. 3. UNITED STATES POLICY AND PURPOSE.

(b) Purpose- It is the intent of Congress that the purpose of this Act is to provide a process for the reorganization of a Native Hawaiian government and for the recognition by the United States of the Native Hawaiian government for purposes of continuing a government-to-government relationship.

Source: Native Hawaiian Government Reorganization Act, S. 381, 111th Congress, 1st Session, 2009. http://www.opencongress.org/bill/111-s381/text. Accessed June 2010.

Part IX
Himalayan American

101. Anonymous, "A College Graduate: To Be or Not to Be," 2005

Migyul is a magazine created by activists in the Himalayan American community in New York City. After the Dalai Lama's visit to New York in 2003, community leaders decided to create a magazine that could be a voice for Bhutanese, Tibetan, Sherpa, and Yolmo Americans. This article discusses the issue of college education in the Himalayan American community. Included is a survey of Himalayan American college students in the New York metropolitan area.

Education plays a vital role within the development context. Its importance is undoubtedly felt in the community level as well. While it is difficult to define a specific face value of education, empirical studies prove that communities with higher percentage of educated members' compared to those without, boasts of better socio-economic conditions.

Education, in today's age of competitiveness, has become a means to take advantage of what is offered. On a daily basis its knowledge is applied to stay abreast with the world around and consequently to make informed choices. On a personal level education is a process of self-growth and realization. On a professional field it qualifies one for competitive positions. All these qualities, directly or indirectly, impacts community development.

Within our Himalayan context it is not uncommon to discover that many of us are first-generation college education seekers. Indeed, we have come a long way from our predecessors, most of them of familial peasant backgrounds. At the same time, as first generation of rural-to-urban migrant, many of us shy from the prospects of higher education.

While it remains true that financial constraints bar many from making this choice, we are aware that large majorities in our communities who, if they choose can afford to go to college, deliberately decide not to. They believe it is not worth investing the time and money when they can start earning right away. Often this means settling for odd jobs and working for less. In their lure of the short-term profit what they fail to consider is the long-term benefits that can be derived from college education.

It is for this majority that Migyul conducted a survey among current college graduates in our community. From the 30 responses we received, an overwhelming majority of our respondents—73 percent, had acquired a bachelor's degree in the US. Interestingly 16 percent had a master's degree and the remaining 11 percent had an associate's degree. Average cost of college tuition amounted to a reasonable $13,434. Although many of our respondents specified having taken loans to complete their respective degrees, the average time to repay them was a mere 2.5 years, whereas a whopping 47% were already earning an income range between $40,000 to $50,000. Our results indicate that overall income range for college graduates far exceeds the average percentage of dollar amount spent for college tuition. You agree not a bad return for the initial investment. It is of little wonder then that none of our respondents' regrets going to college. With patience and time, college education after all seems to pay. Survey results have been broken down to reflect an average percent of all 30 respondents [see Table 1].

Table 1. Migyul Survey of 30 College Graduates

Breakdown of degrees acquired	
Associates	11%
Bachelors	73%
Masters	16%
Doctorate	0%
Years taken to complete studies	3.7 years
Dollar amount spent for college tuition	$13,434.00
Means of paying for school	
Self	62%
Family	69%
Loan	54%
Range of loan taken	
$5,000–10,000	0%
$10,000–15,000	8%
$15,000–20,000	8%
$20,000 and above	39%
Time to repay loan	2.5 years
Was the loan worth taking?	
Yes	47%
No	15%
Did you receive any external funding?	
Yes	39%
No	61%

Table 1. (*continued*)

If yes, funding was received from	
School	38%
Government	8%
Others	8%
Did you work to support yourself through college?	
Yes	85%
No	15%
Hours worked every week	
10–20	31%
20–30	47%
30–40	8%
40 and more	0%
Have you found a job after college?	
Yes	97%
No	3%
Specify income range	
$30,000–40,000	15%
$40,000–50,000	47%
$50,000–60,000	15%
$60,000 and above	8%
Do you regret having gone to college?	
Yes	0%
No	100%

Source: Anonymous. "A College Graduate: To Be or Not to Be." *Migyul: The Himalayan Community Magazine*, no. 5, Spring 2005. Reprinted with permission of the author.

102. Anonymous, "Migyul Youth" Questions and Answers, 2005

"Migyul Youth" is the youth section of *Migyul* magazine, a publication created by activists in the Himalayan American community in New York City. After the Dalai Lama's visit to New York in 2003, community leaders decided to create a magazine that could be a voice for Bhutanese, Tibetan, Sherpa, and Yolmo Americans. This excerpt comes from interviews with three Tibetan American youth in New York. Tenzin Yeshi was a high school senior from New York when this article was published in 2005. Tenzin Lhundup was a second-year student at Stony Brook University and Rinzin Wangmo was a first-year college student in Delhi. MY stands for Migyul Youth in the excerpt below. In these interviews, TY and TL reflect on their Tibetan American identities, culture, and generational relations within the community. Their answers provide a rare glimpse into a very understudied community, a community that in many ways sees itself as a society in exile.

Since Migyul Youth has just come out, we the editors decided to keep it very general with this interview. And since this is our first interview, we thought it would make sense to start off with views from our youth. There is definitely a disparity of thought between generations—not just between parents and children but also between Migyul and Youth and most of all amongst the youth themselves. The interview thus reflects.

We would like to add that we tried our level best in trying to involve all youths of the Himalayan community but there was a lack of participation. For the time being, here are three of our participants. We hope their opinions will get your thinking juices going a little more and we cross our fingers and hope that more of the Himalayan Youth will join us in expressing their ideas in the near future.

- Tenzin Yeshi is a high school senior from New York.
- Tenzin Lhundup is a second-year student at Stony Brook University.
- And lastly, Rinzin Wangmo is a first-year college student in Delhi.

MY: *Define culture in your terms of understanding.*
TY: I define culture as a customary belief and social forms, which has a variety of traits that reflects racial, religious and social groups.
TL: I believe culture is something that defines us—the way we dress, eat, live, think and react with other people from different societies. It is also something that is passed on from one generation to another.
RW: Culture to me is the basic human values, the virtues, the traditions, heritage, religion and the fashion in which our day to day life flows. Or say how we let it flow.
MY: *How do you feel about our culture in exile today?*
TY: Basically, culture had changed a lot in these 50 years after our country was invaded by the Chinese. As compared to early cultures and the modern culture of the Tibetans, it had changed in both ways, negatively as well as positively. From the positive aspect, we (Tibetans) have learned the strategy of developing our ethnic culture and put in a new version, to make it more entertaining and aesthetic, so that new coming generations will find an interest in our culture, in which the culture remains to flow through to the following generations. There is a huge advantage for us to retain the threads of our culture within our society and the nation. We can be proud of being Tibetan and having a unique culture; also we can significantly prove the world that "Tibet was an independent nation" invaded by Chinese. Unfortunately we had also lost our abundance of regional culture in these years. Obviously, most cultures were destroyed by Chinese, after invasion of our country. I believe that it is not that our people are ignorant and unwilling, but owing to desperate situations and harsh livelihood in Tibetan's settlement at the periods of time culture has taken a back seat. Since from the repression and the losing of our country, and being a refugee in these years, Tibetans had advanced greatly in many fields, like finance, education, politics and

religion . . . From that view, I feel that Tibetan culture that is lost or became invisible for a moment, is being revived, even further developed. I believed that Tibetan culture will be develop to a level as earlier when it was unique and rich.

TL: In exile, I think we are not preserving our culture enough which I believe is due to a lack of communication between our elders and younger generation. Our youth are very eager to cope with present advancement in our culture with very little effort. There are more youths at a party compared to other age groups in any Tibetan function.

RW: Our culture in exile is a contaminated version of what I have read in books and heard from my elders about it. Example: A. I feel, much has degraded in terms of values and morality, in the younger generation. B. It is certainly not right environmentally to wear all the traditional dress we know in Tibet. So it is of no point to argue what we wear. But we do a lot to maintain what we had and have.

MY: *What do you feel of the importance to maintain and preserve our culture?*

TY: Culture plays an important role in representing one's diverse nation; for an individual, it represents nationality and that part of a particular nation he/she belongs to. Without culture is without identity, culture defines nationally, identity and ethnic backgrounds. It gives you a voice and defines who you are and what is your right. Speaking through my experience, being a Tibetan, our strong inheritance culture defines my identity, who I am and what my ethnicity and nationally is. Chinese government had already separate propaganda that Tibet is a part of China. In this abstract situation of defending our nation, our unique culture has helped to differentiate and prove that Tibet was a separate independent nation. It is very important to show to the world and let them know that we are totally different from Chinese.

TL: It is important to maintain what our culture is consisted of because, our culture will show the differences between us and the Chinese. If we constantly, try to cope with other cultures then one day, we will have a mixed culture which is clearly shown in the way we speak. I have noticed that people over here in USA constantly speak Tibetan mixing the English words (there must be a reason behind this).

RW: It is appealing to hear the cliché 'we have to preserve our culture'. I think it is very important to maintain what is very little left of our rich heritage. We as refugees need something to relate to. It is not as if a refugee has no identity less. God knows when we have to return back.

MY: *What about the importance in finding a medium between what "our" culture was, is and what "we" aspire it to be?*

TY: Sorry Migyul Youth, I don't know how to answer this Q. or may be I don't like this Q.

TL: What do we mean by a "medium", is it that we are trying to make a new kind of Tibetan culture which is composed of both previous and the cultures which we get by living here in USA or in other countries. I think, we should preserve and keep our old culture which is passed down by our elders.

RW: This is important and I believe Migyul Youth is a very good medium.

MY: *How do you feel about the elder generation? And their opinion towards the younger generation? Whether if they are in tune with younger generation?*

TY: I believe that elderly generations are representing an ideal for the younger generation. I absolutely appreciate and respect those elder generation for showing us the right path. I can't comment on how the previous generation's view the younger generation. But for the moment through my experiences with the elderly, especially my parents; I think they hope for us to sustain our culture and traditions and want us be concerned for our country. I think many elderly are in tune with the younger people but it depends on the individual. Those elderly generations, who are educated and conscious about modernity are more likely to adjust with the younger generation. For elderly generation that are orthodox and unaware in academic fields, are less likely to link with younger generation. I think it is based on modern education.

TL: I think, our elder generation have to take the responsibility to teach and pass our culture to their children. They also have to understand the present necessities of our youth like not judging us by the way we dress or behave (these things can change) and have to find a way to pass our culture on us (youth). Every household should try to preserve our culture starting with speaking clear Tibetan, eating Tibetan food and respecting each other.

RW: I strongly feel that the elder generation has a lot to do with what we accept as culture, they are the roots from whom we absorb information of our culture. I must say that their opinion towards the younger generation other than the metaphor 'Future seed of Tibet' is little less of hope and more of agitation. Of course they are not in tune with the younger generation. It is because they have come in contact with the major culture shock, ever. The transition from Tibet to the rest of the world was so abrupt and quick and shocking.

MY: *Do you feel a need to prove yourself to the elder generation?*

TY: I think that, it is not always necessary always that the elderly show the way first but younger generations can teach lessons to the elderly. Some people are better in one field than others.

TL: I think there is no need to prove anything to anybody but our Tibetan youth have to listen to what our elder generation.

RW: There is the need. In my case, I need to show them that I am more than just a confused refugee girl. That I need to relate somewhere to something. That I can play the parts in the bigger cultural circle, and that even I care.

MY: *Is there a need for a magazine, like the Migyul youth?*

TY: I think we need "Migyul Youth" magazine, I totally agree with it. It is really a good idea of having our own magazine. For me, a magazine symbolizes an inspiration and expression of one's opinions and ideas. To participate in a magazine, gain education in variety of fields, writing, journalism, communication, dealing with the people and etc.. We definitely need a magazine; it's not only to teach ourselves to write in the magazine but it also encourages and invites other readers to participate in our magazine, which will expand our group. So let us start! fellow people . . .

TL: I think it is really a good idea to create a Migyul youth where we can express our thoughts about our current situation and to listen to what other youths think about our culture and about Tibet.

RW: I consider Migyul Youth as a very very important platform to introduce our culture who understand 'the something' we are missing not having a genuine nationality to relate to.

Source: "Questions and Answers." *Migyul: The Himalayan Community Magazine*, no. 5, Spring 2005. Reprinted with permission.

103. Sonam G. Sherpa, "My Identity" and "As American as Apple Pie. What's in a name?" 2005

Originally from Solukhumbu, Nepal, Sonam's father, a Sherpa, and his mother, a Tibetan from Shigatse, made Sonam leave Solu at the age of seven to go to a boarding school in Kathmandu, the capital city of Nepal. He spent a few years at school before he was sent to school in Kalimpong. Concerned about the lack of religious education, Sonam's father sent him to study at the Central Institute of Tibetan Higher Studies in Varanasi, against Sonam's personal wishes. Sonam eventually moved to California in the 1980s in search of a new life. He now resides in New York as a Senior Treasury Analyst for a commuter railroad company there. Sonam is a community activist and leader who has helped form several Himalayan American organizations in the New York/New Jersey region including the Regional Tibetan Youth Congress of NY/NJ, the Tibetan dance group Cholsum, the Sherpa Kyidug, and the United Sherpa Association. In the following two magazine articles for *Migyul* (Himalyan American magazine), Sonam discusses what it means to be a Sherpa and why it is important for him to retain his identity as a Sherpa living in America.

"MY IDENTITY"

On a trip to Dharamsala, India, in the summer of 1991, the wife of my cousin gave birth to a baby boy. On this happy occasion, I went to see her at the Delek hospital. Barely a day old, the bundle of joy, the baby lay beside the exhausted mother. Fruits and cookies or biscuits as they called them in India, brought in by visitors were scattered all around the private room. After exchanging pleasantries, and commenting on how beautiful the little boy she had just given birth to was she remarked, "Sherpa babies look like monkeys!!!".

Not only was I taken aback but, was quite furious to hear such blatant mockery of my people. There were a few questions which came to mind. Did she know that I was a Sherpa too? Just because I spoke Tibetan, did she think I was not a Sherpa? Did she know that many of her husband's relatives were Sherpas? Was it because of a few Sherpas that she had dealt with, she somehow had a negative perception of them and that had made her comment in that manner? Did it even matter to her what ethnic group I preferred to be?

I was a Tibetan for her, and she must have figured, it was ok to make such comments amongst Tibetans.

Her husband, my cousin, was born in Dharamsala. His father is a first cousin of my father and both their grand parents had immigrated from Gyarong, Tibet, to Nepal, gradually becoming Sherpas. My father and most of his relatives still living in Nepal are as pure Sherpas as they come. But my uncle, who had moved to Dharamsala many years ago and settled there with his family, had become

'Tibetan'. Making everyone born to his family and other relatives that moved to India, Tibetans as well. Well, I wouldn't be a bit surprised if their perception were contrary to mine.

From an early age, I joined Tibetan schools and spoke Tibetan but I had never met any relatives of mine who could speak Tibetan. I was in quite a shock when the irst time someone related to me spoke in Tibetan but did not speak Nepali at all or spoke very little of it. My cousins in India grew up as Tibetans, without ties to their relatives in Nepal. . . .

This has always made me wonder that no matter how much I try to blend as a Tibetan, to some Tibetans I'll always be a Nepali, which I am.

This aside, on another occasion, at a get together of Sherpa friends and families, speaking in Tibetan to a Tibetan friend (who's married to a Sherpa lady), a Sherpa friend jumped on me and made a crude remark, "Why are you guys speaking in 'Bhotey Bhasa' (Tibetan language), speak Nepali." This was the same person who on many occasions had labeled me a Tibetan in his attempt to exclude me from attending Sherpa functions. "Sonam is a Bhotey (Tibetan)," was what I overheard him saying to people at a party.

My answer to him at this gathering was that the Nepali language wasn't even our own language and that if he felt that speaking in "our language" was so important why did the fact that not everyone there spoke in our Sherpa language as totally unnoticed by him. Others present quickly resolved the hostilities and we continued to speak in a plethora of languages.

It is not easy for someone like me born as national in one country and growing up in the midst of another to always be defensive (although, I feel I am totally capable of distinguishing my own identity, it is oftentimes, others that make judgements about it).

Being born in Nepal to a Sherpa father and a Tibetan mother, I grew up as a Nepali. As the majority of Nepal's population is of Hindu religion and of a different race, they occasionally called us 'Bhotey' as in Tibetan, to which we would defend ourselves as not being one. Sherpa culture and religion is similar to that of the Tibetan's but by birth and national origin we are Nepalese.

I started life in a boarding school in Kathmandu early. With my sister and I being the only Mongoloid students, we were often teased for being different, as children usually are. The rest of the school population was Nepalese of the Hindu faith, as in the Dravidian race. We were called Bhotey, an innocuous term for people from Tibet, but used derogatorily. My sister and I certainly didn't come from Tibet. That was also a time when many Tibetans started moving to the Boudh Nath area, where a huge stupa stands. It is a holy place for people of Buddhist faith. This was also a neighborhood in the outskirts of Kathmandu, where local alcohol was sold openly. Although prohibited by the local law, officers looked the other way. One day a fight broke out between two Tibetans, who were intoxicated, that resulted in the death of one.

News spread like fire in the Kathmandu valley. Some of the consequences were ugly as children started calling me a 'murderer', which brought out the worst in me and having to fight those who accused me of such.

Just because a Tibetan murdered another Tibetan, my sister and I were teased as Tibetan murderers also. That brought out some kind of negative feelings in me for Tibetans, so much so that, I would play the part of 'brave Chinese soldiers' as depicted in the propaganda comic books and magazines sold in Nepal very cheaply. These were the publications that were heavily subsidized by the government of People's Republic of China and sold in Nepal for a few rupees. As children played in the playgrounds, I would be one of the ruthless Chinese Red Armies, capturing and torturing Japanese (as in the imperial war) and Tibetans.

Playing a "brave Chinese army personnel" was a phase that went through in my boyhood age. No matter how hard I pretended to be a non-Tibetan, walking the streets of Kathmandu always invited catcalls from other boys or bullies in the street to call me, 'Hey Bhotey' which then was similar to calling the African Americans the "N" word.

When I was attending the Central Institute of Higher Tibetan Studies in India, my nationality and being different was something that worked to my advantage. On a Losar day, on being woken up by a teacher to go to a monastery for early prayer ceremony and receiving the traditional share of 'Khapseys', I was able to fool him. Losar is a day to have fun. At that period of my life, nothing was more fun than to sleep late. So, being too lazy to get up early and justify my own crooked way of celebrating Losar by sleeping, when my teacher tried to wake me up, I told him that I was a Sherpa and that we didn't celebrate Losar. He gasped and whispered, "Oh", and left me alone to wake other students up.

From an early age, it seemed like others are always trying to make decisions for me as to what I am. Nepalese call me Tibetan, Tibetans call me Nepali and some call us "monkeys".

Why can't everyone just accept me for who I am? I am just a human being with just one identity, as in the name I was given in my birth?

"AS AMERICAN AS APPLE PIE. WHAT'S IN A NAME?"

When my daughter was in the first grade, I volunteered as a parent-chaperone to go along with her class for a trip to the Bronx Zoo. When the children arrived at the zoo, they were whisked away into a classroom, where an instructor told them all about the animals they were going to see that day. She spoke at great length about the animals, reptiles for that day, and then she began to ask questions. The children's names were all displayed on large index cards hung around their necks, and whoever raised their hand, the instructor would point to and say, "David, do you know the answer?"

There were many questions asked—and I knew for certain that my daughter knew answers to a few of them, as we had discussed some of them in preparation for the class trip. My daughter, even at that young age, was quite an outgoing person and talkative to an extent. To my amazement, she didn't raise her hand even once to questions that I was certain she knew the answers to.

When the information session was over and we got ready to go view the reptiles, I held her hand and asked her if she didn't know any of the answers. She said she did. "Then why didn't you raise your hand to answer?" I asked her. To which, she answered, "Daddy, they can't say my name right."

When my son, who is five years younger than my daughter, was old enough to play with other kids in the park, we spent many hours there. He's the type who would lead other children, some even older than him, to his kind of games. Coming down the slides or on monkey bars, he's the one, usually, leading the pack. On one of these outings, while he seemed to be quite careless, I shouted his name and told him to be careful. Upon hearing his name, he came running to me. Then to my ear, he whispered, "Daddy, my name is MICHAEL. They (his friends in the park) can't say my name right."

As easy as it is for others to pronounce my name, many of my colleagues had asked me if they could call me "Sam". But, knowing Sam would be a short form of Samuel for males and Samantha for females, in general, I declined their request. Just as it falls upon my shoulders to remember my colleagues' names, it is their responsibility to remember mine, if they feel it is worthwhile.

My colleagues have also suggested naming my children "American" names. So, I asked what names would be American. To which they suggested names that were derived from Christian and Jewish faiths. Personally, I have a great deal of respect for all faiths of the world, but to call those names American was a bit too much. I made them aware that the names they suggested were of different religious persuasions than my own and they were most definitely not "American". As America is the land of immigrants, my children's names are "as American as apple pie," I politely reminded them.

On separate occasions, both my children have said to me, "I hate my name". They say people make fun of their names. As a concerned father, I tried to explain them that children are just children. They make fun of any name. I asked them if some of their friends with more common names are also made fun of. Surely, they gave me examples of how other children were made fun of also. After we agreed that children can, when they want, make something up to ridicule any name, not just theirs, I proposed to change their names legally to their desire, if they so wished. I told them that my wife and I gave them their names when they were born based on our cultural background. Now that they are old enough to understand what their special names represent, and they can pick alternate names for themselves, if they desired, and if it would make them happy, I for one was ready to fulfill their wish.

And to my wonderment and pride, they have both declined to change their names. They like their names, they said, as they are unique.

The practice of naming names is different in various part of the world. Some name names that are related to their religion. Some are regional. Some names mean something. Some names are chosen at random.

Most of us from the Himalayan region request a name for our children from a high Lama after the birth of our children. Back home, we would bring the newborns to a Lama and request him to name the child. Lamas are also invited to our own homes for the child's christening.

In today's modern world, many of us simply make a telephone call to the Lama. After giving him the necessary details, such as gender, date and time of birth, the

Lama speaks the name over the phone and the child is named as such. This telephone call could be made weeks or months after a child is born.

Since many of us are now in western countries, where a name is required for newborns at the hospital as soon as they are delivered, we require their names for them before they are even born. In such circumstances, to play safe, we ask the Lama for two names—a male and a female name. Of course, if one is certain of the gender of the child with the advent of Sonogram and other modern technologies, you ask for just one name.

And many of us name our children on our own. When people ask me who named my children, I jokingly tell them, "Pala Rimpoche". My daughter is named after both my wife's and my own mother's—coincidentally, they shared the same name. My son is named after the Indian guru who brought Buddhism to Tibet. My mother said she had prayed to the guru for us to have a male child. So when her prayers came true, we said why not name our son after him?

So, the names my children have are very special to me. Likewise, any name you name your children has a special meaning. Be it a name you name on your own, from a high Lama, or His Holiness the Dalai Lama. These names signify our background, our religion, our culture, and our tradition that defines each and every one of us. Just because we are in the midst of people who aren't familiar with these names, it does not mean that we should abandon our culture of naming our own in our own tradition.

Here's a quiz: Do you know these names and can you pronounce them correctly? George Stephanopoulos, host of "This Week" on Sundays on ABC TV and a former aide to the president Bill Clinton. Michael William Krzyzewski, often referred to as "Coach K", the Basketball Coach at Duke University. Zbigniew Brezinski, former National Security Advisor to the then U.S. President Jimmy Carter. Kweisi Mfume, the former President and Chief Executive Officer of the National Association for the Advancement of Colored People (NAACP). Or how about General John M. Shalikashveli, former Chairman of the Joint Chiefs of Staff.

If the American people can say the above names, they sure will learn to say ours, if only we reach to the positions where everyone is compelled to know our names. Although very important in relation to one's background, names are not that important in comparison to the qualities that the name-bearer possesses. In William Shakespeare's "Romeo and Juliet," the Bard asked, "What's in a name? That which we call a rose by any other name would smell as sweet."

Sources: Sherpa, Sonam G. "My Identity." *Migyul: The Himalayan Community Magazine*, no. 5, Spring 2005, and "As American as Apple Pie. What's in a name?" *Migyul: The Himalayan Community Magazine*, no. 6, Summer 2005. Reprinted with permission.

104. Roshani Adhikary, "Nepali Grrl Blues," 2005

Roshani Adhikary was born in the United States to Nepali parents. A graduate of Eastern Michigan University, Adhikary enjoys teaching English and traveling. Her essay "Nepali Grrl Blues" was originally published in *Viewpoints,* the newsletter of the Association of Nepalese in Midwest America (anma.org). Written from the viewpoint of a Nepali American,

Adhikary's essay touches on themes relevant not only to immigrant and Asian Pacific American communities, but to American families as well. Adhikary shows how the various perspectives held by people in the same family are conditioned by their immigration experiences, generational differences, pressures to Americanize and assimilate, as well as by their political sensibilities. Adhikary also suggests that unconsciously held racial and gender stereotypes can surface sometimes unexpectedly in normal conversation. In 2006, Adhikary began exploring her identity through hip-hop, recording her first album, *Sol Joints*, in the Kathmandu language. Hip-hop is still a part of her daily life, and she continues to feel a connection to both America and Nepal.

I listen to hip hop. Matter of fact, I breathe hip hop. I live it. To me hip hop is a lifestyle. It involves critical thinking, creative solutions, art and entrepreneurship. Most of you might be wondering, "Is she talking about the same rap-music we loathe?" This is where things get slightly complicated. You see, I hate rap. I hate the channel Black Entertainment Television (B.E.T) and furthermore I cannot stand main-stream rap entertainers like 50 Cent or even, dare I say it, Eminem. I only listen to the "good" stuff. Black Star. Dead Prez. Common. Hi-Tek. Talib Kweli. Lauryn Hill. Mos Def. The Coup. Even if some of these artists have not come out with anything new or chart-blazing, I am willing to dig out their old joints and place my walkman (as the vibrations of hip hop can only be felt fully thru a live performance or headphones) on full blast. I guess you could say I am a hip hop puritan.

Hip hop music has a culture that correlates directly with one's sense of style. This is similar to most genres in music. If you're a reggae-head you probably believe in some of the principles of Rastafari, which would lead to much of your wardrobe being red, yellow and green. If you like punk you probably wear Converse's Chuck-Taylors or Doc Martins or something along those lines. While these are sweeping generalizations and there are always exceptions, my point is that people who gravitate towards a certain form of music usually do so because they have like-minds. This is often reflected externally in fashion-trends.

I often wear a head-wrap and an over-sized baseball-cap which reads, "Got Melanin?" This does not sit well with my Nepali-born parents. My dad throws his hands in the air—almost on beat—and my mom looks at me funny. Recently I suppose her silence bothered her too much; she blurted out, "Roshani, do you think you're an African American?" I couldn't help but scoff at her blatant hypocrisy. During my high school years when I really had no sense of self she was the very wombyn who paid $106 for me to get my hair highlighted *blonde*! Peculiar that she never asked did I think I was European-American then. Quite the contrary, she smiled with glee as she said I looked, "so pretty."

At our house the Mahabharata takes place on a daily basis. Of course this day was no exception. As soon as my mom asked me if I thought I was Black I responded with the question, "Why would you think that?"

"You know, you wear that topi-cap and you wear that scarf around your head: these are not parts of our culture," she stated feeling triumphant that her points were valid.

I looked at her up and down. Studying her sweater, jeans and socks. Ann Taylor. Gap. Ralph Lauren. "Hmm. I didn't know denim was a part of Nepali culture," I signaled my eyes towards her jeans. "Furthermore, this *scarf* around my head is from Nepal!"

She shook her head and murmured, "Buck-buck, buck-buck, esko khaali buck-buck whooncha." ["Yap, yap, yap, all you do is yap."] After this debate of ours I dropped the baseball cap, but stuck with my dupata-turned-head-wrap. Our house has had peace for a few months since, but of course, like all good things those fleeting moments of harmony passed.

I'm currently writing a play about the South Asian American experience. Two weeks back I went on my first business trip to the east coast in hopes of interviewing South Asians living in Jersey City so I could interview them about the hate-crime group that terrorized Hindus in the late 1980s. Known as the Dot-Busters this group harassed and even killed some South Asian Americans. Their targets were people they called Dot- Heads: people who looked like they would wear the Tika, or red-dot. After speaking with countless organizers and activists from that era, I felt inspired. I decided to start wearing a Tika in homage to the victims of the Dot Busters.

My mom cringed at the sight of my latest fashion choice. "Chya! Ke gurrya tyo? Keena Tika lugga? Kusto Pakhe justo dehkya chow!" ["Tsk! What're you doing? Why are you wearing that thing on your forehead? You look like a total hick!"]

I gasped, "I thought you wanted me to be more in tune with my culture?" So she frowned her face, unaware of what she could possibly say this time.

"We're only supposed to wear that once we've been married," She said.

I reminded her that both my sister and I had a ceremony in which we were married to the sun once we came of age. [Adhikary is referring to a traditional Nepali ritual for girls once they begin menstruating.] Didn't that count for anything?

In the end we agreed to disagree by sighing and shaking our heads in unison as we always do. I put my headphones back on and was comforted by Rakim's lyrics. "It ain't where you from, it's where you at."

Source: Adhikary, Roshani. "Nepali Grrl Blues." *Viewpoints*, Association of Nepalese in Midwest America, New Year 2005. http://www.anmausa.org/viewpoints.aspx. Accessed February 2010. Used with permission of the Association of Nepalese in Midwest America.

105. Tenzin Shakya, "Living as 'Other' in the U.S.A.," 2008

In recent years, there has been a growing awareness of the dispute between Tibet and China. The Tibetan government in exile claims that the People's Republic of China invaded Tibet in 1949. China maintains that Tibet has always been a part of China. This dispute has reached global proportions, with some Hollywood actors publicly supporting Tibetan independence. However, the issue is mired in a complicated history between the two nations reaching back centuries. In this article written for the Diablo Valley College newspaper, Tenzin Shakya, born in Nepal but of Tibetan ancestry, explains how this long standing political dispute has impacted her own immigrant experience. As a student at the San Francisco Bay Area school, Shakya was a correspondent for her school newspaper. She immigrated to the United States at an early age and like other Tibetans she struggles to retain her cultural heritage and national identity. In the article, Shakya relates one Tibetan American's struggle to retain her identity and cultural heritage, in the face of extreme circumstances.

I am a Tibetan, born in Nepal and raised in India until age 8, when I came to the United States.

Mine is a typical journey for this second generation of Tibetan "refugees," who fight against being extinct in the modern world.

Our parents fled from their homeland to become refugees in neighboring countries to save their families' lives and provide better education for their children.

We try our best to preserve our ancestral culture and beliefs by telling anyone who will listen, about the situation in Tibet.

Located in the central Himalayan, Tibet is also known to many as "Shangrila" meaning "utopian peace." I have never been there myself but it is a priority after finishing my studies.

Growing up in America was difficult but surely not impossible. I spoke four languages—Tibetan, Nepali, Hindi and English—and managed to blend in with the rest in elementary and middle school, never really questioning who I was.

But that changed my first year of high school.

I was filling out a form online, when I noticed there was no selection for "Tibetan" under "ethnicity"

Clicking on the word "Asian," I was led to a list of everything from "Indian" to "Chinese" and even "Taiwanese."

I hit the box for "other" and typed in "Tibetan," thinking how America is one of the top countries in the world, and yet there is no room on a form to acknowledge my identity.

Since then, I have felt the need to specify my ethnicity as Tibetan. Sir Francis Bacon (1561–1626) once said, "Knowledge is power." And I believe knowledge is gained through education.

China claims Tibet to be a part of China. Yet Tibetans are forced to be minorities in their own land and lack many economic and educational resources needed to survive.

The Chinese government repeatedly states its invasion benefited Tibet by bringing it into the modern world. How it is possible then that the educational index for Tibet ranks last against China's other 31 provinces? And why must the youth of Tibet learn to speak Chinese in order to go to school? Many of them fail to do so and drop out after the fifth grade.

Due to this lack of educational opportunities, young Tibetans escape every year across the treacherous Himalayas to join the Tibetan exile community in India. And from there, they try to further their education by coming to the west. Thus, the cycle of my story starts all over again.

The Tibetan Association of Northern California estimates the population of Tibetans here is at about 3,500.

But we were invisible until the controversy surrounding the decision to hold the 2008 Olympic Games in China. Now, just about everyone knows of the "Free Tibet" movement.

When people ask me why Tibet should be free, I answer by saying, "Because everyone has the right to basic freedom."

I am pro Tibetan independence, but more along the lines of "Tibetan freedom." I also favor "Chinese freedom" and "African freedom." It is a matter of focusing on the basic principles of human rights.

People deserve the right to make choices for themselves regarding their lives—to speak when they have ideas to share and to practice the religion in which they believe.

The way to participate in a "modern" civilized society is by making dialogues a necessity. Government's primary role should be to protect the rights of its citizens, not restrict them.

Source: Shakya, Tenzin. "Living as 'Other' in the U.S.A." *The Inquirer: Diablo Valley College Student Voice*, Opinion Section, September 25, 2008. Reprinted with permission.

106. Shilpa Lama, "One Nepalese Woman's Journey to America," 2009

Shilpa Lama is a Nepalese immigrant who moved to the United States several years ago. The following oral history records the experiences of Lama's cousin, who immigrated to the United States about 15 years ago. Lama conducted the interview and wrote this oral history as part of a project for her Asian American history class at City College of San Francisco during the spring semester of 2009. She is currently attending Cañada College in Redwood City, California.

Reema is my mother's sister's daughter and they both come from a very poor family. Unlike my mom who was pretty well-off after she got married to my father, Reema's mother was still facing financial and family problems after her marriage. Reema lived in a joint family with her uncles, aunts, their kids, grandparents and so on. I still remember when I used to go there to visit them, there was only one bathroom and basically it was just a toilet. You had to take a bucket of water to the toilet because there was no source of water and for shower, everybody used to go a place called "dhungedhara" which was an open shower taking public place. Ladies would have to wake up 5 in the morning to take showers just so that no man would see them.

Reema came to America because she married a white American man. Uncle Ryan was an acquaintance of my uncle whom he met in New York. Uncle Ryan had come to Nepal to help build an organization. My mother and father let him stay at our house during his stay in Nepal and he met Reema because she used to baby-sit me. Uncle Ryan developed affection for Reema when he noticed her modest and simple nature. At first, Reema rejected Uncle Ryan's proposal because she thought their culture had a vast difference. After many months, Reema contacted Uncle Ryan and decided to meet him. They met and got married 2 months after that. Reema did not marry Uncle Ryan because she loved him, she married him for financial reasons, she married him so that she could come to America and send money to her poor family in Nepal.

When Reema and Ryan first came to Nevada, they rented a small studio. Reema got a job as a bathroom cleaner at an old home shelter. Life was much better with good food, showers everyday, privacy, and good clothes but inside her heart she was lonely, sad and depressed.

When she went to Wisconsin to visit her mother and father-in-law, she was treated with love and respect. However, when she went to stores and shops she would get stares and glances from white people. This was Reema's first experience with prejudice. A Nepalese living in Wisconsin, Reema came to know discrimination well. At work, she experienced unequal treatment between her and a white female employee. People would not bother talking to her if she did not understand what they were saying the first time.

She decided to do something about her situation and enrolled in college to improve her English skills and empower herself. After Reema and Uncle Ryan moved to San Jose, California, Reema sponsored her mother and father to come to the United States. Both of them are now permanent residents of United States. During these years, Reema also opened a successful day care center with the help of her mother. She has found taking care of children and guiding them her passion. Now, Reema has a very good life. Her husband has a great job and she has two great daughters who mean the world to her.

Even though Reema still sees herself as a true Nepalese inside, she has created a bicultural household. She prays everyday and she has got pictures of several Hindu god's at her house. She makes Nepalese food everyday which her husband and daughters love to eat. Reema has taught her daughters about Nepalese culture and they love knowing their mother's culture. Her daughters who look so white with their blonde and brown hair and white skin actually sing Nepalese songs and have learned the Nepalese language very well. Her family celebrates 'Dasain', the major Nepalese holiday, just as they celebrate Christmas and Thanksgiving every year. She gives equal priorities to both Nepalese and American culture and guides her daughters to do so as well.

For Reema, coming to United States was an extremely difficult decision. She sacrificed the life she knew for the sake of her family. Even with the many hardships she faced in Nepal and America, she feels it was worth it. She has two wonderful daughters and a caring, loving husband. I asked her if she would like to go back to Nepal permanently, but she says that California is her home now. She discovered herself here in the United States. She says that Nepal will always be her cherished homeland, but America made her into a whole person and she wants to continue her blissful life here.

Source: Lama, Shilpa. "One Nepalese Woman's Journey to America." Oral history conducted for City College of San Francisco Asian American Studies 20 class. April 2009.

107. Prem and Kumari Tamang, Interview by Emily Moberg Robinson, 2010

The Nepalese Civil War, which took place between 1996 and 2006, ushered in an era of great instability for the country. The Maoist Communist Party of Nepal fought with the Parliamentarians and the monarchy; thousands of people were killed, and over 100,000 were displaced during the conflict. The tourism industry, which had for decades been one of the largest sources of nonagricultural employment in Nepal, was decimated, and many Nepalese left the country to escape the deprivations of war and to find employment.

Until the Civil War, very few Nepalese immigrated to the United States. However, this changed quickly after 1996 even though it was difficult for Nepalese, especially those with little education and skills, to get visas and passports. Today there is a small but growing Nepali American community, and now that the population is large enough, it is beginning to differentiate along indigenous ethnic lines.

Prem Tamang worked for a trekking company in Kathmandu, where he met and befriended successive groups of American tourists. A dozen of them sponsored his first visit to the United States, a six-month cross-country trip in 1995. Three years later, fleeing persecution from the hands of local Maoists who were targeting his family, Tamang was granted political asylum in the United States. He brought his wife, Kumari, and their two sons, Milan and Suran, to America in 2003. Emily Moberg Robinson interviewed Prem and Kumari Tamang in their home in San Mateo, California, on February 28, 2010. Jessica Ratcliff Kumar, a mutual friend, assisted with the interview. In the following excerpts, the Tamangs talk about their upbringing in Nepal, their immigration stories, and their lives in the United States. Both of them stress the value and necessity of doggedness and hard work in the pursuit of the American dream: owning their own house and providing a college education for their boys.

Emily Moberg Robinson: So tell me about your childhood; where did you grow up; what was it like?

Prem Tamang: I grow up in a little town in my country—my country is name Nepal—I'm from Nepal. And I was grow up in a little home town called Tekanpur. District they called Kavre district . . . And the home town is Tekanpur.

Like back in two hundred years before how was in America. There was no electric, no TV, no car, no telephone . . .

When I was ten years old, there wasn't any school close by my home. There wasn't any school. There was one school which was one hour to go up, one hour to come down. Two hours daily walking . . .

EMR: So you walked an hour to school and an hour back?

PT: Yeah. Then after the first grade . . . second grade . . . one of my relative—their son was going to another school, which is three, four hours away from my home . . .

My father, his cousin was there . . . like a teenager, eighteen years or something like that . . . and I was thirteen years old. I went to there, studied a little bit . . . and then when he graduate from high school, he's gone, right? And I used to live with him and he's gone and I don't have any guardian or friend, right? I have to live there myself from my home town. And it's kind of feel lonely. And other hand was . . . my parents have nine children; I was the oldest boy . . . I see badly they need help from me. Work. And then after that . . . my dad's cousin is gone, after high school graduate, and I feel kind of lonely; and other hand, I see my mom and dad need help; other hand, they don't have money to rent a house there for me an apartment. I see all these problem financial—money –so badly. I see that. And it make me change my life you know. If I study with those struggle, all—I see my future making money is way—I don't know when. But if I run now, I can make some money and my parents can have it. And I decided to run away from home.

Dad doesn't like that. I didn't give any note for dad, but mom knows. I run from home. I still remember that day, when I was just thirteen years old, you know. I was running from home, and I get some construction job which is five rupees a day. Seven AM to six PM.

Jessica Kumar: Where was the construction job?
PT: It's northeast from Kathmandu.
Kumari Tamang: Very far away.
EMR: So you ran away—
PT: A place called Barabise—the road was going toward Khasa Lhasa. Tibet. China. So there—between Nepal and Tibet there was little border that they would take through road—they called Arniko Rajmarg highway road . . .

I was there eighteen month. Within eighteen month . . . I make two hundred–fifty sixty rupee . . . I send that money. Then, first time my dad's like, "Oooh, ok, I got some money from my son." I send money with person. Whoever going home.

KT: That's the culture. To send money.
PT: That was the beginning. That happened.
KT: The Nepal way.
PT: After that . . . my dad—still wants me to go to school, and I said no. I will quit this school, I don't go. Let me challenge my life—I did that, Bahini ["little sister"] . . .

Later on, I went to Kathmandu. By the time I was almost seventeen. And I found job—all kind of job in Kathmandu—and I never back away from any kind of job. ANY kind of job. Restaurant worker, construction, everything, right? Something like road builder, house building, painting, carpenter, all kind of things . . .

Finally, when I come seventeen, eighteen, later . . . people are telling me about mountain climbing. I have a big interest to go there. How to get in there. And I must keep asking with someone whoever goes, from the hometown, they said your age is not enough. You may get hurt. You're young. And I have to wait . . .

Finally, finally I got job there. First year I was temporary porter. Second year, finally after those all kind of struggle—"OK, we need people like Prem as a porter. He work fast, he carry the heavy load, and so, and he can speaks some English, why don't we give him chance to cook in kitchen, serve food for the member . . ." I got chance there, and day by day my English was getting better and better . . .

My first trekking start was in 1984, '85, '86. From '86 for me I was becoming more speaking English and '88 I was permanent assistant guide. '89 assistant guide, '90 we got married with this pumpkin girl . . . [lots of laughing]

KT: I don't like you that much! [laughing] I never! I didn't want to marry him! Yeah, I was getting mad all the time when I see him . . . I was little, like 15 years old!

PT: Yeah, she was 15 years old when we get married. Her parents—her mom did that, mostly.

KT: What they call orange marriage. [lots of laughing] Arranged marriage!

PT: '94, Milan [Prem and Kumari's oldest son] was get born. Milan born '94. '95, finally, I become America, with all the friends [that Prem met while working as a trekking guide] . . .

I always ask them, "How is America. What should I do to go America. I want to go America." So many says, "Difficult. You cannot go there. Number one. You don't know the place. Number two. So difficult. Your English not enough, you don't have any relative there. And number three, four, whatever, hard to get paperwork that you want to be there. But if you want to go, we'll help you. Who knows something about the paperwork?"

[Prem's American friends raised over ten thousand dollars to bring him to the United States for a six-month visit in 1995.]

PT: And after six month, my experience living in America, visiting America, I went back to Nepal, and then my mind: living in America, think America—and how to bring my bride, life, for future and my two boys . . . And situation also getting worse in Nepal; the political situation was worse, and job cutting, tourism is gone because of situation . . . And I come '98 again back to America, and I'm still here. Never went back.

[Prem was able to get his work visa in 2001; by 2003, he had brought Kumari and their two young sons over to the United States.]

EMR: What sorts of things do you do to remember Nepal, and to try to keep Nepali culture alive for your children while in the United States? Is that difficult?

PT: I love my hometown, I love my culture. But my hometown, my culture—the situation did not give me—to live there. Meaning is, it's too small for me. I just like wild pig, I just run, because that [Nepal] is too small for me. I still love culture, people, my family, my parents are still there, my brother, sister there, mom, dad there still. And here, they have special days, now—back in '95 there wasn't a lot of Nepali, but now there are lots of Nepalis here, so, these days they have Nepali gathering committee, one. Next, they is separated here, then. They have a Tamang group, there is a Tamang society here. Brahman society here. Newar society, Guru society here. They have their own community here, they're just sitting down, just starting . . .

KT: I like to live here, Bahini, it's so nice.

EMR: Do you miss anything?

PT: I miss my family, and the place I play, I go—I miss it, of course. But day by day as long as—now, I feel more like I live here, love here. Life you can take anywhere, anywhere you want to be. So now I think if I go there, it's hard for me. I cannot take a hot shower every day . . . So if I go to Nepal—don't have hot shower, don't have even cold water, right, I freeze—because my body change, system change. Anything could be so hard for me now. Anything would be hard. Maybe the food might not going to digest that I used to . . . because my body change now . . .

My boys need to know [about how hard Prem and Kumari have worked]. Every day we have a Monday special dinner. One we can have all together. Otherwise I will be here all at my work. When I come they don't sleep. When I woke they go to school.

Couple years ago I told Bahini, Jessica, "A couple years ago some friend said, 'How is your family, how big are your boys are?' I said, 'One is this big [holds hands apart horizontally] and one is this bigger . . .' When I measure from this side—because when I come they laying down sleeping. One this bigger, and the other one, this bigger, and they growing day by day this way. Because when I come at night, eleven o'clock, they are sleeping right? And when I woke up, they gone. To school. So I never see them this way [holds hands apart vertically]. This is the view that I get from my home—I see them like this all the time. Sleeping. Before I check them I don't go myself bed. Even twelve o'clock. I want to look. I saw them one time. Even sleeping. They grow this way. 2004, '5, '6, '7 I see them like this."

[Prem shows picture of his family's house in Nepal; he sent money from the United States to build it.]

Later on—right here—that's the new house, changing new life. You see that . . . This is the front side of the house. These are all my nieces and nephews, yes. See, compared to the old house—a

	change! This is the first town in the hometown I built . . . First house in that whole town. Fancy nice great house.
EMR:	So they have the American dream, too—they have it in Nepal.

Source: Tamang, Prem, and Tamang, Kumari. Interview by Emily Moberg Robinson. February 28, 2010, San Mateo, California. Transcribed, edited, and excerpted by Emily Moberg Robinson. Used with permission of Prem Tamang and Kumari Tamang.

PART X
Hmong American

108. Pang Xiong Sirirathasuk Sikoun, Interview by Sally Peterson, 2006

Pang Xiong Sirirathasuk Sikoun was born in the mountains of Laos, in the northern province of Zieng Khouang, near Vietnam and China. During her childhood, Xiong learned many forms of Hmong folk art, including traditional storytelling and singing techniques, musical instruments, and appliqué and sewing skills. In the late 1950s, Pathet Lao Communists took over Xiong's village, and she and her family fled south to Thailand. There, several of her brothers, along with many other Hmong mountain people, were trained by the U.S. Central Intelligence Agency and the Thai military to fight the North Vietnamese–backed Pathet Lao in a "secret" war. Five of her brothers were killed in the war, and after the 1973 cease-fire, the Americans pulled out of Laos, abandoning many Hmong soldiers and leaving many more civilians in refugee camps.

In 1979, Xiong and her family resettled in Philadelphia, along with thousands of other Southeast Asian refugees. There, she formed a Hmong dance troupe and then began selling flower cloth, the elaborate needlework depicting scenes from Hmong life and experience, known as *paj ntaub*. *Paj ntaub* was primarily practiced in refugee camps. Xiong brought this art form with her to the United States and successfully introduced it to an American audience.

In her 2006 interview with the Philadelphia Folklore Project's Sally Peterson, Pang Xiong spoke a short prose poem about triumphing over adversity and what it means to make it in America.

We came to this country very sad, and we try to win something.
You cannot win the war. You cannot win the gun. You cannot win the life.
You say, what do I win?
I do not win my brother's life, he died…they killed him. They threw him in the Mekong River.
He died. We do not win their life, I cannot bring them back.
I [can] not win my five brothers' lives.
But I win because my brothers' children are here.
My mother, my father came here, even though they died, but they win, because they already come here.

We win when we can get a house.
We win, we can get a new car.
We win, we can get a new home, we can be an American citizen.
We try to be strong here. We try to be an example people.
We win. My name is in books, articles, so I win that.
People know my name, know Pang Xiong.
I win a lot. My children got bachelor's, master's degrees. That means I win.
Many people win in this country the same way with me. Same way.
But they don't know the meaning.
But my meaning's in my head.

Source: Peterson, Sally. "We Try to Be Strong: Pang Xiong Sirirathasuk Sikoun." In *Works in Progress, The magazine of the Philadelphia Folklore Project*, Winter 2006, pp. 4–7, 21–22, 24. http://www.folkloreproject.org/folkarts/resources/pubs/wip/2006Winter/Sikoun.pdf. Accessed June 2009. Reprinted with permission.

109. and 110. Chao Xiong, "Waiting, 'not knowing if they are even alive,'" 2007 and Sheng Xiong, "Address to the United States National Press Club," 2009

Between 1953 and 1975, the Communist Pathet Lao Party and the Royal Lao government fought a civil war for control over Laos. As in Vietnam, the United States involved itself in the internal conflict. Central Intelligence Agency (CIA) agents covertly supplied money, arms, and military training to ethnic Hmong Laotians. The Hmong formed a special guerrilla unit, led by Hmong General Vang Pao, that rescued American pilots and blocked the Viet Cong's supply lines on the Ho Chi Minh trail that ran through Laos. Thousands of Hmong soldiers were wounded and killed while fighting for the United States in what was known as America's Secret War in Southeast Asia. However, when the Pathet Lao overthrew the Royal Lao government in 1975, the United States abandoned the Hmong, standing aside as the Pathet Lao exacted retribution. Thousands were sent to reeducation camps as political prisoners; thousands escaped to the mountains where they continued to engage in guerrilla warfare against the Communists; and thousands more became refugees, seeking asylum in Thailand, the United States, and the West.

The first wave of Hmong refugees arrived in the United States in 1976, most of them men who had fought in Vang Pao's secret army. In 1980, with the passage of the Refugee Act, their family members were allowed to enter. These migrants formed the core of the growing Hmong American community. They were overwhelmingly anti-Communist and remained very invested in the struggles of their families and countrymen left behind in Laos. In 2007, the American government accused General Vang Pao, who had migrated to the United States in 1975 when he escaped Laos with his CIA case officer, of terrorist activity and of plotting to overthrow the Pathet Lao government. Although the charges were dropped in 2009, the case had far-reaching ramifications. Hmong Americans were dismayed to see their popular and influential leader arrested and put on trial by the government he had aided so loyally during the war. And in Laos, the Pathet Lao, which had for years been attacking the remaining Hmong in their mountain hideouts, grew even more suspicious of Hmong Americans and their perceived support of the embattled rebels.

Hmong Americans traveling to Laos were subject to detention by the Pathet Lao government. Chao Xiong's article, from the Minneapolis newspaper the *Star Tribune,* tells the story of Hakit Yang, Cong Shi Neng Yang, and Trillion Yunhaison, three St. Paul men who were arrested while on a trip to Laos, on suspicion of being associated with Vang Pao. Following the article is Sheng Xiong's address to the U.S. National Press Club, where she describes in more detail what happened to her husband and his friends. She asks the U.S. embassy to act on their behalf. As of 2010, none of the men have been released, and the Laotian government denies their existence.

109. CHAO XIONG, "WAITING, 'NOT KNOWING IF THEY ARE EVEN ALIVE'," 2009

Wives, children and a mother—about 20 relatives in all—lingered at the airport on Sunday on the slim chance that they would see three St. Paul men thought to be imprisoned in Laos.

Sheng Xiong clutched a bouquet of purple and orange flowers at the Minneapolis-St. Paul International Airport on Sunday afternoon—her ninth wedding anniversary—patiently waiting for her husband to return home from a trip to his native Laos.

The slight Xiong watched for an hour and a half as the waves of travelers passing through the international arrivals gate dwindled to a trickle, hoping Hakit Yang would disembark from Northwest Airlines Flight 20 from Tokyo, greet their two children at the baggage claim and head home for a large family gathering.

But in her heart, she knew: Her husband and his two traveling companions, Cong Shi Neng Yang and Trillion Yunhaison, were probably still being held in a Lao jail since their reported arrest Aug. 25. They were all scheduled to arrive on the flight that landed at 11:50 a.m.

"I guess they're not coming," Xiong said. "I was expecting this."

About 20 of the men's relatives showed up at the airport on the slim chance that they'd arrive. No one has heard from them since Aug. 25, when Yunhaison called to say they had been arrested.

Relatives and children carried signs reading, "Daddy, we miss you" and "We love you" and a large poster board pleading with the Lao government to release Hakit Yang, 29, Cong Shi Neng Yang, 31, and Yunhaison, 41. The St. Paul residents left for Laos on July 10 to visit relatives and look into possible business ventures, including opening a guest house, farm and herbal and acupuncture clinic, their family members said.

Xiong, her two children, her older sister and her niece were the last holdouts at the airport, turning away only after the sliding glass doors had grown quiet and the baggage claim nearly empty.

Earlier in the day, Xiong spoke to the media, serving also as a spokeswoman for the other men's wife and mother, who speak little English. "We're hoping to see them," she said before tearing up. "It's been really hard. That's the worst part: not knowing if they are even alive."

Family members said Lao officials have not responded to repeated requests from State Department authorities for confirmation of the arrests. Xiong said she hoped Lao officials would somehow see the men's relatives waiting at the airport and relent.

Philip Smith, executive director of the Center for Public Policy Analysis, which works on human rights issues in Laos, has said that the men were approached by military and security forces and accused of serving as spies for Gen. Vang Pao.

The general led a CIA-backed guerrilla army during the Vietnam War that fought Lao Communists, an alliance that many say has led to persecution of the minority Hmong in Laos. Vang, who has ties to the Twin Cities, was indicted this year by federal authorities on charges of plotting to overthrow the Lao government.

The men's family members said they have no ties to the general and didn't think their safety was at risk because of the case against him. They traveled in Laos on a recent occasion without problems, Xiong said.

Ulond Yang, Xiong and Hakit Yang's 8-year-old son, could barely speak when asked about his father, scrunching up his face as tears welled in his eyes. Ulond and the couple's daughter, Journie Yang, 5, have stopped asking about their father's whereabouts and whether they can call him.

Yunhaison's younger children still ask about him. His 17-year-old son, Feng Yang, said he's always ready with an answer: "He'll be coming home." Although hopeful, Feng Yang said he wasn't expecting a miracle Sunday.

"I'm just here to show support," he said. "If this could happen once, it might not just be my dad. It could be somebody else" next time.

In 2003, the Rev. Naw-Karl Mua of St. Paul was arrested and imprisoned in Laos along with two European journalists who hired him as an interpreter. They were released more than a month later, a fact that Xiong holds onto as hope for her husband's safe return.

Yunhaison's and his wife, Neng Lee, have six children ages 22 to 9. Lee said her husband recently earned a degree in China in herbal medicine and acupuncture.

"I'm heartbroken," Lee said through tears. "I'm just one person. I can't take care of all of my kids."

Cong Shi Neng Yang's 5-year-old son, Dennis Yang, ran in circles about the group's legs, unaware that his father had apparently been jailed overseas. Cong Shi Neng Yang's mother, Sao Xiong, stood bewildered at the thought of raising her two grandchildren without her son, a single father.

"They just know he's gone," Sao Xiong said. "I want him to come home."

110. SHENG XIONG, "ADDRESS TO THE UNITED STATES NATIONAL PRESS CLUB," 2009

I am Sheng Xiong, the wife of Hakit Yang, one of the missing people in Laos.

First of all I would like to thank Kay Danes; Philip Smith, and other speakers and supporters that I have not mentioned.

Today is a very important and special day for me. Without the supporters and help I've received from so many of you, I wouldn't be standing here in front of you all today. I may not be able to represent all families who have lost a love one from imprisonment in a foreign country, but I hope that as I share some of my thoughts and feelings, I will gain a step closer to the answers that I'd been seeking for.

I am here today on the behalf of the families of the missing men in Laos, who were arrested and detained from Lao Authority on August 25th, 2007. These men are Hakit Yang, Congshineng Yang, and Trillion Yunhansion. On July 10, 2007 the men departed the United States for Laos to pursue business investment opportunities. The men were staying at the #5 Guest House in Phousavan, Laos when they were arrested by secret police forces. They were detained in Phonthong Prison and later transferred to an unknown destination. As of today, the families of Congshineng, Trillion and I have not heard from them, since Trillion's phone call indicating that they had been arrested for an unknown cause. These men were last seen on August 29th, 2007 when they were being transported to an unknown location. We have not received any information to what has happened to them since their arrest.

The U.S. Embassy contacted the Lao government who denied having any record of the men entering their country and any U.S. Citizens being detained or arrest. Later, the Lao government changed their previous denials and admitted that the men did indeed entered Laos, but allegedly claimed that they had departed Laos via the Lao-Thai Friendship Bridge on August 29, 2007. Despite repeated requests from the US Embassy no departure cards have ever been produced as evidence for their departure.

It has been over a year not knowing where Hakit may be and I wonder everyday and night if he is okay and or somewhere waiting to be saved to reunite with his family. Not for a second do I not think about him. Everyday and night, I wish and pray for the safety of Hakit's return. I have many supporters who speak positive thoughts and encouragement but at the end of the day, I'm alone with my children who are still so young to understand the situation of their father. It is hard to face my children sometimes knowing that their father may not be able to hold them tight in his arms again. It is difficult to think and wonder when I am not sure if their father will be able to be by their sides growing up, and to see them go through their milestones whether small or large.

Each day I wake up hoping that I will hear the good news that my husband, Hakit was found and that every thing will be okay and he will soon be home. It's hard to concentrate on the things that I usually do daily. I am so frustrated and often times I don't know what to do anymore. However, I am trying to be strong and focus for the sake of Hakit, my children, and myself. It's not easy being a mother and a father to two small children at this time but I have to struggle through it and I have no choice. Sometimes I say to myself, it's my fate and I will have to live with it. Some things happen for a reason but to accept the imprisonment and then disappearance of my husband is too much.

I have tried to connect with other families who are currently in the same situation, to support each other emotionally. I'm continually seeking help from the US Embassy, the State Department, and other departments, but there has been no accomplishment pertaining the arrest/ or disappearance. I respectfully ask the US Embassy and the State Department to continue their further investigation. I just want truthful answers.

Sources: Xiong, Chao. "Waiting, 'Not knowing if they are even alive.'" *Star Tribune*, September 9, 2007. http://www.startribune.com/local/11589131.html. Accessed April 2010. Used with permission of the *Star Tribune*; Xiong, Sheng. "Address to the United States National Press Club." April 2009. http://et-ee.facebook.com/topic.php?uid=56985849716&topic=12052. Accessed November 2010. Used with permission of the author.

111. Critical Hmong Studies Collective, "Persistent Invisibility: Hmong Americans are silenced," 2008

During the Vietnam War, the United States waged a secret war in the mountains of Laos. Hmong guerrilla soldiers, trained by Central Intelligence Agency (CIA) agents, fought the communist Pathet Lao on behalf of the United States. Hmong soldiers attacked and blocked the Viet Cong's supply lines on the Ho Chi Minh Trail and rescued downed American pilots. After the war, however, the United States withdrew from Southeast Asia and largely abandoned the Hmong. When the Communist Pathet Lao party took power in Laos and began to exact retribution from those who had supported the Americans, thousands of Hmong fled to refugee camps in Thailand, where they have lived in squalor for decades. Some of those Hmong who remained in Laos were sent to harsh reeducation camps; others escaped to the mountains where they established guerrilla camps and periodically launched attacks against the Pathet Lao government. A third group of Hmong, primarily soldiers and their families, escaped to the United States in the 1970s and 1980s.

However, despite the great sacrifices made by the Hmong, the United States did not acknowledge their contributions, or even the existence of the Secret War, until 1997. Moreover, it was not until the early 2000s, when it became impossible to ignore both the dangers Hmong faced in Laos and the squalid conditions in the Thai refugee camps, that the United States finally opened its doors to tens of thousands of refugees seeking asylum.

Today, there are over 200,000 Hmong living in the United States, most of whom live in California, Minnesota, and Wisconsin. Their history remains largely unknown to mainstream Americans, and many Hmong Americans fear that they have been defined by vituperative rhetoric about refugees receiving government aid and sensational media reports about maladjusted and violent Hmong soldiers.

In 2007, a University of Wisconsin law professor made some comments about Hmong men and women during a class lecture, setting off a heated debate among Hmong students and the academic community at large. The students objected to the professor's comments because they reinforced broader societal portrayals of Hmong Americans as primitive, militaristic, and violent. The murder of Cha Vang by a white hunter earlier in the year exacerbated fears that racialized images of the Hmong people and culture could result in hate crimes. Vang's killer had told authorities that the Hmong "kill everything." The professor himself first responded with an apology and then, months later, claimed that his remarks had been misinterpreted.

The Critical Hmong Studies Collective, a multidisciplinary network of graduate students and faculty, issued "Persistent Invisibility" in response to the lecture. This editorial provides both the historical and cultural context surrounding the protests, explains why silencing Hmong Americans is particularly damaging, and raises thought-provoking questions about the place of recent immigrant groups in the American heartland and consciousness.

In February of last year, a University of Wisconsin at Madison law professor unwittingly ignited a firestorm when he used Hmong Americans as an example in a lecture on legal formalism.

The exact language and context of his statements are disputed, but no one debates that he depicted Hmong men as warriors and killers and referred to a high level of gang activity among young, second generation Hmong men, among other comments.

Hmong law students in the class protested his portrayal and demanded an apology. Students met with deans and the professor, filed a legal complaint with the university and set up a website. A few weeks later, the Chronicle of Higher Education Newsblog reported [the professor] to be in full apology mode. Suddenly, however, dialogue came to a halt.

[The professor] sent a letter to his Dean for public release denying some of the comments and asserting that context was "critical." The students were increasingly dismissed as being oversensitive and accused of identity politics and ungrounded accusations of racism.

The controversy rekindled in December when [the professor] gave an invitation-only talk at the Madison rotary club. Virtually all press coverage of the event championed [his] courage in exercising academic freedom to pursue controversial issues. [He] criticized his Hmong detractors for a kind of over-eager political correctness: "We are all harmed if professors avoid controversial material in deference to some accepted or imposed correctness or an apprehension that a topic may offend sensitivities."

But political correctness does not apply here in its usual sense; Hmong identities are not sufficiently gelled in the American mainstream for political correctness to be meaningful. Hmong Americans, with only some 30 years in the United States, have not had a civil rights era, a history of campus activism or entries in school textbooks. What is "correct" to say and not say about Hmong hasn't been established.

Instead, there's been a persistent invisibility. Hmong lived as ethnic minority farmers in the northern highlands of Vietnam, Laos, Thailand and Burma for several generations, having emigrated from China. In the late 1970s, fleeing from Laos became a political necessity, as the regime's reprisals were directed specifically at us.

Why was the Laotian government so vindictive? Hmong had been recruited by and given military service to the CIA in the so-called Secret War in Laos. On the frontlines, we were armed and trained by Americans in an effort to battle the North Vietnamese on terrain that was officially neutral.

The secrecy of that effort has meant the enduring invisibility of Hmong veterans. But the situation turned much more serious when the 2001 Patriot Act placed us on the list of immigrant groups to be denied entry or naturalization because we had formerly acted as or materially supported guerillas. Only in January did Congress exempt Hmong from this list, recognizing the injustice of denying us refuge after making us political refugees.

Hmong indignation at the incident in Madison is less about [the individual] than the forces that make experts' voices heard while Hmong are silenced. [The professor] sometimes denied his comments while simultaneously defending their accuracy: "Sometimes you do harm to people's sensitivity by speaking the truth." That [the professor] believed he was sympathetic toward the Hmong, that he presented stereotypes not as slurs but as "truths," is what's alarming.

Before dismissing Hmong reactions as oversensitive, we need to remember the larger experience of hate speech and acts in Wisconsin, where a white man was recently convicted of brutally murdering a Hmong man. He told the sheriff immediately afterwards that he did it because, among other reasons, "Hmong men kill everything that moves."

This is the kind of social context that confronts Hmong Madisonians outside the classroom. What we want to illuminate here is why such statements become even more of a problem when they are validated by the authority of academia.

Source: Critical Hmong Studies Collective. "Persistent Invisibility: Hmong Americans are silenced." September 13, 2008. Edited by Louisa Schein, 2010. A version of this piece can be found at http://www.asianweek.com/2008/09/13/persistent-invisibility-hmong-americans-are-silenced/. Accessed October 2010. Used with permission of Chia Vang and the Critical Hmong Studies Collective.

112. Katie Ka Vang, "Uncle's Visit," 2008

Katie Ka Vang is a Hmong American writer, actress, playwright, and performance artist. She works primarily in the Twin Cities area, where many Southeast Asian refugee migrants settled after the Vietnam War. In addition to performing, she works to support aspiring Hmong and Asian American artists. Vang originally published the following poem in her poetry chapbook *Never Said*. "Uncle's Visit" captures the unspoken but lasting tension and loss of innocence in a refugee family.

My uncle once came to visit
us.

When he came, we the kids,
the younger ones, who didn't
know any better would jump
up with excitement and say
txiv ntxawm koj lug lawm
los!!!!
We would give him hugs as

though he had survived some
kind of war, freed a million
enerations, broke free from
his grave.

Our hearts would praise his
arrival and we'd hop around
him, rejoicing him, as though
he was a king- and he waited
for his feast.

My sisters and my mother
prepared a meal.
They deep fried chicken
and pork.
They made beef jerky.
They made qaab ci.
There were two kinds of rice,
mov txhua and mov nplaum
ntsaav
and one bowl of zaub ntsuab.
which I never ate, that was
something only my parents
ate.
I remember it was a meal
involving mostly oil,

because after uncle ate the
meal, we didn't have any
napkins (at least that's been
my excuse for him to get
through my childhood),
or maybe we did, but he
didn't want to use it, he
had royal hands.

And so he walked over to the
closet,
with his oily hands, from the
qaab ci, and the deep fried
meat

And there in the closet were
Winter coats, my sisters silk
shirt, the one they both
shared, my mom's double

shift, my brother's soccer
potential, my dad's working
hands, my brother and his
video games, my other sister
and her daughter, my
halloween costume, my
mother's handkerchiefs the
ones she used to hide her
beautiful strands, my father's
ties, the ones he only wore to
church and my memory

his Hands, gathered all these
things together, as though he
was rinsing cilantro squeezing
them into bundles but there
were
too many, that his Godly
hands couldn't hold.

So some of them, most of
them slipped away, but the
things that got caught, were
wiped on.

Uncle's prints were oiled
onto these things

my memory one of them-
stained.
I now wonder,
why my parents didn't say
"damn, that's fucked up?" Or
"what the fuck are you doing?"
of course they didn't know
these words, still don't. They
still struggle to speak english.
But I know they feel them.
And 3 decades later
I feel them.

Translations provided by Katie Ka Vang:

xiv ntxawm koj lug lawm los—*uncle you're back*
qaab ci—*baked chicken*
mov txhua—*plain rice*

mov nplaum ntshsaav—sticky rice the color of blood
zaub ntsuab—green vegetables

Source: Vang, Katie. "Uncle's Visit." *Bakka Magazine*. http://www.bakkamagazine.com/site/articles/3_poems_by_katie_vang/. Accessed July 2010. Used with permission of author and *Bakka Magazine*.

113. Noukou Thao, "Dowry," 2009

Noukou Thao was born in Laos; she resettled with her family as Vietnam War refugees in Selma, Alabama, in 1976. Growing up in a small Hmong community, she developed a love and affection for her Hmong heritage, the South, and literature. Thao now lives in Minnesota with her husband and two daughters. She is a cofounder of the Center of Hmong Arts and Talent (CHAT), the first organization dedicated to cultivating Hmong arts. "Dowry" was written between 2004 and 2009, the years when she transitioned from living the life of a single Hmong woman to the life of a married Hmong woman. The five-stanza poem is from her poetry collection, *Lineage*, which traces the spiritual journey of a Hmong woman. It draws from the stories of Hmong women she has been exposed to all her life.

DOWRY

the money, goods, or estate that a woman brings to her husband in marriage

I
Mother spent years
Cross stitching the aida fabric
The longest and most
Complex piece of my wedding dress.

Her sisters sat next to her under the sun's
Nurturing hands, pressing them against her
Arms and back, scarring her with the
Burn of floral impressions.

The sewing ritual hurried her
daughter to find her daughter's
true clan.

But Mother I cannot live this way
Passing from one clan to another . . .
As though I am a vassal for our family history
When I go into marriage,
The story of my father's clan and my husband's
Clan will be discussed

Bad relations will be fined
Along with negotiation of other fees

My brideprice
The fee for my mother's milk
If I am the younger of sisters
A fee to compensate them for going first into marriage

All accounted for, in this
Meticulous bargaining
For all its labor, its tears
Its complexity
A fundamental human contract

Capabilities and infractions upon laws created
By man to be followed by man
But I am a woman, I cannot wear my Hmong skirt
for these reasons

If I must wear my Hmong wedding dress
I will wear it for my own reasons.

   This is why I wear it.

II
I keep the pleated skirt mother spent
Nearly four years laboring over
Inside a cheap suitcase
Along with the rest of my dowry

Each time I take a business trip somewhere
I unpack it
And push it inside a holding place
The dusty closet where I keep my daughter's Easter dresses
Where we keep the vacuum cleaner.

   When I return, I re-suitcase it.

Sometimes I want to bury this tradition
Folksy sentimentality
That my mother has shed so many tears to explain
To me, how she wanted a paj ntaub skirt growing up
Like her sisters, but her mother could not
Afford dresses for all her daughters.

How she got married
Without a dress of her own so she lived

The duration of my life when I still lived with her,
Gathering threads
To craft into my wedding gown.

Seems all her life, all she did
Was to collect things for my dowry.

   The life of a Hmong mother

Today I carry my dowry with me
To each new house I move to
Each new person I become
I carry my colorful sashes

My skirt of two hundred paj ntaub pleats
My paj ntaub panel money belts and purses
My purple turban
The striped wrap-around the turban

   These stitches my mother gave me

This is how it happened, the night I got married,
How I got hold of my dowry.

She started, started to sew
Like this.

III
Sacrifice a cow,
Two pigs, twenty chickens
Mix my blood with the animals,
Put a hen's egg beside my
daughter's head

in the moonlight
she stirs, sees the egg.

It has been there
for centuries.

This Hmong dress was a gift from you
A body wrapped in spirit
Creeping in my closet,
Rolled into bones, its color
folding in a body until I unfolded it

   You said

Bring it back to me
so I can sew it back into
the pleats, the spine.

The newness of the
thread can be yours. It is yours.
Your bloodline.

   This is your lineage.

IV
The pig's blood surrounds me
The room is filled with so many people
Relative voices and words of happiness.

   Now you will go away

   To become someone else.

Don't go too long, come back and visit.
Now you will go and be their person.
Don't go too long, come back and visit.

Is four hundred dollars enough
To compensate my mother for her milk?
They dragged the pig into the kitchen –
What is the brideprice?

What are her parents giving her to take
With her into marriage?

   What does she see?

   What do her relatives give her?

They give me a dusty garden filled
With flowers that have lain down
Under my foot for at least a thousand years

I am carried by their collected fragrance
A smell of death and rot
That at once becomes the color
Purple and fuchsia all at once

Streaming into me, my nose,
My throat, my heart, my art—streaming
Into me, giving me life,

Resuscitating a dusty garden
Into a field of poppies.

   This is my amazing village.

V
When I left my dowry is what you gave me
Four Hmong skirts
Two money belts
Three turbans
Wrapped from five yards
Of hemp died purple
At the end, a splash of cream.
Untangled by a relative aunt
Into my wedding dress.

All this material rolled into tubes
Of craft that Hmong women sewed
With their hands, tending to this material

Hands pressing the folds
Stretching out, until they have fully dressed me,
And I have become,
Like them,

   A Hmong woman.

Source: Thao, Noukou. "Dowry." 2009. Used with permission of the author.

114. Sheng Yang and Sami Scripter, excerpt from *Cooking from the Heart*, 2009

Sheng Yang was born in Laos. After the Communist takeover in 1975, five-year-old Yang and her family fled to Thailand, along with thousands of other Laotians who had supported the United States during the Vietnam War. Four years later, the Yang family moved to the United States, eventually settling in Portland, Oregon, close to Sami Scripter's home. The two families grew close, sharing American and Hmong cultural traditions and teaching each other how to cook. In 2009, after years of collaboration, Yang and Scripter published *Cooking from the Heart: The Hmong Kitchen in America*, a collection of Hmong recipes interspersed with commentary on Hmong practices and traditions. The following recipe for nqaij qaib hau xyaw tshuaj, soup for new mothers, shows the practical ways in which Hmongs in America preserve their rich heritage.

Chickens figure prominently in the Hmong way of life. According to the anthropologist Dr. Dia Cha, they are considered one of the "Eight most important spirits in the Hmong cultural tradition" (*Yim tus tswv dab nyob hauv Hmoob kev cai dab qhuas*). Chickens play a role in many traditional Hmong practices. They help heal the sick, divine providence, and guarantee good fortune. A Hmong shaman may employ a chicken's spirit to assist in dealings with the other world. Chickens have an important part in birth, soul-calling, naming, marriage and death rituals. Ask any Hmong person, old or young, what their favorite Hmong food is and the answer often is, "boiled chicken."

Hmong farmers take pride in raising vigorous, beautiful chickens for their own dinner tables. Hmong professionals who are busy with nine-to-five jobs often treat their families by cooking such a chicken that has been purchased at a Hmong grocery store. These chickens have been hand-raised and butchered quietly and quickly using an age-old technique. Although the meat is tender, it is very lean, and flavorful. The difference between a Hmong-raised chicken and one purchased at a mainstream grocery store is tremendous.

Fresh Chicken with Hmong Herbs (Soup for New Mothers)

Nqaij Qaib Hau Xyaw Tshuaj

If Hmong people have a signature dish, this is it. This very simple soup incorporates a fresh whole chicken cooked gently in a lemongrass-flavored broth. The addition of Hmong herbs—some of which do not have common English names—makes it unique. The herbs help new mothers stay warm and gain strength after the strain of giving birth. Women who eat this soup after bearing a child also maintain strong bones in old age. Hmong custom dictates that, for one month after a baby is born, a mother's diet consists of only this chicken soup, freshly cooked rice, and the warm water drained from the second soaking of rice (*kua ntxhai*), or clear, warm water. Hmong Americans often add vegetables to keep their diet well-balanced. This soup is also eaten at regular meals by the entire family.

Which herbs are used in the soup depend upon a family's customs and what is available. Some of the herbs in the following recipe are not available in any store in America. They are lovingly grown in backyard plots and on the patios and windowsills of most Hmong homes. Many of these plants originated from seeds and starts carefully brought to the United States from Laos in the handbags and pockets of Hmong women striving to preserve their healthful cooking traditions. In Hmong booths at farmers' markets, bouquets of the herbs are sometimes available in season. The herb bundles are called *Tshuaj Rau Qaib* (pronounced "chua chao kai"). This soup will not taste the same if mass-produced and -processed chicken pieces are used.

Ingredients

1 whole fresh chicken (the kind purchased from a Hmong market or home farm)
10 cups water
1 stalk lemongrass, tough outer leaves and root removed
1 tablespoon salt (or to taste)
1/2 teaspoon black pepper

Hmong Herbs

Each cook cites favorite herbs, often including *hmab ntsha ntsuab* (slippery vegetable), *koj liab* (angelica, sometimes called duck-feet herb), *ntiv* (sweet fern), *pawj qaib* (sweet flag), *tseej ntug* (common dayflower), and *ncaug txhav* and *tshab xyoob* (for which no English translations were available).

Preparation

Clean and chop the chicken into about 16 pieces. Refrigerate the giblets in the refrigerator for other uses. Pick or buy herbs shortly before using, and wash them carefully. Several sprigs of each herb is the customary amount. In a medium-sized pot, bring the water to a boil. Add the lemongrass, salt and pepper. Bring the water back to a boil and add the chicken pieces. Boil 15 minutes (do not overcook the chicken). Add the herbs and cook a few more minutes. Remove the lemongrass and serve with rice.

Using Food to Heal

The Hmong prepare another kind of soup, called medicinal chicken (*qaib tsaws tshuaj*), to help heal injuries. They make it with a very small breed of chicken cooked in water along with strictly medicinal herbs (*tshuaj ntsub*). Most elderly Hmong know which herbs treat what illness, and they grow many of them in their backyard gardens. Depending upon the ailment, additional herbs, pods, tree barks, and roots are purchased from Hmong herbalists. Only a few of these plants have common English names. Because healing herbs taste bitter, and because medicinal chicken contains no salt and pepper, this food definitely tastes like medicine!

Food remedies, such as medicinal chicken and medicinal eggs, are used to help heal wounds or ease problems such as indigestion and coughs, but they are not utilized to treat diseases such as cancer or heart problems. Most modern Hmong people supplement Western medicine with herbal food remedies.

A personal experience of Sami and Sheng demonstrates this Hmong practice. When "Little Sami," (Sheng's youngest sister, named in honor of Sami Scripter) suffered at age twenty-four a broken leg and pelvis in a sledding accident, doctors used metal rods and pins to set the bones and hold her leg and pelvis together. Afterward, the medical staff were unsure how well—or even if—she would be able to walk again. When she was finally released from the hospital, Little Sami's family and friends worked together to provide the support she needed. "Big" Sami (this book's co-author) came to help around Little Sami's home and to care for her two young children during the day while Little Sami's husband was at work.

Each morning during the first week that Little Sami was home from the hospital, her father, Gnia Kao, delivered a pot with a cooked medicinal chicken for her breakfast. He also applied a traditional herbal ointment to her many incisions. Gnia Kao instructed his daughter to eat every bit of the chicken, beginning with the chicken's left leg (corresponding to Little Sami's leg most damaged in the accident). The two Samis decided that this must have something to do with restoring the wholeness of her body. But, as is always the case with Hmong healing, the logic and healing properties behind the prescription were not explained. They also laughingly agreed that it was a good thing that Little Sami did not have a broken skull!

Some people scoff at such remedies, but the home-health professionals who visited were astounded at Little Sami's rapid rate of healing and progress. By the end of the third week after her accident, Little Sami was hopping around, only partly supported by her crutches, fixing everyone's dinner and baking her famous chocolate chip cookies. She was even able to dance with her husband at a nephew's wedding reception.

Making medicinal food is a gift of love and skill. To prepare the dish, Little Sami's father had to drive for miles to a farm that raised the right kind of chickens. Her mother knew exactly how to cook the chicken and which herbs to include.

Source: Scripter, Sami, and Yang, Sheng. *Cooking from the Heart: The Hmong Kitchen in America.* Minneapolis: University of Minnesota Press, 2009, pp. 93–97. Reprinted with permission from the University of Minnesota Press.

115. May Lee-Yang and Katie Ka Vang, Interview by *Bakka Magazine*, 2009

May Lee-Yang and Katie Ka Vang are Hmong American authors and performance artists. Yang has written and presented several plays, including *Sia[b]*, a reflection on finding home and community in Hmong America. *Sia* is Hmong for "life," and *Siab* means "liver" (although it often is mistranslated as "heart"). In May 2009, Yang and Vang performed *Sia[b]* together in Minneapolis. *Bakka Magazine* interviewed them later that year. In the following excerpt, the two women talk about how their work impacts their communities and what it means to be an activist.

What led to this latest collaboration?

Katie Ka Vang: I guess the first collaboration, or the first act produced by Mu and I was brought in as an actor to read the script. May and I created an energy for the piece and it worked- and now we're trying to expand on that energy.

May Lee-Yang: About two years ago, I was writing what would later become Sia(b). I had an opportunity to hire an actress to perform my work out loud so I could see how it flowed. By chance, my director Robert Karimi and I decided to ask Katie to come to the table because we'd heard about her. It was a lucky coincidence that Katie and I clicked and though I'm credited as playwright for the show, Katie has played a big part in helping to put the work together. The process of creating this play involved not just writing but also improv work that we did together.

What are some the directions you're trying to take Hmong American performance art?

MLY: For one thing, I'm trying to move beyond the refugee mentality. What I mean by that is that, when people come to a Hmong play, they expect an exposition on who the Hmong people are, how they came to the United States, etc. I want to take us to the next level and talk about real Hmong people who live and breathe beyond just being refugees. Having said this, I should mention that, if you come see the show, you'll notice that, despite what I just said, the "refugee mentality" still finds its way into my show.

KKV: It's quite challenging because I gravitate towards non-traditional processes and I'd like to expose Hmong audiences to non-traditional processes but there is a big pocket of our community that hasn't even seen a traditional plays yet, so I'm still working on finding balance between the two—in many ways, I think Sia(b) does a great job of that...

How do you feel your vision as a community activist intersects with your vision as an artist, if at all?

KKV: Lately, I've been hearing the term "activists" alot. And there are all types of perceptions of what "activists" look like and what they're suppose to do... (like lead a group or something and throw up fists in solidarity for the revolution) but I'm a bit cynical these days, because so many of those who claim to be "activists" actually lead a very different life, or are completely oblivious to the injustices they put on folks around them (folks they work with) because they are so caught up in being recognized as an activists they don't stop to question whether or not it's benefitting a community or just them... and when they create work specifically towards their activism, I question the genuineness of their work. I'd rather not call myself an activists, I prefer to just create work and let those around me decide for themselves. Recently a friend told me something her grandmother said "If you're wearing perfume, you don't have to announce it to everyone, they can smell it for themselves". Sorry for such a long answer, this issue has been in my head for a while now.

MLY: Lately, I've been hesitant to call myself a community activist. When I think of those folks, I think of people who rally in the streets and do grassroots community organizing. But I would also be selling myself short if I didn't acknowledge that my work—whether intentional or not—is a form of community activism. I have to remind myself that the act of someone who has previously not had a voice speaking their stories is powerful.

When I start to create a work, I don't think of how it is a form of activism, but they are. The title of my "Sia(b)" is an example. Some people might say, "Why not choose a title that's more accessible?" My question is, "Accessible to whom?" Of course, the answer is "Non-Hmong people." Why can't I name my show something from a language that is a part of me despite that most people don't know what it means? The activist part of me is always like, "Do what you want to do. Don't compromise."

As a result, even my director, who is an Iranian-Guatemalan by birth, can say my full-length Hmong name (which is way more complex than May Lee-Yang), and can understand enough Hmong to know when I'm talking smack...

Can you talk about what challenges have arisen in embarking down the path of an artist?

KKV: There are many challenges—the first one that sticks out in my head right away is the money. You want to do great work, but great work requires time; rarely will you find a gig where you're being paid adequate money for your time and creative energy; but then for me, it encourages me to seek out my own funding. There is also a heavy admin side to this- its like running your own business.

MLY: One of the biggest challenges has been just plain economics. I've always known I wanted to be an artist. About three years ago, I quit my full-time job to live out my dreams. While I now have a flexible schedule and have accomplished a lot more work than I did while working full-time, I still have to think about things like access to health insurance and a steady income. The great thing, however, is that I have a supportive spouse and family. No one has said to me, "May, grow up. Get a job." Instead, most people have said, "What project are you working on next?"

Aside from subject matter, are you trying to do something different now than you did in your previous works, or do you feel you are trying to extend those performances?

KKV: Well since we're here on behalf of Sia(b) I'll first speak specifically in relation to Sia(b)- I'm trying to dive deeper into these characters—there is a consistency in the content of the script, but the characters have a different journey; there are also a few new characters that invite you into different parts of May's life. It has been a frustratingly useful journey in being a part of this piece because it's really challenging me as an actor and creator in how I handle and portray these characters and situations that are always grabbing for power.

In my personal work I'm trying to find time to work on my own stuff. I have a few projects in the works and hoping to have a few showings by end of year.

MLY: I've been trying to write a memoir (or several ones) for years now and oddly enough, instead of a book, you get a play out of me. But the rules of theater are trickier than books, I think. With theater, there's some wiggle room for playing around whereas, in a book, I'd probably stick to all the rules of keeping it real. I think that I'm also growing as an artist. One of the reasons why Katie was originally cast in my show was that, despite having done acting and performance work, I was apprehensive about being in a show about my own life. Now, having worked through this show, I've already done one solo show through the Naked Stages program at Intermedia Arts and am writing a new one called "The Sex Lady," which is about how we talk about sex in a culture that supposedly doesn't talk about sex. Two years ago, the idea of doing a solo show didn't even click in my head . . .

Where in your work are you trying to push yourself, challenge yourself, risk something?

KKV: I feel like my work comes from a very expository process . . . and I think it comes naturally, even more so when you have a mentor like Laurie Carlos.

MLY: Whether I am conscious of it or not, I am always pushing myself. Because certain pieces of my work needed to exist as a theater piece, I opened myself up to the possibility. It might have been more comfortable for me to not be on stage, but I'm pushing myself to tell my own stories. I've also realized that if I have the nerve to put the audience on the spot, to make themselves vulnerable, I have to do the same. But I think the way in which I have risked the most artistically has just been being honest. I once worked with a sixteen year-old girl. She shared a poem with me and I thought, "That was great. That was wonderful." This was because she was so raw and honest in her piece I couldn't help but gravitate towards it. Since then, I've told myself, I can't keep hiding behind walls. If I want to create something great, I need to risk something too.

When did you fall in love with the arts?

KKV: I think I'd always loved the arts. I think I liked performing in general- but when I was growing up the only type of performances I was exposed to was music and singing, through church. So growing up, I did a lot of singing at church, I used to sing for this contemporary christian rock band called Forgiven. And later I discovered theater, so here I am.

MLY: I was twelve. I was stuck at home with nothing to do. From there, I began reading books. I averaged seven per week. I began watching tons of movies and fantasized about directing them. Since then, I knew that I would be involved in some medium of storytelling.

Source: Excerpt from "From Stage to Sia[b]: An Interview with May Lee Kang and Katie Ka Vang." *Bakka Magazine,* vol. 23, no. 26, June 2009. http://www.bakkamagazine.com/site/articles/siab2009/. Accessed July 2010. Used with permission of May Lee Kang, Katie Ka Vang, and *Bakka Magazine.*

116. Bee Vang and Louisa Schein, "A Conversation On Race and Acting," 2010

Gran Torino, Clint Eastwood's 2008 film about the relationship between an immigrant Hmong family and their white Korean War veteran neighbor, received critical acclaim in the mainstream media for its nuanced portrayal of Asian Americans. However, within Asian American communities, there was significant criticism surrounding the depictions of Hmong men and the archetypical white savior trope that permeated the film. In his 2010 interview with Louisa Schein, lead actor Bee Vang reflects on the film's underlying messages as well his attempt to "redeem" the emasculated character, Thao.

LS: *Talk about yourself and your interests growing up. Especially your exposure to film and acting.*

BV: I was born in Fresno, but moved to the Twin Cities as a baby. I remember getting interested in movies at an early age. But my love for film, when I began to appreciate films on a different level, really started at age 9. My family loved to watch Asian movies that had been dubbed in Hmong. We didn't pay any attention to American movies. We watched Japanese, Hong Kong, Chinese, Thai, Bollywood. It wasn't until much later that I heard of anyone like Brad Pitt or George Clooney . . .

LS: *Do you remember being conscious of race in those early years?*

BV: No, not when I was younger, but it might have had something to do with the fact that I grew up watching predominantly Asian films. Living in America, though, it was inevitable that I would start watching some movies made in the West. From my early teens, I remember Kubrick's *Clockwork Orange,* Peter Jackson's *Heavenly Creature,* Rambo and other war movies. I found the war movies ridiculous: too much action.

Then when I saw *Heaven and Earth*—the Oliver Stone movie based on a Vietnamese woman's memoir of the war—I felt so critical of it as a white man's story about a white savior. I never wanted the Vietnamese woman to give in to Tommy

	Lee Jones—I was always for her independence. And when she spoke broken English with him, it made me more angry because it emphasized her lack of power. I always preferred films about Asians in the original language with subtitles . . .
LS:	*Did you identify the movie with your own history at all?*
BV:	Not really. It just seemed like another war movie. The author hadn't intended to make a movie—she was writing a memoir. The process of turning it into a movie felt like turning it into lies. I objected to the way the cinematography—sweeping shots of landscapes—made the actual war seem more beautiful and diminished that it was a horrible and terrifying experience for her. I remember thinking, though, that if it hadn't been for the war in Vietnam, there wouldn't have been all those war movies and Asians would never have had as much of a presence in Hollywood. Ironically, the war created acting opportunities for us—even if the roles were undeveloped and we stood for the enemy most of the time.
LS:	*How did Americans' chronic confusion of Southeast Asian refugees with Asian enemies play for you personally?*
BV:	Well it always made me think that we, as Asians, had to be saved, but also saved from each other. The only way that we could be saved was through Western intervention. Of course, my response at an early age was that we were backwards, cruel and had to be whitened. I kind of took that on, but at the same time, it was a ridiculous idea to me!
LS:	*So what went through your head when you started to hear about Gran Torino?*
BV:	I never thought I would try out. I heard about the story and the "sides"—the excerpts from the script that were used for auditions—and I was just really repulsed by what I read. I tried to make sense of the characters and their lines. But there were things I couldn't figure out about the relations between Walt and the Hmong characters. For instance, at some point Thao tells Walt "You know you can call me these racist names as much as you want because you know what? I'll take it." I didn't understand why a character like Thao would say that? Why wouldn't he object to being insulted? What does "taking it" even mean? What was intended by the screenwriter or was this just careless writing?
LS:	*The story, as we know, takes place in Detroit and centers on a white man who is probably dying and doesn't have much time left. His Asian neighbors are a backdrop to his search for redemption from acts in the Korean war—*
BV:	Of course, those Asians are nothing but FOBs or youth on the streets killing each other . . .
LS:	*Right. So Walt has to teach them the "right" way to behave, and to save the good ones from the bad. In the process, he valiantly takes the fall. Talk about your impressions of the plot, the script itself.*
BV:	The thing is, the story can't take place without those Hmong characters, especially mine. But in the end, it's Walt that gets glorified. We fade out in favor of his heroism. I felt negated by the script and by extension in my assuming the role. It's almost like a non-role. Strange for a lead . . .
LS:	*What about the script's portrayal of Thao's masculinity?*
BV:	Well first off, the girlfriend part is totally crazy. . . . Walt and the gangsters and the grandma—all of them have nothing but insults about Thao's manliness—or lack thereof. He doesn't cut it in any way and he's not super-hot. So why is it that the gorgeous girl decides to pick him over all the other guys?
LS:	*It sends an incoherent message, doesn't it?*

BV: That the dumb, passive, quiet, loner guy can still get the best girl. It pained me that Thao let his masculinity suffer so badly over the course of the story.

LS: *The only manhood he gains is bestowed by Walt, and that's pretty dubious even up to the end . . . And how did you feel about the character descriptions?*

BV: The Thao character was described as an "Asian Johnny Depp." "A slight, slender Hmong boy with long hair and eyelashes." OK, but I didn't understand the function of those looks in the story. Also I was annoyed at the comparing of Asian men to a white standard of beauty. I mean [chuckles] who's to say we're not even better than Johnny's looks?

LS: *How did you interpret this in terms of your own look?*

BV: I have no idea what look they cast me for. I know I don't look like Johnny Depp. And on set they didn't do anything about my looks, just told me to come as I was . . . it's still a mystery to me.

LS: *So you were uneasy about the lines and character descriptions. Why did you audition and ultimately take the part?*

BV: Friends kept pushing me to try out. I didn't take it seriously. Didn't think I'd get the part. But when I was called back for another round of auditioning, I realized I wanted to be part of the hype, because this would become a great cultural event of our time, especially for Hmong. Most importantly, my intentions were, as I continued to audition and do my best, to try to improve on the script and the ways Hmong were portrayed. I wanted to create a character that people could love. I decided to commit to developing the role of Thao, making him more complex and credible. I imagined a guy who would chafe at his subordination more. So even when he had to obey, he did it with more attitude.

LS: *Did you feel you succeeded in creating this character?*

BV: I added a lot of intonation and gestures to try to give Thao some dignity. For instance, when my sister is offering me to work for Walt, I raised my voice to a shout to indicate I hated the idea of slaving for Walt. That outburst wasn't in the script. But most of the script was not very open to interpretation and it was premised on his not having any dignity. He needs to be clueless and have no self-respect in order for the white elder man to achieve his savior role. He has to hang his head and absorb abuse. So it makes me wonder how a character like Thao could bring any change to Walt.

LS: *Were you able to draw on parts of yourself or your experience for this role?*

BV: Well that was the idea, from what I could tell. The production process didn't include rehearsals or coaching. Eastwood didn't want us to consult with him. He just wanted us to be ourselves. The plan was for us to be so-called "natural actors," just stepping out of our lives and into the frames. This way the production could move efficiently. So we didn't get the scripts until a week before the shooting started and had no prep time to use the method acting process of getting into the psychology of the character.

LS: *How did you feel about the result?*

BV: That's a difficult one. I know I gave it my all, but at the same time, it doesn't look like stellar acting to me. I just wished that perhaps the physical acting aspect would at least be recognizable. Also, it's funny, when I watch the final product of Gran Torino, I often have the impression that the takes they chose for each scene were my weakest. I'm not sure what that's about.

LS: *Say more about the role itself.*

BV: But then I think that maybe it's not about the quality of my acting. It's the fact of the character being unsympathetic because of his weakness. It's an odd thing, as a first time actor, to have to step into a role that's disparaged by the script and humiliated by the other characters. Playing him well is like making a deal with the devil. To the extent that I did a good job, I reinforced that image of effeminate Asian guys who are wimps, geeks and can't advocate for themselves.

LS: *Does Thao become a man in your opinion? Does he get stronger?*

BV: I worked on that. It wasn't easy because the scenes were shot completely out of sequence so it was hard to get a sense of the continuity and the progression. I tried to show Thao's change through the physicality of my performances. I hung my head less and less. In the barbershop scene, I made my voice get a bit raspier and more like Eastwood's as they tried to "man me up." I threw in some sassy gestures. By the time I was getting the job at the construction site, I added more of a swagger to my walk. Things like that.

LS: *Did you feel like you were playing Hmong in Gran Torino? At what points in the story, if any, did you feel you drew on your Hmong identity to play the role?*

BV: I know there were a lot of Hmong references and scenes in the film, but I didn't feel it in my character. What I felt was being called on to perform the pan-Asian stereotype of the submissive, kow-towing geek with no girlfriend. Plus there's no real reason for us to be Hmong in the script. We could be any minority. And not only that, but Walt is always confusing us with Koreans and other Asians. Even with the enemies he fought in Korea. So Hmong culture, Hmong identity didn't end up seeming so relevant.

LS: *How do you feel about what audiences reflect back to you regarding the film?*

BV: Y'know a middle-aged white guy was telling me the thing he loved most about *Gran Torino* was the interactions between Walt and the Hmong people—that the film "rings true" to him in some kind of way. A lot of people say this. Well—"rings true" for who? Maybe to people who live in a world where whites are the only heroes. Or to those who take the film as a documentary about Hmong culture. Even other Asians do this a lot. And then they tell me how much they learned about my culture. Meanwhile, what a lot us Hmong feel is that the film is distorting and un-true. I guess watching *Gran Torino* is really subjective. People get all sorts of different things out of it.

LS: *What's next for you?*

BV: I have a lot of ideas. I'm going to study filmmaking and pursue my acting. And I'm also going to study Chinese and see where it all takes me. Whatever I do, I want to keep social justice work in the mix.

Source: Vang, Bee, and Schein, Louisa. "Gran Torino's Hmong Lead Bee Vang on Race and Acting." 2010. Reprinted with permission.

117. Ly Chong Thong Jalao, "Looking *Gran Torino* in the Eye: A Review," 2010

Ly Chong Thong Jalao is a PhD student in English at the University of California, Santa Barbara. His research focuses on the colonial legacy of the French and the United States after the first and second Indochina conflicts. He is particularly interested in how Hmong American literary and cultural productions intersect with larger history. He is also a member of the Critical Hmong Studies Collective, a group of scholars and activists working on issues of political, cultural, and academic importance to Hmong Americans. This excerpt from his article "Looking *Gran Torino* in the Eye" provides critical historical context for the movie's portrayal of Asian Americans in general and Hmong Americans in particular. Jalao argues that the ostensibly benign—even positive—*Gran Torino* actually traffics in infantilizing and alienating stereotypes, made even more dangerous by the 2005 murder trial of a Hmong hunter and subsequent tension between mainstream and Hmong American communities.

Even before Clint Eastwood's *Gran Torino* was released to critical acclaim and commercial success in 2009, some were apprehensive given Hollywood's past treatment of Asian American communities. When details emerged that the plot would involve Hmong gang members, many Hmong feared the film would exacerbate the stereotyping of Hmong men as naturally violent. Given the context of the sensationalized murder trial of Chai Soua Vang, a Hmong man convicted of killing six white hunters, their fear was well founded even if, this time, only one white person was murdered in the film.

Despite Hmong involvement in the production of *Gran Torino*, from actors to production assistants to "cultural consultants," the film insists on genericizing Hmong Americans into some vaguely Asian group. In one scene, a Hmong grandmother is shown out-spitting Clint Eastwood's character, Walt Kowalski—a sight not so much disgusting as inaccurate, and hence unsettling for Hmong viewers since Hmong people have never chewed betel nut, even in Asia. For Hmong American audiences, then, the experience of watching the film is akin to that of watching dancers who look familiar but are out of sync: the moves are performed and the poses are struck, but the timing is so off that the result is a feeling of malrecognition.

A rather tired Hollywood melodrama, the film's narrative repackages the theme of redemption for our era of change and racial transition. Walt Kowalski, a Korean War veteran with a guilty conscience, is the sort of racist we can all come to love because deep down, he's really a nice guy. Walt watches as his neighborhood is overrun by Asians. This enables him to become a reluctant father figure to the "newcomers," especially Thao, Walt's teen Hmong neighbor. Walt dispenses advice to Thao on how to become a man as freely as he utters racial epithets. In one scene, he takes Thao to the barbershop to "man him up" by teaching him proper racist and sexist banter. The barber plays along and, at one point and seemingly in jest, brandishes a concealed shotgun at Thao to show his disapproval of the young "trainee's" lack of macho and racist etiquette. Meanwhile, the Hmong gang members harass Thao and his sister, Sue, and exchange threats with Walt, prodding him to become the siblings' protector. But unlike Walt's innocuous racism and the barber's pedagogic shotgun threat, the gang members' violence is consummated when they rape Sue in retaliation for Thao's unwillingness to join them.

Gran Torino could almost have been Thao's coming-of-age story, but the redemption of Walt Kowalski takes precedence and turns Thao into a vehicle for Walt's salvation. Likewise, Thao's strong-willed sister starts off as a tough, young woman but ends up as a broken victim of intra-ethnic violence. This act of violence leads to the film's denouement, when Walt sacrifices himself by "tricking" the gang into shooting him, an unarmed man, thereby triggering the Hollywood cliché of police arriving on the scene to drag off the bad guys.

In all of this, the two Hmong siblings exist in a universe where Hmong adults are either dead (the father), present but muted by limited English skills (their mother and grandmother), or relegated to the status of props (the curious elderly Hmong neighbors). The only other major Hmong characters are the gang members, who come off as kids trying to look tough. They embody a line uttered by Sue, one many Hmong viewers found to be the most injurious moment in the film: "Hmong girls over here fit in better. The girls go to college. The boys go to jail." The overall effect is of an infantilized Hmong community severely lacking in the proper tools for success in America, as epitomized by Thao's self-deprecation to Walt, "I don't have a job, a car, or a girlfriend"—i.e. none of the trappings of an ideal American masculinity.

For a well-versed Hmong audience, the plot of *Gran Torino* uncannily follows the broad outline of U.S. intervention in Vietnam. We have in Walt the well-intentioned American who lost his innocence in a foreign war, and we have in Thao an effeminate Asia in need of being saved from itself and from pathological inter-ethnic strife.

Ironically, for many Hmong viewers, the most believable part of the film is when the gang members kill Walt. Believable not because the film's portrayal of Hmong youths as violent and predatory gang members depicts an essential reality, but because the gang members are the only characters in the film who exhibit the kind of agency that approximates the real possibilities and precariousness of life in a Hmong American community. That is to say, despicable as they appear on screen, the Hmong gang members defy the very disciplining the film's plot imposes on Thao. For many younger Hmong Americans, the gang members' deviation from middle-class propriety becomes a pivot whereby America becomes contestable once again.

Of course, therein also lies the divided subjective response to the film by Hmong. Given their relegation to the status of perpetual foreigners/warriors—quasi-genetically predisposed to violence—the predicament most Hmong viewers find themselves in, however inchoately, is that the more liberating and true-to-experience part of the film is also the very negative stereotype which condemns them to life as perpetual aliens. In the process of exploiting the lives and stories of other people, Hollywood imposes the injunctions of a law-abiding, middle-class life for Hmong people while at the same time also obscuring the very extra-legal forms of violence it depends on, beginning with America's amnesic and bellicose relationship with Southeast Asia, and including racial and other forms of discursive violence committed upon the Hmong and other minoritized groups. For Hmong Americans, the legacy of *Gran Torino* will always be a complicated matter as it marks a cultural homecoming of sorts, but one in which all the previous tensions and repressed histories have not been worked through on an equal footing by all parties involved. For many Hmong individuals, the film's refusal to explore the intertwined and complicated history of the Hmong and the U.S. is seen as both a cop-out and a challenge for the Hmong to tell their own story, on their own terms.

Source: Jalao, Ly Chong Thong. "Looking *Gran Torino* in the Eye: A Review." Abridged by Louisa Schein. Originally published in the *Journal for Southeast Asian American Education and Advancement*, vol. 5, 2010. http://jsaaea.coehd.utsa.edu/index.php/JSAAEA/article/view/73/68. Used with permission of the *Journal for Southeast Asian American Education and Advancement* and the author.

PART XI
Indian American

118. Mary Bamford, *Angel Island: The Ellis Island of the West,* 1917

Recent scholarship suggests that post–Civil War American Baptists increasingly attempted to redefine citizenship in terms of religion instead of race as a means of limiting the power of millions of newly emancipated African American slaves and a growing influx of Gold Rush Chinese. And although many subscribed to commonly held white supremacist beliefs about the inferiority of Chinese culture and morality, American Baptists still championed progressive attempts to curb racist and exclusionary legislation in the United States. This mindset permeated their domestic missionary efforts within Asian immigrant communities for the next 50 years. In 1917, Mary Bamford, a member of the Women's American Baptist Home Missionary Society, wrote a book describing the Angel Island Immigration Station and its inmates.

In her foreword to Bamford's book, the Baptist Home Missionary Society's Lillian M. Soares reveals the ways in which religion and civil society were inextricably bound together in early-20th-century America. The following excerpt contains Bamford's description of the Immigration Station at Angel Island. She comments on the widespread Chinese practice of paper families to fraudulently claim legal U.S. residence as a means of circumventing the 1880 Exclusion Act. The final selection describes some of the South Asian immigrants who were detained on Angel Island while they waited to be processed. Like most early-20th-century Americans, Bamford mistakenly calls these migrants "Hindus," even though the majority of early South Asian immigrants were actually Sikhs who moved to the United States to work as agricultural laborers. Some of the young men Bamford describes were likely among the last South Asians to enter the United States until 1946. In 1917, the same year that *Angel Island* was published, Congress passed the 1917 Immigration Act, which created an Asiatic Barred Zone, effectively cut off Indian immigration to the United States. Not until the 1946 Luce-Cellar Act were Indians allowed to immigrate to the United States and become naturalized citizens.

FOREWORD

We are all familiar with Ellis Island on the Atlantic coast, but many do not know of the existence of Angel Island on the Pacific where the incoming orientals are received.

It was a note of the early Christian that he was "given to hospitality." The spirit of the Master teaches us to share with others. Why should not this attitude characterize our national relations with the incomers who cross the seas to sojourn in our land?

Unrestricted and unregulated immigration would not be wise either on our eastern or western coasts. We need the most careful consideration of the character of our future citizenship. But when we have decided who may be admitted to our land, let us receive all who come with a true Christian courtesy. It is not wholly a matter of legislation and officialism. The observant writer of this little story indicates clearly the significance of what should be done to give our new guests a kindly welcome. The Golden Gate and Angel Island should be worthy of their beautiful names. Here is an important task for the Christian women of our Home Mission Societies.

We can always be sure that every bad influence will meet the stranger. All the tribe that seeks to exploit the new-arrival confused in his unfamiliar surroundings, will be alert, and in spite of all the care which the government can exercise, the immigrant will not seldom be cheated and misled. Strangely enough the Christian forces may give no heed to him. Too busy about our own affairs we may not realize that these are folk coming from old Asia, whence our Savior came, who are getting their first impression of a Christian land. They are sure to see our evil side; we must not fail to let them see our purity, faith, patriotism and Christian love.

Foreign missions come over to us at Angel Island. Those folk from the east will learn our tongue. They will also share our faith if we give them a chance. How touching to read the story of their gratitude for a copy of the gospel! How our hearts thrill when we read of the Chinese Boys' Band and the stirring notes of "America" which they played so well!

"Sweet land of liberty." America has ever been a Promised Land. There ought not to be one soul in all our broad country who does not show the loyalty that makes a nation strong. Patriotism is only at its best when it is Christian.

It is our Home Missionary task to help the strangers within our gates to become Christian patriots.

Lillian M. Soares
May, 1917

Angel Island

... Angel Island is a much better place to keep immigrants than the old detention-sheds in San Francisco were, as opportunities for coaching witnesses in fraudulent cases are now prevented by island isolation. Angel Island was first opened as an Immigrant Station in October, 1909. The next report of the Commissioner General of Immigration stated that Angel Island Station had been built largely because the Chinese and their friends and attorneys had persistently complained that the conditions under which the Chinese were detained in San Francisco were unsafe and unsanitary. But when these complainants discovered that the United States Government would have a great advantage in preventing the coaching of applicants and witnesses by occupying the Station at Angel Island, there arose violent protests, which, however, did not prevent the Government from carrying out its plan.

Angel Island is seven miles in circumference, and has an altitude of nine hundred feet. On the south side of the island, the buildings and the khaki-colored tents that we see, do not mark the Immigration Station portion of the island, but comprise what is sometimes called the "Casual Camp," where soldiers from the Philippines are lodged. On the west of the island, out of sight of our boat, is Fort McDowell, the military station. On the north side of the island, is the quarantine station.

The Buildings.—Our boat passes a little further and turns by a wooded bluff. We swing alongside a wharf. Connected with the wharf by a broad wooden walk, is the main building of the eighteen buildings on this section of the island devoted to the United States Immigration Service. Ten acres of the island are fenced in for this purpose. We pass up the walk to the Administration Building and at the door we show our pass to the old doorkeeper. While we wait here for our guide, we notice that this large room in which we stand is railed off into sections.

The Japanese. The Japanese girls with the Japanese young men in one section are "picture-brides," with their prospective bridegrooms and friends. Of the "picture-brides" I shall treat more fully in a later chapter.

Our guide leads us from the main room of the Administration Building into a long curving passageway, made secure by wire netting on the side opening outdoors, and we are ushered into the large dining-room for immigrants. Long, clean rows of tables stretch parallel to one another across the width of the room. . . .

The Indians.—Our guide takes us to the other side of the building to show us the Hindus. Here they come! Fine-looking, stalwart fellows, with white turbans swathing their heads, they come up the long stairway and confront us. Other Indians are in the further room. How different this type of men from the Chinese or Japanese whom we have been seeing! Some authorities hold that the Hindu and the American both belong to the Aryan race, and that whether we like it or not, these Hindus are bone of our bone. Our speech bewrayeth us, according to the philologists. One looks back through the ages, and sees the time when the Aryan forefathers of these Hindus, and our own forefathers parted in central Asia, the Hindu forefathers going south, and in a subsequent emigration, our forefathers going west. The Hindu is not a Mongolian, but our long-lost brother, and the Californian is not usually any more glad to see him coming than the respectable brother was to see the prodigal son in the parable. I recall seeing a small group of Indians beside the entrance to the Pacific Mail Steamship Company's pier in San Francisco, before the sailing of a steamer, and hearing a white man adjure the harmless group, who were not obstructing anything that I could see, "You move on! You fellows can't stand their talking!"

Those Indians were not devoid of human instinct when treated kindly, for when I gave a copy of the Gospel of John written, in the strange oval and horizontal Punjabi characters, to one Hindu of the group, he drew a nickel from his pocket as if to pay me, and on my refusal he uttered an "Ah-h!" of protest. Another time, after I had given a group of four Indians some Gospels in Punjabi, one of them who wore a red turban came after me and held out his sallow hand in which was a little change, as if he would have paid me. When I refused the money, he thanked me.

The kindly hearted American who pleasantly says, "Salaam," in greeting an Indian, hears "Salaam," in return. A missionary from India, while visiting the camps of Indians in northern California, was gladly received when it was discovered he could speak Hindustani. Once on his way to an Indian camp, this same missionary saw a workman in a field and called to him in his own tongue. The man came running, and was full of joy at being spoken to in his native language. His employer called him, but he enthusiastically shouted back, "I can't work now! My brother has come! My brother has come!"

A San Francisco employe[e] of the American Bible Society told me of a friend who had carried gospels to an outgoing steamer, and an Indian was so glad to receive a gospel in his native tongue that he kissed the book. A colporteur is said to have found five Indian laborers at prayer one evening in their hut. Not a word of English could any of them speak, but they were reading from a Bible that a missionary had given to one of them in India, and which he had brought with him to America.

Source: Bamford, Mary. *Angel Island: The Ellis Island of the West.* Chicago: The Woman's American Baptist Home Mission Society, 1917, pp. 5–6, 12, 20–22. The California Historical Society, PAM 1277. http://content.cdlib.org/ark:/13030/hb7t1nb2dc/?&brand=oac. Accessed May 2010. Courtesy of the California Historical Society.

119. *U.S. v. Bhagat Singh Thind*, 1923

In 1790, the U.S. Congress passed a law restricting naturalization rights to "free white persons." Originally, the Naturalization Act of 1790 was meant to prevent African American slaves from becoming U.S. citizens. However, after Chinese laborers began to arrive in California, the restrictions were expanded to apply to successive groups of Asians as well. While strictures to deny Asian immigrants citizenship were reaffirmed in 1870 and 1907, South Asian immigrants occupied a gray area. Anthropologists in the early 20th century had begun classifying South Asians as Caucasians. However, many white Americans saw no commonalities between their white skin and European culture and the dark skinned peoples from India. In 1923, the U.S. Supreme Court eliminated any doubt over Indian citizenship rights in *U.S. v. Bhagat Singh Thind*.

Bhagat Singh Thind was born in 1892 in the Punjab, a region of northern India. He immigrated to the United States in 1913 and enlisted in the U.S. Army during the last few months of World War I. After being honorably discharged, Thind sought and was granted American citizenship on December 9, 1918, in Washington State. Four days later, a judge rescinded Thind's citizenship, on the grounds that he was not a "free white man," as required in the Naturalization Act of 1790. Eleven months later, Thind got his citizenship reinstated in Oregon on the grounds that he was a "high caste Hindu" from the Caucus region in India even though Thind practiced the Sikh religion. At the time, white Americans made no distinctions between the various people from the Indian subcontinent. For the average American, all Indians were "Hindus" or "Hindoos." The Immigration and Naturalization Service appealed the second ruling. On February 19, 1923, the U.S. Supreme Court concluded that Thind—and all Indians—were not Caucasian and that the "common man's" definition of "white," would be the standard used to determine legal racial status, which in turn determined citizenship rights (following the Naturalization Act of 1790). Thind, along with 50 other Indian Americans, retroactively lost their citizenship. Loss of citizenship also meant being subject to restrictive Alien Land Laws in over a dozen states that prevented "aliens ineligible for citizenship" from owning land.

Thind regained his citizenship for the third time in 1936, after Congress decided that veterans of World War I, even ones from the Asian Barred Zone, could become naturalized citizens. For the rest of his life, he wrote and lectured on spirituality and metaphysical theology.

Argued January 11, 12, 1923
Decided February 19, 1923
261 U.S. 204
CERTIFICATE FROM THE CIRCUIT COURT OF APPEALS FOR THE NINTH CIRCUIT
Syllabus

1. A high caste Hindu, of full Indian blood, born at Amrit Sar, Punjab, India, is not a "white person" within the meaning of Rev.Stats., § 2169, relating to the naturalization of aliens.
2. "Free white persons," as used in that section, are words of common speech, to be interpreted in accordance with the understanding of the common man, synonymous with the word "Caucasian" only as that word is popularly understood. *Ozawa v. United States.*
3. The action of Congress in excluding from admission to this country all natives of Asia within designated limits, including all of India, is evidence of a like attitude toward naturalization of Asians within those limits.

Questions certified by the circuit court of appeals, arising upon an appeal to that court from a decree of the district court dismissing, on motion, a bill brought by the United States to cancel a certificate of naturalization.

MR. JUSTICE SUTHERLAND delivered the opinion of the Court.

This cause is here upon a certificate from the Circuit Court of appeals requesting the instruction of this Court in respect of the following questions:

"1. Is a high-caste Hindu, of full Indian blood, born at Amritsar, Punjab, India, a white person within the meaning of § 2169, Revised Statutes?"
"2. Does the Act of February 5, 1917, disqualify from naturalization as citizens those Hindus now barred by that act who had lawfully entered the United States prior to the passage of said act?"

The appellee was granted a certificate of citizenship by the District Court of the United States for the District of Oregon, over the objection of the Naturalization Examiner for the United States. A bill in equity was then filed by the United States seeking a cancellation of the certificate on the ground that the appellee was not a white person, and therefore not lawfully entitled to naturalization. The district court, on motion, dismissed the bill, and an appeal was taken to the circuit court of appeals. No question is made in respect of the individual qualifications of the appellee. The sole question is whether he falls within the class designated by Congress as eligible.

Section 2169, Revised Statutes, provides that the provisions of the Naturalization Act "shall apply to aliens being free white persons and to aliens of African nativity and to persons of African descent."

If the applicant is a white person within the meaning of this section, he is entitled to naturalization; otherwise not. In *Ozawa v. United States*, we had occasion to consider the application of these words to the case of a cultivated Japanese, and were constrained to hold that he was not within their meaning. As there pointed out, the provision is not that any particular class of persons shall be excluded, but it is, in effect, that only white persons shall be included within the privilege of the statute.

"The intention was to confer the privilege of citizenship upon that class of persons whom the fathers knew as white, and to deny it to all who could not be so classified. It is not enough to say that the framers did not have in mind the brown or yellow races of Asia. It is necessary to go farther and be able to say that, had these particular races been suggested, the language of the act would have been so varied as to include them within its privileges"

—citing *17 U. S. 644. Following a long line of decisions of the lower federal courts, we held that the words imported a racial, and not an individual, test, and were meant to indicate only persons of what is popularly known as the Caucasian race. But, as there pointed out, the conclusion that the phrase "white persons" and the word "Caucasian" are synonymous does not end the matter. It enabled us to dispose of the problem as it was there presented, since the applicant for citizenship clearly fell outside the zone of debatable ground on the negative side; but the decision still left the question to be dealt with, in doubtful and different cases, by the "process of judicial inclusion and exclusion." Mere ability on the part of an applicant for naturalization to establish a line of descent from a Caucasian ancestor will not ipso facto and necessarily conclude the inquiry. "Caucasian" is a conventional word of much flexibility, as a study of the literature dealing with racial questions will disclose, and, while it and the words "white persons" are treated as synonymous for the purposes of that case, they are not of identical meaning*—idem per idem.

In the endeavor to ascertain the meaning of the statute, we must not fail to keep in mind that it does not employ the word "Caucasian," but the words "white persons," and these are words of common speech, and not of scientific origin. The word "Caucasian" not only was not employed in the law, but was probably wholly unfamiliar to the original framers of the statute in 1790. When we employ it, we do so as an aid to the ascertainment of the legislative intent, and not as an invariable substitute for the statutory words. Indeed, as used in the science of ethnology, the connotation of the word is by no means clear, and the use of it in its scientific sense as an equivalent for the words of the statute, other considerations aside, would simply mean the substitution of one perplexity for another. But, in this country, during the last half century especially, the word, by common usage, has acquired a popular meaning, not clearly defined to be sure, but sufficiently so to enable us to say that its popular, as distinguished from its scientific, application is of appreciably narrower scope. It is in the popular sense of the word, therefore, that we employ it as an aid to the construction of the statute, for it would be obviously illogical to convert words of common speech used in a statute into words of scientific terminology when neither the latter nor the science for whose purposes they were coined was within the contemplation of the framers of the statute or of the people for whom it was framed. The words of the statute are to be interpreted in accordance with the understanding of the common man from whose vocabulary they were taken.

They imply, as we have said, a racial test; but the term "race" is one which, for the practical purposes of the statute, must be applied to a group of living persons now possessing in common the requisite characteristics, not to groups of persons who are supposed to be or really are descended from some remote common ancestor, but who, whether they both resemble him to a greater or less extent, have at any rate ceased altogether to resemble one another. It may be true that the blond Scandinavian and the brown Hindu have a common ancestor in the dim reaches of antiquity, but the average man knows perfectly well that there are unmistakable and profound differences between them today, and it is not impossible, if that common ancestor could be materialized in the flesh, we should discover that he was himself sufficiently differentiated from both of his descendants to preclude his racial classification with either. The question for determination is not, therefore, whether, by the speculative processes of ethnological reasoning, we may present a probability to the scientific mind that they have the same origin, but whether we can satisfy the common understanding that they are now the same or sufficiently the same to justify the interpreters of a statute—written in the words of common speech, for common understanding, by unscientific men—in classifying them together in the statutory category as white persons. In 1790, the Adamite theory of creation—which gave a common ancestor to all mankind—was generally accepted, and it is not at all probable that it was intended by the legislators of that day to submit the question of the application of the words "white persons" to the mere test of an indefinitely remote common ancestry, without regard to the extent of the subsequent divergence of the various branches from such common ancestry or from one another.

The eligibility of this applicant for citizenship is based on the sole fact that he is of high-caste Hindu stock, born in Punjab, one of the extreme northwestern districts of India, and classified by certain scientific authorities as of the Caucasian or Aryan race. The Aryan theory, as a racial basis, seems to be discredited by most, if not all, modern writers on the subject of ethnology. A review of their contentions would serve no useful purpose. It is enough to refer to the works of Deniker (Races of Man, 317), Keane (Man, Past and Present, 445, 446), and Huxley (Man's Place in Nature, 278), and to the Dictionary of Races, Senate Document 662, 61st Congress, 3d Sess. 1910–1911, p. 17.

The term "Aryan" has to do with linguistic, and not at all with physical, characteristics, and it would seem reasonably clear that mere resemblance in language, indicating a common linguistic root buried in remotely ancient soil, is altogether inadequate to prove common racial origin. There is, and can be, no assurance that the so-called Aryan language was not spoken by a variety of races living in proximity to one another. Our own history has witnessed the adoption of the English tongue by millions of negroes, whose descendants can never be classified racially with the descendants of white persons, notwithstanding both may speak a common root language.

The word "Caucasian" is in scarcely better repute. It is, at best, a conventional term, with an altogether fortuitous origin, which, under scientific manipulation, has come to include far more than the unscientific mind suspects. According to Keane, for example (The World's Peoples 24, 28, 307 et seq.), it includes not only the Hindu, but some of the Polynesians (that is, the Maori, Tahitians, Samoans, Hawaiians, and others), the Hamites of Africa, upon the ground of the Caucasic cast of their features, though in color they range from brown to black. We venture to think that the average well informed white American would learn with some degree of astonishment that the race to which he belongs is made up of such heterogeneous elements.

The various authorities are in irreconcilable disagreement as to what constitutes a proper racial division. For instance, Blumenbach has five races; Keane, following Linnaeus, four; Deniker, twenty-nine. The explanation probably is that "the innumerable varieties of mankind run into one another by insensible degrees," and to arrange them in sharply bounded divisions is an undertaking of such uncertainty that common agreement is practically impossible.

It may be, therefore, that a given group cannot be properly assigned to any of the enumerated grand racial divisions. The type may have been so changed by intermixture of blood as to justify an intermediate classification. Something very like this has actually taken place in India. Thus, in Hindustan and Berar, there was such an intermixture of the "Aryan" invader with the dark-skinned Dravidian.

In the Punjab and Rajputana, while the invaders seem to have met with more success in the effort to preserve their racial purity, intermarriages did occur producing an intermingling of the two and destroying to a greater or less degree the purity of the "Aryan" blood. The rules of caste, while calculated to prevent this intermixture, seem not to have been entirely successful.

It does not seem necessary to pursue the matter of scientific classification further. We are unable to agree with the district court, or with other lower federal courts, in the conclusion that a native Hindu is eligible for naturalization under § 2169. The words of familiar speech, which were used by the original framers of the law, were intended to include only the type of man whom they knew as white. The immigration of that day was almost exclusively from the British Isles and Northwestern Europe, whence they and their forebears had come. When they extended the privilege of American citizenship to "any alien being a free white person," it was these immigrants—bone of their bone and flesh of their flesh—and their kind whom they must have had affirmatively in mind. The succeeding years brought immigrants from Eastern, Southern and Middle Europe, among them the Slavs and the dark-eyed, swarthy people of Alpine and Mediterranean stock, and these were received as unquestionably akin to those already here and readily amalgamated with them. It was the descendants of these, and other immigrants of like origin, who constituted the white population of the country when § 2169, reenacting the naturalization test of 1790, was adopted, and, there is no reason to doubt, with like intent and meaning.

What, if any, people of primarily Asiatic stock come within the words of the section we do not deem it necessary now to decide. There is much in the origin and historic development of the statute to suggest that no Asiatic whatever was included. The debates in Congress during the consideration of the subject in 1870 and 1875 are persuasively of this character. In 1873, for example, the words "free white persons" were unintentionally omitted from the compilation of the Revised Statutes. This omission was supplied in 1875 by the act to correct errors and supply omissions. When this act was under consideration by Congress, efforts were made to strike out the words quoted, and it was insisted, upon the one hand, and conceded upon the other, that the effect of their retention was to exclude Asiatics generally from citizenship. While what was said upon that occasion, to be sure, furnishes no basis for judicial construction of the statute, it is nevertheless an important historic incident which may not be altogether ignored in the search for the true meaning of words which are themselves historic. That question, however, may well be left for final determination until the details have been more completely disclosed by the consideration of particular cases as they from time to time arise. The words of the statute, it must be conceded, do not readily yield to exact interpretation, and it is probably better to leave them as they are than to risk undue extension or undue limitation of their meaning by any general paraphrase at this time.

What we now hold is that the words "free white persons" are words of common speech, to be interpreted in accordance with the understanding of the common man, synonymous with the word "Caucasian" only as that word is popularly understood. As so understood and used, whatever may be the speculations of the ethnologist, it does not include the body of people to whom the appellee belongs. It is a matter of familiar observation and knowledge that the physical group characteristics of the Hindus render them readily distinguishable from the various groups of persons in this country commonly recognized as white. The children of English, French, German, Italian, Scandinavian, and other European parentage quickly merge into the mass of our population and lose the distinctive hallmarks of their European origin. On the other hand, it cannot be doubted that the children born in this country of Hindu parents would retain indefinitely the clear evidence of their ancestry. It is very far from our thought to suggest the slightest question of racial superiority or inferiority. What we suggest is merely racial difference, and it is of such character and extent that the great body of our people instinctively recognize it and reject the thought of assimilation.

It is not without significance in this connection that Congress, by the Act of February 5, 1917, 39 Stat. 874, c. 29, § 3, has now excluded from admission into this country all natives of Asia within designated limits of latitude and longitude, including the whole of India. This not only constitutes conclusive evidence of the congressional attitude of opposition to Asiatic immigration generally, but is persuasive of a similar attitude toward Asiatic naturalization as well, since it is not likely that Congress would be willing to accept as citizens a class of persons whom it rejects as immigrants.

It follows that a negative answer must be given to the first question, which disposes of the case and renders an answer to the second question unnecessary, and it will be so certified.

Source: Excerpt from *U.S. v. Bhagat Singh Thind*, 261 U.S. 204 (1923).

120. Mary T. Mathew, Interview by Rashmi Varna, 1999

In immigrant families, generational differences between parents and children are exacerbated by the cultural expectations of both parties. Tension over the level of Americanization is frequently expressed in conflicts over gender roles and social strictures. Mary Mathew, an immigrant from Kerala, in southern India, moved to North Carolina in 1970. In this excerpt from her 1999 interview with Rashmi Varna, she speaks about how she and her daughters navigate between American and Indian cultural expectations, particularly in respect to dating.

MARY T. MATHEW: Ahm . . . both our children are, temperamentally, very sweet and easy to get along with. And, raising both of them in their childhood was delightful. And as they grow up, and during their early growing years . . . mentally, both of us were still firmly rooted in the cultural expectations of typical Indian parents . . . It was unthinkable to us that girls would wear shorts. It was unthinkable to us that our children would think of dating, boys, and . . . It was unthinkable to us that our children would want to . . . go out on dates and return . . . after nightfall. So, all of these are . . . expectations I should say, that we had so firmly implanted in us, that we could not get reconciled to how our girls were changing before our eyes. So, when our older daughter who was the guinea pig in our, child-rearing, went through these stages, . . . we, had encounters when we would try to explain our respective positions and so on. So, I would say that it took us time and a few years to realize that our children were not extensions of our personalities, even though they were Indian in terms of having Indian parents, they had grown up here and so these children who were, in the real sense of the term, Americans and we could not package them into a predetermined cultural entity.

RASHMI VARMA: Did they have questions for you, as to what, you know, their identities were? Did you ever see any confusion in them? Or do you think that it was easy for them to just see themselves as Americans? Did they come ever with experiences from school, you know, where someone had asked them about their identity and that had led to some confusion?

MARY T. MATHEW: . . . It took us a few years for these issues to get resolved, and then, then we had a few tough years when the girls felt that we were unreasonably strict with them, and that we didn't understand what their, needs were, in these social areas, and so on.

RASHMI VARMA: What about cultural areas? Do you think that they were ever confused about their identity? Did other kids perceive them as different? Did they ever have questions about that, as to why they were different?

MARY T. MATHEW: . . . They didn't. They didn't have problems in that area. One reason could be that their friends loved coming to our house

	and having dinner with us, so they found their cultural background to be a social advantage. [Laughter] Well, and all our spicy food and so on were popular among their friends. Neither of them would wear a sari or, things like that, at that time. Even though now they would.
RASHMI VARMA:	They would now?
MARY T. MATHEW:	Yes.
RASHMI VARMA:	What has made the difference that now they would?
MARY T. MATHEW:	Because when you're in your early and mid teens, you think to be different, is to be, socially inept, and now, now that they're more confident of their, themselves as persons, they see it as a way to look more attractive. [Laughter] They see it as exotic, what once they would have seen as different, you know, in a bad way. So, on the one hand as parents, we realized what our mistakes were, and we began to come out of pre-established cultural behavioral expectations. And, [unclear] we started allowing them to date young men, who of course, always, making sure when we could, that these were young men of good character and, you know, carefully counseling them about the dangers of, not sticking within one's moral boundaries and so on. So, I would say that both girls have benefited from our relaxing that stern grip, on their social life and, they have both been very responsible and, we are proud of the choices they have made.

Source: Excerpted from interview with Mary T. Mathew by Rashmi Varna, April 25, 1999 (K-0815), in the Southern Oral History Program Collection (#4007), Southern Historical Collection, Louis Round Wilson Special Collections Library, University of North Carolina at Chapel Hill. http://docsouth.unc.edu/sohp/K-0815/excerpts/excerpt_8773.html. Accessed November 2009.

121. Anita Chawla, Interview by Peggy Bulger, 2001

Anita Chawla was born in the United States to Punjabi parents and grew up in Atlanta, Georgia. She is now a physician in the Washington, D.C., area. Chawla heard about Al Qaeda's assault on the World Trade Center and the Pentagon while she was stuck on an expressway waiting for a car repair. Because she lived in a very liberal and politically active community, seeing anti-Muslim signs in her community was particularly distressing for Chawla, who remembered the racial profiling and antagonism she experienced as a child during the Iran hostage crisis. In her interview with Peggy Bulger two weeks after 9/11, Chawla discussed how the attacks changed her life as a brown person living in America. Like other South Asians, Chawla experienced a heightened sense of racial identity almost overnight, as Americans came to identify brown skin with the enemy.

CHAWLA:	I'm Anita Chawla; I'm originally from—well, my family's from India and I was born and raised in Atlanta, Georgia, and now I live in Takoma Park, MD. I'm 34 years old and I'm a physician.

BULGER: And, Anita, I'm asking everyone: the horrible events that happened on September 11th impacted all of us . . . Where were you when these events unfolded?

CHAWLA: Well, I was actually on my way—I was on the Beltway on my way to work and right when I had a flat tire—my tire gave out right as the news was coming about well there's a plane that hit the World Trade Center and I pulled over and I spent the next two hours listening to the radio hearing things unfold and news trickling in and waiting for someone to come change my tires so I was just sitting there in total shock listening to these things happen . . . and the confusion and people not sure what exactly had happened . . . and it was very scary. It was very unbelievable, very surreal . . .

BULGER: And you being of Indian descent . . . how is your life changed since that time?

CHAWLA: Well, unfortunately, I've become very much more self-conscious and aware of being a minority and I've become much more aware of racism and how much do I blend in. You know my mother lives with us and I've explained to her what has happened and encouraged her not to wear her shalwar and kameez, her Indian clothes, outside when she goes out, just because I'm afraid for her and she doesn't speak the language. So I worry about her being out and I'm concerned about that. And I'm much more aware of even going into stores and public places. I'm much more self-conscious, and I know, I can feel—sometimes I feel people looking at me and I'm not sure why—like I'll catch people's eyes. And that's unfortunate because in the past I never thought anything of it. But now I'm having to—I feel unsafe, and I feel unsafe for my family . . .

It feels very isolating and it feels almost like I'm in prison. And I feel so bad for the Sikhs who of course they wear turbans and there's so much misunderstanding and it's just heartbreaking. It's really heartbreaking. And everybody's just afraid.

BULGER: . . . Are there any other things that you think should be, could be done by our government?

CHAWLA: Well, I think I've heard things coming out about remembering that Islam is not—Muslims are not bad, that Islam is not bad, it's the people that distort it, and the politics and so forth and I think that that's—if we could hear more of that. And I certainly appreciated when Bush went out and has been saying those kinds of remarks and so forth. But I really think that there has to be a lot done at the community level. There has to be a lot more educating, and just teachings of tolerance . . .

[We're] trying not to feel so imprisoned and trying to take some steps to remember our community and remember the people, that we are connected and people do support us. So that's important, that is reassuring.

Source: Interview with Anita Chawla, conducted by Peggy Bulger, Takoma Park, Maryland, September 24, 2001, in the September 11, 2001, Documentary Project Collection (AFC 2001/015), Archive of Folk Culture, American Folklife Center, Library of Congress Reprinted with permission from Anita Chawla. http://hdl.loc.gov/loc.afc/afc2001015.sr082a02. Accessed October 2009.

122. DJ Rekha, Interview by Demetrius Cheeks, 2007

DJ Rekha is a South Asian American DJ who specialized in mixing bhangra, traditional music and dance from the Punjab region in India, with electronic house music. DJ Rehka's Basement Bhangra music became hugely popular in the New York City club scene in the early 2000s. Rekha, like other South Asian Americans or Asian Indians, is part of a new generation of post-1965 Asian Americans. With the liberalization of U.S. immigration policies in 1965, Asian Indians began coming to the United States in large numbers. The new immigration policies created a preference system for highly educated professionals, particularly in the areas of medicine, the sciences, and engineering. Many of the first post-1965 Indian immigrants arrived in the United States under these preferences or as students in U.S. graduate school programs. Currently, South Asians are the fastest-growing and most educated Asian ethnic group in the United States. Currently, they are the third-largest Asian American ethnic group and are concentrated in California, New York, New Jersey, Texas, and Illinois (though there are significant populations in Pennsylvania, Florida, Michigan, Maryland, Virginia, Georgia, and Ohio). Because of South Asian immigrants' high educational levels, many second-generation South Asian Americans feel pressured to follow in their parents' footsteps and become doctors, engineers, or lawyers. However, a growing number of South Asian Americans, like DJ Rekha, have found success in other avenues. In this interview DJ Rekha describes how her Indian heritage has influenced her artistic development.

Let's assume that the readership is unfamiliar with both Sangament and Bhangra. Can you briefly describe the enterprise and the cultural phenomenon?

Sangament is the name I've given to my company. It's a combination of the words Sangam and entertainment. "Sangam" itself is a North Indian Hindi word meaning the confluence of rivers; it's where the rivers flow, in essence. Sangament Inc. is the entity through which I do all of my work—as a DJ, as a marketer and as a consultant.

How would you describe or characterize Bhangra?

Bhangra is a music and a dance that originally comes from Punjab: a region—and an ethnicity—divided by India and Pakistan. It's one of the forms of music that's indigenous to that area. It was transported to the UK through the immigration of Punjabi peoples that came to the UK post World War II. And now, roughly three generations later, the music has taken in its environment and developed and transformed in a unique way.

What was it that drew you into that cultural space?

The cultural space was my household in many respects. I was exposed to the language via my parents. I didn't have much exposure to that music. I grew up on Bollywood, which is a Hindi language-based music that emerged in the Hindi-language film industry. I was initially exposed to the music by my mother; she brought back a tape from

England after a visit there. This was around the time that the Bhangra scene really started kicking off in the UK. I heard it and it really blew my mind. At the same time, my cousins and I just got interested in DJ-ing and forming a crew.

How was Bhangra initially received in India and how is it received today?

I think initially, in India and maybe even in Pakistan, Bhangra was perceived as sort of regionally based folk music: very specific to a locale, very jubilant, very lively and very festive. It was and is the music of north Indian weddings. In India, that's how people took it; in the UK, in the same way, it was brought over and it kept going through cultural practices. Especially because of the political context in which it sort of incubated in the UK: you had these communities of color that didn't really assimilate or mix and they really held on to their cultural traditions, so they kept it alive. And in terms of its perception, Bhangra has been like house [music]: it keeps having waves in the UK, of breaking and becoming mainstream. There was actually a hit a few years ago with Punjabi MC. This record that broke in Europe, and then Jay-Z actually rapped on it here [in the States] quite by accident. The whole idea has been that this music is really going to break and go somewhere. And it does a little bit and then it doesn't. But there're still a lot of barriers to entry to South Asian artists in the UK. Even though it's a community that's embedded in that cultural landscape, I think that artists there tend to have a hard time breaking out and doing stuff. Society there is still kind of insular and the industry is kind of shallow. I mean it took dancehall 25 years to break outside of Bob Marley. So we have to see the corporate forces that encourage, discourage, exploit and co-opt these cultural forms.

Let me ask you this: India, China and America seem to be the three nations with large enough, and wealthy enough, populations to sustain their own independent cultural forms—commercially speaking. Why hasn't that seemed to happen with Bhangra in India?

Well, it has. But you have to understand that Bhangra is a very specific kind of music, and in India it's popular now, to some degree. But in India, Bollywood and Hindi-language is more accessible to people; it's not simply that Bhangra isn't popular. Also, preferences and taste preferences are different. So where you have a community and you have a large Diaspora, what works in India—and I know first-hand as a DJ—doesn't fly in the UK and it doesn't work here. People's tastes are different. There was a moment in the early 90s where these Bhangra bands were becoming quite popular in the UK. They went to India and no one was feelin' them. Because India is so diverse culturally: so many languages, the largest middle-class in the world, it's hard to generalize people's preferences. Only after Punjabi MC's track broke internationally did it break in India, very much in the same way a Madonna track would break in India. It got put on a soundtrack in a Bollywood movie—one of the first Indian movies to have a soundtrack of music that wasn't in the film. Usually the soundtrack of Bollywood films are musicals: you see the movie, you hear the music, you buy the CD. Here [in the States] when we buy a soundtrack, we know that what gets licensed for the soundtrack may not be in the film; it's more about the idea or the thematic connection. That helped break that record in India. In fact, that record broke before Jay-Z touched it. In fact, the reason that Jay-Z even knew about it is that he went to Europe and he said "what the hell is this?! . . ."

Ok. Let's take a few steps back: Earlier you mentioned that you got exposed to Bhangra music through your family back home [in India], and that, in turn, stimulated your interest in DJ-ing. Is it accurate to say then that this enterprise proceeded from that interest in DJ-ing?

Well, I grew up in a business-oriented family. So I have this little entrepreneurial . . . problem. I've always worked for my dad, growing up; he had several businesses. For several years I worked at his store in midtown Manhattan and, you know, that was my business education. So there's something very innate in me about not working for anyone, having a certain kind of hustle going. So there's that side to me. And having done it a lot—having dealt with cash growing up—that was always inherent. I always found a way to maintain some autonomy. So when I started DJing, it was a business. I always took it seriously as a business. It took a while to get it down on paper, and what have you, but the minute money was exchanged, it was a business to me. It started with my cousins and just grew from there. I have a real keen sense and interest in branding and remaining a viable entity. I came to it through Bhangra music and as a DJ, but I see it as a larger thing, a larger idea.

What's your relationship—and the relationship of Bhangra—to the American music industry?

To the American music industry, if anything, I'm just a squirrel trying to get my nut. To the music industry at large, I'm not overly interested in a "grand success" model. I believe that slow and steady wins the race. After 9 some-odd years, I just signed a deal with Koch Records. And I'm really happy with it. I like the company. I the way that they work. I also don't see it as my meal ticket; it's just adding something to my enterprise. Koch tends to align with artists that already have their own following. And I think that the most important thing that a label can do for you is to get your music on the shelf. One of the benefits of actually having a business of my own is understanding the other side of the equation, is knowing that the label is a company: they have X amount of resources and the things that will give them a return—and the people who are nicest to work with—is where the energy is going to go. So make it easy for them, and it will be easier for you. In the case of the Punjabi MC record, that song was licensed in this territory. The licensing label made tons of money on the song, but you couldn't find it in the stores. I say that to illustrate that several strategies exist for monetizing music; it's key to understand the tendencies of the label you're affiliated with.

In closing, what are your hopes for Bhangra? Would you like to see it become a cultural institution in the way of, say, hip-hop?

I don't know. I find a lot of similarities between Bhangra and Dancehall, insofar as they both come from a very specific cultural experience . . . as does hip-hop. Not to discount hip-hop in any way. Arguably, hip-hop references Dancehall in many ways. Many of the hip-hop pioneers were second-generation Jamaican and Caribbean immigrants. But the whole notion or structure of success may be problematic. The music is powerful; it has a certain aesthetic and I think it will always have an audience. I'd like to see it exposed to a wider audience in whatever way possible.

Have you contemplated an exit strategy for yourself? As a DJ? As a businessperson?

It's funny, for many years I said that I would stop Basement Bhangra after 10 years, because 10 years is good for a club night. . . . And part of me still wants to, believe me.

I am not lying. I'm like: let 'em crave, let 'em want it. Go out when you're on a high note. The party definitely requires a large commitment. People have counseled me to hand it over to someone else to run, but I can't do that. In nine years—and we do eighteen a year—I've only missed two nights. If the party starts to weaken, I'll be the first one to say stop. Everything comes to an end; it all functions on a cycle. If the other facets of the company continue to grow, I'll be more inclined to step back.

Source: Cheeks, Demetrius. "The Outsider." New York University Stern School of Business paper, *Opportunity,* March 6, 2007. Reprinted with permission.

123. Sweta Srivastava Vikram, "Racist or a Victim?" 2009

Sweta Srivastava Vikram is a multigenre writer and the author of two poetry chapbooks, *Kaleidoscope: An Asian Journey of Colors* and *Because All Is Not Lost.* She is the coauthor of *Whispering Woes of Ganges & Zambezi.* Born and raised in India, Vikram now lives in New York City. In her essay "Racist or a Victim?" Vikram challenges the notion that only white Americans are racist, casting a critical eye upon her own community.

"You are *gori-chitthi*. What problems you have," said one of my *desi* associates when in one of my idealistic moments, I said, "I can't believe people, even today, judge others based on their skin color!" This person, disdainfully, assumed that my life was problem-free because I was a relatively lighter shade of brown than her. Ironically, she hired cleaners based on their ethnicity.

It took over 200 years for one of the largest democracies in the world to pretend to look beyond color. Over a year ago, the world witnessed history in the making when Barack Hussein Obama became the first African American to be elected as the President of the United States of America. But did Obama truly redeem the world or was his victory a symbolic step? Obama might have won the majority of the African American votes on election night, but at one point, wasn't he accused, by his own race, of not being truly black? It seems there are "accepted" and "unaccepted" shades of color within each race.

Anyway, on Wednesday morning, November 5th, 2008, the air in NYC smelt different. There were celebratory clouds hovering over the City and at work. In my exhilarated mood, I screamed, "Congratulations," to my coworkers. One of my black colleagues, one of the kindest and professional person otherwise, said, "Congratulations for what?" "Because Obama won," I explained. "Oh, okay," she added in a suspicious tone. Just then, two other African American women walked up to the same coworker and said, "Congratulations! We made it!" In response, they got a warm hug. I felt alienated. I wondered if my words offended her. If they did, was it because I am a shade different—brown as opposed to black?

It's amazing how we, South Asians in the west, complain about racism when a significant number commit acts of bigotry themselves. For instance, even today, some people continue to make trips to India to handpick wives/daughter-in-laws. The key criterion in the screening process is "How fair is she?" The woman could be a witch from Eastwick, but all is forgiven if she is light-skinned.

This pseudo-progressive family I know of went to India a few years ago to find their son the perfect wife—"Fair-skinned." I say pseudo-progressive because on one hand they gave their own children the best education, lifestyle, and exposure possible; on the other, they desired a non-ambitious, extremely fair, convent-educated girl as a trophy daughter-in-law, who they could show off to their socialite friends. On the bride-hunting trip, the family stayed at a luxurious five-star hotel in New Delhi to impress the girls' families, who made the final cut; watched videos of each of the candidates dancing, walking, and talking; and, after days of humiliating, degrading, and rejecting the potential girls, announced their final verdict. The fairest maiden amongst them all was selected as the future daughter-in-law. Mind you, these same Indian-Americans voted for Obama to sound progressive, but ultimately made the commitment of a lifetime based on color.

Across the globe, the situation isn't very different. On seeing my picture on my book's back cover, one of my mother's acquaintance screeched, "Your daughter is fair. Like a foreigner." In the Indian culture, her words would qualify for the elite-class compliment. But I felt nauseated and appalled because my hard work was ignored; the only point noticed was the color of my skin.

On the same trip, as I read Bombay Times, one of the local newspapers in Mumbai, I shuddered with shock. Despite the economic growth and aesthetic modernization of India, certain traditions remain unchanged, like the ritual of rejecting and selecting brides based on the color of their skin. The matrimonial columns read: "Wanted tall, fair, convent-educated, etc." Classified ads on Craigslist have more dignified description for furniture than some of these "Bride-seeking" columns.

Growing up, I remember a cousin aunt, who spent her day rubbing "fairness creams" like Fair & Lovely on her face, hoping her skin would become light. She was considered unsuitable bride material by prospective suitors because her complexion was darker than the benchmark they had in mind. Never mind her astute brain or delicate features or warm personality, her parents had to finally pay dowry so she could settle down.

Bigotry is heinous. But before we accuse another human being of it, shouldn't we ask ourselves a simple question: if there is a bigot in all of us, can we truly expect prejudice to ever die?

Source: Vikram, Sweta Srivastava. "Racist or a Victim?" 2009. Used with permission of the author.

124. Athena Kashyap, Four Poems, 2009

In 1947, the Indian Independence Act dissolved the British Empire in India and led to the creation of the sovereign nation of Pakistan. Conflicts over what regions of India would join Pakistan, coupled with sectarian tension created massive human suffering. As millions of displaced people crossed over the border to join their religious group, long-standing divisions between Hindus and Muslims erupted into tragic violence. Estimates vary, but likely several hundreds of thousands of people were killed in the ensuing riots and massacres, and thousands more died from deprivation produced by the chaos. Memories of the Partition remain strong and traumatic for its survivors and their families in Pakistan, India, and abroad.

Athena Kashyap grew up in Bangalore and Bombay, India and has been living in the United States since she was 18 years old. Her parents are the children of emigrants from Lahore, now in Pakistan, who eventually settled in Delhi and Bombay. A writer, poet, and writing teacher at City College of San Francisco, Kashyap's poems and essays examine the concept of travel and dislocation: the impact of different and changing geographical locations on personal lives. Kashyap's following four poems explore the ways in which history and the homeland remain integral to individuals' new lives in a new land. In particular, "coming down the mountain" is a reflection on the continuing impact of the Partition on South Asian immigrants in the United States. Lahore, the capital of what is now Pakistani Punjab, saw some of the worst sectarian violence between Muslims, Sikhs, and Hindus.

COMING DOWN THE MOUNTAIN

Great-grandfather enters my room in Los Angeles, clutching two clumps of roots still bleeding Himalayan mud. He says he's sorry to come so late at night, but he can't find his way. The family house he built in Lahore still stands, but neighbors have moved in and his family is gone. At the University, the botany lab he founded no longer bears his name. His students have aged terribly—they look right through him. He has trouble with his eyes, sees just half of everything—his students, the map of India on the wall. Even the city landscape is missing parts—temples, sari shops, certain street names. The last thing he remembers is climbing the mountain, up from the city he once knew and loved. He looks so tired, I want to help him but am myself adrift, barely flickering in this city's sea of lights. Our family's dispersed like seeds, searching for each other and their own selves in clouds of lost mountains. *I see*, says Grandfather with his half-blind eyes, but then he's gone, waving dead roots in my face.

WORLD CAFÉ

I'm diluted, my skin grown permeable, breathable.
With Abraham in his cafe, conversation oscillates, a dance—
he suggests I try *dolmas* in his thick desert English,
I vacillate, trying to locate the exact geography of my craving.
My body succumbs, my tongue a compass for distant tastes:
crunchy Korean fish eyes, sugar-chili Gujarati vegetables,
Burmese floating soups—murky ponds with flotsams
of beef and vegetables, red simmering Kerala crab curries,
the salty sweetness of my lover's dark skin.
So many lives I've lived—I revisit them all and more in these cafes,
truck stops for travelers needing to shake off and drink in selves.

THE CORNER STORE

The owner of the corner store does not know my name, nor I his.
He does not even nod when I enter, but stands gruff and still.
When I complain about the price—fifty cents for an onion—

he tells me "buy elsewhere." But when he chats with his children,
just come back from school, his voice melts. For a moment,
the sound of soft clapping, clouds and rain takes me back to Mumbai,
the sea-washed sidewalks, bare feet slipping out of rubber slippers.
The J-Church screeches past. I look up, the children are gone.
Only mounds of tins, moldy produce surround us once again.
I pay for my onion and count the change. We are careful
not to let our fingers touch. Mountains of miles trail both of us—
we have to keep them untangled.

AMERICA

Throat of vase
filled with pebbles
from afar, and memories
plump and sweet, crossing over
continents, thirsty seas, generations
spilling into this living room, bodies
dissolving into each other, strains of music:
o sathi rey, aee, aee, tere bhi nabhi kya jeena—
Soulja boy grew up in this hoe, watch me crank it—
shifting this idea we had about you and me, these worlds
we've built out of paper—visas, passports, bank accounts,
collapsing at the center of time unfolding, the splendor of being—
no fathers and mothers, grandfathers and grandmothers, great grandmothers,
no one, not even our past selves, no one there to catch up, demand explanations.

Source: Kashyap, Athena. "coming down the mountain," "world café," "the corner store," "America." 2009. "coming down the mountain" originally was published in *The Fourth River*, no. 6, 2009. "world café," "the corner store," and "America" originally were published in *The Noe Valley Voice*, May 2009. "world café," "the corner store," and "America" will be published in the forthcoming *Same Difference*, edited by Smita Singh, London: J Publishing Company, 2010. Used with permission of author, *The Fourth River*, and *The Noe Valley Voice*.

125. Sandip Roy, "The Great Diwali Fight and Obama," 2009

Sandip Roy is an editor with New America Media. In his blog essay, he reflects on how different groups in the United States are reacting to multiculturalism and how Hindu Americans are "inserting" themselves into mainstream America via political activism. He argues for official federal recognition of Diwali, or the Festival of Lights, which is celebrated by Hindus, Jains, and Sikhs alike as a national holiday in India. Whether by issuing a postage stamp to commemorate Diwali or by recognizing it in a White House celebration, acknowledging Diwali would signify a redefinition—a broadening—of what it means to be American.

OK, you have to give it to President Obama. He knows how to work the symbol.

President Obama became the first US President to celebrate Diwali, the festival of lights, in the White House.

That's been a long-standing fight of Hindu Americans.

Actually all of Diwali has been the touchstone of multicultural tussles in America.

The first big Diwali fight was about street parking. New York Mayor Bloomberg didn't want to add Diwali to its list of major holidays when street cleaning would be suspended. The City Council passed the bill in 2005 and the Mayor vetoed it. In 2007 it was finally approved. Phew.

Then there was the petition for the Diwali stamp. If Muslims could get the Eid stamp, why not a Diwali stamp? Diwali is our Christmas said the Hindus. There was an online petition for signatures. According to SAJA the petition was started by an Atlanta businessman Bob Ghosh and it even got dead signatories like former Indian prime minister Jawaharlal Nehru. The US Postal Service told them respectfully that the signatures didn't count. But like the NPR funding being cut right now hoax email, the Diwali signature email would pop up in Indian-American mailboxes every year.

That fight started a long time ago. You can tell. The stamp was worth 37 cents. In 2009 the Hindu American Foundation formally asked the US Postal Service's Citizens Stamp Advisory Committee for a Diwali stamp. Earliest that can happen—2012. No one claimed this was express mail.

But the big fight was always about the Presidency.

Next year, Diwali in the White House.

They got close with George W. Bush. But it was always Diwali in the annex to the White House. And it was always with a "senior administration official", never the Big Boss himself.

One can't blame Bush. In 2007 When Rajan Zed, a Hindu priest was invited to offer the morning prayer in the Senate protesters shouted "this is an abomination" from the gallery.

The American Family Association urged its members to protest because Zed would be "seeking the invocation of a non-monotheistic god." (Note the small g). Former Navy Chaplain Gordon Klingenschmitt said Zed "committed the sin of idolatry" with the "permission" of the government.

Now that abomination has moved from the outhouse to the inner sanctum itself. The historic East Room of the White House was the site of the Diwali celebration. Hindu Americans are tickled pink. The Hindu American Foundation has issued a press release saying "Never before had a sitting US President personally celebrated the Diwali holiday, and with that one gesture, two million Hindu-Americans felt a bit more like they belonged—one more reason to feel at home."

Of course for those who think Obama is the anti-christ this is one more proof that godless heathens have taken over the White House. But the president was careful to make sure he didn't make it seem like the ten-armed goddesses were taking over the administration. (But I think a ten-armed kick ass Goddess with a lot of Second-Amendment protected weapons would not be a bad ally to have in pushing through health care reform).

Obama invited people of different faiths to the ceremony. And he talked about the larger significance of a festival of lights—a time for celebration and contemplation.

He explained what Diwali meant for Hindus, and what it meant for Jains and what it meant for Sikhs. I was startled because having grown up in India I didn't know all that myself.

I just knew Diwali as fireworks, oil lamps and platters of sweets. It needed President Obama to explain my culture back to me with professorial authority.

It was a little embarrassing.

But anyway what are the brave Diwali fighters going to do now?

I guess they could always go back to the great battle for the Diwali stamp.

Source: Roy, Sandip. "The Great Diwali Fight and Obama." October 16, 2009. http://blogs.newamericamedia.org/sandip-roy/1801/the-great-diwali-fight-and-obama. Accessed February 2010. Used with permission of the author and New America Media.

126. Rajiv Srinivasan, "My Battle Within: The Identity Crisis of a Hindu Soldier in the US Army," 2009

Rajiv Srinivasan was born in Chennai (formerly known as Madras), on the southeastern coast of India. When he was a child, he and his parents moved to Roanoke, Virginia. He graduated from the U.S. Military Academy at West Point, where he studied Arabic and comparative politics. Srinivasan was commissioned as an armor officer; as a lieutenant in the army and served a yearlong deployment in Kandahar, Afghanistan. While attending West Point, Srinivasan founded Beyond Orders (www.beyondorders.com), a nonprofit organization that provides humanitarian assistance for Afghani and Iraqi communities. American soldiers deployed in Afghanistan and Iraq can request specific items from donors in the United States who ship those items overseas.

Srinivasan wrote "My Battle Within" for the Hindu American Foundation's 2009 NextGen Essay Contest, "The Importance of a Hindu-American Identity." In "My Battle Within," Srinivasan writes about how he reconciles Hindu principles of nonviolence with his occupation as an officer in the army, and how his religion impacts his actions as an American.

The barrel of my M4 assault rifle is slender, black, and cold. The rippled plastic grips fit ergonomically to a mission driven hand; one that aggresses to protect a nation and way of life. With each trigger squeeze, a 5.56 caliber bullet breaches the muzzle at 2,900 feet per second with the sole purpose of taking another's life. Despite its lethality, this weapon is only a piece of metal. It is nothing without the mind and heart of the soldier perched behind it. As I don my body armor, grab my weapon, and prepare to lead my platoon of 32 soldiers into Afghanistan, I hesitate. I turn to the portrait of Krishna in my office and demand of him, "What is the worth of this fight? Is it worth our limbs, our lives, or the heartbreak of our parents? What cause is so important as to merit the coming violence?" And so begins my war within: the quest for an identity.

Like most Indian youth in the U.S., I faced the inner conflict between my Indian and American identities. At home, I watched Bollywood movies and prayed to Hindu deities; but at school, I spoke English, played football, and did whatever I could to emulate a typical American childhood. I felt pulled in two directions: one identity abandoning my Indian heritage, the other neglecting my American way of life. Thus, I went through my most formative years without knowing who I was, nor what I stood for.

As high school came to an end, I hastily made the decision to attend the U.S. Military Academy at West Point, but did so in vain. At the time, I was not sure about being an Army officer. I was just looking for a shining star for my résumé. I was looking for a way to pay for college. Perhaps on a deeper level, I was looking for a sense of belonging. I wanted an identity to which everyone in my immediate surroundings could relate and respect.

The U.S. Army is a rare home for an Indian immigrant, but no other endeavor has ever given me the professional and spiritual fulfillment than the experience of military service. The army challenged my most extreme patriotic influences against my peaceful Hindu beliefs. How could I serve patriotically as a U.S. Army Officer, owning the responsibility of waging war against our national enemies, but remain a man of the Hindu faith believing in the peaceful coexistence of all beings? This was a deep philosophical confrontation, but I accepted it with resolve.

Through days of wet, cold, hot, humid, tired, and hungry, I maintained a vegetarian diet. After a long day of military training, I returned to my barracks to indulge myself in the poetry of the Bhagavad Gita. I found solace in Arjuna's struggle as a shamed warrior fighting against his blood. I found strength in Krishna's assertion of conviction and discipline. I found that, though typical Hindus and Soldiers lead vastly different lives, both share a common purpose: to serve a higher calling for good. Thus, there was no need for a struggle between my American and Hindu identities; rather, finding strength in one made me stronger in the other.

My Hindu-American Identity is now a defining part of my life. As Arjuna beckons of his charioteer, "How can I wage war against my family? I would rather surrender, than commit such atrocities," Krishna affirms that it is our duty as Hindus to do what we believe is right, regardless of the opposition. When peaceful attempts to reconcile fail, we must be prepared to defend the values in which we so wholeheartedly believe. It is this reasoning that convinces Arjuna to fight to protect his kingdom. It is this reasoning that Gandhi used when supporting the British Army's aggression against the Nazis in World War II. This reasoning is why I feel so compelled to defend this nation, that has given my family countless gifts, against those who wish to do it unnecessary harm. I do not fight *in spite* of my religion. I fight *inspired* by it.

The importance of the Hindu-American identity extends beyond a vague resolve to fight for what you believe in. Each of us is faced daily with moral challenges in this country, and our reactions to them define our spiritual resolve. This nation is in an ethical crisis; from the poorest of American ghettos through the wealthiest of corporate banks. Hindu-Americans are a dominant source of influence, wealth, and intellect in this nation, so what does it say of our personal constitutions if we tolerate the ethical degradation around us? We have the means to drastically improve the ethical standards in this country. We owe it to ourselves as Hindu-Americans to defend, as Arjuna does his Kingdom, the moral foundations which have made this country a haven for religious and ethnic tolerance. We could collectively sit on the sidelines and criticize our leadership as many Americans do. But if we aspire to follow Krishna's guidance, it is our duty to proactively defend the integrity that upholds our great society. This is the new importance, the calling, of the Hindu-American identity: inspired by our faith, we must actively rebuild our nation's character and preserve it for our posterity. So I ask of each Hindu-American, what have you done to make America stronger for our children?

Krishna's picture sits in my office as a constant reminder of my Hindu-American Identity; a reminder that strength in principle outweighs the comfort of indifference. No matter what challenges lie ahead of me, I will bear my uniform each day with pride knowing I am defending a nation I truly love, and caring for a platoon of soldiers who do the same. It is through the discharge of my duties to God and Country that I have finally found the identity I was looking for all along; that of a fulfilled Hindu-American.

Source: Srinivasan, Rajiv. "My Battle Within: The Identity Crisis of a Hindu Soldier in the US Army." 2009. Originally published by the Hindu American Foundation. http://www.hafsite.org/media/pr/rajiv-srinivasan. Accessed September 2010. Reprinted with permission.

127. Ainee Fatima, "To My Mother," "Blues from a Black Burqah," and "Graceland Part I," 2009

Ainee Fatima is an Indian American poet and spoken-word artist. She is a two-time winner of Chicago's "Louder Than a Bomb" youth poetry slam, the largest poetry event of its kind in the United States. Fatima's poetry explores her experiences growing up Muslim in the United States and the ways immigrant families navigate the often-opposing pressures of Americanization and tradition. In "To My Mother," Fatima compares the family ideal of arranged marriage with her growing desire to choose her own spouse. In "Blues from a Black Burqah," she considers how familial relationships and structures are changing the longer they live in the United States. "Graceland Part I" is a humorous poem in which Fatima sheds her burqah for Elvis Presley's clothes, a metaphor for accepting her own multifaceted identity.

TO MY MOTHER

My mother is at the garage deflating the tires of my red Schwinn,
Her finger depresses the nozzle.
Over the hiss, *"Zainab Auntie's 18 year old daughter,*
Leila ran away from home on her bike.
Ainee, good Muslim girls don't ride bikes; they stay home."
My ten year old head nods in agreement.
I've been disciplined to agree with everything they say
Because I don't know any better and tradition is always followed.
But why would Leila run away?

For the next eight years,
The red bike lay on its side next to the white garage door,
No one ever rode it again; someone must've thrown it away.
All that remains is the rusted outline of the bike.

October rain falls hard, pressing
Ochre maple leaves on sidewalks.
Wind howls in the ruby Maple
Like the "no" that cyclones my eyes each time they say
"You're ready to get married."
If I am old enough to get married off,
I should be old enough to choose to whom.
A child's soul is more important than tradition being kept.

The wind trips the motion detector of the garage light,
And through the glass, I stare at the rust outline of the bike.
In the window's condensation, I trace away the rims that still stain the cement,
Drawing a stick figure of myself riding away on it.

There is no one home.
I pull the suitcase from my mother's closet.
The traffic light over the intersection of Crawford and Touhy Avenue
Goes from red to green to yellow before I make up my mind to open it.
Inside, all the clothes my mother got for her wedding lie dormant.
Beneath the green, blue, yellow, pink saris and Rajasthani silk,
I remove her red wedding dress.

I want to see if it fits.
If this dress fits me as it hugged my mother's seventeen year old body.
If this idea of an arranged marriage fits.

The traffic light bleeds red down the street,
With my nose soft against the window,
I hear Pachelbel's Canon in D major in my mind.

The lace touches my bare shoulder blades.
Flat folds of red satin,
A casing for a forced love nineteen years ago.
But it's the red of the bike I want touching my skin, not the dress.

Outside, a whoosh of cars pass me in the wake of a life I loathe
I force aged metal hooks tight against my spine,
Fastening me into a future with a stranger.
It doesn't fit; this is not meant for me.
I know I will never love.

My parents' idea of freedom is a ring binding my life to another.
I will never be free to climb onto the Schwinn
And ride through a green light to flee into this October night to join Leila.
The traffic light always remains red in reality.

The autumn rain pops on the window,
The light changes from yellow to red,
Tree limbs sway as the wind howls,
The rusty stain remains.

So much depends
On the memory of a red bike
Glazed by rain,
Beside the white garage.

BLUES FROM A BLACK BURQAH

I.

We moved into our house when I was eight.
My grandfather wanted to ensure the house was blessed, so
He sat at the kitchen table writing prayers on paper rectangles
To place on doorways of the house.
Above door in the green kitchen: *There is no God but Allah.*
On the brown front door: *Thee do we worship, and Thine aid we seek.*
In the doorjam of my room: *Praise to Allah the most Beneficent and Merciful.*
As he wrote this out,
Ink from the word *rahim* bled through the paper,
Tattooing "mercy" onto the table top.

Once the house was blessed
My mother hung a drawing of mine from kindergarten.
It was the same crayon house every kid draws:
A square house, two windows with curtains—
A door, don't forget the knob,
A chimney on the peaked roof with smoke curling out in spite of
the smiley face sun shining in the corner,
3 red tulips against a white picket fence,
Smiling stick figures lined up according to height,
"Home is where the heart is," bubble-lettered along the bottom.
It was a happy home.

II.

In the years following,
Dinners opened with *Bismillahi wa'ala baraka-tillah*

plates passed over my head in a blur,
wooden troughs of basmati rice,
white platters of curries,
silver dishes of tomato chutney, yet
My eyes always fixed on the word *rahim* magnified under my water glass.
an inky fish floating under my glass
Many times they yelled my name because I was lost in the aquarium under my cup
Rahim floated in calligraphy curving spines
Tracing in it with eyes the arc of its tail
I tried to drink mercy from an early age
With every mouthful I drank a bit of it away.
Until it finally faded.
Now there is no mercy for me at the table.

Each night before her bedtime prayers, with tasbih in hand.
My mother walked into our rooms, whispering a string
Of Arabic words I do not know.
As she slides each bead, she leans over our beds
Blowing prayers of protection, praying we wake up each morning.
Hoping, that the gravity of God's words make their way to our souls
So we may forge a path that keeps our faith intact.
Making sure obedience does not falter, for the Prophet once said
"Paradise lies at the feet of your mother."

III.

"Home is where the heart is, Ainee. What happened?!"
She threw the drawing at my feet the day I disobeyed her.
I bit my tongue and resisted to give her an answer.
"I just want to write . . ."

Months following that, Grandfather's prayers were taken down
In result of the wallpaper being torn down.
My mother never bothered to put them back up.
My father never came home for dinner anymore.
Instead of breaking bread, we broke each other's hearts.

Each night before bed, she kisses prayers onto foreheads,
She walks past my bed saying nothing.
Nothing will push her to turn her head towards me.
She doesn't pray for me anymore.
My name is no longer on her tongue.

I was always told to write what I know.
But, I do not know my mother
Nor my father or this home anymore.

GRACELAND: PART I

> "I ain't no saint, but I have tried never to do anything
> that would hurt my family or offend God."
>
> —Elvis Presley

I shift into park, kill the engine, unbuckle my seatbelt.
I've been casing the joint for days.
The Tennessee twilight hangs in pastel orange, blue, purple.
As sweat drips down my temple, the light above the front entrance goes out.
And step out of the minivan into the Memphis evening.
I pop the trunk, grab my guitar case.
(You will breathe in deep through nose now)
The air is clean, close, and sweet.

My black burq'ha conceals me as I climb each music note on the gate and
   drop in.
I move unnoticed past the stone lions, and
Slide in through the window into the kitchen.
Past guitars, past gold and platinum records, past gun collections that glow
   beneath lights:
I pass it all—even the velvet rope that secures the second floor from tourists.
No one is here except me, my guitar case,
And the things of the King I came for.
Inside the double padded doors of his bedroom,
A shoulder high statue of Christ greets me.
I slide Jesus some skin and wink at him.
"Gotta date with the King, Issa."

Pleated red velvet lines the bedroom walls.
Smoked mirrors trimmed in black velvet.
I put my guitar case on the bed, next to the '68 comeback leather jacket.
I'll get that on my way out.
I stroll slowly into his closet:
Hundreds of jumpsuits
I caress them as I pass,
Chinese Dragon, no.
Bengali Tiger, no.
Powder Blue two-piece, maybe.
The '77 Hawai'i gold-studded American Eagle on white, absolutely. 200
I liberate myself from my *Burqah* and slide on the jumpsuit.
Adjust the belt, fasten the cape . . . the cape
I make my way back into the bedroom, and
The drag co-efficient is Elvis awesome.
In the smoky mirror rimmed in black velvet,
arms stretched eagle wing wide

I'm a Muslim woman who must be covered; I accept that,
But I'm also American, baby: You accept that.

Wise men say
only fools rush in
But I can't help
falling in love with you

Source: Fatima, Ainee. "To My Mother," "Blues from a Black Burqah," and "Graceland: Part I." 2009. Used with permission of the author.

128. John, "ABCD's: American-Born Confused Desis," 2009

In recent years, a trend has developed among young American-born South Asians. They are traveling back to India to rediscover their cultural heritage and reconcile their American identity with their ancestral heritage. In the following article, Taiwanese American blogger John explores the difficulties these transnational South Asians encounter when they try to reintegrate and identify with Indian friends and family.

I am an avid fan of National Public Radio (NPR)—and this morning, I heard the story of "Young Indians Abroad Return to Help Better Country" as part of the series on "Climate Connections: Profiles." The story discusses the growing trend of young Indians who grew up in Britain, Australia and America are now going to the new wild west—India, hanging out with Indian friends, and having conversations about climate change and the environment. Indian-Americans are known as "ABCD's"—"American-Born Confused Desis":

"In this broadcast on Morning Edition we talk to a bunch of American-born Indians and their local friends who discuss what it's like to come "home" and what it's like to be invaded by Americans who want to rediscover their "Indian-ness". The locals have a nickname for these Americans—they call them "ABCDs." That's an acronym for American-Born Confused Desis. Desi is slang for an Indian guy or gal, and the term basically means kids from America who return a little mixed-up about who they are. "The conversation, as you'll hear, explores all kinds of issues: the advantages of an American accent in India, the value (and limits) of Western experience in attacking pollution and poverty, the importance (or not) of movies and popular culture in creating social change, and why Indian woman (some of them) like beef-eating men."

NPR interviews a local Indian man, who says he doesn't like ABCD's, since with their Western education and non-Indian accents, are highly sought out for better jobs, status, etc . . . as well as the fact that ABCD men can get local Indian women easier—as he had read in Maxim India (supposedly because ABCD's eat more meat and are bigger, etc..)—which made the NPR reporter laugh.

To be honest, the Indian man's complaints kind of reminded me of the perennial debate of Asian women dating white men. After the laugh, the Indian does say that these ABCD's do provide different and "amazing" perspectives and insights that are helpful. Anyways, I was amused by the ABCD acronym. As a Taiwanese-American,

I've heard the term ABC—American Born Chinese quite often. I did know one person at college who referred to himself as a CBA—Chinese Born American, to emphasize the Chinese part of him, even though he was born in America. Finally, someone in my dorm referred herself as an ABCDEF—American Born, Culturally Deprived, Egyptian Female. I thought that was clever and got a big kick out of that.

Source: John. "ABCD's: American-Born Confused Desis." April 28, 2009. http://www.8asians.com/2008/04/28/abcds-american-born-confused-desis/. Accessed September 2009. Reprinted with permission from John@8asians.com.

129. Sanjay Patel, Interview by Grain edit, 2010

Sanjay Patel moved to the United States in 1980, along with his Gujarati parents, who ran a motel in Southern California. His first book, *The Little Book of Hindu Deities*, includes comic book–style illustrations and short descriptions of Hindu gods. His latest book, *Ramayana: Divine Loophole*, is a graphic design adaptation of the Hindu epic. Patel has discussed his desire to create a bridge between Indian immigrants and their Indian American children and to retell the ancient Indian stories in a way that makes sense to young people today. The following is a 2010 interview with Grain edit, a design blog.

Chronicle Books has just released *Ramayana: Divine Loophole* the latest book from Pixar animator and illustrator Sanjay Patel. As one of the core legends of Hindu mythology, *Ramayana* recounts a tale of Rama, a god-turned-prince, and his quest to rescue his wife Sita after she was kidnapped by a demon king. Sanjay is able to breath new life into this 2500-year-old epic tale with over 150 pages of lush, detailed illustrations.

In this interview, he gives us a glimpse into the making of the book and some of the challenges he faced along the way.

Lets start off with a little bit about your background. Where are you from originally?

I was born in the UK and lived there till I was five. My parents then immigrated to Southern California, and began running and living in a motel off of route 66. So next time you're in San Bernardino be sure to drop in on my folks at the Lido Motel . . . They've been living and running the motel for thirty fucking years now!

When and how did you become interested in illustration?

As far as I can remember I was drawing. In elementary school my third grade teacher gave me a wonderful collection of hard bound vintage Superman comics. She wrote an inscription inside the book about what a wonderful artist I was and how I apparently had so much talent. She must have had me mixed up with someone else. Because the first thing I did with that book was draw all over the pages adding poop and pee coming out of all the great Superman panels. Eventually I began respecting my comics a lot more. I was really obsessed with a marvel artist named Michael Golden and his series called The NAM. From there I started watching a ton of Robotek and Looney tunes. But it was only until my high school art teacher gave me the famous Nicolaides "The

Natural Way To Draw" book, did I finally get what drawing and illustration was all about. I dropped my comics and fell in love with Michelangelo, the Renaissance, and Norman Rockwell. The desire to communicate through a visual language has stayed with me ever since.

What led you to create a book on the Ramayana?

There were a lot of different impulses that led to the decision to tackle the Ramayana. In many ways The Little Book of Hindu Deities was a success and at the same time really didn't capture the full scope of my talent. As I began to read the Ramayana it became very clear that the mythology was loaded with a visually rich world. It was also very clear that no one has tried interpreting the epic story in pictures and illustration with a modern graphic flair. Or at least in a visual language that was in line with my aesthetics and love of mid-century animation.

How much time did you put into researching for the project?

I'm almost embarrassed to say this but I spent close to four years on the project. It took me the better part of a year to read different translations of the story and write my own summarized version. After selling both my manuscript and a full black and white dummy I took a year sabbatical from PIXAR to work on the ridiculously detailed vector illustrations full time. After working day and night for over a year and not leaving my apartment for days at a time I eventually ended up burning out. Luckily I discovered yoga and therapy and was able to finish the project.

How long did it take you to create the illustrations for the book?

Once a pencil sketch was done which took about two days I could jump into Adobe Illustrator and start building vector shapes, which took another three days depending on how complicated the illustration was. If I was lucky I would get things right, but in almost every case I re did things dozens of times.

What were some of the obstacles/challenges that you faced along the way?

The biggest obstacle was of course the scope of the project, The Ramayana has dozens of character and locations, mega war scenes and complicated crowd illustrations. But somehow I was able to get things running fairly quickly that is until till I decided to redo everything top to bottom a few times. I kept fighting to work in a design style that was cute and silly, when the Ramayana is anything but that. As a reaction of too much cute I ended up turning the illustration into something much more grown up and stiff. Eventually the design pendulum settled somewhere in between cute and boring. Somewhere that I hope captures the action and drama in a fun modern style that honors this great mythology.

During the day you work at Pixar, how did you find time to work on this massive project?

That's a long story, but what I can say is this. Growing up in a motel in a grimy part of San Bernardino I had very few friends let alone neighbors. I spent most of my time drawing alone. In many ways once I come home from work I want nothing more than to return to that same comfort of pencil and paper and solitude. Not much has changed in that way.

What artists/ books served as inspiration for your illustrations?

My office at Pixar is covered in Charley Harper pages. I actually bought two copies of the massive monograph that Ammo Books put out. I took one of the books and had it professionally cut and started using all the pages as wall paper for my office. So of course there is a ton of Harper in my everyday life and in my Ramayana. Like many other Cal Arts students I love mid century illustration. My favorites are Saul Steinberg, Provensons, & Sasek. Of course there are tons more artist that I love like Peter Arno, Tezuka, Steig, Boutavant, Lindberg, Wyeth, . . . And of course the great master Mr. Bill Watterson and his Calvin & Hobbes.

In what ways did the initial concepts differ from the finished book?

I wanted the book to be cute and silly like a Richard Scary version of the Ramayana. Instead I think I ended up with a weird Charley Harper, animation hybrid. Hopefully the combination works.

Source: Patel, Sanjay. Interview. 2010. http://grainedit.com/2010/02/26/sanjay-patel-interview/. Accessed April 2010. © 2010 www.grainedit.com.

Part XII
Indonesian American

130. Nadia Syahmalina, "Kamu Bukan Orang Sini," 2001

Historically, only a relatively small number of Indonesians have immigrated to the United States. According to the 2000 census, about 70,000 people of Indonesian heritage were living in the United States. Many of the early migrants from Indonesia arrived during the 1950s to study at U.S. colleges and universities. As with other Asian nations, U.S. foreign aid programs encouraged student exchange as part of American efforts to thwart Communism worldwide. The political upheaval and violence that followed the ousting of Indonesia's first president, Sukarno, resulted in a new wave of Indonesian immigrants to the United States during the mid- to late 1960s. Most of these new arrivals were Indonesians of Chinese descent. As the turmoil in Indonesia subsided, so did immigration. Today, as in the past, most Indonesians come to the United States for educational or economic reasons, and the majority reside in Southern California. Indonesia's cultural, ethnic, and religious diversity and the small number of immigrants may have contributed to the absence of ethnic community development on the scale of the Chinese, Korean, or Indian American communities.

Nadia Syahmalina was born in Jakarta, Indonesia, and raised in Morgantown, West Virginia. Her essay "Kamu Bukan Orang Sini" originally was published by InvAsian in 2001, and again the next year by the (currently inactive) Society of Indonesian Americans (SIA). Syahmalina currently lives in the Washington, D.C., area and is the vice-president of the Indonesian Muslim Association of America (IMAAM). "Kamu Bukan Orang Sini" describes the cultural and generational conflicts in immigrant Indonesian families and the difficulty of finding one's place in either country.

My 17-year-old sister has not set foot in Indonesia since she was four years old. I see her struggling in trying to count the numbers in Indonesian, and I am reminded of myself.

There was a point in my life when I had a hard time pronouncing "satu, dua, tiga, empat" which in English is "one, two, three, four." I still find it hard to even say "selamat pagi" sometimes, but I know that her troubles would far exceed mine because she is just starting out. I know that she would be hassled for having this impairment. People, it seems, find it hard to swallow that this girl who looks like them could be in anyway different.

Their inability to understand is what usually brings out the worst in them. They start with asking questions, and when they find the answers unsatisfactory, they find other ways to satisfy themselves; and this is usually at the expense of the one being questioned. How do I know this? Because I had been the one questioned, the one at the end of gibes and mockeries. The sole reason behind all this is that I was different—internally.

Being different on the inside is more hard to grasp because you can't really see it, and usually people judge you on the exterior. So it was therefore accepted if you were different physically, and it was appalling to some that one who looks so similar outwardly could be so different inwardly.

My parents also had similar opinions all throughout my childhood. They usually never forget to remind me of how different I was from my friends because they were not Indonesian. I was not an "orang sini" whenever I wanted to spend the night or go to a party at friends. I was not an "orang sini" whenever I wanted to date boys. Most of the things that I wanted to do with my friends that were foreign to them were answered with "kamu bukan orang sini, jadi kamu tidak boleh."

As the years went by the invitations to parties and sleepovers slowly decreased, and my friends became afraid of inviting me to anything because I usually wasn't allowed to go. At this, I distanced myself from my friends and became extremely confused. My parents, though, didn't seem to notice the change in my attitude, so they continued with their remarks, unaware of how belittling they were.

They then added that my real friends would be in Indonesia because Indonesians could understand me more. Confused and hurt, I wanted to go to Indonesia and be an "orang sini," be among my "true friends," and just be accepted.

I got the chance to go to Indonesia in the summer of 1997. I was a very eager person when I boarded that plane in Singapore. "In a couple of hours I would be home," I said to myself. I kept checking the on-flight map just to see how close the plane got to Jakarta. As soon as the rice paddies (farm lands) below came to view, this up-till-now-unexplainable feeling came over me.

When I had stepped out of that plane and breathed in the air that was perfumed with the smell of wet grass and rice growing in the fields, I did feel home. I couldn't wait to meet my relatives and old childhood friends again, and especially make new lifelong friendships (just like my parents said). Everything was fine during the first few weeks. Only after a couple of months had passed I noticed something was not right.

I longed for the smell of my house in the States and to gab with the friends who I had distanced myself from, but I shrugged this off as homesickness; and besides, I was "home," right? So I suppressed my longing and tried so hard to adjust to my new surroundings. It was never enough though, because no matter how hard I tried, I could never really fit in. Everything I did got a disapproving look and every word I said got a snicker or a smirk because it was odd to them how an Indonesian spoke or acted like a foreigner. Some even found it insulting.

I couldn't walk around my neighborhood without hearing whispers or catcalls. The cab drivers would look at me funny once I spoke even a "hello." They'd ask my mom or whoever was with me at the time, "Bu, nih anak kok susah amat yah ngomong. Mang dari mana sih?" My relatives were pretty hostile to me too because

I disrupted their seemingly quiet life. I could never do anything right, and making friends was even harder than I thought.

Most parents were afraid that I would have a bad influence on their children, since I came from a country that had an enticingly bad culture and reputation. I once heard a rumor that I was the cause behind a friend's present non-diligent behavior. The adopted belief among my neighbors was that I was "an unruly child with no manners."

I then realized how much of an outsider I really was, how I wasn't accepted at all. It hurt, and it hurt a lot. This was supposed to be my "home," the place where I would feel like I belonged, but I didn't feel like I belonged at all. Instead I felt the complete opposite. "What am I supposed to do, aku mo kemana lagi? Ini kan home saya, tapi kenapa aku gak merasa demikian?" I'd say to myself over and over again. I resorted to crying almost every single night because I was so confused.

I wanted to go back to America, but in America I'm not accepted—well that's what my parents said. And I couldn't stay here: I wasn't accepted here also. I felt like I had nowhere to go, since I wasn't accepted in either of the two countries that I had resided in.

After a year and a half in Indonesia of trying so hard to conform and almost succeeding, a twist of fate came and I returned to America. Did this solve my problem? Nope, it only added to it. I was very wary of how people acted towards me and remained very distant, maybe even more so. Someone summed it all up when he said that "I was here, yet wasn't here."

My parents' words replayed itself in my mind almost on an everyday basis. I could not understand what brought them to say those things to me at such an impressionable age. After many arguments and bitter quarrels, though, I finally understood the reasons behind their actions. I realized that this all came about because they were afraid that I would lose my Indonesian heritage, forget who I was and where I came from.

Their apprehension increased by the fact that they were amateurs in this: They had no one to consult with about family matters, especially on how to raise children in a foreign land. So they reared their children the best way they knew how. After this moment of realization, I no longer harbored deep anger for my parents; now it is more like sympathy. They were trying their best after all.

From all this I've concluded that you don't need to be almost mirror images of someone for you to be "kindred spirits" with them. Dissimilarity isn't so bad nor is it a thing for ridicule. You do not generally need to be skilled in the native language to have pride in your country nor do you have to act like everyone else does over there to be proud of where you come from. That should not be what gives you pride. If it is then that is a false sense of pride, because true pride comes from within.

There are many people who talk Indonesian fluently and eat bakmi and somay on a regular basis who aren't proud of being an Indonesian. What makes them better than those Indonesians who were born and/or raised out of Indonesia who do have pride yet speak in broken Indonesian and eat pancakes and pizza almost everyday?

Neither is this whole cultural conflict the fault of the parent who brought the child to a foreign land. This kind of assumption is wrong too. It's not their fault.

It is just a risk a family takes when emigrating or immigrating to another country. Cultures will clash, identity crises will happen. It's just a matter of whether a family handles it or not; and sadly for me, my family couldn't.

In the end, though, I think going through the rough and turbulent times was worth it. My parents realized their mistakes and now embrace a more open attitude towards strange and new things, and a communication line is now open between parent and child. They realize that maybe their children are also an "orang sini" as well as an Indonesian.

And maybe because of my stay in Indonesia, my relatives won't be as hostile and my neighbors will have a more understanding attitude towards my sister when she goes there. Seeing her struggle with the numbers "delapan, sembilan, sepuluh" I sincerely hope so.

Translations from Indonesian:

Selamat pagi: Good morning
Kamu bukan orang sini: You are not someone from here.
Orang sini: Someone here
Kamu bukan orang sini, jadi kamu tidak boleh: You are not someone here; therefore you can't.
Bu, nih anak kok susah amat yah ngomong. Mang dari mana sih?: Mam, this child has a lot of difficulty in talking. Where is she from anyway?
Aku mo kemana lagi? Ini kan home saya, tapi kenapa aku gak merasa demikian?: What . . . where am I supposed to go now? This is my home, but how come it doesn't feel like it?
delapan, sembilan, sepuluh: eight, nine, ten

Source: Syahmalina, Nadia. "Kamu Bukan Orang Sini." 2001. Used with permission of the author.

131. Peter Phwan, "Game of Chance: Chinese Indonesians Play Asylum Roulette in the United States," 2009

In May 1998, following decades of institutionalized discrimination and state-ignored violence against ethnic Chinese Indonesians, yet another series of race riots broke out in Jakarta, Indonesia's capital city. The collapse of the Indonesian currency in the Asian economic crisis, exacerbated by government corruption under President Suharto, led to widespread protests in 1998, which then erupted into violence targeting Chinese Indonesians. Although they comprised only a small percentage of the Indonesian population, Chinese Indonesians controlled a disproportionate amount of the country's wealth and thus consistently were held up as scapegoats. During the May 1998 riots, over 1,000 Chinese were killed, over 100 women were raped, and shops and homes were looted and burned. As a result, more than 70,000 Chinese Indonesians fled to countries in Asia and the Pacific and to the United States.

Peter Phwan, under the pseudonym Damai Sukmana, wrote the following article for *Inside Indonesia,* describing the plight of the Chinese Indonesian refugees and their reception in the United States.

Ten years after winning his asylum interview, Victor Liem (not his real name) is now a permanent resident of the US and one step away from becoming a US citizen. Despite the improved situation for ethnic Chinese in Indonesia, Liem—who has built and runs his own business in Silicon Valley—and his wife still feel nervous about returning. In the 1990s Liem was a hopeful businessman in Jakarta. He was a London School of Engineering graduate and owned two companies in West Jakarta. On 14 May 1998, driving home along the Kebon Jeruk highway, Liem was confronted by an angry mob attacking motorists with rocks, wooden bats and metal bars. The thugs were checking motorists' identity cards. He saw light skin-coloured men being dragged from their cars and beaten. Liem made the decision to drive at high speed through the makeshift blockage rather than risk being stopped. He finally reached Serpong Gate and was saved by locals who secured the area. His car was severely damaged by rocks. There were serious cuts on his face and hands. He then realised that a long sharp metal bar, which had broken the windscreen, had fallen just next to his stomach.

Liem and his family got the first available flight out of Indonesia. They landed in the United States in June 1998. The whole family applied for political asylum, and their application was approved soon after. Today there are at least 7000 Chinese Indonesians—former asylum seekers—living in United States.

* * *

Fleeing after May 1998

Thousands of Chinese Indonesians left Indonesia after the anti-Chinese violence in Jakarta and other major Indonesian cities in May 1998. Many fled to the US seeking sanctuary either temporarily or with the hope of permanent settlement. Indonesia is currently one of the top 25 countries whose citizens seek asylum in the United States, peaking at 12th ranking in 2004. According to the US Department of Justice, over twenty thousand Indonesian asylum cases have been filed since 1998. In 1998 alone, at least 1972 Indonesians were granted asylum in the United States; the highest number granted for Indonesians as a result of the relatively fast and non-adversarial process of 'affirmative asylum interviews', in a decade. The majority of these political asylum seekers from Indonesia were of ethnic Chinese descent.

This unusually high number of successful asylum applicants was greatly influenced by considerable and high-profile lobbying on their behalf by Chinese American groups. In the wake of the May riots members of the ethnic Chinese diaspora, particularly those in the United States, were outraged at the targeting of ethnic Chinese Indonesians and lobbied their own governments to condemn the inaction of the Indonesian government to protect them. Those approached by Chinese American groups included high profile politicians such as the present Speaker of the House, Nancy Pelosi, and Gavin Newsom, currently Mayor of San Francisco. Liem and his family were beneficiaries of this effort. But as the political heat around this issue cooled, so too did the relative ease with which asylum applications were granted. Now Chinese Indonesians whose claims are yet to be resolved face a game of asylum roulette.

* * *

Asylum roulette

In the ten years to 2007, 7359 asylum cases involving Chinese Indonesians were approved and 5848 cases denied. Chinese Indonesians commonly relate their asylum claims to the history of government-sponsored discrimination, persecution and violence towards the minority. While many may not have experienced personal physical harm, they have feared persecution in the past, and now fear present and possibly future persecution.

A decade after the May riots and despite important changes in law and the lack of anti-Chinese violence in this time, Chinese Indonesians continue to seek asylum overseas because they fear persecution. Many continue to suffer trauma as a consequence of events in the past and maintain a continued sense of vulnerability about their situation in Indonesia, seeing these legal changes as simply cosmetic. Recent arrivals to the United States indicate that they simply do not trust the government to provide them with the protection they will need in a time of potential future crisis and targeting of ethnic Chinese. Although, all hope that these new legal and cultural freedoms will help more ethnic Chinese feel safe at home, and when they don't, asylum should always be an option.

Proving a credible fear of persecution is crucial to winning an asylum case. As the political system in Indonesia and the legal conditions for ethnic Chinese have improved, including the repeal of discriminatory legislation in recent years, proving such a fear has become less straightforward than it was in 1998. Moreover, in recent times applicants have found the asylum seeking process to be considerably more difficult. If their application is denied at the first hurdle by the Asylum office, an applicant's case is then referred to an Immigration Judge. This process is usually called a Defensive Asylum Hearing and applicants must find legal representation. If they lose their case before the Immigration Court they may then appeal at the Board of Immigration Appeal (BIA) and Circuit Courts.

The lives of Chinese Indonesians currently in the US with asylum cases still pending in the Courts remain in limbo. For many years now they have counted the days until the US Circuit Courts issue the final order for them to, in all probability, leave the country. Some are even detained for immigration violations before being deported. Outcomes depend on how individual judges interpret the case, how convincingly an applicant's story is presented to the court, if they can afford or find pro-bono counsel willing to provide representation, as well as the standard of such representation.

However, an important and relatively recent precedent for these later Chinese Indonesian asylum cases is that of Sael vs Ashcroft, decided in October 2004 by the Ninth Circuit Court. This court covers many states, including California, Washington, Oregon, Nevada and Hawaii. It is the largest circuit court in the United States and overall second only in size to the US Supreme Court. The Court ruled that Taty Sael and her husband were eligible for political asylum after finding that the woman faced likely persecution in Indonesia. The US Court of Appeal gave three reasons for finding Taty would be in danger if she were deported. These were the historical pattern of anti-Chinese violence that dates back to 1740, laws still on the books that prohibit Chinese schools and other institutions, and mob attacks and threats against the applicant before she fled with her husband. Her husband's asylum claim was based on her situation.

This marks the first time a US Court has ruled there to be government-sanctioned discrimination against Indonesia's Chinese minority. Despite this precedent however, many Chinese Indonesian asylum seekers still face challenging legal battles in US immigration courts. Those who lose face the reality of returning to Indonesia.

Source: Phwan, Peter. "Game of Chance: Chinese Indonesians Play Asylum Roulette in the United States." *Inside Indonesia* 95, January–March 2009. http://www.insideindonesia.org/edition-95/game-of-chance. Accessed November 2010. Reprinted with permission.

132. William Wright, "Indonesian Makes New Life in America," 2009

The following article published in the *Cleveland (Tennessee) Daily Banner* recounts the story of one Indonesian woman's journey to America. Unlike most Indonesian Americans, Dianingrum does not live in Southern California and did not come to the United States for education or economic opportunities. She moved from her home in Indonesia to Cleveland, Ohio, in 2006 because she married an American soldier. Her marriage soon ended in divorce, and with no family in the United States, she found herself alone in a country she never expected to call home. Nevertheless, Dianingrum decided to remain in the United States despite her difficulties adjusting. She found strength in her Indonesian cultural heritage, which values diversity, something she has also found true of America. Her story highlights some of the difficulties experienced by individuals in cross-cultural marriages and is a reminder of the diversity within the immigrant experience.

Growing up in Indonesia, Wilis Dianingrum never thought she would go live in the United States or be married to an American, but she did.

Three years ago the 33-year-old Cleveland State Community College student moved from her homeland in Southeast Asia and married a U.S. soldier only to become a divorced woman striving to make a new life for herself in a new country.

Dianingrum admits her life has been one struggle after another after losing her full-time job at Rubbermaid and her part-time job at a local restaurant six months ago. To top it off, her father died last year in a motorcycle accident and she was unable to attend his funeral.

With no family in the states and few friends to rely on, she said she took the matter to the highest authority.

"I believe God will help take care of me. He gave me the wisdom to go back to school. Cleveland State accepted me and I received financial aid," said Dianingrum. "I'm trying to survive here."

With the dramatic change in the U.S. economy and a more casual view of divorce in Western civilization, Dianingrum had to learn about life in America the hard way, from reality.

"I never dreamed of living in America," admits Dianingrum. "It was too far away. I never dreamed I would marry an American. Now I am the first in my family to get divorced."

Dianingrum said it seems people give up too quickly on marriage, adding, "In Asia we believe marriage is to be respected. Husbands take care of their wives and wives respect their husbands. There is not a lot of divorce there."

Raised Catholic but attending a Baptist church in Cleveland, Dianingrum said it was a shock to learn her husband wanted a divorce and did not want to work out their differences. It was another painful disappointment to learn she was losing her only means of making a living.

"When I lost both my jobs I was very sad but I went back to school," said Dianingrum. "Maybe the economy will get better soon and I will be able to find a job or get a better one. I cannot give up. I'm trying to be a strong, tough woman."

Although she said it is not easy for her to trust men after what happened in her cross cultural marriage, Dianingrum said she hopes to find lasting love one day but no time soon. When the time comes, however, she said she will be aware of how cultural differences can affect relationships.

"Living together is not part of my culture," said Dianingrum. "Having children out of wedlock is not my culture, but I do not judge others. I realize the culture here is different."

The Republic of Indonesia comprises 17,508 islands. With a population of more than 240 million people, it is the world's fourth most populous country, with the world's largest population of Muslims.

"We have 26 states and every state has a different language," said Dianingrum who speaks two languages. "Our national language is Bahasa."

Indonesia's national slogan, "Bhinneka Tunggal Ika" is translated "unity in diversity" which expresses the diversity that shapes her country. Dianingrum said she noticed a similar unity in diversity developing in Cleveland which she likes.

"I decided to stay here because I like to learn the language and the culture," she said. "I love traveling. I went to Europe for three months as an exchange student. I like the adventure. I like to try new things. Since I don't have any kids I would love to visit every state in the U.S. some day."

Of all the things that make her happy, Dianingrum said she is happiest when people accept her as she is.

"Most educated people are open-minded," she said. "I like living in Cleveland. People try to reach out to others."

Dianingrum said she still likes to eat with her hands although she sometimes uses a spoon. She has never eaten cereal. A favorite dish of Indonesians is a mixture of rice, coconut milk, meat and vegetables. According to Dianingrum, Indonesians also eat less bread than Americans.

"I come from Jakarta, the capital of Indonesia. They don't hunt animals where I live and I've never eaten deer," she said. "Also, we don't drink much beer, wine or liquor in Indonesia. You can get it everywhere here but not there. It's very expensive."

Dianingrum, who is majoring in accounting, said she carries the hope that more people will understand the importance of embracing diversity and avoid stereotyping others as they strive to become more united.

In her own struggle for survival in a land far from home, Dianingrum reflected on the American Dream that is still within her grasp and wondered why some people only see the negative rather than focus on the positive in life.

"I live by myself and I'm doing good," she said. "You can go to school and make a better life for yourself. It's easier when you already know the language. I have to learn a different language, a different culture with different values. It's harder for me but it's the most important thing right now. If I can do it, so can others."

Dianingrum said she is making no plans to return to Indonesia where her mother lives with one of her three brothers. She has a 10 year green card she must carry before she can apply to become a U.S. citizen.

Despite her challenges to make a life in America, Dianingrum said she is positive her life will be a learning experience full of adventure, happiness and love, things that also flourish in America.

Source: Wright, William. "Indonesian Makes New Life in America." *Cleveland Daily Banner* (TN), October 28, 2009. Reprinted with permission from the *Cleveland Daily Banner* of Cleveland, Tennessee.